Global One Health Index Report 2022

Xiao-Nong Zhou · Xiaokui Guo
Xiaoxi Zhang
Editors

Global One Health Index Report 2022

Springer

Editors
Xiao-Nong Zhou
School of Global Health
Chinese Center for Tropical Diseases
Research, Shanghai Jiao Tong
University School of Medicine
Shanghai, China

Xiaokui Guo
School of Global Health
Chinese Center for Tropical Diseases
Research, Shanghai Jiao Tong
University School of Medicine
Shanghai, China

Xiaoxi Zhang
School of Global Health
Chinese Center for Tropical Diseases
Research, Shanghai Jiao Tong
University School of Medicine
Shanghai, China

ISBN 978-981-97-4823-5   ISBN 978-981-97-4824-2   (eBook)
https://doi.org/10.1007/978-981-97-4824-2

Shanghai Jiao Tong University 2020JCPT01

Foreword

The globe faces a prominent and public health threat at the human-animal-environment interface, with respect to emerging diseases such as avian influenza viruses, the viruses associated with the severe acute respiratory syndrome (SARS-Cov-1), and COVID-19, that underlines a vulnerability exacerbated by dense human populations and human-animal interactions. Simultaneously, it grapples with zoonotic infections and a burden of neglected tropical diseases (NTDs), which strongly affect community health and economic stability, yet receive insufficient attention and resources. Adding to these concerns, challenges with antimicrobial resistance and food security issues have been exacerbated by the interaction of diverse ecological landscape and social-economic patterns.

The significance of One Health approach in addressing these challenges is well-recognized. However, at the national and sub-national levels, challenges in implementing One Health remain, and this imposes an urgent need for executive protocols to guide One Health actions. Addressing this critical gap, the global One Health index (GOHI), pioneered by the team from School of Global Health, Chinese Center for Tropical Diseases Research, Shanghai Jiao Tong University School of Medicine, is not just an academic pursuit but a groundbreaking initiative.

Global One Health Index Report 2022 provides comprehensive insights into One Health metrics across an impressive scope of global countries/territories. The narrative navigates crucial scenarios—from the intricate dynamics of zoonotic disease control, the vast landscape of food security, the profound implications of climate change, to the escalating challenge of antimicrobial resistance. Each segment is anchored in scientific evidence, offering a vista of the prevailing global health landscape.

We hope this report may serve a catalytic role in improving One Health implementational paradigms, benefiting various stakeholders in: (i) promoting exchanges in theoretical knowledge, innovative technologies, and research breakthroughs, thereby driving the advancement of scientific frontiers in One Health; (ii) facilitating the establishment of One Health practice pilot projects and cooperating with local governments to establish One Health solutions, helping to design prototypes suitable for tailoring into local scenarios; (iii) building One Health educational curricula and professional training systems to cultivate One Health professionals. Overall, by pursuing these initiatives, we together can contribute to the advancement of scientific frontiers, the implementation of effective One Health solutions, and the development of a skilled workforce capable of addressing the complex health challenges we face today.

French Academy of Sciences   Yvon Le Maho
Paris, France

Academia Europaea
London, UK

French National Academy of Pharmacy
Paris, France

Norwegian Academy of Art and Letters
Strasbourg, France

Preface

The publication of the "Global One Health Index Report 2022" could not have come at a better time. As the world grapples with increasingly complex health challenges, ranging from zoonotic disease outbreaks to the spread of antimicrobial resistance, climate change-induced threats, and food insecurity, there is a palpable need for an integrative perspective. This publication aims to fill that gap, offering not just an understanding of these multifaceted issues but, more crucially, a transformative framework—the global One Health index (GOHI)—designed to address them holistically.

The pressing question remains: Why this book? The answer lies in the intersection of necessity and innovation. While the One Health concept, emphasizing the interrelation between human, animal, and environmental health, has gained traction globally, there remains a dearth of comprehensive tools and resources to operationalize it. This report aspires to be that seminal guide, elucidating the intricacies of the One Health approach, and offering actionable insights through the GOHI framework.

Intended for a broad spectrum of readers, this volume is not restricted to the ivory towers of academia. While it undoubtedly serves as an academic touchstone, the report is also tailored for policymakers, international health organizations' authorities, public health practitioners, and even grassroots community leaders. The goal is to arm these diverse stakeholders with knowledge and strategies, fostering a unified, global response to the multifarious health challenges we face.

The herculean task of compiling this report was undertaken by a consortium of luminaries. Spearheaded by the School of Global Health, Chinese Center for Tropical Diseases Research, Shanghai Jiao Tong University School of Medicine, the core team was composed of experts from a global coalition. Their multidisciplinary backgrounds and vast reservoirs of expertise echo through every chapter, from theoretical expositions to pragmatic case studies.

The creation of this report was truly a collaborative odyssey. The guidance and insights from international entities like the World Health Organization, the Food and Agriculture Organization of the United Nations, the World Organization for Animal Health, the World Bank, and the World Meteorological Organization were instrumental in shaping its content. These partnerships not only enriched the narrative but also ensured its global relevance.

In closing, heartfelt appreciation is extended to every individual and institution that contributed to this endeavor, to the dedicated research teams, international collaborators, meticulous reviewers, and all who offered their insights, wisdom, and time. Your unwavering commitment has birthed a seminal work that promises to redefine the contours of global One Health strategy for years to come.

Shanghai, China   Xiao-Nong Zhou
Shanghai, China   Xiaokui Guo
Shanghai, China   Xiaoxi Zhang

Statistical Team

Chief

Team Members

1. School of Global Health, Chinese Center for Tropical Diseases Research, Shanghai Jiao Tong University School of Medicine, Shanghai, People's Republic of China
2. Institute of One Health, Shanghai Jiao Tong University, Shanghai, People's Republic of China
3. National Institute of Parasitic Diseases at Chinese Center for Disease Control and Prevention (Chinese Center for Tropical Diseases Research), NHC Key Laboratory of Parasite and Vector Biology, WHO Collaborating Centre for Tropical Diseases, Shanghai, People's Republic of China
4. Walter and Eliza Hall Institute, Parkville, VIC, Australia
5. Department of Medical Biology, University of Melbourne, Melbourne, VIC, Australia

Acknowledgements

We extend our sincerest gratitude to Qian Ye, Liz Grant, Geoff Simm, Jürg Utzinger, Junxia Song, and the experts from Shanghai Jiao Tong University (Koguan School of Law), Shanxi Agricultural University, Sun Yat-Sen University (School of Public Health), China Agricultural University (College of Veterinary Medicine and College of Humanities and Development Studies), Lanzhou Veterinary Research Institute at the Chinese Academy of Agricultural Sciences, China Pharmaceutical University, National Institute of Parasitic Diseases at the Chinese Center for Diseases Control and Prevention (Chinese Center for Tropical Diseases Research), School of Life Science at Inner Mongolia University, Northeast Forestry University, Huazhong Agricultural University (College of Biomedicine and Health), Huazhong University of Science and Technology (School of Public Health, Tongji Medical College), South China Agricultural University (College of Veterinary Medicine), Jilin University, Kunming Medical University, Nanjing Agricultural University, Hainan University, Hainan Medical University, Hainan Tropical Diseases Research Center, the World Health Organization, the Food and Agriculture Organization of the United Nations, the World Bank, and the World Meteorological Organization for their valuable comments and suggestions.

This work was supported by the Bill & Melinda Gates Foundation (No. INV-046218), the National Natural Science Foundation of China (No. 72204160), and the China Medical Board (No. 20-365).

Contents

About the Editors[1]

Xiao-Nong Zhou is the Chief Scientist for parasitic diseases control at Chinese Center for Disease Control and Prevention (China CDC) and the Director of the World Health Organization (WHO) Collaborating Centre for Tropical Diseases. He also serves as Vice Dean of the School of Global Health, Chinese Center for Tropical Diseases Research, Shanghai Jiao Tong University School of Medicine, and as Director of the One Health Center, Shanghai Jiao Tong University-The University of Edinburgh. He serves as the Chairman of Global Health Society of Chinese Preventive Medicine Association, the Member of Quadripartite One Health High-Level Expert Panel, the Chair of One Health Working Group for the World Federation of Public Health Associations, as well as the founding Editor-in-Chief of *Infectious Diseases of Poverty*, the founding Editor-in-Chief of *Science in One Health*, and Editor-in-Chief of *Chinese Journal for Schistosomiasis Control*. Professor Zhou is a leading international expert in the research and control of tropical diseases, with over 40 years of experience in implementing One Health approaches to control tropical diseases. In particular, his research interests focus on the spatial epidemiology of parasitic diseases, leading to innovative strategies to support national control programs. With great efforts in implementation research, his contribution to the establishment of surveillance-response systems for parasitic diseases at national level has significantly promoted the elimination of parasitic diseases in China.

Xiaokui Guo is a Distinguished Professor at Shanghai Jiao Tong University, Deputy Director of the National Center for Tropical Disease Research, Director of the Global Center for Medical Education Research, and Director of the Biomedical Science Program. He also serves as the Chairman of the Medical Microbiology and Immunology Committee of the Chinese Society of Microbiology, Deputy Chairman of the Microecology and Health Committee of the China Medicine Education Association, and Secretary-General of the Chinese Consortium for One Health. He serves as the Editor-

---

[1]The authors are from the Global One Health Index (GOHI) research team. This team comprises more than 40 experts from the School of Global Health, Chinese Center for Tropical Diseases Research, Shanghai Jiao Tong University School of Medicine. Members of this team specialize in various One Health-related fields, such as epidemiology, antimicrobial resistance, governance and policy, environmental health, and others. The team has made significant contributions to the field of One Health through interdisciplinary research and advocacy for the integration of human, animal, and environmental health.

in-Chief of *Global Medical Education* and the Director of the Editorial Department of *Science in One Health*. The main focus of his scientific research is on microbiology and One Health. His team was the first one to complete the genomic sequence analysis of leptospires globally. They established a genomic-based probiotic safety evaluation technology service platform and promoted the first clinical practice in China on phage therapy for drug-resistant bacterial infections, following approval by institutional ethics committees. He has been awarded the National Outstanding Teacher, National-Level Teaching Master, and National Advanced Individual in Education and Scientific Research. He has also received the first prize of the National Textbook Award, a Special Award for National Education Research Achievement, and two first prizes and one second prize for national teaching achievements.

Xiaoxi Zhang is an Associate Research Professor at the School of Global Health, Chinese Center for Tropical Diseases Research, Shanghai Jiao Tong University School of Medicine. Xiaoxi holds a PhD in economics, MSc in global health, and a bachelor's degree in clinical medicine. Currently, she serves as the member of Global Health Governance Expert Working Group for the National Disease Control and Prevention Administration of China, the consultant on Health Nutrition & Population for the World Bank, the consultant for the World Health Organization Academy, and the secretary general for One Health Action Commission. She has strong research interests in global health governance and health policy research, with a specific focus on performance evaluation and decision-making simulation in One Health scenarios. She has publications in impactful academic journals including *The Lancet Regional Health*, *Infectious Diseases of Poverty*, *Nature* (correspondence letter), *One Health*, and *Global Health Research and Policy, etc*. Her work has been selected as one of the Top 100 China's Medical Science paper of 2022 by Chinese Medical Association. She hopes that her research could bring real-world impact to the system building of One Health.

In the last two decades, the globe has faced numerous significant public health crises triggered by zoonotic diseases. Notable instances include the severe acute respiratory syndrome (SARS) outbreak from 2002 to 2004, the Ebola virus epidemic in West Africa between 2013 and 2016, the spread of the Zika virus in the Americas from 2015 to 2016, and the COVID-19 pandemic starting in 2019. These events underscore the pressing need for a holistic, integrated approach to address these health threats. The global One Health index (GOHI) was introduced to meet this need, emphasizing a collaborative strategy across human, animal, and environmental health domains. The GOHI project aims to assess the application and development status of the One Health approach in over 160 countries/territories, intending to enhance its global implementation. The GOHI framework evaluates various aspects, including external, intrinsic, and core drivers of One Health development. Emphasizing a multidisciplinary collaboration, GOHI offers insights into the global performance of the One Health approach, highlighting areas for improvement. Its ultimate goal is to guide nations in adopting effective strategies, optimizing health practices, and formulating policies that encompass the intricate interplay between humans, animals, and the environment.

1 Why Is the Global One Health Index (GOHI) Needed?

Over the past 20 years, the emergence of zoonotic diseases has precipitated significant public health emergencies worldwide. Since the 1970s, these diseases have been responsible for more than three-quarters of all new and re-emerging infectious diseases, resulting in approximately 2.5 billion cases and 2.7 million fatalities annually [1]. As of late February 2022, the COVID-19 pandemic alone has led to around 440 million confirmed cases and nearly 6 million deaths [2]. Despite unprecedented access to advanced technology for managing, preventing, treating, and monitoring diseases, the threat posed by new and re-emerging zoonotic diseases persists. The COVID-19 crisis has particularly highlighted the critical challenges in early diagnosis, prevention, and control of epidemics, exacerbated by a lack of coordination among human, animal, and environmental health sectors [3, 4].

To tackle the intricate health challenges at the nexus of humans, animals, and the environment, a One Health approach has been advocated. This strategy emphasizes the need for interdisciplinary and cross-sectoral collaboration across borders. On December 1, 2021, the Food and Agriculture Organization of the United Nations (FAO), the World Organization for Animal Health

X.-N. Zhou et al. (eds.), *Global One Health Index Report 2022*,
https://doi.org/10.1007/978-981-97-4824-2_1

(WOAH), the World Health Organization (WHO), and the United Nations Environment Programme (UNEP) (the Quadripartite)'s One Health High-Level Expert Panel (OHHLEP) formally defined One Health as "an integrated, unifying approach that aims to sustainably balance and optimize the health of people, animals and ecosystems" [5].

In 2022, the Quadripartite developed the One Health Joint Plan of Action (2022–2026) (OH JPA) to respond to international requests to prevent future pandemics and to promote health sustainability through the One Health approach. Since the launch of the Quadripartite OH JPA, OHHLEP has been actively preparing an implementation guide to compact the planning schedule for activities and resources. It has been devoted to building up One Health community on global level and regional level.

Despite widespread recognition of the One Health approach, its key drivers and mechanisms for practical implementation remain ambiguous. A lack of empirical evidence has made it difficult to pinpoint deficiencies within the interconnected health of humans, animals, and the environment, obstructing the effective integration of One Health principles into policy and practice. There's a pressing need for a well-devised framework to enhance One Health practices.

Consequently, we are conducting the GOHI project, aiming to assess the progress and ability of 160 countries/territories in adopting One Health strategies. This initiative seeks to elevate the global execution of One Health concepts. Through disseminating exemplary One Health practices, we aspire to assist each country/territory in implementing robust actions to address identified shortcomings, thereby broadening the real-world application of One Health methodologies.

2 What Does GOHI Contribute?

GOHI represents a pioneering step toward an integrated, multifaceted approach to health, as defined by the core principles of One Health [6].

We devised a cell-like GOHI evaluation framework to identify the gaps in One Health policy and practice across various nations and territories. This novel tool stands as the first of its kind, offering a comprehensive evaluation of One Health from a global standpoint and employing empirical data for analysis. Primarily, GOHI reflects the current state of One Health's evolution, revealing challenges like uneven global progress, regional disparities, and governance issues, aligning with existing literature. Furthermore, GOHI serves as a guide for resource allocation and strategic planning, with its analytical capabilities suggesting its usefulness in forecasting intervention outcomes and health trends. Lastly, its adaptability and mixed-methods approach in assimilating both qualitative and quantitative data make it flexible for diverse scenarios across different countries.

The construction of GOHI unfolds in five stages: conceptualizing the framework, choosing indicators, creating a database, assigning weights, and calculating GOHI scores. Within its cell-like structure, a multitiered weighted indicator system was developed. To guarantee index accuracy, a GOHI expert advisory panel was formed to refine the framework. Through extensive expert consultations, recommendations were made on indicator selection, weight allocation, data analysis and interpretation strategies. After rounds of consultations, a robust indicator system was developed, encompassing three categories, 13 primary indicators, 50 secondary indicators, and 170 sub-indicators.

3 What Are the Key Findings of GOHI?

Globally, GOHI scores indicate significant potential for improvement. The average global GOHI score stands at 54.82, with the external drivers index (EDI), intrinsic drivers index (IDI), and core drivers index (CDI) showing averages of 46.57, 58.01, and 57.25, respectively. This reflects a substantial gap from the ideal scores, exceeding 40 points. Among the 160 countries analyzed, none achieved the top rank across all CDI dimensions.

GOHI scores reveal extensive variability, with marked differences across regions and individual countries. The scoring ranges for each region, from high to low, are North America (62.94–66.65), Europe and Central Asia (45.50–66.75), Latin America and the Caribbean (42.31–59.26), South Asia (41.00–55.33), Middle East and North Africa (38.61–55.39), East Asia and Pacific (38.34–64.04), and sub-Saharan Africa (36.53–52.05).

The scores of Governance (C1) (26.75–80.52), Zoonoses diseases (C2) (43.01–84.86), Food security (C3) (24.84–73.09) and Antimicrobial resistance (C4) (14.75–81.43) in different countries/territories span a wide range. Some data stands out including:

(i) In governance dimension (C1), the indicator of "Consensus-oriented" outperforms others, with a mere 9 (5.63%) of nations scoring below 30.00, which suggests a global propensity toward consensus in One Health governance, underscored by a collective readiness to enhance it;

(ii) Zoonotic diseases (C2) ranks as the most proficient among the CDI key indicators, spotlighting the global focus on managing zoonotic illnesses, the "Route of transmission" component exhibits the lowest efficiency (59.30), which reveals gaps in blocking zoonotic disease spread through transmission pathways;

(iii) "Government support and response" notably underperforms within the Food Security sector (C3), dragging its average to 52.89 with a score of 16.85, which underachievement highlights potential shortcomings in governmental actions toward food security from a One Health standpoint;

(iv) Antimicrobial resistance (C4) unveils global vulnerabilities in antimicrobial resistance (AMR) surveillance and management, particularly in two indicators: the AMR surveillance system and the antimicrobial resistance rate for critical antibiotics, with median scores of 32.61 and 31.62, respectively, which indicates a significant lag compared to the overall median of 43.09.

4   What Are the Policy Recommendations from GOHI?

Enhancing global collaboration among countries through the establishment of One Health networks or partnerships is essential. This includes strengthening ties between countries in the Global South and between those in the Global South and North, leveraging intradisciplinary, multisectoral, and interregional cooperation. To achieve this, there's a need to dismantle existing bottlenecks and construct a comprehensive One Health framework geared toward societal action. In this process, it has been always vital to place a greater focus on improving communication, coordination, collaboration, and capacity building in redefining both national development strategies and international cooperation efforts within the One Health context.

Fundamentally, the enhancement of the global data sharing framework for One Health is paramount. It is recommended that international entities collaborate with nations to foster greater transparency, accessibility, and integration of global One Health governance data. Establishing a cross-sectoral, high-level database, underpinned by extensive surveillance systems, is advocated to support this objective. Alongside advancing data sharing protocols, bridging the gaps in animal and environmental monitoring systems is essential for prompt identification and reaction to zoonotic disease outbreaks, natural disasters, and other urgent health crises. In the realm of technological advancement, there is a pressing need to enhance capabilities in laboratory diagnostics, epidemiological tracking, as well as in the monitoring and evaluation processes. National governments must bolster health worker training at the grassroots level and ensure the upkeep of laboratory equipment.

It has been beneficial to strategically promote the One Health concept by integrating the One Health approach into global governance and setting a high-level agenda with One Health. It is essential to engage as many stakeholders as possible, including international organizations, nongovernmental organizations (NGOs), civil society organizations (CSOs), the private sector, and academia, to ensure that the cooperation network can operate sustainably. At the current stage, intergovernment dialogue should be actively promoted to build long-term financing mechanisms, establish early global warning and response mechanisms, and prepare for the next pandemic with global partners.

Eventually, turning One Health research into actionable policies and practices across different levels necessitates sustained investment in funding, personnel, and infrastructure. It is critical to refine concrete implementation strategies, which include delineating government and stakeholder duties and crafting incentive mechanisms, all under a strategic overarching design. Utilizing insights from GOHI, nations can pinpoint their strengths and areas for improvement, fostering growth in their strong suits while formulating strategies to mitigate weaknesses, aiming for a balanced approach to global One Health governance.

The global One Health index (GOHI) is a comprehensive measure developed to assess the integrated approach to human, animal, and environmental health. The construction of GOHI involves five steps: (i) framework formulation, (ii) indicator selection, (iii) database building, (iv) weight determination, and (v) GOHI score calculation. To ensure its reliability, a GOHI expert advisory committee was established, drawing expertise from diverse fields such as human medicine, veterinary science, and environmental science. The foundational principles of GOHI are based on the interconnectedness of human, animal, and environmental health, the holistic perspective required to address global health challenges, and the promotion of coordinated development within these systems. The GOHI framework consists of three layers: external drivers index (EDI) assessing factors influencing One Health's evolution, intrinsic drivers index (IDI) evaluating practices across human, animal, and environmental interfaces, and core drivers index (CDI) measuring the management of key scientific areas, such as zoonotic diseases, antimicrobial resistance, food security, climate change, and governance, etc. Indicator selection was guided by expert consultations and literature reviews, ensuring they are relevant, accessible, and globally comparable. The fuzzy analytical hierarchy process (FAHP) was used to assign weights to the indicators, and scores were normalized using specific equations to derive the overall GOHI score. The GOHI serves as a pivotal tool for global health evaluation, promoting a more integrated approach to address health challenges.

GOHI is constructed in five steps, including (i) framework formulation; (ii) indicator selection; (iii) database building; (iv) weight determination; and (v) GOHI scores calculation (Fig. 2.1).

1 Expert Advisory Committee

The School of Global Health, Chinese Center for Tropical Diseases Research, Shanghai Jiao Tong University School of Medicine, maintains a database of cooperating partners with expertise in relevant research fields. We selected 29 experts from the expert database to construct the GOHI expert advisory committee by convenience sampling based on professional expertise, research relevance and willingness to participate (Table 2.1).

2 Conceptual Framework

In developing the index framework, we assumed three essential components of a One Health approach [6]. Our framework is founded upon a three-layer structure comprising external, intrinsic, and core layers, in accordance with the structure-process-outcome thinking [7]. The external layer of One Health should be an appropriate setting for One Health's development, the intrinsic layer of One Health should

X.-N. Zhou et al. (eds.), *Global One Health Index Report 2022*,
https://doi.org/10.1007/978-981-97-4824-2_2

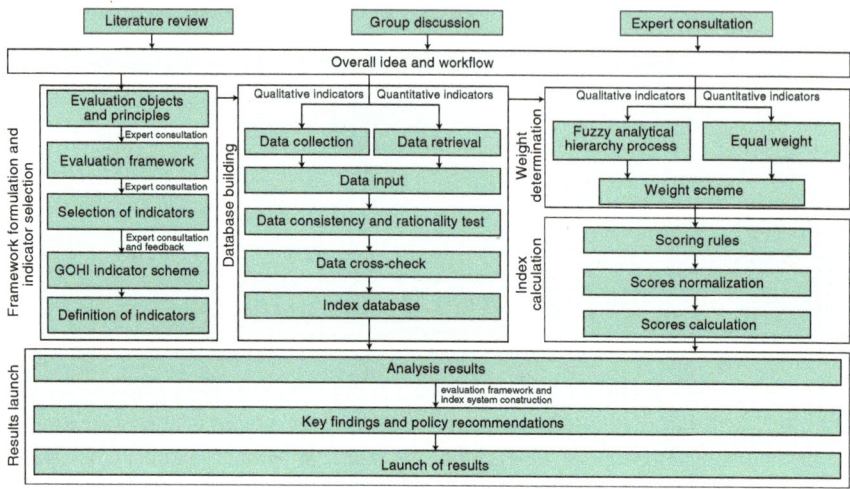

Fig. 2.1 Flowchart for the construction of the global One Health index (GOHI)

Table 2.1 Characteristics of the expert advisory committee assisting with the development of the global One Health index (GOHI) [n = 29][a]

Item	Category	Counts	Percentage (%)
Gender	Male	16	55.2
	Female	13	44.8
Age (years)	21–30	6	20.7
	31–40	12	41.4
	41–50	8	27.6
	>50	3	10.3
Education	Doctoral degree	20	69.0
	Master degree	9	31.0
	Bachelor degree	0	0.0
	College degree	0	0.0
	Other	0	0.0
Professional level	Senior level	10	34.5
	Vice-senior level	8	27.6
	Middle level	9	31.0
	Primary level	2	6.9
Type of work	Medical institutions	11	37.9
	Colleges and universities	15	51.7
	Governments	3	10.3
Working experience (in years)	<10 years	14	48.3
	10–20 years	8	27.6
	>20 years	7	24.1
Primary research area	Human medicine	12	41.4
	Veterinary science	7	24.1
	Environmental science	7	24.1
	Social science	1	3.4
	Political science	1	3.4
	Management science	1	3.4

Table 2.1 (continued)

Item	Category	Counts	Percentage (%)
Secondary research area	Human medicine	7	24.1
	Veterinary science	1	3.4
	Environmental science	1	3.4
	Social science	3	10.3
	Political science	3	10.3
	Management science	5	17.2

[a] The committee expansion is under way

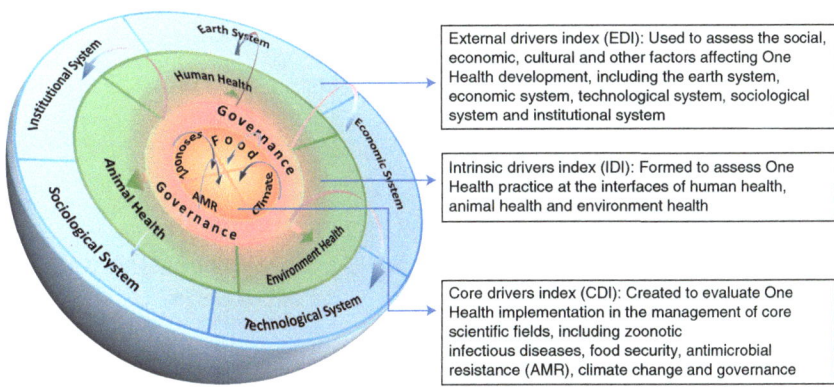

External drivers index (EDI): Used to assess the social, economic, cultural and other factors affecting One Health development, including the earth system, economic system, technological system, sociological system and institutional system

Intrinsic drivers index (IDI): Formed to assess One Health practice at the interfaces of human health, animal health and environment health

Core drivers index (CDI): Created to evaluate One Health implementation in the management of core scientific fields, including zoonotic infectious diseases, food security, antimicrobial resistance (AMR), climate change and governance

Fig. 2.2 Cell-like framework of the global One Health index (GOHI)

Table 2.2 Data selection criteria of the global One Health index (GOHI)

Principle	Criteria
Relevance	Data should represent the content of corresponding indicators
Authoritative sources	Data is retrieved from authoritative global/countries agencies
Open access	Data is available from public, open sources with transparent collection and statistical methods under comprehensive scrutiny
Completeness	Data used for indicators should cover a sufficient proportion of countries/territories
Timeliness	Data should cover a recent temporal period and be updated annually
Comparability	For single indicators, data should be measured with an established and unified method and peer-reviewed across countries/territories
Country-level data	Data should describe the status of indicators at the country-level

be the integrated development of human-animal-environmental systems, and the core layer should be the response to the challenges of key One Health issues.

Therefore, a cell-like framework of GOHI (Fig. 2.2) had been developed, which comprises the EDI, IDI and CDI. Our previous published work described the concept of three layers and the selection of the core scientific fields of the CDI. We also defined what the good One Health performance required to set the evaluation standard appropriately [6].

3 Indicator Selection

We carried out multiple rounds of expert consultation to provide suggestions on the selection of indicators, the determination of weights, and the strategies for data processing and interpretation. The indicators were selected according to the principles of relevance, authoritative sources, open access, completeness, timeliness, comparability, and country-level data availability (Table 2.2). In the four rounds of expert advisory committee consultations, we have determined the

Fig. 2.3 Indicator structure of the global One Health index (GOHI)

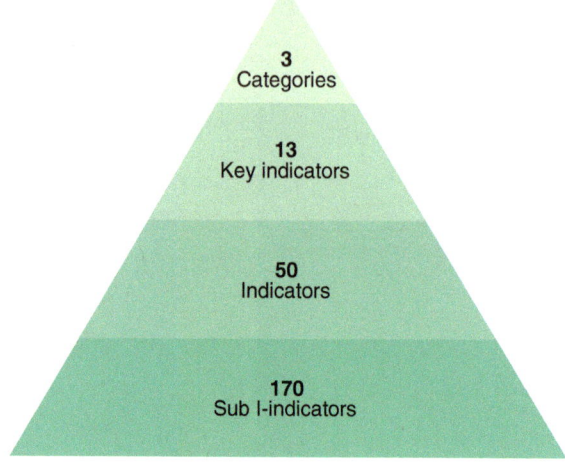

indicator scheme and its demonstration. The indicator system included 3 categories, 13 key indicators, 50 indicators and 170 sub I-indicators (Fig. 2.3).

4 Weight Determination

An FAHP [8] was adopted to assign the weights for most of the indicators. We conducted two rounds of investigations among our expert advisory committee to collect opinions by questionnaire on the relative importance between indicators. Table 2.3 shows the indicator and weight scheme of GOHI. The full details of the indicators and weights of GOHI are shown in the special reports.

5 Data Processing and Score Calculation

For missing data, we interpolated the missing value using the mean of the counterparts from three countries with the most similar conditions. For those indicators with values of 0 or 1, we generate random numbers in the specified interval to replace them to deal with the bias from over-polarization. We also deleted indicators and countries with high missing data rates in the calculation based on certain standards. Based on our explanation of One Health performance, the EDI, IDI and CDI scores were weighted and summed to obtain the final GOHI score. For details on the content above, see our previous published work [6].

Table 2.3 Indicator and weight scheme of the global One Health index (GOHI)

Category			Key indicator			Indicator		
Name	Code	Weight (%)	Name	Code	Weight (%)	Name	Code	Weight (%)
External drivers index (EDI)	A	15.2	Earth system	A1	20.0	Land	A1.1	19.0
						Forest	A1.2	18.0
						Water	A1.3	24.0
						Air	A1.4	23.0
						Natural disasters	A1.5	17.0
			Institutional system	A2	20.0	Justice	A2.1	46.0
						Governance	A2.2	54.0
			Economical system	A3	20.0	Finance	A3.1	38.0
						Work	A3.2	30.0
						Housing	A3.3	32.0
			Sociological system	A4	20.0	Demographic	A4.1	33.0
						Education	A4.2	38.0
						Inequalities	A4.3	29.0
			Technological system	A5	20.0	Transport	A5.1	31.0
						Technology adoption	A5.2	35.0
						Consumption and production	A5.3	34.0
Internal drivers index (IDI)	B	16.3	Human health	B1	33.3	Health coverage	B1.1	33.0
						Diseases burden	B1.2	33.0
						Injury and violence	B1.3	33.0
			Animal health and ecosystem diversity	B2	33.3	Animal epidemic disease	B2.1	50.0
						Wildlife and marine life biodiversity	B2.2	50.0
			Environmental health	B3	33.3	Air quality and climate change	B3.1	33.0
						Environmental biodiversity	B3.2	33.0
						Environmental resources	B3.3	33.0

(continued)

Table 2.3 (continued)

Category			Key indicator			Indicator		
Name	Code	Weight (%)	Name	Code	Weight (%)	Name	Code	Weight (%)
Core drivers index (CDI)	C	68.5	Governance	C1	21.7	Participation	C1.1	14.3
						Rule of law	C1.2	0.0
						Transparency	C1.3	14.3
						Responsiveness	C1.4	14.3
						Consensus oriented	C1.5	14.3
						Equity and inclusiveness	C1.6	14.3
						Effectiveness and efficiency	C1.7	14.3
						Political support	C1.8	14.3
			Zoonotic diseases	C2	20.4	Source of infection	C2.1	23.7
						Route of transmission	C2.2	25.3
						Targeted population	C2.3	19.1
						Capacity building	C2.4	16.8
						Outcomes (case-studies)	C2.5	15.1
			Food security	C3	21.4	Food demand and supply	C3.1	20.0
						Food safety	C3.2	20.0
						Nutrition	C3.3	20.0
						Natural and social circumstances	C3.4	20.0
						Government support and response	C3.5	20.0
			Antimicrobial resistance	C4	18.1	AMR surveillance system	C4.1	20.0
						AMR laboratory network and coordination capacity	C4.2	20.0
						Antimicrobial control and optimization	C4.3	20.0
						Improve awareness and understanding	C4.4	20.0
						AMR rate for important antibiotics	C4.5	20.0
			Climate change	C5	18.5	Climate change risks	C5.1	33.0
						Health outcome	C5.2	33.0
						Mitigation and adaptation capacity	C5.3	33.0

Note: Part of the indicators utilized for previous publications have been refined with updated data. For details see special reports

The global One Health index (GOHI) assesses One Health approaches across human, animal, and environmental sectors. Significant disparities in GOHI performance exist worldwide, with the United States achieving the highest score (70.61) and Guinea-Bissau the lowest (39.03). Overall, the global average score stands at 54.82, suggesting considerable room for improvement in One Health practice. Notably, income levels correlate with One Health performance, with high-income regions like North America, Europe, and East Asia achieving better scores than low-income regions such as sub-Saharan Africa. Despite variations, no country reached the optimal score in all indicators of core drivers index. The study further emphasizes the importance of international cooperation, especially between high- and low-income countries, to enhance One Health outcomes. The pandemic has highlighted the significance of global collaboration in tackling health crises. Moreover, there is an evident need to bolster data capacity at a global level, ensuring transparency and comprehensive data coverage, particularly in animal and environmental health sectors. Lastly, a more unified and consolidated governance structure for One Health is recommended, underscoring the urgency of translating One Health policies into actionable strategies across different levels of governance.

1 Main Results

1.1 Global Score

The GOHI analysis highlights notable variations across different countries and territories, with the United States achieving the highest score (70.61) and Guinea-Bissau the lowest (39.03), and a median score across all countries being 54.00. The analysis identifies a clear correlation between economic prosperity and One Health performance, with the top-scoring countries predominantly located in wealthier regions such as North America, Europe and Central Asia, and the East Asia and Pacific, contrasted by the lower scores found primarily in sub-Saharan Africa, a region with countries ranging from upper middle-income to low-income. This distribution underscores a global need for enhanced One Health governance capabilities, as the overall international performance falls short of optimal standards (Fig. 3.1).

The average GOHI score stands at 54.82, with component scores for the External Drivers Index (EDI, A), Intrinsic Drivers Index (IDI, B), and Core Drivers Index (CDI, C), alongside specific indicators such as Governance (C1), Zoonotic diseases (C2), Food Security (C3), Antimicrobial Resistance (C4), and Climate Change (C5)

X.-N. Zhou et al. (eds.), *Global One Health Index Report 2022*,
https://doi.org/10.1007/978-981-97-4824-2_3

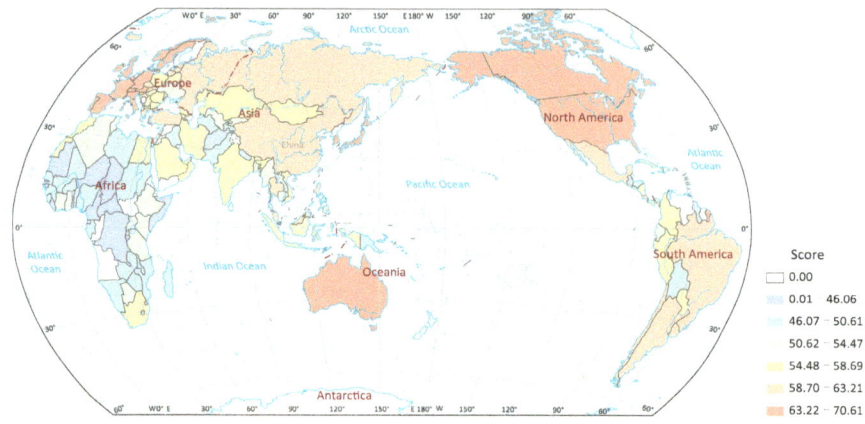

Fig. 3.1 Global score map of the global One Health index (GOHI)

Fig. 3.2 The global One Health index (GOHI) score distribution by category

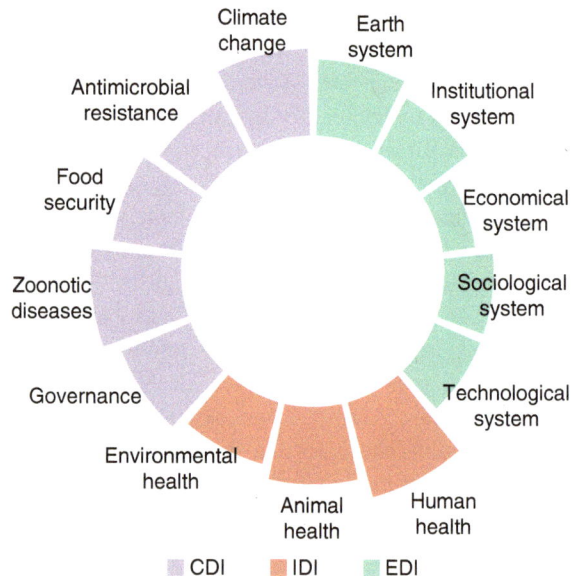

reflecting varied averages: 46.57, 58.01, 57.25, 56.51, 68.06, 52.89, 44.05, and 64.19, respectively (Fig. 3.2).

The distribution of scores across different components and regions reveals both strengths and areas for improvement. For instance, the median scores in various categories—EDI, IDI, and CDI—along with specific indicators such as Governance and Zoonotic diseases, display a broad range of outcomes, underscoring the diverse performance levels across the 160 countries evaluated.

Specifically, the regional distribution of GOHI scores, detailed in the analysis, highlights North America and Europe and Central Asia as regions with higher median scores, followed by East Asia and Pacific, and Latin America and the Caribbean, with sub-Saharan Africa ranking lowest (Fig. 3.3). This regional performance reflects in the average scores for each category, with North America often leading in aspects such as Governance, Zoonotic diseases, Food Security, and Antimicrobial resistance.

The regional average score is highest in North America (48.66) and lowest in South Asia (36.21). Similarly, for the regional average score of IDI, North America has the highest score (67.35) and sub-Saharan Africa has the lowest score (52.01). Among the average scores of Governance by region, North America (78.45),

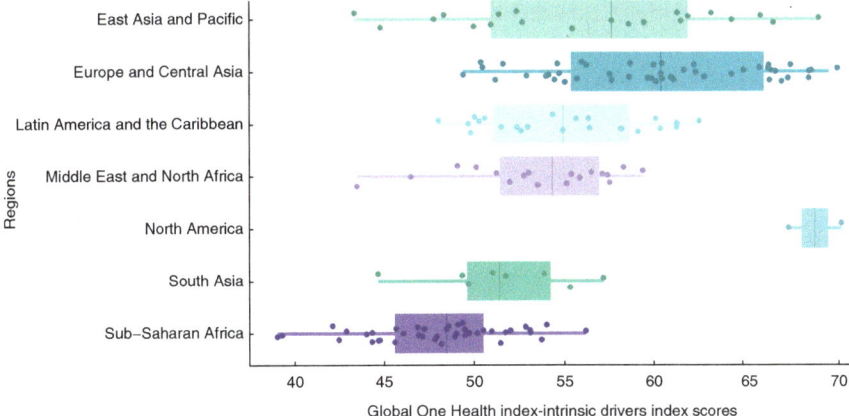

Fig. 3.3 Regional score distribution of the global One Health index (GOHI)

Fig. 3.4 Dimensional
score distribution of the
global One Health index
(GOHI)

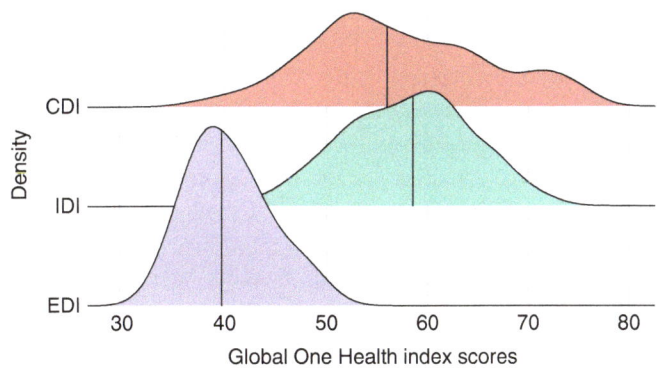

Europe and Central Asia (57.79) scored higher.
By their scores of Zoonotic diseases, North
America (82.76), Europe and Central Asia
(75.49) scored higher. For the average scores of
Food security by region, North America (69.97)
and Europe and Central Asia (59.71) score higher.
For Antimicrobial resistance, North America
(65.53) has the highest regional average score.
The median score of Climate change for 160
countries is 64.12. The average scores for coun-
tries in North America (72.40), Europe and
Central Asia (66.47) are higher than that in
Middle East and North Africa (58.57), and sub-
Saharan Africa (63.38).

In EDI, Earth system (A1) has the highest
average score (56.21) and the highest median
(56.29), while Economical system (A3) has the
lowest average score (24.62) and the lowest
median (24.64). In IDI, Human health (B1) has

the highest average score (72.35), in which
Diseases burden (B1.2), Animal epidemic disease
(B2.1), Air quality and climate change (B3.1) has
the highest average score in their corresponding
dimensions with 80.74, 94.57 and 53.72 respectively. In CDI, the highest median scores of the
indicators under the Governance is awarded to
Consensus oriented (C1.5, median: 94.58). For
Zoonotic diseases, the scores of Case studies
(C2.5) are the highest, with most distributed in
the 80.00–90.00 range. In Antimicrobial resistance, Laboratory network and coordination
capacity (C4.2, median: 54.37) has the highest
median score. For Climate change, Health outcome has the highest median score (C5.2, median:
85.40).

The components of GOHI scores from high to
low are as follows (sorted by median): IDI
(58.50), CDI (55.91), and EDI (39.72) (Fig. 3.4),

while the scores span from high to low are as follows: CDI (39.46), IDI (29.89), and EDI (17.45).

For the CDI and IDI, the distribution of scores
among countries/territories is relatively scattered,
indicating that there are large gaps in the scores
between countries/territories in the two key indicators (Fig. 3.4). Based on Shapiro-Wilk's normality test, IDI (B) ($P = 0.4854$) and Environment
Health ($P = 0.1621$) scores follow a normal
distribution.

1.2   Global Ranking

Table 3.1 presents a global ranking of the GOHI
index scores for 160 assessed countries/territo-
ries. Countries from North America, Europe and
Central Asia, East Asia and Pacific show higher
scores, while countries in sub-Saharan Africa,
Middle East and North Africa, East Asia and
Pacific, and South Asia have lower scores. The 16
top-performing countries for the total score of
GOHI are the United States, the United Kingdom,
Australia, Norway, Germany, France,
Switzerland, Canada, Sweden, Finland, the
Netherlands, Japan, Austria, Italy, Spain, and
Denmark. However, the bottom 16 mainly com-
prises sub-Saharan African countries, indicating
significant disparities in One Health ability
(Table 3.1).

Global Ranking in EDI
In the analysis of 160 countries/territories,
Table 3.2 highlights the top 25 countries. This
elite group includes 2 from North America
(Canada and the United States), 16 frontrunners
from Europe and Central Asia (constituting
10.00% of that region's total), 6 from East Asia
and Pacific, and a single representative, Uruguay,
from Latin America and the Caribbean. On the
opposite end, the lowest 25 countries, as presented in Table 3.2, feature 11 from sub-Saharan
Africa, 5 from the Middle East and North Africa,
and 5 from South Asia.

The three countries with lowest scores (Libya,
Iraq, and Kuwait) are all from the Middle East
and North Africa region.

Global Ranking in IDI
Of the 160 countries under evaluation, the top 25
countries are in Table 3.3. Among these, 11 are
countries from Europe and Central Asia (repre-
senting 6.88% of the region), 3 are from East
Asia and Pacific, 3 from Latin America and the
Caribbean, 3 countries from South Asia, 3 countries from the Middle East and North Africa, and
2 countries (the United States and Canada) from
North America.

Among the bottom 25 countries in the ranking, as shown in Table 3.3, 18 are from sub-
Saharan Africa. Also, the ten countries with the
lowest scores (Niger, Dem. Rep. Congo, Burundi,
Cameroon, the Central African Republic, Chad,
Somalia, Liberia, Namibia, and Lesotho) are all
from the sub-Saharan Africa.

Global Ranking in CDI
In the evaluation of 160 countries/territories, the
leading 25 are detailed in Table 3.4. Of these, 16
hail from Europe and Central Asia, accounting
for 10.00% of the region's representation, 7 originate from East Asia and Pacific, and 2 (the United
States and Canada) are from North America.
Conversely, the lower 25 countries, as depicted in
Table 3.4, comprise 16 from sub-Saharan Africa
and 4 from the East Asia and Pacific region. The
two nations with the lowest evaluations (Somalia
and Guinea-Bissau) are both situated in sub-
Saharan Africa.

1.3   Regional Performance

The scores and rankings of GOHI in the seven
territories are listed in Table 3.5. The average
total scores of the GOHI by region from high to
low are: North America (64.80), Europe and
Central Asia (56.19), East Asia and Pacific
(51.56), Latin America and the Caribbean
(49.81), Middle East and North Africa (48. 81),
South Asia (48.33), sub-Saharan Africa (42.98).

North America
The average score of the two countries included
in the report is 64.80. These two, highly devel-

Table 3.1 The global scores and ranking of the global One Health index (GOHI)

Global rank			Global rank			Global rank			Global rank		
Rank	Country	Score	Rank	Country	Score	Rank	Country	Score	Rank	Country	Score
1	United States	70.61	41	Estonia	59.99	81	Ukraine	53.99	121	Guyana	49.69
2	United Kingdom	69.90	42	Slovakia	59.88	82	Sri Lanka	53.88	122	Mali	49.49
3	Australia	69.30	43	Turkey	59.66	83	Ghana	53.73	123	Burkina Faso	49.49
4	Norway	68.89	44	Philippines	59.45	84	Jordan	53.53	124	Turkmenistan	49.42
5	Germany	68.75	45	Israel	59.38	85	Rwanda	53.11	125	Nepal	49.35
6	France	68.74	46	Uruguay	59.12	86	Cote d'Ivoire	53.10	126	Nigeria	49.35
7	Switzerland	67.70	47	Hungary	58.69	87	Lebanon	53.03	127	Zimbabwe	49.10
8	Canada	67.60	48	Belarus	58.63	88	Jamaica	52.99	128	Bahrain	49.09
9	Sweden	67.56	49	Indonesia	58.60	89	Kyrgyzstan	52.92	129	Gabon	49.03
10	Finland	67.21	50	Malta	58.32	90	Uganda	52.85	130	Namibia	48.93
11	Netherlands	66.86	51	Peru	58.24	91	Tunisia	52.75	131	Sudan	48.57
12	Japan	66.72	52	Colombia	58.16	92	Myanmar	52.68	132	Mozambique	48.46
13	Austria	66.61	53	Romania	57.65	93	El Salvador	52.62	133	Timor-Leste	48.33
14	Italy	66.52	54	Viet Nam	57.63	94	Dominican Republic	52.39	134	Seychelles	48.18
15	Spain	66.47	55	Qatar	57.52	95	Brunei Darussalam	52.37	135	Guatemala	48.03
16	Denmark	66.44	56	Poland	57.51	96	Ethiopia	52.01	136	Madagascar	47.92
17	Singapore	66.00	57	United Arab Emirates	57.42	97	Kuwait	51.98	137	Guinea	47.82
18	Belgium	65.95	58	India	57.17	98	Bangladesh	51.75	138	Papua New Guinea	47.77
19	Portugal	65.05	59	Oman	57.11	99	Bangladesh	51.73	139	Sierra Leone	47.23
20	Ireland	64.38	60	Saudi Arabia	56.49	100	Azerbaijan	51.61	140	Benin	47.12
21	South Korea	64.38	61	Panama	56.40	101	Belize	51.51	141	Malawi	46.92
22	China	63.21	62	Cuba	56.34	102	Botswana	51.46	142	Cabo Verde	46.87
23	Iceland	62.82	63	Armenia	56.22	103	Laos	51.38	143	Libya	46.49
24	Chile	62.53	64	South Africa	56.18	104	Algeria	51.24	144	Cameroon	46.06
25	Slovenia	62.32	65	Georgia	55.95	105	Uzbekistan	51.19	145	Togo	45.66
26	Czech Republic	62.22	66	Iran	55.84	106	Maldives	51.03	146	Liberia	45.59
27	Malaysia	61.89	67	Kazakhstan	55.70	107	Tanzania	50.96	147	Vanuatu	44.81
28	Greece	61.66	68	Nicaragua	55.66	108	Cambodia	50.94	148	Niger	44.77
29	Thailand	61.49	69	Mongolia	55.44	109	Honduras	50.61	149	Equatorial Guinea	44.69
30	New Zealand	61.29	70	Morocco	55.38	110	Eswatini	50.51	150	Afghanistan	44.67
31	Argentina	61.27	71	Bhutan	55.31	111	Montenegro	50.49	151	Lesotho	44.34

(continued)

Table 3.1 (continued)

Global rank			Global rank			Global rank		
Rank	Country	Score	Rank	Country	Score	Rank	Country	Score
32	Brazil	61.26	**72**	Egypt	55.12	**112**	Tajikistan	50.39	**152**	Burundi	44.33
33	Latvia	61.09	**73**	Serbia	55.03	**113**	Bolivia	50.28	**153**	Dem. Rep. Congo	44.02
34	Lithuania	60.95	**74**	Paraguay	54.93	**114**	Senegal	50.17	**154**	Djibouti	43.49
35	Cyprus	60.47	**75**	North Macedonia	54.72	**115**	Iraq	50.13	**155**	Solomon Islands	43.34
36	Russia	60.44	**76**	Bulgaria	54.62	**116**	Trinidad and Tobago	50.04	**156**	Chad	42.88
37	Luxembourg	60.39	**77**	Moldova	54.47	**117**	Fiji	49.99	**157**	Mauritania	42.46
38	Mexico	60.36	**78**	Ecuador	54.36	**118**	Barbados	49.83	**158**	Central African Republic	42.10
39	Costa Rica	60.12	**79**	Albania	54.14	**119**	Zambia	49.73	**159**	Somalia	39.29
40	Croatia	60.12	**80**	Kenya	54.01	**120**	Pakistan	49.70	**160**	Guinea-Bissau	39.03

Table 3.2 The global score and ranking of the global One Health index (GOHI) in EDI

Global rank			Global rank			Global rank			Global rank		
Rank	Country	Score	Rank	Country	Score	Rank	Country	Score	Rank	Country	Score
1	Finland	50.28	41	Brazil	42.71	81	Cote d'Ivoire	39.66	121	Uganda	37.58
2	Sweden	49.53	42	Mongolia	42.63	82	Zambia	39.49	122	Egypt	37.51
3	Canada	49.50	43	Czech Republic	42.61	83	Seychelles	39.44	123	Guinea-Bissau	37.50
4	Denmark	49.44	44	Guyana	42.51	84	Belize	39.39	124	Madagascar	37.42
5	Switzerland	48.75	45	Mauritius	42.32	85	Trinidad and Tobago	39.37	125	Kenya	37.35
6	Australia	48.64	46	Gabon	42.26	86	Timor-Leste	39.37	126	Saudi Arabia	37.23
7	Norway	48.13	47	Peru	42.07	87	Brunei Darussalam	39.36	127	Tanzania	37.20
8	Iceland	47.92	48	Kazakhstan	42.00	88	Sri Lanka	39.27	128	Mozambique	37.17
9	New Zealand	47.86	49	Thailand	41.97	89	Maldives	39.17	129	Honduras	37.15
10	United States	47.82	50	Bhutan	41.93	90	Myanmar	39.15	130	Ethiopia	37.08
11	Singapore	47.71	51	Georgia	41.89	91	South Africa	39.04	131	Liberia	37.03
12	Estonia	47.51	52	Colombia	41.85	92	Moldova	39.01	132	Eswatini	37.02
13	South Korea	47.35	53	Panama	41.83	93	Ukraine	38.97	133	Senegal	36.98
14	Germany	47.13	54	Montenegro	41.81	94	Jordan	38.97	134	Uzbekistan	36.90
15	Ireland	46.91	55	Fiji	41.81	95	Solomon Islands	38.92	135	Lebanon	36.86
16	Japan	46.38	56	Jamaica	41.73	96	Rwanda	38.79	136	Kyrgyzstan	36.70
17	Spain	46.14	57	Cyprus	41.67	97	Namibia	38.77	137	India	36.60
18	Netherlands	46.09	58	Paraguay	41.67	98	Serbia	38.74	138	Dem. Rep. Congo	36.46
19	Lithuania	46.03	59	Romania	41.66	99	Papua New Guinea	38.65	139	Tajikistan	36.45
20	Austria	45.66	60	Israel	41.64	100	North Macedonia	38.58	140	Cameroon	36.44
21	France	45.48	61	Hungary	41.52	101	Armenia	38.57	141	Zimbabwe	36.17
22	United Kingdom	45.45	62	Slovakia	41.46	102	Qatar	38.52	142	Cambodia	36.10
23	Malaysia	45.29	63	Viet Nam	41.40	103	Guatemala	38.52	143	Mali	36.08
24	Uruguay	44.98	64	China	41.31	104	El Salvador	38.50	144	Sudan	35.87
25	Belgium	44.93	65	Botswana	41.30	105	Nigeria	38.50	145	Sudan	35.83
26	Russia	44.64	66	Mexico	41.27	106	Central African Republic	38.48	146	Nepal	35.82
27	Portugal	44.56	67	Barbados	41.09	107	Nicaragua	38.25	147	Niger	35.54
28	Latvia	44.30	68	Vanuatu	40.92	108	Azerbaijan	38.10	148	Mauritania	35.27

(continued)

Table 3.2 (continued)

Global rank			Global rank			Global rank			Global rank		
Rank	Country	Score	Rank	Country	Score	Rank	Country	Score	Rank	Country	Score
29	Luxembourg	44.01	69	Belarus	40.79	109	Bolivia	38.06	149	Bahrain	35.14
30	Argentina	43.98	70	Croatia	40.78	110	Sierra Leone	37.93	150	Chad	35.09
31	United Arab Emirates	43.75	71	Cuba	40.54	111	Iran	37.91	151	Pakistan	34.82
32	Chile	43.67	72	Dominican Republic	40.50	112	Benin	37.88	152	Somalia	34.67
33	Malta	43.40	73	Ghana	40.41	113	Oman	37.81	153	Djibouti	34.64
34	Indonesia	43.33	74	Tunisia	40.31	114	Burkina Faso	37.77	154	Bangladesh	34.45
35	Costa Rica	43.32	75	Laos	40.24	115	Cabo Verde	37.77	155	Turkmenistan	34.18
36	Italy	43.26	76	Turkey	40.22	116	Togo	37.76	156	Burundi	34.17
37	Bulgaria	43.19	77	Morocco	40.15	117	Equatorial Guinea	37.76	157	Afghanistan	34.04
38	Poland	43.15	78	Albania	40.10	118	Algeria	37.75	158	Libya	34.00
39	Slovenia	43.13	79	Philippines	39.98	119	Malawi	37.73	159	Iraq	33.97
40	Greece	42.72	80	Ecuador	39.78	120	Guinea	37.64	160	Kuwait	32.83

Table 3.3 The global scores and ranking of the global One Health index (GOHI) in IDI

Global rank			Global rank			Global rank			Global rank		
Rank	Country	Score	Rank	Country	Score	Rank	Country	Score	Rank	Country	Score
1	France	71.88	41	Ireland	62.06	81	Morocco	58.47	121	Pakistan	53.34
2	Oman	70.98	42	Belize	61.96	82	Finland	58.35	122	Ethiopia	53.11
3	Switzerland	70.58	43	Viet Nam	61.93	83	Moldova	58.16	123	Latvia	53.08
4	United Kingdom	70.55	44	Albania	61.86	84	Mongolia	58.12	124	Bolivia	52.87
5	Austria	68.82	45	Sweden	61.80	85	North Macedonia	57.91	125	Paraguay	52.66
6	India	68.55	46	Slovakia	61.59	86	Denmark	57.84	126	Serbia	52.60
7	Australia	68.21	47	Germany	61.54	87	Honduras	57.69	127	Botswana	52.57
8	Cyprus	67.49	48	Belarus	61.47	88	Hungary	57.52	128	Poland	52.47
9	United States of America	67.40	49	Djibouti	61.41	89	Kenya	57.50	129	Guinea	52.47
10	Iceland	67.35	50	Tajikistan	61.40	90	Eswatini	57.40	130	Guyana	52.37
11	Canada	67.30	51	Ghana	61.38	91	Trinidad and Tobago	57.27	131	Montenegro	52.31
12	Italy	67.06	52	Kazakhstan	61.16	92	Brazil	56.89	132	Mauritania	52.01
13	Bahrain	66.93	53	Jamaica	61.15	93	Azerbaijan	56.88	133	Mozambique	51.89
14	Sri Lanka	66.90	54	Egypt	61.15	94	Thailand	56.79	134	Togo	51.76
15	Panama	66.62	55	United Arab Emirates	61.12	95	Vanuatu	56.56	135	Ukraine	51.70
16	Czech Republic	66.53	56	Saudi Arabia	61.12	96	Uzbekistan	56.36	136	Libya	51.60
17	Nicaragua	66.53	57	Kyrgyzstan	61.11	97	Iraq	56.27	137	Georgia	51.27
18	Luxembourg	66.22	58	Turkey	61.09	98	Senegal	56.14	138	South Africa	51.08
19	Costa Rica	65.89	59	Spain	60.92	99	Dominican Republic	56.11	139	Mali	51.05
20	Singapore	65.79	60	Armenia	60.72	100	China	56.02	140	Bangladesh	50.56
21	Belgium	65.60	61	Israel	60.71	101	Timor-Leste	55.77	141	Nigeria	50.36
22	Qatar	65.03	62	Cuba	60.64	102	Lithuania	55.76	142	Cambodia	50.33
23	Maldives	64.90	63	Seychelles	60.48	103	Tanzania	55.76	143	Afghanistan	50.32
24	Portugal	64.81	64	Barbados	60.21	104	Uganda	55.66	144	Zimbabwe	49.50
25	Japan	64.66	65	Bulgaria	59.93	105	El Salvador	55.46	145	Guinea-Bissau	49.12
26	Croatia	64.50	66	Kuwait	59.93	106	Malaysia	55.39	146	Benin	48.94
27	Slovenia	64.44	67	Malta	59.69	107	Nepal	55.36	147	Myanmar	48.89
28	Lebanon	64.21	68	Jordan	59.50	108	Sudan	55.31	148	Malawi	48.57

(continued)

Table 3.3 (continued)

Global rank			Global rank			Global rank			Global rank		
Rank	Country	Score	Rank	Country	Score	Rank	Country	Score	Rank	Country	Score
29	Chile	64.19	69	Papua New Guinea	59.43	109	Rwanda	54.93	149	Burkina Faso	48.41
30	New Zealand	63.83	70	Russia	59.19	110	Fiji	54.52	150	Indonesia	48.40
31	Uruguay	63.82	71	Guatemala	59.14	111	Equatorial Guinea	54.37	151	Niger	48.35
32	Brunei Darussalam	63.63	72	Argentina	59.02	112	Iran	54.24	152	Dem. Rep. Congo	48.33
33	Mexico	62.69	73	Philippines	59.00	113	Turkmenistan	54.20	153	Burundi	48.32
34	Norway	62.62	74	South Korea	58.96	114	Gabon	54.13	154	Cameroon	46.67
35	Ecuador	62.58	75	Romania	58.84	115	Greece	54.09	155	Central African Republic	46.33
36	Solomon Islands	62.43	76	Algeria	58.81	116	Netherlands	53.97	156	Chad	46.27
37	Cabo Verde	62.40	77	Estonia	58.73	117	Cote d'Ivoire	53.84	157	Somalia	45.78
38	Tunisia	62.32	78	Mauritius	58.68	118	Laos	53.74	158	Liberia	44.96
39	Peru	62.24	79	Sierra Leone	58.58	119	Zambia	53.61	159	Namibia	44.76
40	Bhutan	62.07	80	Colombia	58.52	120	Madagascar	53.59	160	Lesotho	41.99

Table 3.4 The global and ranking of the global One Health index (GOHI) in CDI

Global rank			Global rank			Global rank			Global rank		
Rank	Country	Score	Rank	Country	Score	Rank	Country	Score	Rank	Country	Score
1	United States of America	76.44	41	Croatia	63.37	81	Cote d'Ivoire	55.91	121	Zambia	51.08
2	Germany	75.26	42	Estonia	63.06	82	Bangladesh	55.88	122	Nepal	50.93
3	United Kingdom	75.18	43	Israel	63.01	83	Rwanda	55.87	123	Tajikistan	50.87
4	Norway	74.99	44	Cyprus	62.98	84	Ecuador	55.64	124	Fiji	50.73
5	Netherlands	74.54	45	Hungary	62.78	85	Uganda	55.58	125	Trinidad and Tobago	50.70
6	Australia	74.15	46	Luxembourg	62.65	86	Albania	55.44	126	Guyana	50.65
7	France	73.17	47	Costa Rica	62.49	87	Jordan	55.34	127	Maldives	50.38
8	Finland	73.08	48	Belarus	61.93	88	El Salvador	55.09	128	Mozambique	50.16
9	Sweden	72.94	49	Poland	61.89	89	Ethiopia	55.07	129	Sudan	49.79
10	Spain	72.31	50	Colombia	61.70	90	Ghana	54.88	130	Gabon	49.33
11	Denmark	72.26	51	Malta	61.30	91	Kyrgyzstan	54.58	131	Barbados	49.31
12	Japan	71.73	52	South Africa	61.20	92	Cambodia	54.39	132	Guinea	48.98
13	Canada	71.69	53	Uruguay	61.14	93	Kuwait	54.35	133	Madagascar	48.91
14	Italy	71.56	54	Romania	60.91	94	Dominican Republic	54.15	134	Benin	48.74
15	Switzerland	71.22	55	Peru	60.88	95	Sri Lanka	54.04	135	Malawi	48.57
16	Austria	70.75	56	Viet Nam	60.22	96	Lebanon	53.98	136	Timor-Leste	48.55
17	Belgium	70.71	57	Iran	60.21	97	Jamaica	53.56	137	Cameroon	48.05
18	Singapore	70.11	58	Georgia	60.18	98	Botswana	53.45	138	Libya	48.05
19	China	69.79	59	Qatar	59.97	99	Azerbaijan	53.36	139	Bahrain	47.96
20	Portugal	69.67	60	Saudi Arabia	59.67	100	Laos	53.30	140	Liberia	47.64
21	South Korea	69.45	61	United Arab Emirates	59.58	101	Tunisia	53.24	141	Guatemala	47.51
22	Ireland	68.82	62	Serbia	59.23	102	Uzbekistan	53.14	142	Seychelles	47.20
23	Greece	67.66	63	Armenia	59.08	103	Tanzania	52.88	143	Papua New Guinea	47.03
24	Malaysia	67.12	64	India	59.04	104	Brunei Darussalam	52.59	144	Lesotho	46.80
25	Thailand	66.95	65	Cuba	58.83	105	Algeria	52.44	145	Sierra Leone	46.60
26	Latvia	66.72	66	Paraguay	58.42	106	Bolivia	52.38	146	Niger	45.97
27	Brazil	66.42	67	Oman	58.11	107	Burkina Faso	52.35	147	Togo	45.97
28	Chile	66.32	68	Morocco	58.03	108	Iraq	52.26	148	Afghanistan	45.70
29	Slovenia	66.08	69	Ukraine	57.87	109	Mauritius	52.18	149	Burundi	45.65

(continued)

Table 3.4 (continued)

Global rank			Global rank			Global rank			Global rank		
Rank	Country	Score	Rank	Country	Score	Rank	Country	Score	Rank	Country	Score
30	Argentina	65.65	70	Mongolia	57.65	110	Namibia	52.18	150	Cabo Verde	45.21
31	Czech Republic	65.56	71	Egypt	57.61	111	Pakistan	52.15	151	Dem. Rep. Congo	44.68
32	Lithuania	65.49	72	North Macedonia	57.54	112	Mali	52.11	152	Equatorial Guinea	43.94
33	Iceland	65.06	73	Kazakhstan	57.45	113	Montenegro	51.99	153	Chad	43.80
34	Indonesia	64.42	74	Panama	57.21	114	Honduras	51.92	154	Vanuatu	42.88
35	Russia	64.25	75	Moldova	57.03	115	Zimbabwe	51.88	155	Central African Republic	41.90
36	Mexico	64.05	76	Nicaragua	56.95	116	Eswatini	51.87	156	Mauritania	41.79
37	Philippines	63.89	77	Kenya	56.88	117	Belize	51.73	157	Djibouti	41.21
38	New Zealand	63.68	78	Bhutan	56.68	118	Senegal	51.69	158	Solomon Islands	39.79
39	Turkey	63.65	79	Myanmar	56.58	119	Turkmenistan	51.67	159	Somalia	38.78
40	Slovakia	63.56	80	Bulgaria	55.91	120	Nigeria	51.53	160	Guinea-Bissau	36.98

Table 3.5 Regional rankings of the global One Health index (GOHI)

East Asia and Pacific

Rank	Country	Score
1	Australia	64.04
2	Thailand	61.01
3	Japan	60.93
4	Singapore	60.29
5	China	58.00
6	South Korea	58.90
7	Malaysia	57.10
8	New Zealand	57.68
9	Indonesia	55.29
10	Philippines	54.46
11	Mongolia	51.30
12	Myanmar	50.61
13	Viet Nam	50.55
14	Cambodia	48.85
15	Fiji	47.53
16	Laos	45.49
17	Timor-Leste	44.25
18	Papua New Guinea	42.54
19	Samoa	42.31
20	Tonga	42.98
21	Vanuatu	41.83
22	Solomon Islands	38.34

Middle East and North Africa

Rank	Country	Score
1	Israel	55.39
2	Malta	53.66
3	Egypt	52.52
4	Iran	52.48
5	United Arab Emirates	52.38
6	Morocco	52.26
7	Saudi Arabia	51.76
8	Qatar	51.26
9	Jordan	50.74
10	Oman	50.19
11	Tunisia	49.17
12	Lebanon	48.77
13	Iraq	48.66
14	Kuwait	46.97
15	Bahrain	44.95
16	Algeria	44.68
17	Libya	44.28
18	Yemen	38.75
19	Djibouti	38.61

Table 3.5 (continued)

Europe and Central Asia

Rank	Country	Score
1	Finland	66.75
2	Germany	66.40
3	Sweden	65.72
4	Netherlands	65.35
5	Norway	65.17
6	France	64.85
7	Spain	64.62
8	Denmark	63.57
9	United Kingdom	63.35
10	Belgium	62.51
11	Austria	61.55
12	Switzerland	60.81
13	Ireland	60.53
14	Italy	60.10
15	Portugal	59.76
16	Slovenia	59.54
17	Latvia	58.62
18	Greece	58.54
19	Lithuania	57.98
20	Czech Republic	57.83
21	Slovakia	56.90
22	Iceland	56.10
23	Estonia	56.07
24	Hungary	55.90
25	Cyprus	55.34
26	Russia	55.10
27	Turkey	54.93
28	Romania	54.29
29	Belarus	53.71
30	Luxembourg	53.48
31	Poland	53.39
32	Serbia	53.14
33	Bulgaria	53.00
34	Croatia	52.39
35	Georgia	52.29
36	Ukraine	52.15
37	North Macedonia	51.53
38	Albania	50.12
39	Moldova	49.93
40	Kazakhstan	49.80
41	Armenia	49.78
42	Azerbaijan	49.53
43	Uzbekistan	48.68
44	Montenegro	48.44
45	Kyrgyzstan	48.39
46	Bosnia and Herzegovina	47.07
47	Turkmenistan	46.70
48	Tajikistan	45.50

(continued)

Table 3.5 (continued)

Sub-Saharan Africa

Rank	Country	Score
1	South Africa	52.05
2	Cote d'Ivoire	47.98
3	Burkina Faso	47.85
4	Uganda	47.74
5	Ghana	47.72
6	Mauritius	47.33
7	Ethiopia	47.17
8	Kenya	47.16
9	Rwanda	46.84
10	Botswana	46.21
11	Nigeria	45.81
12	Sudan	45.73
13	Senegal	45.57
14	Tanzania	45.45
15	Zimbabwe	45.39
16	Eswatini	45.22
17	Mali	44.40
18	Malawi	44.40
19	Zambia	44.21
20	Cabo Verde	44.21
21	Seychelles	44.07
22	Namibia	43.69
23	Gabon	43.51
24	Mozambique	42.54
25	Madagascar	42.49
26	Benin	41.91
27	Guinea	41.67
28	Sierra Leone	41.52
29	Togo	41.45
30	Liberia	41.26
31	Burundi	41.22
32	Niger	40.84
33	Cameroon	40.64
34	Lesotho	40.41
35	Angola	40.01
36	Eritrea	39.90
37	Mauritania	39.88
38	Comoros	39.17
39	Sao Tome and Principe	38.94
40	Gambia	38.69
41	Equatorial Guinea	38.54
42	Guinea-Bissau	38.43
43	Chad	37.46
44	Somalia	37.04
45	Central African Republic	36.87
46	South Sudan	36.53

Table 3.5 (continued)

South Asia

Rank	Country	Score
1	India	55.33
2	Bangladesh	51.24
3	Bhutan	50.26
4	Sri Lanka	48.37
5	Pakistan	47.48
6	Maldives	46.48
7	Nepal	46.44
8	Afghanistan	41.00

Latin America and the Caribbean

Rank	Country	Score
1	Brazil	59.26
2	Chile	58.67
3	Mexico	57.27
4	Argentina	56.95
5	Peru	55.58
6	Colombia	55.12
7	Costa Rica	53.13
8	Cuba	52.86
9	Paraguay	52.56
10	Uruguay	52.45
11	El Salvador	52.29
12	Nicaragua	51.70
13	Panama	50.44
14	Jamaica	49.60
15	Ecuador	49.46
16	Dominican Republic	48.80
17	Honduras	46.40
18	Trinidad and Tobago	46.15
19	Suriname	45.91
20	Guyana	45.90
21	Belize	45.13
22	Bolivia	45.07
23	Guatemala	44.97
24	Saint Lucia	44.77
25	Barbados	44.45
26	Venezuela	43.90
27	Bahamas	43.60
28	Haiti	42.31

North America

Rank	Country	Score
1	United States of America	66.65
2	Canada	62.94

oped countries (the United States and Canada), which both earn high scores for Food security, top the global ranking and perform well in the five sub-indicators. The United States ranks 1st with a score of 70.61, 1st with 76.44 points, and 2nd with a score of 72.34, in the global rankings of GOHI, CDI, and Food security respectively. Canada, another top performer, places 3rd with 67.6 points in GOHI, and scores 67.61, ranked 9th in the Food security. Despite its strong performance, the United States can still improve its capacity of EDI, in which it ranks 10th with a score of 47.82.

Europe and Central Asia

The average score of 48 countries included in the report is 56.19. Five of the best-performing countries in the region are Finland, Germany, Sweden, Netherlands, and Norway, with a score range of 65.17–66.75. Finland earns the highest score in EDI with a score of 50.28. Italy ranks 3rd, 5th, and 8th, in the global rankings of Food security, Climate change, and Zoonotic diseases, respectively.

Latin America and the Caribbean

The 28 countries included in this discussion have an average score of 49.81. The top five performers are Brazil, Chile, Mexico, Argentina, and Peru, with scores ranging from 55.58 to 59.26. Brazil ranks first in this region with a score of 65.01 and ranks 16th in the global ranking of Food security.

East Asia and Pacific

The 22 countries included from East Asia and Pacific have an average score of 51.56. Within the region, the top five are Australia, Thailand, Japan, Singapore, and China, with scores ranging from 58.00 to 64.04. Australia ranks first in this region with a score of 73.08 and ranks first in the global ranking of Food security.

Middle East and North Africa

The average score of 19 countries included in the report is 48.81. In this region, the top five coun-tries are Israel, Malta, Egypt, Iran, and the United Arab Emirates, whose scores range is 52.38–55.39. The best-performing country in this region is Israel with a score of 66.59, which places it 35th in the global ranking of Governance.

South Asia

There are 8 countries in the South Asian region, with an average score of 48.33. The top five are India, Bangladesh, Bhutan, Sri Lanka, and Pakistan, with scores ranging from 47.48 to 55.33. India ranks first in the region with a score of 68.55 and ranks 6th in the IDI.

Sub-Saharan Africa

Of the 46 countries included in the report from this region, the average score is 42.98. The top five are South Africa, Cote d'Ivoire, Burkina Faso, Uganda, and Ghana, whose scores range is 47.72–52.05. South Africa ranks first in this region with a score of 60.15 and ranks 47th in Food security.

2 Key Findings

2.1 Room for Improvement in the GOHI Scores

Overall, there is potential for enhancement in the GOHI scores worldwide. The worldwide average for the GOHI stands at 54.82, with the average scores for the EDI, IDI, and CDI recorded at 46.57, 58.01, and 57.25, respectively. This high-lights a discrepancy exceeding 40 points from the ideal, as depicted in Fig. 3.3. Within the scope of the 160 nations evaluated in this analysis, not a single one achieves a leading position across all principal CDI indicators.

Even with the United States ranking first (with a total score of 70.61), it is still 30 points away from the optimal state; Guinea-Bissau ranks 160th (with a total score of 39.03), which is 31.58 points lower than the top country (Table 3.1). The average scores of five key indicators in CDI are all below the 70.00.

2.2 Regional Disparities in GOHI Scores

The global scores of GOHI are highly disparate, with considerable variations among different regions. The scoring range of each region, from high to low are: North America (62.94–66.65), Europe and Central Asia (45.50–66.75), Latin America and the Caribbean (42.31–59.26), South Asia (41.00–55.33), Middle East and North Africa (38.61–55.39), East Asia and Pacific (38.34–64.04), and sub-Saharan Africa (36.53–52.05) (Table 3.5).

The range of scores for each country/territory varies from 39.03 to 70.61. Specifically, the scores for EDI (A) range between 32.83 and 50.28, for Governance between 26.75 and 80.52, for Zoonotic diseases between 43.01 and 84.86, for Food security between 24.84 and 73.09, and for Antimicrobial resistance between 14.75 and 81.43, demonstrating a broad spectrum across different countries/territories. Sub-Saharan Africa, in particular, ranks lowest in terms of Governance and Food security, underscoring significant challenges in One Health governance and food security within this region.

3 Policy Suggestions

3.1 Strengthening International Cooperation and Regional Coordination on One Health

Improving international cooperation between high-income and low-income countries and strengthening the regional coordination mechanism for One Health is urgent and essential issue. The lessons learned from COVID-19 remind us that in an interconnected world, no country can survive a global health crisis alone without international cooperation and coordination. Variations of international/regional performance on One Health are apparent.

According to our key findings, low-income countries generally ranked low in the control of zoonotic sources of infection, while high-income countries performed better. It was recommended that high-income and upper-middle-income countries cooperate with low-income and lower-

middle-income countries in relation to the prevention and control of Zoonotic diseases. In addition, it was notable that the spread of zoonoses respected no national boundaries, and collaboration and exchange among countries in the same region can improve the efficiency of prevention and control.

Data capacity is a strong predictor of cooperation/coordination performance.

3.2 Improving the Data Capacity of One Health at the Global Level

Our investigation reveals a general lack of effort toward data transparency among countries, highlighted by numerous essential global One Health governance indicators either missing or having opaque data. The scarcity of available data sources for assessing animal health within the IDI meant that only 160 out of 220 countries/territories could be considered in the final analysis. There is a critical need for the establishment of an accessible, well-structured database or platform dedicated to One Health data sharing. Moreover, the restricted availability of data on animals and the environment posed a significant hurdle in the assessment of Food security, leading to diminished scores in the C3.5 category and approximately 20.20% of missing values across all sub-indicators of Category I.

3.3 Translating One Health Policies into Practice on Various Levels

To date, a scant number of countries have created dedicated government agencies to oversee the coordination of One Health strategies, indicating a fragmented approach to One Health governance. The OHHLEP suggests that prioritizing actions to foster a globally unified vision for One Health could be an essential step forward. This strategy emphasizes the importance of collaborative efforts and integrated policies to address health challenges across human, animal, and environmental domains effectively.

The One Health approach is a comprehensive framework that integrates the health of humans, animals, and the environment. It utilizes tools like the external drivers index (EDI) and intrinsic drivers index (IDI) to evaluate and measure health performance across nations. Governance, defined by principles such as transparency and accountability, plays a crucial role in managing global health crises. Zoonotic diseases, which account for a significant proportion of all infectious diseases, underscore the urgency of adopting a multisectoral approach to health. Another pressing concern is food security, which, despite global initiatives, reveals stark disparities when viewed through the One Health lens. Antimicrobial resistance (AMR) has emerged as a formidable global challenge, with misuse of drugs leading to increased resistance. It necessitates a holistic, One Health-based strategy. Climate change, primarily driven by human activities, poses multidimensional threats to biodiversity, health, and ecological balance. The repercussions of climate change, combined with other health challenges, emphasize the need for nations to collaborate, innovate, and commit to sustainable solutions. In sum, the global challenges underscored in the text highlight the indispensable role of the One Health approach in fostering a healthier future for all.

1 External Drivers Index

1.1 Background

The concept and practice of One Health is an integrated approach that encompasses human beings, animals, food, climate change, environment, and urban construction, etc. [5]. The book *Health Economics and Policy*, written by James W. Henderson, Professor of Economics at Baylor University, deals not only with the impact of health care on health, but also with other factors that affect health, such as socio-cultural, aging, legal, and technological factors, which are not health care [9]. From the book, we can see that the economic and social environment can influence human health. Information technology can influence human and animal health. The article [10] describes the current metrics, policies, and legislation for the protection of public health from ambient particles. That means institutional systems can influence human and environmental health. Furthermore, the geographical environment of the earth influences animal and environmental health. Thus, it is evident that the health of humans, animals, and the environment are closely related [11]. Hence, it is possible to assess One Health from the perspective of external environmental factors in five dimensions: earth system, institutional system, economical system,

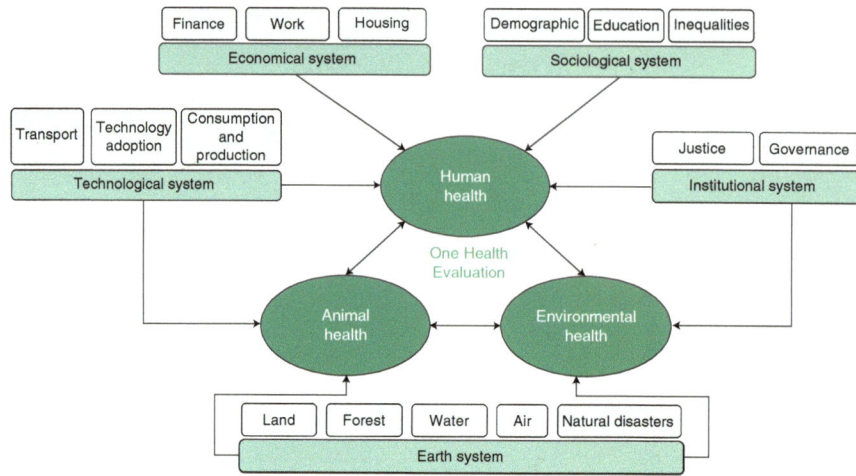

Fig. 4.1 The structural diagram of the global One Health index-external drivers index (GOHI-EDI)

sociological system, and technological system. These five dimensions together constitute five key indicators in EDI.

1.2 The Necessity to Evaluate External Drivers Index from One Health Perspective

The external drivers index is used to assess the status of One Health in each country from the perspective of the external environment. In the global One Health index-external drivers index (GOHI-EDI), we collect relevant indicators and data in order to further assess the overall performance of each country/region for One Health. The structure of the GOHI-EDI is shown in Fig. 4.1.

1.3 Framework Construction of External Drivers Index

Framework

GOHI-EDI indicators are expected to characterize the macro social, economic, cultural, and other external conditions of One Health development in the evaluated region, whose system is analyzed from five pillars: the earth system, institutional system, economical system, sociological system, and technological system. The earth system is used to show the natural, ecological, and geographical environmental characteristics that

affect the healthy development of an area. The institutional system is used to reflect the characteristics of the organizational system; for instance, the form of social organization, management mechanism, and policy implementation capabilities of the region. The Economical system is used to characterize the economic characteristics of the region's fiscal revenue and expenditure, production development, and distribution mechanism. The sociological system describes the characteristics of social development, such as population structure, social equity, and education distribution. The technological system evaluates the scientific development of the area, such as the application of advanced products and technologies or other scientific and technological characteristics.

Indicators

According to the classification of the indicators in the early stage of the project, the GOHI-EDI includes five key indicators: the earth system, institutional system, economical system, sociological system, and technological system. Four factors of the data, scientific rigor, logic, integrity and availability, were considered while determining the indicators and sub I-indicators. Using the internal expert consultations, group discussions and data reviews, the final GOHI-EDI covers 5 key indicators, 16 indicators, and 69 sub I-indicators. The specific indicators of the GOHI-EDI are shown in Table 4.1 under the GOHI-EDI framework.

Table 4.1 Indicator and weight scheme of the global One Health index-external drivers index (GOHI-EDI)

Key indicator		Indicator			Sub 1-indicator			
Name	Weight (%)	Name	Code	Weight (%)	Weight (%)	Name	Code	Weight (%)
Earth system	20.0	Land	A1.1	19.0		Country area	A1.1.1	25.0
						Cultivated area	A1.1.2	25.0
						Arable land area	A1.1.3	25.0
						Terrain ruggedness index	A1.1.4	25.0
		Forest	A1.2	18.0		Forest area	A1.2.1	33.3
						Forest transition phase	A1.2.2	33.3
						Trees per capita	A1.2.3	33.3
		Water	A1.3	24.0		Renewable water resources	A1.3.1	33.3
						Water dependency ratio	A1.3.2	33.3
						Water stress	A1.3.3	33.3
		Air	A1.4	23.0		CO_2 emissions	A1.4.1	50.0
						Air pollution index	A1.4.2	50.0
		Natural disasters	A1.5	17.0		Disasters death rate	A1.5.1	33.3
						Disaster economic loss	A1.5.2	0.0
						Disasters affected population	A1.5.3	33.3
Institutional system	20.0	Justice	A2.1	46.0		Unsentenced detainees	A2.1.1	20.0
						Property rights	A2.1.2	20.0
						Corruption perception index	A2.1.3	20.0
						Press freedom index	A2.1.4	20.0
						Affordability of justice	A2.1.5	20.0
		Governance	A2.2	54.0		Voice and accountability	A2.2.1	10.0
						Government spending	A2.2.2	0.0
						Public social expenditure	A2.2.3	0.0
						Public education expenditure	A2.2.4	10.0
						Public health expenditure	A2.2.5	0.0
						Political stability	A2.2.6	10.0
						Government effectiveness	A2.2.7	10.0
						Regulatory quality	A2.2.8	10.0
						Rule of law	A2.2.9	10.0
						Control of corruption	A2.2.10	10.0

(continued)

Table 4.1 (continued)

Key indicator Name	Weight (%)	Indicator Name	Code	Sub I-indicator Weight (%)	Name	Code	Weight (%)
Economical system	20.0	Finance	A3.1	38.0	Gross domestic product	A3.1.1	25.0
					GDP deflator	A3.1.2	25.0
					Revenue excluding grants	A3.1.3	25.0
					Grants and other revenue	A3.1.4	25.0
		Work	A3.2	30.0	Labor force participation	A3.2.1	25.0
					Unemployment	A3.2.2	25.0
					Annual working hours	A3.2.3	0.0
					Youth condition	A3.2.4	0.0
		Housing	A3.3	32.0	Own outright	A3.3.1	0.0
					Rent at reduced/subsidized price	A3.3.2	0.0
Sociological system	20.0	Demographic	A4.1	33.0	Natural population growth	A4.1.1	20.0
					Life expectancy	A4.1.2	20.0
					Child and infant mortality	A4.1.3	20.0
					Total fertility rate	A4.1.4	20.0
					Urbanization	A4.1.5	20.0
		Education	A4.2	38.0	Education enrollment	A4.2.1	14.3
					Literacy	A4.2.2	0.0
					Pisa score	A4.2.3	14.3
					Science performance	A4.2.4	14.3
					Expenditure on research	A4.2.6	14.3
					Female graduates	A4.2.7	0.0
					Researcher population	A4.2.8	0.0
		Inequalities	A4.3	29.0	Gini coefficient	A4.3.1	20.0
					Palma ratio	A4.3.2	0.0
					Human development index	A4.3.3	20.0
					Poverty rate	A4.3.4	0.0
					Gender inequality index	A4.3.5	20.0

Technological system	20.0	Transport	31.0	A5.1		Railway travel	A5.1.1	0.0
						Air travel	A5.1.2	50.0
		Technology adoption	35.0	A5.2		Internet population	A5.2.1	16.7
						Motor vehicle ownership	A5.2.2	16.7
						Mobile cellular subscriptions	A5.2.3	16.7
						Logistics performance index	A5.2.4	16.7
						Access to electricity	A5.2.5	16.7
						Share of renewable energy	A5.2.6	0.0
		Consumption and production	34.0	A5.3		Energy consumption	A5.3.1	25.0
						Electricity consumption	A5.3.2	25.0
						Electronic waste	A5.3.4	25.0
						SO_2 emissions	A5.3.5	0.0

Data Sources

In the GOHI-EDI, quantitative indicators are derived from statistics from international agencies, including the Food and Agriculture Organization of the United Nations (FAO), the World Bank Group, the Organization for Economic Co-operation and Development (OECD), Our World in Data, the International Energy Agency (IEA), the International Telecommunication Union (ITU), and other international organizations. Among the qualitative indicators, some are statistically assigned based on information provided in national annual reports, while others are based on a series of literature surveys adjusted by the panel of experts.

Limitations

For the evaluation of the same indicator, the consistency of the results can be guaranteed due to the same methodology. However, there are limitations in the data sources adopted, resulting in the possibility of some errors in the estimation of the final results. Firstly, for instance, some of the data are from the OECD, which is an intergovernmental international economic organization composed of 38 countries with market economies, whose data do not cover all countries in the world. Similar situations occur in other indicators. Secondly, to ensure the timeliness of the evaluation, data were selected for inclusion in the calculations for the most recent year currently available. The years adopted for each indicator in the five systems vary due to the different methods of obtaining the original data. Most of the data is focused on the period 2016–2020, with a small amount of data lagging behind, which may cause some bias in the estimation of the final results. For example, the indicator Terrain Ruggedness Index only contains data from 1996 and the indicator Science Performance contains data from 2015.

In addition, the total amount of missing data in the GOHI-EDI is 40.88%, mainly due to the lack of data sources, resulting in a potentially incomplete evaluation. In the earth system, the missing data is mainly related to economic loss from disasters; in the institutional system, the missing data mainly focus on government spending, public social expenditure, and public health expenditure; as for the economic system,

the missing data are mainly in annual working hours, youth condition, outright ownership, and rent at reduced/subsidized prices; in the sociological system, the missing data mainly relate to literacy, female graduates, researcher population, Palma ratio, and poverty rate; as for the technological system, the missing data mainly relate to railway travel, share of renewable energy, and SO_2 emissions. The missing rate of those 16 sub I-indicators are all over 75%; thus, they were ignored in the calculation of the GOHI-EDI scores.

1.4   Main Results

Global Score

The total scores of GOHI-EDI worldwide are generally sub-optimal. The score of each country/territory ranges from 32.83 to 50.28 in Fig. 4.2, which shows that the scores over 46.15 are distributed in Europe and Central Asia, North America, and East Asia and Pacific. Scores below 35.87 are distributed in sub-Saharan Africa, South Asia, Middle East and North Africa, Europe, and Central Asia.

Total scores of GOHI-EDI by region are as follows (sorted by median): North America (48.66), Europe and Central Asia (43.13), East Asia and Pacific (41.40), Latin America and the Caribbean (41.27), the Middle East and North Africa (37.78), sub-Saharan Africa (37.58) and South Asia (36.21). Of these, North America and European countries/territories score highest, followed by East Asia and Pacific and Latin America and the Caribbean. Countries/territories with the lowest scores are concentrated in the sub-Saharan Africa (Fig. 4.3).

Air (A1.4), as one of indicators, has the highest average score (71.93). Transport (A5.1) has the lowest score (6.54) (Fig. 4.4). Housing (A3.3) is not presented in this figure because the missing rate of housing is over 80.00%.

Figure 4.4 shows the score distribution of the global One Health index-external drivers index (GOHI-EDI) by indicator. (LAN: Land, FST: Forest, WAT: Water, AIR: Air, NLD: Natural disasters, JUS: Justice, GOV: Governance, FIN: Finance, WOR: Work, DEM: Demographic,

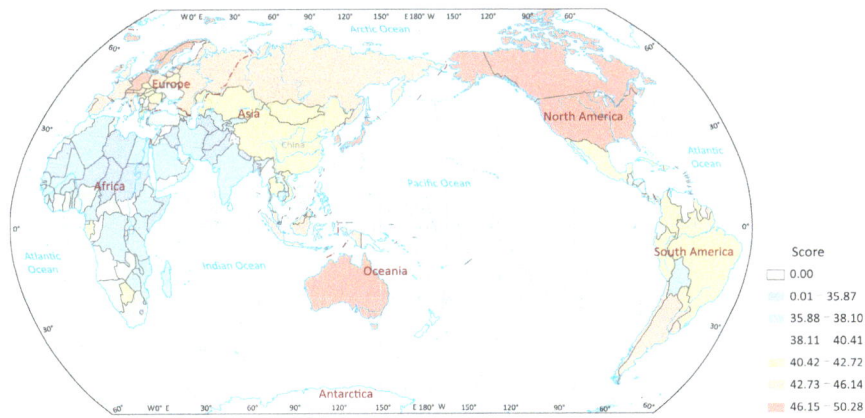

Fig. 4.2 Global score map of the global One Health index-external drivers index (GOHI-EDI)

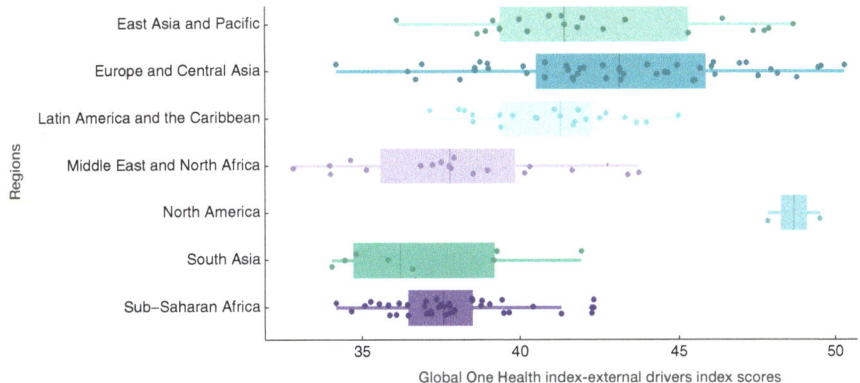

Fig. 4.3 Regional score distribution of the global One Health index-external drivers index (GOHI-EDI)

EDU: Education, INE: Inequalities, TRP: Transport, TEC: Technology adoption, CAP: Consumption and production.)

The scores of indicators in GOHI-EDI, from high to low, are as follows (sorted by median): Earth system (56.29), Institutional system (44.33), Sociological system (37.50), Technological system (37.39) and Economical system (24.64). As for the Institutional system and the Earth system, the distribution of scores among countries/territories is relatively scattered, indicating that there is a large variation in the scores between countries/territories in the two key indicators (Fig. 4.5).

Global Ranking

The scores and rankings of countries/territories of GOHI-EDI components are shown in

Table 4.2. The average score of the GOHI-EDI is 40.45. Among the 160 assessed countries/territories, the highest score is Finland (50.28) and the lowest is Kuwait (32.83).

Leaders and Laggards

Table 4.2 shows the top 25 countries and the bottom 25 countries of GOHI-EDI scores.

The top 25 countries are Finland (50.28), Sweden, Canada, Denmark, Switzerland, Australia, Norway, Iceland, New Zealand, the United States, Singapore, Estonia, South Korea, Germany, Ireland, Japan, Spain, Netherlands, Lithuania, Austria, France, the United Kingdom, Malaysia, Uruguay and Belgium (44.93). The top rankings are mostly countries in Europe and Central Asia (16 in total) followed by East Asia and Pacific (6 in total).

Fig. 4.4 The score distribution of the global One Health index-external drivers index (GOHI-EDI) by indicators. (*LAN* land, *FST* forest, *WAT* water, *AIR* air, *NLD* natural disasters, *JUS* justice, *GOV* governance, *FIN* finance, *WOR* work, *DEM* demographic, *EDU* education, *INE* inequalities, *TRP* transport, *TEC* technology adoption, *CAP* consumption and production)

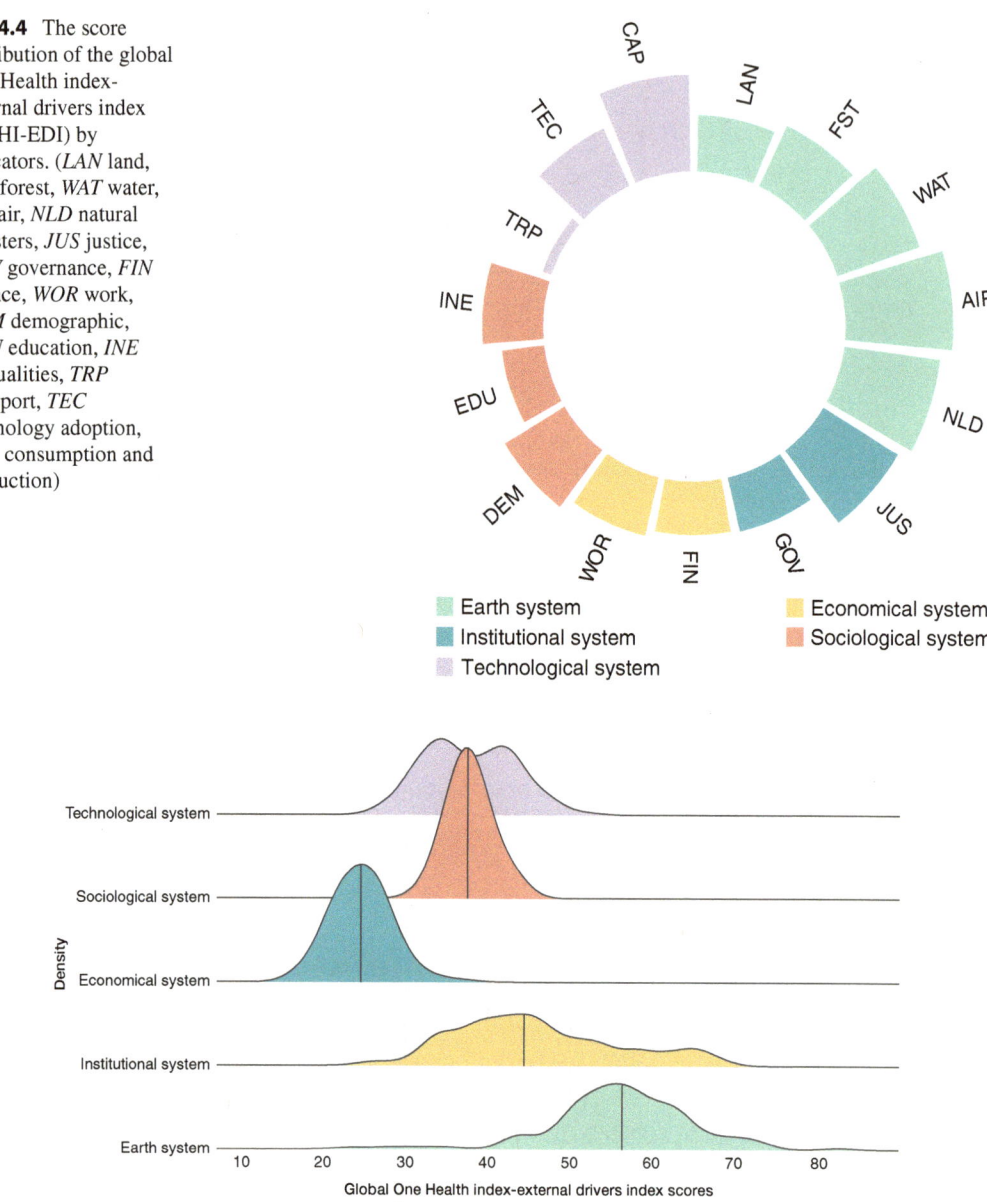

Fig. 4.5 Dimensional score distribution of the global One Health index-external drivers index (GOHI-EDI)

The bottom 25 countries are Kyrgyzstan (36.70), India, Dem. Rep. Congo, Tajikistan, Cameroon, Zimbabwe, Cambodia, Mali, Sudan, Lesotho, Nepal, Niger, Mauritania, Bahrain, Chad, Pakistan, Somalia, Djibouti, Bangladesh, Turkmenistan, Burundi, Afghanistan, Libya, Iraq, and Kuwait (32.83), which mainly distributed in sub-Saharan Africa (11 in total), fol-lowed by the Middle East and North Africa (5 in total) and South Asia (5 in total).

From the Table 4.3, Finland, as the top country of total score, ranks 4th in the Earth system (72.76), ranks 1st in the Institutional system (69.04); ranks 76th in the Economic system (24.93); ranks 8th in the Sociological system (42.84); ranks 42nd in the Technological system (41.81). Kuwait, with the lowest total score,

Table 4.2 Country ranking of total score in the global One Health index-external drivers index (GOHI-EDI)

Total rank	Country/territory	Total	Reg rank
1	Finland	50.28	1
2	Sweden	49.53	2
3	Canada	49.50	3
4	Denmark	49.44	3
5	Switzerland	48.75	4
6	Australia	48.64	1
7	Norway	48.13	5
8	Iceland	47.92	6
9	New Zealand	47.86	2
10	United States of America	47.82	2
11	Singapore	47.71	7
12	Estonia	47.51	7
13	South Korea	47.35	4
14	Germany	47.13	8
15	Ireland	46.91	9
16	Japan	46.38	5
17	Spain	46.14	10
18	Netherlands	46.09	11
19	Lithuania	46.03	12
20	Austria	45.66	13
21	France	45.48	14
22	United Kingdom	45.45	15
23	Malaysia	45.29	6
24	Uruguay	44.98	1
25	Belgium	44.93	16
26	Russia	44.64	17
27	Portugal	44.56	18
28	Latvia	44.30	19
29	Luxembourg	44.01	20
30	Argentina	43.98	2
31	United Arab Emirates	43.75	1
32	Chile	43.67	3
33	Malta	43.40	2
34	Indonesia	43.33	7
35	Costa Rica	43.32	4
36	Italy	43.26	21
37	Bulgaria	43.19	22
38	Poland	43.15	23
39	Slovenia	43.13	24
40	Greece	42.72	25
41	Brazil	42.71	5
42	Mongolia	42.63	8
43	Czech Republic	42.61	26
44	Guyana	42.51	6
45	Mauritius	42.32	1
46	Gabon	42.26	2
47	Peru	42.07	7
48	Kazakhstan	42.00	27
49	Thailand	41.97	9
50	Bhutan	41.93	1
51	Georgia	41.89	28
52	Colombia	41.85	8
53	Panama	41.83	9
54	Fiji	41.81	10
55	Montenegro	41.81	29
56	Jamaica	41.73	10
57	Cyprus	41.67	30
58	Paraguay	41.67	11
59	Romania	41.66	31
60	Israel	41.64	3
61	Hungary	41.52	32
62	Slovakia	41.46	33
63	Viet Nam	41.40	11
64	China	41.31	12
65	Botswana	41.30	3
66	Mexico	41.27	12
67	Barbados	41.09	13
68	Vanuatu	40.92	13
69	Belarus	40.79	34
70	Croatia	40.78	35
71	Cuba	40.54	14
72	Dominican Republic	40.50	15
73	Ghana	40.41	4
74	Tunisia	40.31	4
75	Laos	40.24	14
76	Turkey	40.22	36
77	Morocco	40.15	5
78	Albania	40.10	37
79	Philippines	39.98	15
80	Ecuador	39.78	16
81	Cote d'Ivoire	39.66	5
82	Zambia	39.49	6
83	Seychelles	39.44	7
84	Belize	39.39	17
85	Timor-Leste	39.37	16
86	Trinidad and Tobago	39.37	18
87	Brunei Darussalam	39.36	17
88	Sri Lanka	39.27	2
89	Maldives	39.17	3
90	Myanmar	39.15	18
91	South Africa	39.04	8
92	Moldova	39.01	38
93	Ukraine	38.97	39
94	Jordan	38.97	6
95	Solomon Islands	38.92	19
96	Rwanda	38.79	9
97	Namibia	38.77	10
98	Serbia	38.74	40
99	Papua New Guinea	38.65	20
100	North Macedonia	38.58	41
101	Armenia	38.57	42
102	Guatemala	38.52	19
103	Qatar	38.52	7
104	El Salvador	38.50	20
105	Nigeria	38.50	11
106	Central African Republic	38.48	12
107	Nicaragua	38.25	21
108	Azerbaijan	38.10	43
109	Bolivia	38.06	22
110	Sierra Leone	37.93	13
111	Iran	37.91	8
112	Benin	37.88	14
113	Oman	37.81	9
114	Burkina Faso	37.77	15
115	Cabo Verde	37.77	16
116	Togo	37.76	17
117	Equatorial Guinea	37.76	18
118	Algeria	37.75	10
119	Malawi	37.73	19
120	Guinea	37.64	20
121	Uganda	37.58	21
122	Egypt	37.51	11
123	Guinea-Bissau	37.50	22
124	Madagascar	37.42	23
125	Kenya	37.35	24
126	Saudi Arabia	37.23	12
127	Tanzania	37.20	25
128	Mozambique	37.17	26
129	Honduras	37.15	23
130	Ethiopia	37.08	27
131	Liberia	37.03	28
132	Eswatini	37.02	29
133	Senegal	36.98	30
134	Uzbekistan	36.90	44
135	Lebanon	36.86	13
136	Kyrgyzstan	36.70	45
137	India	36.60	4
138	Dem. Rep. Congo	36.46	31
139	Tajikistan	36.45	46
140	Cameroon	36.44	32
141	Zimbabwe	36.17	33
142	Cambodia	36.10	21
143	Mali	36.08	34
144	Sudan	35.87	35
145	Lesotho	35.83	36
146	Nepal	35.82	5
147	Niger	35.54	37
148	Mauritania	35.27	38
149	Bahrain	35.14	14
150	Chad	35.09	39
151	Pakistan	34.82	6
152	Somalia	34.67	40
153	Djibouti	34.64	15
154	Bangladesh	34.45	7
155	Turkmenistan	34.18	47
156	Burundi	34.17	41
157	Afghanistan	34.04	8
158	Libya	34.00	16
159	Iraq	33.97	17
160	Kuwait	32.83	18

Legend: East Asia and Pacific · Europe and Central Asia · Latin America and the Caribbean · Middle East and North Africa · North America · South Asia · Sub-Saharan Africa

Table 4.3 Country ranking of key indicator score in the global One Health index-external drivers index (GOHI-EDI)

Total rank	Country/territory	Earth system		Institutional system		Economical system		Sociological system		Technological system	
		Sub-rank	Sub-score	Sub-rank	Sub-score	Sub-rank	Sub-score	Sub-rank	Sub-score	Sub-rank	Sub-score
1	Finland	4	72.76	1	69.04	76	24.93	8	42.84	42	41.81
2	Sweden	6	71.01	9	64.96	28	27.56	4	43.52	56	40.58
3	Canada	1	82.47	13	63.23	11	29.85	29	39.66	131	32.27
4	Denmark	29	62.98	3	67.1	46	26.64	7	42.93	6	47.53
5	Switzerland	95	54.72	7	65.33	2	35.46	23	40.45	4	47.78
6	Australia	8	70.74	14	63.08	16	28.68	42	39.15	49	41.56
7	Norway	21	64.37	2	67.6	18	28.42	20	40.93	64	39.32
8	Iceland	14	66.88	18	61.24	47	26.44	19	40.97	19	44.09
9	New Zealand	22	64.36	5	65.83	45	26.68	50	38.85	21	43.6
10	United States	16	66.44	23	58.25	5	32.17	9	42.53	63	39.7
11	Singapore	107	53.5	6	65.82	3	33.9	11	42.42	27	42.93
12	Estonia	9	69.61	15	61.96	143	20.37	58	38.39	7	47.24
13	South Korea	10	69.45	25	58.14	49	26.35	15	41.86	53	40.94
14	Germany	77	56.63	11	64.74	57	25.81	9	42.53	11	45.93
15	Ireland	72	57.04	8	65.04	4	32.49	62	38.18	45	41.8
16	Japan	56	59.06	10	64.88	72	25.12	16	41.84	51	41.03
17	Spain	31	62.78	26	58	104	23.2	52	38.56	3	48.16
18	Netherlands	138	49.58	4	67.09	86	24.35	12	42.26	8	47.18
19	Lithuania	13	67.62	21	58.76	138	20.89	64	38.15	16	44.74
20	Austria	83	56.1	12	64.27	117	22.34	17	41.25	18	44.33
21	France	33	62.57	22	58.64	136	21	24	40.33	15	44.85
22	United Kingdom	49	59.99	24	58.19	44	26.75	32	39.62	33	42.7
23	Malaysia	35	62.28	43	51.97	23	28.04	47	38.97	14	45.19
24	Uruguay	20	64.4	17	61.77	119	22.33	66	38.12	76	38.29
25	Belgium	102	53.97	16	61.82	117	22.34	3	43.74	32	42.76
26	Russia	2	73.53	78	44.56	88	24.1	40	39.21	46	41.78
27	Portugal	74	56.91	20	59.46	142	20.4	60	38.33	5	47.69
28	Latvia	12	68.02	36	53.63	152	19.16	85	37.37	24	43.34
29	Luxembourg	133	50.38	19	61.12	26	27.88	21	40.61	61	40.06
30	Argentina	29	62.98	69	46.12	14	29.34	71	37.8	20	43.66
31	United Arab Emirates	157	33.03	29	55.95	1	37.52	27	39.77	1	52.5
32	Chile	47	60.14	28	56.82	109	22.66	25	40.17	72	38.56

33	Malta	100	54.22	41	52.05	124	21.97	53	38.54	2	50.22
34	Indonesia	18	64.97	73	45.98	27	27.76	126	35.87	37	42.07
35	Costa Rica	38	61.69	49	49.77	79	24.65	95	36.95	22	43.55
36	Italy	65	58.03	33	54.11	148	20.02	79	37.55	9	46.58
37	Bulgaria	27	63.1	50	49.63	93	23.77	75	37.71	47	41.72
38	Poland	61	58.24	38	52.9	139	20.88	54	38.48	13	45.24
39	Slovenia	81	56.22	30	55.86	132	21.24	31	39.64	34	42.67
40	Greece	60	58.32	45	50.94	147	20.2	61	38.29	12	45.85
41	Brazil	5	71.71	85	43.87	111	22.52	66	38.12	81	37.33
42	Mongolia	25	63.61	84	44.15	29	27.38	80	37.5	57	40.52
43	Czech Republic	115	52.82	27	57.38	140	20.68	38	39.28	28	42.9
44	Guyana	3	73.21	81	44.26	75	24.99	142	34.73	96	35.37
45	Mauritius	64	58.13	34	54.02	121	22.25	135	35.25	39	41.95
46	Gabon	7	70.97	117	39.02	82	24.63	33	39.47	83	37.2
47	Peru	26	63.44	98	42	55	25.82	87	37.26	41	41.84
48	Kazakhstan	46	60.34	93	42.81	8	30.88	127	35.8	60	40.18
49	Thailand	78	56.59	72	46.06	77	24.89	123	35.96	10	46.33
50	Bhutan	63	58.16	39	52.68	98	23.67	133	35.39	62	39.72
51	Georgia	59	58.41	37	53.36	96	23.75	145	34.61	64	39.32
52	Colombia	11	68.72	112	40.33	78	24.86	103	36.72	69	38.66
53	Panama	36	62.18	63	46.77	88	24.1	132	35.51	54	40.62
54	Montenegro	52	59.78	60	47.02	130	21.59	115	36.31	17	44.36
55	Fiji	23	63.93	69	46.12	105	23.01	86	37.34	70	38.65
56	Jamaica	45	60.62	54	48.87	120	22.27	112	36.34	57	40.52
57	Cyprus	93	54.78	44	51.92	128	21.8	101	36.74	25	43.1
58	Paraguay	17	65.85	131	37.35	24	27.99	118	36.1	51	41.03
59	Romania	62	58.21	40	52.5	149	20	141	34.78	30	42.82
60	Israel	144	47.25	32	54.19	58	25.68	13	41.96	67	39.1
61	Hungary	86	55.85	48	49.96	150	19.64	36	39.35	31	42.81
62	Slovakia	88	55.58	46	50.7	141	20.46	65	38.13	35	42.44
63	Viet Nam	73	56.93	68	46.21	101	23.38	51	38.66	42	41.81
64	China	69	57.55	91	43.26	80	24.64	22	40.51	54	40.62
65	Botswana	67	57.83	47	50.4	135	21.02	30	39.65	79	37.58

(continued)

Table 4.3 (continued)

Total rank	Country/territory	Earth system Sub-rank	Earth system Sub-score	Institutional system Sub-rank	Institutional system Sub-score	Economical system Sub-rank	Economical system Sub-score	Sociological system Sub-rank	Sociological system Sub-score	Technological system Sub-rank	Technological system Sub-score
66	Mexico	47	60.14	122	38.53	35	27.19	55	38.44	38	42.04
67	Barbados	90	55.44	42	52.04	21	28.18	154	33.52	86	36.25
68	Vanuatu	19	64.94	52	49.54	61	25.59	159	32.36	134	32.17
69	Belarus	24	63.76	140	34.68	84	24.52	44	39.13	40	41.85
70	Croatia	85	55.94	53	49.48	156	18.36	90	37.11	26	43.02
71	Cuba	28	63.04	101	41.6	95	23.76	106	36.53	78	37.77
72	Dominican Republic	49	59.99	79	44.53	43	26.78	91	37.09	115	34.11
73	Ghana	117	52.31	57	47.36	80	24.64	56	38.42	64	39.32
74	Tunisia	76	56.67	88	43.81	22	28.17	82	37.44	95	35.47
75	Laos	37	62.16	99	41.98	63	25.55	130	35.67	91	35.83
76	Turkey	132	50.42	97	42.16	40	26.92	26	39.96	48	41.64
77	Morocco	89	55.45	88	43.81	124	21.97	116	36.13	23	43.36
78	Albania	58	58.61	90	43.37	151	19.2	108	36.5	29	42.85
79	Philippines	57	58.64	113	39.73	34	27.21	129	35.79	73	38.55
80	Ecuador	42	61.25	94	42.6	110	22.63	110	36.45	89	35.96
81	Cote d'Ivoire	129	50.66	103	41.24	50	26.23	5	43.06	84	37.12
82	Zambia	54	59.35	100	41.76	115	22.42	39	39.24	105	34.69
83	Seychelles	120	51.74	35	53.7	64	25.53	136	35.07	144	31.15
84	Belize	38	61.69	102	41.32	99	23.49	122	35.98	109	34.45
85	Trinidad and Tobago	104	53.76	55	48.85	41	26.9	138	35.01	130	32.31
86	Timor-Leste	51	59.79	83	44.17	90	23.89	148	34.03	101	34.96
87	Brunei Darussalam	125	50.86	62	46.88	17	28.45	134	35.35	98	35.24
88	Sri Lanka	92	55.22	96	42.25	31	27.28	156	32.97	71	38.64
89	Maldives	82	56.13	86	43.84	69	25.23	146	34.59	88	36.06
90	Myanmar	53	59.46	154	32.38	6	31.75	83	37.43	103	34.72
91	South Africa	128	50.69	61	46.91	157	17.62	14	41.9	77	38.08
92	Moldova	43	61.15	82	44.25	153	18.98	155	33.47	82	37.22
93	Ukraine	34	62.36	104	41.2	158	17.05	77	37.68	85	36.53
94	Jordan	127	50.77	58	47.33	53	26.04	98	36.83	117	33.91
95	Solomon Islands	32	62.74	106	41.01	70	25.21	160	30.94	104	34.71
96	Rwanda	118	51.86	51	49.62	25	27.92	147	34.11	149	30.44

97	Namibia	67	57.83	59	47.15	159	16.5	34	39.45	126	32.94
98	Serbia	108	53.48	74	45.93	160	16.42	106	36.53	50	41.37
99	Papua New Guinea	41	61.42	86	43.84	38	27	157	32.89	157	28.08
100	North Macedonia	71	57.14	66	46.33	155	18.42	121	35.99	100	35.01
101	Armenia	112	53.26	65	46.4	123	21.99	117	36.12	99	35.06
102	Qatar	158	29.89	31	54.37	15	28.94	89	37.14	36	42.25
103	Guatemala	87	55.74	132	36.97	60	25.64	127	35.8	74	38.47
104	El Salvador	98	54.31	92	43.13	97	23.7	120	36.05	97	35.3
105	Nigeria	136	49.93	126	38	10	29.98	2	44.4	152	30.19
106	Central African Republic	15	66.7	139	34.73	134	21.19	42	39.15	148	30.61
107	Nicaragua	44	61.1	141	34.56	68	25.31	124	35.89	111	34.36
108	Azerbaijan	126	50.8	105	41.18	51	26.16	99	36.81	94	35.52
109	Bolivia	38	61.69	157	30.44	64	25.53	49	38.86	119	33.78
110	Sierra Leone	80	56.36	126	38	41	26.9	59	38.34	153	30.03
111	Iran	121	51.69	147	33.56	87	24.31	62	38.18	42	41.81
112	Benin	122	51.53	95	42.27	106	23	45	39.1	124	33.5
113	Oman	151	43.86	75	45.37	32	27.26	68	38.08	108	34.5
114	Burkina Faso	113	53.09	110	40.54	91	23.83	100	36.75	106	34.62
115	Cabo Verde	130	50.5	56	48.81	114	22.46	158	32.5	107	34.59
116	Togo	109	53.44	123	38.45	55	25.82	104	36.63	110	34.44
117	Equatorial Guinea	70	57.47	155	31.64	85	24.39	18	40.98	112	34.34
118	Algeria	96	54.42	126	38	102	23.22	88	37.19	90	35.94
119	Malawi	84	56.04	77	44.78	39	26.98	152	33.61	159	27.24
120	Guinea	101	54.07	125	38.08	74	25.03	28	39.7	143	31.32
121	Uganda	111	53.28	114	39.47	37	27.04	102	36.73	142	31.38
122	Egypt	153	43.12	64	46.7	58	25.68	109	36.47	93	35.56
123	Guinea-Bissau	135	50.2	107	40.94	36	27.07	73	37.75	139	31.52
124	Madagascar	55	59.21	129	37.98	48	26.36	96	36.94	160	26.63
125	Kenya	91	55.35	118	38.98	107	22.85	125	35.88	120	33.72
126	Saudi Arabia	156	35.68	76	44.79	30	27.36	35	39.38	68	38.94
127	Tanzania	106	53.55	119	38.89	108	22.84	48	38.94	137	31.79
128	Mozambique	75	56.85	143	34.4	72	25.12	78	37.63	135	31.88
129	Honduras	66	57.93	136	35.9	61	25.59	140	34.89	140	31.46

(continued)

Table 4.3 (continued)

Total rank	Country/territory	Earth system		Institutional system		Economical system		Sociological system		Technological system	
		Sub-rank	Sub-score	Sub-rank	Sub-score	Sub-rank	Sub-score	Sub-rank	Sub-score	Sub-rank	Sub-score
130	Ethiopia	94	54.75	137	35.79	12	29.61	150	33.81	140	31.46
131	Liberia	99	54.28	108	40.86	100	23.41	76	37.7	155	28.91
132	Eswatini	110	53.35	111	40.49	137	20.98	105	36.58	122	33.68
133	Senegal	142	48	71	46.08	83	24.61	144	34.64	138	31.56
134	Uzbekistan	148	44.28	120	38.8	13	29.44	93	37.07	102	34.9
135	Lebanon	123	51.32	153	32.73	91	23.83	69	38.03	75	38.37
136	Kyrgyzstan	103	53.8	124	38.16	112	22.48	139	34.98	116	34.08
137	India	116	52.6	115	39.34	154	18.91	112	36.34	92	35.81
138	Dem. Rep. Congo	124	51.04	138	35.04	133	21.22	1	44.74	151	30.28
139	Tajikistan	143	47.95	142	34.47	7	30.89	142	34.73	113	34.21
140	Cameroon	105	53.7	145	34.15	126	21.95	41	39.16	125	33.26
141	Zimbabwe	79	56.44	156	31.27	121	22.25	70	38.01	127	32.87
142	Cambodia	97	54.33	130	37.6	103	23.21	153	33.55	136	31.83
143	Mali	134	50.36	134	36.19	66	25.5	118	36.1	132	32.24
144	Sudan	145	46.79	150	33.41	20	28.33	92	37.08	120	33.72
145	Lesotho	131	50.47	121	38.72	146	20.27	46	38.99	146	30.68
146	Nepal	141	48.7	109	40.84	129	21.78	131	35.61	133	32.2
147	Niger	119	51.84	116	39.09	131	21.42	137	35.02	150	30.34
148	Mauritania	152	43.48	133	36.66	52	26.1	114	36.33	118	33.8
149	Bahrain	159	27.37	80	44.4	71	25.18	56	38.42	59	40.32
150	Chad	139	49.28	144	34.38	54	25.92	81	37.49	156	28.37
151	Pakistan	155	41.81	135	35.92	67	25.38	84	37.41	123	33.56
152	Somalia	149	44.13	159	25.98	9	30.45	6	43.02	154	29.76
153	Djibouti	140	49	151	33.4	113	22.47	74	37.72	147	30.63
154	Bangladesh	147	44.41	148	33.53	127	21.81	110	36.45	87	36.07
155	Turkmenistan	146	46.46	160	25.74	19	28.37	72	37.78	128	32.57
156	Burundi	114	52.89	152	33	93	23.77	151	33.75	158	27.46
157	Afghanistan	150	44.05	146	34.01	33	27.22	149	34.02	145	30.9
158	Libya	137	49.88	158	28.08	143	20.37	37	39.33	129	32.35
159	Iraq	154	42.85	149	33.47	116	22.4	94	36.97	114	34.18
160	Kuwait	160	23.24	67	46.26	145	20.35	97	36.86	80	37.45

ranks 160th in the Earth system (23.24); ranks 67th in the Institutional system (46.26); ranks 145th in the Economic system (20.35); ranks 97th in the Sociological system (36.86); ranks 80th in the Technological system (37.45). Therefore, no country performance best in all indicators and vice versa.

Regional Ranking

The regional ranking of GOHI-EDI is shown in Table 4.4.

Table 4.4 Regional ranking of the global One Health index-external drivers index (GOHI-EDI)

East Asia and Pacific

Rank	Country	Score
1	Australia	48.64
2	New Zealand	47.86
3	Singapore	47.71
4	South Korea	47.35
5	Japan	46.38
6	Malaysia	45.29
7	Indonesia	43.33
8	Mongolia	42.63
9	Thailand	41.97
10	Fiji	41.81
11	Viet Nam	41.40
12	China	41.31
13	Vanuatu	40.92
14	Laos	40.24
15	Philippines	39.98
16	Timor-Leste	39.37
17	Brunei Darussalam	39.36
18	Myanmar	39.15
19	Solomon Islands	38.92
20	Papua New Guinea	38.65
21	Cambodia	36.10
22	Solomon Islands	38.34

Middle East and North Africa

Rank	Country	Score
1	United Arab Emirates	43.75
2	Malta	43.40
3	Israel	41.64
4	Tunisia	40.31
5	Morocco	40.15
6	Jordan	38.97
7	Qatar	38.52
8	Iran	37.91
9	Oman	37.81
10	Algeria	37.75

Table 4.4 (continued)

Middle East and North Africa

Rank	Country	Score
11	Egypt	37.51
12	Saudi Arabia	37.23
13	Lebanon	36.86
14	Bahrain	35.14
15	Djibouti	34.64
16	Libya	34.00
17	Iraq	33.97
18	Kuwait	32.83
19	Djibouti	38.61

Europe and Central Asia

Rank	Country	Score
1	Finland	50.28
2	Sweden	49.53
3	Denmark	49.44
4	Switzerland	48.75
5	Norway	48.13
6	Iceland	47.92
7	Estonia	47.51
8	Germany	47.13
9	Ireland	46.91
10	Spain	46.14
11	Netherlands	46.09
12	Lithuania	46.03
13	Austria	45.66
14	France	45.48
15	United Kingdom	45.45
16	Belgium	44.93
17	Russia	44.64
18	Portugal	44.56
19	Latvia	44.30
20	Luxembourg	44.01
21	Italy	43.26
22	Bulgaria	43.19
23	Poland	43.15
24	Slovenia	43.13
25	Greece	42.72
26	Czech Republic	42.61
27	Kazakhstan	42.00
28	Georgia	41.89
29	Montenegro	41.81
30	Cyprus	41.67
31	Romania	41.66
32	Hungary	41.52
33	Slovakia	41.46
34	Belarus	40.79
35	Croatia	40.78
36	Turkey	40.22

(continued)

Table 4.4   (continued)

Europe and Central Asia

Rank	Country	Score
37	Albania	40.10
38	Moldova	39.01
39	Ukraine	38.97
40	Serbia	38.74
41	North Macedonia	38.58
42	Armenia	38.57
43	Azerbaijan	38.10
44	Uzbekistan	36.90
45	Kyrgyzstan	36.70
46	Tajikistan	36.45
47	Turkmenistan	34.18
48	Tajikistan	45.50

Sub-Saharan Africa

Rank	Country	Score
1	Mauritius	42.32
2	Gabon	42.26
3	Botswana	41.30
4	Ghana	40.41
5	Cote d'Ivoire	39.66
6	Zambia	39.49
7	Seychelles	39.44
8	South Africa	39.04
9	Rwanda	38.79
10	Namibia	38.77
11	Nigeria	38.50
12	Central African Republic	38.48
13	Sierra Leone	37.93
14	Benin	37.88
15	Cabo Verde	37.77
16	Burkina Faso	37.77
17	Togo	37.76
18	Equatorial Guinea	37.76
19	Malawi	37.73
20	Guinea	37.64
21	Uganda	37.58
22	Guinea-Bissau	37.50
23	Madagascar	37.42
24	Kenya	37.35
25	Tanzania	37.20
26	Mozambique	37.17
27	Ethiopia	37.08
28	Liberia	37.03
29	Eswatini	37.02
30	Senegal	36.98
31	Dem. Rep. Congo	36.46
32	Cameroon	36.44
33	Zimbabwe	36.17
34	Mali	36.08

Table 4.4   (continued)

Sub-Saharan Africa

Rank	Country	Score
35	Sudan	35.87
36	Lesotho	35.83
37	Niger	35.54
38	Mauritania	35.27
39	Chad	35.09
40	Somalia	34.67
41	Burundi	34.17
42	Guinea-Bissau	38.43
43	Chad	37.46
44	Somalia	37.04
45	Central African Republic	36.87
46	South Sudan	36.53

South Asia

Rank	Country	Score
1	Bhutan	41.93
2	Sri Lanka	39.27
3	Maldives	39.17
4	India	36.60
5	Nepal	35.82
6	Pakistan	34.82
7	Bangladesh	34.45
8	Afghanistan	34.04

Latin America and the Caribbean

Rank	Country	Score
1	Uruguay	44.98
2	Argentina	43.98
3	Chile	43.67
4	Costa Rica	43.32
5	Brazil	42.71
6	Guyana	42.51
7	Peru	42.07
8	Colombia	41.85
9	Panama	41.83
10	Jamaica	41.73
11	Paraguay	41.67
12	Mexico	41.27
13	Barbados	41.09
14	Cuba	40.54
15	Dominican Republic	40.50
16	Ecuador	39.78
17	Belize	39.39
18	Trinidad and Tobago	39.37
19	Guatemala	38.52
20	El Salvador	38.50
21	Nicaragua	38.25
22	Bolivia	38.06
23	Honduras	37.15

Table 4.4 (continued)

Latin America and the Caribbean

Rank	Country	Score
24	Saint Lucia	44.77
25	Barbados	44.45
26	Venezuela	43.90
27	Bahamas	43.60
28	Haiti	42.31

North America

Rank	Country	Score
1	Canada	49.50
2	United States	47.82

In rankings of regions, the top five countries in East Asia and Pacific are Australia, New Zealand, Singapore, South Korea, and Japan, with a score range of 46.38–48.64; in sub-Saharan Africa, the top five are Mauritius, Gabon, Botswana, Ghana, and Cote d'Ivoire, the score range is 39.66–42.32. In Middle East and North Africa, the top five are the United Arab Emirates, Malta, Israel, Tunisia and Morocco whose score range is 40.15–43.75. In South Asia, the top five are Bhutan, Sri Lanka, Maldives, India, and Nepal, with a score range of 35.82–41.93. In Latin America and the Caribbean, the top five are Uruguay, Argentina, Chile, Costa Rica, and Brazil, with a score range of 59.58–54.56. In North America, the United States scores 47.82 and Canada 49.50. In Europe and Central Asia, the top five are Finland, Sweden, Denmark, Switzerland, and Norway, with a score range of 48.13–50.28.

From the Tables 4.2 and 4.4, we can draw the following conclusions.

In East Asia and Pacific, Australia scores highest (48.64) and ranks 6th in total score globally. Cambodia scores lowest (36.10) and ranks 142nd in total score globally, with a dispersal distribution.

In sub-Saharan Africa, of the 41 countries included in the discussion, the average score is 37.67, with the top five countries in the region being Mauritius, Gabon, Botswana, Ghana, and Cote d'Ivoire in that order. Mauritius scores highest (42.32) and ranks 45th globally.

In the Middle East and North Africa, of the 18 countries included in the discussion, the average

score is 37.91, with the top three countries, United Arab Emirates, Malta, and Israel in that order. The United Arab Emirates scores highest (43.75) and ranks 31st globally.

In South Asia, of the eight countries included in the discussion, the average score is 37.01 and the countries are ranked in order of Bhutan, Sri Lanka, Maldives, India, Nepal, Pakistan, Bangladesh, and Afghanistan. Bhutan scores highest (41.93) and ranks 50th globally.

In Latin America and the Caribbean, of the 23 countries included in the discussion, the average score is 40.99, with the top three countries being Uruguay, Argentina, and Chile in that order. Uruguay scores highest (44.98) and ranks 24th globally.

In North America, two countries included in the discussion are the United States and Canada, with an average score of 48.66. Canada, scores 49.50, ranks 3rd in total score globally. The United States, scores 47.82, ranks 10th globally.

In Europe and Central Asia, out of 47 countries included in the discussion, the average score is 37.67, with the top five countries in the region being Finland, Sweden, Denmark, Switzerland, Norway in that order. Finland scores highest (50.28) and ranks 1st globally.

The scores of each region under different indicators are shown in Table 4.5.

When looking at all 16 indicators, the scores of each region are not exclusively above or below the global average, meaning that the gap in the Table 4.5 is displayed as a positive excess or a negative deficit to the global average. In the 5 key indicators, the scores in South Asia are all below the global average. The scores of other 6 regions vary, both above and below the global average.

1.5 Key Findings

The Total Scores of GOHI-EDI Around the World Are Far From Ideal

We used 100 points to characterize the optimal state of the GOHI-EDI performance. In terms of total scores, no country scores over 60.00. Even with Finland ranking first (with a total score of 50.28), it is still more than 40 points away from

Table 4.5 Regional performance of the global One Health index-external drivers index (GOHI-EDI)

Indicator Code	Title	Global	East Asia and Pacific Average	Gap	Europe and Central Asia Average	Gap	Latin America and the Caribbean Average	Gap	Middle East and North Africa Average	Gap	North America Average	Gap	South Asia Average	Gap	Sub-Saharan Africa Average	Gap
A.1	Earth system	56.21	60.82	4.61	58.44	2.22	61.78	5.57	44.43	−11.79	74.46	18.24	50.14	−6.08	53.65	−2.56
A.1.1	Land	36.41	36.31	−0.10	38.85	2.44	38.50	2.09	28.75	−7.66	60.69	24.27	22.50	−13.91	37.39	0.98
A.1.2	Forest	43.43	49.69	6.25	47.62	4.18	46.63	3.20	32.03	−11.41	65.67	22.24	38.92	−4.52	38.45	−4.99
A.1.3	Water	58.09	69.56	11.47	55.03	−3.06	65.73	7.63	44.14	−13.95	97.16	39.07	57.48	−0.61	55.78	−2.31
A.1.4	Air	71.93	75.02	3.09	78.69	6.75	83.22	11.29	50.40	−21.54	71.71	−0.23	62.26	−9.68	67.63	−4.30
A.1.5	Natural disasters	64.65	64.89	0.24	65.75	1.10	65.64	0.99	64.80	0.15	66.44	1.79	63.19	−1.47	62.85	−1.80
A.2	Institutional system	46.01	48.51	2.50	52.63	6.63	43.84	−2.16	43.24	−2.77	60.74	14.73	40.30	−5.71	39.96	−6.05
A.2.1	Justice	58.25	59.72	1.47	65.10	6.85	55.03	−3.22	56.31	−1.94	72.52	14.26	50.29	−7.96	53.17	−5.08
A.2.2	Governance	35.58	38.95	3.37	42.02	6.44	34.32	−1.26	32.10	−3.48	50.71	15.13	31.79	−3.79	28.70	−6.88
A.3	Economical system	24.62	26.56	1.93	23.50	−1.12	25.05	0.43	25.15	0.53	31.01	6.39	23.91	−0.71	24.28	−0.35
A.3.1	Finance	34.35	38.29	3.94	31.64	−2.70	35.49	1.15	36.19	1.84	50.64	16.29	32.21	−2.13	33.59	−0.75
A.3.2	Work	38.58	40.03	1.45	38.27	−0.31	38.55	−0.03	38.00	−0.58	39.22	0.64	38.90	0.32	38.38	−0.20
A.3.3	Housing	0.00	0.00	0.00	0.00	0.00	0.00	0.00	0.00	0.00	0.00	0.00	0.00	0.00	0.00	0.00
A.4	Sociological system	37.70	37.00	−0.71	38.53	0.82	36.62	−1.08	38.02	0.32	41.10	3.39	35.35	−2.36	37.88	0.18
A.4.1	Demographic	46.31	43.24	−3.07	39.92	−6.39	46.67	0.36	47.45	1.14	42.41	−3.91	44.35	−1.96	55.07	8.76
A.4.2	Education	28.26	28.97	0.71	30.91	2.65	26.45	−1.81	27.35	−0.91	36.28	8.02	27.30	−0.96	26.06	−2.20
A.4.3	Inequalities	40.28	40.42	0.13	46.91	6.63	38.53	−1.76	41.28	0.99	45.92	5.64	35.65	−4.64	33.80	−6.48
A.5	Technological system	37.72	38.64	0.92	41.90	4.19	37.64	−0.08	38.71	1.00	35.99	−1.73	35.37	−2.35	32.60	−5.12
A.5.1	Transport	6.54	7.70	1.16	6.42	−0.13	4.32	−2.22	10.28	3.73	12.77	6.22	1.98	−4.56	6.29	−0.25
A.5.2	Technology adoption	41.23	44.03	2.80	55.97	14.73	39.61	−1.62	45.80	4.57	50.36	9.13	31.79	−9.45	23.22	−18.02
A.5.3	Consumption and production	62.53	61.28	−1.24	59.79	−2.74	65.99	3.46	57.35	−5.18	42.36	−20.17	69.51	6.98	66.19	3.67

the optimal state; Kuwait ranks 160th (with a total score of 32.82), which is 17.46 points lower than Finland. There is also a large variation in the scores across countries/territories. No country performances best in all dimensions and vice versa.

Significant Variations Exist in GOHI-EDI Scores Among Different Countries/Territories

The scoring range of each region, from high to low (sorted by the lowest score in region) are: North America, with a score range of 47.82–49.50; Latin America and the Caribbean, with a score range of 37.15–44.98; East Asia and Pacific, with a score range of 36.1–48.64; Europe and Central Asia, with a score range of 34.18–50.28; sub-Saharan Africa, with a score range of 34.17–42.32; South Asia, with a score range of 34.04–41.93; Middle East and North Africa, with a score range of 32.83–43.75. The smallest difference of total score between countries in one region is 1.68 points between North America and the largest difference is 16.10 points between Europe and Central Asia.

1.6   Conclusion

No country ranks first in all dimensions in the GOHI-EDI. Each country needs to improve in its own way due to various shortfalls. The GOHI-EDI organizes and analyzes data through the earth system, institutional system, economic system, sociological system, and technological system, which constructs objective indicators to measure One Health performance. It assesses the performance of each indicator in the EDI, which helps countries to realize their local status and therefore strengthen global action for One Health. Therefore, the performance of each country in the earth system, institutional system, economic system, sociological system, and technological system can achieve a balanced development.

2   Intrinsic Drivers Index

2.1   Background

As a global One Health assessment framework, the global One Health index (GOHI) comprises three components: EDI, IDI and CDI. The global One Health index-intrinsic drivers index (GOHI-IDI) is an index that describes the status of One Health globally for various countries. The GOHI-IDI focuses on the broad scope of human health, animal health, ecosystem diversity, and environmental health. The IDI describes the outcome of implementing One Health approach.

2.2   The Necessity to Evaluate Intrinsic Drivers of One Health

Taking a One Health perspective, evaluating intrinsic drivers is essential understanding the scope and interconnections between the health of humans, animals, and the environment. Intrinsic drivers are the underlying factors that shape and influence the health of these three interconnected domains.

Evaluating intrinsic drivers of One Health enables to identification the root causes of health issues that affect humans, animals, and the environment. For example, the emergence of zoonotic diseases like COVID-19 is driven by intrinsic factors such as pathogen spillover, animal habitat destruction, climate change, and wildlife trade. By understanding these factors, we can develop more effective strategies for preventing and controlling zoonotic diseases.

The GOHI project requires an indicator assessment framework that accurately reflects the global situation. Faithfully describing the situation of the ecological environment and the intervention measures taken by each country can help policymakers make informed decisions.

2.3 Framework of GOHI-IDI Constructed

Framework

As illustrated, the GOHI-IDI is for evaluating the human-animal-environmental health conditions. In a previous study, a three-level evaluation framework of the GOHI-IDI was developed based on a literature review, group discussions, and the analysis of 82 studies using Grounded Theory (GT), a qualitative research method proposed by American scholars Anselm Strauss and Barney Glaser in 1967 [12]. The GT includes open coding, axial coding, and selective coding to establish the framework. This framework was further developed through semi-structured interviews with health-related experts, and the indicators were integrated and simplified according to their inclusion criteria. To assign weights to these indicators, the Fuzzy Analytical Hierarchy Process (FAHP) was used, combined with the entropy weight method, forming the evaluation indicator framework of the human, animal, and environmental health development processes. The GOH-IDI scheme consists of 3 first-level indicators, 8 second-level indicators, and 22 third-level indicators, with weightings for each (Table 4.6).

Indicators

In this study, our group has structured the GOHI-IDI with the following indicators. The "Human health", "Animal health" and "Environmental health" indicators sit at the first level. "Universal health", "Diseases burden", "Injury and violence", "Animal epidemic disease", "Wildlife and marine life biodiversity", "Air quality and climate change", "Environmental biodiversity", and "Environmental resource" are the second-level indicators. "Life expectancy", "Health service coverage", "Domestic health expenditure", "Health risks", "Noncommunicable diseases", "Road traffic", "Homicide", "Diseases of domestic animal", "Diseases of wild animal", "Red list index", "Fisheries", "Air quality", "Climate risk index", "Biodiversity conditions", "Ecological services", "Water resources", "Acidification", "Clean water", "Waste reduction", "Heavy metal pollutants" are the selected third-level indicators.

Indicators of IDI-Human health cover the broad scope of human health from the macroscopic perspective. The potential individual health harm to humans, including reproductive, maternal, newborn and child health, infectious diseases, noncommunicable diseases, and mental health are synthesized into a key indicator as the Diseases burden. Health coverage which includes the two sub I-indicators, Health service coverage, Life expectancy, and Domestic health expenditure has been set as the key indicator as they are more concise and of generality; Health risks from all diseases are also categorized into this key indicator. The key indicator of external harm is formed with the two indicators, Road traffic and Homicide, to reflect health threats from the social context.

In the animal health section, two aggregated indicators from the Fisheries and Red list index (RLI) are used to reflect wildlife and marine health. The fisheries measure the health and sustainability of the world's fisheries. It is made up of three parts, which are fish stock status, marine trophic index, and fish caught by trawling. The RLI shows trends in overall extinction risk for groups of species. A declining RLI indicates that the risk of extinction among the species indexed is increasing and links the performance of countries with Sustainable Development Goals (SDG) targets.

In Environmental health, based on practical circumstances and expert consultation, an Environmental resources category has been included. The environmental resource is a combination of Sanitation and water resources, Hazardous chemicals, and Environmental biodiversity. Climate risk is an indicator reflecting the impact of climate change on countries globally; however, there was no data update for 2023. The Environmental Performance Index of Yale (EPI) is the main database used.

Data Sources

The raw data collection and calculation were constructed in five steps, including framework formulation, indicator selection, database building, weight determination, and GOHI scores calculation. In the GOHI-IDI, indicators are derived from statistics from international agencies and

Table 4.6 Indicator and weight scheme of the global One Health index-intrinsic drivers index (GOHI-IDI)

Indicator			Sub I-indicator			Sub II-indicator		
Name	Code	Weight (%)	Name	Code	Weight (%)	Name	Code	Weight (%)
Human health	B1	33.3	Health coverage	B1.1	33.3	Life expectancy	B1.1.1	25.0
						Health service coverage	B1.1.2	25.0
						Domestic health expenditure	B1.1.3	25.0
						Health risks	B1.1.4	25.0
			Diseases burden	B1.2	33.3	Infectious diseases	B1.2.1	33.0
						Noncommunicable diseases	B1.2.2	33.0
						Metal health	B1.2.3	33.0
			Injury and violence	B1.3	33.3	Road traffic	B1.3.1	50.0
						Homicide	B1.3.2	50.0
Animal health	B2	33.3	Animal epidemic disease	B2.1	50.0	Diseases of domestic animal	B2.1.1	50.0
						Diseases of wild animal	B2.1.2	50.0
			Wildlife and marine life biodiversity	B2.2	50.0	Fisheries	B2.2.1	50.0
						Red list index	B2.2.2	50.0
Environmental health	B3	33.3	Air quality and climate change	B3.1	33.3	Air quality	B3.1.1	50.0
						Climate risk index	B3.1.2	50.0
			Environmental biodiversity	B3.2	33.3	Biodiversity conditions	B3.2.1	50.0
						Ecological services	B3.2.2	50.0
			Environmental resources	B3.3	33.3	Water resources	B3.3.1	20.0
						Acidification	B3.3.2	20.0
						Clean water	B3.3.3	20.0
						Waste reduction	B3.3.4	20.0
						Heavy metal pollutants	B3.3.5	20.0

their databases, such as the World Bank, WHO, the SDGs dashboard, Our World in Data from the United Nations, EPI, World Animal Information System of the World Animal Health Organization (WOAH-WAHIS), and other international organizations.

Limitations

There are some limitations of this study. Firstly, data sources that have been adopted may have their own limitations. The in-depth analysis of original data or materials could not be repeated to evaluate the quality and rationality of the data included in this report, which may result in the possibility of errors in the estimation of the results. The intrinsic dynamics of the GOH-IDI have not been investigated to learn the underlying connections when developing the GOH-IDI as an indicator system.

2.4   Main Results

An indicator framework for GOHI-IDI was established in this study. The framework is universal, balanced, and scientific, and will hopefully be a tool for the evaluation of the joint development of human, animal, and environmental health in different countries/territories around the world.

A total of 160 countries/territories worldwide were included in this study, of which 21 were in East Asia and Pacific, 47 were in Europe and Central Asia, 23 were in Latin America and the Caribbean, 18 were in the Middle East and North Africa, 2 were in North America, 8 were in South Asia, and 41 were in sub-Saharan Africa.

Global Score

The numbers in Table 4.7 represent the scores of each country/territory, and the depth of color represents the ranking of the country/territory. The mean (SD) score of GOHI-IDI is 58.04 (6.20), the lowest score is 41.99, and the highest score is 71.88. The mean (SD) score of Human health is 72.35(10.74). The mean (SD) score of Animal health is 56.58 (4.27). The mean (SD) score of Environmental health is 46.87 (12.84). In Fig. 4.6

showing the scores of GOHI-IDI for countries and regions around the world, lighter colors indicate higher scores. The average score in North America (67.35) is the highest.

The total scores of GOHI-IDI by regions are as follows (sorted by median): North America (67.35), South Asia (62.07), Latin America and the Caribbean (61.12), Europe and Central Asia (61.09), the Middle East and Africa (60.92), East Asia and Pacific (58.12) and sub-Saharan Africa (52.01). The total scores by region are shown in Fig. 4.6, illustrating that among the seven regions around the world, North America's situation is significantly better than other regions, while sub-Saharan Africa lags behind (Fig. 4.7).

The scores of key indicators from high to low are as follows: Human health (B1, score: 73.60), Animal health (B2, score: 55.99), Environmental health (B3, score: 45.76). Diseases burden (B1.3), Animal epidemic disease (B2.1), and Air quality and climate change (B3.1) each have the highest average score in their corresponding dimensions with 80.74, 94.57 and 53.72 respectively (Fig. 4.8).

Based on Shapiro-Wilk's normality test, Human health ($P = 0.002$) and Animal health ($P = 4.874e - 08$) do not follow a normal distribution, while IDI ($P = 0.49$) and Environment health ($P = 0.1621$) do follow a normal distribution (Fig. 4.9).

Global Ranking

The GOH-IDI scores for 160 countries/territories are evaluated to generate the global ranking, it is shown in Table 4.7. France (71.89) and Lesotho (41.99) rank first and last, respectively, in GOHI-IDI. Generally, countries/territories from North America, Europe and Central Asia have higher GOHI-IDI scores, while countries/territories in sub-Saharan Africa and South Asia reveal lower scores. The top 25 countries/territories are France, Oman, Switzerland, the United Kingdom, Austria, India, Australia, Cyprus, the United States, Iceland, Canada, Italy, Bahrain, Sri Lanka, Panama, Nicaragua, Czech Republic, Luxembourg, Costa Rica, Singapore, Belgium, Qatar, Maldives, Portugal, and Japan. The top rankings contain nine countries/territories in Europe and Central Asia.

Table 4.7 The score of the global One Health index-intrinsic drivers index (GOHI-IDI) for countries

Country	Human health	B 1.1 Health coverage	B 1.2 Diseases burden	B 1.3 Injury and violence	Animal health	B 2.1 Animal epidemic disease	B 2.2 Wildlife and marine life biodiversity	Environmental health	B 3.1 Air quality and climate change	B 3.2 Environmental biodiversity	B 3.3 Environmental resources	Global one health intrinsic drivers index
Afghanistan	63.15	30.08	79.97	81.33	56.74	94.82	18.65	32.58	38.89	46.25	13.6	50.32
Albania	77.39	61.41	84.37	88.74	59.29	94.26	24.32	50.76	68.75	44.06	41.02	61.86
Algeria	79.71	70.08	90.24	81.21	54.67	95.59	13.75	43.84	64.14	23.2	45.5	58.81
Argentina	79.31	72.67	83.87	84	54.11	97.32	10.9	45.44	50.86	32.7	54.14	59.02
Armenia	72.75	55.75	81.79	82.93	57.9	97.58	18.22	53.36	57.45	66.5	37.74	60.72
Australia	87.91	88.13	82.94	95.32	55.95	95.11	16.8	62.84	56.53	51.1	82.8	66.21
Austria	84.2	81.59	78.27	95.3	55.27	92.41	18.13	69.08	60.98	57	91.36	66.82
Azerbaijan	74.03	49.27	82.38	92.68	50.69	89.63	12.15	47.43	61.05	52.15	30.52	56.88
Bahrain	81.34	67.56	89.99	88.93	58.8	98.14	19.45	62.66	67.35	57.65	64.94	66.93
Bangladesh	72.5	46.31	87.53	86.84	61.02	91.98	30.05	19.69	16.23	26.15	17.3	50.56
Barbados	76.74	64.11	80.15	84.29	55.28	89.41	15.15	53.45	82.65	24.75	54.56	60.21
Belarus	72.1	60.56	66.15	91.79	54.98	96.01	13.9	59.2	73.05	42.3	64.04	61.47
Belgium	83.34	83.2	76.1	93.25	51.65	94.09	9.2	63.82	64.76	49.35	79.28	65.6
Belize	75.04	63.11	88.96	76.41	56.33	90.81	21.85	56.38	68.8	60.8	41.24	61.96
Benin	57.92	25.88	73.19	76.43	50.84	91.52	10.15	39.55	61.15	39.7	19	48.94
Bhutan	76.46	58.58	86.78	88.33	62.53	93.86	31.2	49.09	59.8	56.45	32.52	62.07
Bolivia	72.84	58.81	84.29	77.62	53.73	93.9	13.57	33.64	22.37	47.8	31.78	52.87
Botswana	58.52	42.24	70.8	64.29	51.34	95.5	7.18	49.44	50.67	74.05	26.1	52.57
Brazil	69.66	66.12	83.71	61.26	57.63	99.11	16.15	45.12	35.69	47.65	53.18	56.89
Brunei Darussalam	81.86	66.31	90.96	90.77	62.13	92.56	11.7	58.84	80.85	39.6	57.84	63.63
Bulgaria	68.76	55.15	61.63	91.59	56.59	98.28	14.9	56.25	56.93	56.25	57.26	59.93
Burkina Faso	50.05	31.41	65.39	54.88	54.73	97.02	12.45	41.91	63.05	44.1	19.84	48.41
Burundi	59.45	35.18	77.34	67.62	55.02	92.94	17.1	31.97	41	32.25	23.62	48.32
Cabo Verde	73.32	64.76	84.67	72.73	73.37	92.23	54.5	42.41	49.16	46.45	32.9	62.4
Cambodia	62.73	51.14	83.62	55.33	55.97	95.29	16.65	33.8	44.67	37.75	20.02	50.33
Cameroon	56.9	25.92	75.91	70.6	55.01	96.81	13.2	29.52	34.63	30.55	24.26	46.67
Canada	86.94	88.38	80.89	94.16	61.09	93.77	8.4	65.93	71.31	46.35	82.12	67.3
Central African Republic	42.36	9.61	52.9	66.87	60.04	93.58	26.5	38	37.61	59.95	17.6	46.33
Chad	47.91	10.58	62.92	71.67	53.59	92.73	14.44	38.73	62.15	35.7	19.52	46.27
Chile	83.25	82.48	85.56	84.23	60.52	97.39	23.65	50.74	37.35	44.85	71.56	64.19
China	79.38	71.2	83.3	86.06	60.65	98.94	22.35	29.74	27.71	15.5	46.9	56.02
Colombia	76.18	76.34	90.81	63.7	54.4	92.49	16.3	46.74	36.59	54	51.04	56.52
Costa Rica	83.54	87.13	88.29	77.74	58.68	99.11	18.25	57.43	75.7	45.7	52.64	65.89
Cote d'Ivoire	61.31	30.82	75.37	79.58	56.17	92.69	19.65	45.69	56.36	56.85	25.24	53.84
Croatia	76.65	67.24	71.74	93.29	57.42	96.64	18	61.39	54.33	57.95	73.76	64.5
Cuba	79.47	73.44	76.98	90.4	58.46	92.96	23.95	45.83	64.44	32.65	41.78	60.64
Cyprus	84.79	74.97	87.64	94.34	49.64	95.68	3.6	70.06	84.15	55.4	72.8	67.49
Czech Republic	81.22	73.83	78.07	94.21	57.21	97.65	16.77	63.19	62.61	51.2	77.68	66.53
Dem. Rep. Congo	59.5	30.04	79.8	70.46	53.38	92.28	14.47	33.58	36.83	43	21.94	48.33
Denmark	85.38	83.81	78.75	96.17	50.8	94.66	6.95	39.09	53.52	43	21.94	57.84

Tab. 4.7 (continued)

Country	Human health	B 1.1 Health coverage	B 1.2 Diseases burden	B 1.3 Injury and violence	Animal health	B 2.1 Animal epidemic disease	B 2.2 Wildlife and marine life biodiversity	Environmental health	B 3.1 Air quality and climate change	B 3.2 Environmental biodiversity	B 3.3 Environmental resources	Global one health intrinsic drivers index
Djibouti	63.5	34.99	80.03	77.41	52.74	92.23	13.25	69.84	71.82	46.65	93.16	61.41
Dominican Republic	63.46	66.76	85.2	40.34	61.61	84.01	39.2	44.97	54.52	34.4	47.36	56.11
Ecuador	79.61	73.82	88.54	78.87	62.16	98.22	26.1	47.86	66.75	48.8	29.48	62.58
Egypt	76.98	55.5	86.93	90.85	54.65	99.51	9.8	53.66	65.91	50.5	46.2	61.15
El Salvador	63.77	72.12	87.28	33.85	56.02	96.04	16	48.26	60.36	48.8	37.08	55.46
Equatorial Guinea	63.32	32.61	83.97	75.29	56.5	92.05	20.95	44.94	57	34.85	44.32	54.37
Estonia	78.2	70.09	72.35	94.51	55.99	91.09	20.9	43.76	59.65	49.45	23.52	58.73
Eswatini	53.05	34.47	60.8	65.48	56.01	90.96	21.05	64.89	68.96	50.6	77.1	57.4
Ethiopia	61.6	33.92	85.06	67.69	57.84	89.44	26.25	41.48	58.45	24.8	42.46	53.11
Fiji	67.48	48.34	75	81.13	61.88	92.61	31.15	35.87	47.63	28.87	32.19	54.52
Finland	83.12	79.88	76.58	95.42	59.26	96.83	21.7	34.42	45.64	19.55	39.12	58.35
France	85.45	83.51	80.54	94.88	57.27	96.3	18.25	75.08	88.01	45.6	93.92	71.88
Gabon	62.19	45.31	81.27	61.88	51.21	96.41	6	50.62	55.37	56.48	41.53	54.13
Georgia	70.19	53.92	70.53	88.26	53.87	95.64	12.1	31.3	32.24	35.35	27.26	51.27
Germany	84.91	86.04	75.09	96.16	56.18	95.91	14.45	46.39	53.19	45.8	41.6	61.54
Ghana	62.42	38.5	80.59	70.07	55.19	95.99	14.4	68.38	63.03	53.2	90.98	61.38
Greece	78.89	68.67	77.74	92.66	54.43	92.55	16.3	30.59	29.61	31.6	31.48	54.09
Guatemala	69.66	62.51	87.93	60.65	59.21	91.67	26.75	50.34	71.75	32.4	48.4	59.14
Guinea	55.73	25.78	68.36	74.72	56.51	96.52	16.5	46.75	61.8	51.33	28.54	52.47
Guinea-Bissau	54.87	22.8	74.06	69.4	57.16	93.82	20.5	36.83	52.34	37.25	22.02	49.12
Guyana	61.42	55.83	61.28	69.01	52.93	92.56	13.3	44.34	59.7	52.25	22.4	52.37
Honduras	66.04	59.88	90.14	50.1	60.86	95.32	26.4	47.91	52.51	54.72	37.95	57.69
Hungary	72.25	60.45	67.67	90.83	57.67	98.2	17.13	44.39	56.77	37.35	40.39	57.52
Iceland	89.33	87.55	85.61	97.56	57.38	98.67	16.1	57.36	55.15	53	65.66	67.35
India	69.33	45.51	79.68	85	62.93	97.11	28.75	75.43	85.35	67.2	76.02	68.55
Indonesia	71.76	51.42	84.51	81.53	59.31	97.96	20.65	15.61	9.97	15.4	21.92	48.4
Iran	80.15	81.23	89.21	72.43	57.85	99.51	20.2	26.38	20.36	32.4	27.18	54.24
Iraq	72.91	51.37	91.64	77.91	58.35	93.62	23.08	39.26	31.35	47.15	40.48	56.27
Ireland	89.12	88.74	84.58	96.74	54.58	96.06	13.1	44.36	51.3	49.25	33.86	62.06
Israel	89.11	82.29	91.43	96.32	60.68	93.56	27.8	34.17	39.87	41.73	21.96	60.71
Italy	84.22	80.27	79.62	95.34	53.53	93.17	13.9	65.46	80.02	40.95	77.38	67.06
Jamaica	65.14	64.76	86.45	46.19	59.66	93.88	25.45	60.51	52.4	51.3	79.66	61.15
Japan	89.23	66.33	78.12	96.96	56.84	93.88	19.8	49.86	69.9	41.65	64.66	64.66
Jordan	80.6	66.4	96.56	83.27	62.48	94.41	10.56	47.23	62.66	39.18	41.28	59.5
Kazakhstan	74.15	59.79	76.96	87.95	55.9	97.89	13.91	55.29	75.36	43.66	48.54	61.16
Kenya	66.29	43.26	84.27	73.35	57.09	95.47	18.7	50.86	64.3	44.35	45.46	57.5
Kuwait	82.87	60.73	95.72	85.67	56.81	95.83	17.8	41.92	45.2	42.4	39.44	59.93
Kyrgyzstan	77.06	58.03	87.37	88.1	51.34	94.15	8.53	56.8	73.5	44.5	54.12	61.11
Laos	67.09	41.95	83.12	78.23	55.57	92.4	18.73	40.2	43.11	45.1	33.62	53.74
Latvia	70.9	60.07	65.2	89.58	57.54	95.38	19.7	32.42	34.06	46.05	18.14	53.08
Lebanon	79.5	69.44	86.58	84.88	52.66	94.12	11.2	62.42	62.04	50.05	77.06	64.21

Country	Human health	B 1.1 Health coverage	B 1.2 Diseases burden	B 1.3 Injury and violence	Animal health	B 2.1 Animal epidemic disease	B 2.2 Wildlife and marine life biodiversity	Environmental health	B 3.1 Air quality and climate change	B 3.2 Environmental biodiversity	B 3.3 Environmental resources	Global one health intrinsic drivers index
Rwanda	68.43	47.6	85.18	74.58	55.2	95.42	14.99	42.81	45.21	31.55	52.98	54.93
Saudi Arabia	77.24	71.06	92.02	70.98	55.33	95.91	14.75	52.65	46.71	79.55	33.3	61.12
Senegal	61.92	40.31	82.78	64.55	54.92	94.59	14.95	53.28	46.89	64.65	49.92	56.14
Serbia	74.41	61.85	70.6	93.04	52.19	94.27	10.11	32.81	39.16	40.3	19.96	52.6
Seychelles	74.91	60.91	80.41	85.67	59.56	92.47	26.65	48.8	53.43	43.2	51.26	60.48
Sierra Leone	54.45	28.54	69.6	66.87	56.28	92.06	20.5	66.8	77.4	73.9	51.12	58.58
Singapore	90.65	86.31	90.15	98.23	76.64	95.77	57.5	32.09	42.81	33.5	20.92	65.79
Slovakia	79.08	68.85	76.6	94.21	55.64	97.96	13.32	51.91	61.87	43.68	51.75	61.59
Slovenia	81.28	76.27	74.4	95.63	54.49	97.49	11.48	59.52	59.63	51.3	69.44	64.44
Solomon Islands	64.44	45.64	67.36	82.28	55.54	92.22	18.85	69.19	66.2	59.3	84.16	62.43
Somalia	53.12	20.16	66.95	73.87	53.25	92.03	14.47	32.35	64.3	9.9	23.82	45.78
South Africa	54.99	50.88	67.96	47.82	61.07	95.68	26.45	38.73	38.13	54.18	25.07	51.08
South Korea	85.69	85.84	83.97	89.87	59.23	96.57	21.9	33.74	24.03	34.55	43.66	58.96
Spain	86.83	84.77	81.98	96.38	56.27	96.84	15.7	41.51	31.29	41.83	52.67	60.92
Sri Lanka	75.67	63.96	82.9	82.43	65.01	92.13	37.9	62.04	54.41	49.6	83.98	66.9
Sudan	65.62	39.45	85.99	73.42	55.06	98.12	12	46.93	54.74	50.92	36.55	55.31
Sweden	87.55	88.99	79.79	96.53	51.09	94.04	8.15	48.64	68.45	46.3	32.64	61.8
Switzerland	86.18	81.96	81.49	97.69	51.24	95.02	7.47	76.47	89.41	49.05	93.26	70.58
Tajikistan	75.15	56.13	86.72	84.89	52.05	96.86	7.23	58.85	73.1	43.05	62.18	61.4
Tanzania	64.24	42.36	77.92	74.38	58.83	92.6	25.05	45.91	50.17	70.3	18.66	55.76
Thailand	76.87	77.42	82.6	72.9	56.75	95.56	17.95	38.47	44.27	44.45	27.84	56.79
Timor-Leste	71.42	44.39	86.61	85.44	58.81	92.97	24.65	38.76	34.76	33.35	49.34	55.77
Togo	60.13	32.61	77.61	71.97	52.15	93.75	10.55	44.57	66.25	44.65	24.16	51.76
Trinidad and Tobago	67	62.61	78.11	62.31	56.77	95.3	18.25	49.76	70.95	31.62	48.21	57.27
Tunisia	78.76	67.26	88.07	83.33	53.39	94.23	12.55	56.71	77.15	50.65	44.04	62.32
Turkey	82.82	70.17	88.47	92.34	53.67	96.58	10.75	48.63	71.65	28.05	47.66	61.09
Turkmenistan	73.86	58.13	81.72	83.97	52.82	96.3	9.34	37.55	49.76	14.75	49.28	54.2
Uganda	60.72	35.42	81.43	67.14	62.3	96.84	27.76	45.65	61.26	50.23	26.85	55.66
Ukraine	65.63	52.66	57.2	89	57.01	99.16	14.85	34.04	30.82	45.2	27.14	51.7
United Arab Emirates	78.29	70.11	89.86	77.26	59.02	97.44	20.6	47.91	49.82	42.5	52.86	61.12
United Kingdom	86.09	87.35	77.69	95.84	53.73	96.96	10.5	73.95	70.85	90.15	63.1	70.55
United States of America	79.76	83.81	72.46	85.43	51.51	85.92	17.1	72.97	77.52	52.55	91.04	67.4
Uruguay	76.4	80.01	74.53	76.97	53.9	97.45	10.35	63.08	75.94	40.35	74.88	63.62
Uzbekistan	75.76	58.41	82.93	88.25	51.33	93.56	9.09	43.71	65.18	16.75	50.52	56.36
Vanuatu	66.16	43.8	73.64	83.03	60.18	92.87	27.5	45.04	58.35	47.75	30.38	56.56
Viet Nam	73.45	63.53	85.41	73.65	60.66	94.73	26.6	53.55	73.35	52.55	36.36	61.93
Zambia	60.43	38.55	78.05	66.53	58.33	98.66	18	43.7	39.91	50.42	42.09	53.61
Zimbabwe	56.56	37.15	72.74	61.51	56.04	90.91	21.17	37.39	38.1	55.45	19.76	49.5

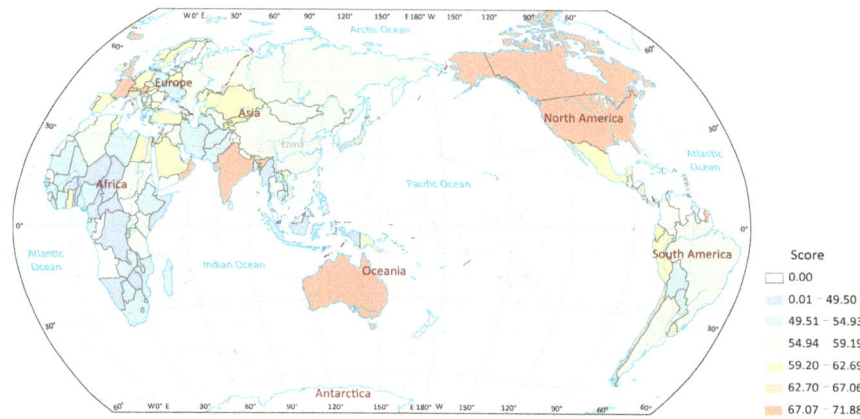

Fig. 4.6 Global score map of the global One Health index-intrinsic drivers index (GOHI-IDI)

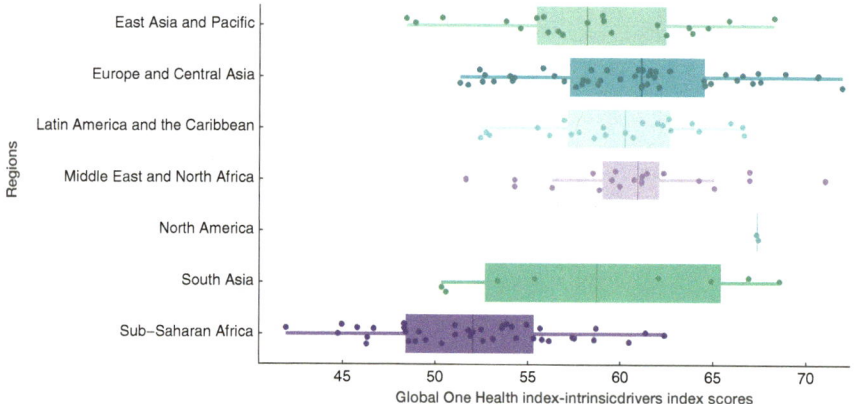

Fig. 4.7 Regional score distribution of the global One Health index-intrinsic drivers index (GOHI-IDI)

Fig. 4.8 Score distribution of the global One Health index-intrinsic drivers index (GOHI-IDI) by indicators. (*HCR* health coverage, *DBD* diseases burden, *INV* injury and violence, *AED* animal epidemic disease, *WMB* wildlife and marine life biodiversity, *AQC* air quality and climate change, *EBO* environmental biodiversity, *ERE* environmental resources)

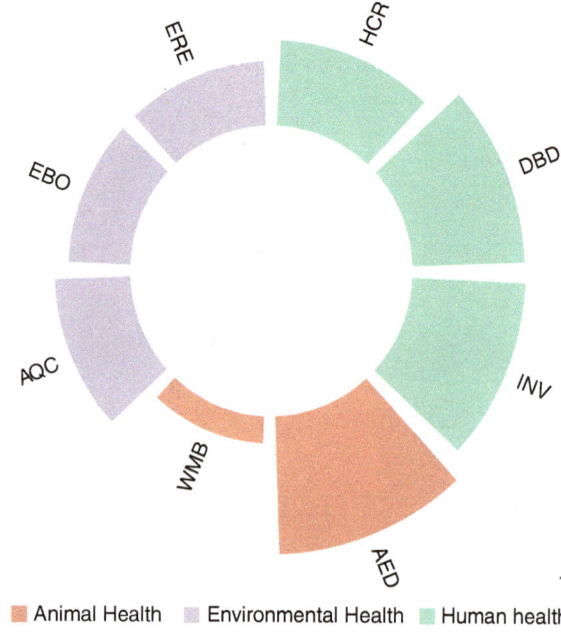

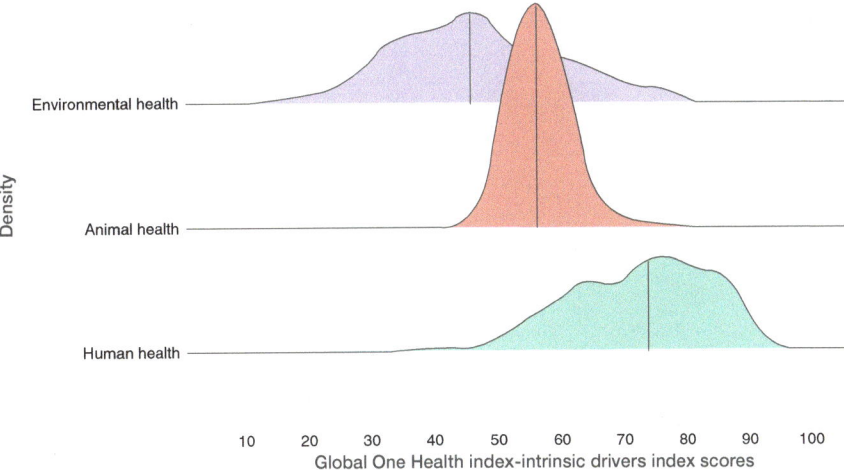

Environmental health

Density

Animal health

Human health

10   20   30   40   50   60   70   80   90   100
Global One Health index-intrinsic drivers index scores

Fig. 4.9 Dimensional score distribution of the global One Health index-intrinsic drivers index (GOHI-IDI)

The bottom 20 countries/territories are Lesotho, Namibia, Liberia, Somalia, Chad, Central African Republic, Cameroon, Burundi, and Dem. Rep. Congo, Niger, Indonesia, Burkina Faso, Malawi, Myanmar, Benin, Guinea-Bissau, Zimbabwe, Afghanistan, Cambodia, and Nigeria. Among them, the majority [16] are from sub-Sahara Africa.

Regional Ranking

The scores of GOH-IDI vary even within regions in most circumstances. The scoring range of different regions, from high to low are East Asia and Pacific, with a score range of 68.21 to 48.40; the Middle East and North Africa, with a score range of 70.98 to 51.60; Europe and Central Asia, with a score range of 71.88 to 51.27; Latin America and the Caribbean, with a score range of 66.62 to 52.37; South Asia, with a score range of 46.76 to 37.16; and sub-Saharan Africa, with a score range of 62.4 to 41.99. North America's situation is significantly better than the other 6 regions of the world, scoring 67.40 (America) and 67.30 (Canada) (Table 4.8).

1. *East Asia and Pacific*

   The best-performing countries/territories in East Asia and Pacific are Australia (68.21), ranking 7th globally. Singapore (65.79) ranks 20th in the world and Japan (64.66) ranks 25th the world. Indonesia (48.40)

ranks last in the region with a global ranking of 150th.

2. *Europe and Central Asia*

   There are 47 countries/territories evaluated in Europe and Central Asia. The best-performing countries are France (71.88) which ranks 1st in the world, Switzerland (70.58), and the United Kingdom (70.55). Georgia (51.27) ranks last in this region and ranks 138th in the world.

3. *Latin America and the Caribbean*

   Of the 23 countries/territories evaluated in the region, the best-performing countries are Panama (66.62), Nicaragua (66.53), and Costa Rica (65.89). Panama ranks 15th in the world. Guyana (52.37) ranks last in Latin America and The Caribbean region, and 130th in the world.

4. *Middle East and North Africa*

   There are 18 countries/territories in the Middle East and North Africa. The best-performing countries are Oman (70.98), which ranks 2nd in the world, Bahrain (66.93), and Qatar (65.03). Libya (51.60) ranks last in the region and 136th in the world.

5. *North America*

   The best-performing country/territory in North America is the United States (67.40) ranks 9th in the world. As there are only 2 countries, Canada (67.30) ranks second and 11th in the world.

Table 4.8 Regional ranking of the global One Health index-intrinsic drivers index (GOHI-IDI)

East Asia and Pacific

Rank	Country	Score
1	Australia	68.21
2	Singapore	65.79
3	Japan	64.66
4	New Zealand	63.83
5	Brunei Darussalam	63.63
6	Solomon Islands	62.43
7	Viet Nam	61.93
8	Papua New Guinea	59.43
9	Philippines	59
10	South Korea	58.96
11	Mongolia	58.12
12	Thailand	56.79
13	Vanuatu	56.56
14	China	56.02
15	Timor-Leste	55.77
16	Malaysia	55.39
17	Fiji	54.52
18	Laos	53.74
19	Cambodia	50.33
20	Myanmar	48.89
21	Indonesia	48.4
22	Solomon Islands	38.34

Middle East and North Africa

Rank	Country	Score
1	Oman	70.98
2	Bahrain	66.93
3	Qatar	65.03
4	Lebanon	64.21
5	Tunisia	62.32
6	Djibouti	61.41
7	Egypt	61.15
8	Saudi Arabia	61.12
9	United Arab Emirates	61.12
10	Israel	60.71
11	Kuwait	59.93
12	Malta	59.69
13	Jordan	59.5
14	Algeria	58.81
15	Morocco	58.47
16	Iraq	56.27
17	Iran	54.24
18	Libya	51.6
19	Djibouti	38.61

Table 4.8 (continued)

Europe and Central Asia

Rank	Country	Score
1	France	71.88
2	Switzerland	70.58
3	United Kingdom	70.55
4	Austria	68.82
5	Cyprus	67.49
6	Iceland	67.35
7	Italy	67.06
8	Czech Republic	66.53
9	Luxembourg	66.22
10	Belgium	65.6
11	Portugal	64.81
12	Croatia	64.5
13	Slovenia	64.44
14	Norway	62.62
15	Ireland	62.06
16	Albania	61.86
17	Sweden	61.8
18	Slovakia	61.59
19	Germany	61.54
20	Belarus	61.47
21	Tajikistan	61.4
22	Kazakhstan	61.16
23	Kyrgyzstan	61.11
24	Turkey	61.09
25	Spain	60.92
26	Armenia	60.72
27	Bulgaria	59.93
28	Russia	59.19
29	Romania	58.84
30	Estonia	58.73
31	Finland	58.35
32	Moldova	58.16
33	North Macedonia	57.91
34	Denmark	57.84
35	Hungary	57.52
36	Azerbaijan	56.88
37	Uzbekistan	56.36
38	Lithuania	55.76
39	Turkmenistan	54.2
40	Greece	54.09
41	Netherlands	53.97
42	Latvia	53.08
43	Serbia	52.6
44	Poland	52.47
45	Montenegro	52.31
46	Ukraine	51.7
47	Georgia	51.27
48	Tajikistan	45.50

Table 4.8 (continued)

Sub-Saharan Africa

Rank	Country	Score
1	Cabo Verde	62.4
2	Ghana	61.38
3	Seychelles	60.48
4	Mauritius	58.68
5	Sierra Leone	58.58
6	Kenya	57.5
7	Eswatini	57.4
8	Senegal	56.14
9	Tanzania	55.76
10	Uganda	55.66
11	Sudan	55.31
12	Rwanda	54.93
13	Equatorial Guinea	54.37
14	Gabon	54.13
15	Cote d'Ivoire	53.84
16	Zambia	53.61
17	Madagascar	53.59
18	Ethiopia	53.11
19	Botswana	52.57
20	Guinea	52.47
21	Mauritania	52.01
22	Mozambique	51.89
23	Togo	51.76
24	South Africa	51.08
25	Mali	51.05
26	Nigeria	50.36
27	Zimbabwe	49.5
28	Guinea-Bissau	49.12
29	Benin	48.94
30	Malawi	48.57
31	Burkina Faso	48.41
32	Niger	48.35
33	Dem. Rep. Congo	48.33
34	Burundi	48.32
35	Cameroon	46.67
36	Central African Republic	46.33
37	Chad	46.27
38	Somalia	45.78
39	Liberia	44.96
40	Namibia	44.76
41	Lesotho	41.99
42	Guinea-Bissau	38.43
43	Chad	37.46
44	Somalia	37.04
45	Central African Republic	36.87
46	South Sudan	36.53

Table 4.8 (continued)

South Asia

Rank	Country	Score
1	India	68.55
2	Sri Lanka	66.9
3	Maldives	64.9
4	Bhutan	62.07
5	Nepal	55.36
6	Pakistan	53.34
7	Bangladesh	50.56
8	Afghanistan	50.32

Latin America and the Caribbean

Rank	Country	Score
1	Panama	66.62
2	Nicaragua	66.53
3	Costa Rica	65.89
4	Chile	64.19
5	Uruguay	63.82
6	Mexico	62.69
7	Ecuador	62.58
8	Peru	62.24
9	Belize	61.96
10	Jamaica	61.15
11	Cuba	60.64
12	Barbados	60.21
13	Guatemala	59.14
14	Argentina	59.02
15	Colombia	58.52
16	Honduras	57.69
17	Trinidad and Tobago	57.27
18	Brazil	56.89
19	Dominican Republic	56.11
20	El Salvador	55.46
21	Bolivia	52.87
22	Paraguay	52.66
23	Guyana	52.37
24	Saint Lucia	44.77
25	Barbados	44.45
26	Venezuela	43.90
27	Bahamas	43.60
28	Haiti	42.31

North America

Rank	Country	Score
1	United States	67.4
2	Canada	67.3

6. *Southern Asia*

There are 8 countries/territories included in the region. The best-performing countries/ territories in South Asia are India (68.55) with a global ranking 6th, Sri Lanka (66.90), and Maldives (64.90). Afghanistan (50.32) scores the lowest in the region, and its global ranking is 143rd.

7. *Sub-Saharan Africa*

41 countries/territories in the sub-Saharan Africa were include. The best-performing countries are Cabo Verde (62.40), Ghana (61.38), and Seychelles (60.48). Lesotho (41.99) scores the lowest, both in the region and the world.

The regional average scores for the GOHI-IDI indicators and comparisons with the global average scores are shown in Table 4.9. North America performs the best in most indicators, including Human health (B1, average 83.35; gap 11.00), Health coverage (B1.1, average 86.10; gap 27.44), Injury and violence (B1.3, average 89.81; gap 9.06), Environmental health (B3, average 69.45; gap 22.58), Air quality and climate change (B3.1, average 74.42; gap 20.69), Environmental biodiversity (B3.2, average 49.45; gap 5.40) and Environmental resources (B3.3, average 86.58; gap 43.33). Middle East and North Africa perform the best in Diseases burden (B1.2, average 89.37; gap 9.54). Europe and Central Asia perform the best in Animal epidemic disease (B2.1, average 95.49; gap 0.92). South Asia performs the best in Animal health (B2, average 61.25; gap 4.68) and Wildlife and marine life biodiversity (B2.2, average 28.38; gap 9.8).

2.5   Key Findings

The Total Score of GOHI-IDI Shows Disparity Within Regions

The total score range of GOHI-IDI is 71.89–41.99. Generally, by regions, countries that score higher than 60.00, are 64 countries/territories in total, they are mostly distributed in North America, West and North Europe, and East Asia and Pacific, such as France, Switzerland, the United Kingdom, Austria, and Australia. The score

between 50.00 and 60.00 is those developing countries/territories in Europe and Central Asia, Middle East and North Africa, Latin America and the Caribbean, East Asia and Pacific, 79 in total, such as Bulgaria, Malta, Romania, Guatemala, Philippines, and Pakistan. Scores under 50.00 are mostly resource-limited countries/territories in sub-Saharan Africa and East Asia and Pacific, of 17 countries/territories in total, including Zimbabwe, Guinea-Bissau, Benin, Myanmar and so on.

The Performance in Human Health, Animal Health, and Environmental Health Is Not Balanced Well Even Within the Top-Ranking Countries

Take Oman and Singapore for example, for total scores of GOHI-IDI, Oman ranks 2nd in the Middle East and North Africa and Singapore ranks 20th in East Asia and Pacific. Oman performs well in animal health and environmental health indicators. As the government of Oman pays much attention to environmental protection, the natural ecology is well preserved, and the territory has a famous turtle, bird habitat and protected area. However, the human health-related indicators do not score that well, which may pin the poor performance of human health on the low health expenditure. Singapore ranks 1st in human health with the best clinical facilities and health system in the region but ranks 142nd in environmental health, since the low-lying island nation is highly urbanized and has a very fragile ecological environment.

3   Governance

3.1   Background

Definitions

Governance is the process by which the public and private sectors manage their affairs and reconcile conflicting interests to take joint action. According to the United Nations, good governance involves "creating well-functioning and accountable institutions—political, juridical and administrative—that citizens regard as legitimate, through which they participate in decisions

Table 4.9 Regional performance of the global One Health index-intrinsic drivers index (GOHI-IDI)

Indicator		Global	East Asia and Pacific		Europe and Central Asia		Latin America and the Caribbean		Middle East and North Africa		North America		South Asia		Sub-Saharan Africa	
Code	Title		Average	Gap	Average	Gap	Average	Gap	Average	Gap	Average	Gap	Average	Gap	Average	Gap
B	IDI	58.01	58.21	0.20	60.56	2.55	59.85	1.84	60.75	2.74	67.35	9.34	59.00	0.99	52.11	−5.90
B.1	Human Health	72.35	74.72	2.37	78.89	6.55	74.11	1.77	78.91	6.56	83.35	11.00	72.41	0.07	59.21	−13.14
B.1.1	Health Coverage	58.65	61.82	3.17	70.06	11.41	69.85	11.20	66.15	7.49	86.10	27.44	50.58	−8.08	34.62	−24.03
B.1.2	Diseases burden	79.83	82.35	2.52	76.81	−3.02	84.88	5.04	89.37	9.54	76.68	−3.16	83.93	4.10	74.34	−5.49
B.1.3	Injury and violence	80.75	82.25	1.50	92.20	11.45	69.86	10.89	83.58	2.84	89.81	9.06	84.93	4.18	70.45	−10.30
B.2	Animal Health	56.58	58.79	2.22	54.67	−1.91	57.67	1.09	56.13	−0.45	51.30	−5.28	61.25	4.68	56.56	−0.02
B.2.1	Animal Epidemic Disease	94.57	94.48	−0.09	95.49	0.92	94.49	−0.08	94.60	0.03	89.85	−4.72	94.12	−0.45	93.91	−0.66
B.2.2	Wildlife and Marine life biodiversity	18.59	23.11	4.52	13.85	−4.74	20.84	2.25	17.67	−0.92	12.75	−5.84	28.38	9.80	19.22	0.63
B.3	Environmental Health	46.87	42.88	−3.99	49.96	3.09	49.58	2.71	49.06	2.19	69.45	22.58	45.12	−1.75	42.13	−4.74
B.3.1	Air Quality and Climate Change	53.72	47.97	−5.75	56.13	2.40	57.14	3.42	55.89	2.16	74.42	20.69	51.08	−2.65	50.56	−3.17
B.3.2	Environmental biodiversity	44.05	40.20	−3.85	45.85	1.80	43.77	−0.28	43.90	−0.15	49.45	5.40	44.59	0.54	43.81	−0.24
B.3.3	Environmental resources	44.25	41.77	−2.49	49.40	5.15	49.32	5.07	48.87	4.62	86.58	42.33	41.05	−3.20	33.31	−10.94

that affect their lives, and by which they are empowered" [13]. Good governance should possess eight key characteristics: participation, consensus orientation, accountability, transparency, responsiveness, effectiveness and efficiency, equity and inclusivity, and lawfulness [14].

Global governance refers to the process of implementing international regulations and fostering effective international cooperation to address global political, economic, ecological and security issues, aiming to maintain normal international political and economic order. It extends governance from the national level to the international level, advocating for democratic consultation and cooperation between governments, international organizations, and citizens to maximize mutual benefits [15].

Global One Health governance should be an integrated process in which actors worldwide collaborate to develop and implement international regulations with a global perspective to better respond to health crises and continually promote One Health at the human-animal-environment interface.

Essential Components

The five essential components of One Health governance include:

Firstly, the regulation of One Health governance: This includes the system of rules used to maintain normal order in global One Health governance and realize universal human values. It encompasses transnational principles, norms, standards, policies, agreements, procedures, etc., used to regulate international relations and standardize international order.

Secondly, the One Health governance objective: This refers to health issues that have, or will, impact the well-being of the human-animal-environment system and are difficult to solve by a single discipline, institution, or country. These include zoonotic diseases, food security, AMR, climate change, etc. According to the OH JPA by the Quadripartite (WHO, FAO, WOAH, UNEP), the six action tracks for One Health promotion include key working areas in health system strengthening, risk management of zoonotic epidemics, disease control of

zoonotic, neglected tropical, and vector-borne diseases, food safety enhancement, AMR control, and environmental health [16].

Thirdly, the structure of One Health governance: This refers to a governance structure formed by the interaction of supply-side subsystems (such as resource supply, service provision, financing and payment), and demand-side subsystems (such as people, animals, and the environment) at local, national, regional, and global levels. Community-based health risk management is the recommended structure.

Fourthly, the subjects of One Health governance: This includes organizations that formulate and implement health regulations, such as national governments, sub-national authorities, intergovernmental international organizations, NGOs, etc. Domestic subjects mainly include government, academic groups, and relevant industries.

Finally, the mechanisms of One Health governance: This refers to mechanisms used to promote organizational leadership, social management, and technical support to address One Health issues. Stakeholders at various community, city, regional, national, and international levels should cooperate to implement a One Health governance system. The top-level design, management mechanism, and technical mechanism should be coordinated to improve the efficiency of the One Health governance system.

3.2   Developing GOHI-Governance

Research Design

The global One Health index-Governance (GOHI-Governance) is constructed in four steps: framework formulation, indicator selection, database building, and GOHI-Governance score calculation. The calculation of the GOHI-Governance score is in accordance with the GOHI score calculation method.

Framework Formulation

The framework of the GOHI-Governance is based on the eight characteristics of good governance by the UN. The framework comprises 8

Table 4.10 Indicator and weight scheme of global One Health index-governance (GOHI-Governance)

Key indicator	Indicator			Sub I-indicator		
Name	Name	Code	Weight (%)	Name	Code	Weight (%)
Governance	Participation	C1.1	14.3	Global connectivity	C1.1.1	33.3
				One Health association	C1.1.2	33.3
				One Health forums	C1.1.3	33.3
	Rule of law	C1.2	0.0	One Health specialized laws and regulations	C1.2.1	0.0
	Transparency	C1.3	14.3	Transparency of surveillance data	C1.3.1	50.0
	Responsiveness	C1.4	14.3	Emergency response operation	C1.4.1	50.0
				Risk communication	C1.4.2	50.0
	Consensus oriented	C1.5	14.3	One Health education	C1.5.1	50.0
	Equity and inclusiveness	C1.6	14.3	Biodiversity protection	C1.6.1	50.0
				Social inclusion	C1.6.2	50.0
	Effectiveness and efficiency	C1.7	14.3	Zoonotic disease governance	C1.7.1	33.3
				Climate change governance	C1.7.2	0.0
				Government effectiveness	C1.7.3	33.3
	Political support	C1.8	14.3	One Health official department	C1.8.1	33.3
				Regulatory quality	C1.8.2	33.3
				Financial input	C1.8.3	33.3

dimensions: public participation, rule of law, transparency, responsiveness, consensus orientation, equity and inclusiveness, effectiveness and efficiency, and policy support. All these dimensions and relevant elements provide the basis of the GOHI-Governance framework.

Indicator Selection

Under the GOHI-Governance framework, a three-level indicator framework was developed, including 8 key indicators and 16 indicators (Table 4.10).

Key indicators are weighted based on the FAHP and indicators are equally weighted. Table 4.10 shows the indicators and weighting scheme of the GOHI-Governance: Participation (14.29%), Transparency (14.26%), Responsiveness (14.29%), Consensus oriented (14.29%), Equity and inclusiveness (14.29%), Effectiveness and efficiency (14.29%), and Political support (14.29%).

Database Building

Eleven indicators were extracted from existing databases, including the Global Health Security Index (GHS Index), EPI, SDG reports, and official World Bank data, depending on the indicator. Five indicators were obtained by our research members who screened official websites from

160 countries/territories. These websites were from different institutions, such as official national education departments, national health departments, and national universities, as well as international and nongovernmental organizations such as One Health organizations, One Health forums, special legislatures on One Health, One Health education, and One Health government departments.

Limitations

Firstly, the GOHI-Governance aims to provide a reference for every country/territory in the world for global One Health governance. However, most data come from literature reviews, which may cause bias in the results.

Secondly, data transparency varies in different countries/territories, with some data considered confidential and not publicly available. However, since we consider data transparency an important factor in good governance, higher GOHI-Governance scores, measured by publicly available data, also represent the efforts made by that country/territory in data sharing. Moreover, with multiple cultures and different official scripts of countries around the world, language also has an impact on data accessibility. Governance is largely influenced by cultural contexts, and in some countries/territories where GOHI-Governance exists at the national level, we may be unable to obtain it through internationally common channels due to linguistic or policy reasons.

Thirdly, the GOHI-Governance aims to include as many countries/territories as possible to provide an international reference. Based on the exclusion criteria, the GOHI-Governance 2022 study covers 160 countries/territories. However, challenges in finding comprehensive metrics that cover key aspects of governance such as coordination mechanisms, social mobilization capacity, and resource inputs affect the representativeness of the GOHI-Governance scores.

3.3 Results

Global Score

GOHI-Governance scores are widely imbalanced between countries/regions, and there is still much

room to improve One Health governance capacities. Scores for each country/region range from 26.75 to 80.52 (Fig. 4.10).

The total scores of GOHI-Governance by regions, sorted by median, are: North America (78.46), Europe and Central Asia (67.00), East Asia and Pacific (60.53), Latin America and the Caribbean (54.59), the Middle East and Africa (54.30), South Asia (48.30), and sub-Saharan Africa (46.40). North America and European countries/territories score higher, followed by East Asia and Pacific, and South Asia. Countries/territories with lower scores are concentrated in the sub-Saharan African region (Fig. 4.11).

The average score of GOHI-Governance is 56.51. The average scores for each key indicator are: 41.70 (C1.1 Participation), 65.15 (C1.3 Transparency), 44.42 (C1.4 Responsiveness), 86.45 (C1.5 Consensus oriented), 73.61 (C1.6 Equity and inclusiveness), 28.38 (C1.7 Effectiveness and efficiency), and 55.89 (C1.8

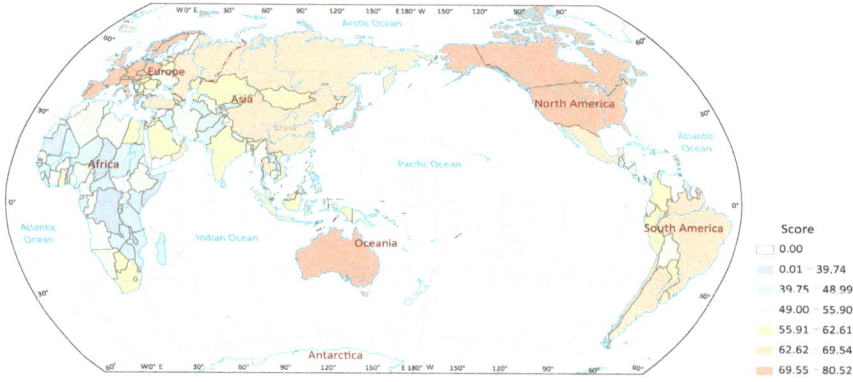

Fig. 4.10 Global score map of the global One Health index-governance (GOHI-Governance)

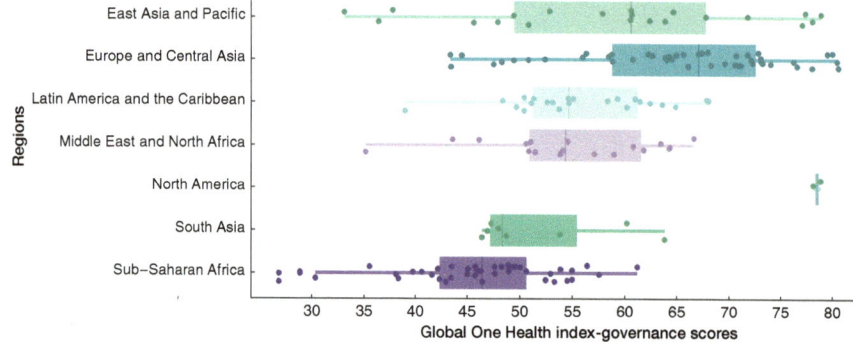

Fig. 4.11 Regional score distribution of the global One Health index-governance (GOHI-Governance)

Political support). In C1.6, Biodiversity protection has the highest average score (85.43). In C1.8, One Health official department has the highest average score (88.71) (Fig. 4.12).

The distribution of the national scores by band is shown in Fig. 4.13, with 26 countries in the (70, 100] band, 39 countries in the (60, 70] band, 43 countries in the (50, 60] band, 40 countries in the (40, 50] band, 10 countries in the (30, 40]

band, and 2 countries in the 30-and-below band. Most scores are concentrated in the [40–70] interval.

The detailed scores of GOHI-Governance components from high to low, sorted by median, are: Consensus oriented (94.58), Equity and inclusiveness (71.57), Transparency (63.85), Political support (54.04), Responsiveness (43.75), Participation (42.59), and Effectiveness

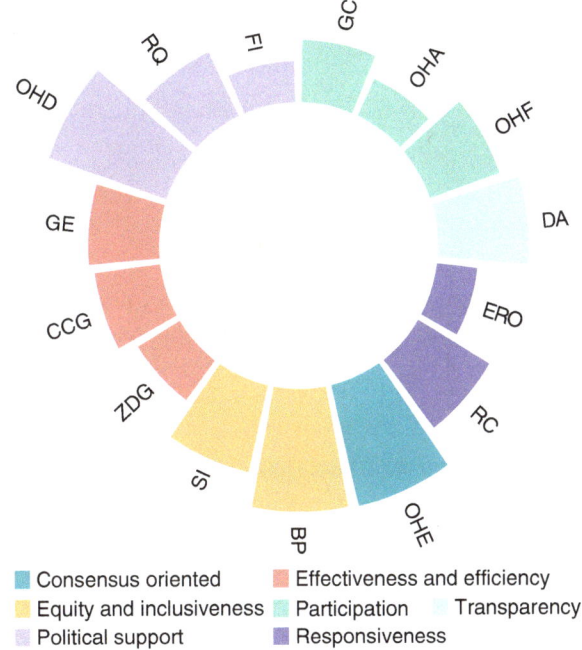

Fig. 4.12 Score distribution of GOHI-Governance by indicators. (*GC* global connectivity, *OHA* One Health association, *OHF* One Health forums, *DA* data availability of national statistical systems, *ERO* emergency response operation, *RC* risk communication, *OHE* One Health edu-

cation, *BP* biodiversity protection, *SI* social inclusion, *ZDG* zoonotic disease governance, *CCG* climate change governance, *GE* government effectiveness, *OHD* One Health official department, *RQ* regulatory quality, *FI* financial input)

Fig. 4.13 Score distribution of the global One Health index-governance (GOHI-Governance) by number of countries

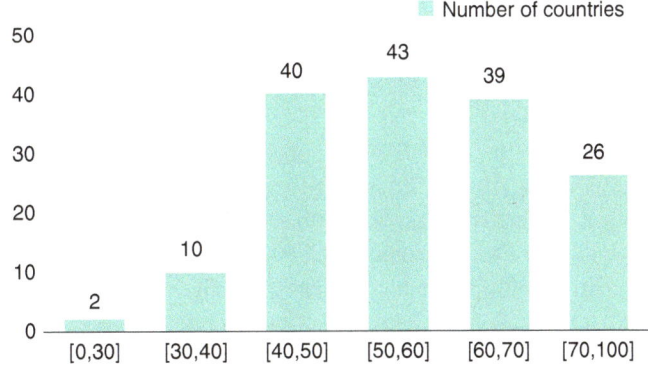

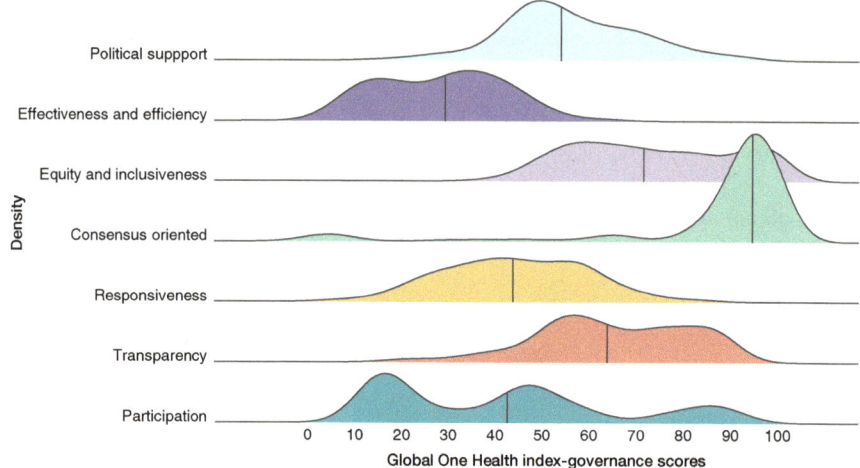

Fig. 4.14 Dimensional score distribution of the global One Health index-governance (GOHI-Governance)

and efficiency (29.30). The distributions of scores for Political support, Equity and inclusiveness and Participation are relatively scattered, indicating large disparities between countries/territories in those three key indicators (Fig. 4.14).

Global Ranking

Among the 160 assessed countries/territories, Norway scores the highest (80.52), and Somalia scores the lowest (26.75).

The top 25 countries/territories are Norway, the Netherlands, the United Kingdom, Germany, Japan, the United States, Canada, Australia, Switzerland, New Zealand, Singapore, Sweden, Denmark, Finland, Poland, Italy, Greece, Slovenia, Luxembourg, Belgium, Portugal, South Korea, France, Spain, the Czech Republic. These are mostly in Europe and Central Asia [18], followed by East Asia and Pacific [5].

Of the top 25 countries/territories, no country/ territory ranks in the top 10 on all GOHI-Governance components. For example, Norway, which ranks first overall, has these components: 1st in Transparency, 2nd in Effectiveness and efficiency, 8th in Political support, 10th in Participation, 19th in Equity and inclusiveness, 54th in Responsiveness, and 89th in Consensus oriented. As another example, China ranks 10th in Effectiveness and efficiency, 10th in Participation, 12th in Consensus oriented, 39th in

Responsiveness, 47th in Political support, 102nd in Equity and inclusiveness, and 102nd in Transparency (Table 4.11).

The bottom 20 countries/territories are Mozambique, Turkmenistan, Tajikistan, Eswatini, Tanzania, Cabo Verde, Guinea, Burundi, Chad, Guatemala, Malawi, the Dem. Rep. Congo, Vanuatu, Solomon Islands, Togo, Bahrain, Timor-Leste, Guinea-Bissau, Mauritania, and Somalia. These countries/territories are mainly distributed in sub-Saharan Africa (13 in total).

Regional Performance

The regional average scores for the seven GOHI-Governance indicators and comparisons and the global average scores for each GOHI-Governance indicator are shown in Table 4.12, with all regions receiving the highest regional scores on the Consensus oriented (C1.5). While Effectiveness and efficiency (C1.7) is the indicator with the lowest average score across all regions, North America and Europe and Central Asia scores better in all indicators, with regional averages all above global levels. Sub-Saharan Africa performs poorly across the seven indicators, with average scores below the global average for all indicators. For Participation (C1.1), the regions that score above the global average (41.70) are North America (90.92), East Asia and Pacific

Table 4.11 Performance of top 25 in the global One Health index-governance (GOHI-Governance)

Rank	Country	Governance	Participation	Transparency	Responsiveness	Consensus	Inclusiveness	Efficiency	Politic
1	Norway	80.52	87.77	90.10	50.00	93.93	97.27	62.27	82.32
2	Netherlands	80.39	87.48	88.00	58.30	93.36	96.91	45.13	93.55
3	United Kingdom	79.95	88.57	83.20	83.35	89.67	98.04	41.87	74.94
4	Germany	79.44	88.50	87.50	58.30	99.39	99.09	50.53	72.77
5	Japan	78.81	88.46	85.80	58.30	99.11	82.74	51.00	86.29
6	United States	78.81	94.82	77.17	70.85	98.37	91.22	42.27	76.96
7	Canada	78.10	87.01	87.50	66.65	86.65	98.14	44.00	76.76
8	Australia	77.97	88.64	88.20	66.65	88.12	90.82	43.40	79.98
9	Switzerland	77.97	85.17	87.00	58.30	96.63	98.63	46.87	73.19
10	New Zealand	77.30	88.26	85.30	58.30	99.03	81.07	50.67	78.48
11	Singapore	77.01	92.40	75.10	58.30	98.99	81.43	40.27	92.56
12	Sweden	76.52	89.56	88.50	50.00	90.31	99.56	44.33	73.35
13	Denmark	76.17	88.76	86.10	45.80	88.88	98.65	55.00	69.97
14	Finland	73.96	58.44	88.50	58.30	83.13	99.45	63.07	66.86
15	Poland	73.16	78.93	89.10	45.80	99.33	98.48	35.27	65.19
16	Italy	73.04	85.54	89.80	25.00	98.55	94.30	44.07	74.04
17	Greece	73.00	81.94	85.40	41.65	97.13	83.24	36.27	85.34
18	Slovenia	72.75	53.46	88.90	66.65	87.73	96.42	49.53	66.55
19	Luxembourg	72.22	85.83	78.20	33.35	97.58	99.15	28.13	83.33
20	Belgium	72.07	60.66	82.40	41.65	97.37	99.14	32.53	90.75
21	Portugal	71.73	53.18	85.50	66.65	93.91	93.12	39.93	69.78
22	South Korea	71.72	57.93	84.63	75.00	92.37	70.98	51.07	70.07
23	France	71.09	57.30	86.30	50.00	97.08	92.04	33.47	81.44
24	Spain	70.88	51.91	88.90	58.30	99.94	83.77	39.67	73.70
25	Czech Republic	70.64	61.37	85.10	35.40	95.53	98.53	40.73	77.81

Table 4.12 Regional performance of the global One Health index-governance (GOHI-Governance)

Region	Indicator		Average score		
	Code	Title	Regional	Global	Gap
Europe and Central Asia	C1.1	Participation	48.53	41.70	6.83
	C1.1.1	Global connectivity	53.41	43.56	9.85
	C1.1.2	One Health association	35.39	28.61	6.78
	C1.1.3	One Health forums	56.79	52.93	3.86
	C1.3	Transparency	79.02	65.15	13.86
	C1.3.1	Data availability of national statistical systems	79.02	65.15	13.86
	C1.4	Responsiveness	46.75	44.42	2.34
	C1.4.1	Emergency response operation	29.76	29.15	0.62
	C1.4.2	Risk communication	63.74	59.69	4.05
	C1.5	Consensus oriented	87.01	86.45	0.55
	C1.5.1	One Health education	87.01	86.45	0.55
	C1.6	Equity and inclusiveness	91.97	73.61	18.36
	C1.6.1	Biodiversity protection	92.79	85.43	7.36
	C1.6.2	Social inclusion	91.14	61.79	29.35
	C1.7	Effectiveness and efficiency	38.29	28.38	9.91
	C1.7.1	Zoonotic disease governance	52.13	34.53	17.60
	C1.7.2	Climate change governance	51.90	47.11	4.79
	C1.7.3	Government effectiveness	62.74	50.60	12.14
	C1.8	Political support	64.46	55.89	8.58
	C1.8.1	One Health official department	91.68	88.71	2.97
	C1.8.2	Regulatory quality	63.60	50.00	13.60
	C1.8.3	Financial input	38.11	28.95	9.16

Region	Indicator		Average score		
	Code	Title	Regional	Global	Gap
Latin America and the Caribbean	C1.1	Participation	41.97	41.70	0.27
	C1.1.1	Global connectivity	40.36	43.56	−3.20
	C1.1.2	One Health association	26.51	28.61	−2.10
	C1.1.3	One Health forums	59.04	52.93	6.10
	C1.3	Transparency	64.10	65.15	−1.06
	C1.3.1	Data availability of national statistical systems	64.10	65.15	−1.06
	C1.4	Responsiveness	47.26	44.42	2.85
	C1.4.1	Emergency response operation	28.96	29.15	−0.19
	C1.4.2	Risk communication	65.57	59.69	5.88
	C1.5	Consensus oriented	90.00	86.45	3.55
	C1.5.1	One Health education	90.00	86.45	3.55
	C1.6	Equity and inclusiveness	68.52	73.61	−5.09
	C1.6.1	Biodiversity protection	78.50	85.43	−6.93
	C1.6.2	Social inclusion	58.54	61.79	−3.25
	C1.7	Effectiveness and efficiency	26.51	28.38	−1.87
	C1.7.1	Zoonotic disease governance	32.61	34.53	−1.92
	C1.7.2	Climate change governance	45.46	47.11	−1.66
	C1.7.3	Government effectiveness	46.92	50.60	−3.67
	C1.8	Political support	54.24	55.89	−1.64
	C1.8.1	One Health official department	93.44	88.71	4.73
	C1.8.2	Regulatory quality	46.49	50.00	−3.51
	C1.8.3	Financial input	22.80	28.95	−6.16

Table 4.12 (continued)

Region	Indicator Code	Title	Average score Regional	Global	Gap
Sub-Saharan Africa	C1.1	Participation	29.49	41.70	−12.21
	C1.1.1	Global connectivity	31.95	43.56	−11.61
	C1.1.2	One Health association	18.57	28.61	−10.04
	C1.1.3	One Health forums	37.97	52.93	−14.97
	C1.3	Transparency	52.85	65.15	−12.31
	C1.3.1	Data availability of national statistical systems	52.85	65.15	−12.31
	C1.4	Responsiveness	37.09	44.42	−7.33
	C1.4.1	Emergency response operation	21.12	29.15	−8.03
	C1.4.2	Risk communication	53.05	59.69	−6.63
	C1.5	Consensus oriented	82.30	86.45	−4.15
	C1.5.1	One Health education	82.30	86.45	−4.15
	C1.6	Equity and inclusiveness	58.16	73.61	−15.45
	C1.6.1	Biodiversity protection	86.00	85.43	0.56
	C1.6.2	Social inclusion	30.33	61.79	−31.46
	C1.7	Effectiveness and efficiency	17.60	28.38	−10.78
	C1.7.1	Zoonotic disease governance	17.07	34.53	−17.46
	C1.7.2	Climate change governance	43.17	47.11	−3.94
	C1.7.3	Government effectiveness	35.72	50.60	−14.87
	C1.8	Political support	46.27	55.89	−9.61
	C1.8.1	One Health official department	83.18	88.71	−5.53
	C1.8.2	Regulatory quality	36.53	50.00	−13.46
	C1.8.3	Financial input	19.10	28.95	−9.85

Region	Indicator Code	Title	Average score Regional	Global	Gap
North America	C1.1	Participation	90.92	41.70	49.22
	C1.1.1	Global connectivity	78.50	43.56	34.94
	C1.1.2	One Health association	97.06	28.61	68.45
	C1.1.3	One Health forums	97.20	52.93	44.26
	C1.3	Transparency	82.34	65.15	17.18
	C1.3.1	Data availability of national statistical systems	82.34	65.15	17.18
	C1.4	Responsiveness	68.75	44.42	24.33
	C1.4.1	Emergency response operation	50.00	29.15	20.85
	C1.4.2	Risk communication	87.50	59.69	27.81
	C1.5	Consensus oriented	92.51	86.45	6.06
	C1.5.1	One Health education	92.51	86.45	6.06
	C1.6	Equity and inclusiveness	94.68	73.61	21.07
	C1.6.1	Biodiversity protection	89.81	85.43	4.37
	C1.6.2	Social inclusion	99.55	61.79	37.76
	C1.7	Effectiveness and efficiency	43.14	28.38	14.76
	C1.7.1	Zoonotic disease governance	50.00	34.53	15.47
	C1.7.2	Climate change governance	47.81	47.11	0.70
	C1.7.3	Government effectiveness	79.40	50.60	28.80
	C1.8	Political support	76.86	55.89	20.97
	C1.8.1	One Health official department	95.58	88.71	6.86
	C1.8.2	Regulatory quality	80.70	50.00	30.71
	C1.8.3	Financial input	54.31	28.95	25.35

Table 4.12 (continued)

| Region | Indicator | | Average score | | |
	Code	Title	Regional	Global	Gap
East Asia and Pacific	C1.1	Participation	52.76	41.70	11.06
	C1.1.1	Global connectivity	47.53	43.56	3.97
	C1.1.2	One Health association	37.36	28.61	8.75
	C1.1.3	One Health forums	73.40	52.93	20.47
	C1.3	Transparency	66.24	65.15	1.08
	C1.3.1	Data availability of national statistical systems	66.24	65.15	1.08
	C1.4	Responsiveness	50.89	44.42	6.47
	C1.4.1	Emergency response operation	39.67	29.15	10.52
	C1.4.2	Risk communication	62.10	59.69	2.42
	C1.5	Consensus oriented	83.39	86.45	−3.06
	C1.5.1	One Health education	83.39	86.45	−3.06
	C1.6	Equity and inclusiveness	67.66	73.61	−5.95
	C1.6.1	Biodiversity protection	76.95	85.43	−8.48
	C1.6.2	Social inclusion	58.36	61.79	−3.42
	C1.7	Effectiveness and efficiency	32.71	28.38	4.34
	C1.7.1	Zoonotic disease governance	41.67	34.53	7.14
	C1.7.2	Climate change governance	38.81	47.11	−8.31
	C1.7.3	Government effectiveness	56.48	50.60	5.88
	C1.8	Political support	57.75	55.89	1.86
	C1.8.1	One Health official department	84.71	88.71	−4.00
	C1.8.2	Regulatory quality	54.15	50.00	4.16
	C1.8.3	Financial input	34.38	28.95	5.42

| Region | Indicator | | Average score | | |
	Code	Title	Regional	Global	Gap
Middle East and North Africa	C1.1	Participation	36.07	41.70	−5.63
	C1.1.1	Global connectivity	43.62	43.56	0.06
	C1.1.2	One Health association	23.78	28.61	−4.83
	C1.1.3	One Health forums	40.81	52.93	−12.13
	C1.3	Transparency	58.01	65.15	−7.14
	C1.3.1	Data availability of national statistical systems	58.01	65.15	−7.14
	C1.4	Responsiveness	42.12	44.42	−2.29
	C1.4.1	Emergency response operation	27.76	29.15	−1.38
	C1.4.2	Risk communication	56.48	59.69	−3.20
	C1.5	Consensus oriented	89.90	86.45	3.45
	C1.5.1	One Health education	89.90	86.45	3.45
	C1.6	Equity and inclusiveness	78.48	73.61	4.87
	C1.6.1	Biodiversity protection	86.93	85.43	1.49
	C1.6.2	Social inclusion	70.04	61.79	8.25
	C1.7	Effectiveness and efficiency	24.09	28.38	−4.28
	C1.7.1	Zoonotic disease governance	22.22	34.53	−12.31
	C1.7.2	Climate change governance	52.49	47.11	5.37
	C1.7.3	Government effectiveness	50.06	50.60	−0.54
	C1.8	Political support	55.58	55.89	−0.31
	C1.8.1	One Health official department	88.48	88.71	−0.23
	C1.8.2	Regulatory quality	46.79	50.00	−3.21
	C1.8.3	Financial input	31.47	28.95	2.51

Table 4.12 (continued)

Region	Indicator Code	Title	Average score Regional	Global	Gap
South Asia	C1.1	Participation	34.68	41.70	−7.02
	C1.1.1	Global connectivity	35.07	43.56	−8.48
	C1.1.2	One Health association	17.03	28.61	−11.58
	C1.1.3	One Health forums	51.94	52.93	−0.99
	C1.3	Transparency	58.76	65.15	−6.39
	C1.3.1	Data availability of national statistical systems	58.76	65.15	−6.39
	C1.4	Responsiveness	42.18	44.42	−2.24
	C1.4.1	Emergency response operation	37.48	29.15	8.33
	C1.4.2	Risk communication	46.88	59.69	−12.81
	C1.5	Consensus oriented	93.04	86.45	6.59
	C1.5.1	One Health education	93.04	86.45	6.59
	C1.6	Equity and inclusiveness	58.96	73.61	−14.65
	C1.6.1	Biodiversity protection	77.04	85.43	−8.39
	C1.6.2	Social inclusion	40.88	61.79	−20.91
	C1.7	Effectiveness and efficiency	25.30	28.38	−3.08
	C1.7.1	Zoonotic disease governance	31.25	34.53	−3.28
	C1.7.2	Climate change governance	53.50	47.11	6.38
	C1.7.3	Government effectiveness	44.65	50.60	−5.95
	C1.8	Political support	50.06	55.89	−5.82
	C1.8.1	One Health official department	95.28	88.71	6.56
	C1.8.2	Regulatory quality	37.80	50.00	−12.20
	C1.8.3	Financial input	17.12	28.95	−11.84

(52.76), Europe and Central Asia (48.53) and Latin America and the Caribbean (41.97). The best to worst gaps to the global average are obtained for North America (47.49), East Asia and Pacific (11.06), Europe and Central Asia (6.83), and Latin America and the Caribbean (0.27), the Middle East and North Africa (−5.63), South Asia (−7.02), and sub-Saharan Africa (−12.21).

In Transparency (C1.3), the regions that score above the global average (65.15) are North America (82.34), Europe and Central Asia (79.02), and East Asia and Pacific (66.24). After comparison with the global average scores, the highest to lowest gap values are obtained for North America (17.18), Europe and Central Asia (13.86), East Asia and Pacific (1.08), Latin America and the Caribbean (−1.06), South Asia (−6.39), the Middle East and North Africa (−7.14) and sub-Saharan Africa (−12.31).

In Responsiveness (C1.4), there are three regions with average scores below the global average (44.42), namely South Asia (42.18), the

Middle East and North Africa (42.12), and sub-Saharan Africa (37.09). Compared with the global average, the gap values from best to worst are: North America (24.33), East Asia and Pacific (6.47), Latin America and the Caribbean (2.85), Europe and Central Asia (2.34), South Asia (−2.24), the Middle East and North Africa (−2.29), and sub-Saharan Africa (−7.33).

In Consensus oriented (C1.5), only two regional averages are lower than the global average (86.45), namely East Asia and Pacific (83.39) and sub-Saharan Africa (82.30). The gap values obtained when compared to the global average are, in descending order, South Asia (6.59), North America (6.06), Latin America and the Caribbean (3.55), the Middle East and North Africa (3.45), Europe and Central Asia (0.55), East Asia and Pacific (−3.06), and sub-Saharan Africa (−4.15).

Three regions score higher on average than the global average (73.61) for indicator C1.6 Equity and inclusiveness: North America (94.68), Europe and Central Asia (91.97), and the Middle East and North Africa (78.48). The highest to lowest gap values when compared to the global average are North America (21.07), Europe and Central Asia (18.36), the Middle East and North Africa (4.87), Latin America and the Caribbean (−5.09), East Asia and Pacific (−5.95), South Asia (−14.65), and sub-Saharan Africa (−15.45).

For Effectiveness and efficiency (C1.7), three regions score above the global average (28.38): North America (43.14), Europe and Central Asia (38.29), and East Asia and Pacific (32.71). Compared to the global average, the highest to lowest gap values are obtained for North America (14.76), Europe and Central Asia (9.91), East Asia and Pacific (4.34), Latin America and the Caribbean (−1.87), South Asia (−3.08), the Middle East and North Africa (−4.28), and sub-Saharan Africa (−10.78).

For Political support (C1.8), three regions score above the global average (55.89): North America (76.86), Europe and Central Asia (64.46), and East Asia and Pacific (57.75). The highest to lowest gap values obtained when compared to the global average are North America (20.97), Europe and Central Asia (8.58), East Asia and Pacific (1.86), the Middle East and North Africa (−0.31), Latin America and the Caribbean (−1.64), South Asia (−5.82), and sub-Saharan Africa (−9.61). Table 4.12 Regional performance of the GOHI-Governance.

1. *East Asia and Pacific*

Among countries/territories in East Asia and Pacific, the gaps of indicators are in the range of −5.95–11.06. Participation (C1.1), the average score has the largest gap (11.06) above the global average with an average score of 41.70. Equity and inclusiveness (C1.6) has the largest gap (−5.95) below the global average with an average score of 73.61. The gaps of the other indicators are in order, 1.56 (C1.8 Political support), 8.83 (C1.7 Effectiveness and efficiency), 6.47 (C1.4 Responsiveness), 1.09 (C1.3 Transparency), −3.06 (C1.5 Consensus oriented). However, C1.5 has highest score among the indicators in the region. Among the sub I-indicators, the gaps are in the range of −8.30–20.47, with five of them (C1.5.1 One Health education,

C1.6.1 Biodiversity protection, C1.6.2 Social inclusion, C1.7.2 Climate change governance and C1.8.1 One Health official department) scoring below the global average.

2. *Europe and Central Asia*

Among countries/territories in European and Central Asia, the gaps of indicators range from −3.06 to 18.37. Consensus oriented has the smallest gap (−3.06) below the global average with an average score of 86.45. Equity and inclusiveness has the largest gap (18.37) above the global average with an average score of 73.61. The gaps of the other indicators are in order, 1.09 (Transparency), 6.47 (Responsiveness), 1.86 (Political support), 6.83 (Participation), and 4.33 (Effectiveness and efficiency). Among sub I-indicators, the gaps range from 0.56–29.35. All the sub I-indicators scores are above the global average, with Social inclusion having the biggest gap above the global average (29.35).

3. *Latin America and the Caribbean*

Among countries/territories in Latin America and the Caribbean, the gaps of indicators range from −5.09 to 3.55. This shows that the performances of Latin America and the Caribbean are below the global average. Equity and inclusiveness has the largest gap (−5.09) below the global average with an average score of 73.61. Participation has the smallest gap (0.27) above the global average with an average score of 41.70. The gaps of the other indicators are in order, −1.65 (Political support), −1.05 (Transparency), −1.87 (Effectiveness and efficiency), 2.84 (Responsiveness), 3.55 (Consensus oriented). Among the sub I-indicators, the gaps range from −6.93 to 6.11. The score of Biodiversity protection is 6.93 points lower than the global average, which is the largest gap among all sub I-indicators.

4. *Middle East and North Africa*

Among countries/territories in Middle East and North Africa, the gaps of indicators range from −7.14 to 4.87. Transparency has the largest gap (−7.14) below the global average with an average score of 65.15. Equity and inclusiveness has the smallest gap (4.87) above the global average with an average score of 73.61. The gaps of other indicators are in order, −4.29 (Effectiveness and efficiency), 3.45 (Consensus oriented), −0.31 (Political support), −5.63 (Participation), −2.30 (Responsiveness). Among the sub I-indicators, the gaps range from −12.31 to 8.25, with only six (C1.1.1 Global connectivity, One Health education, Biodiversity protection, Social inclusion, Climate change governance, and C1.8.3 Financial Input) scoring higher than the global average.

5. *North America*

Among countries/territories in North America, the gaps of indicators range from 6.06 to 49.22, showing that the North America performs better than the global average in all seven indicators. Participation has the largest gap (49.22) above the global average with an average score of 41.70. Consensus oriented has the smallest gap (6.06) above the global average with an average score of 86.45. The gaps of other indicators are in order, 24.33 (Responsiveness), 14.75 (Effectiveness and efficiency), 21.07 (Equity and inclusiveness), 17.19 (Transparency), and 20.97 (Political support). Among all sub I-indicators, the gaps range from 0.70 to 68.45, all of which scores above the global average. Five sub I-indicators score above 30.00, and C1.1.2 One Health association has the largest gap above the global average.

6. *South Asia*

Among countries/territories in South Asia, the gaps of indicators range from −14.65 to 6.59. Equity and inclusiveness has the largest gap (−14.65) below the global average with an average score of 73.61. C1.4 Responsiveness has the smallest gap (−2.24) below the global average with an average score of 44.42. The gaps of the other indicators are in order, −6.39 (Transparency), 6.59 (Consensus oriented), −14.65 (Participation), −3.08 (Effectiveness and efficiency) and −5.83 (Political support). Among the three levels of indicators, the gaps range from −20.91 to 8.33, with only four indicators (C1.4.1 Emergency response operation, One Health education,

Climate change governance and One Health official department) scoring better than the global average.

7. *Sub-Saharan Africa*

Among countries/territories in sub-Saharan Africa, the gaps of indicators range from −15.45 to −4.15, and all are less than 0.00. This means that all seven indicators are below the global average. Equity and inclusiveness has the largest gap (−15.45) below the global average with an average score of 73.61. Consensus oriented has the smallest gap (−4.15) below the global average with an average score of 86.45. The gaps of the other indicators are in order, −12.30 (Transparency), −7.33 (Responsiveness), −12.21 (Participation), −10.78 (Effectiveness and efficiency), and −9.62 (Political support). Among all sub I-indicators, the gaps range from −31.46 to −0.57, only one of which scored above the global average (Biodiversity protection), while Social inclusion has the largest gap below the global average (−31.46).

3.4 Key Findings

The Total Scores of GOHI-Governance Worldwide Are Far from Optimal (100 Points)

Overall, it is unsatisfactory that the average score for all countries in GOHI-Governance 2022 is 56.51 out of 100.00, and no country ranks among the top three out of 160 countries/territories in more than two indicators. The highest GOHI-Governance score is Norway (80.52) and the lowest score is Somalia (26.75). The difference in score of GOHI-Governance across countries is about 53.77, indicating that One Health governance capacity is significantly polarized.

GOHI-Governance Scores Are Highly Disparate, with Considerable Variations Among Different Regions

In the regional analysis, the average scores vary considerably. Of the seven regions, the North America and Europe and Central Asia score outstandingly in all indicators and achieve above the global average, indicating that these two regions are leaders in One Health governance. In the North America, three indicators score above 90.00, including Participation, Consensus oriented, and Equity and inclusiveness, with Equity and inclusiveness scoring the highest (94.68). This indicates that the United States and Canada perform better in promoting and educating the concept of One Health. To contrast, sub-Saharan Africa shows unsatisfactory results that its average scores in all seven indicators are below the global average.

Among the top 50 countries/territories in the total scores, 31 countries (62%) are from Europe and Central Asia. Among the bottom 50, 28 countries/territories (56%) are from sub-Saharan Africa.

Of the Indicators of GOHI-Governance, Consensus Oriented and Equity and Inclusiveness Score Highest

Of the indicators, Consensus oriented performs best in the average scores, with only 9, or 5.63%, of countries/territories scoring below 30.00. This is followed by Equity and inclusiveness. Effectiveness and efficiency performs worst, with 83 countries/territories (51.88%) scoring below 30.00. Throughout the GOHI-Governance study, evidence shows that most countries around the world have higher performance in consensus and orientation, reflecting a global consensus of One Health governance and a willingness of contribution to improving One Health governance.

The Scores of Sub I-Indicators Reveal Weakness in Establishing Specialized Institutions and Promoting Social Inclusion

Among the sub I-indicators of Participation, One Health association has the lowest average score of 28.61. This indicates a global weakness in establishing specialized institutions to promote One Health governance capacity. Though the sub I-indicators, One Health forums, has the highest average score (52.93), there are only 83 out of 160 countries/territories assessed (51.88%) have held One Health forums. This shows the inadequate academic communication and technical

exchange in One Health worldwide. Countries still need to strengthen the intensity of One Health promotion and communication.

However, among the sub I-indicators of Consensus oriented, One Health education performs well, with only 13 out of the 160 countries/territories (8.13%) not having One Health-related education activities. This suggests that most countries around the world have been serious about increasing public awareness and promoting talent fostering in One Health practice.

In the regional rankings, the top five countries/territories in East Asia and Pacific are Japan, Australia, New Zealand, Singapore, and South Korea, with scores in the range of 71.72–78.81. In sub-Saharan Africa, the top five are South Africa, Ghana, Botswana, Senegal, and Uganda, with scores in the range of 54.95–61.20. In the Middle East and North Africa, the top five are Israel, the United Arab Emirates, Qatar, Oman, and Malta, whose score in the range of 61.79–66.59. In South Asia, the top five are Bhutan, India, Bangladesh, Sri Lanka, and Afghanistan, with scores in the range of 47.91–63.81. In Latin America and the Caribbean, the top five are Brazil, Chile, Argentina, Mexico, and Colombia, with scores in the range of 62.38–67.97. In North America, the United States scores 78.81, and Canada 78.10. In Europe and Central Asia, the top five are Norway, the Netherlands, the United Kingdom, Germany, and Switzerland, with scores in the range of 77.97–80.52 (Table 4.13).

In the East Asian and Pacific, Japan ranks 1st (and 5th globally) with a score of 78.81. The last country in the region, Timor-Leste, ranks 157th in the global ranking, with a more spread out and disparate distribution.

In the European and Central Asia with 47 countries/territories included, the average score is 65.15. The top five countries in order are Norway, the Netherlands, the United Kingdom, Germany, and Switzerland. Norway ranks 1st in the region with a score of 80.52 and also 1st globally.

In the Latin American and the Caribbean with 23 countries/territories included, the average score is 56.08. The top three countries are Brazil,

Table 4.13 Regional ranking of the global One Health index-governance (GOHI-Governance)

East Asia and Pacific

Rank	Global rank	Country	Score
1	5	Japan	78.81
2	8	Australia	77.97
3	10	New Zealand	77.30
4	11	Singapore	77.01
5	22	South Korea	71.72
6	32	China	67.69
7	40	Malaysia	64.60
8	47	Thailand	63.82
9	53	Mongolia	62.33
10	61	Indonesia	60.62
11	62	Brunei Darussalam	60.53
12	63	Philippines	60.48
13	72	Viet Nam	57.79
14	93	Cambodia	52.80
15	102	Papua New Guinea	50.78
16	112	Myanmar	49.37
17	122	Laos	47.83
18	135	Fiji	45.55
19	153	Vanuatu	37.74
20	154	Solomon Islands	36.38
21	157	Timor-Leste	33.08

Middle East and North Africa

Rank	Global rank	Country	Score
1	35	Israel	66.59
2	42	United Arab Emirates	64.30
3	43	Qatar	64.23
4	50	Oman	63.42
5	55	Malta	61.79
6	59	Saudi Arabia	60.78
7	67	Egypt	58.93
8	74	Jordan	57.04
9	82	Tunisia	54.53
10	85	Iran	54.06
11	88	Kuwait	53.81
12	97	Morocco	51.44
13	100	Lebanon	50.99
14	101	Algeria	50.81
15	105	Libya	50.56
16	131	Iraq	46.08
17	139	Djibouti	43.58
18	156	Bahrain	35.13

Europe and Central Asia

Rank	Global rank	Country	Score
1	1	Norway	80.52
2	2	Netherlands	80.39
3	3	United Kingdom	79.95
4	4	Germany	79.44

Table 4.13 (continued)

Europe and Central Asia

Rank	Global rank	Country	Score
5	9	Switzerland	77.97
6	12	Sweden	76.52
7	13	Denmark	76.17
8	14	Finland	73.96
9	15	Poland	73.16
10	16	Italy	73.04
11	17	Greece	73.00
12	18	Slovenia	72.75
13	19	Luxembourg	72.22
14	20	Belgium	72.07
15	21	Portugal	71.73
16	23	France	71.09
17	24	Spain	70.88
18	25	Czech Republic	70.64
19	26	Austria	70.51
20	27	Iceland	69.54
21	28	Ireland	68.20
22	30	Cyprus	67.88
23	33	Lithuania	67.33
24	34	Estonia	67.00
25	36	Slovakia	66.03
26	37	Georgia	65.58
27	38	Latvia	64.89
28	41	Turkey	64.48
29	44	Croatia	64.18
30	45	Armenia	64.02
31	46	Russia	63.85
32	51	Romania	62.61
33	54	Hungary	62.21
34	60	Kazakhstan	60.72
35	68	North Macedonia	58.76
36	69	Belarus	58.67
37	70	Serbia	58.39
38	76	Moldova	56.26
39	77	Ukraine	55.90
40	96	Montenegro	52.37
41	103	Bulgaria	50.77
42	111	Uzbekistan	49.38
43	120	Azerbaijan	48.21
44	125	Albania	47.44
45	138	Kyrgyzstan	44.43
46	142	Turkmenistan	43.42
47	143	Tajikistan	43.34

Sub-Saharan Africa

Rank	Global rank	Country	Score
1	57	South Africa	61.20
2	73	Ghana	57.52
3	75	Botswana	56.39

(continued)

Table 4.13 (continued)

Sub-Saharan Africa

Rank	Global rank	Country	Score
4	79	Senegal	54.96
5	80	Uganda	54.95
6	84	Cote d'Ivoire	54.50
7	86	Mauritius	53.87
8	90	Ethiopia	53.31
9	92	Nigeria	52.93
10	95	Burkina Faso	52.46
11	104	Cameroon	50.62
12	108	Namibia	50.04
13	110	Lesotho	49.57
14	113	Seychelles	49.33
15	114	Sierra Leone	48.99
16	115	Kenya	48.93
17	116	Gabon	48.89
18	119	Zimbabwe	48.25
19	123	Rwanda	47.58
20	124	Mali	47.58
21	128	Zambia	46.40
22	130	Niger	46.27
23	132	Benin	45.89
24	133	Sudan	45.74
25	134	Liberia	45.74
26	136	Equatorial Guinea	45.07
27	137	Madagascar	45.01
28	140	Central African Republic	43.53
29	141	Mozambique	43.48
30	144	Eswatini	42.96
31	145	Tanzania	42.35
32	146	Cabo Verde	42.18
33	147	Guinea	41.62
34	148	Burundi	40.62
35	149	Chad	39.74
36	151	Malawi	38.32
37	152	Dem. Rep. Congo	38.09
38	155	Togo	35.51
39	158	Guinea-Bissau	30.34
40	159	Mauritania	28.83
41	160	Somalia	26.75

South Asia

Rank	Global rank	Country	Score
1	48	Bhutan	63.81
2	64	India	60.17
3	87	Bangladesh	53.81
4	117	Sri Lanka	48.68
5	121	Afghanistan	47.91
6	126	Maldives	47.23
7	127	Nepal	46.87
8	129	Pakistan	46.35

Table 4.13 (continued)

Latin America and the Caribbean

Rank	Global rank	Country	Score
1	29	Brazil	67.97
2	31	Chile	67.79
3	39	Argentina	64.83
4	49	Mexico	63.57
5	52	Colombia	62.38
6	56	El Salvador	61.42
7	58	Uruguay	60.94
8	65	Costa Rica	60.13
9	66	Paraguay	59.24
10	71	Peru	58.30
11	78	Panama	55.01
12	81	Dominican Republic	54.59
13	83	Trinidad and Tobago	54.53
14	89	Bolivia	53.69
15	91	Ecuador	53.09
16	94	Cuba	52.56
17	98	Honduras	51.28
18	99	Nicaragua	51.04
19	106	Jamaica	50.37
20	107	Barbados	50.37
21	109	Belize	49.62
22	118	Guyana	48.29
23	150	Guatemala	38.94

North America

Rank	Global rank	Country	Score
1	6	United States	78.81
2	7	Canada	78.10

Chile, and Argentina. Brazil ranks 48th globally, with a score of 67.97.

In the Middle Eastern and North Africa with 18 countries/territories included, the average score is 54.89, with the top three countries being Israel, the United Arab Emirates and Qatar. 1st-ranked Israel also ranks 35th globally, with a score of 66.59.

In the North America (the United States and Canada), the two countries have an average score of 78.46. The United States scores 78.81 and is 6th globally. Canada ranks 7th globally, with a score of 78.10.

In the South Asia with eight countries/territories included, the average score is 51.85. The countries, in ranking order, are Bhutan, India, Bangladesh, Sri Lanka, Afghanistan, the Maldives, Nepal, and Pakistan. Bhutan ranks 1st in the region with a score of 63.81, also placing 45th globally.

In the sub-Saharan Africa with 41 countries included, the average score is 46.25. The top five countries in the region are South Africa, Ghana, Botswana, Senegal, and Uganda, in that order. South Africa ranks 1st in the region with a score of 61.20 and ranks 57th globally.

4 Zoonotic Diseases

4.1 Background

Zoonoses are diseases that are naturally transmitted between humans and other vertebrates [17] and can be transmitted to humans through droplets, droplet nuclei, aerosols, food, soil, and arthropods.

Zoonoses, which originate in animals and infect humans, account for 60% of all known infectious diseases [18]. At least six out of every ten infectious diseases in humans are known to be transmitted by animals [19], while three out of every four emerging human infectious diseases are transmitted by animals [1]. The pathogens of zoonoses include viruses, bacteria, parasites, fungi, and prions [20]. Zoonoses pose a serious threat to global health security, causing 2.5 billion infections and 2.7 million deaths per year, and these diseases are a serious threat to human health and agricultural development as well as food safety [21].

In 2002, a previously unknown coronavirus was transmitted from animals to humans in an outbreak of severe acute respiratory syndrome (SARS) and later spread globally, with studies finding that masked palm civets occasionally served as a direct source of human infection [22]. In 2012, an outbreak of Middle East respiratory syndrome (MERS), possibly originating in bats and with camels serving as intermediate hosts, was transmitted to humans [23]. The coronavirus disease 2019 (COVID-19) outbreak, similar to other coronaviruses, was presumed to be transmitted from wildlife to humans, and there is substantial evidence that the virus originated in horseshoe bats (*Rhinolophus* spp.) and that pangolins are likely to be intermediate hosts [24].

The virus may undergo recombination events in intermediate hosts before entering human populations [25]. During the COVID-19 pandemic, there were several reports of COVID-19 infection in pets such as dogs and cats owned by COVID-19 patients, with cats appearing to be highly susceptible to the virus [26]. In 2021, COVID-19 was detected in 129 of 360 white-tailed deer (*Odocoileus virginianus*) in northeastern Ohio, USA [27]. More recently, India reported that animals can also be affected by the "Delta" strain which was confirmed in nine lions at Chennai Zoo in Tamil Nadu, India [28].

Since the twentieth century, the emergence of drug-resistant strains and mutant strains, ecological changes, global climate change, frequent population movements, industrialization of food production, and increased movement of animals and animal product markets have accelerated the occurrence and spread of zoonotic infections [29]. In addition, emerging zoonotic diseases have a significant negative socioeconomic impact across the world and are threats to global public health.

4.2 The Necessity to Evaluate Zoonoses from One Health Perspective

Humans interact with animals within the ecosystem and are susceptible to zoonotic infections. For example, herders are susceptible to brucellosis through direct contact with goats infected with *Brucella*, or by consuming unpasteurized goat milk. In recent years, due to global warming and the continuous development of human society, a large number of wild animals have left their territories to find new habitats. The constant development of cities and farms facilitated direct and frequent direct contact between humans and wild animals, posing a new challenge for human society. The impact of viruses and parasites carried by wild animals on humans is unpredictable, and new infectious agents and intermediate hosts are emerging in this context.

Since 2020, the COVID-19 pandemic has raised questions about the ability of public health departments worldwide to deal with the spread of zoonoses and whether government departments have appropriate policies, regulations, and guidelines to guide health preparedness. In the past, people may have thought that their own country's epidemic prevention measures were sufficient. However, as global trade and transportation have developed, countries have become more connected and new challenges have emerged. These include the faster spread and broader impact of epidemics. Simultaneously, the COVID-19 pandemic has put significant pressure on the political, economic, and health aspects of each country.

To respond to zoonotic threats, the FAO, WOAH, and WHO published the guideline "Taking a Multisectoral, One Health Approach: A Tripartite Guide to Addressing Zoonotic Diseases in Countries" [30]. One Health uses an integrated, unifying approach that mobilizes multiple sectors, disciplines, and communities at varying levels of society to work together to balance and optimize the health of people, animals, and the environment [31]. Currently, One Health is receiving increasing attention in zoonosis prevention and control. The US Centers for Disease Control and Prevention have developed the One Health Zoonotic Disease Prioritization (OHZDP) tool based on One Health's three dimensions of people, animals, and the environment. This tool ranks zoonotic diseases in a country, optimizes the allocation of prevention and control resources, and strengthens monitoring [32]. The Generalizable One Health Framework (GOHF) presented five steps for how countries should use a One Health approach to improve multisectoral collaboration and enhance the prevention and control of zoonotic diseases [33]. However, there is currently no framework based on the One Health approach to assessing the level of zoonotic disease control worldwide.

Recently, we developed an evaluation tool for One Health performance through GOHI [6]. Based on the concept of One Health, the global One Health index-zoonotic diseases (GOHI-Zoonoses) assesses the performance in controlling zoonoses and the ability to respond to zoonotic threats in countries worldwide from various aspects. It aims to provide evidence-based guidance to different stakeholders, public

health departments, and research institutions in each country to optimize the health of people, animals, and the environment. This report identified the highlights and shortcomings in the control and responses to zoonotic events and provided evidence-based suggestions.

4.3 Framework Construction for GOHI-Zoonoses

Framework

We have established a GOHI-Zoonoses framework by using the databases of WHO, WOAH, World Bank, GHS index and Global Health Data Exchange (GHDx) [34]. The design of the framework starts from the basic modes of zoonotic transmission and is divided into three indicators: Sources of infection (SI), Route of transmission (RT), and Target populations (TP). Since the data obtained were expected to reflect the response capacity of a country or region to zoonoses, Capacity building (CB) and Case studies (CS) were added to provide an overall assessment that uses a total of five indicators.

During the process of constructing the logical framework and subsequent data search and analysis, we selected the indicators according to the principles of relevance, authoritative sources, open access, completeness, timeliness, comparability, and country-level data. We referred to the contents of authoritative databases, such as the WHO, GHS index, WOAH, World Bank, and GHDx, when constructing the indicator. We then organized the core data sources and used them to establish indicators and underlying data.

Indicators

We initially organized a logical framework containing four indicators and 16 sub I-indicators. Thereafter, we conducted rounds of consultations with expert advisory committees and several key informants from multiple UN agencies, including experts from the WHO, WOAH, FAO, World Bank, and World Meteorological Organization (WMO). We also referred to the OH JPA (2022–2026) [35] and validated the final indicator framework. The selected indicators align with the OH JPA guidelines: (i) focus on the detection, monitoring, and assessment of risk factors for human, livestock, and wildlife health, vectors, and natural environment; (ii) include an evaluation of national guidelines, laws, and regulations related to zoonotic diseases; (iii) focus on the control of neglected tropical diseases (NTDs) and vector-borne diseases; (iv) concentrate on the coverage and accessibility of basic sanitation facilities and health services; and (v) select representative zoonotic diseases (e.g., echinococcosis, leishmaniasis, tuberculosis, yellow fever) for case studies. After integration and expert discussion, the final indicator construction pathway includes five indicators, 16 sub I-indicators and 31 sub II-indicators. It uses multiple dimensions to comprehensively assess the capacity of countries to deal with zoonoses and their ability to respond to zoonotic events (Table 4.14).

Data Sources

The datasets used for calculating the zoonotic capacity score, policy adoption of insecticide-treated mosquito nets, policy adoption of indoor residual spraying, preventive chemotherapy coverage of zoonoses, costs related to chemotherapy/vaccination of humans, legislation of zoonosis educational activities, zoonotic vaccine national programs, zoonotic events and the human-animal interface, Universal Health Coverage (UHC) service sub-index on infectious diseases, NTD control and prevention, surveillance, COVID-19 infections numbers, COVID-19 deaths, COVID-19 vaccination coverage, and yellow fever vaccination were obtained from the WHO.

The datasets used for general surveillance, vector control, and wildlife reservoir control were obtained from the WOAH.

Table 4.14 Indicator and weight scheme of the global One Health index-zoonotic diseases (GOHI-Zoonoses)

Indicator Name	Code	Weight	Sub I-indicator Name	Code	Weight	Sub II-indicator Name	Code	Weight
Source of infection	C2.1	23.70%	Strategy and regulation	C2.1.1	50.0%	National guidelines for surveillance/control	C2.1.1.1	35.0%
						National legislation on animal reservoirs	C2.1.1.2	35.0%
						Zoonotic capacity score	C2.1.1.3	30.0%
			Monitoring and feedback	C2.1.2	25.0%	General surveillance	C2.1.2.1	34.0%
						Vector control	C2.1.2.2	33.0%
						Wildlife reservoirs control	C2.1.2.3	33.0%
			Hygiene	C2.1.3	25.0%	Basic sanitation services	C2.1.3.1	100.0%
Route of transmission	C2.2	25.30%	Conventional intervention	C2.2.1	45.2%	Laboratory testing for zoonotic reservoirs	C2.2.1.1	100.0%
			Ecological interventions	C2.2.2	54.9%	Policy adoption of insecticide-treated mosquito nets	C2.2.2.1	33.3%
						Policy adoption of indoor residual spraying	C2.2.2.2	33.3%
						Preventive chemotherapy coverage of zoonoses	C2.2.2.3	33.3%
Target population	C2.3	19.10%	Vaccination coverage	C2.3.1	29.0%	National strategy and regulation for human/animal vaccination	C2.3.1.1	100.0%
			Population coverage and cost of interventions	C2.3.2	39.4%	Proportion of population having basic drinking water and sanitation facilities	C2.3.2.1	50.0%
						Costs directed to chemotherapy/vaccination of humans	C2.3.2.2	50.0%
			Inhabitants below 5 m above sea level	C2.3.3	31.6%	Proportion of population living in the areas where elevation is below 5 meters	C2.3.3.1	100.0%
Capacity building	C2.4	16.80%	Guidelines for the control and supervision of zoonotic diseases	C2.4.1	56.9%	Legislation of zoonosis educational activities	C2.4.1.1	16.7%
						Zoonosis vaccine national plan	C2.4.1.2	16.7%
						Zoonotic events and the human-animal interface	C2.4.1.3	16.7%
						Universal health coverage Service sub-index on infectious diseases	C2.4.1.4	16.7%
						NTD control and prevention	C2.4.1.5	16.7%
						Surveillance	C2.4.1.6	16.7%
			Nature reserves	C2.4.2	43.1%	Proportion of natural protected areas	C2.4.2.1	100.0%
Case studies	C2.5	15.10%	COVID-19	C2.5.1	20.0%	COVID-19 infection number	C2.5.1.1	33.3%
						COVID-19 deaths	C2.5.1.2	33.3%
						COVID-19 vaccination coverage	C2.5.1.3	33.3%
			Echinococcosis	C2.5.2	15.6%	Echinococcosis human DALYS	C2.5.2.1	100.0%
			Leishmaniasis	C2.5.3	13.4%	Leishmaniasis human DALYS	C2.5.3.1	100.0%
			Rabies	C2.5.4	17.1%	Rabies human DALYS	C2.5.4.1	100.0%
			Tuberculosis	C2.5.5	20.8%	Tuberculosis human DALYS	C2.5.5.1	100.0%
			Yellow fever	C2.5.6	13.2%	Yellow fever DALYS	C2.5.6.1	50.0%
						Yellow fever vaccination	C2.5.6.2	50.0%

Note: According to the "structure-process-outcome" model, each indicator was divided into sub I-indicators that were then divided into sub II-indicators: blue represents "structure" or resource allocation, green represents "process" or intervention measures, and pink represents "outcome" or performance after intervention

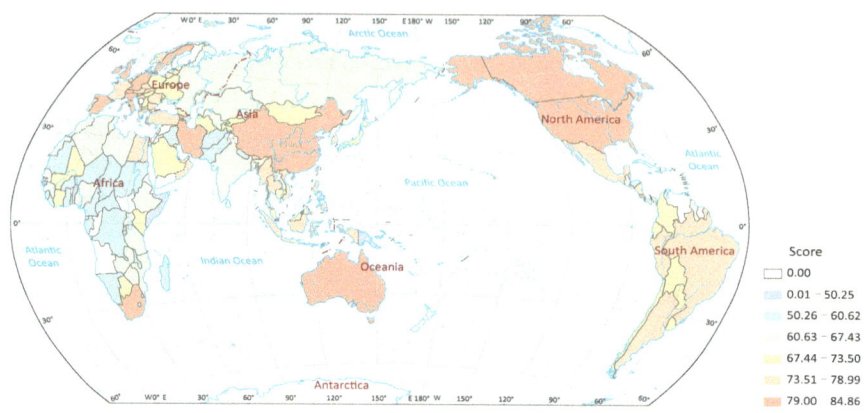

Fig. 4.15 Global score map of the global One Health index-zoonotic diseases (GOHI-Zoonoses)*

The datasets used for national guidelines for surveillance/control, national legislation on animal surveillance/control, national legislation on animal reservoirs, laboratory testing for zoonotic reservoirs, vaccination strategy, and regulation of vaccination were derived from the GHS index.

Finally, the dataset of human DALYs for echinococcosis, leishmaniasis, rabies, tuberculosis, and yellow fever was obtained from GHDx.

Limitations

Indicators at each level are set following a logical framework that refers to the OH JPA (2022–2026) [35], However, the logical framework need to be continuously adjusted with global zoonoses development trend, which will require subsequent data updates.

Limitations exist in the data sources. Most of the data used for these indicators only come from English-language databases, and information from databases in other languages could not be searched and used for some countries or territories. In addition, some of the databases were less up-to-date, and recent data could not be found. Some countries with less-developed economies lack data, so we interpolate for countries with missing data based on GDP levels, which may lead to biased results. The total amount of missing data in this report was 20.10%, and C2.3.2.2 was not included in the calculation due to missing data proportions of up to 80.00%.

4.4   Main Results

Global Score

The performance of GOHI-Zoonoses is at a medium level, with only a few countries or territories scoring above 70, mostly concentrated in East Asia, North America, and Europe. Zoonosis prevention and control in other regions needs to be improved. The total scores of countries or territories range from 43.01 to 84.86 (Fig. 4.15).

The total scores of GOHI-Zoonoses by region are as follows (sorted by median): North America (82.76), Europe and Central Asia (75.49), East Asia and Pacific (73.25), Latin America and the Caribbean (69.22), the Middle East and North Africa (68.71), South Asia (60.93), and sub-Saharan Africa (58.76). North America and European countries or territories score higher, followed by East Asia and Pacific, then Latin America and the Caribbean. Countries or territories with lower scores are concentrated in sub-Saharan Africa (Fig. 4.16).

The average score of the GOHI-Zoonoses is 68.06. The average scores for SI, RT, TP, CB, and CS key indicators were 69.22, 59.30, 59.90, 72.85, and 85.89, respectively. In SI, Monitoring and feedback (MF) has the highest average score of 83.56. In RT, Ecological interventions (ECI) has the highest average score (69.84); in TP, Inhabitants below 5 m above sea level (IHB) has the highest average score (86.77); in CB, Nature reserves (NR) has the highest average score

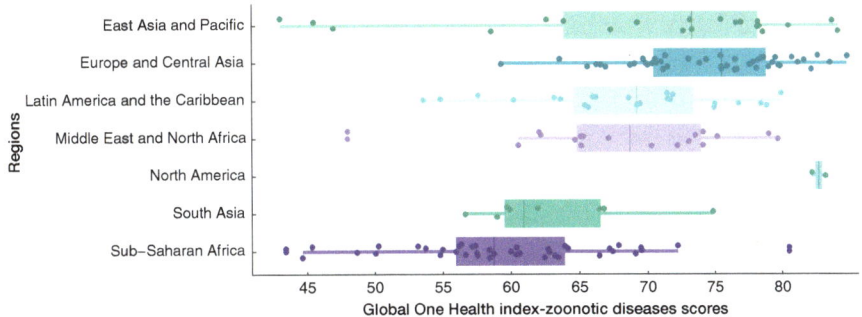

Fig. 4.16 Regional score distribution of the global One Health index-zoonotic diseases (GOHI-Zoonoses)

Fig. 4.17 The GOHI-Zoonoses score distribution by sub I-indicators. (*SR* strategy and regulation, *MF* monitoring and feedback, *HYG* hygiene, *CI* conventional interventions, *ECI* ecological interventions, *VAC* vaccination coverage, *PIC* population coverage and cost of interventions, *IHB* inhabitants below 5 m above sea level, *GCS* guidelines for the control and supervision of zoonotic diseases, *NR* nature reserves, *COV* COVID-19, *ECHIN* echinococcosis, *LEISH* leishmaniasis, *RHL* rabies, *TUB* tuberculosis, *YF* yellow fever)

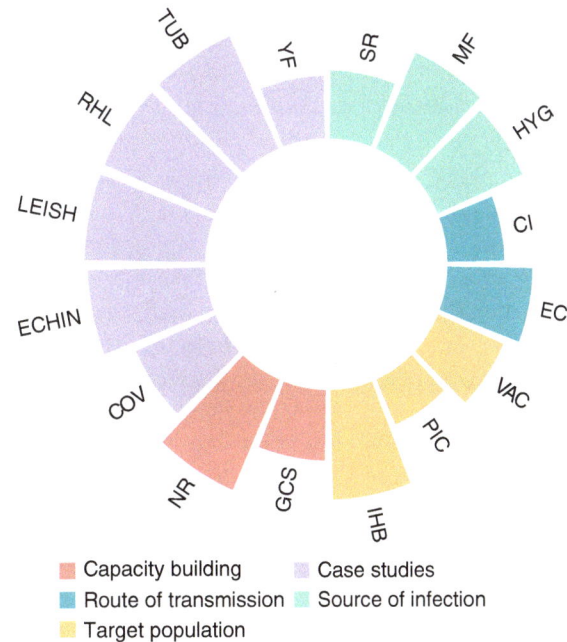

(95.36); finally, in CS, the average score (98.18) of Tuberculosis (TB) is highest (Fig. 4.17).

The overall distribution of the five indicators of zoonoses is shown in Fig. 4.18. In terms of the SI, most countries are distributed in the range of 50.00–80.00, a few countries have scores above 90.00, and variability is wide. For the RT, the average score is 59.30, with most countries lying in the range of 40.00–80.00. For the TP, the scores are mostly distributed in the ranges of 40.00–50.00 and 70.00–80.00. Most of the scores for CB are concentrated in the 70.00–80.00 range. Overall, the scores for the CS are high, with most distributed in the 80.00–90.00 range.

Global Ranking

The overall ranking of the 160 countries is shown in Table 4.15. The top 10 countries/territories are Germany (84.86), Singapore (84.18), Australia (83.74), Finland (83.59), the United States (83.27), the United Kingdom (82.67), Canada (82.25), Italy (82.19), Switzerland (81.64), and Slovenia (81.17). The bottom 10 countries or territories are Lesotho (50.25), Somalia (50.04), Benin (48.69), Djibouti (48.00), Papua New Guinea (46.96), Vanuatu (45.50), Cabo Verde (45.36), Equatorial Guinea (44.64), Guinea-Bissau (43.40), and Solomon Islands (43.01).

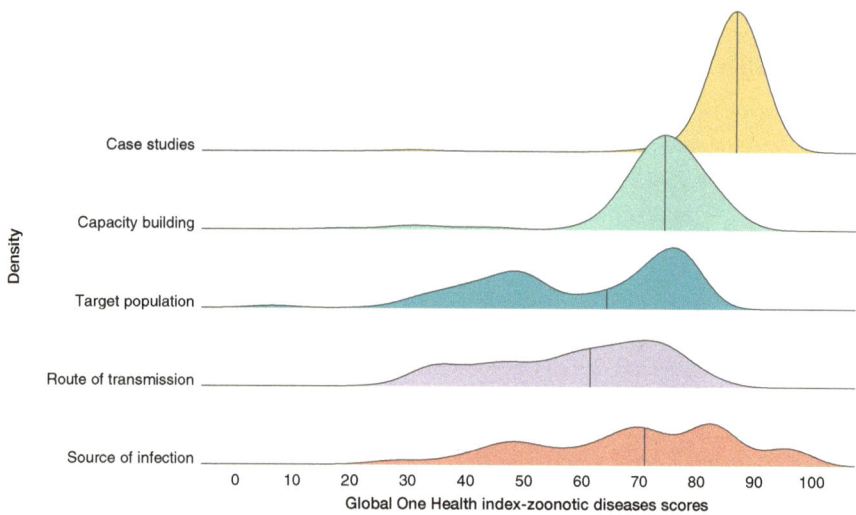

Fig. 4.18 Dimensional score distribution of the global One Health index-zoonotic diseases (GOHI-Zoonoses)

In rankings of regions, the top five in Europe and Central Asia are Germany, Finland, United Kingdom, Italy, and Switzerland, ranging from 81.64 to 84.86; in sub-Saharan Africa, the top five are South Africa, Rwanda, Mali, Cote d'Ivoire, and Kenya, ranging from 69.10 to 80.51; in Latin America and the Caribbean, the top five are Costa Rica, Argentina, Brazil, Nicaragua, and Mexico, with a range of 74.99–79.92; in East Asia and Pacific, the top five countries are Singapore, Australia, China, South Korea, and Thailand, with a score range of 78.28–84.18; in the Middle East and North Africa, the top five are Iran, Egypt, United Arab Emirates, Kuwait, and Oman, with a score range of 74.09–79.69; in South Asia, the top five are Bhutan, India, Bangladesh, Sri Lanka, and Pakistan, with a range of 59.91–74.84; in North America, the United States scores 83.27 and Canada scores 82.25 (Table 4.16).

Regional Performance

The scores of each region under different indicators are shown in Table 4.17.

In terms of SI, countries in East Asia and Pacific and South Asia need to improve their monitoring and feedback (gap: −11.91). The scores for other indicators differ slightly from the global average. Countries or territories in Europe and Central Asia do not score well for COVID-19 control and prevention (gap: −21.96). In Latin America and the Caribbean countries and territories, the vaccination strategy and regulation scores of zoonotic diseases are significantly lower than the global average (gap: −13.24). The Middle East and North Africa score lower in terms of strategy and regulation and conventional interventions, with gaps of −5.06 and −8.29 respectively. North America scores better overall. South Asia differs significantly from the global average in terms of strategy and regulation adoption for zoonoses (gap: −15.53) and vaccination coverage (gap: −27.78). There is a need to strengthen zoonotic disease legislation, surveillance, and control of wildlife reservoirs, as well as to focus on the prevention and treatment of echinococcosis (gap: −15.66), leishmaniasis (−18.80), rabies (gap: −15.42), and tuberculosis (−14.25). Sub-Saharan Africa scores low on the strategy and regulation of zoonoses (gap: −14.75), basic sanitation services (gap: −37.53), conventional interventions (gap: −16.61), vaccination coverage (−22.31), and population coverage with basic sanitation and cost of interventions (gap: −19.23), which are inadequate. Many countries lack basic drinking water and basic sanitation services. Table 4.17 can be used as a reference for the health priorities of each region or country.

Table 4.15   Country ranking of total score in the global One Health index-zoonotic diseases (GOHI-Zoonoses)

Rank	Country	Score	Rank	Country	Score	Rank	Country	Score
				Global rank				
1	Germany	84.86	55	Malaysia	73.25	109	Cuba	63.64
2	Singapore	84.18	56	Japan	73.11	110	Montenegro	63.56
3	Australia	83.74	57	Saudi Arabia	73.02	111	Togo	63.45
4	Finland	83.59	58	Turkmenistan	73.00	112	Mozambique	63.19
5	United States of America	83.27	59	Mongolia	72.6	113	Guyana	63.17
6	United Kingdom	82.67	60	Israel	72.18	114	Zambia	62.80
7	Canada	82.25	61	Rwanda	72.18	115	Guinea	62.70
8	Italy	82.19	62	Colombia	71.85	116	Timor-Leste	62.61
9	Switzerland	81.64	63	Bolivia	71.63	117	Zimbabwe	62.44
10	Slovenia	81.17	64	Panama	71.47	118	Tunisia	62.19
11	Ireland	80.72	65	Georgia	71.44	119	Jordan	62.06
12	South Africa	80.51	66	Chile	71.41	120	Sri Lanka	61.95
13	China	80.46	67	Moldova	71.28	121	Cameroon	60.62
14	Costa Rica	79.92	68	Poland	71.13	122	Iraq	60.55
15	Netherlands	79.85	69	Belarus	70.98	123	Seychelles	60.40
16	Spain	79.72	70	North Macedonia	70.62	124	Eswatini	60.38
17	Iran	79.69	71	Hungary	70.53	125	Honduras	60.22
18	Armenia	79.50	72	Kyrgyzstan	70.33	126	Burkina Faso	59.99
19	Sweden	79.28	73	Lebanon	70.27	127	Pakistan	59.91
20	Egypt	78.99	74	Serbia	70.00	128	Nepal	59.71
21	Albania	78.98	75	Luxembourg	69.87	129	Azerbaijan	59.30
22	Argentina	78.86	76	Ukraine	69.66	130	Maldives	58.99
23	Norway	78.62	77	Mali	69.53	131	Niger	58.76
24	South Korea	78.54	78	Cote d'Ivoire	69.48	132	Brunei Darussalam	58.58
25	Austria	78.46	79	Ecuador	69.44	133	Namibia	58.44
26	Brazil	78.42	80	Cambodia	69.24	134	Dem. Rep. Congo	58.42
27	Thailand	78.28	81	Paraguay	69.22	135	Belize	57.63
28	Belgium	78.18	82	Kenya	69.10	136	Ghana	57.56
29	Viet Nam	78.18	83	Tajikistan	69.05	137	Malawi	57.51
30	Myanmar	78.14	84	Estonia	68.74	138	Liberia	57.41
31	Croatia	78.09	85	Uruguay	68.63	139	Central African Republic	57.15
32	Turkey	77.82	86	Botswana	67.88	140	Sudan	56.67
33	Bulgaria	77.57	87	Uganda	67.43	141	Afghanistan	56.66
34	Indonesia	76.93	88	Laos	67.31	142	Madagascar	56.36
35	Nicaragua	76.76	89	Tanzania	67.20	143	Chad	56.19
36	Greece	76.64	90	Morocco	67.15	144	Sierra Leone	55.96
37	Philippines	76.57	91	Kazakhstan	66.94	145	Burundi	54.98
38	Portugal	76.53	92	India	66.8	146	Trinidad and Tobago	54.84
39	Latvia	76.49	93	Russia	66.57	147	Mauritania	54.79
40	Slovakia	76.47	94	Bangladesh	66.47	148	Gabon	53.73
41	Lithuania	75.90	95	Nigeria	66.45	149	Barbados	53.59
42	Denmark	75.49	96	Iceland	66.26	150	Mauritius	53.17
43	Romania	75.45	97	El Salvador	66.23	151	Lesotho	50.25
44	New Zealand	75.44	98	Guatemala	65.98	152	Somalia	50.04
45	Czech Republic	75.41	99	Jamaica	65.67	153	Benin	48.69
46	United Arab Emirates	75.16	100	Uzbekistan	65.59	154	Djibouti	48.00
47	Mexico	74.99	101	Dominican Republic	65.40	155	Papua New Guinea	46.96
48	Peru	74.93	102	Libya	65.29	156	Vanuatu	45.50
49	Bhutan	74.84	103	Algeria	65.14	157	Cabo Verde	45.36
50	France	74.34	104	Malta	65.10	158	Equatorial Guinea	44.64
51	Kuwait	74.09	105	Bahrain	64.67	159	Guinea-Bissau	43.40
52	Oman	74.09	106	Senegal	64.14	160	Solomon Islands	43.01
53	Cyprus	73.82	107	Ethiopia	63.92			
54	Qatar	73.50	108	Fiji	63.87			

East Asia and Pacific   Europe and Central Asia   Latin America and the Caribbean   Middle East and North Africa

North America   South Asia   Sub-Saharan Africa

Table 4.16 Regional ranking of the global One Health index-zoonotic diseases (GOHI-Zoonoses)

East Asia and Pacific

Rank	Country	Score
1	Singapore	84.18
2	Australia	83.74
3	China	80.46
4	South Korea	78.54
5	Thailand	78.28
6	Viet Nam	78.18
7	Myanmar	78.14
8	Indonesia	76.93
9	Philippines	76.57
10	New Zealand	75.44
11	Malaysia	73.25
12	Japan	73.11
13	Mongolia	72.60
14	Cambodia	69.24
15	Laos	67.31
16	Fiji	63.87
17	Timor-Leste	62.61
18	Brunei Darussalam	58.58
19	Papua New Guinea	46.96
20	Vanuatu	45.50
21	Solomon Islands	43.01

Middle East and North Africa

Rank	Country	Score
1	Iran	79.69
2	Egypt	78.99
3	United Arab Emirates	75.16
4	Kuwait	74.09
5	Oman	74.09
6	Qatar	73.50
7	Saudi Arabia	73.02
8	Israel	72.18
9	Lebanon	70.27
10	Morocco	67.15
11	Libya	65.29
12	Algeria	65.14
13	Malta	65.10
14	Bahrain	64.67
15	Tunisia	62.19
16	Jordan	62.06
17	Iraq	60.55
18	Djibouti	48.00

Europe and Central Asia

Rank	Country	Score
1	Germany	84.86
2	Finland	83.59
3	United Kingdom	82.67

Table 4.16 (continued)

Europe and Central Asia

Rank	Country	Score
4	Italy	82.19
5	Switzerland	81.64
6	Slovenia	81.17
7	Ireland	80.72
8	Netherlands	79.85
9	Spain	79.72
10	Armenia	79.50
11	Sweden	79.28
12	Albania	78.98
13	Norway	78.62
14	Austria	78.46
15	Belgium	78.18
16	Croatia	78.09
17	Turkey	77.82
18	Bulgaria	77.57
19	Greece	76.64
20	Portugal	76.53
21	Latvia	76.49
22	Slovakia	76.47
23	Lithuania	75.90
24	Denmark	75.49
25	Romania	75.45
26	Czech Republic	75.41
27	France	74.34
28	Cyprus	73.82
29	Turkmenistan	73.00
30	Georgia	71.44
31	Moldova	71.28
32	Poland	71.13
33	Belarus	70.98
34	North Macedonia	70.62
35	Hungary	70.53
36	Kyrgyzstan	70.33
37	Serbia	70.00
38	Luxembourg	69.87
39	Ukraine	69.66
40	Tajikistan	69.05
41	Estonia	68.74
42	Kazakhstan	66.94
43	Russia	66.57
44	Iceland	66.26
45	Uzbekistan	65.59
46	Montenegro	63.56
47	Azerbaijan	59.3

Sub-Saharan Africa

Rank	Country	Score
1	South Africa	80.51
2	Rwanda	72.18

Table 4.16 (continued)

Sub-Saharan Africa

Rank	Country	Score
3	Mali	69.53
4	Cote d'Ivoire	69.48
5	Kenya	69.10
6	Botswana	67.88
7	Uganda	67.43
8	Tanzania	67.20
9	Nigeria	66.45
10	Senegal	64.14
11	Ethiopia	63.92
12	Togo	63.45
13	Mozambique	63.19
14	Zambia	62.80
15	Guinea	62.70
16	Zimbabwe	62.44
17	Cameroon	60.62
18	Seychelles	60.40
19	Eswatini	60.38
20	Burkina Faso	59.99
21	Niger	58.76
22	Namibia	58.44
23	Dem. Rep. Congo	58.42
24	Ghana	57.56
25	Malawi	57.51
26	Liberia	57.41
27	Central African Republic	57.15
28	Sudan	56.67
29	Madagascar	56.36
30	Chad	56.19
31	Sierra Leone	55.96
32	Burundi	54.98
33	Mauritania	54.79
34	Gabon	53.73
35	Mauritius	53.17
36	Lesotho	50.25
37	Somalia	50.04
38	Benin	48.69
39	Cabo Verde	45.36
40	Equatorial Guinea	44.64
41	Guinea-Bissau	43.40

South Asia

Rank	Country	Score
1	Bhutan	74.84
2	India	66.80
3	Bangladesh	66.47
4	Sri Lanka	61.95
5	Pakistan	59.91
6	Nepal	59.71
7	Maldives	58.99
8	Afghanistan	56.66

Table 4.16 (continued)

Latin America and the Caribbean

Rank	Country	Score
1	Costa Rica	79.92
2	Argentina	78.86
3	Brazil	78.42
4	Nicaragua	76.76
5	Mexico	74.99
6	Peru	74.93
7	Colombia	71.85
8	Bolivia	71.63
9	Panama	71.47
10	Chile	71.41
11	Ecuador	69.44
12	Paraguay	69.22
13	Uruguay	68.63
14	El Salvador	66.23
15	Guatemala	65.98
16	Jamaica	65.67
17	Dominican Republic	65.40
18	Cuba	63.64
19	Guyana	63.17
20	Honduras	60.22
21	Belize	57.63
22	Trinidad and Tobago	54.84
23	Barbados	53.59

North America

Rank	Country	Score
1	United States	83.27
2	Canada	82.25

4.5 Key Findings

The Indicator of Route of Transmission Has to Be Strengthened Further

Global performance of GOHI-Zoonoses is the highest among five key indicators of CDI, indicating that zoonotic disease control has been paid attention by global communities and UN member countries. But the route of transmission scores lowest (59.30) compared with other indicators (SI: 69.22, TP: 59.90, CB: 72.85, CS: 85.89), which means the route of transmission is the weakest component in the prevention and control of zoonotic diseases worldwide.

Table 4.17 Regional performance of the global One Health index-zoonotic diseases (GOHI-Zoonoses)

Code	Title	Global	East Asia and Pacific		Europe and Central Asia		Latin America and the Caribbean		Middle East and North Africa		North America		South Asia		Sub-Saharan Africa	
			Average	Gap	Average	Gap	Average	Gap	Average	Gap	Average	Gap	Average	Gap	Average	Gap
C2.1.1	Strategy and regulation	53.85	56.05	2.20	68.91	15.06	52.81	−1.04	48.79	−5.06	98.64	44.79	38.32	−15.53	39.10	−14.75
C2.1.2	Monitoring and feedback	83.56	71.65	−11.91	88.56	5.00	90.91	7.35	83.55	−0.01	93.72	10.16	74.21	−9.35	81.14	−2.42
C2.1.3	Hygiene	76.40	77.57	1.16	96.20	19.79	87.96	11.55	92.70	16.29	99.36	22.95	73.78	−2.62	38.88	−37.53
C2.2.1	Conventional interventions	46.48	52.38	5.90	61.44	14.95	41.85	−4.64	38.19	−8.29	75.00	28.52	53.13	6.64	29.88	−16.61
C2.2.2	Ecological intervention	69.84	71.07	1.23	68.86	−0.98	66.07	−3.77	67.38	−2.46	69.32	−0.52	71.81	1.97	73.18	3.34
C2.3.1	Vaccination coverage	58.67	79.34	20.67	80.04	21.36	45.43	−13.24	54.88	−3.79	94.58	35.91	30.90	−27.78	36.36	−22.31
C2.3.2	Population coverage and cost of interventions	39.26	40.36	1.10	48.05	8.79	46.62	7.35	47.03	7.77	49.58	10.32	42.09	2.83	20.03	−19.23
C2.3.3	Inhabitants below 5 m above sea level	86.77	89.38	2.60	86.25	−0.52	81.76	−5.02	90.39	3.61	94.71	7.93	81.64	−5.14	87.88	1.11
C2.4.1	Guidelines for the control and supervision of zoonotic diseases	55.77	58.22	2.45	55.51	−0.26	60.55	4.78	59.99	4.22	67.97	12.20	53.81	−1.96	50.07	−5.70
C2.4.2	Nature reserves	95.36	90.21	−5.15	100.00	4.64	95.69	0.33	94.58	−0.77	100.00	4.64	88.35	−7.00	93.97	−1.39
C2.5.1	COVID-19	70.91	79.12	8.21	59.07	−11.84	72.04	1.13	74.59	3.68	70.28	−0.63	84.46	13.55	75.42	4.50
C2.5.2	Echinococcosis	95.38	97.80	2.42	94.30	−1.09	99.72	4.34	94.32	−1.07	99.52	4.14	79.73	−15.66	96.27	0.89
C2.5.3	Leishmaniasis	97.97	100.00	2.03	99.95	1.98	98.04	0.07	99.34	1.37	100.00	2.03	79.17	−18.80	97.59	−0.38
C2.5.4	Rabies	98.11	98.17	0.06	99.97	1.87	99.99	1.88	99.93	1.82	99.97	1.86	82.68	−15.42	96.99	−1.11
C2.5.5	Tuberculosis	98.18	97.87	−0.31	99.87	1.69	99.82	1.64	99.87	1.70	99.91	1.73	83.93	−14.25	97.43	−0.74
C2.5.6	Yellow fever	49.93	50.00	0.07	50.02	0.09	50.99	1.06	50.00	0.07	50.00	0.07	50.00	0.07	49.16	−0.78
C2.1	Source of infection	69.22	66.45	−2.77	82.07	12.84	74.13	4.91	71.20	1.98	96.86	27.63	59.03	−10.19	52.94	−16.28
C2.2	Route of transmission	59.30	62.63	3.34	65.51	6.21	55.13	−4.16	54.20	−5.09	71.89	12.59	63.37	4.08	53.63	−5.67
C2.3	Target population	59.90	67.14	7.25	69.39	9.49	57.38	−2.52	63.00	3.11	76.88	16.98	51.34	−8.56	46.20	−13.70
C2.4	Capacity building	72.85	72.02	−0.83	74.70	1.85	75.71	2.86	74.92	2.07	81.79	8.94	68.71	−4.14	69.01	−3.84
C2.5	Case studies	85.89	88.13	2.24	84.31	−1.58	87.60	1.71	87.32	1.42	87.37	1.47	78.05	−7.84	86.43	0.54
C2	Total	68.06	69.83	1.77	74.56	6.50	68.43	0.37	68.40	0.33	82.76	14.70	63.17	−4.90	59.59	−8.47

The Performance of GOHI-Zoonoses Is Much Better in the Agricultural Countries

C2.1: South Africa scores highest (96.21) in sub-Saharan region and ranks 10th globally, which far exceeds the global average score of 69.22.

C2.2: Uganda and India are the only sub-Saharan African countries and South Asian countries, in the top ten countries with scores of 74.19 and 78.28 respectively.

C2.3: Spain ranks first and is the only country with a score above 80. The top ten countries are upper-middle-income or high-income countries.

C2.4: Germany ranks first, with a score of 88.16. EI Salvador is a low-income country, it performs well in legislation related to zoonotic disease control and formulation of national guidelines, with a score of 84.35.

C2.5: The top 10 countries are mainly located in Latin America and the Caribbean, the Middle East and North Africa, East Asia and Pacific, South Asia, and sub-Saharan Africa.

It Is Urgent to Strengthen the Laboratory Capacity Testing for Infections Both in Human and Zoonotic Reservoir

There are two sub I-indicators under RT, which are Conventional interventions (CI) and Ecological interventions (ECI), with average scores of 46.48 and 69.84, respectively. Therefore, the lower score for CI in RT indicates an inadequate ability of laboratory testing for zoonotic reservoirs. We also find that 45.30% of the countries with scores below the average of 46.48 are in sub-Saharan Africa, 31.25% of the countries or territories in Latin America and the Caribbean and Middle East and North Africa, implying that these regions in particular need to improve their zoonotic disease detection capacity.

There Is a Significant Gap in Total Score Between Different Countries Within a Region, Indicating That Country-Based Intervention Policy Has to Be Promoted and Implemented

Each region has top-ranked countries or territories, for example, South Africa in sub-Saharan Africa ranks 12th in the world with a GOHI-Zoonoses score of 80.51. However, the average GOHI-Zoonoses score for sub-Saharan Africa is only 59.59. Similarly, Argentina and Mexico are the only two Latin American and the Caribbean countries in the top 10, both scoring 87.50, significantly above the average score of this region (68.43). All these reflect the unbalanced GOHI-Zoonoses scores within the region, indicating the large gap in the performance of responding to zoonotic diseases within the region.

4.6   Conclusion

To reduce disparities in the ability to deal with zoonotic diseases among regions or countries, it is necessary to understand the route of transmission for each zoonotic disease at the local level and transfer information to decision-makers to improve the capacity of control programs. International cooperation and communication to reduce the price of vaccines and drugs are essential approaches to lower the cost of preventing zoonotic diseases. Legislation related to zoonotic disease surveillance should be improved to fill legal gaps. In addition, it is urgent to promote upstream prevention in zoonoses and enhance the ability of zoonotic pathogen testing. Finally, various departments should reduce "data barriers," adopt the One Health approach, and carry out cross-sectoral cooperation to increase the transparency, credibility, and public availability of data.

5   Food Security

5.1   Background

Food security refers to the state in which people have physical, social, and economic access to safe and nutritious food that meets their dietary needs and preferences for an active and healthy life [36]. It holds significant implications for economic growth, social harmony, and environmental preservation [37]. According to the latest definition by the High-Level Panel of Experts on Food Security and Nutrition (HLPE-FSN) of the UN, ensuring food security not only means providing people and communities with adequate amounts of wholesome and safe food, promoting overall health, preventing malnutrition and associated illnesses, and supporting general well-being, but also transforming food systems in the direction needed to meet the SDGs. This requires action at various levels to ensure food system availability, accessibility, utilization, stability, agency, and sustainability [38].

Food security holds significant importance, as demonstrated by its prominence in numerous international agreements and national policies. The UN Millennium Development Goals initially aimed to halve the proportion of hungry people in the total population by 2015, while the 2030 Agenda for Sustainable Development further prioritized the elimination of hunger, achievement of food security and improved nutrition, and promotion of sustainable agriculture as one of the SDGs [39]. From July 2022 to February 2023, the heads of the FAO, International Monetary Fund (IMF), the World Bank, World Food Programme (WFP), and World Trade Organization (WTO) issued three joint statements calling for urgent and continued action to address the global food and nutrition security crisis and to avoid further setbacks to the SDGs. Facilitating trade and improving the function and resilience of global markets for food and agriculture, including cereals, fertilizers, and other agricultural production inputs, have also been prioritized. These measures, along with the collaborative efforts of international organizations and governments, are vital in addressing the challenges posed by the food and nutrition security crisis [40–42].

Despite these efforts, food security is facing increasing threats from human, animal, and environmental factors in this new era [6]. Increased food demand contributes to resource depletion, soil erosion, and pollution, negatively affecting food security [43]. Natural disasters can disrupt agriculture and food stability while also causing zoonotic diseases that harm human and animal health, further impacting food security [6]. The 2022 edition of the UN SOFI (The State of Food Security and Nutrition in the World) report revealed that 828 million people suffered from hunger in 2021, an increase of 46 million from the previous year and 150 million from 2019. The proportion of people affected by hunger rose in 2020 and continued to increase in 2021, reaching 9.80% of the world population [44].

Therefore, the "One Health" concept was introduced in areas such as food security, food safety, AMR, nutrition, and animal and plant health to better address global food security crises. The latest report published by the HLPE emphasizes the importance of adopting an analytical and policy framework for food systems, which acknowledges the complexity and interconnectedness of various factors affecting food security and nutrition [38]. Additionally, the FAO has been working in partnership with international organizations like the WHO and the WOAH to develop joint action strategies and programs that address food safety and other One Health issues [45]. In addressing One Health, one also addresses environmental health issues such as soil fertility decline, land desertification, and crop irrigation, which directly impact food production and quality; improves the prevention and control of zoonotic diseases, promoting both human and animal health, increasing food productivity, and reducing biosecurity risks; and encourages research on food security-related issues at the human-animal-environment interface, leading to cumulative beneficial effects on food security. Thus, implementing One Health measures is essential for ensuring food security, preventing environment-related health threats, and tackling various challenges [46].

5.2   Necessity to Evaluate Food Security from One Health Perspective

Food security has been assessed using various tools. Several primary indices are widely employed to evaluate food security, such as the Global Food Security Index (GFSI) [47], Global Hunger Index (GHI) [48], and Food Sustainability Index (FSI) [49]. While these existing indices emphasize distinct aspects of food security, they might not be adequate to tackle the challenges and threats posed to food security in the new era, particularly those arising at the human-animal-environment interface.

To address these challenges, we argue that the One Health concept should be at the basis of the food security index. One Health provides a holistic perspective based on the human-animal-environment interface, promoting cross-sectoral and multidisciplinary collaboration for effectively tackling food security issues [11]. The new index system built on the One Health concept offers three main advantages over traditional indices:

Comprehensive Coverage: The new index system addresses the six aspects of food security, including availability, accessibility, utilization, stability, sustainability, and agency. It does so by incorporating dimensions such as food demand and supply, food safety, nutritional status, natural and social environment, and government support and response [38, 50].

Resilience indicators: The system introduces new indicators that reflect a country's or region's food system resilience against extreme weather, disasters, or crises, providing a better understanding of their ability to cope with external threats.

Sustainability indicators: The new index also adds indicators that reflect the sustainability of natural resources required for food production, such as the proportion of organic agricultural land and the percentage of agricultural water withdrawal from total renewable water resources.

By incorporating the One Health concept, we developed the global One Health index-food security (GOHI-FS) that systematically reflects the food security status of different countries. It considers the extent to which countries can effectively meet their population's energy and nutritional needs and examines the impact of various factors, including agricultural infrastructure, natural resource sustainability, government support, economic support, technical support, and environmental disasters.

5.3 Framework Construction of GOHI-FS

Framework

The framework was developed based on the mainstream international food security evaluation framework. We collected and collated relevant evaluation indicators and data from existing databases to establish a three-level framework and database. The binary fuzzy evaluation method was used to determine the indicator weights. The underlying data of each country was normalized and then used to calculate the score and total value of each evaluation indicator for each country. We also carried out further analyses on evaluation categories and regions.

The construction of the GOHI-FS framework was based on a large body of literature and reports from internationally recognized organizations on the subject. A series of key themes were extracted, and after group discussions and expert consultation in conjunction with evaluations on the purposes of the indicators, five indicators were established to evaluate food security from a One Health perspective. To construct the sub II-indicators, a preliminary database of alternative indicators was formed after extensive brainstorming and searching of authoritative databases. The team members condensed ideas from the underlying data to establish the sub II-indicators while ensuring the scientific and logical integrity of evaluation system. Indicators in the framework were classified according to the "structure (blue)—process (green)—outcome (pink)" framework, as shown in Table 4.18.

Indicators

After repeated discussions, information review, indicator selection, two rounds of expert consultation, and consideration of data accessibility and completeness, a new round of consolidation of indicators was carried out to capture the safety of livestock and the environment and measure government responses.

To evaluate food security indicators from a One Health perspective, the system analyzes food security through five different indicators: food demand and supply, food safety, nutrition, natural and social circumstances, government support and response. There are 5 main indicators, 20 sub I-indicators and 54 sub II-indicators.

Data Sources

In the GOHI-FS, quantitative indicators are derived from statistics from international agencies, including the FAO of the UN, World Bank,

Table 4.18 Indicator and weight scheme of the global One Health index-food security (GOHI-FS)

Indicator			Sub I-indicator			Sub II-indicator		
Name	Code	Weight	Name	Code	Weight	Name	Code	Weight
Food demand and supply	C3.1	20.0%	Food demand score	C3.1.1	21.8%	Ratio of population growth	C3.1.1.1	40.0%
						Ratio of refugees and internally displaced people	C3.1.1.2	20.0%
						Ratio of moderately or severely food insecure people	C3.1.1.3	40.0%
			Food loss and waste	C3.1.2	20.2%	Food loss	C3.1.2.1	50.0%
						Food waste	C3.1.2.2	50.0%
			Infrastructures score	C3.1.3	19.4%	Logistic performance index	C3.1.3.1	33.3%
						Net capital stocks	C3.1.3.2	33.3%
						Percent of arable land equipped for irrigation	C3.1.3.3	33.3%
			Food aid	C3.1.4	14.7%	Food aid	C3.1.4.1	100.0%
			Food production score	C3.1.5	23.9%	Average value of food production	C3.1.5.1	33.3%
						Food production viability	C3.1.5.2	33.3%
						Livestock production index	C3.1.5.3	33.3%
Food safety	C3.2	20.0%	Food safety governance	C3.2.1	18.8%	Food safety agency	C3.2.1.1	50.0%
						Food policy, legal and regulatory framework	C3.2.1.2	50.0%
			Food control and surveillance	C3.2.2	19.2%	Inspections in farm-to-fork food chain	C3.2.2.1	50.0%
						Food recalls	C3.2.2.2	50.0%
			Food safety evaluation	C3.2.3	20.3%	Food safety score	C3.2.3.1	100.0%
			Foodborne illness burden	C3.2.4	25.8%	DALY of diarrhoea	C3.2.4.1	100.0%
			Safety of livestock production	C3.2.5	13.6%	Livestock density	C3.2.5.1	33.3%
						Domestic animal disease outbreak	C3.2.5.2	33.3%
						Manure management	C3.2.5.3	33.3%
Nutrition	C3.3	20.0%	Food balance	C3.3.1	39.3%	Average dietary energy supply adequacy	C3.3.1.1	33.3%
						Average protein supply	C3.3.1.2	33.3%
						Per capita food supply variability	C3.3.1.3	33.3%
			Nutrition promoting capacity	C3.3.2	30.1%	Nutrition labeling	C3.3.2.1	33.3%
						Nutrition guideline	C3.3.2.2	33.3%
						Nutrition education programme	C3.3.2.3	33.3%
			Nutrition score	C3.3.3	30.6%	Undernourishment	C3.3.3.1	25.0%
						Stunting in children under five	C3.3.3.2	25.0%
						Anemia among women of reproductive age	C3.3.3.3	25.0%
						Ratio of overweight children	C3.3.3.4	25.0%
Natural and social circumstances	C3.4	20.0%	Famine warning	C3.4.1	20.6%	Food affected by extreme weather conditions, disasters or crisis	C3.4.1.1	100.0%
			Natural sources sustainability	C3.4.2	28.9%	Per person land under cereal production	C3.4.2.1	12.5%
						Agricultural water withdrawal as % of total renewable water resources	C3.4.2.2	12.5%
						Agriculture area under organic agric	C3.4.2.3	12.5%
						Naturally regenerating forest	C3.4.2.4	12.5%
						Percentage of agriculture land area affected by soil erosion	C3.4.2.5	12.5%
						Livestock diversity	C3.4.2.6	12.5%
						Crop diversity	C3.4.2.7	12.5%
						Agricultural nitrous oxide emissions	C3.4.2.8	12.5%
			Economic performance index	C3.4.3	18.6%	Trade balance indicators	C3.4.3.1	25.0%
						Economic vulnerability index	C3.4.3.2	25.0%
						Cereal import dependency ratio	C3.4.3.3	25.0%
						Value of food imports over total merchandise exports	C3.4.3.4	25.0%
			Agriculture value added per worker	C3.4.4	18.2%	Agriculture value added per worker	C3.4.4.1	100.0%
			Food price indicators	C3.4.5	13.7%	Agricultural import tariffs	C3.4.5.1	33.3%
						Consumer prices food indices	C3.4.5.2	33.3%
						Food price inflation	C3.4.5.3	33.3%
Government support and response	C3.5	20.0%	Investment and financial support score	C3.5.1	55.4%	Government investment on agriculture	C3.5.1.1	10.0%
						Credit to agriculture, forestry, fishing	C3.5.1.2	40.0%
						Research and development (R&D) expenses	C3.5.1.3	10.0%
						Agricultural R&D investment intensity	C3.5.1.4	40.0%
			Training and AI agriculture performance score	C3.5.2	44.6%	Training programme	C3.5.2.1	50.0%
						Smart and digital agriculture	C3.5.2.2	50.0%

WHO, UN data, UNHCR, UNEP, and other international organizations. Among the qualitative indicators, some are statistically assigned based on information provided in national annual reports, while others are based literature surveys adjusted by a pool of experts.

Limitations

There were some limitations in the data sources adopted, which can lead to underestimation for some countries. First, some data were widely missing in less economically developed countries, posing a challenge to the complete evaluation of food security in those counties. To address this, we interpolated the data for the missing countries with the average estimation of three other countries with similar GDP levels. This approach avoids underestimation due to missing data being assigned a value of zero, but the accuracy of the data still needs improvement. Second, the total data missing rate was 20.20%, mainly for quantitative indicators, resulting in an incomplete evaluation. We excluded data from our estimates if it had a missing rate over 60.00% from countries, mainly related to Government support and response, and outcome indicators, including Government investment on agriculture (C3.5.1.1), Research and development (R&D) expenses (C3.5.1.3), and Training programme (C3.5.2.1). Additionally, the years adopted for each of the sub II-indicators varied due to differences in the method of obtaining the original data. To ensure the timeliness of the evaluation, data were selected from the most recent year when available for evaluation. Most data were from years 2016–2021, with a small amount of data with a time lag. This may bias the estimation of the results. Finally, the current evaluation of qualitative indicators was not fine-detailed due to the

lack of national One Health-related policies. For example, some indicators in C3.2 were simply expressed by a binary variable that did not capture the granularity in the effectiveness or efficiency of the specific implementation.

5.4   Main Results

Global Score

Overall, GOHI-FS indicates an overall low level of One Health food security worldwide. The scores, ranging from 73.08 (Australia) to 24.83 (Central African Republic) with a standard deviation of 9.80, reveal that there is significant variation in the level of food security across the 160 countries evaluated (Fig. 4.19).

The total scores of GOHI-FS by regions are as follows (sorted by median): North America (69.97), Europe and Central Asia (59.71), Latin America and the Caribbean 56.09), East Asia and Pacific (55.41), the Middle East and Africa (53.57), South Asia (49.41), sub-Saharan Africa (41.53). Of the seven major geographic regions evaluated, North America has the highest average score while sub-Saharan Africa has the lowest average score of 41.53. Of them, North America and European countries/territories score higher, followed by Latin America and the Caribbean, and East Asia and Pacific. Countries/territories with lower scores are mostly in the sub-Saharan Africa (Fig. 4.20).

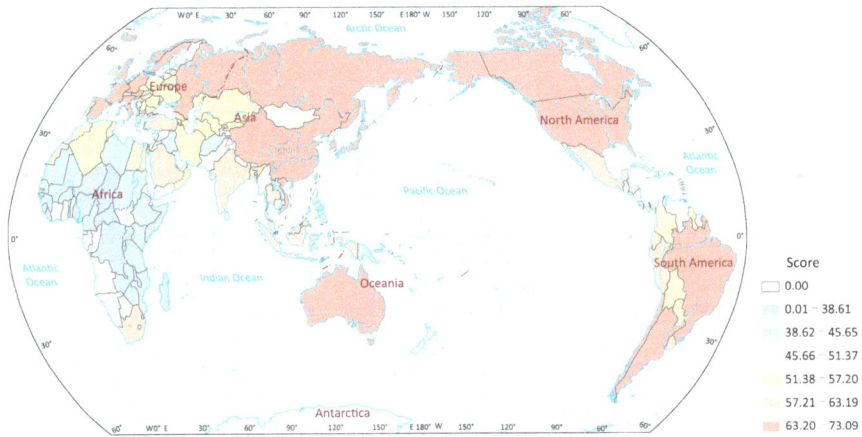

Fig. 4.19 Global score map of the global One Health index-food security (GOHI-FS)

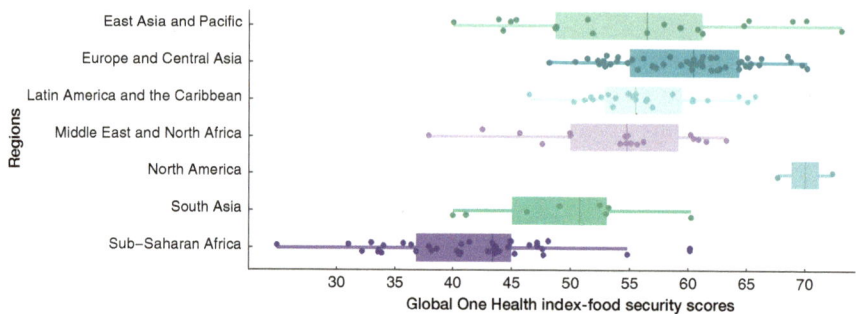

Fig. 4.20 Regional score distribution of the global One Health index-food security (GOHI-FS)

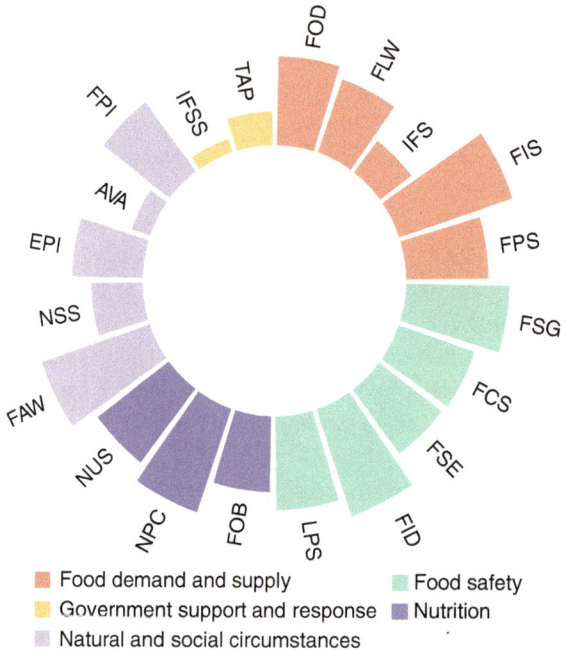

Fig. 4.21 The global One Health index-food security (GOHI-FS) score distribution by categories. (*FOD* food demand score, *FLW* food loss and waste, *IFS* infrastructures score, *FIS* food aid, *FPS* food production score, *FSG* food safety governance, *FCS* food control and surveillance, *FSE* food safety evaluation, *FID* foodborne illness burden, *LPS* safety of livestock production, *FOB* food balance, *NPC* nutrition promoting capacity, *NUS* nutrition score, *FAW* famine warning, *NSS* natural sources sustainability, *EPI* economic performance index, *AVA* agriculture value added per worker, *FPI* food price indicators, *IFSS* investment and financial support score, *TAP* training and AI agriculture performance score)

The average score of the GOHI-FS is 52.89. The detailed scores of the five GOHI-FS sub-dimensions from high to low are as follows (sorted by median): Nutritional status (C3.3, median: 70.78), Food security (C3.2, median: 66.95), Natural and social environment (C3.4, median: 63.26), Food demand and supply (C3.1, median: 57.02), and Government support and response (C3.5, median: 31.16). In each second-level dimension, the highest average scores are attained in Food aid (C3.1.4), Foodborne illness burden (C3.2.4), Nutrition promoting capacity (C3.3.2), Famine warning (C3.4.1), Training and AI agriculture performance score (C3.5.2), with 89.98, 83.28, 80.65, 87.85, and 24.81 respectively (Fig. 4.21).

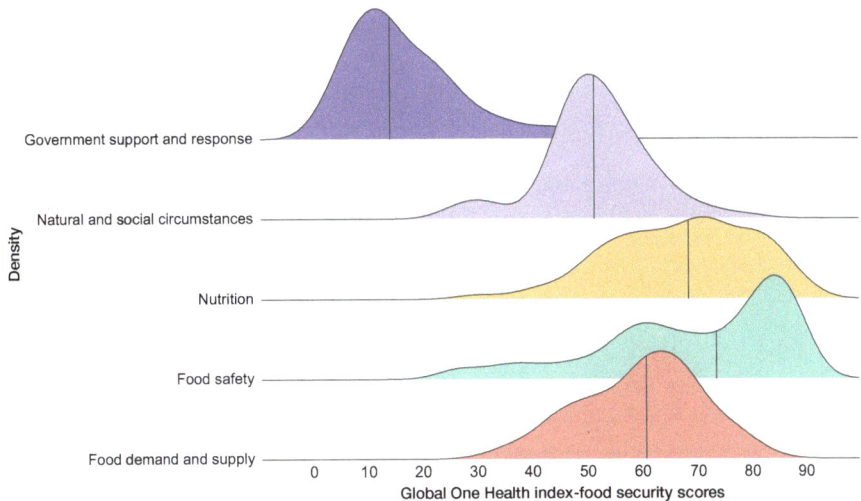

Fig. 4.22 Dimensional score distribution of the global One Health index-food security (GOHI-FS)

The results of the five indicators in GOHI-FS also show significant variation across evaluated countries/regions. When analyzing Food security (C3.2) and Nutritional status (C3.3), the distributions of scores among countries/territories are scattered with standard deviations of 16.87 and 13.03, respectively, indicating large disparities between countries/territories (Fig. 4.22).

Global Rankings

Based on the GOHI-FS scores for 160 countries/territories evaluated, the global rankings is shown in Table 4.19. Generally, countries/territories from East Asia and Pacific, Europe and Central Asia, and North America tend to have higher GOHI-FS scores, whereas countries in sub-Saharan Africa, South Asia, and some parts of the Middle East and North Africa exhibit lower scores. The top 10 includes Australia, the United States, Italy, China, Germany, Japan, France, the United Kingdom, Canada, and Norway, while the bottom 10 is predominantly occupied by the sub-Saharan African countries/territories, emphasizing the disparities in global food security. This analysis underscores the need for targeted efforts and policies to improve the food security with One Health measures in these countries/territories and work toward global equity in development and well-being.

1. *Leaders and laggards*

In the 160 countries/territories under evaluation, the top 25 countries are listed in Table 4.19. Both countries/territories in North America (the United States and Canada) are also in the top 10. The other 23 include 14 countries/territories from Europe and Central Asia (29.79% of the region), five from East Asia and Pacific (23.81% of the region), three from Latin America and the Caribbean (13.04% of the region), and only one country, Qatar, from the Middle East and North Africa region (5.56% of the region). The bottom 20 countries/territories are Chad (32.01), Central African Republic, Mauritania, Yemen, Niger, Burundi, Gabon, Madagascar, Afghanistan, Dem. Rep. Congo, Libya, Benin, Sierra Leone, Pakistan, Togo, Nigeria, Senegal, Papua New Guinea, Iraq, and Guinea (38.32). These countries/territories mainly distributed in sub-Saharan Africa (14 in total), followed by the Middle East and North Africa (three in total).

The bottom 25 countries/territories in the rankings, as shown in Table 4.19 include 20 from the sub-Saharan Africa. The five countries with lowest score (Burundi, Central African Republic, Dem. Rep. Congo, Madagascar, and Somalia) are

Table 4.19 Global score and regional ranking of the global One Health index-food security (GOHI-FS)

Total rank	Country/territory	Total	Reg ranking	Total rank	Country/territory	Total	Reg ranking	Total rank	Country/territory	Total	Reg ranking	Total rank	Country/territory	Total	Reg ranking
1	Australia	73.09	1	41	Luxembourg	60.39	24	81	Belize	53.72	15	121	Senegal	45.27	10
2	United States of America	72.34	1	42	Peru	60.32	5	82	Honduras	53.51	16	122	Tanzania	44.96	11
3	Italy	70.11	1	43	Uruguay	60.31	6	83	Moldova	53.28	39	123	Cabo Verde	44.87	12
4	China	70.03	2	44	Albania	60.24	25	84	Bangladesh	53.18	2	124	Timor-Leste	44.83	18
5	Germany	69.67	2	45	India	60.22	1	85	Dominican Republic	53.11	17	125	Kenya	44.77	13
6	Japan	68.83	3	46	Israel	60.16	5	86	Azerbaijan	52.97	40	126	Burkina Faso	44.7	14
7	France	68.68	3	47	South Africa	60.15	1	87	Sri Lanka	52.97	3	127	Laos	44.19	19
8	United Kingdom	68.42	4	48	Bulgaria	60.13	26	88	Slovakia	52.84	41	128	Equatorial Guinea	43.95	15
9	Canada	67.61	2	49	Cyprus	59.81	27	89	Kyrgyzstan	52.71	42	129	Zambia	43.85	16
10	Norway	66.17	5	50	Hungary	59.32	28	90	Jamaica	52.51	18	130	Papua New Guinea	43.81	20
11	Austria	65.99	6	51	Indonesia	59.28	8	91	Maldives	52.45	4	131	Zimbabwe	43.67	17
12	Chile	65.66	1	52	Thailand	59.23	9	92	Uzbekistan	52.35	43	132	Guinea	43.59	18
13	Belgium	65.28	7	53	Costa Rica	58.6	7	93	Turkmenistan	52.23	44	133	Mozambique	43.51	19
14	Netherlands	65.16	8	54	Estonia	58.38	29	94	Guyana	51.82	19	134	Rwanda	43.44	20
15	Viet Nam	65.09	4	55	Malaysia	57.87	10	95	Brunei Darussalam	51.8	12	135	Uganda	43.35	21
16	Brazil	65.01	2	56	Slovenia	57.83	30	96	Bolivia	51.64	20	136	Mali	42.99	22
17	Finland	64.99	9	57	Czech Republic	57.2	31	97	Cambodia	51.37	13	137	Libya	42.46	17
18	Iceland	64.83	10	58	Kazakhstan	56.88	32	98	North Macedonia	51.35	45	138	Mauritania	41.4	23
19	South Korea	64.66	5	59	Colombia	56.88	8	99	Nicaragua	51.12	21	139	Bhutan	41.1	7
20	Spain	64.44	11	60	Ecuador	56.41	9	100	Montenegro	50.34	46	140	Eswatini	40.72	24
21	Sweden	64.25	12	61	Philippines	56.39	11	101	Trinidad and Tobago	50.22	22	141	Ethiopia	40.69	25
22	Russia	64.25	13	62	Panama	56.32	10	102	Bahrain	49.95	13	142	Sudan	40.55	26
23	Argentina	64.24	3	63	Tunisia	56.14	6	103	Lebanon	49.91	14	143	Cameroon	40.36	27
24	Qatar	63.19	1	64	Romania	56.1	33	104	Pakistan	49.07	5	144	Solomon Islands	40	21
25	Switzerland	63.07	14	65	Ukraine	55.6	34	105	Fiji	48.75	14	145	Afghanistan	39.98	8
26	Denmark	62.58	15	66	Egypt	55.59	7	106	Myanmar	48.72	15	146	Malawi	38.61	28
27	Ireland	62.39	16	67	Paraguay	55.45	11	107	Mongolia	48.65	16	147	Togo	38.2	29
28	Turkey	62.29	17	68	El Salvador	55.44	12	108	Tajikistan	48.15	47	148	Nigeria	37.95	30
29	Croatia	61.91	18	69	Cuba	55.17	13	109	Ghana	48.14	3	149	Djibouti	37.88	18
30	Latvia	61.83	19	70	Serbia	55.12	35	110	Seychelles	47.73	4	150	Lesotho	36.84	31
31	Mexico	61.57	4	71	Algeria	55.05	8	111	Namibia	47.65	5	151	Sierra Leone	36.4	32
32	United Arab Emirates	61.49	2	72	Barbados	54.8	14	112	Jordan	47.59	15	152	Niger	35.71	33
33	Lithuania	61.17	20	73	Mauritius	54.79	2	113	Gabon	47.25	6	153	Guinea-Bissau	34	34
34	Belarus	61.14	21	74	Oman	54.79	9	114	Botswana	47.19	7	154	Chad	33.83	35
35	Singapore	61.13	6	75	Poland	54.75	36	115	Benin	47.19	8	155	Liberia	33.58	36
36	Portugal	61.02	22	76	Iran	54.66	10	116	Cote d'Ivoire	46.53	9	156	Burundi	33.54	37
37	Malta	60.82	3	77	Kuwait	54.55	11	117	Guatemala	46.45	23	157	Madagascar	32.95	38
38	New Zealand	60.72	7	78	Morocco	54.14	12	118	Nepal	46.32	6	158	Somalia	32.16	39
39	Greece	60.63	23	79	Armenia	53.92	37	119	Iraq	45.65	16	159	Dem. Rep. Congo	31.01	40
40	Saudi Arabia	60.4	4	80	Georgia	53.83	38	120	Vanuatu	45.32	17	160	Central African Republic	24.84	41

East Asia and Pacific   Europe and Central Asia   Latin America and the Caribbean   Middle East and North Africa   North America   South Asia   Sub-Saharan Africa

all from the North African region and score poorly in all five indicators.

Regional Performance

This chapter reports the GOHI-FS scores and rankings in seven geographical regions, as shown in Table 4.20. To gain a deeper understanding of the food system performance, Table 4.21 compares the average score of each region with the global average. A negative gap, which indicates that the region's score is below the global average, highlights areas where the food system needs improvement.

1. *East Asia and Pacific*

    The 19 countries/territories included in the East Asia and Pacific region have an average score of 55.41. The top five countries in this region are Australia, China, Japan, Viet Nam, and South Korea. Australia ranks first in this region with a score of 73.08 and ranks 1st in the global rankings, while Solomon Islands bottoms the rankings with a score of 40.00 and ranks 144th globally. There is a significant disparity in scores among countries in the region, with over 30 points between Australia and the Solomon Islands.

    The negative gaps identified for East Asia and Pacific include Safety of livestock production, Food balance, Natural sources sustainability, and Economic performance index, suggesting room for improvement in these areas to enhance the overall performance of the food system. Among these, Safety of livestock production indicator has the most significant gap, being 9.65 points below the global average.

2. *Europe and Central Asia*

    The 46 countries/territories included in the Europe and Central Asia region have an average score of 59.70. The top five countries in this region are Italy, Germany, France, the United Kingdom, and Norway. Italy ranks first in this region with a score of 70.10 and ranks 3rd globally.

    The negative gap identified in the Food production score, Safety of livestock production, Food price indicators, and Training and

AI agriculture performance score in this region suggest that policies and investments are needed to address these areas for better food system performance in the region. Among these, Safety of livestock production indicator has the largest gap and is 8.17 points below the global average.

3. *Latin America and the Caribbean*

    The 19 countries/territories included in the Latin America and the Caribbean region have an average score of 56.10. The top five countries are Chile, Brazil, Argentina, Mexico, and Peru. Chile ranks first in the region with a score of 65.66 and ranks 12th globally.

    Several negative gaps identified in Latin America and the Caribbean include issues with Food demand and supply, Food loss and waste, Infrastructure, Food production, Safety of livestock production, Food balance, Economic performance, Agriculture value added per worker, Food price indicators, Government support and response, and Investment and financial support. Among these, Food loss and waste has the largest gap and is 4.96 points below the global average.

4. *Middle East and North Africa*

    The 18 countries/territories included in the Middle East and North Africa region have an average score of 53.57. The top five countries in this region are Qatar, United Arab Emirates, Malta, Saudi Arabia, and Israel. Qatar ranks first in this region with a score of 63.19 and ranks 24th globally.

    The negative gaps identified suggest Middle East and North Africa needs to improve its efforts in reducing food waste and ensuring food safety, strengthening nutrition-promoting programs, ensuring sustainable use of natural resources, and investing in training and AI technologies for more resilient and sustainable food system(s). Among these, Food control and surveillance has the most significant gap and is 14.62 points below the global average.

5. *North America*

    The United States and Canada perform well in each of the five sub I-indicators and together have an average score of 69.98, plac-

Table 4.20 Regional ranking of the global One Health index-food security (GOHI-FS)

East Asia and Pacific

Rank	Country	Score
1	Australia	73.09
2	China	70.03
3	Japan	68.83
4	Viet Nam	65.09
5	South Korea	64.66
6	Singapore	61.13
7	New Zealand	60.72
8	Indonesia	59.28
9	Thailand	59.23
10	Malaysia	57.87
11	Philippines	56.39
12	Brunei Darussalam	51.80
13	Cambodia	51.37
14	Fiji	48.75
15	Myanmar	48.72
16	Mongolia	48.65
17	Vanuatu	45.32
18	Timor-Leste	44.83
19	Laos	44.19
20	Papua New Guinea	43.81
21	Solomon Islands	40.00

Middle East and North Africa

Rank	Country	Score
1	Qatar	63.19
2	United Arab Emirates	61.49
3	Malta	60.82
4	Saudi Arabia	60.40
5	Israel	60.16
6	Tunisia	56.14
7	Egypt	55.59
8	Algeria	55.05
9	Oman	54.79
10	Iran	54.66
11	Kuwait	54.55
12	Morocco	54.14
13	Bahrain	49.95
14	Lebanon	49.91
15	Jordan	47.59
16	Iraq	45.65
17	Libya	42.46
18	Djibouti	37.88

Europe and Central Asia

Rank	Country	Score
1	Italy	70.11
2	Germany	69.67
3	France	68.68
4	United Kingdom	68.42
5	Norway	66.17
6	Austria	65.99
7	Belgium	65.28
8	Netherlands	65.16
9	Finland	64.99
10	Iceland	64.83
11	Spain	64.44
12	Sweden	64.25
13	Russia	64.25
14	Switzerland	63.07
15	Denmark	62.58
16	Ireland	62.39
17	Turkey	62.29
18	Croatia	61.91
19	Latvia	61.83
20	Lithuania	61.17
21	Belarus	61.14
22	Portugal	61.02
23	Greece	60.63
24	Luxembourg	60.39
25	Albania	60.24
26	Bulgaria	60.13
27	Cyprus	59.81
28	Hungary	59.32
29	Estonia	58.38
30	Slovenia	57.83
31	Czech Republic	57.20
32	Kazakhstan	56.88
33	Romania	56.10
34	Ukraine	55.60
35	Serbia	55.12
36	Poland	54.75
37	Armenia	53.92
38	Georgia	53.83
39	Moldova	53.28
40	Azerbaijan	52.97
41	Slovakia	52.84
42	Kyrgyzstan	52.71
43	Uzbekistan	52.35
44	Turkmenistan	52.23
45	North Macedonia	51.35
46	Montenegro	50.34
47	Tajikistan	48.15

Sub-Saharan Africa

Rank	Country	Score
1	South Africa	60.15
2	Mauritius	54.79
3	Ghana	48.14
4	Seychelles	47.73
5	Namibia	47.65
6	Gabon	47.25
7	Botswana	47.19
8	Benin	47.19
9	Cote d'Ivoire	46.53
10	Senegal	45.27
11	Tanzania	44.96
12	Cabo Verde	44.87
13	Kenya	44.77
14	Burkina Faso	44.70
15	Equatorial Guinea	43.95
16	Zambia	43.85
17	Zimbabwe	43.67
18	Guinea	43.59
19	Mozambique	43.51
20	Rwanda	43.44
21	Uganda	43.35
22	Mali	42.99
23	Mauritania	41.40
24	Eswatini	40.72
25	Ethiopia	40.69
26	Sudan	40.55
27	Cameroon	40.36
28	Malawi	38.61
29	Togo	38.20
30	Nigeria	37.95
31	Lesotho	36.84
32	Sierra Leone	36.40
33	Niger	35.71
34	Guinea-Bissau	34.00
35	Chad	33.83
36	Liberia	33.58
37	Burundi	33.54
38	Madagascar	32.95
39	Somalia	32.16
40	Dem. Rep. Congo	31.01
41	Central African Republic	24.84

South Asia

Rank	Country	Score
1	India	60.22
2	Bangladesh	53.18
3	Sri Lanka	52.97
4	Maldives	52.45
5	Pakistan	49.07
6	Nepal	46.32
7	Bhutan	41.10
8	Afghanistan	39.98

Latin America and the Caribbean

Rank	Country	Score
1	Chile	65.66
2	Brazil	65.01
3	Argentina	64.24
4	Mexico	61.57
5	Peru	60.32
6	Uruguay	60.31
7	Costa Rica	58.60
8	Colombia	56.88
9	Ecuador	56.41
10	Panama	56.32
11	Paraguay	55.45
12	El Salvador	55.44
13	Cuba	55.17
14	Barbados	54.80
15	Belize	53.72
16	Honduras	53.51
17	Dominican Republic	53.11
18	Jamaica	52.51
19	Guyana	51.82
20	Bolivia	51.64
21	Nicaragua	51.12
22	Trinidad and Tobago	50.22
23	Guatemala	46.45

North America

Rank	Country	Score
1	United States of America	72.34
2	Canada	67.61

Table 4.21 Reginal performance of the global One Health index-food security (GOHI-FS)

Code	Indicator Title	Global Average	East Asia and Pacific Average	Gap	Europe and Central Asia Average	Gap	Latin America and the Caribbean Average	Gap	Middle East and North Africa Average	Gap	North America Average	Gap	South Asia Average	Gap	Sub-Saharan Africa Average	Gap
C3	Food security	52.89	55.42	2.53	59.70	6.81	56.10	3.21	53.58	0.69	69.98	17.08	49.41	−3.48	41.53	−11.36
C3.1	Food demand and supply	59.53	64.25	4.72	67.44	7.91	59.14	−0.39	60.13	0.60	64.99	5.46	62.24	2.71	47.20	−12.33
C3.1.1	Food demand score	65.33	71.90	6.57	84.00	18.67	66.88	1.55	66.88	1.55	83.15	17.82	64.51	−0.82	38.30	−27.03
C3.1.2	Food loss and waste	57.11	61.06	3.95	62.07	4.96	56.39	−0.72	48.85	−8.26	42.22	−14.88	68.41	11.30	51.94	−5.17
C3.1.3	Infrastructures score	29.41	34.53	5.12	42.25	12.84	24.67	−4.74	37.51	8.10	43.24	13.83	26.99	−2.43	10.97	−18.44
C3.1.4	Food aid	89.98	96.67	6.68	99.88	9.90	92.42	2.44	91.56	1.58	100.00	10.02	91.35	1.37	72.40	−17.58
C3.1.5	Food production score	62.00	64.15	2.15	57.36	−4.64	61.92	−0.08	62.53	0.53	63.79	1.78	65.66	3.66	65.23	3.23
C3.2	Food safety	69.36	71.31	1.94	80.04	10.67	79.79	10.43	71.40	2.04	85.18	15.82	58.59	−10.78	50.72	−18.64
C3.2.1	Food safety governance	77.94	79.98	2.04	79.62	1.67	82.04	4.09	71.06	−6.88	87.62	9.67	74.15	−3.80	75.98	−1.97
C3.2.2	Food control and surveillance	60.35	60.67	0.32	87.61	27.26	79.64	19.29	45.73	−14.62	96.52	36.17	26.81	−33.54	29.32	−31.03
C3.2.3	Food safety evaluation	59.10	63.49	4.39	70.92	11.82	73.07	13.97	63.43	4.33	100.00	40.90	37.50	−21.60	35.77	−23.32
C3.2.4	Foodborne illness burden	83.28	90.79	7.51	98.24	14.96	95.37	12.10	95.57	12.30	98.44	15.16	84.99	1.71	49.02	−34.26
C3.2.5	Safety of livestock production	69.31	59.66	−9.65	61.15	−8.17	69.31	−0.01	84.34	15.02	32.02	−37.29	71.56	2.24	78.41	9.10
C3.3	Nutrition	67.17	67.95	0.78	76.40	9.23	72.97	5.80	66.59	−0.58	86.17	19.00	59.10	−8.07	53.83	−13.34
C3.3.1	Food balance	55.87	55.50	−0.37	68.76	12.88	55.65	−0.23	60.21	4.34	82.12	26.24	42.04	−13.84	40.94	−14.94
C3.3.2	Nutrition promoting capacity	80.65	81.48	0.83	84.45	3.80	92.24	11.59	75.53	−5.12	94.71	14.07	82.19	1.54	70.62	−10.03
C3.3.3	Nutrition score	68.42	70.64	2.22	78.29	9.88	76.27	7.86	65.98	−2.44	82.97	14.55	58.31	−10.10	53.88	−14.54

(continued)

Table 4.21 (continued)

Code	Indicator Title	Global	East Asia and Pacific		Europe and Central Asia		Latin America and the Caribbean		Middle East and North Africa		North America		South Asia		Sub-Saharan Africa	
			Average	Gap	Average	Gap	Average	Gap	Average	Gap	Average	Gap	Average	Gap	Average	Gap
C3.4	Natural and social circumstances	51.54	53.92	2.37	57.20	5.66	52.19	0.65	51.09	−0.45	76.04	24.50	47.81	−3.74	43.21	−8.34
C3.4.1	Famine warning	87.85	94.82	6.96	95.40	7.55	91.89	4.03	89.18	1.33	95.98	8.13	84.85	−3.01	72.98	−14.87
C3.4.2	Natural sources sustainability	40.21	40.01	−0.20	43.22	3.01	42.86	2.65	33.97	−6.23	60.00	19.79	43.29	3.08	36.55	−3.66
C3.4.3	Economic performance index	54.71	53.83	−0.88	62.02	7.32	54.18	−0.53	56.34	1.63	67.45	12.75	47.46	−7.24	47.14	−7.57
C3.4.4	Agriculture value added per worker	15.48	16.85	1.37	25.83	10.35	11.67	−3.81	20.22	4.74	88.14	72.66	2.40	−13.08	1.98	−13.50
C3.4.5	Food price indicators	64.45	71.11	6.65	64.37	−0.08	63.34	−1.12	63.80	−0.65	75.46	11.01	62.43	−2.02	61.91	−2.55
C3.5	Government support and response	16.85	19.65	2.80	17.43	0.58	16.39	−0.46	18.68	1.83	37.50	20.65	19.32	2.47	12.71	−4.14
C3.5.1	Investment and financial support score	10.44	11.83	1.38	12.83	2.39	7.51	−2.93	19.30	8.86	32.35	21.91	5.15	−5.29	4.72	−5.72
C3.5.2	Training and AI agriculture performance score	24.81	29.38	4.57	23.15	−1.65	27.43	2.62	17.90	−6.91	43.89	19.08	36.91	12.11	22.63	−2.18

ing them highly. United States ranks 2nd in the global rankings with a score of 72.34, and Canada ranks 9th with a score of 67.61.

The negative gaps identified for the region imply weaknesses in Food loss and waste at −14.88 and Safety of livestock production at −37.29. Addressing these gaps could lead to improvements in the North American food system performance.

6. *South Asia*

The eight countries included in the South Asian region have an average score of 49.41. The top five countries are India, Bangladesh, Sri Lanka, Maldives, and Pakistan. India ranks first, with a score of 60.22 and is ranked 45th globally. Aside from India, Bangladesh, and Sri Lanka, the remaining 8 countries in this region score below the global average (52.89).

The negative gaps identified suggest that the food systems in South Asia face several challenges, including issues with food safety governance, food control and surveillance, nutrition, and economic performance. These challenges may hinder the region's ability to meet the growing demand for food and address issues related to food security and malnutrition. Addressing these gaps is crucial for improving the food systems' performances in South Asia.

7. *Sub-Saharan Africa*

The 41 countries/territories included in the sub-Saharan Africa region have an average score of 41.53. The top five countries in this region are South Africa, Mauritius, Ghana, Seychelles, and Namibia. South Africa ranks first in this region with a score of 60.15 and is ranked 47th globally. Aside from South Africa and Mauritius, the scores of the remaining 39 countries/territories in this region are below the global average (52.89). The scores of the five sub-indicators of the region are generally low, with 39 of the countries ranked 100th–160th of 160 countries/territories coming from the sub-Saharan Africa and possessing

gaps in all indicators except government support and response.

Correlation Analysis

As shown in Fig. 4.23, countries with higher SDI, GDP per capita, and HDI scores tend to have better GOHI-FS rankings. The countries ranked higher are mostly from Europe and Central Asia. High incomes, combined with relatively low inequality rates, mean more equitable access to resources and better ability to cope with the various unexpected economic shocks that may lead to food insecurity.

The countries with lower rankings mostly come from sub-Saharan Africa, which is the poorest region in the world. Thirty-one countries in this region are listed by the United Nations as "Least Developed Countries." These countries experience rapid population growth, low levels of urbanization, low technological quality, slow agricultural development, and are unable to achieve food self-sufficiency. As a result, their overall performance in the GOHI-FS is poor.

5.5 Key Findings

Significant Low Performance of Government Support and Response Drags Down the Total Score of GOHI-FS

Among all five indicators of Food Security, Government support and response has the worst performance with an average score of 16.84, contributing to the average GOHI-FS score of 52.89. This low performance in Government support and response is particularly concerning, as it suggests potential inadequacy in government efforts to address food security issues from a One Health perspective. A closer examination of raw data reveals that the low score could be partially explained by missing data. The low score performance and missing data may be attributed to several factors. First, there could be challenges in data collection and reporting processes within government agencies, leading to gaps in

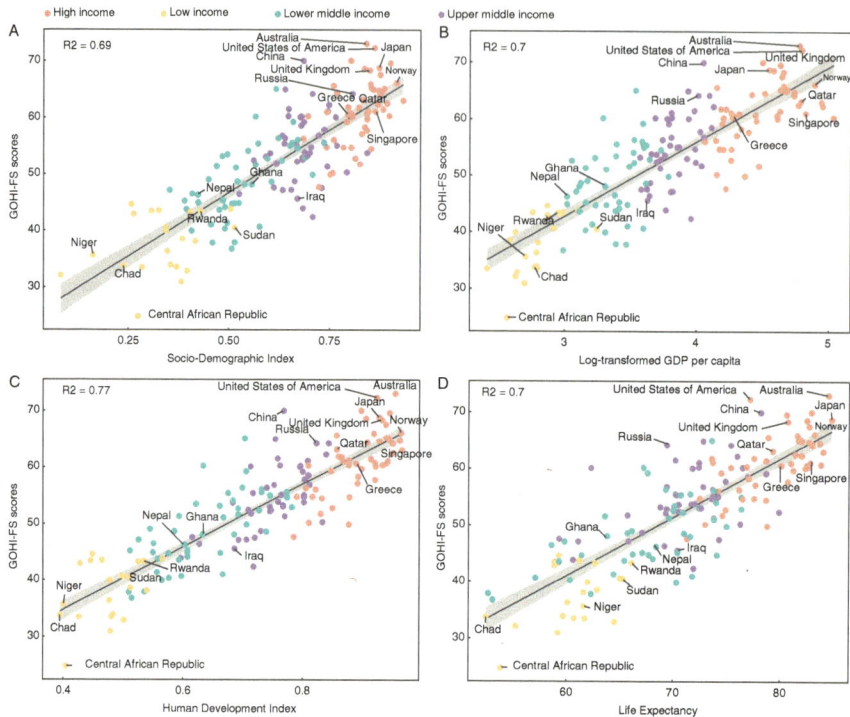

Fig. 4.23 Correlation analysis of the global One Health index-food security (GOHI-FS) score with (**a**) Socio-Demographic Index (SDI), (**b**) GDP per capita, (**c**) Human Development Index (HDI), and (**d**) Life expectancy

the information required to accurately evaluate their support and response efforts. This issue might be further exacerbated by the lack of standardized data collection methods, making it difficult to compile and compare information across different regions or countries. Additionally, the COVID-19 pandemic has placed considerable strain on governments worldwide, potentially diverting resources away from food security initiatives and toward more immediate public health concerns. Consequently, the reduced focus on food security may have resulted in decreased data availability and a weaker government response, which, in turn, contributed to the low C3.5 score. Further investigation is needed to confirm these hypotheses and to better under-

stand the underlying reasons behind the low score and missing data.

Potential Trade-Off Exists Between Production Efficiency and Safety

The low scores in agricultural infrastructure (C3.1.3) and production efficiency (C3.4.4) and the relatively higher score in the safety of livestock production (C3.2.5) suggest a potential trade-off between production efficiency and safety.

The agricultural infrastructure (C3.1.3) indicator assesses the availability and quality of physical infrastructure, such as irrigation systems, storage facilities, and transportation networks, that support agricultural production. A low score in this indicator suggests that countries may face challenges in ensuring that the necessary infrastructure is available to support agricultural production.

The production efficiency (C3.4.4) indicator measures the efficiency of agricultural production, such as the yield per hectare, labor productivity, and the use of fertilizers and pesticides. A low score in this indicator suggests that countries may face challenges in optimizing their agricultural production processes to maximize output.

The safety of livestock production (C3.2.5) indicator assesses the safety of animal-based food products, such as meat, milk, and eggs, and the measures in place to ensure their safety. A high score in this indicator suggests that countries have effective systems in place to ensure the safety of livestock production, minimizing the risks of foodborne illnesses.

The trade-off between production efficiency and safety can be influenced by various factors, such as pressure to meet production targets, lack of investment in safety equipment and training, the complexity of production processes, employee fatigue or complacency, and the regulatory environment.

Large Gaps Present in Performance for Food Safety and Nutrition

There are significant variations in the performance of Food security (C3.2) and Nutrition (C3.3) among countries, with standard deviations of 16.87 and 13.03, respectively. According to results shown in Table 4.22, Australia ranks first in overall food safety with a sub-ranking of 2 and a sub-score of 89.96, while Chile has the highest score in the nutrition category with a sub-ranking of 1 and a sub-score of 90.59. Conversely, Central African Republic has the lowest scores in both food safety (sub-ranking: 25.25) and nutrition (sub-score: 28.90).

The large gaps in scores between countries for Food security and Nutrition can be attributed to various factors such as differences in economic development, income levels, political stability, agricultural productivity, and access to resources. Countries with higher income levels and more equitable distribution of resources tend to have better food security and nutritional status. Additionally, political stability and effective government policies play a crucial role in ensuring food security and proper nutrition. On the other hand, countries facing rapid population growth, low levels of urbanization, poor technological infrastructure, slow agricultural development, and inadequate government support often struggle with food security and achieving optimal nutritional status for their populations.

5.6   Conclusion

In conclusion, the GOHI-FS utilizes the One Health approach to provide a more comprehensive assessment of food security in different countries. The findings of this year's evaluation indicate that there is poor performance in food security overall and significant disparities in food security exist between the 160 countries/territories evaluated. To tackle this issue, we recommend the adoption of the One Health approach to enhance data collection, promote sustainable food production, and improve food security. In the future, the GOHI-FS will continue to enhance its evaluation capabilities to offer better assessments of food systems as a critical One Health aspect.

Table 4.22 Country ranking of total score in the global One Health index-food security (GOHI-FS)

Total ranking	Country/territory	Food demand and supply Sub-ranking	Sub-score	Food safety Sub-ranking	Sub-score	Nutrition Sub-ranking	Sub-score	Natural and social circumstances Sub-ranking	Sub-score	Government support and response Sub-ranking	Sub-score
1	Australia	54	65.49	2	89.96	16	83.68	1	79.51	2	46.79
2	United States	55	65.38	30	85.06	3	89.50	3	73.55	1	48.19
3	Italy	2	79.87	9	88.46	19	82.60	13	63.56	9	36.06
4	China	14	73.96	52	82.36	6	86.82	20	61.67	3	45.33
5	Germany	15	73.87	57	80.80	2	90.02	26	59.91	5	43.74
6	Japan	1	84.24	10	88.39	34	79.78	40	56.51	11	35.25
7	France	26	70.07	61	80.55	20	82.26	9	66.57	4	43.92
8	United Kingdom	10	76.17	13	87.20	13	85.14	41	56.49	8	37.08
9	Canada	61	64.59	28	85.31	18	82.84	2	78.52	25	26.81
10	Norway	3	79.76	4	89.07	14	84.08	4	71.48	142	6.45
11	Austria	4	79.56	17	87.06	15	83.86	29	59.46	55	20.02
12	Chile	18	72.93	1	90.59	23	81.97	64	53.71	19	29.10
13	Belgium	17	73.36	21	86.61	4	89.31	28	59.53	63	17.56
14	Netherlands	7	78.21	69	77.78	10	85.53	19	62.14	39	22.15
15	Viet Nam	32	68.52	41	83.76	35	79.69	78	51.76	6	41.73
16	Brazil	78	61.03	3	89.92	28	80.92	36	58.03	12	35.14
17	Finland	8	76.84	16	87.07	9	85.85	10	65.61	121	9.57
18	Iceland	6	78.22	32	84.59	11	85.28	17	62.68	87	13.40
19	South Korea	11	76.14	18	87.05	43	76.53	67	53.56	16	30.04
20	Spain	37	67.93	31	84.91	32	80.37	12	65.38	33	23.61
21	Sweden	23	70.92	50	82.64	8	86.05	7	68.59	92	13.05
22	Russia	12	75.12	14	87.18	61	72.71	22	61.00	28	25.22
23	Argentina	111	53.73	48	82.79	33	80.10	5	71.36	14	33.21
24	Qatar	19	72.77	40	83.83	57	73.07	62	53.78	15	32.49
25	Switzerland	5	79.52	76	75.89	5	86.96	27	59.83	90	13.15
26	Denmark	27	69.38	11	87.78	24	81.66	11	65.56	130	8.51
27	Ireland	13	74.01	5	88.91	17	83.54	32	58.59	136	6.92
28	Turkey	76	61.44	26	85.69	1	90.70	70	52.82	49	20.80
29	Croatia	88	59.59	37	83.99	41	76.81	48	55.35	13	33.83
30	Latvia	65	63.25	39	83.88	25	81.61	23	60.81	56	19.62
31	Mexico	91	59.18	38	83.90	21	82.18	45	55.88	26	26.70

32	United Arab Emirates	24	70.88	12	87.38	78	68.83	42	56.48	32	23.87
33	Lithuania	93	58.87	6	88.67	52	74.38	24	60.54	36	23.38
34	Belarus	66	63.11	7	88.67	69	70.66	68	53.23	17	30.02
35	Singapore	16	73.55	66	78.97	46	76.02	6	71.28	147	5.84
36	Portugal	29	68.92	46	83.26	12	85.20	49	55.22	96	12.51
37	Malta	67	62.39	59	80.68	26	81.39	55	54.44	29	25.18
38	New Zealand	35	68.05	99	66.30	30	80.51	21	61.42	23	27.34
39	Greece	36	67.95	65	79.01	29	80.86	25	60.34	76	14.99
40	Saudi Arabia	52	65.60	98	66.31	39	77.91	16	62.82	18	29.37
41	Luxembourg	9	76.57	15	87.14	55	73.15	15	63.30	160	1.79
42	Peru	79	61.01	19	86.85	47	75.88	46	55.82	41	22.04
43	Uruguay	110	53.87	24	86.21	38	78.48	18	62.20	48	20.80
44	Albania	58	65.03	49	82.71	22	81.98	93	49.79	43	21.71
45	India	21	71.25	86	70.85	109	60.87	37	56.86	7	41.29
46	Israel	46	66.01	95	67.80	7	86.72	8	67.20	91	13.06
47	South Africa	28	69.08	29	85.31	81	68.20	59	54.09	31	24.07
48	Bulgaria	50	65.89	42	83.75	51	74.44	44	56.18	52	20.37
49	Cyprus	95	58.76	22	86.55	37	78.87	38	56.73	60	18.12
50	Hungary	39	67.13	70	77.75	31	80.47	30	59.35	103	11.89
51	Indonesia	30	68.57	78	75.62	104	61.57	51	54.69	10	35.92
52	Thailand	41	66.70	35	84.10	75	69.25	52	54.55	45	21.56
53	Costa Rica	59	64.96	27	85.39	49	74.64	74	52.23	71	15.79
54	Estonia	68	62.34	62	80.25	40	77.78	14	63.31	132	8.20
55	Malaysia	49	65.91	63	80.16	80	68.45	66	53.58	47	21.25
56	Slovenia	34	68.13	67	78.70	44	76.36	57	54.26	106	11.71
57	Czech Republic	22	71.14	54	81.10	113	60.22	35	58.08	73	15.47
58	Kazakhstan	72	61.74	43	83.62	95	64.58	47	55.80	59	18.66
59	Colombia	90	59.25	33	84.47	63	72.39	82	51.12	64	17.15
60	Ecuador	43	66.53	44	83.55	105	61.42	56	54.27	67	16.29
61	Philippines	75	61.46	64	79.73	89	66.86	86	50.42	35	23.47
62	Panama	42	66.63	23	86.43	87	67.13	87	50.36	110	11.06
63	Tunisia	130	48.93	8	88.50	62	72.45	58	54.22	66	16.59
64	Romania	48	65.93	105	62.63	36	79.34	43	56.44	70	16.17
65	Ukraine	69	62.32	68	78.38	98	64.14	31	58.81	80	14.32
66	Egypt	70	62.10	47	82.95	91	65.95	107	48.15	58	18.79

(continued)

Table 4.22 (continued)

Total ranking	Country/territory	Food demand and supply		Food safety		Nutrition		Natural and social circumstances		Government support and response	
		Sub-ranking	Sub-score	Sub-ranking	Sub-score	Sub-ranking	Sub-score	Sub-ranking	Sub-score	Sub-ranking	Sub-score
67	Paraguay	96	58.70	34	84.11	66	71.84	53	54.52	133	8.08
68	El Salvador	85	60.08	20	86.70	53	74.25	100	49.19	135	6.97
69	Cuba	97	58.58	73	76.41	54	73.40	94	49.53	62	17.92
70	Serbia	82	60.63	55	81.01	85	67.72	79	51.61	79	14.62
71	Algeria	99	58.24	36	84.02	90	66.33	77	51.91	77	14.77
72	Barbados	25	70.11	116	60.44	45	76.11	124	46.73	51	20.63
73	Mauritius	40	66.92	92	68.31	88	67.11	131	46.11	27	25.53
74	Oman	81	60.70	94	68.04	83	68.06	95	49.46	22	27.70
75	Poland	53	65.58	113	61.27	27	81.18	75	52.03	85	13.70
76	Iran	74	61.47	93	68.29	70	70.46	129	46.25	24	26.84
77	Kuwait	31	68.54	103	63.78	74	69.31	112	47.65	34	23.48
78	Morocco	108	54.77	87	70.07	72	70.23	61	54.02	44	21.61
79	Armenia	94	58.84	80	73.47	82	68.06	106	48.59	50	20.64
80	Georgia	71	62.04	72	76.83	60	72.73	111	47.66	115	9.87
81	Belize	100	58.09	60	80.58	67	71.35	99	49.25	123	9.34
82	Honduras	119	51.96	51	82.47	73	69.39	88	50.33	88	13.39
83	Moldova	121	51.59	56	80.83	50	74.52	122	47.04	98	12.40
84	Bangladesh	38	67.81	118	60.00	111	60.58	54	54.45	37	23.08
85	Dominican Republic	112	53.66	58	80.80	65	72.07	73	52.30	140	6.74
86	Azerbaijan	51	65.80	25	86.06	122	57.32	98	49.31	143	6.39
87	Sri Lanka	57	65.16	127	56.64	56	73.08	109	48.03	42	21.92
88	Slovakia	45	66.25	75	76.06	139	52.81	33	58.19	111	10.90
89	Kyrgyzstan	60	64.70	82	72.39	101	62.29	85	50.65	86	13.52
90	Jamaica	56	65.33	97	67.43	59	72.85	139	44.70	100	12.23
91	Maldives	20	72.67	74	76.24	108	61.09	130	46.22	145	6.02
92	Uzbekistan	63	63.72	91	68.32	96	64.56	65	53.71	108	11.43
93	Turkmenistan	47	65.95	115	60.84	64	72.34	69	53.17	128	8.85
94	Guyana	149	42.71	84	71.87	42	76.73	34	58.11	120	9.66
95	Brunei Darussalam	62	63.84	81	73.33	110	60.69	39	56.58	152	4.54
96	Bolivia	92	58.92	96	67.50	68	71.20	63	53.76	137	6.82
97	Cambodia	101	57.39	79	74.78	92	65.50	89	50.24	126	8.91

98	North Macedonia	107	54.91	117	60.21	48	75.45	91	49.96	68	16.21
99	Nicaragua	129	49.75	45	83.45	121	57.37	81	51.24	83	13.80
100	Montenegro	44	66.35	104	63.09	93	65.10	142	43.07	81	14.08
101	Trinidad and Tobago	64	63.38	112	61.29	77	68.87	134	45.30	99	12.27
102	Bahrain	73	61.62	106	62.62	103	61.58	92	49.90	82	14.02
103	Lebanon	77	61.26	108	62.20	94	64.95	143	42.25	57	18.87
104	Pakistan	89	59.25	138	50.32	135	53.71	60	54.06	21	28.02
105	Fiji	80	60.74	129	55.86	71	70.33	121	47.11	119	9.69
106	Myanmar	87	59.65	125	57.34	86	67.62	102	49.14	116	9.83
107	Mongolia	131	48.73	107	62.38	58	73.04	110	48.02	109	11.07
108	Tajikistan	118	52.37	90	69.06	115	59.95	125	46.56	94	12.82
109	Ghana	105	56.34	135	53.58	106	61.38	116	47.25	40	22.15
110	Seychelles	33	68.22	101	64.12	116	59.55	141	43.82	155	2.97
111	Namibia	103	56.93	130	55.85	107	61.21	103	48.88	74	15.35
112	Jordan	109	54.47	77	75.77	151	46.62	72	52.34	129	8.74
113	Gabon	117	52.39	100	65.98	102	62.01	113	47.54	131	8.33
114	Botswana	113	53.54	89	69.61	142	51.43	135	45.20	69	16.17
115	Benin	137	46.18	110	61.74	76	68.93	114	47.42	107	11.68
116	Cote d'Ivoire	115	52.56	144	45.15	99	63.15	80	51.50	54	20.26
117	Guatemala	128	49.91	83	72.07	84	67.84	154	30.53	102	11.89
118	Nepal	86	59.84	140	49.50	79	68.80	119	47.19	144	6.26
119	Iraq	125	50.46	126	56.92	123	56.87	50	54.86	125	9.13
120	Vanuatu	84	60.09	114	61.08	119	57.72	137	44.98	156	2.73
121	Senegal	151	42.26	120	59.13	129	54.87	115	47.39	38	22.68
122	Tanzania	139	45.33	132	55.34	141	51.54	83	51.11	46	21.50
123	Cabo Verde	123	50.76	53	81.47	144	50.50	147	39.85	159	1.80
124	Timor-Leste	98	58.52	88	69.81	150	47.29	132	45.92	157	2.61
125	Kenya	141	44.97	128	56.13	125	56.38	148	37.80	20	28.57
126	Burkina Faso	143	44.75	122	57.57	132	54.54	128	46.35	53	20.29
127	Laos	122	51.37	137	50.38	118	57.75	96	49.43	101	12.00
128	Equatorial Guinea	116	52.54	136	51.62	136	53.56	123	47.01	75	15.02
129	Zambia	120	51.72	133	54.90	137	53.05	90	50.05	122	9.54
130	Papua New Guinea	106	55.93	134	54.88	149	48.85	138	44.72	78	14.67
131	Zimbabwe	132	47.79	124	57.57	127	56.16	126	46.44	113	10.39

(continued)

Table 4.22 (continued)

Total ranking	Country/territory	Food demand and supply		Food safety		Nutrition		Natural and social circumstances		Government support and response	
		Sub-ranking	Sub-score	Sub-ranking	Sub-score	Sub-ranking	Sub-score	Sub-ranking	Sub-score	Sub-ranking	Sub-score
132	Guinea	152	41.60	109	62.02	128	55.99	105	48.63	118	9.73
133	Mozambique	144	44.34	71	76.86	130	54.67	157	27.99	84	13.71
134	Rwanda	136	47.20	102	63.92	140	51.90	140	43.83	114	10.33
135	Uganda	133	47.64	141	47.62	126	56.27	118	47.21	61	18.02
136	Mali	156	36.82	85	71.74	114	59.95	149	33.51	93	12.94
137	Libya	102	57.24	121	58.55	154	43.27	117	47.22	146	6.00
138	Mauritania	150	42.64	145	43.34	112	60.47	108	48.13	97	12.40
139	Bhutan	104	56.78	131	55.40	156	40.67	97	49.33	154	3.29
140	Eswatini	134	47.48	143	45.41	138	52.89	84	50.82	134	6.99
141	Ethiopia	148	42.78	119	59.76	117	59.04	155	28.68	89	13.22
142	Sudan	157	36.72	111	61.56	124	56.76	150	32.11	72	15.60
143	Cameroon	138	45.69	149	37.40	134	54.03	76	52.02	95	12.67
144	Solomon Islands	83	60.41	146	41.22	148	49.09	120	47.13	158	2.17
145	Afghanistan	140	45.16	139	49.74	133	54.04	159	26.30	30	24.66
146	Malawi	153	40.01	150	37.18	120	57.70	127	46.36	104	11.79
147	Togo	124	50.75	155	31.82	143	50.70	104	48.84	127	8.88
148	Nigeria	127	49.95	157	26.72	97	64.34	152	31.86	65	16.89
149	Djibouti	142	44.91	123	57.57	131	54.60	158	26.65	150	5.65
150	Lesotho	114	53.46	142	46.09	158	36.04	145	41.80	139	6.79
151	Sierra Leone	145	44.32	151	37.12	145	49.97	146	41.44	124	9.16
152	Niger	158	35.75	156	28.60	146	49.95	71	52.50	105	11.76
153	Guinea-Bissau	147	43.54	154	33.33	153	43.60	133	45.61	153	3.92
154	Chad	159	35.03	159	25.27	147	49.13	101	49.19	112	10.52
155	Liberia	154	37.96	147	39.81	155	41.24	144	42.19	141	6.71
156	Burundi	146	44.03	158	26.56	152	46.43	136	45.00	149	5.68
157	Madagascar	126	50.40	152	35.57	157	40.00	151	31.99	138	6.80
158	Somalia	160	30.42	153	33.52	100	63.12	160	23.98	117	9.77
159	Dem. Rep. Congo	135	47.44	148	39.76	159	30.40	153	31.63	148	5.83
160	Central African Republic	155	37.08	160	25.25	160	28.90	156	28.32	151	4.64

6 Antimicrobial Resistance

6.1 Background

A multitude of bacterial infectious diseases have been successfully treated since the discovery of penicillin and the widespread clinical application of antibiotics. According to the WHO, antimicrobial drugs include antibacterial, antiviral, antifungal, and antiparasitic medications used to prevent and treat infections in humans, animals, and plants [51].

AMR refers to the phenomenon in which bacteria, viruses, fungi, and parasites evolve and become less responsive to drugs over time, resulting in increased difficulty in treating infections and increased risks of disease transmission, severe illness, and mortality. Such resistance may be innate or acquired, and is frequently the result of improper usage of medications [52]. Resistance can spread rapidly between various bacteria due to the exchange of genetic material, and resistant bacteria can spread continuously through food, water, and air in humans, animals, and plants [53]. AMR yields antimicrobial drugs ineffective, making the treatment of infectious diseases increasingly difficult or impossible. AMR impedes progress in crucial areas such as economic growth, eradication of poverty, agricultural security, environmental health, and global health [54].

Antimicrobial drugs have been an integral component of modern medicine for over 80 years [55]. However, in recent years, a growing number of pathogens have demonstrated resistance to one or more medications, necessitating the urgent development of new drugs, as identified on the WHO-published lists [56]. Antimicrobial drugs serve an important role in livestock farming, not only for disease treatment but also for growth promotion. In the past, certain drugs were extensively used in industrial animal feeds as growth promoters and drug additives for infection prevention. In September 2016, the United Nations General Assembly reported that the inappropriate use of antimicrobial drugs in animals was one of the primary causes of AMR [57].

The widespread use of antimicrobial drugs in human activities and livestock farming has increased the growth rate of farmed animals, but the issue of environmental pollution from improper waste disposal has become a topic of intense international research, especially on environmental pollution caused by the misuse of antimicrobial drugs in livestock and aquaculture [58]. Due to heavy use of antimicrobial drugs, not only will many unmetabolized antimicrobial drugs be excreted with animal feces, but resistant bacteria and resistance genes developed can be spread to the environment, and thus further spread among humans, animals, plants, and the environment.

AMR continues to pose a grave hazard to public health despite its colossal burden [59]. According to a global survey, 4.95 million fatalities were associated to bacterial AMR in 2019, with 1.27 million deaths attributable to bacterial AMR [60]. Additionally, AMR not only complicates the treatment and eradication of bacterial infections but also raises the risk of disease transmission, severe illness, and mortality [61].

AMR is a significant global threat that affects, among others, the human, animal, plant, food, and environmental sectors. The presence of AMR in multiple sources of infection poses a severe threat to public health security. Hence, countries and multiple sectors in the One Health field are taking this threat very seriously [51]. Addressing AMR requires a comprehensive, cross-sectoral, and collaborative approach. The Global Action Plan on Antimicrobial Resistance (GAP), adopted by the WHO in 2015, proposes joint multisectoral action on AMR using the One Health concept. This approach involves developing multisectoral and cross-national policies, guidelines, and guidance to achieve human, animal, and environmental health at the regional, national, and global levels [53, 62].

6.2   The Necessity to Evaluate Antimicrobial Resistance from One Health Perspective

There is currently no accepted evaluation standard for AMR [63, 64]. Nonetheless, AMR has been monitored and evaluated in a variety of ways, most notably through the country Self-Assessment Survey (TrACSS) jointly sponsored by WHO, FAO, WOAH, UNEP. Additionally, the Global Antimicrobial Resistance and Use Surveillance System (GLASS) by WHO, and regional AMR surveillance networks, such as the Pan American Health Organization's (PAHO) surveillance of AMR are notable examples. However, they may not provide a comprehensive analysis of the current global AMR situation in accordance with the One Health principle.

To resolve these challenges, the AMR index system should be based on the One Health concept [65]. One Health provides a holistic perspective based on the interface between humans, animals, and the environment, fostering cross-sectoral and multidisciplinary collaboration for effectively addressing AMR issues. The new index system, based on the concept of One Health, offers three major advantages over current assessment methods:

Following One Health strategy: Pay particular attention to the AMR situation in humans, animals, and the environment from the perspective of One Health, including antimicrobial use, AMR surveillance, and legal regulations.

Comprehensive coverage: The new index system addresses the five aspects of AMR, including the AMR surveillance system, the AMR laboratory network and coordination, antimicrobial control and optimization, awareness and comprehension, and the AMR rate for important antibiotics.

Quantitative surveillance indicators: Surveillance data on resistance rates of important antimicrobial drugs and pathogens are included in the AMR index system to accurately reflect the prevalence of AMR in different countries, including carbapenems, glycopeptides, β-lactams, macrolides, aminoglycosides, and quinolones.

Incorporating the One Health concept into the AMR index system will allow it to better reflect the AMR status across countries and examine the impact of various factors, such as the control and optimization of antimicrobial drugs in humans, animals, and the environment, the implementation of AMR surveillance, the mechanism for multisectoral coordination, the national laws, and the level of public awareness of AMR.

6.3   Framework Construction of GOHI-AMR

Framework

Indicator construction begins with the existing database, refers to AMR surveillance reports, collects and collates relevant evaluation sub II-indicator and data, establishes the three-level AMR evaluation framework and database, applies the binary fuzzy evaluation method to determine the sub II-indicator weights, normalizes the underlying data for each country, and calculates the scores and total values of each evaluation indicator.

The construction of the global One Health index-antimicrobial resistance (GOHI-AMR) framework was founded on an extensive body of literature and reports from internationally renowned organizations, from which several key themes were extracted. In accordance with the purpose of the evaluation and following group discussions and expert consultations, it was determined that AMR should be evaluated from a One Health perspective across six pillars. After extensive brainstorming and scouring of authoritative databases, a preliminary database of 70 sub II-indicator candidates was compiled. Finally, through discussions, information review, selection of indicators, two rounds of expert consultation, and consideration of data accessibility and completeness, 5 indicators, 17 sub I-indicators, and 54 sub II-indicators were established (Table 4.23).

Indicators

To evaluate the global AMR situation, the GOHI-AMR analyzes AMR in five pillars: AMR surveillance system, AMR laboratory network and coordination capacity, antimicrobial control and optimization, improving awareness and understanding, and the resistance rate for important antimicrobials. There are five indicators, 17 sub I-indicators, and 54 sub II-indicators, categorized with the "structure (blue)—process (green)—outcome (pink)" framework.

In the 2022 report, five sub II-indicators were divided and refined. As a result of panel discussions and expert consultation, a distinction is made between aquatic and terrestrial animals, separated into two sub II-indicators, and the reference laboratory for AMR has been divided into separate reference laboratories for fungi and bacteria to provide a more comprehensive response to AMR under the One Health concept.

Data Sources

Quantitative indicators in the GOHI-AMR are derived from global, regional, and national surveillance networks, such as the GLASS by WHO, European Antimicrobial resistance Surveillance Network (EARS-net), and the Chinese antimicrobial resistance surveillance system (CARSS). Among the qualitative indicators are those derived from WHO, FAO, WOAH, and UNEP's TrACSS data. To reduce the subjectivity of qualitative indicators in the TrACSS database, all qualitative indicators were averaged over data from 2021 and 2022. If an indicator was absent for a given year, it was allocated the value 0 before averaging.

Limitations

The most recent data on global AMR were compiled from authoritative databases, which contain temporal differences between qualitative and quantitative data. Qualitative sub II-indicators were derived from the TrACSS, which annually reports statistical data from the previous year. Quantitative information was collected from each AMR surveillance system. Currently, except for European Centre for Disease Prevention and Control (ECDC), which will update its data in 2021, the other surveillance databases, including

GLASS, have only updated their data to 2020, indicating a lag in AMR surveillance data. Therefore, all quantitative data involved in the calculation are from the year 2020.

Furthermore, the COVID-2019 pandemic made it challenging to implement AMR surveillance [66]. When processing the data, we averaged the previous 2 years of qualitative data, so countries with 1 year of lacking data received a lower score.

When the rate of missing data for an indicator exceeds 72.73%, the indicator is not included in the calculation. Unfortunately, some indicators have a high rate of missing data, especially for the quantitative AMR rate for important antibiotics (C4.5), including Vancomycin-resistant *Enterococcus faecalis* (C4.5.2.2), Third-generation β-lactams-resistant *Streptococcus pneumoniae* (C4.5.3.4), Third-generation β-lactams-resistant *Pseudomonas aeruginosa* (C4.5.3.5), Vancomycin-resistant *Enterococcus faecalis* (C4.5.4.2), Aminoglycosides-resistant *Klebsiella pneumoniae* (C4.5.5.1), and Quinolone-resistant *Acinetobacter baumannii* (C4.5.6.3). Although these sub II-indicators still carry some weight in the framework, they were not included in the calculation due to the absence of participation, resulting in a low score.

It is necessary to enhance the weight distribution of each sub II-indicator or to balance the number of sub II-indicators under each key sub II-indicator in the GOHI-AMR framework system, primarily due to the difference in the number of sub II-indicators included in some of the sub I-indicators. For instance, among the AMR surveillance system (C4.1), Environmental AMR surveillance (C4.1.3) has only one sub II-indicator, while Antimicrobial consumption surveillance (C4.1.1) has three. In the C4.1, C4.1.1 constitutes 27.60% of the weight, while C4.1.3 constitutes 30.80%. The only sub II-indicator under C4.1.3 constitutes 30.80%, while C4.1.1.1 constitutes only 9.20% of the total. Consequently, the C4.1 score is highly influenced by Environmental surveillance system (C4.1.3.1).

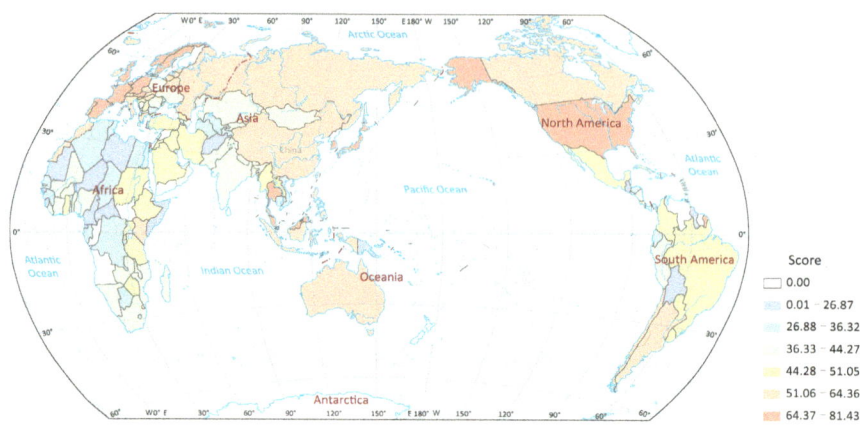

Fig. 4.24 Global score map of the global One Health index-antimicrobial resistance (GOHI-AMR)

6.4   Main Results

Global Score

Overall, GOHI-AMR scores of countries and territories are low. There is still considerable potential for One Health AMR improvement. The scores range between 14.75 and 81.43 (Fig. 4.24, Table 4.24).

The total scores of GOHI-AMR for each region are as follows (sorted by median): North America (65.53), Europe and Central Asia (54.40), East Asia and Pacific (45.34), the Middle East and Africa (43.37), South Asia (41.95), the sub-Saharan Africa (39.50), and Latin America and the Caribbean (36.22). The regions of the North America and the Europe and Central Asia have the outstanding scores, followed by East Asia and Pacific and the Middle East and Africa. Lower-scoring nations and territories are concentrated in Latin America and the Caribbean (Fig. 4.25).

The average GOHI-AMR score is 44.05. The average scores for AMR surveillance system (C4.1), AMR laboratory network and coordination capacity (C4.2), Antimicrobial control and optimization (C4.3), Improve awareness and understanding (C4.4), and AMR rate for important antibiotics (C4.5) are 34.79, 55.57, 48.76, 48.09, and 33.03, respectively. AMR status surveillance (C4.1.2) (average score: 46.99) has the highest average score in AMR surveillance system. In AMR laboratory network and coordination capacity, the average score is highest for the National plan (C4.2.3, score: 62.00). In Antimicrobial control and optimization, the average score is highest for National law(s) for antibiotic use (C4.3.1, score: 67.69). Public health awareness (C4.4.1, score: 55.63) has the highest average score within Improve awareness and understanding. Carbapenems (C4.5.1) have a higher score of GOHI-AMR compared to other important antibiotics, with an average score of 68.13 (Fig. 4.26).

The scores of sub II-indicator in GOHI-AMR from high to low are as follows (sorted by median): AMR laboratory network and coordination capacity (C4.2, score: 54.37), Improve awareness and understanding (C4.4, score: 48.44), Antimicrobial control and optimization (C4.3, score: 47.21), AMR surveillance system (C4.1, score: 32.61), and AMR rate for important antibiotics (C4.5, score: 31.62). Except for AMR rate for important antibiotics, the distribution of scores among countries/territories is dispersed, indicating disparities between countries/territories (Fig. 4.27).

Global Ranking

As shown in Table 4.24, it displays the GOHI-AMR scores and rankings of 160 countries and territories. The median GOHI-AMR score for the 160 countries is 44.05, and the interquartile range is 22.43. Overall, more than 70% of countries worldwide scored below 50. France has the greatest score out of the 160 countries/territories evaluated (81.43), while Djibouti has the lowest (14.75).

Table 4.23 Indicator and weight scheme of the global One Health index-antimicrobial resistance (GOHI-AMR)

Indicator			Sub I-indicator			Sub II-indicator		
Name	Code	Weight	Name	Code	Weight	Name	Code	Weight
AMR surveillance system	C4.1	20.0%	Antimicrobial consumption surveillance	C4.1.1	27.6%	Antimicrobial consumption in human	C4.1.1.1	33.3%
						Antimicrobial consumption in animals	C4.1.1.2	33.3%
						Pesticide use	C4.1.1.3	33.3%
			Antimicrobial resistance status surveillance	C4.1.2	41.6%	AMR in human	C4.1.2.1	25.0%
						AMR in terrestrial animals	C4.1.2.2	25.0%
						AMR in aquatic animals	C4.1.2.3	25.0%
						AMR in food	C4.1.2.4	25.0%
			Environmental antimicrobial resistance	C4.1.3	30.8%	Environmental surveillance system	C4.1.3.1	100.0%
AMR laboratory network and coordination capacity	C4.2	20.0%	National AMR capacity	C4.2.1	37.0%	National reference laboratory for bacteria	C4.2.1.1	33.3%
						National reference laboratory for fungi	C4.2.1.2	33.3%
						Effective integration of laboratories	C4.2.1.3	33.3%
			Technical level	C4.2.2	30.2%	Multi-sector working on AMR	C4.2.2.1	25.0%
						Standardization and harmonization of laboratories	C4.2.2.2	25.0%
						Relevance of diagnostic techniques	C4.2.2.3	25.0%
						Technical level of data management	C4.2.2.4	25.0%
			National plan	C4.2.3	32.7%	National action plan on monitoring and evaluation	C4.2.3.1	25.0%
						National action plan on AMR	C4.2.3.2	25.0%
						National action plan on AMR linked to any other existing action plans	C4.2.3.3	25.0%
						Publishment of action plan	C4.2.3.4	25.0%
Antimicrobial control and optimization	C4.3	20.0%	National law(s) for antibiotic use	C4.3.1	38.3%	National law(s) for antibiotic use in humans	C4.3.1.1	20.0%
						National law(s) for antibiotic use in terrestrial animals	C4.3.1.2	20.0%
						National law(s) for antibiotic use in aquatic animals	C4.3.1.3	20.0%
						National law(s) on marketing of pesticides	C4.3.1.4	20.0%
						National law(s) on prohibits the use of antibiotics	C4.3.1.5	20.0%
			Antimicrobial use optimization	C4.3.2	30.2%	Optimizing antimicrobial use in human health	C4.3.2.1	40.0%
						Optimizing antimicrobial use in terrestrial animal health	C4.3.2.2	15.0%
						Optimizing antimicrobial use in aquatic animal health	C4.3.2.4	15.0%
						Optimizing antimicrobial pesticide use in plant	C4.3.2.3	30.0%
			Antimicrobial use control	C4.3.3	31.5%	Infection Prevention and Control in human	C4.3.3.1	40.0%
						Reduce transmission of AMR in terrestrial animal production	C4.3.3.2	15.0%
						Reduce transmission of AMR in aquatic animal production	C4.3.3.3	15.0%
						Reduce transmission of AMR in food processing	C4.3.3.4	30.0%
Improve awareness and understanding	C4.4	20.0%	Raising awareness and understanding	C4.4.1	50.0%	Food affected by extreme weather conditions, disasters or crisis	C4.4.1.1	100.0%
			Professional training	C4.4.2	50.0%	Training in the human health sector	C4.4.2.1	25.0%
						Training in the veterinary sector	C4.4.2.2	25.0%
						Training in farming sector	C4.4.2.3	25.0%
						Progress with strengthening veterinary services	C4.4.2.4	25.0%
Antimicrobial resistance rate for important antibiotics	C4.5	20.0%	Carbapenems	C4.5.1	19.3%	Carbapenems-resistant *Klebsiella pneumoniae*	C4.5.1.1	25.0%
						Carbapenems-resistant *Acinetobacter baumannii*	C4.5.1.2	25.0%
						Carbapenems-resistant *Escherichia coli*	C4.5.1.3	25.0%
						Carbapenems-resistant *Pseudomonas aeruginosa*	C4.5.1.4	25.0%
			Glycopeptide	C4.5.2	15.1%	Vancomycin-resistant *Enterococcus faecium*	C4.5.2.1	50.0%
						Vancomycin-resistant *Enterococcus faecalis*	C4.5.2.2	0.0%
			β-lactams	C4.5.3	17.8%	Methicillin-resistant Staphylococcus aureus	C4.5.3.1	20.0%
						Third-generation β-lactams-resistant *Klebsiella pneumoniae*	C4.5.3.2	20.0%
						Third-generation β-lactams-resistant *Escherichia coli*	C4.5.3.3	20.0%
						Third-generation β-lactams-resistant *Streptococcus pneumoniae*	C4.5.3.4	0.0%
						Third-generation β-lactams-resistant *Pseudomonas aeruginosa*	C4.5.3.5	0.0%
			Macrolides	C4.5.4	14.0%	Macrolides-resistant *Streptococcus pneumoniae*	C4.5.4.1	0.0%
			Aminoglycosides	C4.5.5	16.5%	Aminoglycosides-resistant *Klebsiella pneumoniae*	C4.5.5.1	0.0%
						Aminoglycosides-resistant *Acinetobacter baumannii*	C4.5.5.2	50.0%
			Quinolone	C4.5.6	17.3%	Quinolone-resistant *Klebsiella pneumoniae*	C4.5.6.1	33.3%
						Quinolone-resistant *Escherichia coli*	C4.5.6.2	33.3%
						Quinolone-resistant *Acinetobacter baumannii*	C4.5.6.3	0.0%

Note: Blue represents structure; green represents process; pink represents outcome

1. *Leaders and laggards*

The top 25 countries out of the 160 being evaluated are shown in Table 4.24. France (score: 81.43), Norway, Malaysia, Denmark, the United States, the United Kingdom, Sweden, the Netherlands, Finland, Belgium, Austria, Spain, Thailand, Japan, Germany, Portugal, Singapore, South Korea, Australia, Ireland, Latvia, Switzerland, China, Hungary, and Russia are the top 25 coun-

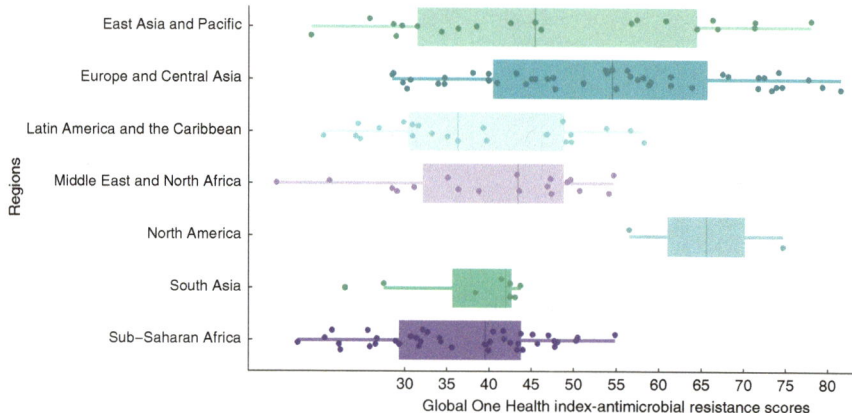

Fig. 4.25 Regional score distribution of the global One Health index-antimicrobial resistance (GOHI-AMR)

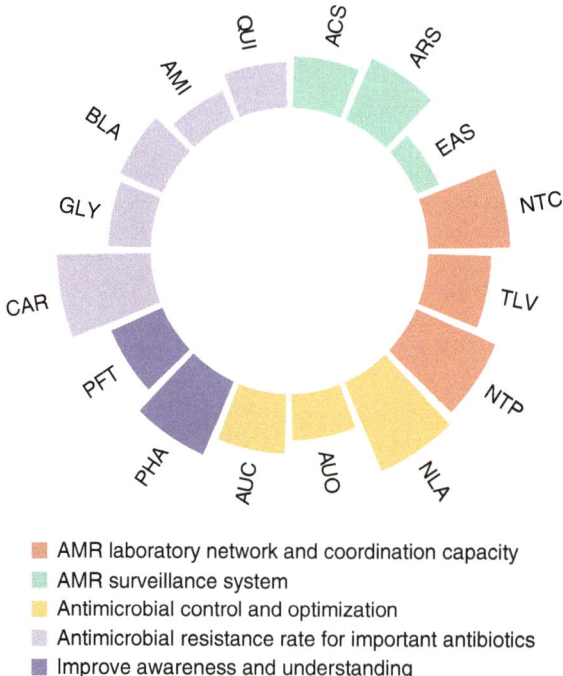

- ■ AMR laboratory network and coordination capacity
- ■ AMR surveillance system
- ■ Antimicrobial control and optimization
- ■ Antimicrobial resistance rate for important antibiotics
- ■ Improve awareness and understanding

Fig. 4.26 The score distribution of global One Health index-antimicrobial resistance (GOHI-AMR) by indicators. (*ACS* antimicrobial consumption surveillance, *ARS* antimicrobial resistance status surveillance, *EAS* environmental antimicrobial resistance surveillance, *NTC* national AMR capacity, *TLV* technical level, *NTP* national plan, *NLA* national law(s) for antibiotic use, *AUO* antimicrobial use optimization, *AUC* antimicrobial use control, *PHA* public health awareness, *PFT* professional training, *CAR* carbapenems, *GLY* glycopeptide, *BLA* β-lactams, *AMI* aminoglycosides, *QUI* quinolone)

tries/territories (58.85). Most of the top territories are in Europe and Central Asia (17 in total), followed by the East Asia and Pacific (7 in total).

The lowest 25 of the 160 countries being evaluated are shown in Table 4.24. Brunei Darussalam (28.88), Vanuatu, Tajikistan, Algeria, Bulgaria, Maldives, El Salvador, Niger, Mauritania, Sierra

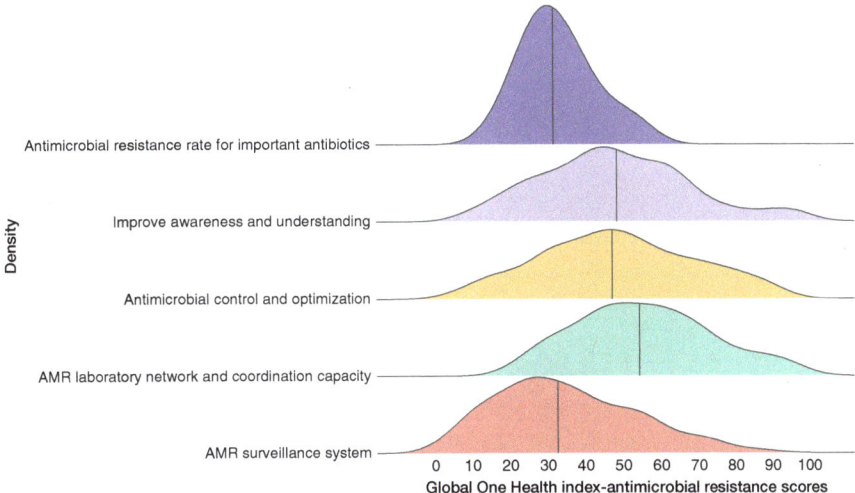

Fig. 4.27 Dimensional score distribution of the global One Health index-antimicrobial resistance (GOHI-AMR)

Leone, Papua New Guinea, Cameroon, Guyana, Barbados, Afghanistan, Equatorial Guinea, Central African Republic, Seychelles, Libya, Somalia, Guatemala, Solomon Islands, Guinea-Bissau, Djibouti (14.75). The sub-Saharan Africa occupy the majority of the top positions (9 in total), followed by the Latin America and the Caribbean (5in total).

Regional Ranking

1. *East Asia and Pacific*

The average score for the 21 countries included is 47.53, as shown in Table 4.25. Malaysia, Thailand, Japan, Singapore, and South Korea are the top five countries in this region. Malaysia ranks first in this region with a score of 77.89 and is ranked third globally, while Solomon Islands ranks last with a score of 18.84 and is ranked 158th.

There is a difference of over 50 points between Malaysia and the Solomon Islands, indicating a vast disparity in the region. As depicted in Table 4.26, East Asia and Pacific scored below the global average on only two sub I-indicators: National AMR capacity (C4.2.1) and National antibiotic use laws (C4.3.1). The apparent deficiencies are concentrated on national governance capacity and related regulatory development in relation to

AMR, primarily as a result of the wide variation within the region.

2. *Europe and Central Asia*

The average score of the 47 countries included is 53.46, as shown in Table 4.25. France, Norway, Denmark, the United Kingdom, and Sweden comprise the top five nations in this region. France ranks first in this region with a score of 81.43 and ranks first globally, while Bulgaria ranks last with a score of 28.42 and ranks 140th.

There is a large disparity in scores between countries in the region, with a difference of over 50 points between France and Bulgaria, indicating a huge disparity in the region. As depicted in Table 4.26, with the exception of Environmental AMR surveillance, the Europe and Central Asia region exceeds the global average in all sub II-indicator, which suggests that the Europe and Central Asia should place a greater emphasis on environmental AMR monitoring.

3. *Latin America and the Caribbean*

The average score for the 23 countries included is 38.49, as shown in Table 4.25. Chile, Cuba, Argentina, Brazil, and Colombia are the top five countries in this region. Chile, which ranks first in this region with a score of 58.18, is ranked 27th globally. As depicted in

Table 4.24 Country ranking of total score in the global One Health index-antimicrobial resistance (GOHI-AMR)

Total rank	Country/territory	Total	Reg ranking	Total rank	Country/territory	Total	Reg ranking	Total rank	Country/territory	Total	Reg ranking	Total rank	Country/territory	Total	Reg ranking
1	France	81.43	1	41	Slovenia	53.8	25	81	Pakistan	43.05	2	121	Trinidad and Tobago	31.52	15
2	Norway	79.25	2	42	Argentina	53.74	3	82	Malawi	42.5	14	122	Fiji	31.39	16
3	Malaysia	77.89	1	43	Belarus	53.67	26	83	India	42.47	3	123	Mauritius	31.39	29
4	Denmark	77.59	3	44	Serbia	51.05	27	84	Nepal	42.46	4	124	Egypt	31.07	14
5	United States of America	74.63	1	45	Saudi Arabia	50.65	3	85	Mongolia	42.45	12	125	Dominican Republic	30.84	16
6	United Kingdom	74.48	4	46	Ethiopia	50.47	2	86	Zambia	41.76	15	126	Honduras	30.83	17
7	Sweden	74.06	5	47	Ghana	50.28	3	87	Mozambique	41.67	16	127	Cabo Verde	30.7	30
8	Netherlands	73.78	6	48	Brazil	49.65	4	88	Bhutan	41.44	5	128	Turkmenistan	30.59	43
9	Finland	73.22	7	49	Colombia	49.6	5	89	Poland	40.85	35	129	Albania	30.17	44
10	Belgium	72.33	8	50	Iran	49.58	4	90	Benin	40.48	17	130	Ecuador	29.79	18
11	Austria	71.65	9	51	Israel	49.21	5	91	Mali	40.13	18	131	Armenia	29.68	45
12	Spain	71.61	10	52	Uruguay	49.03	6	92	South Africa	39.94	19	132	Viet Nam	29.59	17
13	Thailand	71.25	2	53	Mexico	48.64	7	93	Romania	39.87	36	133	Chad	29.33	31
14	Japan	71.18	3	54	Eswatini	48.1	4	94	Kazakhstan	39.84	37	134	Tunisia	29.04	15
15	Germany	68.06	11	55	Rwanda	47.79	5	95	Ukraine	39.84	38	135	Lesotho	28.9	32
16	Portugal	67.39	12	56	Croatia	47.75	28	96	Namibia	39.67	20	136	Brunei Darussalam	28.88	18
17	Singapore	66.76	4	57	Zimbabwe	47.73	6	97	Nicaragua	39.62	10	137	Vanuatu	28.57	19
18	South Korea	66.19	5	58	Turkey	47.55	29	98	Liberia	39.5	21	138	Tajikistan	28.55	46
19	Australia	64.36	6	59	Jordan	47.35	6	99	Peru	39.24	11	139	Algeria	28.46	16
20	Ireland	63.8	13	60	Iraq	47.23	7	100	Bahrain	38.74	11	140	Bulgaria	28.42	47
21	Latvia	61.32	14	61	Uganda	47.05	7	101	Timor-Leste	38.41	13	141	Maldives	27.47	7
22	Switzerland	61.31	15	62	Cyprus	46.88	30	102	Sri Lanka	38.36	6	142	El Salvador	26.87	19
23	China	60.71	7	63	Qatar	46.87	8	103	Kyrgyzstan	37.99	39	143	Niger	26.66	33
24	Hungary	58.96	16	64	Costa Rica	46.8	8	104	Kuwait	36.32	12	144	Mauritania	26.5	34
25	Russia	58.85	17	65	Paraguay	46.74	9	105	Cambodia	36.25	14	145	Sierra Leone	25.81	35
26	Italy	58.74	18	66	Myanmar	46.07	10	106	Panama	36.22	12	146	Papua New Guinea	25.72	20
27	Chile	58.18	1	67	Sudan	45.73	8	107	Senegal	35.58	22	147	Cameroon	25.57	36
28	Greece	58.08	19	68	Georgia	45.37	31	108	Lebanon	35.08	13	148	Guyana	24.62	20
29	Iceland	57.4	20	69	Laos	45.34	11	109	Belize	35.02	13	149	Barbados	24.35	21
30	Philippines	57.29	8	70	Tanzania	45.15	9	110	Uzbekistan	34.66	40	150	Bolivia	24.06	22
31	Indonesia	56.63	9	71	Luxembourg	44.98	32	111	Moldova	34.63	41	151	Afghanistan	22.85	8
32	Cuba	56.56	2	72	North Macedonia	44.27	33	112	Gabon	34.31	23	152	Equatorial Guinea	22.32	37
33	Slovakia	56.54	21	73	Nigeria	44	10	113	New Zealand	34.28	15	153	Central African Republic	22.15	38
34	Canada	56.43	2	74	Madagascar	43.76	11	114	Guinea	34.12	24	154	Seychelles	21.34	39
35	Czech Republic	56.15	22	75	Bangladesh	43.68	1	115	Montenegro	33.87	42	155	Libya	21	17
36	Lithuania	54.87	23	76	United Arab Emirates	43.52	9	116	Jamaica	33.13	14	156	Somalia	20.49	40
37	Kenya	54.82	1	77	Cote d'Ivoire	43.46	12	117	Botswana	32.68	25	157	Guatemala	20.28	23
38	Morocco	54.59	1	78	Burkina Faso	43.29	13	118	Dem. Rep. Congo	32.13	26	158	Solomon Islands	18.84	21
39	Estonia	54.4	24	79	Oman	43.22	10	119	Togo	31.9	27	159	Guinea-Bissau	17.32	41
40	Malta	54.05	2	80	Azerbaijan	43.13	34	120	Burundi	31.68	28	160	Djibouti	14.75	18

East Asia and Pacific   Europe and Central Asia   Latin America and the Caribbean   Middle East and North Africa   North America   South Asia   Sub-Saharan Africa

Table 4.25 Regional ranking of the global One Health index-antimicrobial resistance (GOHI-AMR)

East Asia and Pacific (EAP)

Ranking	Country	Score
1	Malaysia	77.89
2	Thailand	71.25
3	Japan	71.18
4	Singapore	66.76
5	South Korea	66.19
6	Australia	64.36
7	China	60.71
8	Philippines	57.29
9	Indonesia	56.63
10	Myanmar	46.07
11	Laos	45.34
12	Mongolia	42.45
13	Timor-Leste	38.41
14	Cambodia	36.25
15	New Zealand	34.28
16	Fiji	31.39
17	Viet Nam	29.59
18	Brunei Darussalam	28.88
19	Vanuatu	28.57
20	Papua New Guinea	25.72
21	Solomon Islands	18.84

Middle East and North Africa (MENA)

Ranking	Country	Score
1	Morocco	54.59
2	Malta	54.05
3	Saudi Arabia	50.65
4	Iran	49.58
5	Israel	49.21
6	Jordan	47.35
7	Iraq	47.23
8	Qatar	46.87
9	United Arab Emirates	43.52
10	Oman	43.22
11	Bahrain	38.74
12	Kuwait	36.32
13	Lebanon	35.08
14	Egypt	31.07
15	Tunisia	29.04
16	Algeria	28.46
17	Libya	21.00
18	Djibouti	14.75

Europe and Central Asia (ECA)

Ranking	Country	Score
1	France	70.11
2	Norway	69.67
3	Denmark	68.68
4	United Kingdom	68.42

Table 4.25 (continued)

Europe and Central Asia (ECA)

Ranking	Country	Score
5	Sweden	66.17
6	Netherlands	65.99
7	Finland	65.28
8	Belgium	65.16
9	Austria	64.99
10	Spain	64.83
11	Germany	64.44
12	Portugal	64.25
13	Ireland	64.25
14	Latvia	63.07
15	Switzerland	62.58
16	Hungary	62.39
17	Russia	62.29
18	Italy	61.91
19	Greece	61.83
20	Iceland	61.17
21	Slovakia	61.14
22	Czech Republic	61.02
23	Lithuania	60.63
24	Estonia	60.39
25	Slovenia	60.24
26	Belarus	60.13
27	Serbia	59.81
28	Croatia	59.32
29	Turkey	58.38
30	Cyprus	57.83
31	Georgia	57.20
32	Luxembourg	56.88
33	North Macedonia	56.10
34	Azerbaijan	55.60
35	Poland	55.12
36	Romania	54.75
37	Kazakhstan	53.92
38	Ukraine	53.83
39	Kyrgyzstan	53.28
40	Uzbekistan	52.97
41	Moldova	52.84
42	Montenegro	52.71
43	Turkmenistan	52.35
44	Albania	52.23
45	Armenia	51.35
46	Tajikistan	50.34
47	Bulgaria	48.15

Sub-Saharan Arica (SSA)

Ranking	Country	Score
1	Kenya	54.82
2	Ethiopia	50.47
3	Ghana	50.28

(continued)

Table 4.25 (continued)

Sub-Saharan Arica (SSA)

Ranking	Country	Score
4	Eswatini	48.10
5	Rwanda	47.79
6	Zimbabwe	47.73
7	Uganda	47.05
8	Sudan	45.73
9	Tanzania	45.15
10	Nigeria	44.00
11	Madagascar	43.76
12	Cote d'Ivoire	43.46
13	Burkina Faso	43.29
14	Malawi	42.50
15	Zambia	41.76
16	Mozambique	41.67
17	Benin	40.48
18	Mali	40.13
19	South Africa	39.94
20	Namibia	39.67
21	Liberia	39.50
22	Senegal	35.58
23	Gabon	34.31
24	Guinea	34.12
25	Botswana	32.68
26	Dem. Rep. Congo	32.13
27	Togo	31.90
28	Burundi	31.68
29	Mauritius	31.39
30	Cabo Verde	30.70
31	Chad	29.33
32	Lesotho	28.90
33	Niger	26.66
34	Mauritania	26.50
35	Sierra Leone	25.81
36	Cameroon	25.57
37	Equatorial Guinea	22.32
38	Central African Republic	22.15
39	Seychelles	21.34
40	Somalia	20.49
41	Guinea-Bissau	17.32

South Asia (SA)

Ranking	Country	Score
1	Bangladesh	43.68
2	Pakistan	43.05
3	India	42.47
4	Nepal	42.46
5	Bhutan	41.44
6	Sri Lanka	38.36
7	Maldives	27.47
8	Afghanistan	22.85

Table 4.25 (continued)

Latin America and the Caribbean (LAC)

Ranking	Country	Score
1	Chile	58.18
2	Cuba	56.56
3	Argentina	53.74
4	Brazil	49.65
5	Colombia	49.60
6	Uruguay	49.03
7	Mexico	48.64
8	Costa Rica	46.80
9	Paraguay	46.74
10	Nicaragua	39.62
11	Peru	39.24
12	Panama	36.22
13	Belize	35.02
14	Jamaica	33.13
15	Trinidad and Tobago	31.52
16	Dominican Republic	30.84
17	Honduras	30.83
18	Ecuador	29.79
19	El Salvador	26.87
20	Guyana	24.62
21	Barbados	24.35
22	Bolivia	24.06
23	Guatemala	20.28

North America (NA)

Ranking	Country	Score
1	United States	74.63
2	Canada	56.43

Table 4.26, the Latin America and the Caribbean scored slightly higher than the global average on only two sub I-indicators: National AMR Capacity (C4.2.1) and Carbapenems (C4.5.1).

4. *Middle East and North Africa*

The average score of the 18 countries included is 40.04, as shown in Table 4.25. Morocco, Malta, Saudi Arabia, Iran, and Israel are the top five nations in this region. With a score of 54.59, Morocco is first in this region and 38th in the global ranking. As depicted in Table 4.26, the Middle East and North Africa scored slightly higher than the global average on only two sub I-indicators: Public health awareness (C4.4.1) and Glycopeptide (C4.5.2).

Table 4.26 Regional performance of the global One Health index-antimicrobial resistance (GOHI-AMR)

Code	Indicator Title	Global Average	East Asia and Pacific		Europe and Central Asia		Latin America and the Caribbean		Middle East and North Africa		North America		South Asia		Sub-Saharan Africa	
			Average	Gap	Average	Gap	Average	Gap	Average	Gap	Average	Gap	Average	Gap	Average	Gap
C4.1	AMR surveillance system	34.79	39.77	4.98	44.01	9.22	26.10	−8.69	30.86	−3.93	59.41	24.62	28.16	−6.63	28.37	−6.42
C4.1.1	Antimicrobial consumption surveillance	36.02	37.70	1.68	50.88	14.86	28.86	−7.16	32.48	−3.54	62.50	26.48	20.32	−15.71	25.47	−10.55
C4.1.2	Antimicrobial resistance status surveillance	46.99	50.59	3.61	63.96	16.98	36.96	−10.03	45.08	−1.91	82.82	35.83	43.75	−3.24	31.02	−15.96
C4.1.3	Environmental antimicrobial resistance surveillance	17.20	26.98	9.78	10.87	−6.32	8.94	−8.26	10.19	−7.01	25.00	7.80	14.12	−3.08	27.37	10.17
C4.2	AMR laboratory network and coordination capacity	55.57	57.54	1.97	63.82	8.26	51.80	−3.77	48.33	−7.24	76.93	21.36	52.32	−3.25	49.97	−5.59
C4.2.1	National AMR capacity	58.57	57.27	−1.29	66.99	8.42	60.87	2.30	53.63	−4.94	79.17	20.60	58.85	0.29	49.39	−9.18
C4.2.2	Technical level	44.93	51.49	6.55	61.37	16.43	31.48	−13.46	35.59	−9.34	78.13	33.19	37.89	−7.04	34.15	−10.79
C4.2.3	National plan	62.00	63.44	1.44	62.52	0.52	60.32	−1.69	54.10	−7.91	73.30	11.29	58.26	−3.74	65.27	3.27
C4.3	Antimicrobial control and optimization	48.76	50.34	1.58	62.45	13.68	45.08	−3.69	43.56	−5.21	77.39	28.62	38.22	−10.55	37.29	−11.48
C4.3.1	National law(s) for antibiotic use	67.69	66.67	−1.02	85.32	17.63	60.72	−6.96	61.48	−6.21	100.00	32.31	60.00	−7.69	54.55	−13.13
C4.3.2	Antimicrobial use optimization	32.27	33.18	0.91	44.31	12.04	31.75	−0.53	27.49	−4.79	60.94	28.67	21.09	−11.18	21.19	−11.08
C4.3.3	Antimicrobial use control	41.54	46.93	5.38	51.99	10.45	38.81	−2.73	37.15	−4.39	65.63	24.08	28.12	−13.42	31.71	−9.84

(continued)

Table 4.26 (continued)

Code	Title	Global	East Asia and Pacific		Europe and Central Asia		Latin America and the Caribbean		Middle East and North Africa		North America		South Asia		Sub-Saharan Africa	
	Indicator		Average	Gap	Average	Gap	Average	Gap	Average	Gap	Average	Gap	Average	Gap	Average	Gap
C4.4	Improve awareness and understanding	48.09	52.60	4.51	60.64	12.55	37.16	−10.93	47.54	−0.55	77.35	29.25	41.02	−7.08	37.73	−10.36
C4.4.1	Public health awareness	55.63	62.50	6.88	68.35	12.73	42.39	−13.23	58.33	2.71	75.00	19.38	48.44	−7.19	44.21	−11.42
C4.4.2	Professional training	40.56	42.71	2.15	52.93	12.37	31.93	−8.63	36.75	−3.81	79.69	39.12	33.59	−6.97	31.25	−9.31
C4.5	Antimicrobial resistance rate for important antibiotics	33.03	37.37	4.35	36.39	3.36	32.33	−0.70	29.91	−3.12	36.60	3.57	28.90	−4.13	29.34	−3.69
C4.5.1	Carbapenems	68.13	76.85	8.73	70.45	2.32	69.41	1.28	62.18	−5.95	82.95	14.82	61.29	−6.84	63.50	−4.63
C4.5.2	Glycopeptide	31.24	33.29	2.05	34.45	3.21	30.53	−0.71	32.78	1.54	16.02	−15.22	31.24	0.00	27.19	−4.05
C4.5.3	β-lactams	33.76	36.31	2.55	41.19	7.43	32.95	−0.81	28.94	−4.82	37.98	4.22	25.17	−8.59	27.98	−5.78
C4.5.4	Macrolides	0.00	0.00	0.00	0.00	0.00	0.00	0.00	0.00	0.00	0.00	0.00	0.00	0.00	0.00	0.00
C4.5.5	Aminoglycosides	21.92	30.67	8.76	22.63	0.71	20.37	−1.55	19.48	−2.43	31.08	9.16	20.69	−1.23	18.35	−3.57
C4.5.6	Quinolone	31.99	34.61	2.62	37.71	5.72	29.45	−2.54	26.56	−5.44	40.06	8.07	25.72	−6.27	28.74	−3.26

5. *North America*

The average score for the two countries (the United States and Canada) is 65.53, as shown in Table 4.25. These two countries are ranked among the world's top. The United States ranks 5th in the global ranking with a score of 74.63, while Canada ranks 34th with a score of 56.43. As shown in Table 4.26, North America is well above the global average in all sub I-indicators, except for Glycopeptide (C4.5.2), suggesting that performance can be improved.

6. *South Asia*

The average score for the eight countries included is 37.72, as shown in Table 4.25. Bangladesh, Pakistan, India, Nepal, and Bhutan are the top five countries in this region. Bangladesh, which ranks first in this region with a score of 43.68, is ranked 75th globally. All eight countries in this region have scores below the global regional average (44.05). As depicted in Table 4.26, the South Asia scores similarly to the global average on only two sub I-indicators: National AMR capacity (C4.2.1) and Carbapenems (C4.5.1).

7. *Sub-Saharan Africa*

The average score for the 41 countries included is 36.54, as shown in Table 4.25. Kenya, Ethiopia, Ghana, Eswatini, and Rwanda are the leading five nations in this region. Kenya, which ranks first in the Sub-Saharan Africa with a score of 54.82, is ranked 37th globally. More than 75% of the region's countries scored below the global average (44.05). As depicted in Table 4.26, the Sub-Saharan Africa scored higher than the global average on two sub I-indicators, Environmental AMR surveillance (C4.1.3) and National plan (C4.2.3), above more than 3 points, whereas the remaining sub II-indicator scored significantly below the global average.

6.5 Key Findings

The Total Score of GOHI-AMR Worldwide Is Unsatisfactory

We characterized the optimal state of One Health performance on AMR with a score of 100 points. The global median score of GOHI-AMR is 43.09

(95% CI: 39.87–45.37), with more than 70% of countries scoring below 50. There is also a substantial difference between the first France (with a GOHI-AMR score of 81.43) and the last Djibouti (with a GOHI-AMR score of 14.75).

There Are Substantial Geographic Regional Disparities and Large Intra-regional Disparities

The score range of GOHI-AMR for each region (from high to low, sorted by the lower limits) is: North America, with a score range of 56.43–74.63; Europe and Central Asia, with a score range of 28.42–81.43; South Asia, with a score range of 22.85–43.68; Latin America and the Caribbean, with a score range of 20.28 to 58.18; East Asia and Pacific, with a score range of 18.84–77.89; and sub-Saharan Africa, with a score range of 17.32–54.82. Nine of the top 25 countries/territories with the highest GOHI scores are located in Europe and Central Asia, while the remaining 14 are located in North America, East Asia, and the Pacific. Nine of the 25 countries/territories with the lowest GOHI scores are located in sub-Saharan Africa. The remaining countries/territories are located in Latin America and the Caribbean, East Asia and Pacific, the Middle East and South Africa, South Asia, Europe, and Central Asia.

The Lower Scores of Two Sub II-Indicators in GOHI-AMR Reveal Weakness in AMR Surveillance and Control

Two of the five GOHI-AMR sub II-indicators, namely AMR surveillance system and AMR rate on important antibiotics, appear to be significantly lagging behind the others. The median scores for these two sub II-indicators are considerably lower than the global median score (43.09), coming in at 32.61 and 31.62, respectively, a difference of more than 10 points from the global level.

6.6 Conclusion

When viewed from the perspective of One Health, AMR remains a serious threat to global health, particularly in the Latin America and the

Caribbean and Sub-Saharan Africa; therefore, additional efforts are required to strengthen AMR governance in these regions. In addition, there are disparities in the status of AMR in the same geographic regions, indicating that regional coordination of AMR must be enhanced. Concurrently, it is necessary to continuously improve the policies and implement AMR governance in humans, animals, and the environment, to refine relevant basic monitoring facilities, to strengthen multisectoral communication and cooperation to jointly address AMR, and to increase public awareness and understanding of AMR.

7 Climate Change

7.1 Background

Socio-economic development and human activities constantly impact the ecology, leading to global climate change and a sharp decline in biodiversity. Extreme weather events under the influence of global climate change have widespread and complex effects on the health of human beings [67, 68] and animals [69]. Natural resources depletion, soil erosion, desertification, carbon stocks decline, and reduction in water and air quality also pose serious threats to ecological and human health [70–74]. Therefore, global climate change profoundly affects human survival and development and is a significant challenge faced by all countries [73, 75, 76].

Climate change refers to long-term changes in average patterns of temperatures and weather [77], including global warming, acid rain, ozone layer depletion, and extreme weather events. Climate change affects human health directly and indirectly through a variety of pathways. The direct impacts of climate change are mainly in the form of acute injuries, diseases, mental health problems, and premature deaths caused by frequent extreme weather events. For example, the frequency of extreme weather events is strongly associated with population mortality, with both high and low temperatures increasing the risk of death. In general, the health effects of extremely high temperatures are acute, while those of

extremely low temperatures are long-term. People with chronic underlying diseases, low-income groups, and older people are more vulnerable to extreme weather events [78–80]. Other extreme weather events such as droughts, floods, and wildfires can also increase the risk of mortality in populations. Each year, approximately 340,000 people die worldwide as a result of wildfires [81].

The indirect effects of climate change on human health are felt through socio-economic or natural systems. Frequent climatic hazards cause poverty and mental health problems. Moreover, climate change affects the prevalence of infectious diseases by influencing the geographical distribution, population density, pathogen infection, and transmission of host and vector organisms. The effect of global warming include changes in migratory patterns, leading to pathogen sharing between previously unconnected species and increasing the chances of pathogen spillover to humans via intermediate hosts [82]. Another effect is that warmer climates can accelerate the life cycle of mosquitoes and thus increase the rate of disease transmission. A 1 °C increase in temperature can increase the risk of mosquito-borne dengue infections by approximately 12% [83]. Similarly, a 1-mm increase in precipitation increases the risk of infection with the rodent-borne disease epidemic hemorrhagic fever by 0.2% [84]. Climate change can also alter the environment by providing more suitable habitats and shelters for hosts and vectors, increasing the pathogen-carrying capacity of the ecosystem [85, 86].

7.2 The Existing Problems of Global Climate Change

The Lancet Countdown report states that climate change is a major threat to human health [87, 88]. Climate change poses an even greater and more permanent global health threat than the COVID-19 epidemic. Without intervention, extreme weather and emerging infectious diseases will become more frequent [88]. The international community and organizations are urging humanity to act urgently on climate change to reduce the risk of future epidemics. For example, the WHO has identified climate change as one of the most important threats to global health since the beginning of the twenty-first century. The WHO has urged national health authorities to pay attention to climate change and develop relevant policies [89]. In 2007, China reported "Responding to Climate Change: China's Policies and Actions", which introduced a series of climate change adaptation policies and shared experiences and approaches with the international community.

Although significant progress has been made globally in addressing climate change health risks, there is still much room for improvement [90–92]. In particular, there are significant challenges in global research on climate change and population health, such as difficulties in obtaining basic data, inadequate health information systems, and lagging prevention and control measures. The existing early warning and prediction models for climate-related diseases in various countries are incomplete, and the accuracy of the models needs to be improved due to the lack of relevant information and data for modeling. Additionally, the low accuracy of early warning and forecasting systems hinders the implementation of climate change control policies.

7.3   Our Goals

To address the risks of global climate change to human health, scientists have attempted to promote the concept of One Health in the fields of environmental safety, ecological health, and climate change. One Health is an integrated that recognizes the relationship between humans, animals, plants, and their shared environment while working at the local, regional, national, and international levels to achieve better health outcomes. Climate change has significant impacts on humans, animals, and the environment and is undeniably linked to human activities on the environment. The One Health approach is, therefore, a good fit to address climate change [69].

To improve the assessment of climate change and consequent health risks, we have developed the global One Health index-climate change (GOHI-CC) based on the concept of One Health, which consists of 30 key indicators covering 160 countries and regions worldwide. The GOHI-CC explores the causes of climate change, its impact on population health, and the health benefits of mitigating climate change by using climate-related data. The GOHI-CC tracks the outcomes of climate change and health risks faced by countries or regions. It then provides policy recommendations based on the results of the indicators, which can support the efficient formulation of climate-related policies.

7.4   Framework Construction of GOHI-CC

Framework

Here, we have constructed the GOHI-CC using One Health theory. Firstly, the level of climate change risks refers to the degree of exposure and vulnerability of a region or population to hazards such as extreme weather events (e.g., hurricanes, floods, and droughts), sea level rise, and temperature changes. The CCR indicator helps assess the physical risks associated with climate change, including the frequency and intensity of climate-related events and their potential impacts on natural resources, infrastructure, and population. By evaluating CCR factors, decision-makers can prioritize areas or population that are most vulnerable to climate change and allocate resources accordingly for mitigation and adaptation efforts.

Secondly, climate change has significant implications for public health, as it can exacerbate existing health risks and create new ones. Health outcomes of climate change include heat-related illnesses, respiratory diseases from air pollution, and vector-borne diseases (e.g., malaria and dengue fever) influenced by changing ecological patterns. Monitoring health outcomes helps policymakers understand the direct and indirect consequences of climate change on human well-being and can inform the develop-

Fig. 4.28 Indicator framework of the global One Health index-climate change (GOHI-CC)

ment of targeted strategies to protect public health and improve resilience.

Mitigation and adaptation refer to the measures and policies implemented by governments at various levels (local, regional, and national) to address climate change. This indicator reflects the level of political will, policy responses, and actions taken by governments to mitigate greenhouse gas emissions, adapt to changing climate conditions, and protect vulnerable populations. Government intervention can include regulations, legislation, incentives, funding, and other policy instruments that influence behavior change, promote renewable energy, support sustainable practices, and build climate resilience. Monitoring government intervention helps assess the effectiveness of climate policies and actions and provides insights into the readiness and capacity of governments to address climate change impacts. After repeated discussions and brainstorming, our group selected data from recent years from authoritative databases to develop a system of 3 indicators, 10 sub I-indicators, and 30 sub II-indicators (Fig. 4.28). By using three-level

framework, our climate change effect reports provide a holistic assessment of the multifaceted impacts of climate change on different sectors of society, including the environmental, social, economic, and public health dimensions. This comprehensive approach enables policymakers, researchers, and stakeholders to better understand the complex interactions between climate change and various sectors and develop evidence-based strategies for climate change mitigation, adaptation, and resilience-building efforts. Based on the One Health concept, this index system comprehensively evaluated the climate change performance of 160 countries and regions regarding their climate risk factors, health impacts, and government intervention.

Indicators

Comprehensive and high-quality data is essential for monitoring global climate change and developing effective climate policies. As shown in Table 4.27, our climate change index system has summarized 30 key climate change indicators, covering Climate Change Risks (CCR), Health

Table 4.27 Indicator and weight scheme of the global One Health index-climate change (GOHI-CC)

| Indicator | | | Sub I-indicator | | | Sub II-indicator | | |
Name	Code	Weight (%)	Name	Code	Weight (%)	Name	Code	Weight (%)
Climate change risks	C5.1	33.3	Greenhouse gases emissions	C5.1.1	25.0	CO_2 emissions	C5.1.1.1	25.0
						Methane emissions	C5.1.1.2	25.0
						Nitrous oxide	C5.1.1.3	25.0
						Other greenhouse gas	C5.1.1.4	25.0
			Energy use	C5.1.2	25.0	Oil	C5.1.2.1	25.0
						Natural gas	C5.1.2.2	25.0
						Coal	C5.1.2.3	25.0
						Energy intensity	C5.1.2.4	25.0
			Air quality	C5.1.3	25.0	Ozone exposure	C5.1.3.1	50.0
						Inhalable particles	C5.1.3.2	50.0
			Natural disaster and extreme weather	C5.1.4	25.0	Wildfires	C5.1.4.1	25.0
						Droughts, floods, and storms	C5.1.4.2	25.0
						Extreme high temperature	C5.1.4.3	25.0
						Extreme low temperature	C5.1.4.4	25.0
Health outcome	C5.2	33.3	Air quality DALYs	C5.2.1	50.0	Inhalable particles burden	C5.2.1.1	100.0
			Climate-related illnesses	C5.2.2	50.0	Heat-related illness' burden	C5.2.2.1	33.3
						Vulnerability to extremes of heat	C5.2.2.2	33.3
						Disasters' death	C5.2.2.3	33.3
Mitigation and adaptation capacity	C5.3	33.3	Mitigation and adaptation achievements	C5.3.1	25.0	Low-carbon energy use	C5.3.1.1	20.0
						Hydro energy use	C5.3.1.2	20.0
						Solar energy use	C5.3.1.3	20.0
						Wind energy use	C5.3.1.4	20.0
						Renewable energy capacity	C5.3.1.5	20.0
			Financial support	C5.3.2	25.0	Climate adaptation spending	C5.3.2.1	0.0
						Renewable energy finance flows	C5.3.2.2	50.0
			Propaganda and education	C5.3.3	25.0	Climate health education	C5.3.3.1	50.0
						Climate health research	C5.3.3.2	50.0
			Forestation	C5.3.4	25.0	Forest change	C5.3.4.1	33.3
						Reforestation	C5.3.4.2	33.3
						Deforestation	C5.3.4.3	33.3

Outcome of climate change (HOC), and Mitigation and Adaptation Capacity (MAC).

CCR is a central component of climate change, where greenhouse gas emissions and energy usage have been identified as major contributors. These factors have resulted in a reduction in air quality, increased natural disasters, and extreme weather events. Climate risk indicators therefore pose a significant health risk and play an important role in the climate change index.

HOC includes air quality DALYs (disability-adjusted life years) and climate-related illnesses. Due to the direct and indirect impacts of climate change on human health, HOC is an essential component in evaluating performance related to climate change.

MAC encompasses policy and intervention-related indicators aimed at assessing responsiveness to climate change. An effective response to climate change and its resulting health threats requires climate governance at both the global and national levels. Based on the One Health concept, MAC emphasizes evaluating responsiveness by integrating climate change-related knowledge systems, policies, and intervention strategies. This approach promotes green and sustainable development, which is crucial in meeting the challenges posed by climate change.

Data Sources

In these 30 key climate change indicators, quantitative data are sourced from the WHO, Our World in Data, Lancet Countdown, OECD BP Statistical Review of World Energy and Ember, Global Health Data Exchange, and State of Global Air, while qualitative indicators are obtained by counting the number of related papers in Web of Science.

Limitations

This indicator system has three main shortcomings. Firstly, some countries do not pay enough attention to the issue of climate change and its social and public health implications due to differences in national policy-making and development levels. For example, indicators for climate change-related education and research are currently only available in a small number of developed countries, reflecting the fact that the level of

development of an economy and the way it considers policymaking play a decisive role in the way to respond to climate change.

Additionally, although we have normalized the data, confounding effects between the data may influence the results. Europe and Central Asia, North and East Asia, and the Pacific tend to perform better due to their inherent strengths. They have greater access to funding, technology, and infrastructure to implement climate-friendly policies and initiatives. As leaders in technological advancement, including renewable energy technologies, energy efficiency measures, and climate-smart agriculture practices, they are able to adopt and implement innovative solutions for mitigating and adapting to climate change more effectively. Furthermore, different databases have varying approaches to data collection, leading to national or geographical differences in the way data is integrated. Given imbalances in population, land area, and economic development among different countries and regions, some indicators cannot be compared directly between different countries and need to be homogenized.

Finally, the global COVID-19 epidemic has raged for the past 3 years. The stagnation of industries due to the epidemic, the decline in economic development in various countries, and the inaccessibility of researchers' work could lead to delays in data collection and integration. Consequently, climate correlation studies have been severely hampered.

7.5   Main Results

Global Scores

The GOHI-CC scores 160 countries from seven regions for assessment, including East Asia and Pacific, Europe and Central Asia, Latin America and the Caribbean, Middle East and North Africa, North America, South Asia, and sub-Saharan Africa. Figure 4.29 visualizes the GOHI-CC scores, indicating that Europe and Central Asia, North America, and East Asia and Pacific perform better in the GOHI-CC Index system, while the Middle East and North Africa and sub-Saharan Africa perform less well.

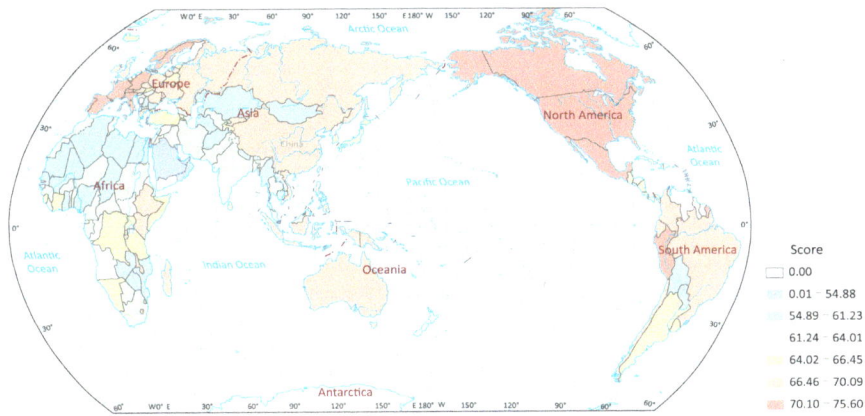

Fig. 4.29 Global score map of the global One Health index-climate change (GOHI-CC)

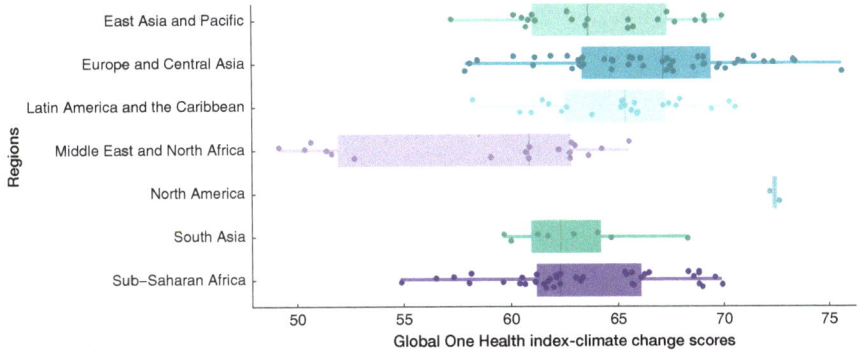

Fig. 4.30 Regional score distribution of the global One Health index-climate change (GOHI-CC)

The average score of GOHI-CC is 64.19, with a median score of 64.12. The average scores for countries in North America (72.40), and Europe and Central Asia (66.47) are higher than those in the Middle East and North Africa (58.57), and sub-Saharan Africa (63.38) (Fig. 4.30).

Figures 4.31 and 4.32 show the distribution of GOHI-CC scores by indicators and categories. The average score for Mitigation and adaptation capacity (MAC, score: 28.24) is significantly lower than that of Climate change risks (CCR, score: 80.87) and Health outcome (HOC, score: 85.40), indicating that there is still much action that should be taken to tackle climate change.

Global Ranking

In this assessment of the global GOHI-CC scores in 160 countries/territories, the top-scoring country is Spain from Europe and Central Asia, with a score of 75.60, and the lowest-scoring country is Qatar from the Middle East and North Africa with a score of 49.16. Table 4.28 lists the rankings of GOHI-CC scores in 160 countries/territories.

1. *Top-ranking countries*

The top 10 countries are mostly from Europe and Central Asia (Table 4.28), such as Spain (75.60), Netherlands (73.39), Germany (73.29), Italy (72.34), and Portugal (71.92). The North American nations of the United States (72.63) and Canada (72.17).

2. *Ranking lagging countries*

The bottom 10 countries in the ranking are from the Middle East and North Africa, sub-Saharan Africa and East Asia and Pacific (Table 4.28). They include Qatar (49.16), United Arab Emirates (50.37), Kuwait (50.66), Bahrain (51.38), Saudi Arabia (51.63), and Oman (52.71).

Fig. 4.31 The global One Health index-climate change (GOHI-CC) scores distribution by indicators. (*GGE* greenhouse gases emissions, *EGU* energy use, *AQT* air quality, *DEW* natural disaster and extreme weather, *AQD* air quality DALYs, *CRI* climate-related illnesses, *MAA* mitigation and adaptation achievements, *FRT* financial support, *PGE* propaganda and education, *FOR* forestation)

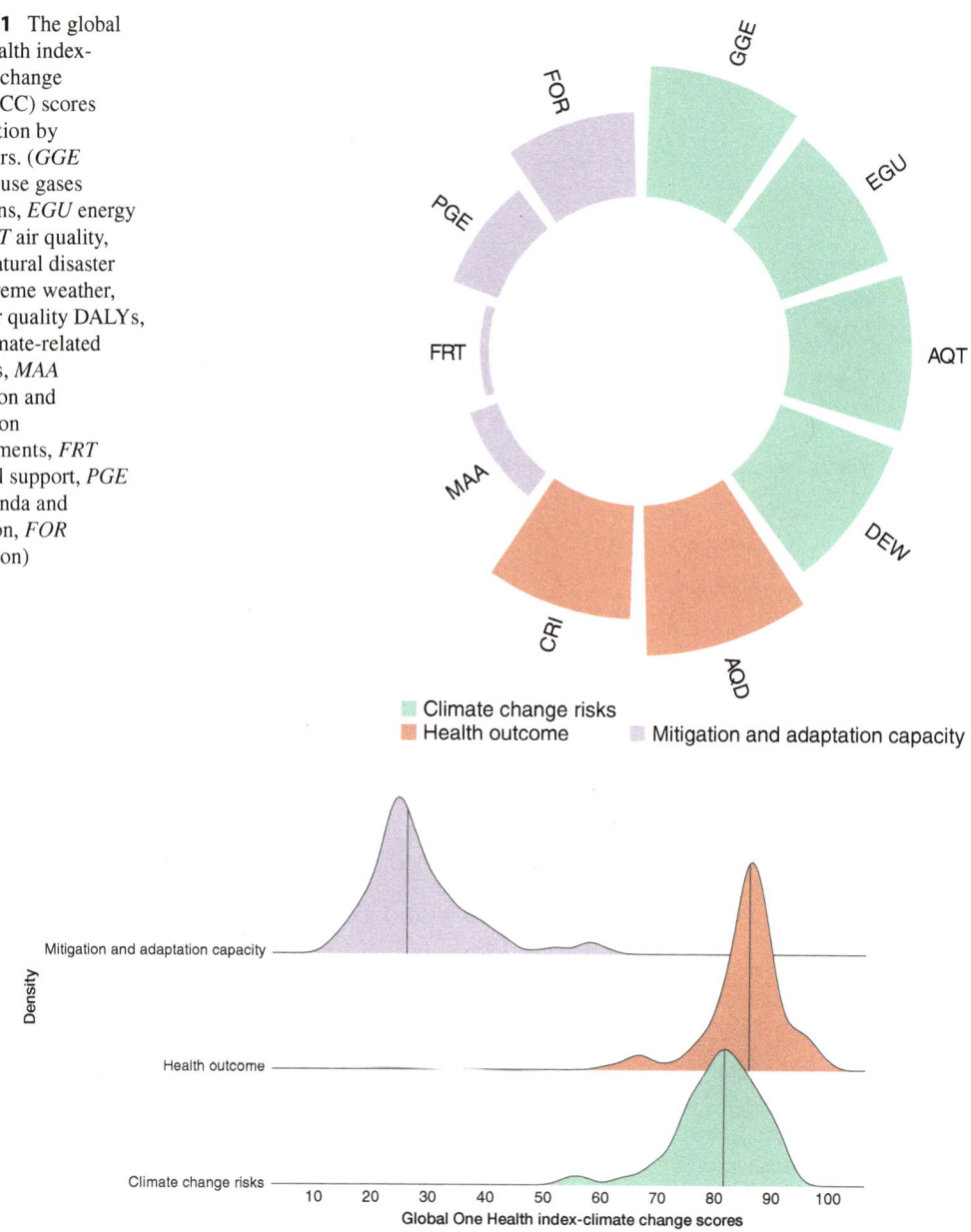

Fig. 4.32 Dimensional score distribution of the global One Health index-climate change (GOHI-CC)

Regional Rankings

GOHI-CC scores are uneven among different regions (Table 4.29). Europe and Central Asia, and North America score higher, while the Middle East and North Africa and sub-Saharan Africa generally score lower. The overall GOHI-CC scores are relatively similar in the East Asia and Pacific, Latin America and the Caribbean, and South Asia.

The average scores for CCR are relatively close between the seven regions, although those in Latin America and the Caribbean are slightly higher than in other regions.

In the HOC component, the Middle East and North Africa has the lowest average score. Otherwise, the average scores in other regions are similar.

Table 4.28 Country ranking of the global One Health index-climate change (GOHI-CC)

Rank	Region	Country	Score
1	Europe and Central Asia	Spain	75.60
2	Europe and Central Asia	Netherlands	73.39
3	Europe and Central Asia	Germany	73.29
4	North America	United States	72.63
5	Europe and Central Asia	Italy	72.34
6	North America	Canada	72.17
7	Europe and Central Asia	Portugal	71.92
8	Europe and Central Asia	France	71.44
9	Europe and Central Asia	Switzerland	70.95
10	Europe and Central Asia	Sweden	70.70
11	Latin America and the Caribbean	Mexico	70.55
12	Europe and Central Asia	Norway	70.54
13	Latin America and the Caribbean	Peru	70.28
14	Europe and Central Asia	Denmark	70.09
15	East Asia and Pacific	Australia	69.93
16	Sub-Saharan Africa	Rwanda	69.92
17	Europe and Central Asia	United Kingdom	69.80
18	Europe and Central Asia	Finland	69.69
19	Sub-Saharan Africa	Eswatini	69.56
20	Latin America and the Caribbean	Brazil	69.42
21	East Asia and Pacific	China	69.12
22	Europe and Central Asia	Romania	69.08
23	East Asia and Pacific	Philippines	69.07
24	Europe and Central Asia	Greece	69.04
25	Europe and Central Asia	Latvia	69.04
26	Sub-Saharan Africa	Burundi	68.95
27	Sub-Saharan Africa	Madagascar	68.79
28	Europe and Central Asia	Ireland	68.78
29	Sub-Saharan Africa	Kenya	68.77
30	Sub-Saharan Africa	Lesotho	68.77
31	East Asia and Pacific	Indonesia	68.66
32	Europe and Central Asia	Moldova	68.53
33	Sub-Saharan Africa	Ethiopia	68.52
34	Sub-Saharan Africa	Malawi	68.26
35	South Asia	Sri Lanka	68.24
36	Latin America and the Caribbean	Ecuador	67.89
37	Latin America and the Caribbean	Chile	67.73
38	East Asia and Pacific	Viet Nam	67.67
39	Europe and Central Asia	Czech Republic	67.58
40	Europe and Central Asia	Kyrgyzstan	67.58
41	Europe and Central Asia	Ukraine	67.47
42	Europe and Central Asia	Russia	67.45
43	Latin America and the Caribbean	Cuba	67.39
44	Europe and Central Asia	Poland	67.33
45	East Asia and Pacific	Papua New Guinea	67.31
46	Europe and Central Asia	Lithuania	67.27
47	Latin America and the Caribbean	Colombia	67.12
48	Europe and Central Asia	Austria	67.12
49	East Asia and Pacific	New Zealand	66.90
50	Sub-Saharan Africa	Mauritius	66.45

Table 4.28 (continued)

Rank	Region	Country	Score
51	Sub-Saharan Africa	Tanzania	66.24
52	Europe and Central Asia	Iceland	66.22
53	Europe and Central Asia	Estonia	66.08
54	Sub-Saharan Africa	Somalia	66.08
55	Latin America and the Caribbean	Uruguay	65.96
56	Latin America and the Caribbean	Costa Rica	65.91
57	Latin America and the Caribbean	Nicaragua	65.81
58	East Asia and Pacific	Japan	65.76
59	Sub-Saharan Africa	Uganda	65.73
60	Europe and Central Asia	Slovakia	65.70
61	Sub-Saharan Africa	Cote d'Ivoire	65.65
62	Latin America and the Caribbean	Panama	65.65
63	Sub-Saharan Africa	Sierra Leone	65.64
64	Europe and Central Asia	Belgium	65.58
65	Middle East and North Africa	Israel	65.53
66	Europe and Central Asia	Armenia	65.53
67	East Asia and Pacific	South Korea	65.52
68	East Asia and Pacific	Timor-Leste	65.51
69	Sub-Saharan Africa	Dem. Rep. Congo	65.37
70	Latin America and the Caribbean	Argentina	65.35
71	Sub-Saharan Africa	Namibia	65.31
72	Latin America and the Caribbean	Dominican Republic	65.26
73	Latin America and the Caribbean	Jamaica	65.21
74	Latin America and the Caribbean	Guatemala	65.15
75	Europe and Central Asia	Belarus	64.78
76	Europe and Central Asia	Cyprus	64.73
77	Europe and Central Asia	Tajikistan	64.73
78	South Asia	Maldives	64.66
79	Europe and Central Asia	Turkey	64.38
80	Middle East and North Africa	Malta	64.22
81	South Asia	India	64.01
82	Latin America and the Caribbean	Guyana	63.79
83	East Asia and Pacific	Fiji	63.60
84	Middle East and North Africa	Morocco	63.60
85	East Asia and Pacific	Malaysia	63.50
86	Europe and Central Asia	Luxembourg	63.38
87	Europe and Central Asia	Azerbaijan	63.34
88	Sub-Saharan Africa	Liberia	63.32
89	Sub-Saharan Africa	Guinea	63.30
90	Europe and Central Asia	Georgia	63.28
91	Sub-Saharan Africa	Cabo Verde	63.22
92	Europe and Central Asia	Croatia	63.21
93	Europe and Central Asia	Slovenia	63.15
94	Sub-Saharan Africa	Equatorial Guinea	63.00
95	Middle East and North Africa	Iraq	62.98
96	South Asia	Pakistan	62.90
97	Europe and Central Asia	Uzbekistan	62.87
98	East Asia and Pacific	Thailand	62.86
99	Middle East and North Africa	Iran	62.81
100	Middle East and North Africa	Lebanon	62.75

Table 4.28 (continued)

Rank	Region	Country	Score
101	Middle East and North Africa	Jordan	62.74
102	Europe and Central Asia	Hungary	62.65
103	East Asia and Pacific	Laos	62.63
104	Latin America and the Caribbean	El Salvador	62.61
105	Latin America and the Caribbean	Honduras	62.37
106	Sub-Saharan Africa	Niger	62.27
107	Sub-Saharan Africa	Central African Republic	62.26
108	Middle East and North Africa	Tunisia	62.21
109	Sub-Saharan Africa	Gabon	62.11
110	Sub-Saharan Africa	Cameroon	62.10
111	Sub-Saharan Africa	Benin	62.06
112	Sub-Saharan Africa	South Africa	61.97
113	Europe and Central Asia	North Macedonia	61.87
114	Sub-Saharan Africa	Togo	61.79
115	Latin America and the Caribbean	Belize	61.77
116	South Asia	Bangladesh	61.70
117	Sub-Saharan Africa	Botswana	61.7
118	Sub-Saharan Africa	Sudan	61.61
119	Sub-Saharan Africa	Burkina Faso	61.50
120	Latin America and the Caribbean	Barbados	61.47
121	South Asia	Bhutan	61.23
122	Sub-Saharan Africa	Zambia	61.17
123	East Asia and Pacific	Cambodia	61.15
124	Sub-Saharan Africa	Ghana	61.12
125	Europe and Central Asia	Serbia	61.12
126	Europe and Central Asia	Kazakhstan	61.06
127	East Asia and Pacific	Mongolia	61.00
128	Latin America and the Caribbean	Trinidad and Tobago	60.96
129	Middle East and North Africa	Algeria	60.86
130	Middle East and North Africa	Egypt	60.82
131	East Asia and Pacific	Brunei Darussalam	60.82
132	East Asia and Pacific	Myanmar	60.71
133	Middle East and North Africa	Djibouti	60.70
134	Sub-Saharan Africa	Chad	60.64
135	East Asia and Pacific	Solomon Islands	60.54
136	Sub-Saharan Africa	Mali	60.50
137	Latin America and the Caribbean	Paraguay	60.43
138	Sub-Saharan Africa	Guinea-Bissau	60.40
139	East Asia and Pacific	Singapore	60.15
140	Europe and Central Asia	Bulgaria	60.14
141	South Asia	Afghanistan	60.00
142	South Asia	Nepal	59.68
143	Sub-Saharan Africa	Mozambique	59.63
144	Middle East and North Africa	Libya	59.08
145	Europe and Central Asia	Montenegro	58.47
146	Latin America and the Caribbean	Bolivia	58.24
147	Sub-Saharan Africa	Mauritania	58.14
148	Europe and Central Asia	Albania	58.10
149	Sub-Saharan Africa	Zimbabwe	58.05
150	Europe and Central Asia	Turkmenistan	57.88

Table 4.28 (continued)

Rank	Region	Country	Score
151	Sub-Saharan Africa	Senegal	57.33
152	East Asia and Pacific	Vanuatu	57.25
153	Sub-Saharan Africa	Nigeria	56.51
154	Sub-Saharan Africa	Seychelles	54.88
155	Middle East and North Africa	Oman	52.71
156	Middle East and North Africa	Saudi Arabia	51.63
157	Middle East and North Africa	Bahrain	51.38
158	Middle East and North Africa	Kuwait	50.66
159	Middle East and North Africa	United Arab Emirates	50.37
160	Middle East and North Africa	Qatar	49.16

Table 4.29 Regional ranking of the global One Health index-climate change (GOHI-CC)

East Asia and Pacific (EAP)

Rank	Country	Score
1	Australia	69.93
2	China	69.12
3	Philippines	69.07
4	Indonesia	68.66
5	Viet Nam	67.67
6	Papua New Guinea	67.31
7	New Zealand	66.90
8	Japan	65.76
9	South Korea	65.52
10	Timor-Leste	65.51
11	Fiji	63.60
12	Malaysia	63.50
13	Thailand	62.86
14	Laos	62.63
15	Cambodia	61.15
16	Mongolia	61.00
17	Brunei Darussalam	60.82
18	Myanmar	60.71
19	Solomon Islands	60.54
20	Singapore	60.15
21	Vanuatu	57.25

Middle East and North Africa (MENA)

Rank	Country	Score
1	Israel	65.53
2	Malta	64.22
3	Morocco	63.6
4	Iraq	62.98
5	Iran	62.81
6	Lebanon	62.75
7	Jordan	62.74
8	Tunisia	62.21
9	Algeria	60.86
10	Egypt	60.82

Table 4.29 (continued)

Middle East and North Africa (MENA)

Rank	Country	Score
11	Djibouti	60.7
12	Libya	59.08
13	Oman	52.71
14	Saudi Arabia	51.63
15	Bahrain	51.38
16	Kuwait	50.66
17	United Arab Emirates	50.37
18	Qatar	49.16

Europe and Central Asia (ECA)

Rank	Country	Score
1	Spain	75.60
2	Netherlands	73.39
3	Germany	73.29
4	Italy	72.34
5	Portugal	71.92
6	France	71.44
7	Switzerland	70.95
8	Sweden	70.70
9	Norway	70.54
10	Denmark	70.09
11	United Kingdom	69.80
12	Finland	69.69
13	Romania	69.08
14	Greece	69.04
15	Latvia	69.04
16	Ireland	68.78
17	Moldova	68.53
18	Czech Republic	67.58
19	Kyrgyzstan	67.58
20	Ukraine	67.47
21	Russia	67.45
22	Poland	67.33
23	Lithuania	67.27

Table 4.29 (continued)

Europe and Central Asia (ECA)

Rank	Country	Score
24	Austria	67.12
25	Iceland	66.22
26	Estonia	66.08
27	Slovakia	65.70
28	Belgium	65.58
29	Armenia	65.53
30	Belarus	64.78
31	Cyprus	64.73
32	Tajikistan	64.73
33	Turkey	64.38
34	Luxembourg	63.38
35	Azerbaijan	63.34
36	Georgia	63.28
37	Croatia	63.21
38	Slovenia	63.15
39	Uzbekistan	62.87
40	Hungary	62.65
41	North Macedonia	61.87
42	Serbia	61.12
43	Kazakhstan	61.06
44	Bulgaria	60.14
45	Montenegro	58.47
46	Albania	58.10
47	Turkmenistan	57.88

Sub-Saharan Arica (SSA)

Rank	Country	Score
1	Rwanda	69.92
2	Eswatini	69.56
3	Burundi	68.95
4	Madagascar	68.79
5	Kenya	68.77
6	Lesotho	68.77
7	Ethiopia	68.52
8	Malawi	68.26
9	Mauritius	66.45
10	Tanzania	66.24
11	Somalia	66.08
12	Uganda	65.73
13	Cote d'Ivoire	65.65
14	Sierra Leone	65.64
15	Dem. Rep. Congo	65.37
16	Namibia	65.31
17	Liberia	63.32
18	Guinea	63.3
19	Cabo Verde	63.22
20	Equatorial Guinea	63
21	Niger	62.27
22	Central African Republic	62.26

Table 4.29 (continued)

Sub-Saharan Arica (SSA)

Rank	Country	Score
23	Gabon	62.11
24	Cameroon	62.1
25	Benin	62.06
26	South Africa	61.97
27	Togo	61.79
28	Botswana	61.7
29	Sudan	61.61
30	Burkina Faso	61.5
31	Zambia	61.17
32	Ghana	61.12
33	Chad	60.64
34	Mali	60.5
35	Guinea-Bissau	60.4
36	Mozambique	59.63
37	Mauritania	58.14
38	Zimbabwe	58.05
39	Senegal	57.33
40	Nigeria	56.51
41	Seychelles	54.88

South Asia (SA)

Rank	Country	Score
1	Sri Lanka	68.24
2	Maldives	64.66
3	India	64.01
4	Pakistan	62.9
5	Bangladesh	61.7
6	Bhutan	61.23
7	Afghanistan	60
8	Nepal	59.68

Latin America and the Caribbean (LAC)

Rank	Country	Score
1	Mexico	70.55
2	Peru	70.28
3	Brazil	69.42
4	Ecuador	67.89
5	Chile	67.73
6	Cuba	67.39
7	Colombia	67.12
8	Uruguay	65.96
9	Costa Rica	65.91
10	Nicaragua	65.81
11	Panama	65.65
12	Argentina	65.35
13	Dominican Republic	65.26
14	Jamaica	65.21
15	Guatemala	65.15
16	Guyana	63.79

Table 4.29 (continued)

Latin America and the Caribbean (LAC)

Rank	Country	Score
17	El Salvador	62.61
18	Honduras	62.37
19	Belize	61.77
20	Barbados	61.47
21	Trinidad and Tobago	60.96
22	Paraguay	60.43
23	Bolivia	58.24

North America (NA)

Rank	Country	Score
1	United States	72.63
2	Canada	72.17

In the MAC component, the score in North America is significantly higher than in other regions, demonstrating that the governments take firm actions on climate change in this region (Figs. 4.33 and 4.34).

1. *East Asia and Pacific*

    A total of 21 countries/territories in this region were evaluated, with Australia scoring the highest score of 69.93 and ranking 15th in the world, and with Vanuatu at the bottom of the region. As a developing country, China ranks 21st in the world with a score of 69.12.

2. *Europe and Central Asia*

    Europe and Central Asia has eight countries/territories in the top 10 and 16 countries in the top 30, with a maximum score of 75.60 and a minimum score of 57.88. With more developed countries and a more advanced economy than the rest of the world, this region places more emphasis on developing climate policies, climate related education and research. Furthermore, Europe and Central Asia have a high level of public awareness of climate change.

3. *Latin America and the Caribbean*

    A total of 23 countries/territories in the region participated, with Mexico being the highest scorer in the region with a score of 70.55 and ranking 11th in the world, while the lowest score in the region is Bolivia with 58.24, ranking 147th in the world.

4. *Middle East and North Africa*

    There are 18 countries/territories evaluated in the Middle East and North Africa region, with the highest score of 65.53 from Israel ranking 65th in the world and the lowest score of 49.16 from Qatar ranking 160th in the world.

5. *North America*

    The United States scores 72.63, ranking 4th in the world, while Canada scores 72.17, ranking 6th in the world. North American countries are among the leading developed countries in the world, both in terms of research, education, and economic investment.

6. *South Asia*

    Eight countries/territories in the region were evaluated, with the highest scoring country being Sri Lanka, ranking 35th in the world and scoring 68.24, and the lowest scoring country being Nepal, ranking 143rd in the world.

7. *Sub-Saharan Africa*

    A total of 41 countries/territories in the region were evaluated, with the highest scoring country being Rwanda at 69.92, ranking 16th in the world. The lowest score in the region is 54.88 from Seychelles. Of the territories in this region, most of them score poorly. The main reason may be that the region has the largest number of developing countries, many of whom have large poor performance in economic, scientific, and technological aspects compared to other regions. There is still much room for improvement in various areas such as climate change policies and education.

7.6 Key Findings

The GOHI-CC 2022 global report analyses and discusses 30 indicators related to climate change and its related population health, drawing the following key conclusions.

Climate Change Exacerbates Health Impacts

The indicators of climate change risks demonstrate that no country is immune to the health

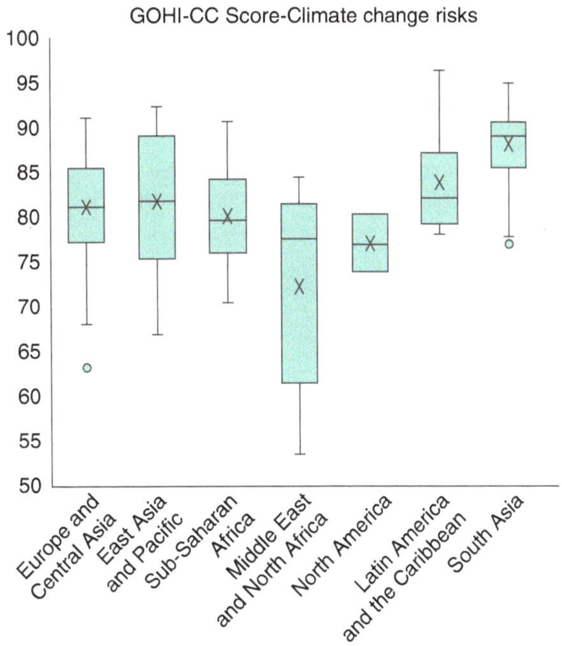

Fig. 4.33 Regional score distribution of Climate change risks by seven regions

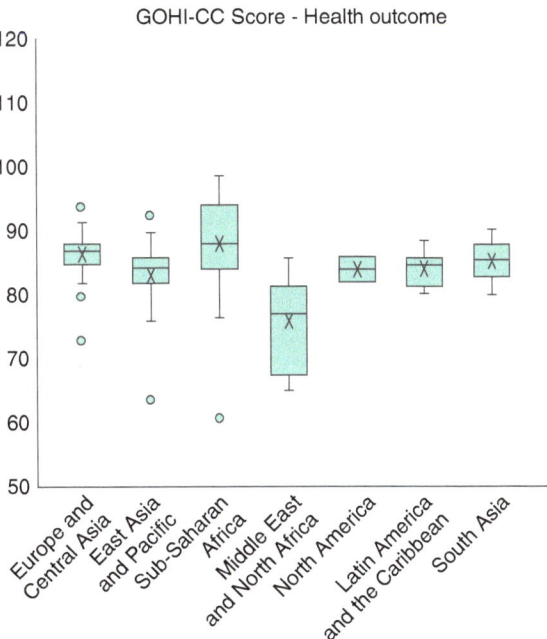

Fig. 4.34 Regional score distribution of Health outcome by seven regions

impacts of climate change. Climate change is likely to exacerbate existing health inequalities, both within and between countries, leading to disproportionate health burdens on marginalized populations. Climate change impacts are expected to worsen existing health disparities within countries. GOHI-CC shows that countries in tropical regions and coastal regions are experiencing higher climate risks, such as Senegal (57.33), South Africa (61.97), Benin (62.06), and Gabon (62.11). While efforts made in response to the concerns of climate change, these climate-related risks frequently have serious negative health effects. People living in urban heat islands,

Fig. 4.35 Regional score distribution of Mitigation and adaptation capacity by seven regions

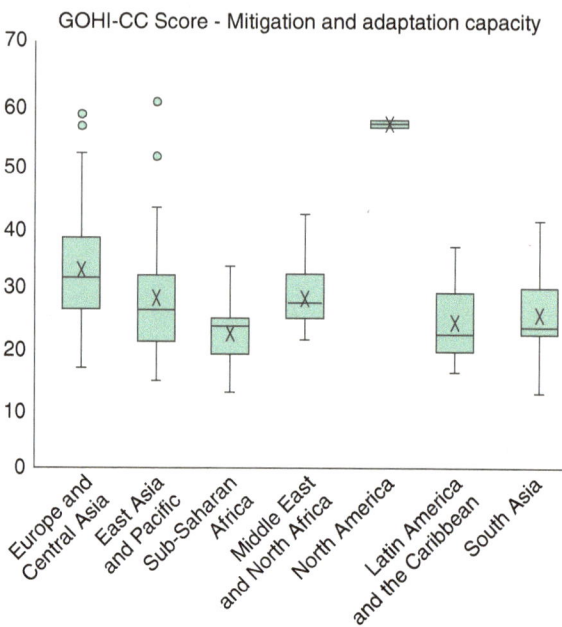

where temperatures are higher due to the concentration of buildings and infrastructure, may face increased risks of heat-related illnesses, such as heatstroke and dehydration. People in lower-income neighborhoods may have less access to air conditioning, green spaces, and other heat-mitigation measures, leading to higher vulnerability to heat-related health risks compared to wealthier areas. Moreover, climate change can disrupt livelihoods, particularly those dependent on agriculture, fisheries, and other climate-sensitive sectors. This can lead to loss of income, food insecurity, and malnutrition, which disproportionately affect marginalized populations, including smallholder farmers, indigenous communities, and coastal communities. These disruptions can have significant impacts on physical and mental health, leading to increased risks of undernutrition, mental health disorders, and other health issues (Fig. 4.35).

Mitigation and Adaptation to Address Impacts of Climate Change

GOHI-CC scores vary widely, not only by region, but also by category. The average score of Mitigation and adaptation capacity (28.24) is much lower than that of Climate change risks (80.87) and Health outcome (85.40), showing that

more efforts need to be done to combat climate change and the government is not doing enough to develop policies, laws, research, and response measures. Even so, developed countries in North American (72.38) and Europe and Central Asia (64.91) perform better than other developing countries, which is related to the level of government attention. Figure 4.29 shows a positive correlation between GOHI-CC scores and national development levels, indicating wealthier countries located in Europe and North America make more efforts on climate change mitigation.

Climate change caused by greenhouse gas emissions has a strong lag. Even if all greenhouse gas emissions were stopped now, global warming would still affect future generations. Therefore, mitigation and adaptation are the two main directions that we should take to address climate change.

Mitigation refers to stabilizing the level of greenhouse gases in the atmosphere by reducing emissions of greenhouse gases such as carbon dioxide or increasing carbon storage by enhancing carbon sequestration [93]. Ways to reduce emissions include reducing the burning of fossil fuels such as coal, oil, and natural gas and using clean energy sources such as wind, water, and solar power. On the other hand, ways to increase carbon storage refer to enhancing forest areas, improving the carbon sequestration capacity of oceans and soils, and storing atmospheric carbon dioxide as organic matter.

Adaptation means anticipating trends in climate change and taking action to reduce potential adverse impacts [93]. Countries should assess the potential health impacts of climate change and develop adaptation plans that are incorporated into national adaptation plans in the United Nations Framework Convention on Climate Change (UNFCCC). Countries should also develop closely linked health systems and systems for monitoring and controlling human-animal diseases. For example, in 2015, WHO proposed the Operational Framework for building Climate-Resilient Health System, which set out ten specific elements of climate resilience and integrates them into the six existing modules of the WHO Health Systems Framework. Strong and close intersectoral alignment makes the various health-related elements more resilient to changing climate conditions and promotes health.

In addition, global cooperation is essential. It is a great opportunity to foster multisectoral collaborations and partnerships to address the complex challenges posed by climate change and its impacts on health, including engagement with climate, health, and policy stakeholders at national and international levels.

Restructuring Energy Use

Global national energy use needs focus and continued restructuring. The GOHI-CC report analyses the clean energy use levels of countries from global energy use indicator data, and finds that the restructuring of energy use needs to be reformed, especially the countries in Asia and Africa with lower than 50 scores, such as the United Arab Emirates (31.78) and Kuwait (37.98). It is recommended that national-level consideration should be given to focusing on the development of clean energy sources such as nuclear power, hydropower and other non-fossil energy sources, including wind, solar, and biomass. In addition, national governments need to develop national energy development plans, promote the construction of national energy bases, and accelerate the construction of large wind power bases and solar photovoltaic power bases. By prioritizing increased health-friendly investments such as renewable energy, clean transport, and other alternatives to fossil fuel dependency, there will be a significant impact on the process of controlling climate change in the future, thereby realizing the health synergies of carbon reduction.

In conclusion, our earth is entering an era in which we must adapt to climate change. Instead of waiting passively, countries need to take strong and proactive action to build resilient socio-economic patterns that reduce the vulnerability of human and natural systems to climate impacts. For a sustainable future, policymakers of all nations around the world must to demonstrate extraordinary political in the interests of humanity.

The global One Health index (GOHI) study provides an extensive assessment of health interrelations among humans, animals, and the environment. Globally, the average GOHI score is 54.82, signaling substantial room for improvement. The study reveals marked disparities in GOHI scores across various regions and countries, suggesting uneven performances in managing health issues in the interface of human, animal and ecosystem. In examining specific nations, Oman's commendable efforts in animal and environmental health contrast its human health performance, while Singapore excels in human health but lags in environmental health. Among the GOHI-Governance indicators, consensus-oriented methods score highest, but the formation of specialized One Health associations is lacking. The GOHI-Zoonoses score is notable, but the route of transmission indicator highlights weaknesses in managing zoonotic disease pathways. These findings underscore the need for robust international cooperation, enhanced data sharing mechanisms, and the translation of One Health research into actionable policies. The study's limitations include potential data collection biases and the need for further validation of the GOHI framework.

1 Key Findings of GOHI

1.1 Improvement Needs of the GOHI Scores

The analysis indicates considerable potential for improvement in the GOHI scores across the board. The worldwide average for the GOHI stands at 54.82, with the external drivers index (EDI), intrinsic drivers index (IDI), and core drivers index (CDI) presenting averages of 46.57, 58.01, and 57.25, respectively. These figures underscore a deviation of more than 40 points from the ideal benchmarks. Within the scope of our study, encompassing 160 nations, not a single country achieves top marks across all facets of the CDI. Even the United States, which leads with a composite score of 70.61, falls short of the ideal by 30 points. On the lower end, Guinea-Bissau is positioned at 160th place, with a score of 39.03—indicating a further deficit of 31.58 points from the bottom ranker. Moreover, the peak scores across five dimensions within the CDI fail to breach the 85.00 mark.

1.2   Disparities of GOHI Scores Among Regions and Countries

The GOHI scores exhibit significant disparities, reflecting a wide spectrum of health outcomes across various regions and countries. The range of scores per region, ordered from highest to lowest, places North America (62.94–66.65) at the forefront, followed by Europe and Central Asia (45.50–66.75), Latin America and the Caribbean (42.31–59.26), South Asia (41.00–55.33), Middle East and North Africa (38.61–55.39), East Asia and Pacific (38.34–64.04), and finally, Sub-Saharan Africa (36.53–52.05). This segmentation highlights the significant variation in health governance, resources, and outcomes globally, pointing to the need for targeted improvements and strategic interventions in underperforming areas.

The scores of each country/territory range from 39.03 to 70.61. The scores of the GOHI-EDI (32.83–50.28), GOHI-Governance (26.75–80.52), GOHI-Zoonoses (43.01–84.86), GOHI-FS (24.84–73.09) and GOHI-AMR (14.75–81.43) in different countries/territories span a wide range.

Each region has top-ranked countries. For example, South Africa in sub-Saharan Africa ranks 12th globally with a GOHI-Zoonoses score of 80.51. However, the average GOHI-Zoonoses score for sub-Saharan Africa is only 59.59. Similarly, Argentina and Mexico are the only two Latin American and Caribbean countries in the top 10, with both scoring 87.50, significantly above the average score of this region (68.43). These disparities highlight the unbalanced GOHI-Zoonoses scores within regions, indicating considerable gaps in the performance against zoonotic diseases between neighbors.

1.3   Unbalanced GOHI-IDI in Different Fields and Countries

The GOHI-IDI showcases an imbalance in the performance across human health, animal health, and environmental health, even among the highest-ranking countries. For instance, within the GOHI-IDI, Oman is positioned as the second highest in the Middle East and North Africa, thanks to its strong performance in animal health and environmental health. This success is largely attributed to the government's commitment to environmental conservation, which has been instrumental in preserving its natural ecosystems. Oman is renowned for its conservation efforts, particularly in safeguarding habitats for turtles and birds, as well as its designated protected areas. Despite these achievements, the country's human health indicators lag behind, potentially due to insufficient healthcare spending.

1.4   Big Variations of GOHI-Governance

Among the GOHI-Governance indicators, those pertaining to consensus-oriented achievements score the highest. On the other hand, within the subset of indicators (sub-I-indicators), the ones related to One Health association scores are the lowest. The consensus-oriented indicator excels in average scores, with merely 9 countries, or 5.63%, registering scores below 30.00. This demonstrates that a majority of nations around the globe show strong performance in achieving consensus and orientation, signifying a worldwide agreement on One Health governance and a collective readiness to enhance it. Conversely, among the Participation sub-I-indicators, the One Health association indicator records the lowest average score at 28.61. This underscores a prevalent challenge in forming specialized entities designed to bolster One Health governance capabilities.

1.5   Lowest Score of Transmission Route Reflected in the GOHI-Zoonoses Scores

The GOHI-Zoonoses indicator emerges as the most outstanding among the five principal indicators of the CDI, underscoring the global commitment to managing zoonotic diseases as recognized by communities worldwide and United Nations members. Nevertheless, within this commendation, the Route of transmission

(RT) indicator reveals a gap, with a lower average score of 59.30 compared to its counterparts. This discrepancy highlights the existing challenges in curtailing zoonotic diseases by addressing their transmission pathways.

Delving deeper, the sub-indicators under RT, namely Conventional intervention (CI) and Ecological interventions (ECI), present average scores of 46.48 and 69.84, respectively. The CI's relatively lower score points to a deficiency in laboratory testing for zoonotic disease reservoirs, suggesting a critical area for improvement. Additionally, the distribution of scores reveals regional disparities, with 45.3% of countries scoring below the CI average located in sub-Saharan Africa, followed by 31.25% in both Latin America and the Caribbean and the Middle East and North Africa. These figures underscore the urgent need for these regions to enhance their capabilities in detecting and managing zoonotic diseases.

1.6 Low Performance of Government Support and Response in the GOHI-FS Scores

The GOHI-FS assessment reveals that the weakest link among its five indicators is Government support and response, averaging a score of 16.84. This significantly affects the overall GOHI-FS average score of 52.89. The underperformance in this area highlights potential gaps in governmental actions toward food security, suggesting a need for a more integrated One Health approach. The low scoring may also be partly due to incomplete data, indicating a further need for comprehensive data collection and analysis.

1.7 Weakness in Antimicrobial Resistance (AMR) Surveillance and Control in GOHI-AMR

The GOHI-AMR scores underscore global shortcomings in AMR surveillance and control. Among the five indicators of GOHI-AMR, the AMR surveillance system and AMR rate on

essential antibiotics are notably lower, with median scores of 32.61 and 31.62, respectively. These figures are over 10 points below the global median of 43.09, pointing to significant areas for global health improvement in monitoring and managing AMR.

1.8 More Efforts in Mitigation and Adaptation to Climate Change Worldwide

There is a pressing need for increased mitigation and adaptation efforts in response to climate change, especially in tropical and coastal regions facing higher climate risks. The Mitigation and adaptation capacity score (28.24) is significantly lower than those for Climate change risks (80.87) and Health outcome (85.40), indicating a gap in effective governmental policies, legal frameworks, research, and response actions. Despite this, high-income countries in North America (72.38) and Europe and Central Asia (64.91) show better performance, reflecting a stronger commitment to addressing climate change issues compared to lower-income counterparts. This disparity underscores the necessity for a global, concerted effort in climate change mitigation and adaptation strategies.

2 Policy Recommendations from GOHI

2.1 Policy Recommendations to UN Agencies

Improving International Cooperation Between South-South and South-North Countries Through Intradisciplinary, Multisectoral, and Interregional Cooperation by Establishment of One Health Networks or Partnerships

The COVID-19 pandemic has underscored the vital importance of global cooperation in tackling health crises. No nation can effectively combat such challenges in isolation.

In our analysis, it was observed that low- and middle-income nations within Latin America and the Caribbean experienced suboptimal vaccination rates. The notable success of the COVID-19 Vaccine Global Access (COVAX) initiative serves as a valuable lesson, emphasizing the importance of collaboration among national leaders and international entities to address vaccine scarcities for zoonotic diseases. Spearheaded by the Coalition for Epidemic Preparedness Innovations (CEPI), Gavi, WHO, and with the United Nations International Children's Emergency Fund (UNICEF) playing a crucial role in implementation, COVAX aimed to accelerate the development and equitable distribution of COVID-19 vaccines globally. Through this initiative, numerous low- and middle-income countries gained timely access to vaccines, benefiting from both financial aid and technical support. This model suggests a feasible approach to enhancing vaccination efforts against other zoonotic diseases in similar economic contexts.

Another instance is global climate change and air quality, which are pressing problems. The countries that emit the most greenhouse gases are not necessarily the most affected. Climate change has a significant impact on all creatures worldwide, calling for close collaboration among all countries. Unfortunately, many underdeveloped regions face extreme climate impacts and numerous socioeconomic challenges, requiring financial assistance and technical guidance from developed entities.

Hence, there is a pressing need to bolster the science-policy-implementation nexus within the One Health framework to promote and improve the collaborative exchange of scientific knowledge, methodologies, and practices across countries. Building global One Health capabilities demands an international cooperation framework, encouraging widespread sharing of information and experiences on mutual concerns. Specifically, on critical issues, leading regions are urged to extend support to those in need by contributing resources, deploying experts, and initiating pilot projects, thereby expediting the formulation of a unified global strategy to tackle One Health challenges.

There is a need to remove obstacles in governance that hinder the effective implementation of the One Health approach. Strengthening communication, coordination, collaboration, and capacity development [94] is crucial in reformulating both national and international strategies.

Improving the Data Sharing Mechanism of One Health at the Global Level

Our research indicates a widespread shortfall in data transparency across numerous nations, with essential indicators for global One Health governance often missing or obscured. The scarcity of data sources for assessing animal health in the GOHI-IDI necessitated the limitation of our final analysis to only 160 of the 220 countries and territories. Furthermore, the evaluation of the GOHI-FS was hindered by restricted access to animal and environmental data, resulting in lower scores in the E.5 dimension and a 20.20% rate of missing values across all indicators. For the GOHI-AMR, although data were sourced from systems like GLASS, EARS-Net, and CARSS, the issue of missing data remains prominent, with over 50.00% of data points missing.

Data infrastructure plays a crucial role in the effective governance and monitoring of One Health. The development of data platforms is crucial for the real-time tracking of progress and advancements in global One Health issues. However, data barriers and gaps in many countries complicate cooperation efforts. The absence of precise and current data challenges policymakers in evaluating the status quo, pinpointing areas for improvement, and enacting efficient policies and initiatives. Governments and stakeholders are urged to enhance data sharing related to food security to bolster transparency, coordination, and cooperation among various entities. This might entail the creation of secure data exchange mechanisms, such as agreements or platforms designed to facilitate data sharing within the scope of One Health initiatives.

International organizations are encouraged to collaborate with countries to improve the transparency, accessibility, and integration of global One Health governance data. The establishment of a high-level, intersectoral database, underpinned by exhaustive surveillance, is recommended. Augmenting animal and environmental surveillance systems and fostering standardized, transparent data sharing will be instrumental in swiftly addressing zoonotic diseases, natural disasters, and other urgent situations.

Promoting the One Health Concept by Integrating the One Health Approach into Global Governance and Setting a High-Level Agenda with One Health

The international consensus on the importance of One Health governance is growing year after year, with the United Nations releasing Sustainable Development Goals (SDGs) in 2015. In 2022, the OHHLEP [25] established by the FAO-WHO-UNEP-WOAH Quadripartite released the One Health Joint Plan of Action (OH JPA), which provides a clear roadmap and shared vision for One Health.

Although recent initiatives and studies on One Health have focused primarily on the interfaces of human-animal-environmental health, they have overlooked the wide-ranging aspects of One Health. Therefore, a robust, coordinated One Health governance structure, featuring high-level leadership and accountable functions and policies, is essential. This structure should foster collaboration across various sectors and disciplines [95]. The coordinated mechanism for One Health in the global health governance process should have enhanced leadership to reinforce the practical application of the concept of One Health and emphasize the collaborative role of multiple disciplines and sectors. Prioritizing actions that align with political will, inter-sector governance, and regulatory frameworks as advised by the One Health High-Level Expert Panel (OHHLEP) is critical to achieving a unified One Health vision globally.

Integrating One Health Implementation into Regional Coordination System

The spread of zoonoses knows no national boundaries, making collaboration and exchange among countries crucial to improve the efficiency of prevention and control. Implementing existing global strategies on zoonoses and ensuring synergy and cohesiveness at a global, regional, and national level are of great value. For example, while the overall performance of the sub-Saharan African region was poor, South Africa, also located in sub-Saharan Africa, performed excellently. South Africa's experience and technology exchange against zoonotic events can be observed by other countries in the region, demonstrating the potential of cooperation at the regional and national levels.

The FAO-WHO-UNEP-WOAH Quadripartite has cooperated with the One Health Group of Friends that composed of Member States, to advocate for the One Health approach in political and global agendas. One Health is positioned as a guiding principle in the intergovernmental negotiating body (INB) process and Pandemic instrument. The Quadripartite has planned the Asia-Pacific Regional Quadripartite Coordination Group to provide full-time attention to One Health coordination at the regional and country levels, along with the Regional Platform Working Groups' efforts on One Health tools, zoonotic influenza, rabies, AMR, and food safety.

To ensure a sustainable cooperative network, it is essential to engage as many stakeholders as possible, including international organizations, nongovernmental organizations (NGOs), civil society organizations (CSOs), the private sector, and academia. At present, it is necessary to promote intergovernmental dialogue actively to build long-term financing mechanisms, establish early global warning and response mechanisms, and develop a coordinated regional One Health system.

2.2 Policy Recommendations to Country Government

Translation of One Health Research into Policy and Practice at Various Levels

The One Health governance framework has evolved, yet the absence of effective governance mechanisms remains a significant hurdle [96]. Few countries have dedicated agencies for One Health coordination, leading to fragmentation.

Therefore, a global, cross-departmental, and multidisciplinary collaboration platform is suggested to integrate human, animal, and environmental health.

Local authorities and stakeholders must break down barriers of regionalism and departmentalism, fostering cross-sector, cross-discipline, and cross-regional cooperation. Sustainable investments and the enhancement of implementation mechanisms are required, alongside improving communication among stakeholders [97].

Countries can use the results and key findings of the GOHI to identify their strengths and weaknesses, continue to develop in areas they excel at, and develop plans to address their weaknesses to achieve balanced global One Health governance.

Strengthen the Governance Capacity on One Health with Emphasis on Synchronous Development, Joint Action on Health Improvement, and Upstream Prevention Action to Improve the Holistic Health of Humans, Animals, and the Environment

The GOHI-IDI score highlights that the IDI performance varies greatly among different countries and regions, as well as among the indicators of human, animal, and environmental health. Therefore, prioritizing the One Health concept, which focuses on ensuring the healthy and balanced development of people, animals, and the environment, is crucial for global health governance. Developed countries generally have higher IDI scores and higher IDI-human health scores, with more attention given to human health, resulting in better overall outcomes, while relatively less attention is given to animal and environmental health. To minimize the impact on human health, countries should prioritize animal, environmental, and climate issues. In countries with low IDI scores, resources are often scarce, resulting in insufficient attention given to human, animal, and environmental health. Hence, it is crucial to coordinate and collaborate with countries with high IDI scores to develop effective human health governance while also promoting

the development of animal and environmental health.

Our findings highlight weak sanitation and insufficient management and control of infectious agents in low- and middle-income countries. Some countries still engage in deforestation, wild animal trapping, and bushmeat trade, which not only leads to direct contact between humans and wild animals but also destroys animal habitats, making it easier for zoonotic diseases to be transmitted to humans [98]. Therefore, these countries should improve relevant laws and regulations to protect the ecological environment, strengthen law enforcement, reduce illegal logging, protect the ecological environment, and reduce ecological and environmental risk factors related to zoonotic diseases. In addition, countries should increase the construction of basic medical and health facilities, rationally allocate health resources, improve the living environment of the masses, and reduce the social risk factors of zoonotic diseases. Upstream prevention aims to reduce the occurrence and spread of zoonotic diseases and reduce the risk at the source by controlling the risk factors of society and the natural environment [99].

Strengthening Technology Innovation in Laboratory Detection, Epidemiological Surveillance, Monitoring, and Evaluation

The global zoonotic pathogen detection score is only 46.48, making it urgent for countries to strengthen their laboratory capacity to detect zoonotic pathogens. The lack of sustainable funding is the biggest challenge for zoonotic disease testing in wildlife [100]. Inadequate laboratory capacity, insufficient human resources, and limited cross-sectoral coordination also contribute to poor zoonotic laboratory testing capacity [100]. To improve the detection capacity of zoonotic pathogens, especially in grassroots health facilities, governments need to strengthen the skills training for health personnel in grassroots health facilities and maintain laboratory instruments. To improve the efficiency of testing, cross-sectoral collaboration should be developed, involving laboratory scientists, diagnosticians, and wildlife specialists in the conception and laboratory program design stages [101].

2.3 Policy Recommendations to Community

Improving the Community-Based Strategies to Improve the Public Awareness of One Health and Efficiency of Actions

Based on our findings, the average score for Improving awareness and understanding of AMR is 48.09, which leaves room for improvement. Community hospitals can play a vital role in promoting science and increasing public awareness and understanding of AMR. This can improve cooperation with the government and relevant departments, both to achieve comprehensive supervision at all levels, and also improve public feedback, resulting in improved AMR governance.

While One Health needs widespread social engagement, many countries lack comprehensive One Health educational initiatives. However, models like the Fukuoka Health Action Plan and China's "Healthy China 2030" strategy can serve as references enhancing, public awareness and establishing effective health education channels.

Community participation in the governance of health services is an essential component for engaging stakeholders. In the United States, Minnesota has implemented a zoonoses education campaign for youth that has improved stakeholder relationships and strengthened responses to major public health and animal health issues. This was achieved through collaboration between the government and NGOs, involving the state Department of Health and others [102]. Through community-based governance strategies, it is possible to engage more partners and promote an equitable distribution of resources among regions, making the strategies more adaptive and sustainable. These provide the initial foundation for mobilizing a One Health society.

Improving Capacity Building on Designing, Implementation, and Evaluation at Local Settings

To address disparities in One Health issues, it is important to recognize the complex interplay between human, animal, and environmental health. The One Health approach emphasizes the need for collaboration among various sectors and stakeholders to identify and address underlying issues that contribute to health outcomes. However, to effectively implement the One Health approach, there is a need for capacity-building efforts to enhance the skills, knowledge, and resources of individuals and institutions involved.

Capacity-building efforts can focus on enhancing the skills and knowledge of health professionals, veterinarians, food scientists, and other relevant stakeholders on the principles and practices of One Health. This can involve developing training programs and workshops that promote interdisciplinary collaboration, data sharing, and evidence-based decision-making. By equipping these stakeholders with the necessary skills and knowledge, they can work together to identify and address the underlying factors that contribute to health outcomes.

Furthermore, capacity-building efforts can focus on strengthening institutional and policy frameworks that promote One Health. This can involve supporting the development of regulations, policies, and programs that promote sustainable food production, processing, and distribution, support small-scale farmers, and enhance access to healthcare services, clean water, and sanitation. By strengthening the institutional and policy frameworks, stakeholders can work together to address the root causes of disparities in food safety and nutrition.

It is also crucial to consider different cultural contexts and economic realities when organizing key events, meetings, and consultations. Governments should adapt their strategies to local socioeconomic and cultural contexts. This is particularly important in addressing unique challenges in rural and urban settings. For instance, in some rural areas, zoonotic diseases and AMR are more prominent, while urban areas face more challenges in addressing air pollution and food safety. The feasibility and cost-effectiveness of One Health strategies should be evaluated, especially in rural and resource-limited areas [103]. Innovative financial mechanisms should be employed to reconcile stakeholder conflicts. The complexity of eco-environmental changes continues to pose challenges to One Health development, both domestically and globally.

3   Limitations

There are several limitations of our study. Firstly, we primarily utilized global official data that is publicly accessible for GOHI, ensuring data validity. However, this approach may have omitted certain indicators. Critical indicators like animal disease rates, burden, and vaccine use were excluded due to data unavailability. Additionally, our data search, primarily in English and French, might introduce a bias in the selection process.

Secondly, the experts on our advisory committee, as shown in Table 2.1, are predominantly from China, potentially affecting the global representation of the committee. Yet, our team comprises experts from international bodies and institutions outside China, and we have interviewed several UN agency experts, adding an international dimension to our research. Moving forward, we plan to involve more international experts in GOHI to enhance the committee's global diversity.

Thirdly, the initial validation of GOHI is an early stage, serving as a case study for potential uses. The current GOHI model requires thorough validation. For instance, we might develop a consensus parameter through data modeling to assess the correlation between GOHI scores and existing literature on One Health.

Moreover, in subsequent studies, we aim to delve deeper into data mining and expand mathematical models using the GOHI framework and database. This will allow us to evaluate the effectiveness of the One Health approach in real-world scenarios, such as zoonosis control, and determine the extent to which it achieves a Pareto improvement in the combined welfare of human, animal, and environmental systems.

Appendix

Country Profile

United States of America
North America | High income

Index Score **001**/160 — 70.61

Global average: 54.82

Regional average: 69.11

Income group average: 61.66

Country performance: 70.61

Missing rate in GOHI database: 15.90%

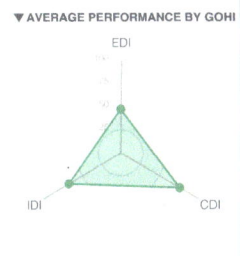

▼ AVERAGE PERFORMANCE BY GOHI

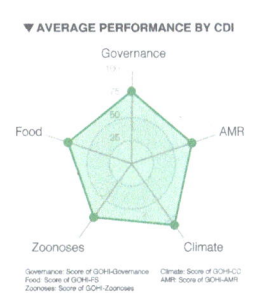

▼ AVERAGE PERFORMANCE BY CDI

Governance: Score of GOHI-Governance   Climate: Score of GOHI-CC
Food: Score of GOHI-FS   AMR: Score of GOHI-AMR
Zoonoses: Score of GOHI-Zoonoses

	Country Score	Global Average
A External drivers index	47.82	40.45
A1 Earth system	66.44	56.21
A1.1 Land	25.92	36.41
A1.2 Forest	50.34	43.43
A1.3 Water	95.17	58.09
A1.4 Air	79.80	71.93
A1.5 Natural disasters	66.25	64.65
A2 Institutional system	58.25	46.01
A2.1 Justice	70.00	57.89
A2.2 Governance	48.24	35.58
A3 Economical system	32.17	24.62
A3.1 Finance	53.83	34.35
A3.2 Work	39.05	38.58
A4 Sociological system	42.53	37.70
A4.1 Demographic	44.79	46.31
A4.2 Education	39.06	28.26
A4.3 Inequalities	44.50	40.28
A5 Technological system	39.70	37.72
A5.1 Transport	13.55	6.54
A5.2 Technology adoption	53.52	41.23
A5.3 Consumption and production	49.31	62.53
B Intrinsic drivers index	67.40	58.01
B1 Human health	79.76	72.35
B1.1 Health coverage	83.81	58.65
B1.2 Diseases burden	72.46	79.83
B1.3 Injury and violence	85.43	80.75
B2 Animal health and ecosystem diversity	51.51	56.58
B2.1 Animal epidemic disease	85.92	94.57
B2.2 Wildlife and marine life biodiversity	17.10	18.59
B3 Environmental health	72.97	46.87
B3.1 Air quality and climate change	77.52	53.72
B3.2 Environmental biodiversity	52.55	44.05
B3.3 Environmental resources	91.04	44.25

	Country Score	Global Average
C Core drivers index	76.44	57.25
C1 Governance	78.81	56.51
C1.1 Participation	94.82	41.70
C1.3 Transparency	77.17	65.15
C1.4 Responsiveness	70.85	44.42
C1.5 Consensus oriented	98.37	86.45
C1.6 Equity and inclusiveness	91.22	73.61
C1.7 Effectiveness and efficiency	42.27	28.38
C1.8 Political support	76.96	55.89
C2 Zoonotic diseases	83.27	68.06
C2.1 Source of infection	96.94	69.22
C2.2 Route of transmission	72.61	59.30
C2.3 Targeted population	76.10	59.90
C2.4 Capacity building	86.38	72.85
C2.5 Case studies	85.26	85.89
C3 Food security	72.34	52.89
C3.1 Food demand and supply	65.38	59.53
C3.2 Food safety	85.06	69.36
C3.3 Nutrition	89.50	67.17
C3.4 Natural and social circumstances	73.55	51.54
C3.5 Government support and response	48.19	16.85
C4 Antimicrobial resistance	74.63	44.05
C4.1 AMR surveillance system	67.76	34.79
C4.2 AMR laboratory network and coordination on capacity	86.89	55.57
C4.3 Antimicrobial control and optimization	79.86	48.76
C4.4 Improve awareness and understanding	96.88	48.09
C4.5 Antimicrobial resistance rate for important antibiotics	41.76	33.03
C5 Climate change	72.63	64.19
C5.1 Mitigation and adaptation capacity	56.97	28.24
C5.2 Climate change risks	80.64	80.87
C5.3 Health outcome	82.47	85.41

Scores are normalized (0-100, where 100 = most favorable)

© The Editor(s) (if applicable) and The Author(s) 2025
X.-N. Zhou et al. (eds.), *Global One Health Index Report 2022*,
https://doi.org/10.1007/978-981-97-4824-2

United Kingdom
Europe & Central Asia | High income

Index Score 002/160

Global average: 54.82

Regional average: 60.26

Income group average: 61.66

Country performance: 69.90

Missing rate in GOHI database: 14.50%

▼ AVERAGE PERFORMANCE BY GOHI

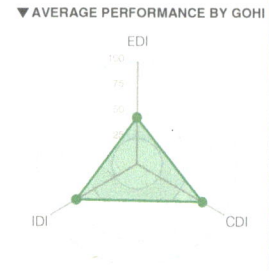

▼ AVERAGE PERFORMANCE BY CDI

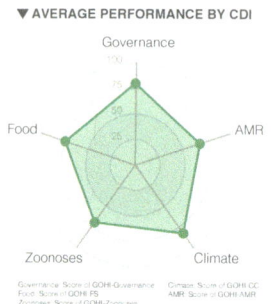

	Country Score	Global Average
A External drivers index	45.45	40.45
A1 Earth system	59.99	56.21
A1.1 Land	34.30	36.41
A1.2 Forest	38.48	43.43
A1.3 Water	65.35	58.09
A1.4 Air	84.92	71.93
A1.5 Natural disasters	66.67	64.65
A2 Institutional system	58.19	46.01
A2.1 Justice	67.48	57.89
A2.2 Governance	50.28	35.58
A3 Economical system	26.75	24.62
A3.1 Finance	40.24	34.35
A3.2 Work	38.20	38.58
A4 Sociological system	39.62	37.70
A4.1 Demographic	40.63	46.31
A4.2 Education	33.99	28.26
A4.3 Inequalities	45.86	40.28
A5 Technological system	42.70	37.72
A5.1 Transport	11.69	6.54
A5.2 Technology adoption	50.40	41.23
A5.3 Consumption and production	63.06	62.53
B Intrinsic drivers index	70.55	58.01
B1 Human health	86.09	72.35
B1.1 Health coverage	87.35	58.65
B1.2 Diseases burden	77.69	79.83
B1.3 Injury and violence	95.84	80.75
B2 Animal health and ecosystem diversity	53.73	56.58
B2.1 Animal epidemic disease	96.96	94.57
B2.2 Wildlife and marine life biodiversity	10.50	18.59
B3 Environmental health	73.95	46.87
B3.1 Air quality and climate change	70.85	53.72
B3.2 Environmental biodiversity	90.15	44.05
B3.3 Environmental resources	63.10	44.25

	Country Score	Global Average
C Core drivers index	75.18	57.25
C1 Governance	79.95	56.51
C1.1 Participation	88.57	41.70
C1.3 Transparency	83.20	65.15
C1.4 Responsiveness	83.35	44.42
C1.5 Consensus oriented	89.67	86.45
C1.6 Equity and inclusiveness	98.04	73.61
C1.7 Effectiveness and efficiency	41.87	28.38
C1.8 Political support	74.94	55.89
C2 Zoonotic diseases	82.67	68.06
C2.1 Source of infection	95.96	69.22
C2.2 Route of transmission	74.58	59.30
C2.3 Targeted population	73.78	59.90
C2.4 Capacity building	83.97	72.85
C2.5 Case studies	85.14	85.89
C3 Food security	68.42	52.89
C3.1 Food demand and supply	76.17	59.53
C3.2 Food safety	87.20	69.36
C3.3 Nutrition	85.14	67.17
C3.4 Natural and social circumstances	56.49	51.54
C3.5 Government support and response	37.08	16.85
C4 Antimicrobial resistance	74.48	44.05
C4.1 AMR surveillance system	87.90	34.79
C4.2 AMR laboratory network and coordination capacity	80.39	55.57
C4.3 Antimicrobial control and optimization	76.95	48.76
C4.4 Improve awareness and understanding	75.00	48.09
C4.5 Antimicrobial resistance rate for important antibiotics	52.17	33.03
C5 Climate change	69.80	64.19
C5.1 Mitigation and adaptation capacity	39.02	28.24
C5.2 Climate change risks	87.22	80.87
C5.3 Health outcome	85.28	85.41

Scores are normalized (0-100, where 100 = most favorable)

Australia

East Asia & Pacific | High income

Index
Score **003**/160

Global average: 54.82

Regional average: 56.52

Income group average: 61.66

Country performance: 69.30

Missing rate in GOHI database: 9.40%

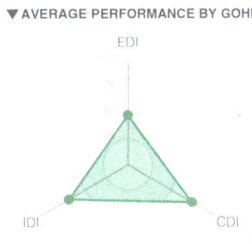

▼ AVERAGE PERFORMANCE BY GOHI

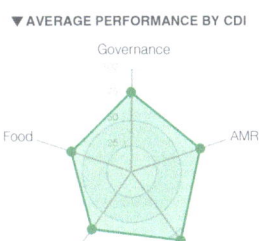

▼ AVERAGE PERFORMANCE BY CDI

	Country Score	Global Average
A External drivers index	48.64	40.45
A1 Earth system	70.74	56.21
A1.1 Land	99.37	36.41
A1.2 Forest	49.01	43.43
A1.3 Water	74.08	58.09
A1.4 Air	60.66	71.93
A1.5 Natural disasters	66.53	64.65
A2 Institutional system	63.08	46.01
A2.1 Justice	75.92	57.89
A2.2 Governance	52.13	35.58
A3 Economical system	28.68	24.62
A3.1 Finance	43.75	34.35
A3.2 Work	40.18	38.58
A4 Sociological system	39.15	37.70
A4.1 Demographic	40.63	46.31
A4.2 Education	30.16	28.26
A4.3 Inequalities	49.25	40.28
A5 Technological system	41.56	37.72
A5.1 Transport	19.94	6.54
A5.2 Technology adoption	52.33	41.23
A5.3 Consumption and production	50.16	62.53
B Intrinsic drivers index	68.21	58.01
B1 Human health	87.91	72.35
B1.1 Health coverage	88.13	58.65
B1.2 Diseases burden	82.94	79.83
B1.3 Injury and violence	95.32	80.75
B2 Animal health and ecosystem diversity	55.95	56.58
B2.1 Animal epidemic disease	95.11	94.57
B2.2 Wildlife and marine life biodiversity	16.80	18.59
B3 Environmental health	62.84	46.87
B3.1 Air quality and climate change	56.53	53.72
B3.2 Environmental biodiversity	51.10	44.05
B3.3 Environmental resources	82.80	44.25

	Country Score	Global Average
C Core drivers index	74.15	57.25
C1 Governance	77.97	56.51
C1.1 Participation	88.64	41.70
C1.3 Transparency	88.20	65.15
C1.4 Responsiveness	66.65	44.42
C1.5 Consensus oriented	88.12	86.45
C1.6 Equity and inclusiveness	90.82	73.61
C1.7 Effectiveness and efficiency	43.40	28.38
C1.8 Political support	79.98	55.89
C2 Zoonotic diseases	83.74	68.06
C2.1 Source of infection	96.49	69.22
C2.2 Route of transmission	75.41	59.30
C2.3 Targeted population	75.13	59.90
C2.4 Capacity building	84.97	72.85
C2.5 Case studies	87.21	85.89
C3 Food security	73.09	52.89
C3.1 Food demand and supply	65.49	59.53
C3.2 Food safety	89.96	69.36
C3.3 Nutrition	83.68	67.17
C3.4 Natural and social circumstances	79.51	51.54
C3.5 Government support and response	46.79	16.85
C4 Antimicrobial resistance	64.36	44.05
C4.1 AMR surveillance system	65.31	34.79
C4.2 AMR laboratory network and coordination on capacity	53.50	55.57
C4.3 Antimicrobial control and optimization	75.06	48.76
C4.4 Improve awareness and understanding	75.00	48.09
C4.5 Antimicrobial resistance rate for important antibiotics	52.95	33.03
C5 Climate change	69.93	64.19
C5.1 Mitigation and adaptation capacity	61.01	28.24
C5.2 Climate change risks	70.21	80.87
C5.3 Health outcome	80.68	85.41

Scores are normalized (0-100, where 100 = most favorable)

Norway
Europe & Central Asia | High income

68.89 **Index Score 004**/160

Global average: 54.82

Regional average: 60.26

Income group average: 61.66

Country performance: 68.89

Missing rate in GOHI database: 8.70%

▼ AVERAGE PERFORMANCE BY GOHI

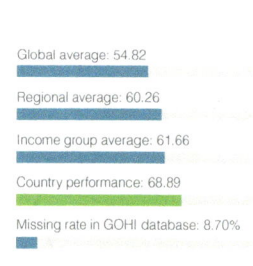

▼ AVERAGE PERFORMANCE BY CDI

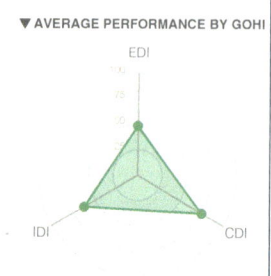

Governance: Score of GOHI-Governance   Climate: Score of GOHI-CC
Food: Score of GOHI-FS   AMR: Score of GOHI-AMR
Zoonoses: Score of GOHI-Zoonoses

	Country Score	Global Average
A External drivers index	48.13	40.45
A1 Earth system	64.37	56.21
A1.1 Land	29.77	36.41
A1.2 Forest	62.98	43.43
A1.3 Water	71.58	58.09
A1.4 Air	82.30	71.93
A1.5 Natural disasters	66.30	64.65
A2 Institutional system	67.60	46.01
A2.1 Justice	82.10	57.89
A2.2 Governance	55.26	35.58
A3 Economical system	28.42	24.62
A3.1 Finance	42.92	34.35
A3.2 Work	40.38	38.58
A4 Sociological system	40.93	37.70
A4.1 Demographic	39.41	46.31
A4.2 Education	33.65	28.26
A4.3 Inequalities	52.19	40.28
A5 Technological system	39.32	37.72
A5.1 Transport	12.07	6.54
A5.2 Technology adoption	68.62	41.23
A5.3 Consumption and production	33.99	62.53
B Intrinsic drivers index	62.62	58.01
B1 Human health	88.70	72.35
B1.1 Health coverage	88.23	58.65
B1.2 Diseases burden	82.66	79.83
B1.3 Injury and violence	97.91	80.75
B2 Animal health and ecosystem diversity	60.49	56.58
B2.1 Animal epidemic disease	98.63	94.57
B2.2 Wildlife and marine life biodiversity	22.35	18.59
B3 Environmental health	40.58	46.87
B3.1 Air quality and climate change	31.99	53.72
B3.2 Environmental biodiversity	40.95	44.05
B3.3 Environmental resources	50.02	44.25

Scores are normalized (0-100, where 100 = most favorable)

	Country Score	Global Average
C Core drivers index	74.99	57.25
C1 Governance	80.52	56.51
C1.1 Participation	87.77	41.70
C1.3 Transparency	90.10	65.15
C1.4 Responsiveness	50.00	44.42
C1.5 Consensus oriented	93.93	86.45
C1.6 Equity and inclusiveness	97.27	73.61
C1.7 Effectiveness and efficiency	67.27	28.38
C1.8 Political support	82.32	55.89
C2 Zoonotic diseases	78.62	69.06
C2.1 Source of infection	97.91	69.22
C2.2 Route of transmission	60.03	59.30
C2.3 Targeted population	71.55	59.90
C2.4 Capacity building	78.88	72.85
C2.5 Case studies	88.11	85.89
C3 Food security	66.17	52.89
C3.1 Food demand and supply	79.76	59.53
C3.2 Food safety	89.07	69.36
C3.3 Nutrition	84.08	67.17
C3.4 Natural and social circumstances	71.48	51.54
C3.5 Government support and response	6.45	16.85
C4 Antimicrobial resistance	79.25	44.05
C4.1 AMR surveillance system	56.42	34.79
C4.2 AMR laboratory network and coordinati on capacity	95.33	55.57
C4.3 Antimicrobial control and optimization	92.37	48.76
C4.4 Improve awareness and understanding	96.88	48.09
C4.5 Antimicrobial resistance rate for important antibiotics	55.26	33.03
C5 Climate change	70.54	64.19
C5.1 Mitigation and adaptation capacity	39.36	28.24
C5.2 Climate change risks	88.57	80.87
C5.3 Health outcome	85.81	85.41

Germany
Europe & Central Asia | High income

Index
Score 005/160

68.75

Global average: 54.82

Regional average: 60.26

Income group average: 61.66

Country performance: 68.75

Missing rate in GOHI database: 5.80%

▼ AVERAGE PERFORMANCE BY GOHI

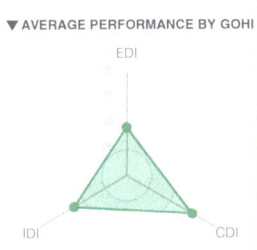

▼ AVERAGE PERFORMANCE BY CDI

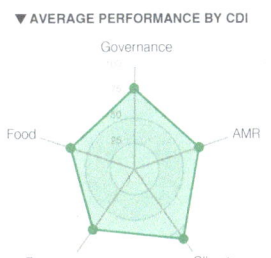

	Country Score	Global Average
A External drivers index	47.13	40.45
A1 Earth system	56.63	56.21
A1.1 Land	31.70	36.41
A1.2 Forest	46.10	43.43
A1.3 Water	55.66	58.09
A1.4 Air	76.61	71.93
A1.5 Natural disasters	66.67	64.65
A2 Institutional system	64.74	46.01
A2.1 Justice	78.23	57.89
A2.2 Governance	53.24	35.58
A3 Economical system	25.81	24.62
A3.1 Finance	36.92	34.35
A3.2 Work	39.25	38.58
A4 Sociological system	42.53	37.70
A4.1 Demographic	37.80	46.31
A4.2 Education	40.86	28.26
A4.3 Inequalities	50.11	40.28
A5 Technological system	45.93	37.72
A5.1 Transport	6.66	6.54
A5.2 Technology adoption	89.30	41.23
A5.3 Consumption and production	50.13	62.53
B Intrinsic drivers index	61.54	58.01
B1 Human health	84.91	72.35
B1.1 Health coverage	86.04	58.65
B1.2 Diseases burden	75.09	79.83
B1.3 Injury and violence	96.16	80.75
B2 Animal health and ecosystem diversity	55.18	56.58
B2.1 Animal epidemic disease	95.91	94.57
B2.2 Wildlife and marine life biodiversity	14.45	18.59
B3 Environmental health	46.39	46.87
B3.1 Air quality and climate change	53.19	53.72
B3.2 Environmental biodiversity	45.80	44.05
B3.3 Environmental resources	41.60	44.25

	Country Score	Global Average
C Core drivers index	75.26	57.25
C1 Governance	79.44	56.51
C1.1 Participation	88.50	41.70
C1.3 Transparency	87.50	65.15
C1.4 Responsiveness	58.30	44.42
C1.5 Consensus oriented	99.39	86.45
C1.6 Equity and inclusiveness	99.09	73.61
C1.7 Effectiveness and efficiency	50.53	28.38
C1.8 Political support	72.77	55.89
C2 Zoonotic diseases	84.86	68.06
C2.1 Source of infection	96.63	69.22
C2.2 Route of transmission	79.48	59.30
C2.3 Targeted population	74.16	59.90
C2.4 Capacity building	88.16	72.85
C2.5 Case studies	85.22	85.89
C3 Food security	69.67	52.89
C3.1 Food demand and supply	73.87	59.53
C3.2 Food safety	80.80	69.36
C3.3 Nutrition	90.02	67.17
C3.4 Natural and social circumstances	59.91	51.54
C3.5 Government support and response	43.74	16.85
C4 Antimicrobial resistance	68.06	44.05
C4.1 AMR surveillance system	57.41	34.79
C4.2 AMR laboratory network and coordination capacity	74.18	55.57
C4.3 Antimicrobial control and optimization	80.69	48.76
C4.4 Improve awareness and understanding	76.56	48.09
C4.5 Antimicrobial resistance rate for important antibiotics	51.47	33.03
C5 Climate change	73.29	64.19
C5.1 Mitigation and adaptation capacity	52.44	28.24
C5.2 Climate change risks	83.81	80.87
C5.3 Health outcome	85.83	85.41

Scores are normalized (0-100, where 100 = most favorable)

France

Europe & Central Asia | High income

68.74 Index Score **006**/160

Global average: 54.82

Regional average: 60.26

Income group average: 61.66

Country performance: 68.74

Missing rate in GOHI database: 8.30%

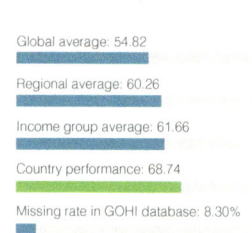

▼ AVERAGE PERFORMANCE BY GOHI

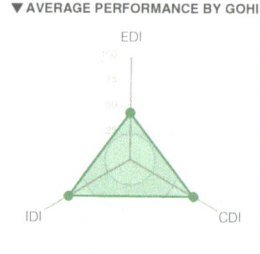

▼ AVERAGE PERFORMANCE BY CDI

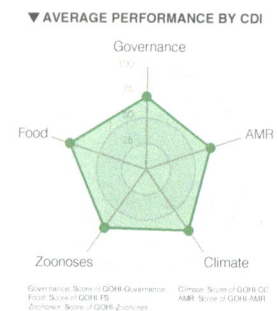

	Country Score	Global Average
A External drivers index	45.48	40.45
A1 Earth system	62.57	56.21
A1.1 Land	38.50	36.41
A1.2 Forest	46.13	43.43
A1.3 Water	66.30	58.09
A1.4 Air	85.67	71.93
A1.5 Natural disasters	66.66	64.65
A2 Institutional system	58.64	46.01
A2.1 Justice	70.96	57.89
A2.2 Governance	48.13	35.58
A3 Economical system	21.00	24.62
A3.1 Finance	26.15	34.35
A3.2 Work	36.95	38.58
A4 Sociological system	40.33	37.70
A4.1 Demographic	37.78	46.31
A4.2 Education	36.26	28.26
A4.3 Inequalities	47.27	40.28
A5 Technological system	44.85	37.72
A5.1 Transport	7.55	6.54
A5.2 Technology adoption	64.53	41.23
A5.3 Consumption and production	58.60	62.53
B Intrinsic drivers index	71.86	53.01
B1 Human health	85.45	72.35
B1.1 Health coverage	83.51	58.65
B1.2 Diseases burden	80.54	79.83
B1.3 Injury and violence	94.88	80.75
B2 Animal health and ecosystem diversity	57.27	56.58
B2.1 Animal epidemic disease	96.30	94.57
B2.2 Wildlife and marine life biodiversity	18.25	18.59
B3 Environmental health	75.08	46.87
B3.1 Air quality and climate change	88.01	53.72
B3.2 Environmental biodiversity	45.60	44.05
B3.3 Environmental resources	93.92	44.25

	Country Score	Global Average
C Core drivers index	73.17	57.25
C1 Governance	71.09	56.51
C1.1 Participation	57.30	41.70
C1.3 Transparency	86.30	65.15
C1.4 Responsiveness	50.00	44.42
C1.5 Consensus oriented	97.08	86.45
C1.6 Equity and inclusiveness	92.04	73.61
C1.7 Effectiveness and efficiency	33.47	28.38
C1.8 Political support	81.44	55.89
C2 Zoonotic diseases	74.34	68.06
C2.1 Source of infection	82.29	69.22
C2.2 Route of transmission	71.62	59.30
C2.3 Targeted population	51.39	59.90
C2.4 Capacity building	84.95	72.85
C2.5 Case studies	83.61	85.89
C3 Food security	68.68	52.89
C3.1 Food demand and supply	70.07	59.53
C3.2 Food safety	80.55	69.36
C3.3 Nutrition	82.26	67.17
C3.4 Natural and social circumstances	66.57	51.54
C3.5 Government support and response	43.92	16.85
C4 Antimicrobial resistance	81.43	44.05
C4.1 AMR surveillance system	71.81	34.79
C4.2 AMR laboratory network and coordination capacity	99.17	55.57
C4.3 Antimicrobial control and optimization	88.67	48.76
C4.4 Improve awareness and understanding	95.31	48.09
C4.5 Antimicrobial resistance rate for important antibiotics	52.21	33.03
C5 Climate change	71.44	64.19
C5.1 Mitigation and adaptation capacity	42.82	28.24
C5.2 Climate change risks	85.35	80.87
C5.3 Health outcome	88.30	85.41

Scores are normalized (0-100, where 100 = most favorable)

Switzerland

Europe & Central Asia | High income

67.7 | Index Score **007**/160

Global average: 54.82

Regional average: 60.26

Income group average: 61.66

Country performance: 67.70

Missing rate in GOHI database: 12.00%

▼ AVERAGE PERFORMANCE BY GOHI

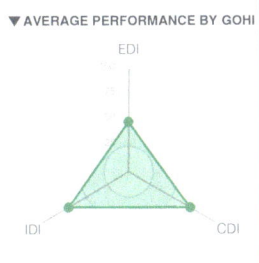

▼ AVERAGE PERFORMANCE BY CDI

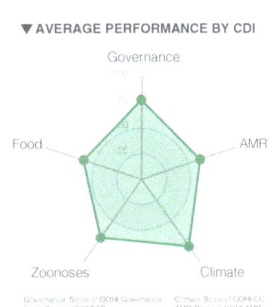

	Country Score	Global Average
A External drivers index	48.75	40.45
A1 Earth system	54.72	56.21
A1.1 Land	5.57	36.41
A1.2 Forest	46.07	43.43
A1.3 Water	58.67	58.09
A1.4 Air	86.86	71.93
A1.5 Natural disasters	66.54	64.65
A2 Institutional system	65.33	46.01
A2.1 Justice	76.49	57.89
A2.2 Governance	55.83	35.58
A3 Economical system	35.46	24.62
A3.1 Finance	61.34	34.35
A3.2 Work	40.51	38.58
A4 Sociological system	40.45	37.70
A4.1 Demographic	37.31	46.31
A4.2 Education	34.79	28.26
A4.3 Inequalities	51.43	40.28
A5 Technological system	47.78	37.72
A5.1 Transport	13.51	6.54
A5.2 Technology adoption	68.13	41.23
A5.3 Consumption and production	58.08	62.53
B Intrinsic drivers index	70.58	58.01
B1 Human health	86.18	72.35
B1.1 Health coverage	81.96	58.65
B1.2 Diseases burden	81.49	79.83
B1.3 Injury and violence	97.69	80.75
B2 Animal health and ecosystem diversity	51.24	56.58
B2.1 Animal epidemic disease	95.02	94.57
B2.2 Wildlife and marine life biodiversity	7.47	18.59
B3 Environmental health	76.47	46.87
B3.1 Air quality and climate change	89.41	53.72
B3.2 Environmental biodiversity	49.05	44.05
B3.3 Environmental resources	93.26	44.25

	Country Score	Global Average
C Core drivers index	71.22	57.25
C1 Governance	77.97	56.51
C1.1 Participation	85.17	41.70
C1.3 Transparency	87.00	65.15
C1.4 Responsiveness	58.30	44.42
C1.5 Consensus oriented	96.63	86.45
C1.6 Equity and inclusiveness	98.63	73.61
C1.7 Effectiveness and efficiency	46.87	28.38
C1.8 Political support	73.19	55.89
C2 Zoonotic diseases	81.64	68.06
C2.1 Source of infection	94.86	69.22
C2.2 Route of transmission	75.48	59.30
C2.3 Targeted population	78.38	59.90
C2.4 Capacity building	73.23	72.85
C2.5 Case studies	84.68	85.89
C3 Food security	63.07	52.89
C3.1 Food demand and supply	79.52	59.53
C3.2 Food safety	75.89	69.36
C3.3 Nutrition	86.96	67.17
C3.4 Natural and social circumstances	59.83	51.54
C3.5 Government support and response	18.15	16.85
C4 Antimicrobial resistance	61.31	44.05
C4.1 AMR surveillance system	55.81	34.79
C4.2 AMR laboratory network and coordination on capacity	61.68	55.57
C4.3 Antimicrobial control and optimization	73.06	48.76
C4.4 Improve awareness and understanding	62.50	48.09
C4.5 Antimicrobial resistance rate for important antibiotics	53.49	33.03
C5 Climate change	70.95	64.19
C5.1 Mitigation and adaptation capacity	35.99	28.24
C5.2 Climate change risks	91.52	80.87
C5.3 Health outcome	87.51	85.41

Scores are normalized (0-100, where 100 = most favorable)

Canada
North America | **High income**

Index Score **008**/160

67.6

Global average: 54.82

Regional average: 69.11

Income group average: 61.66

Country performance: 67.60

Missing rate in GOHI database: 12.70%

▼ AVERAGE PERFORMANCE BY GOHI

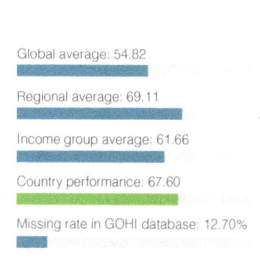

▼ AVERAGE PERFORMANCE BY CDI

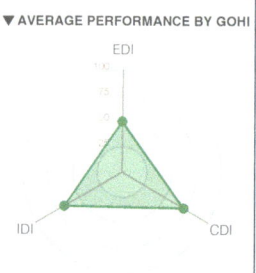

Governance: Score of GOHI-Governance   Climate: Score of GOHI-CC
Food: Score of GOHI-FS   AMR: Score of GOHI-AMR
Zoonoses: Score of GOHI-Zoonoses

	Country Score	Global Average
A External drivers index	49.50	40.45
A1 Earth system	82.47	56.21
A1.1 Land	95.45	36.41
A1.2 Forest	81.00	43.43
A1.3 Water	99.15	58.09
A1.4 Air	63.61	71.93
A1.5 Natural disasters	66.63	64.65
A2 Institutional system	63.23	46.01
A2.1 Justice	75.03	57.89
A2.2 Governance	53.18	35.58
A3 Economical system	29.85	24.62
A3.1 Finance	47.44	34.35
A3.2 Work	39.39	38.58
A4 Sociological system	39.66	37.70
A4.1 Demographic	40.02	46.31
A4.2 Education	33.50	28.26
A4.3 Inequalities	47.34	40.28
A5 Technological system	32.27	37.72
A5.1 Transport	11.98	6.54
A5.2 Technology adoption	47.20	41.23
A5.3 Consumption and production	35.40	62.53
B Intrinsic drivers index	67.30	58.01
B1 Human health	86.94	72.35
B1.1 Health coverage	88.38	58.65
B1.2 Diseases burden	80.89	79.83
B1.3 Injury and violence	94.18	80.75
B2 Animal health and ecosystem diversity	51.09	56.58
B2.1 Animal epidemic disease	93.77	94.57
B2.2 Wildlife and marine life biodiversity	8.40	18.59
B3 Environmental health	65.93	46.87
B3.1 Air quality and climate change	71.31	53.72
B3.2 Environmental biodiversity	46.35	44.05
B3.3 Environmental resources	82.12	44.25

Scores are normalized (0-100, where 100 = most favorable)

	Country Score	Global Average
C Core drivers index	71.89	57.25
C1 Governance	78.10	56.51
C1.1 Participation	87.01	41.70
C1.3 Transparency	87.50	65.15
C1.4 Responsiveness	66.65	44.42
C1.5 Consensus oriented	86.65	86.45
C1.6 Equity and inclusiveness	98.14	73.61
C1.7 Effectiveness and efficiency	44.00	28.38
C1.8 Political support	76.76	55.89
C2 Zoonotic diseases	82.25	68.06
C2.1 Source of infection	96.77	69.22
C2.2 Route of transmission	71.16	59.30
C2.3 Targeted population	77.65	59.90
C2.4 Capacity building	77.20	72.85
C2.5 Case studies	89.47	85.89
C3 Food security	67.61	52.89
C3.1 Food demand and supply	64.59	59.53
C3.2 Food safety	85.31	69.36
C3.3 Nutrition	82.84	67.17
C3.4 Natural and social circumstances	78.52	51.54
C3.5 Government support and response	26.81	16.85
C4 Antimicrobial resistance	56.43	44.05
C4.1 AMR surveillance system	51.06	34.79
C4.2 AMR laboratory network and coordination capacity	66.96	55.57
C4.3 Antimicrobial control and optimization	74.91	48.76
C4.4 Improve awareness and understanding	57.81	48.09
C4.5 Antimicrobial resistance rate for important antibiotics	31.43	33.03
C5 Climate change	72.17	64.19
C5.1 Mitigation and adaptation capacity	57.93	28.24
C5.2 Climate change risks	74.28	80.87
C5.3 Health outcome	86.48	85.41

Sweden
Europe & Central Asia | **High income**

 Index Score **009**/160
67.56

Global average: 54.82

Regional average: 60.26

Income group average: 61.66

Country performance: 67.56

Missing rate in GOHI database: 7.20%

▼ AVERAGE PERFORMANCE BY GOHI

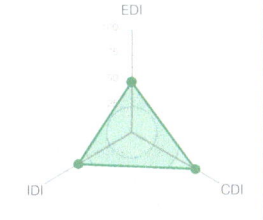

▼ AVERAGE PERFORMANCE BY CDI

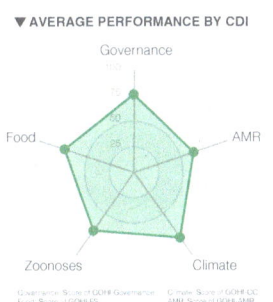

	Country Score	Global Average
A External drivers index	49.53	40.45
A1 Earth system	71.01	56.21
A1.1 Land	41.71	36.41
A1.2 Forest	78.77	43.43
A1.3 Water	68.53	58.09
A1.4 Air	91.94	71.93
A1.5 Natural disasters	66.56	64.65
A2 Institutional system	64.96	46.01
A2.1 Justice	79.81	57.89
A2.2 Governance	52.31	35.58
A3 Economical system	27.56	24.62
A3.1 Finance	41.33	34.35
A3.2 Work	39.51	38.58
A4 Sociological system	43.52	37.70
A4.1 Demographic	39.70	46.31
A4.2 Education	40.54	28.26
A4.3 Inequalities	51.79	40.28
A5 Technological system	40.58	37.72
A5.1 Transport	7.46	6.54
A5.2 Technology adoption	66.00	41.23
A5.3 Consumption and production	44.61	62.53
B Intrinsic drivers index	61.80	58.01
B1 Human health	87.55	72.35
B1.1 Health coverage	88.99	58.65
B1.2 Diseases burden	79.79	79.83
B1.3 Injury and violence	96.53	80.75
B2 Animal health and ecosystem diversity	51.09	56.58
B2.1 Animal epidemic disease	94.04	94.57
B2.2 Wildlife and marine life biodiversity	8.15	18.59
B3 Environmental health	48.64	46.87
B3.1 Air quality and climate change	68.45	53.72
B3.2 Environmental biodiversity	46.30	44.05
B3.3 Environmental resources	32.64	44.25

	Country Score	Global Average
C Core drivers index	72.94	57.25
C1 Governance	76.52	56.51
C1.1 Participation	89.56	41.70
C1.3 Transparency	88.50	65.15
C1.4 Responsiveness	50.00	44.42
C1.5 Consensus oriented	90.31	86.45
C1.6 Equity and inclusiveness	99.56	73.61
C1.7 Effectiveness and efficiency	44.33	28.38
C1.8 Political support	73.35	55.89
C2 Zoonotic diseases	79.28	68.06
C2.1 Source of infection	86.94	69.22
C2.2 Route of transmission	69.07	59.30
C2.3 Targeted population	77.07	59.90
C2.4 Capacity building	79.90	72.85
C2.5 Case studies	86.47	85.89
C3 Food security	64.25	52.89
C3.1 Food demand and supply	70.92	59.53
C3.2 Food safety	82.64	69.36
C3.3 Nutrition	86.05	67.17
C3.4 Natural and social circumstances	68.59	51.54
C3.5 Government support and response	13.05	16.85
C4 Antimicrobial resistance	74.06	44.05
C4.1 AMR surveillance system	62.16	34.79
C4.2 AMR laboratory network and coordination capacity	82.68	55.57
C4.3 Antimicrobial control and optimization	90.40	48.76
C4.4 Improve awareness and understanding	81.25	48.09
C4.5 Antimicrobial resistance rate for important antibiotics	53.80	33.03
C5 Climate change	70.70	64.19
C5.1 Mitigation and adaptation capacity	38.58	28.24
C5.2 Climate change risks	90.42	80.87
C5.3 Health outcome	85.25	85.41

Scores are normalized (0-100, where 100 = most favorable)

Finland

Europe & Central Asia | High income

67.21 | **Index Score 010**/160

Global average: 54.82

Regional average: 60.26

Income group average: 61.66

Country performance: 67.21

Missing rate in GOHI database: 8.00%

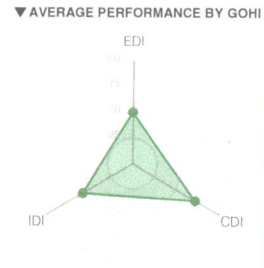
▼ AVERAGE PERFORMANCE BY GOHI

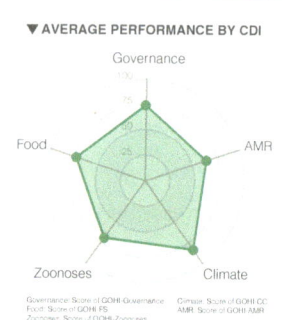
▼ AVERAGE PERFORMANCE BY CDI

	Country Score	Global Average
A External drivers index	50.28	40.45
A1 Earth system	72.76	56.21
A1.1 Land	55.80	36.41
A1.2 Forest	88.50	43.43
A1.3 Water	66.92	58.09
A1.4 Air	82.97	71.93
A1.5 Natural disasters	65.19	64.65
A2 Institutional system	69.04	46.01
A2.1 Justice	84.32	57.89
A2.2 Governance	56.02	35.58
A3 Economical system	24.93	24.62
A3.1 Finance	35.43	34.35
A3.2 Work	38.22	38.58
A4 Sociological system	42.84	37.70
A4.1 Demographic	39.47	46.31
A4.2 Education	39.18	28.26
A4.3 Inequalities	51.47	40.28
A5 Technological system	41.81	37.72
A5.1 Transport	10.78	6.54
A5.2 Technology adoption	69.27	41.23
A5.3 Consumption and production	41.84	62.53
B Intrinsic drivers index	59.35	59.01
B1 Human health	83.12	72.35
B1.1 Health coverage	79.88	58.65
B1.2 Diseases burden	76.58	79.83
B1.3 Injury and violence	95.42	80.75
B2 Animal health and ecosystem diversity	59.26	56.58
B2.1 Animal epidemic disease	96.83	94.57
B2.2 Wildlife and marine life biodiversity	21.70	18.59
B3 Environmental health	34.42	46.87
B3.1 Air quality and climate change	45.64	53.72
B3.2 Environmental biodiversity	19.55	44.05
B3.3 Environmental resources	39.12	44.25

	Country Score	Global Average
C Core drivers index	73.08	57.25
C1 Governance	73.96	56.51
C1.1 Participation	58.44	41.70
C1.3 Transparency	88.50	65.15
C1.4 Responsiveness	58.30	44.42
C1.5 Consensus oriented	88.13	86.45
C1.6 Equity and inclusiveness	99.45	73.61
C1.7 Effectiveness and efficiency	63.07	28.38
C1.8 Political support	66.86	55.89
C2 Zoonotic diseases	83.59	68.06
C2.1 Source of infection	96.64	69.22
C2.2 Route of transmission	78.85	59.30
C2.3 Targeted population	77.09	59.90
C2.4 Capacity building	75.96	72.85
C2.5 Case studies	87.71	85.89
C3 Food security	64.99	52.89
C3.1 Food demand and supply	76.84	59.53
C3.2 Food safety	87.07	69.36
C3.3 Nutrition	85.85	67.17
C3.4 Natural and social circumstances	65.61	51.54
C3.5 Government support and response	9.57	16.85
C4 Antimicrobial resistance	73.22	44.05
C4.1 AMR surveillance system	65.16	34.79
C4.2 AMR laboratory network and coordination capacity	92.61	55.57
C4.3 Antimicrobial control and optimization	87.61	48.76
C4.4 Improve awareness and understanding	65.62	48.09
C4.5 Antimicrobial resistance rate for important antibiotics	55.10	33.03
C5 Climate change	69.69	64.19
C5.1 Mitigation and adaptation capacity	39.16	28.24
C5.2 Climate change risks	86.21	80.87
C5.3 Health outcome	85.82	85.41

Scores are normalized (0-100, where 100 = most favorable)

Netherlands

Europe & Central Asia | High income

66.86 Index **011**/160
Score

Global average: 54.82

Regional average: 60.26

Income group average: 61.66

Country performance: 66.86

Missing rate in GOHI database: 6.90%

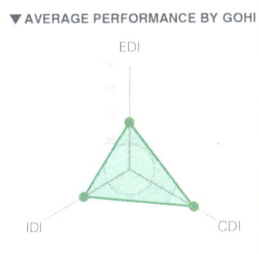

▼ AVERAGE PERFORMANCE BY GOHI

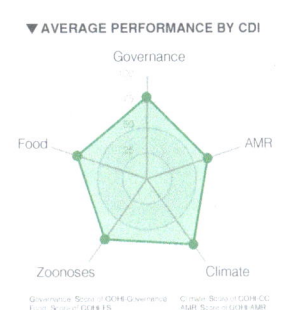

▼ AVERAGE PERFORMANCE BY CDI

	Country Score	Global Average
A External drivers index	46.09	40.45
A1 Earth system	49.58	56.21
A1.1 Land	28.69	36.41
A1.2 Forest	37.49	43.43
A1.3 Water	36.27	58.09
A1.4 Air	75.41	71.93
A1.5 Natural disasters	66.67	64.65
A2 Institutional system	67.09	46.01
A2.1 Justice	81.69	57.89
A2.2 Governance	54.65	35.58
A3 Economical system	24.35	24.62
A3.1 Finance	31.92	34.35
A3.2 Work	40.74	38.58
A4 Sociological system	42.26	37.70
A4.1 Demographic	41.28	46.31
A4.2 Education	35.98	28.26
A4.3 Inequalities	51.59	40.28
A5 Technological system	47.18	37.72
A5.1 Transport	14.70	6.54
A5.2 Technology adoption	66.88	41.23
A5.3 Consumption and production	56.52	62.53
B Intrinsic drivers index	53.97	58.01
B1 Human health	85.93	72.35
B1.1 Health coverage	84.35	58.65
B1.2 Diseases burden	79.69	79.83
B1.3 Injury and violence	96.36	80.75
B2 Animal health and ecosystem diversity	52.71	56.58
B2.1 Animal epidemic disease	95.92	94.57
B2.2 Wildlife and marine life biodiversity	9.50	18.59
B3 Environmental health	24.90	46.87
B3.1 Air quality and climate change	12.26	53.72
B3.2 Environmental biodiversity	45.25	44.05
B3.3 Environmental resources	17.94	44.25

	Country Score	Global Average
C Core drivers index	74.54	57.25
C1 Governance	80.39	56.51
C1.1 Participation	87.48	41.70
C1.3 Transparency	88.00	65.15
C1.4 Responsiveness	58.30	44.42
C1.5 Consensus oriented	93.96	86.45
C1.6 Equity and inclusiveness	96.91	73.61
C1.7 Effectiveness and efficiency	45.13	28.38
C1.8 Political support	93.55	55.89
C2 Zoonotic diseases	79.85	68.06
C2.1 Source of infection	83.51	69.22
C2.2 Route of transmission	76.28	59.30
C2.3 Targeted population	76.59	59.90
C2.4 Capacity building	78.93	72.85
C2.5 Case studies	85.24	85.89
C3 Food security	65.16	52.89
C3.1 Food demand and supply	78.21	59.53
C3.2 Food safety	77.78	69.36
C3.3 Nutrition	85.53	67.17
C3.4 Natural and social circumstances	62.14	51.54
C3.5 Government support and response	22.15	16.85
C4 Antimicrobial resistance	73.76	44.05
C4.1 AMR surveillance system	72.51	34.79
C4.2 AMR laboratory network and coordination on capacity	70.41	55.57
C4.3 Antimicrobial control and optimization	78.88	48.76
C4.4 Improve awareness and understanding	92.19	48.09
C4.5 Antimicrobial resistance rate for important antibiotics	54.91	33.03
C5 Climate change	73.39	64.19
C5.1 Mitigation and adaptation capacity	58.90	28.24
C5.2 Climate change risks	78.91	80.87
C5.3 Health outcome	84.58	85.41

Scores are normalized (0-100, where 100 = most favorable)

Japan
East Asia & Pacific | High income

66.72 **Index Score** 012/160

Global average: 54.82

Regional average: 56.52

Income group average: 61.66

Country performance: 66.72

Missing rate in GOHI database: 10.90%

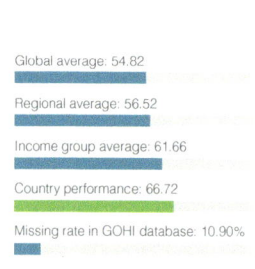

▼ AVERAGE PERFORMANCE BY GOHI

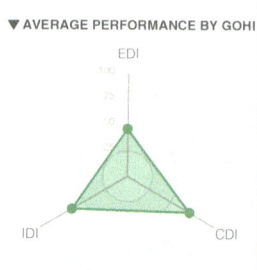

▼ AVERAGE PERFORMANCE BY CDI

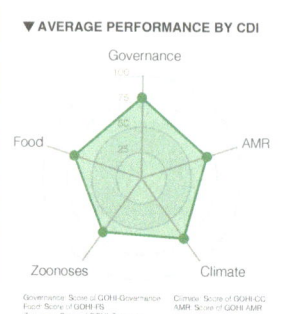

Governance: Score of GOHI-Governance   Climate: Score of GOHI-CC
Food: Score of GOHI-FS   AMR: Score of GOHI-AMR
Zoonoses: Score of GOHI-Zoonoses

	Country Score	Global Average
A External drivers index	46.38	40.45
A1 Earth system	59.06	56.21
A1.1 Land	17.03	36.41
A1.2 Forest	59.62	43.43
A1.3 Water	70.66	58.09
A1.4 Air	73.19	71.93
A1.5 Natural disasters	66.49	64.65
A2 Institutional system	64.88	46.01
A2.1 Justice	77.85	57.89
A2.2 Governance	53.83	35.58
A3 Economical system	25.12	24.62
A3.1 Finance	34.67	34.35
A3.2 Work	39.83	38.58
A4 Sociological system	41.84	37.70
A4.1 Demographic	37.90	46.31
A4.2 Education	40.77	28.26
A4.3 Inequalities	47.72	40.28
A5 Technological system	41.03	37.72
A5.1 Transport	4.62	6.54
A5.2 Technology adoption	57.41	41.23
A5.3 Consumption and production	57.35	62.53
B Intrinsic drivers index	64.66	58.01
B1 Human health	89.23	72.35
B1.1 Health coverage	95.33	58.65
B1.2 Diseases burden	78.12	79.83
B1.3 Injury and violence	96.96	80.75
B2 Animal health and ecosystem diversity	56.84	56.58
B2.1 Animal epidemic disease	93.88	94.57
B2.2 Wildlife and marine life biodiversity	19.80	18.59
B3 Environmental health	49.86	46.87
B3.1 Air quality and climate change	6.99	53.72
B3.2 Environmental biodiversity	41.65	44.05
B3.3 Environmental resources	39.54	44.25

Scores are normalized (0-100, where 100 = most favorable)

	Country Score	Global Average
C Core drivers index	74.54	57.25
C1 Governance	78.81	56.51
C1.1 Participation	88.46	41.70
C1.3 Transparency	85.80	65.15
C1.4 Responsiveness	58.30	44.42
C1.5 Consensus oriented	99.11	86.45
C1.6 Equity and inclusiveness	82.74	73.61
C1.7 Effectiveness and efficiency	51.00	28.38
C1.8 Political support	86.29	55.89
C2 Zoonotic diseases	73.11	68.06
C2.1 Source of infection	83.90	69.22
C2.2 Route of transmission	49.79	59.30
C2.3 Targeted population	73.81	59.90
C2.4 Capacity building	78.08	72.85
C2.5 Case studies	88.81	85.89
C3 Food security	68.83	52.89
C3.1 Food demand and supply	84.24	59.53
C3.2 Food safety	88.39	69.36
C3.3 Nutrition	79.78	67.17
C3.4 Natural and social circumstances	56.51	51.54
C3.5 Government support and response	35.25	16.85
C4 Antimicrobial resistance	71.78	44.05
C4.1 AMR surveillance system	58.26	34.79
C4.2 AMR laboratory network and coordination on capacity	77.73	55.57
C4.3 Antimicrobial control and optimization	81.75	48.76
C4.4 Improve awareness and understanding	85.94	48.09
C4.5 Antimicrobial resistance rate for important antibiotics	52.21	33.03
C5 Climate change	65.76	64.19
C5.1 Mitigation and adaptation capacity	33.04	28.24
C5.2 Climate change risks	81.68	80.87
C5.3 Health outcome	84.56	85.41

Austria

Europe & Central Asia | **High income**

66.61 Index **013**/160
Score

Global average: 54.82

Regional average: 60.26

Income group average: 61.66

Country performance: 66.61

Missing rate in GOHI database: 6.90%

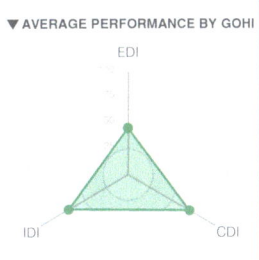

▼ AVERAGE PERFORMANCE BY GOHI

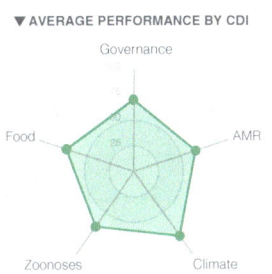

▼ AVERAGE PERFORMANCE BY CDI

	Country Score	Global Average
A External drivers index	45.66	40.45
A1 Earth system	56.10	56.21
A1.1 Land	18.94	36.41
A1.2 Forest	53.09	43.43
A1.3 Water	57.08	58.09
A1.4 Air	78.11	71.93
A1.5 Natural disasters	66.37	64.65
A2 Institutional system	64.27	46.01
A2.1 Justice	78.54	57.89
A2.2 Governance	52.12	35.58
A3 Economical system	22.34	24.62
A3.1 Finance	28.24	34.35
A3.2 Work	38.71	38.58
A4 Sociological system	41.25	37.70
A4.1 Demographic	34.79	46.31
A4.2 Education	39.27	28.26
A4.3 Inequalities	51.18	40.28
A5 Technological system	44.33	37.72
A5.1 Transport	6.14	6.54
A5.2 Technology adoption	67.74	41.23
A5.3 Consumption and production	55.06	62.53
B Intrinsic drivers index	68.82	53.01
B1 Human health	84.20	72.35
B1.1 Health coverage	81.59	58.65
B1.2 Diseases burden	78.27	79.83
B1.3 Injury and violence	95.30	80.75
B2 Animal health and ecosystem diversity	55.27	56.58
B2.1 Animal epidemic disease	92.41	94.57
B2.2 Wildlife and marine life biodiversity	18.13	18.59
B3 Environmental health	69.08	46.87
B3.1 Air quality and climate change	60.98	53.72
B3.2 Environmental biodiversity	57.00	44.05
B3.3 Environmental resources	91.36	44.25

	Country Score	Global Average
C Core drivers index	70.75	57.25
C1 Governance	70.51	56.51
C1.1 Participation	56.89	41.70
C1.3 Transparency	89.10	65.15
C1.4 Responsiveness	50.00	44.42
C1.5 Consensus oriented	85.83	86.45
C1.6 Equity and inclusiveness	94.65	73.61
C1.7 Effectiveness and efficiency	52.13	28.38
C1.8 Political support	64.98	55.89
C2 Zoonotic diseases	78.46	68.06
C2.1 Source of infection	97.93	69.22
C2.2 Route of transmission	58.90	59.30
C2.3 Targeted population	79.25	59.90
C2.4 Capacity building	75.52	72.85
C2.5 Case studies	82.97	85.89
C3 Food security	65.99	52.89
C3.1 Food demand and supply	79.56	59.53
C3.2 Food safety	87.06	69.36
C3.3 Nutrition	83.86	67.17
C3.4 Natural and social circumstances	59.46	51.54
C3.5 Government support and response	20.02	16.85
C4 Antimicrobial resistance	71.65	44.05
C4.1 AMR surveillance system	49.76	34.79
C4.2 AMR laboratory network and coordinati on capacity	88.96	55.57
C4.3 Antimicrobial control and optimization	77.90	48.76
C4.4 Improve awareness and understanding	89.06	48.09
C4.5 Antimicrobial resistance rate for important antibiotics	52.58	33.03
C5 Climate change	67.12	64.19
C5.1 Mitigation and adaptation capacity	32.35	28.24
C5.2 Climate change risks	84.02	80.87
C5.3 Health outcome	87.03	85.41

Scores are normalized (0-100, where 100 = most favorable)

Italy
Europe & Central Asia | High income

Index Score **014**/160 · 66.52

Global average: 54.82

Regional average: 60.26

Income group average: 61.66

Country performance: 66.52

Missing rate in GOHI database: 7.60%

▼ AVERAGE PERFORMANCE BY GOHI

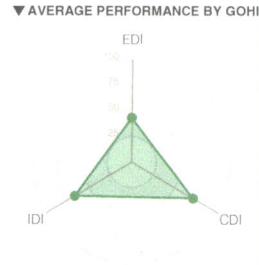

▼ AVERAGE PERFORMANCE BY CDI

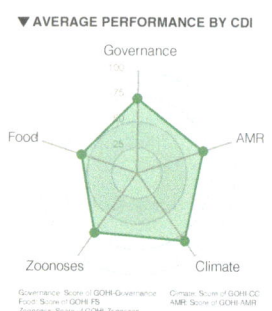

Governance: Score of GOHI-Governance   C-major: Score of GOHI-CC
Food: Score of GOHI-FS   AMR: Score of GOHI-AMR
Zoonoses: Score of GOHI-Zoonoses

	Country Score	Global Average
A External drivers index	43.26	40.45
A1 Earth system	58.03	56.21
A1.1 Land	22.45	36.41
A1.2 Forest	46.12	43.43
A1.3 Water	65.74	58.09
A1.4 Air	79.81	71.93
A1.5 Natural disasters	66.65	64.65
A2 Institutional system	54.11	46.01
A2.1 Justice	66.69	57.89
A2.2 Governance	43.40	35.58
A3 Economical system	20.02	24.62
A3.1 Finance	25.31	34.35
A3.2 Work	34.68	38.58
A4 Sociological system	37.55	37.70
A4.1 Demographic	35.33	46.31
A4.2 Education	31.86	28.26
A4.3 Inequalities	47.52	40.28
A5 Technological system	46.58	37.72
A5.1 Transport	4.94	6.54
A5.2 Technology adoption	67.26	41.23
A5.3 Consumption and production	63.26	62.53
B Intrinsic drivers index	67.06	58.01
B1 Human health	84.22	72.35
B1.1 Health coverage	80.27	58.65
B1.2 Diseases burden	79.62	79.83
B1.3 Injury and violence	95.34	80.75
B2 Animal health and ecosystem diversity	53.53	56.58
B2.1 Animal epidemic disease	93.17	94.57
B2.2 Wildlife and marine life biodiversity	13.90	18.59
B3 Environmental health	65.46	46.87
B3.1 Air quality and climate change	80.02	53.72
B3.2 Environmental biodiversity	40.95	44.05
B3.3 Environmental resources	77.38	44.25

	Country Score	Global Average
C Core drivers index	71.56	57.25
C1 Governance	73.04	56.51
C1.1 Participation	85.54	41.70
C1.3 Transparency	89.80	65.15
C1.4 Responsiveness	25.00	44.42
C1.5 Consensus oriented	98.55	86.45
C1.6 Equity and inclusiveness	94.30	73.61
C1.7 Effectiveness and efficiency	44.07	28.38
C1.8 Political support	74.04	55.89
C2 Zoonotic diseases	82.19	68.06
C2.1 Source of infection	95.89	69.22
C2.2 Route of transmission	71.62	59.30
C2.3 Targeted population	78.72	59.90
C2.4 Capacity building	81.61	72.85
C2.5 Case studies	83.45	85.89
C3 Food security	70.11	52.89
C3.1 Food demand and supply	79.87	59.53
C3.2 Food safety	88.46	69.36
C3.3 Nutrition	82.60	67.17
C3.4 Natural and social circumstances	63.56	51.54
C3.5 Government support and response	36.06	16.85
C4 Antimicrobial resistance	58.74	44.05
C4.1 AMR surveillance system	54.51	34.79
C4.2 AMR laboratory network and coordination capacity	73.88	55.57
C4.3 Antimicrobial control and optimization	64.33	48.76
C4.4 Improve awareness and understanding	68.75	48.09
C4.5 Antimicrobial resistance rate for important antibiotics	32.23	33.03
C5 Climate change	72.34	64.19
C5.1 Mitigation and adaptation capacity	48.26	28.24
C5.2 Climate change risks	84.54	80.87
C5.3 Health outcome	86.41	85.41

Scores are normalized (0-100, where 100 = most favorable)

Spain
Europe & Central Asia | High income

 Index Score **015**/160

Global average: 54.82

Regional average: 60.26

Income group average: 61.66

Country performance: 66.47

Missing rate in GOHI database: 9.80%

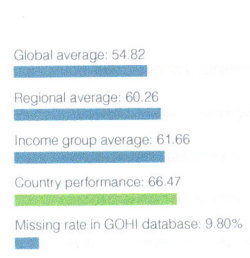

▼ AVERAGE PERFORMANCE BY GOHI

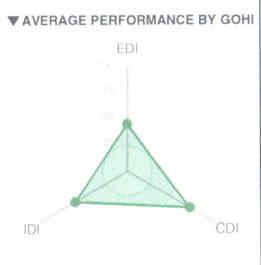

▼ AVERAGE PERFORMANCE BY CDI

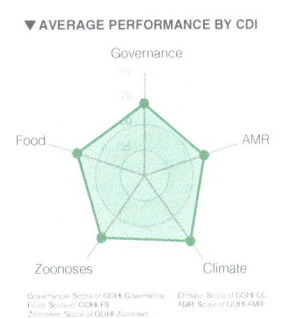

Governance Score of GOHI-Governance   Climate Score of GOHI-CC
Food Score of GOHI-FS   AMR Score of GOHI-AMR
Zoonoses Score of GOHI-Zoonoses

	Country Score	Global Average
A External drivers index	46.14	40.45
A1 Earth system	62.78	56.21
A1.1 Land	37.73	36.41
A1.2 Forest	48.63	43.43
A1.3 Water	65.30	58.09
A1.4 Air	86.30	71.93
A1.5 Natural disasters	66.67	64.65
A2 Institutional system	58.00	46.01
A2.1 Justice	71.94	57.89
A2.2 Governance	46.12	35.58
A3 Economical system	23.20	24.62
A3.1 Finance	32.82	34.35
A3.2 Work	35.76	38.58
A4 Sociological system	38.56	37.70
A4.1 Demographic	38.41	46.31
A4.2 Education	30.64	28.26
A4.3 Inequalities	49.09	40.26
A5 Technological system	48.16	37.72
A5.1 Transport	11.14	6.54
A5.2 Technology adoption	67.26	41.23
A5.3 Consumption and production	62.25	62.53
B Intrinsic drivers index	60.92	58.01
B1 Human health	86.83	72.35
B1.1 Health coverage	84.77	58.65
B1.2 Diseases burden	81.98	79.83
B1.3 Injury and violence	96.38	80.75
B2 Animal health and ecosystem diversity	56.27	56.58
B2.1 Animal epidemic disease	96.84	94.57
B2.2 Wildlife and marine life biodiversity	15.70	18.59
B3 Environmental health	41.51	46.87
B3.1 Air quality and climate change	31.29	53.72
B3.2 Environmental biodiversity	41.83	44.05
B3.3 Environmental resources	52.67	44.25

	Country Score	Global Average
C Core drivers index	72.31	57.25
C1 Governance	70.88	56.51
C1.1 Participation	51.91	41.70
C1.3 Transparency	88.90	65.15
C1.4 Responsiveness	58.30	44.42
C1.5 Consensus oriented	99.94	86.45
C1.6 Equity and inclusiveness	83.77	73.61
C1.7 Effectiveness and efficiency	39.67	28.38
C1.8 Political support	73.70	55.89
C2 Zoonotic diseases	79.72	68.06
C2.1 Source of infection	81.07	69.22
C2.2 Route of transmission	76.45	59.30
C2.3 Targeted population	80.14	59.90
C2.4 Capacity building	76.05	72.85
C2.5 Case studies	86.63	85.89
C3 Food security	64.44	52.89
C3.1 Food demand and supply	67.93	59.53
C3.2 Food safety	84.91	69.36
C3.3 Nutrition	80.37	67.17
C3.4 Natural and social circumstances	65.38	51.54
C3.5 Government support and response	23.61	16.85
C4 Antimicrobial resistance	71.61	44.05
C4.1 AMR surveillance system	55.96	34.79
C4.2 AMR laboratory network and coordination capacity	85.92	55.57
C4.3 Antimicrobial control and optimization	82.77	48.76
C4.4 Improve awareness and understanding	90.62	48.09
C4.5 Antimicrobial resistance rate for important antibiotics	42.77	33.03
C5 Climate change	75.60	64.19
C5.1 Mitigation and adaptation capacity	56.97	28.24
C5.2 Climate change risks	85.82	80.87
C5.3 Health outcome	86.32	85.41

Scores are normalized (0-100, where 100 = most favorable)

Denmark
Europe & Central Asia | High income

66.44 Index Score **016**/160

Global average: 54.82

Regional average: 60.26

Income group average: 61.66

Country performance: 66.44

Missing rate in GOHI database: 8.70%

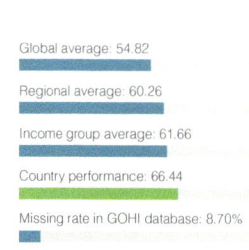

▼ AVERAGE PERFORMANCE BY GOHI

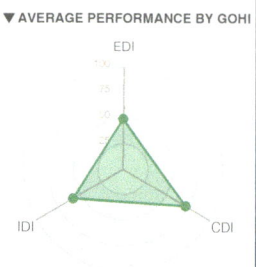

▼ AVERAGE PERFORMANCE BY CDI

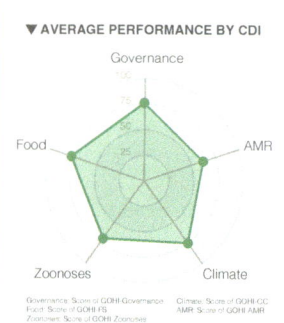

Governance: Score of GOHI Governance
Food: Score of GOHI FS
Zoonoses: Score of GOHI Zoonoses
Climate: Score of GOHI CC
AMR: Score of GOHI AMR

	Country Score	Global Average
A External drivers index	49.44	40.45
A1 Earth system	62.98	56.21
A1.1 Land	51.96	36.41
A1.2 Forest	39.46	43.43
A1.3 Water	64.90	58.09
A1.4 Air	85.35	71.93
A1.5 Natural disasters	63.52	64.65
A2 Institutional system	67.10	46.01
A2.1 Justice	81.29	57.89
A2.2 Governance	55.01	35.58
A3 Economical system	26.64	24.62
A3.1 Finance	38.98	34.35
A3.2 Work	39.44	38.58
A4 Sociological system	42.93	37.70
A4.1 Demographic	40.31	46.31
A4.2 Education	38.22	28.26
A4.3 Inequalities	52.09	40.28
A5 Technological system	47.53	37.72
A5.1 Transport	11.21	6.54
A5.2 Technology adoption	66.73	41.23
A5.3 Consumption and production	60.87	62.53
B Intrinsic drivers index	57.84	58.01
B1 Human health	85.38	72.35
B1.1 Health coverage	83.81	58.65
B1.2 Diseases burden	78.75	79.83
B1.3 Injury and violence	96.17	80.75
B2 Animal health and ecosystem diversity	50.80	56.58
B2.1 Animal epidemic disease	94.66	94.57
B2.2 Wildlife and marine life biodiversity	6.95	18.59
B3 Environmental health	39.09	46.87
B3.1 Air quality and climate change	53.52	53.72
B3.2 Environmental biodiversity	43.00	44.05
B3.3 Environmental resources	21.94	44.25

	Country Score	Global Average
C Core drivers index	72.26	57.25
C1 Governance	76.17	56.51
C1.1 Participation	88.76	41.70
C1.3 Transparency	86.10	65.15
C1.4 Responsiveness	45.80	44.42
C1.5 Consensus oriented	88.88	86.45
C1.6 Equity and inclusiveness	98.65	73.61
C1.7 Effectiveness and efficiency	55.00	28.38
C1.8 Political support	69.97	55.89
C2 Zoonotic diseases	75.49	68.06
C2.1 Source of infection	72.72	69.22
C2.2 Route of transmission	75.29	59.30
C2.3 Targeted population	72.02	59.90
C2.4 Capacity building	75.16	72.85
C2.5 Case studies	84.91	85.89
C3 Food security	62.58	52.89
C3.1 Food demand and supply	69.38	59.53
C3.2 Food safety	87.78	69.36
C3.3 Nutrition	81.66	67.17
C3.4 Natural and social circumstances	65.56	51.54
C3.5 Government support and response	8.51	16.85
C4 Antimicrobial resistance	77.59	44.05
C4.1 AMR surveillance system	58.26	34.79
C4.2 AMR laboratory network and coordination capacity	93.95	55.57
C4.3 Antimicrobial control and optimization	86.70	48.76
C4.4 Improve awareness and understanding	95.31	48.09
C4.5 Antimicrobial resistance rate for important antibiotics	53.75	33.03
C5 Climate change	70.09	64.19
C5.1 Mitigation and adaptation capacity	36.64	28.24
C5.2 Climate change risks	90.68	80.87
C5.3 Health outcome	85.09	85.41

Scores are normalized (0-100, where 100 = most favorable)

Singapore
East Asia & Pacific | High income

Index Score **017**/160

Global average: 54.82

Regional average: 56.52

Income group average: 61.66

Country performance: 66.00

Missing rate in GOHI database: 18.50%

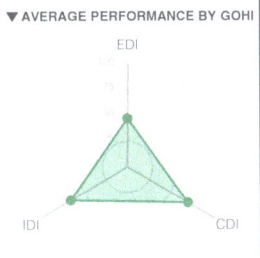

▼ AVERAGE PERFORMANCE BY GOHI

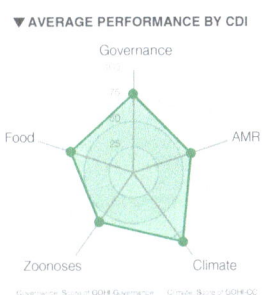

▼ AVERAGE PERFORMANCE BY CDI

	Country Score	Global Average
A External drivers index	47.71	40.45
A1 Earth system	53.50	56.21
A1.1 Land	24.98	36.41
A1.2 Forest	41.45	43.43
A1.3 Water	60.48	58.09
A1.4 Air	69.41	71.93
A1.5 Natural disasters	63.61	64.65
A2 Institutional system	65.82	46.01
A2.1 Justice	74.03	57.89
A2.2 Governance	58.82	35.58
A3 Economical system	33.90	24.62
A3.1 Finance	56.38	34.35
A3.2 Work	41.59	38.58
A4 Sociological system	42.42	37.70
A4.1 Demographic	44.75	46.31
A4.2 Education	34.17	28.26
A4.3 Inequalities	50.60	40.28
A5 Technological system	42.93	37.72
A5.1 Transport	46.83	6.54
A5.2 Technology adoption	46.98	41.23
A5.3 Consumption and production	35.20	62.53
B Intrinsic drivers index	65.79	58.01
B1 Human health	90.65	72.35
B1.1 Health coverage	86.31	58.65
B1.2 Diseases burden	90.15	79.83
B1.3 Injury and violence	98.23	80.75
B2 Animal health and ecosystem diversity	76.64	56.58
B2.1 Animal epidemic disease	95.77	94.57
B2.2 Wildlife and marine life biodiversity	57.50	18.59
B3 Environmental health	32.09	46.87
B3.1 Air quality and climate change	42.81	53.72
B3.2 Environmental biodiversity	33.50	44.05
B3.3 Environmental resources	20.92	44.25

	Country Score	Global Average
C Core drivers index	70.11	57.25
C1 Governance	77.01	56.51
C1.1 Participation	92.40	41.70
C1.3 Transparency	75.10	65.15
C1.4 Responsiveness	58.30	44.42
C1.5 Consensus oriented	98.99	86.45
C1.6 Equity and inclusiveness	81.43	73.61
C1.7 Effectiveness and efficiency	40.27	28.38
C1.8 Political support	92.56	55.89
C2 Zoonotic diseases	84.18	68.06
C2.1 Source of infection	85.86	69.22
C2.2 Route of transmission	84.08	59.30
C2.3 Targeted population	79.94	59.90
C2.4 Capacity building	83.15	72.85
C2.5 Case studies	88.23	85.89
C3 Food security	61.13	52.89
C3.1 Food demand and supply	73.55	59.53
C3.2 Food safety	78.97	69.36
C3.3 Nutrition	76.02	67.17
C3.4 Natural and social circumstances	71.28	51.54
C3.5 Government support and response	5.84	16.85
C4 Antimicrobial resistance	66.76	44.05
C4.1 AMR surveillance system	70.21	34.79
C4.2 AMR laboratory network and coordination capacity	94.40	55.57
C4.3 Antimicrobial control and optimization	63.70	48.76
C4.4 Improve awareness and understanding	60.94	48.09
C4.5 Antimicrobial resistance rate for important antibiotics	44.54	33.03
C5 Climate change	60.15	64.19
C5.1 Mitigation and adaptation capacity	26.20	28.24
C5.2 Climate change risks	73.23	80.87
C5.3 Health outcome	82.83	85.41

Scores are normalized (0-100, where 100 = most favorable)

Belgium

Europe & Central Asia | High income

65.95 Index Score 018 /160

Global average: 54.82

Regional average: 60.26

Income group average: 61.66

Country performance: 65.95

Missing rate in GOHI database: 7.20%

▼ AVERAGE PERFORMANCE BY GOHI

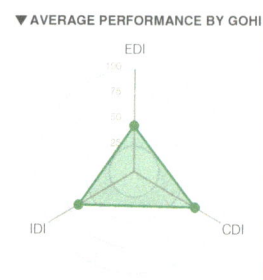

▼ AVERAGE PERFORMANCE BY CDI

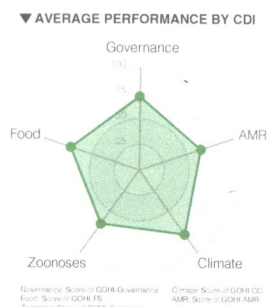

	Country Score	Global Average
A External drivers index	44.93	40.45
A1 Earth system	53.97	56.21
A1.1 Land	28.13	36.41
A1.2 Forest	42.04	43.43
A1.3 Water	51.31	58.09
A1.4 Air	75.72	71.93
A1.5 Natural disasters	66.65	64.65
A2 Institutional system	61.82	46.01
A2.1 Justice	78.44	57.89
A2.2 Governance	47.66	35.58
A3 Economical system	22.34	24.62
A3.1 Finance	29.56	34.35
A3.2 Work	37.02	38.58
A4 Sociological system	43.74	37.70
A4.1 Demographic	42.39	46.31
A4.2 Education	38.87	28.26
A4.3 Inequalities	51.67	40.28
A5 Technological system	42.76	37.72
A5.1 Transport	6.34	6.54
A5.2 Technology adoption	64.83	41.23
A5.3 Consumption and production	53.24	62.53
B Intrinsic drivers index	65.60	59.01
B1 Human health	85.34	72.35
B1.1 Health coverage	83.20	58.65
B1.2 Diseases burden	76.10	79.83
B1.3 Injury and violence	93.25	80.75
B2 Animal health and ecosystem diversity	51.65	56.58
B2.1 Animal epidemic disease	94.09	94.57
B2.2 Wildlife and marine life biodiversity	9.20	18.59
B3 Environmental health	63.82	46.87
B3.1 Air quality and climate change	64.76	53.72
B3.2 Environmental biodiversity	49.35	44.05
B3.3 Environmental resources	79.28	44.25

	Country Score	Global Average
C Core drivers index	70.71	57.25
C1 Governance	72.07	56.51
C1.1 Participation	60.66	41.70
C1.3 Transparency	82.40	65.15
C1.4 Responsiveness	41.65	44.42
C1.5 Consensus oriented	97.37	86.45
C1.6 Equity and inclusiveness	99.14	73.61
C1.7 Effectiveness and efficiency	32.53	28.38
C1.8 Political support	90.75	55.89
C2 Zoonotic diseases	78.18	68.06
C2.1 Source of infection	84.01	69.22
C2.2 Route of transmission	71.11	59.30
C2.3 Targeted population	78.85	59.90
C2.4 Capacity building	74.99	72.85
C2.5 Case studies	84.86	85.89
C3 Food security	65.28	52.89
C3.1 Food demand and supply	73.36	59.53
C3.2 Food safety	86.61	69.36
C3.3 Nutrition	89.31	67.17
C3.4 Natural and social circumstances	59.53	51.54
C3.5 Government support and response	17.56	16.85
C4 Antimicrobial resistance	72.33	44.05
C4.1 AMR surveillance system	72.35	34.79
C4.2 AMR laboratory network and coordination capacity	82.73	55.57
C4.3 Antimicrobial control and optimization	88.52	48.76
C4.4 Improve awareness and understanding	65.62	48.09
C4.5 Antimicrobial resistance rate for important antibiotics	52.40	33.03
C5 Climate change	65.58	64.19
C5.1 Mitigation and adaptation capacity	36.74	28.24
C5.2 Climate change risks	77.47	80.87
C5.3 Health outcome	84.53	85.41

Scores are normalized (0-100, where 100 = most favorable)

Portugal

Europe & Central Asia | High income

Index Score **019**/160

65.05

Global average: 54.82

Regional average: 60.26

Income group average: 61.66

Country performance: 65.05

Missing rate in GOHI database: 8.00%

▼ AVERAGE PERFORMANCE BY GOHI

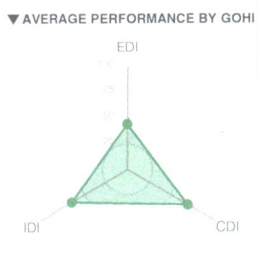

▼ AVERAGE PERFORMANCE BY CDI

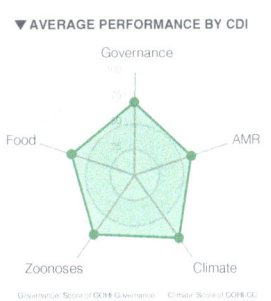

	Country Score	Global Average
A External drivers index	44.46	40.45
A1 Earth system	56.91	56.21
A1.1 Land	27.75	36.41
A1.2 Forest	48.60	43.43
A1.3 Water	49.39	58.09
A1.4 Air	88.95	71.93
A1.5 Natural disasters	62.21	64.65
A2 Institutional system	59.46	46.01
A2.1 Justice	73.73	57.89
A2.2 Governance	47.30	35.58
A3 Economical system	20.40	24.62
A3.1 Finance	23.84	34.35
A3.2 Work	37.79	38.58
A4 Sociological system	38.33	37.70
A4.1 Demographic	35.65	46.31
A4.2 Education	33.10	28.26
A4.3 Inequalities	48.20	40.26
A5 Technological system	47.69	37.72
A5.1 Transport	11.63	6.54
A5.2 Technology adoption	63.63	41.23
A5.3 Consumption and production	64.15	62.53
B Intrinsic drivers index	64.81	56.01
B1 Human health	84.02	72.35
B1.1 Health coverage	79.48	58.65
B1.2 Diseases burden	82.24	79.83
B1.3 Injury and violence	92.89	80.75
B2 Animal health and ecosystem diversity	53.49	56.58
B2.1 Animal epidemic disease	92.62	94.57
B2.2 Wildlife and marine life biodiversity	14.35	18.59
B3 Environmental health	58.89	46.87
B3.1 Air quality and climate change	53.73	53.72
B3.2 Environmental biodiversity	52.50	44.05
B3.3 Environmental resources	72.22	44.25

Scores are normalized (0-100, where 100 = most favorable)

	Country Score	Global Average
C Core drivers index	69.67	57.25
C1 Governance	71.73	56.51
C1.1 Participation	53.18	41.70
C1.3 Transparency	85.50	65.15
C1.4 Responsiveness	66.65	44.42
C1.5 Consensus oriented	93.91	86.45
C1.6 Equity and inclusiveness	93.12	73.61
C1.7 Effectiveness and efficiency	39.93	28.38
C1.8 Political support	69.78	55.89
C2 Zoonotic diseases	76.53	68.06
C2.1 Source of infection	84.34	69.22
C2.2 Route of transmission	69.63	59.30
C2.3 Targeted population	73.10	59.90
C2.4 Capacity building	72.31	72.85
C2.5 Case studies	84.85	85.89
C3 Food security	61.02	52.89
C3.1 Food demand and supply	68.92	59.53
C3.2 Food safety	83.26	69.36
C3.3 Nutrition	85.20	67.17
C3.4 Natural and social circumstances	55.22	51.54
C3.5 Government support and response	12.51	16.85
C4 Antimicrobial resistance	67.39	44.05
C4.1 AMR surveillance system	54.51	34.79
C4.2 AMR laboratory network and coordination on capacity	82.63	55.57
C4.3 Antimicrobial control and optimization	86.59	48.76
C4.4 Improve awareness and understanding	67.19	48.09
C4.5 Antimicrobial resistance rate for important antibiotics	46.02	33.03
C5 Climate change	71.92	64.19
C5.1 Mitigation and adaptation capacity	40.29	28.24
C5.2 Climate change risks	90.16	80.97
C5.3 Health outcome	87.49	85.41

Ireland

Europe & Central Asia | **High income**

64.38 Index **020**/160
Score

Global average: 54.82

Regional average: 60.26

Income group average: 61.66

Country performance: 64.38

Missing rate in GOHI database: 8.70%

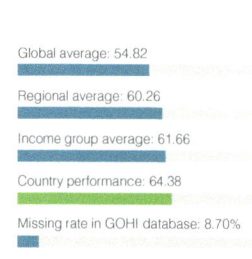

▼ AVERAGE PERFORMANCE BY GOHI

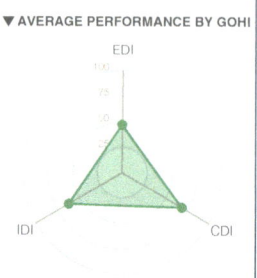

▼ AVERAGE PERFORMANCE BY CDI

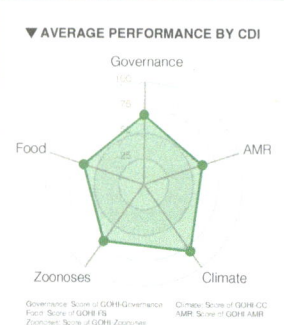

Governance: Score of GOHI-Governance   Climate: Score of GOHI-CC
Food: Score of GOHI-FS   AMR: Score of GOHI-AMR
Zoonoses: Score of GOHI-Zoonoses

	Country Score	Global Average
A External drivers index	46.91	40.45
A1 Earth system	57.04	56.21
A1.1 Land	29.55	36.41
A1.2 Forest	38.46	43.43
A1.3 Water	64.02	58.09
A1.4 Air	81.61	71.93
A1.5 Natural disasters	60.98	64.65
A2 Institutional system	65.04	46.01
A2.1 Justice	76.51	57.89
A2.2 Governance	55.27	35.58
A3 Economical system	32.49	24.62
A3.1 Finance	54.58	34.35
A3.2 Work	39.17	38.58
A4 Sociological system	38.18	37.70
A4.1 Demographic	36.43	46.31
A4.2 Education	30.02	28.26
A4.3 Inequalities	50.88	40.28
A5 Technological system	41.80	37.72
A5.1 Transport	15.38	6.54
A5.2 Technology adoption	46.78	41.23
A5.3 Consumption and production	60.76	62.53
B Intrinsic drivers index	62.06	58.01
B1 Human health	89.12	72.35
B1.1 Health coverage	88.74	58.65
B1.2 Diseases burden	84.58	79.83
B1.3 Injury and violence	96.74	80.75
B2 Animal health and ecosystem diversity	54.58	56.58
B2.1 Animal epidemic disease	96.06	94.57
B2.2 Wildlife and marine life biodiversity	13.10	18.59
B3 Environmental health	44.36	46.87
B3.1 Air quality and climate change	51.30	53.72
B3.2 Environmental biodiversity	49.25	44.05
B3.3 Environmental resources	33.86	44.25

Scores are normalized (0-100, where 100 = most favorable)

	Country Score	Global Average
C Core drivers index	68.82	57.25
C1 Governance	68.20	56.51
C1.1 Participation	53.32	41.70
C1.3 Transparency	87.00	65.15
C1.4 Responsiveness	33.35	44.42
C1.5 Consensus oriented	96.63	86.45
C1.6 Equity and inclusiveness	95.71	73.61
C1.7 Effectiveness and efficiency	43.33	28.38
C1.8 Political support	68.04	55.89
C2 Zoonotic diseases	80.72	68.06
C2.1 Source of infection	91.93	69.22
C2.2 Route of transmission	75.56	59.30
C2.3 Targeted population	78.20	59.90
C2.4 Capacity building	69.85	72.85
C2.5 Case studies	86.99	85.89
C3 Food security	62.39	52.89
C3.1 Food demand and supply	74.01	59.53
C3.2 Food safety	88.91	69.36
C3.3 Nutrition	83.54	67.17
C3.4 Natural and social circumstances	58.59	51.54
C3.5 Government support and response	6.92	16.85
C4 Antimicrobial resistance	63.80	44.05
C4.1 AMR surveillance system	83.85	34.79
C4.2 AMR laboratory network and coordination capacity	53.50	55.57
C4.3 Antimicrobial control and optimization	81.71	48.76
C4.4 Improve awareness and understanding	50.00	48.09
C4.5 Antimicrobial resistance rate for important antibiotics	49.95	33.03
C5 Climate change	66.78	64.19
C5.1 Mitigation and adaptation capacity	32.34	28.24
C5.2 Climate change risks	87.24	80.87
C5.3 Health outcome	88.82	85.41

South Korea

East Asia & Pacific | High income

64.38 Index Score **021** /160

Global average: 54.82

Regional average: 56.52

Income group average: 61.66

Country performance: 64.38

Missing rate in GOHI database: 21.70%

▼ AVERAGE PERFORMANCE BY GOHI

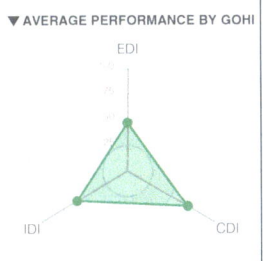

▼ AVERAGE PERFORMANCE BY CDI

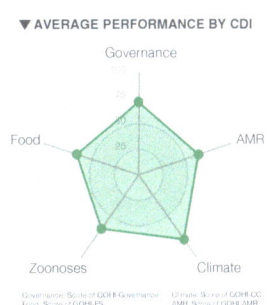

	Country Score	Global Average
A External drivers index	47.35	40.45
A1 Earth system	69.45	56.21
A1.1 Land	72.73	36.41
A1.2 Forest	57.72	43.43
A1.3 Water	87.21	58.09
A1.4 Air	56.43	71.93
A1.5 Natural disasters	66.67	64.65
A2 Institutional system	58.14	46.01
A2.1 Justice	70.74	57.89
A2.2 Governance	47.41	35.58
A3 Economical system	26.35	24.62
A3.1 Finance	37.86	34.35
A3.2 Work	39.89	38.58
A4 Sociological system	41.86	37.70
A4.1 Demographic	39.32	46.31
A4.2 Education	41.14	28.26
A4.3 Inequalities	45.69	40.28
A5 Technological system	40.94	37.72
A5.1 Transport	5.79	6.54
A5.2 Technology adoption	64.59	41.23
A5.3 Consumption and production	48.64	62.53
B Intrinsic drivers index	58.96	58.01
B1 Human health	85.69	72.35
B1.1 Health coverage	85.84	58.65
B1.2 Diseases burden	83.97	79.83
B1.3 Injury and violence	85.87	80.75
B2 Animal health and ecosystem diversity	59.23	56.58
B2.1 Animal epidemic disease	96.67	94.57
B2.2 Wildlife and marine life biodiversity	21.90	18.59
B3 Environmental health	33.74	46.87
B3.1 Air quality and climate change	24.03	53.72
B3.2 Environmental biodiversity	34.55	44.05
B3.3 Environmental resources	43.66	44.25

	Country Score	Global Average
C Core drivers index	69.45	57.25
C1 Governance	71.72	56.51
C1.1 Participation	57.93	41.70
C1.3 Transparency	84.63	65.15
C1.4 Responsiveness	75.00	44.42
C1.5 Consensus oriented	92.37	86.45
C1.6 Equity and inclusiveness	70.98	73.61
C1.7 Effectiveness and efficiency	51.07	28.38
C1.8 Political support	70.07	55.89
C2 Zoonotic diseases	78.54	68.06
C2.1 Source of infection	87.78	69.22
C2.2 Route of transmission	63.14	59.30
C2.3 Targeted population	77.96	59.90
C2.4 Capacity building	82.74	72.85
C2.5 Case studies	85.89	85.89
C3 Food security	64.66	52.89
C3.1 Food demand and supply	76.14	59.53
C3.2 Food safety	87.05	69.36
C3.3 Nutrition	78.53	67.17
C3.4 Natural and social circumstances	53.56	51.54
C3.5 Government support and response	30.04	16.85
C4 Antimicrobial resistance	66.19	44.05
C4.1 AMR surveillance system	68.60	34.79
C4.2 AMR laboratory network and coordination capacity	90.17	55.57
C4.3 Antimicrobial control and optimization	76.12	48.76
C4.4 Improve awareness and understanding	62.50	48.09
C4.5 Antimicrobial resistance rate for important antibiotics	33.55	33.03
C5 Climate change	65.52	64.19
C5.1 Mitigation and adaptation capacity	43.54	28.24
C5.2 Climate change risks	69.10	80.87
C5.3 Health outcome	85.89	85.41

Scores are normalized (0-100, where 100 = most favorable)

China
East Asia & Pacific | **Upper middle income**

63.21 Index Score **022**/160

Global average: 54.82

Regional average: 56.52

Income group average: 54.54

Country performance: 63.21

Missing rate in GOHI database: 15.60%

▼ AVERAGE PERFORMANCE BY GOHI

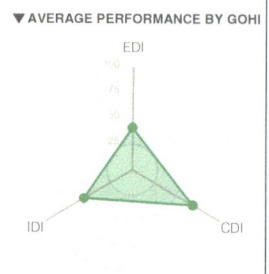
▼ AVERAGE PERFORMANCE BY CDI

	Country Score	Global Average
A External drivers index	41.31	40.45
A1 Earth system	57.55	56.21
A1.1 Land	22.38	36.41
A1.2 Forest	42.60	43.43
A1.3 Water	96.43	58.09
A1.4 Air	49.30	71.93
A1.5 Natural disasters	65.58	64.65
A2 Institutional system	43.26	46.01
A2.1 Justice	53.47	57.89
A2.2 Governance	34.56	35.58
A3 Economical system	24.64	24.62
A3.1 Finance	33.92	34.35
A3.2 Work	39.15	38.58
A4 Sociological system	40.51	37.70
A4.1 Demographic	40.37	46.31
A4.2 Education	38.20	28.26
A4.3 Inequalities	43.71	40.28
A5 Technological system	40.62	37.72
A5.1 Transport	1.67	6.54
A5.2 Technology adoption	51.45	41.23
A5.3 Consumption and production	64.97	62.53
B Intrinsic drivers index	56.02	53.01
B1 Human health	79.38	72.35
B1.1 Health coverage	71.20	58.65
B1.2 Diseases burden	83.30	79.83
B1.3 Injury and violence	86.06	80.75
B2 Animal health and ecosystem diversity	60.65	56.58
B2.1 Animal epidemic disease	98.94	94.57
B2.2 Wildlife and marine life biodiversity	22.35	18.59
B3 Environmental health	29.74	46.87
B3.1 Air quality and climate change	27.71	53.72
B3.2 Environmental biodiversity	15.50	44.05
B3.3 Environmental resources	46.90	44.25

	Country Score	Global Average
C Core drivers index	69.79	57.25
C1 Governance	67.69	56.51
C1.1 Participation	82.97	41.70
C1.3 Transparency	58.20	65.15
C1.4 Responsiveness	58.30	44.42
C1.5 Consensus oriented	98.66	86.45
C1.6 Equity and inclusiveness	64.59	73.61
C1.7 Effectiveness and efficiency	47.27	28.38
C1.8 Political support	63.81	55.89
C2 Zoonotic diseases	80.46	68.06
C2.1 Source of infection	83.36	69.22
C2.2 Route of transmission	77.27	59.30
C2.3 Targeted population	75.94	59.90
C2.4 Capacity building	83.07	72.85
C2.5 Case studies	84.05	85.89
C3 Food security	70.03	52.89
C3.1 Food demand and supply	73.96	59.53
C3.2 Food safety	82.36	69.36
C3.3 Nutrition	86.82	67.17
C3.4 Natural and social circumstances	61.67	51.54
C3.5 Government support and response	45.33	16.85
C4 Antimicrobial resistance	60.71	44.05
C4.1 AMR surveillance system	42.95	34.79
C4.2 AMR laboratory network and coordination capacity	67.31	55.57
C4.3 Antimicrobial control and optimization	71.58	48.76
C4.4 Improve awareness and understanding	75.00	48.09
C4.5 Antimicrobial resistance rate for important antibiotics	46.69	33.03
C5 Climate change	69.12	64.19
C5.1 Mitigation and adaptation capacity	51.86	28.24
C5.2 Climate change risks	67.31	80.87
C5.3 Health outcome	90.30	85.41

Scores are normalized (0-100, where 100 = most favorable)

Iceland

Europe & Central Asia | High income

Index Score **023**/160

62.82

Global average: 54.82

Regional average: 60.26

Income group average: 61.66

Country performance: 62.82

Missing rate in GOHI database: 13.00%

▼ AVERAGE PERFORMANCE BY GOHI

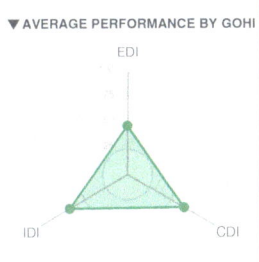

▼ AVERAGE PERFORMANCE BY CDI

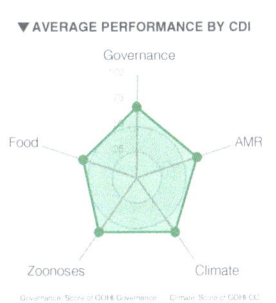

	Country Score	Global Average
A External drivers index	47.92	40.45
A1 Earth system	66.88	56.21
A1.1 Land	65.01	36.41
A1.2 Forest	34.98	43.43
A1.3 Water	69.32	58.09
A1.4 Air	89.73	71.93
A1.5 Natural disasters	64.43	64.65
A2 Institutional system	61.24	46.01
A2.1 Justice	73.40	57.89
A2.2 Governance	50.88	35.58
A3 Economical system	26.44	24.62
A3.1 Finance	36.39	34.35
A3.2 Work	42.02	38.58
A4 Sociological system	40.97	37.70
A4.1 Demographic	42.33	46.31
A4.2 Education	32.66	28.26
A4.3 Inequalities	50.30	40.28
A5 Technological system	44.09	37.72
A5.1 Transport	50.00	6.54
A5.2 Technology adoption	68.45	41.23
A5.3 Consumption and production	13.62	62.53
B Intrinsic drivers index	67.35	58.01
B1 Human health	89.33	72.35
B1.1 Health coverage	87.55	58.65
B1.2 Diseases burden	85.61	79.83
B1.3 Injury and violence	97.56	80.75
B2 Animal health and ecosystem diversity	57.38	56.58
B2.1 Animal epidemic disease	98.67	94.57
B2.2 Wildlife and marine life biodiversity	16.10	18.59
B3 Environmental health	57.36	46.87
B3.1 Air quality and climate change	55.15	53.72
B3.2 Environmental biodiversity	53.00	44.05
B3.3 Environmental resources	65.66	44.25

	Country Score	Global Average
C Core drivers index	65.06	57.25
C1 Governance	69.54	56.51
C1.1 Participation	47.10	41.70
C1.3 Transparency	77.80	65.15
C1.4 Responsiveness	58.30	44.42
C1.5 Consensus oriented	97.25	86.45
C1.6 Equity and inclusiveness	93.29	73.61
C1.7 Effectiveness and efficiency	35.93	28.38
C1.8 Political support	77.08	55.89
C2 Zoonotic diseases	66.26	68.06
C2.1 Source of infection	46.47	69.22
C2.2 Route of transmission	61.31	59.30
C2.3 Targeted population	78.86	59.90
C2.4 Capacity building	69.65	72.85
C2.5 Case studies	85.87	85.89
C3 Food security	64.83	52.89
C3.1 Food demand and supply	78.22	59.53
C3.2 Food safety	84.59	69.36
C3.3 Nutrition	85.28	67.17
C3.4 Natural and social circumstances	62.68	51.54
C3.5 Government support and response	13.40	16.85
C4 Antimicrobial resistance	57.40	44.05
C4.1 AMR surveillance system	58.26	34.79
C4.2 AMR laboratory network and coordination on capacity	66.67	55.57
C4.3 Antimicrobial control and optimization	64.21	48.76
C4.4 Improve awareness and understanding	50.00	48.09
C4.5 Antimicrobial resistance rate for important antibiotics	47.87	33.03
C5 Climate change	66.22	64.19
C5.1 Mitigation and adaptation capacity	35.64	28.24
C5.2 Climate change risks	79.48	80.87
C5.3 Health outcome	85.53	85.41

Scores are normalized (0-100, where 100 = most favorable)

Chile

Latin America & Caribbean | **High income**

Index Score **024**/160

Global average: 54.82

Regional average: 55.08

Income group average: 61.66

Country performance: 62.53

Missing rate in GOHI database: 12.70%

▼ AVERAGE PERFORMANCE BY GOHI

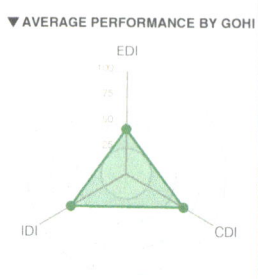

▼ AVERAGE PERFORMANCE BY CDI

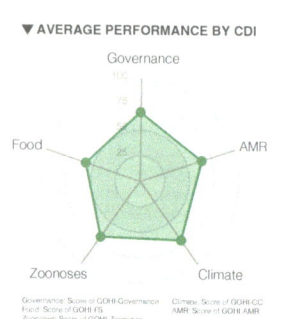

	Country Score	Global Average
A External drivers index	43.67	40.45
A1 Earth system	60.14	56.21
A1.1 Land	21.43	36.41
A1.2 Forest	49.12	43.43
A1.3 Water	77.52	58.09
A1.4 Air	75.23	71.93
A1.5 Natural disasters	66.59	64.65
A2 Institutional system	56.82	46.01
A2.1 Justice	69.33	57.89
A2.2 Governance	46.17	35.58
A3 Economical system	22.66	24.62
A3.1 Finance	30.32	34.35
A3.2 Work	37.11	38.58
A4 Sociological system	40.17	37.70
A4.1 Demographic	45.08	46.31
A4.2 Education	33.00	28.26
A4.3 Inequalities	43.99	40.28
A5 Technological system	38.56	37.72
A5.1 Transport	4.49	6.54
A5.2 Technology adoption	42.12	41.23
A5.3 Consumption and production	65.96	62.53
B Intrinsic drivers index	64.19	58.01
B1 Human health	83.25	72.35
B1.1 Health coverage	82.48	58.65
B1.2 Diseases burden	85.56	79.83
B1.3 Injury and violence	84.23	80.75
B2 Animal health and ecosystem diversity	60.52	56.58
B2.1 Animal epidemic disease	97.39	94.57
B2.2 Wildlife and marine life biodiversity	23.65	18.59
B3 Environmental health	50.74	46.87
B3.1 Air quality and climate change	37.35	53.72
B3.2 Environmental biodiversity	44.85	44.05
B3.3 Environmental resources	71.56	44.25

	Country Score	Global Average
C Core drivers index	66.32	57.25
C1 Governance	67.79	56.51
C1.1 Participation	81.05	41.70
C1.3 Transparency	82.40	65.15
C1.4 Responsiveness	50.00	44.42
C1.5 Consensus oriented	96.04	86.45
C1.6 Equity and inclusiveness	79.84	73.61
C1.7 Effectiveness and efficiency	29.20	28.38
C1.8 Political support	55.87	55.89
C2 Zoonotic diseases	71.41	68.06
C2.1 Source of infection	70.80	69.22
C2.2 Route of transmission	74.84	59.30
C2.3 Targeted population	53.10	59.90
C2.4 Capacity building	74.35	72.85
C2.5 Case studies	86.46	85.89
C3 Food security	65.66	52.89
C3.1 Food demand and supply	72.93	59.53
C3.2 Food safety	90.59	69.36
C3.3 Nutrition	81.97	67.17
C3.4 Natural and social circumstances	53.71	51.54
C3.5 Government support and response	29.10	16.85
C4 Antimicrobial resistance	58.18	44.05
C4.1 AMR surveillance system	33.91	34.79
C4.2 AMR laboratory network and coordinati on capacity	83.10	55.57
C4.3 Antimicrobial control and optimization	80.02	48.76
C4.4 Improve awareness and understanding	60.94	48.09
C4.5 Antimicrobial resistance rate for important antibiotics	32.91	33.03
C5 Climate change	67.73	64.19
C5.1 Mitigation and adaptation capacity	32.76	28.24
C5.2 Climate change risks	86.53	80.87
C5.3 Health outcome	85.96	85.41

Scores are normalized (0-100, where 100 = most favorable)

Slovenia
Europe & Central Asia | **High income**

Index Score **025**/160

Global average: 54.82

Regional average: 60.26

Income group average: 61.66

Country performance: 62.32

Missing rate in GOHI database: 12.00%

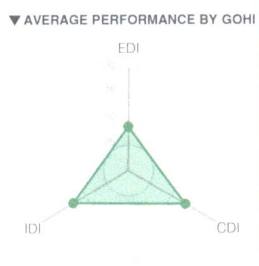

▼ AVERAGE PERFORMANCE BY GOHI

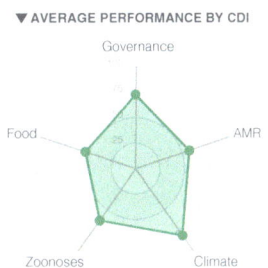

▼ AVERAGE PERFORMANCE BY CDI

	Country Score	Global Average
A External drivers index	43.13	40.45
A1 Earth system	56.22	56.21
A1.1 Land	20.28	36.41
A1.2 Forest	60.43	43.43
A1.3 Water	52.69	58.09
A1.4 Air	76.17	71.93
A1.5 Natural disasters	66.61	64.65
A2 Institutional system	55.86	46.01
A2.1 Justice	68.06	57.89
A2.2 Governance	45.48	35.58
A3 Economical system	21.24	24.62
A3.1 Finance	25.50	34.35
A3.2 Work	38.51	38.58
A4 Sociological system	39.64	37.70
A4.1 Demographic	33.18	46.31
A4.2 Education	35.20	28.26
A4.3 Inequalities	52.83	40.28
A5 Technological system	42.67	37.72
A5.1 Transport	1.29	6.54
A5.2 Technology adoption	64.17	41.23
A5.3 Consumption and production	58.27	62.53
B Intrinsic drivers index	64.44	58.01
B1 Human health	81.28	72.35
B1.1 Health coverage	76.27	58.65
B1.2 Diseases burden	74.40	79.83
B1.3 Injury and violence	95.63	80.75
B2 Animal health and ecosystem diversity	54.49	56.58
B2.1 Animal epidemic disease	97.49	94.57
B2.2 Wildlife and marine life biodiversity	11.48	18.59
B3 Environmental health	59.52	46.87
B3.1 Air quality and climate change	59.63	53.72
B3.2 Environmental biodiversity	51.30	44.05
B3.3 Environmental resources	69.44	44.25

	Country Score	Global Average
C Core drivers index	66.08	57.25
C1 Governance	72.75	56.51
C1.1 Participation	53.46	41.70
C1.3 Transparency	88.90	65.15
C1.4 Responsiveness	66.65	44.42
C1.5 Consensus oriented	87.73	86.45
C1.6 Equity and inclusiveness	96.42	73.61
C1.7 Effectiveness and efficiency	49.53	28.38
C1.8 Political support	66.55	55.89
C2 Zoonotic diseases	81.17	68.06
C2.1 Source of infection	96.50	69.22
C2.2 Route of transmission	74.85	59.30
C2.3 Targeted population	79.56	59.90
C2.4 Capacity building	71.82	72.85
C2.5 Case studies	80.14	85.89
C3 Food security	57.83	52.89
C3.1 Food demand and supply	68.13	59.53
C3.2 Food safety	78.70	69.36
C3.3 Nutrition	76.36	67.17
C3.4 Natural and social circumstances	54.26	51.54
C3.5 Government support and response	11.71	16.85
C4 Antimicrobial resistance	53.60	44.05
C4.1 AMR surveillance system	48.00	34.79
C4.2 AMR laboratory network and coordination capacity	53.95	55.57
C4.3 Antimicrobial control and optimization	69.01	48.76
C4.4 Improve awareness and understanding	48.44	48.09
C4.5 Antimicrobial resistance rate for important antibiotics	49.62	33.03
C5 Climate change	63.15	64.19
C5.1 Mitigation and adaptation capacity	22.23	28.24
C5.2 Climate change risks	80.63	80.87
C5.3 Health outcome	88.50	85.41

Scores are normalized (0-100, where 100 = most favorable)

Czech Republic
Europe & Central Asia | High income

62.22 Index **026**/160
Score

Global average: 54.82

Regional average: 60.26

Income group average: 61.66

Country performance: 62.22

Missing rate in GOHI database: 18.80%

▼ AVERAGE PERFORMANCE BY GOHI

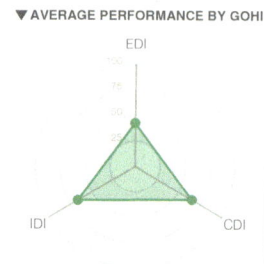

▼ AVERAGE PERFORMANCE BY CDI

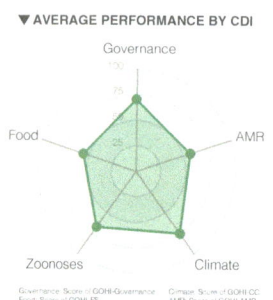

	Country Score	Global Average
A External drivers index	42.61	40.45
A1 Earth system	52.82	56.21
A1.1 Land	45.31	36.41
A1.2 Forest	47.38	43.43
A1.3 Water	37.63	58.09
A1.4 Air	69.86	71.93
A1.5 Natural disasters	62.24	64.65
A2 Institutional system	57.38	46.01
A2.1 Justice	68.12	57.89
A2.2 Governance	48.23	35.58
A3 Economical system	20.68	24.62
A3.1 Finance	23.45	34.35
A3.2 Work	39.24	38.58
A4 Sociological system	39.28	37.70
A4.1 Demographic	36.99	46.31
A4.2 Education	36.16	28.26
A4.3 Inequalities	45.98	40.28
A5 Technological system	42.90	37.72
A5.1 Transport	2.71	6.54
A5.2 Technology adoption	62.92	41.23
A5.3 Consumption and production	58.95	62.53
B Intrinsic drivers index	68.53	58.01
B1 Human health	81.22	72.35
B1.1 Health coverage	73.83	58.65
B1.2 Diseases burden	78.07	79.83
B1.3 Injury and violence	94.21	80.75
B2 Animal health and ecosystem diversity	57.21	56.58
B2.1 Animal epidemic disease	97.65	94.57
B2.2 Wildlife and marine life biodiversity	16.77	18.59
B3 Environmental health	63.19	46.87
B3.1 Air quality and climate change	62.61	53.72
B3.2 Environmental biodiversity	51.20	44.05
B3.3 Environmental resources	77.68	44.25

	Country Score	Global Average
C Core drivers index	65.56	57.25
C1 Governance	70.64	56.51
C1.1 Participation	61.37	41.70
C1.3 Transparency	85.10	65.15
C1.4 Responsiveness	35.40	44.42
C1.5 Consensus oriented	95.53	86.45
C1.6 Equity and inclusiveness	98.53	73.61
C1.7 Effectiveness and efficiency	40.73	28.38
C1.8 Political support	77.61	55.89
C2 Zoonotic diseases	75.41	68.06
C2.1 Source of infection	84.20	69.22
C2.2 Route of transmission	63.95	59.30
C2.3 Targeted population	75.75	59.90
C2.4 Capacity building	73.34	72.85
C2.5 Case studies	82.68	85.89
C3 Food security	57.20	52.89
C3.1 Food demand and supply	71.14	59.53
C3.2 Food safety	81.10	69.36
C3.3 Nutrition	60.22	67.17
C3.4 Natural and social circumstances	58.08	51.54
C3.5 Government support and response	15.47	16.85
C4 Antimicrobial resistance	56.15	44.05
C4.1 AMR surveillance system	53.36	34.79
C4.2 AMR laboratory network and coordination capacity	59.39	55.57
C4.3 Antimicrobial control and optimization	65.43	48.76
C4.4 Improve awareness and understanding	57.81	48.09
C4.5 Antimicrobial resistance rate for important antibiotics	44.76	33.03
C5 Climate change	67.58	64.19
C5.1 Mitigation and adaptation capacity	39.11	28.24
C5.2 Climate change risks	82.73	80.87
C5.3 Health outcome	82.96	85.41

Scores are normalized (0-100, where 100 = most favorable)

Malaysia

East Asia & Pacific | Upper middle income

Index Score **027** /160

Global average: 54.82

Regional average: 56.52

Income group average: 54.54

Country performance: 61.89

Missing rate in GOHI database: 12.70%

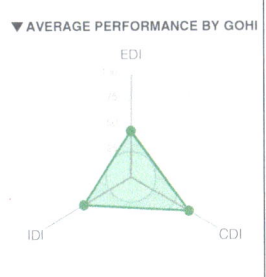

▼AVERAGE PERFORMANCE BY GOHI

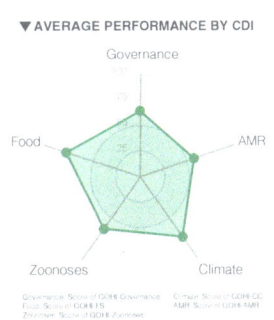

▼AVERAGE PERFORMANCE BY CDI

	Country Score	Global Average
A External drivers index	45.29	40.45
A1 Earth system	62.28	56.21
A1.1 Land	30.03	36.41
A1.2 Forest	58.03	43.43
A1.3 Water	75.50	58.09
A1.4 Air	72.79	71.93
A1.5 Natural disasters	66.26	64.65
A2 Institutional system	51.97	46.01
A2.1 Justice	63.74	57.89
A2.2 Governance	41.95	35.58
A3 Economical system	28.04	24.62
A3.1 Finance	43.31	34.35
A3.2 Work	38.60	38.58
A4 Sociological system	38.97	37.70
A4.1 Demographic	47.03	46.31
A4.2 Education	26.80	28.26
A4.3 Inequalities	45.76	40.28
A5 Technological system	45.19	37.72
A5.1 Transport	6.20	6.54
A5.2 Technology adoption	62.46	41.23
A5.3 Consumption and production	62.96	62.53
B Intrinsic drivers index	55.39	58.01
B1 Human health	77.91	72.35
B1.1 Health coverage	67.12	58.65
B1.2 Diseases burden	88.14	79.83
B1.3 Injury and violence	80.82	80.75
B2 Animal health and ecosystem diversity	58.60	58.58
B2.1 Animal epidemic disease	95.04	94.57
B2.2 Wildlife and marine life biodiversity	22.15	18.59
B3 Environmental health	31.35	46.87
B3.1 Air quality and climate change	23.27	53.72
B3.2 Environmental biodiversity	48.70	44.05
B3.3 Environmental resources	23.02	44.25

	Country Score	Global Average
C Core drivers index	67.12	57.26
C1 Governance	64.60	56.51
C1.1 Participation	48.96	41.70
C1.3 Transparency	77.10	65.15
C1.4 Responsiveness	66.70	44.42
C1.5 Consensus oriented	97.06	86.45
C1.6 Equity and inclusiveness	74.29	73.61
C1.7 Effectiveness and efficiency	39.93	28.38
C1.8 Political support	54.16	55.89
C2 Zoonotic diseases	73.25	68.06
C2.1 Source of infection	46.76	69.22
C2.2 Route of transmission	82.10	59.30
C2.3 Targeted population	77.78	59.90
C2.4 Capacity building	77.74	72.85
C2.5 Case studies	89.23	85.89
C3 Food security	57.87	52.89
C3.1 Food demand and supply	65.91	59.53
C3.2 Food safety	80.16	69.36
C3.3 Nutrition	68.45	67.17
C3.4 Natural and social circumstances	53.58	51.54
C3.5 Government support and response	21.25	16.85
C4 Antimicrobial resistance	77.89	44.05
C4.1 AMR surveillance system	73.66	34.79
C4.2 AMR laboratory network and coordination on capacity	91.23	55.57
C4.3 Antimicrobial control and optimization	85.80	48.76
C4.4 Improve awareness and understanding	95.31	48.09
C4.5 Antimicrobial resistance rate for important antibiotics	43.43	33.03
C5 Climate change	63.50	64.19
C5.1 Mitigation and adaptation capacity	24.93	28.24
C5.2 Climate change risks	82.23	80.87
C5.3 Health outcome	85.25	85.41

Scores are normalized (0-100, where 100 = most favorable)

Greece

Europe & Central Asia | **High income**

 Index Score **028**/160

Global average: 54.82

Regional average: 60.26

Income group average: 61.66

Country performance: 61.66

Missing rate in GOHI database: 9.10%

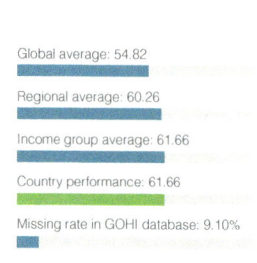
▼ AVERAGE PERFORMANCE BY GOHI

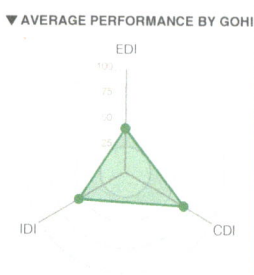
▼ AVERAGE PERFORMANCE BY CDI

Governance: Score of GOHI-Governance   Climate: Score of GOHI-CC
Food: Score of GOHI-FS   AMR: Score of GOHI-AMR
Zoonoses: Score of GOHI-Zoonoses

	Country Score	Global Average
A External drivers index	42.72	40.45
A1 Earth system	58.32	56.21
A1.1 Land	27.58	36.41
A1.2 Forest	46.37	43.43
A1.3 Water	60.98	58.09
A1.4 Air	81.64	71.93
A1.5 Natural disasters	66.61	64.65
A2 Institutional system	50.94	46.01
A2.1 Justice	62.03	57.89
A2.2 Governance	41.49	35.58
A3 Economical system	20.20	24.62
A3.1 Finance	26.32	34.35
A3.2 Work	33.99	38.58
A4 Sociological system	38.29	37.70
A4.1 Demographic	38.42	46.31
A4.2 Education	30.84	28.26
A4.3 Inequalities	47.89	40.28
A5 Technological system	45.85	37.72
A5.1 Transport	9.31	6.54
A5.2 Technology adoption	61.30	41.23
A5.3 Consumption and production	63.27	62.53
B Intrinsic drivers index	54.09	58.01
B1 Human health	78.89	72.35
B1.1 Health coverage	68.67	58.65
B1.2 Diseases burden	77.74	79.83
B1.3 Injury and violence	92.66	80.75
B2 Animal health and ecosystem diversity	54.43	56.58
B2.1 Animal epidemic disease	92.55	94.57
B2.2 Wildlife and marine life biodiversity	16.30	18.59
B3 Environmental health	30.59	46.87
B3.1 Air quality and climate change	26.91	53.72
B3.2 Environmental biodiversity	31.60	44.05
B3.3 Environmental resources	31.48	44.25

	Country Score	Global Average
C Core drivers index	67.66	57.25
C1 Governance	73.00	56.51
C1.1 Participation	81.94	41.70
C1.3 Transparency	85.40	65.15
C1.4 Responsiveness	41.65	44.42
C1.5 Consensus oriented	97.13	86.45
C1.6 Equity and inclusiveness	83.24	73.61
C1.7 Effectiveness and efficiency	36.27	28.38
C1.8 Political support	85.34	55.89
C2 Zoonotic diseases	76.64	68.06
C2.1 Source of infection	83.06	69.22
C2.2 Route of transmission	66.83	59.30
C2.3 Targeted population	78.61	59.90
C2.4 Capacity building	74.21	72.85
C2.5 Case studies	83.17	85.89
C3 Food security	60.63	52.89
C3.1 Food demand and supply	67.95	59.53
C3.2 Food safety	79.01	69.36
C3.3 Nutrition	80.86	67.17
C3.4 Natural and social circumstances	60.34	51.54
C3.5 Government support and response	14.99	16.85
C4 Antimicrobial resistance	58.08	44.05
C4.1 AMR surveillance system	52.36	34.79
C4.2 AMR laboratory network and coordination capacity	60.27	55.57
C4.3 Antimicrobial control and optimization	78.96	48.76
C4.4 Improve awareness and understanding	75.00	48.09
C4.5 Antimicrobial resistance rate for important antibiotics	23.79	33.03
C5 Climate change	69.04	64.19
C5.1 Mitigation and adaptation capacity	43.50	28.24
C5.2 Climate change risks	79.52	80.87
C5.3 Health outcome	86.19	85.41

Scores are normalized (0-100, where 100 = most favorable)

Thailand

East Asia & Pacific | Upper middle income

61.49 Index Score **029**/160

Global average: 54.82

Regional average: 56.52

Income group average: 54.54

Country performance: 61.49

Missing rate in GOHI database: 11.60%

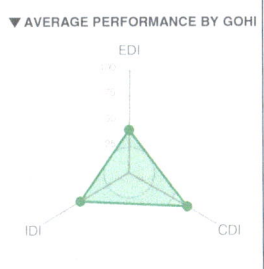

▼ AVERAGE PERFORMANCE BY GOHI

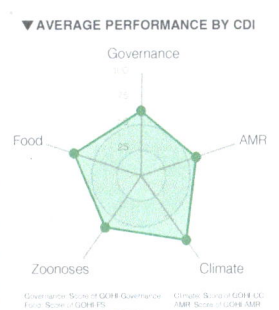

▼ AVERAGE PERFORMANCE BY CDI

	Country Score	Global Average
A External drivers index	41.97	40.45
A1 Earth system	56.59	56.21
A1.1 Land	38.09	36.41
A1.2 Forest	48.52	43.43
A1.3 Water	52.19	58.09
A1.4 Air	73.73	71.93
A1.5 Natural disasters	65.54	64.65
A2 Institutional system	46.06	46.01
A2.1 Justice	58.49	57.89
A2.2 Governance	35.48	35.58
A3 Economical system	24.89	24.62
A3.1 Finance	32.82	34.35
A3.2 Work	41.38	38.58
A4 Sociological system	35.96	37.70
A4.1 Demographic	37.81	46.31
A4.2 Education	30.70	28.26
A4.3 Inequalities	40.73	40.28
A5 Technological system	46.33	37.72
A5.1 Transport	4.88	6.54
A5.2 Technology adoption	61.31	41.23
A5.3 Consumption and production	68.70	62.53
B Intrinsic drivers index	56.79	58.01
B1 Human health	76.87	72.35
B1.1 Health coverage	77.42	58.65
B1.2 Diseases burden	82.60	79.83
B1.3 Injury and violence	72.90	80.75
B2 Animal health and ecosystem diversity	56.75	56.58
B2.1 Animal epidemic disease	95.56	94.57
B2.2 Wildlife and marine life biodiversity	17.95	18.59
B3 Environmental health	38.47	46.87
B3.1 Air quality and climate change	44.27	53.72
B3.2 Environmental biodiversity	44.45	44.05
B3.3 Environmental resources	27.84	44.25

	Country Score	Global Average
C Core drivers index	66.95	57.25
C1 Governance	63.82	56.51
C1.1 Participation	47.47	41.70
C1.3 Transparency	76.10	65.15
C1.4 Responsiveness	83.35	44.42
C1.5 Consensus oriented	89.36	86.45
C1.6 Equity and inclusiveness	66.69	73.61
C1.7 Effectiveness and efficiency	35.00	28.38
C1.8 Political support	48.76	55.89
C2 Zoonotic diseases	78.28	68.06
C2.1 Source of infection	80.90	69.22
C2.2 Route of transmission	74.38	59.30
C2.3 Targeted population	68.47	59.90
C2.4 Capacity building	80.92	72.85
C2.5 Case studies	90.17	85.89
C3 Food security	59.23	52.89
C3.1 Food demand and supply	66.70	59.53
C3.2 Food safety	84.10	69.36
C3.3 Nutrition	69.25	67.17
C3.4 Natural and social circumstances	54.55	51.54
C3.5 Government support and response	21.56	16.85
C4 Antimicrobial resistance	71.25	44.05
C4.1 AMR surveillance system	78.10	34.79
C4.2 AMR laboratory network and coordination on capacity	82.38	55.57
C4.3 Antimicrobial control and optimization	71.31	48.76
C4.4 Improve awareness and understanding	82.81	48.09
C4.5 Antimicrobial resistance rate for important antibiotics	41.65	33.03
C5 Climate change	62.86	64.19
C5.1 Mitigation and adaptation capacity	28.45	28.24
C5.2 Climate change risks	79.71	80.87
C5.3 Health outcome	82.33	85.41

Scores are normalized (0-100, where 100 = most favorable)

New Zealand

East Asia & Pacific | High income

61.29 Index Score **030**/160

Global average: 54.82

Regional average: 56.52

Income group average: 61.66

Country performance: 61.29

Missing rate in GOHI database: 18.50%

▼ AVERAGE PERFORMANCE BY GOHI

▼ AVERAGE PERFORMANCE BY CDI

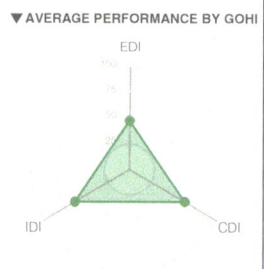

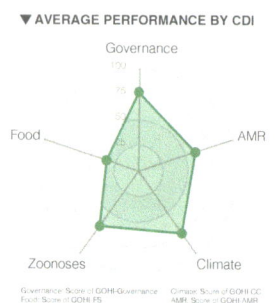

Governance: Score of GOHI-Governance   Climate: Score of GOHI-CC
Food: Score of GOHI-FS   AMR: Score of GOHI-AMR
Zoonoses: Score of GOHI-Zoonoses

	Country Score	Global Average
A External drivers index	47.86	40.45
A1 Earth system	64.36	56.21
A1.1 Land	27.69	36.41
A1.2 Forest	63.10	43.43
A1.3 Water	71.19	58.09
A1.4 Air	84.08	71.93
A1.5 Natural disasters	66.54	64.65
A2 Institutional system	65.83	46.01
A2.1 Justice	78.79	57.89
A2.2 Governance	54.78	35.58
A3 Economical system	26.68	24.62
A3.1 Finance	37.32	34.35
A3.2 Work	41.67	38.58
A4 Sociological system	38.85	37.70
A4.1 Demographic	41.40	46.31
A4.2 Education	29.48	28.26
A4.3 Inequalities	48.23	40.28
A5 Technological system	43.60	37.72
A5.1 Transport	20.93	6.54
A5.2 Technology adoption	53.85	41.23
A5.3 Consumption and production	53.71	62.53
B Intrinsic drivers index	63.83	53.01
B1 Human health	86.28	72.35
B1.1 Health coverage	88.24	58.65
B1.2 Diseases burden	82.53	79.83
B1.3 Injury and violence	90.68	80.75
B2 Animal health and ecosystem diversity	56.57	56.58
B2.1 Animal epidemic disease	96.45	94.57
B2.2 Wildlife and marine life biodiversity	22.70	18.59
B3 Environmental health	47.58	46.87
B3.1 Air quality and climate change	54.60	53.72
B3.2 Environmental biodiversity	38.27	44.05
B3.3 Environmental resources	51.33	44.25

Scores are normalized (0-100, where 100 = most favorable)

	Country Score	Global Average
C Core drivers index	63.63	57.25
C1 Governance	77.30	56.51
C1.1 Participation	88.26	41.70
C1.3 Transparency	85.30	65.15
C1.4 Responsiveness	58.30	44.42
C1.5 Consensus oriented	99.03	86.45
C1.6 Equity and inclusiveness	81.07	73.61
C1.7 Effectiveness and efficiency	50.67	28.38
C1.8 Political support	78.48	55.89
C2 Zoonotic diseases	75.44	68.06
C2.1 Source of infection	86.86	69.22
C2.2 Route of transmission	55.48	59.30
C2.3 Targeted population	79.86	59.90
C2.4 Capacity building	73.53	72.85
C2.5 Case studies	87.49	85.89
C3 Food security	60.72	52.89
C3.1 Food demand and supply	68.05	59.53
C3.2 Food safety	66.30	69.36
C3.3 Nutrition	80.51	67.17
C3.4 Natural and social circumstances	61.42	51.54
C3.5 Government support and response	27.34	16.85
C4 Antimicrobial resistance	34.28	44.05
C4.1 AMR surveillance system	11.40	34.79
C4.2 AMR laboratory network and coordination capacity	46.51	55.57
C4.3 Antimicrobial control and optimization	45.93	48.76
C4.4 Improve awareness and understanding	29.69	48.09
C4.5 Antimicrobial resistance rate for important antibiotics	37.85	33.03
C5 Climate change	66.90	64.19
C5.1 Mitigation and adaptation capacity	35.12	28.24
C5.2 Climate change risks	82.37	80.87
C5.3 Health outcome	85.24	85.41

Argentina

Latin America & Caribbean | **Upper middle income**

Index Score **031**/160

Global average: 54.82

Regional average: 55.08

Income group average: 54.54

Country performance: 61.27

Missing rate in GOHI database: 10.90%

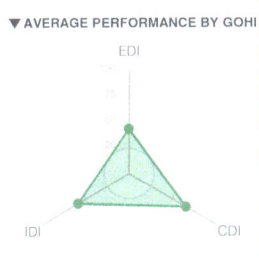

▼ AVERAGE PERFORMANCE BY GOHI

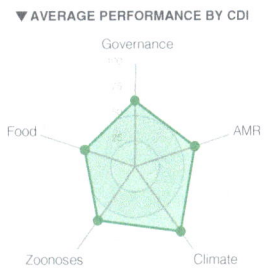

▼ AVERAGE PERFORMANCE BY CDI

	Country Score	Global Average
A External drivers index	43.98	40.45
A1 Earth system	62.98	56.21
A1.1 Land	75.67	36.41
A1.2 Forest	33.55	43.43
A1.3 Water	48.24	58.09
A1.4 Air	85.46	71.93
A1.5 Natural disasters	66.66	64.65
A2 Institutional system	46.12	46.01
A2.1 Justice	61.57	57.89
A2.2 Governance	32.96	35.58
A3 Economical system	29.34	24.62
A3.1 Finance	47.72	34.35
A3.2 Work	37.36	38.58
A4 Sociological system	37.80	37.70
A4.1 Demographic	47.44	46.31
A4.2 Education	27.36	28.26
A4.3 Inequalities	40.51	40.28
A5 Technological system	43.66	37.72
A5.1 Transport	2.29	6.54
A5.2 Technology adoption	56.92	41.23
A5.3 Consumption and production	67.72	62.53
B Intrinsic drivers index	59.02	58.01
B1 Human health	79.31	72.35
B1.1 Health coverage	72.67	58.65
B1.2 Diseases burden	83.67	79.83
B1.3 Injury and violence	84.00	80.75
B2 Animal health and ecosystem diversity	54.11	56.58
B2.1 Animal epidemic disease	97.32	94.57
B2.2 Wildlife and marine life biodiversity	10.90	18.59
B3 Environmental health	45.44	46.87
B3.1 Air quality and climate change	50.85	53.72
B3.2 Environmental biodiversity	32.70	44.05
B3.3 Environmental resources	54.14	44.25

	Country Score	Global Average
C Core drivers index	65.65	57.25
C1 Governance	64.83	56.51
C1.1 Participation	77.63	41.70
C1.3 Transparency	64.60	65.15
C1.4 Responsiveness	50.00	44.42
C1.5 Consensus oriented	98.03	86.45
C1.6 Equity and inclusiveness	86.42	73.61
C1.7 Effectiveness and efficiency	30.93	28.38
C1.8 Political support	46.19	55.89
C2 Zoonotic diseases	78.86	68.06
C2.1 Source of infection	80.19	69.22
C2.2 Route of transmission	72.44	59.30
C2.3 Targeted population	78.97	59.90
C2.4 Capacity building	79.44	72.85
C2.5 Case studies	86.71	85.89
C3 Food security	64.24	52.89
C3.1 Food demand and supply	53.73	59.53
C3.2 Food safety	82.79	69.36
C3.3 Nutrition	80.10	67.17
C3.4 Natural and social circumstances	71.36	51.54
C3.5 Government support and response	33.21	16.85
C4 Antimicrobial resistance	53.74	44.05
C4.1 AMR surveillance system	48.16	34.79
C4.2 AMR laboratory network and coordination on capacity	75.75	55.57
C4.3 Antimicrobial control and optimization	57.68	48.76
C4.4 Improve awareness and understanding	48.44	48.09
C4.5 Antimicrobial resistance rate for important antibiotics	38.68	33.03
C5 Climate change	65.35	64.19
C5.1 Mitigation and adaptation capacity	30.17	28.24
C5.2 Climate change risks	82.29	80.87
C5.3 Health outcome	85.56	85.41

Scores are normalized (0-100, where 100 = most favorable)

Brazil

Latin America & Caribbean | **Upper middle income**

Index Score **032**/160

Global average: 54.82

Regional average: 55.08

Income group average: 54.54

Country performance: 61.26

Missing rate in GOHI database: 12.30%

▼ AVERAGE PERFORMANCE BY GOHI

▼ AVERAGE PERFORMANCE BY CDI

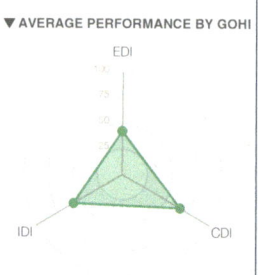

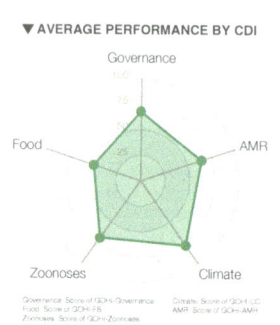

Governance: Score of GOH-Governance
Food: Score of GOH-FS
Zoonoses: Score of GOH-Zoonosis

Climate: Score of GOH-CC
AMR: Score of GOH-AMR

	Country Score	Global Average
A External drivers index	42.71	40.45
A1 Earth system	71.71	56.21
A1.1 Land	45.96	36.41
A1.2 Forest	43.57	43.43
A1.3 Water	88.40	58.09
A1.4 Air	90.86	71.93
A1.5 Natural disasters	66.02	64.65
A2 Institutional system	43.87	46.01
A2.1 Justice	56.57	57.89
A2.2 Governance	33.05	35.58
A3 Economical system	22.52	24.62
A3.1 Finance	30.07	34.35
A3.2 Work	36.97	38.58
A4 Sociological system	38.12	37.70
A4.1 Demographic	50.13	46.31
A4.2 Education	29.79	28.26
A4.3 Inequalities	35.38	40.28
A5 Technological system	37.33	37.72
A5.1 Transport	1.66	6.54
A5.2 Technology adoption	37.98	41.23
A5.3 Consumption and production	69.18	62.53
B Intrinsic drivers index	56.88	58.01
B1 Human health	69.66	72.35
B1.1 Health coverage	66.12	58.65
B1.2 Diseases burden	83.71	79.83
B1.3 Injury and violence	61.26	80.75
B2 Animal health and ecosystem diversity	57.63	56.58
B2.1 Animal epidemic disease	99.11	94.57
B2.2 Wildlife and marine life biodiversity	16.15	18.59
B3 Environmental health	45.12	46.87
B3.1 Air quality and climate change	35.89	53.72
B3.2 Environmental biodiversity	47.65	44.05
B3.3 Environmental resources	53.18	44.25

Scores are normalized (0-100, where 100 = most favorable)

	Country Score	Global Average
C Core drivers index	66.42	57.25
C1 Governance	67.97	56.51
C1.1 Participation	79.44	41.70
C1.3 Transparency	76.80	65.15
C1.4 Responsiveness	45.80	44.42
C1.5 Consensus oriented	95.48	86.45
C1.6 Equity and inclusiveness	80.45	73.61
C1.7 Effectiveness and efficiency	38.60	28.38
C1.8 Political support	59.25	55.89
C2 Zoonotic diseases	78.42	68.06
C2.1 Source of infection	83.25	69.22
C2.2 Route of transmission	65.43	59.30
C2.3 Targeted population	79.09	59.90
C2.4 Capacity building	86.05	72.85
C2.5 Case studies	83.27	85.89
C3 Food security	65.01	52.89
C3.1 Food demand and supply	61.03	59.53
C3.2 Food safety	89.92	69.36
C3.3 Nutrition	80.92	67.17
C3.4 Natural and social circumstances	58.03	51.54
C3.5 Government support and response	35.14	16.85
C4 Antimicrobial resistance	49.65	44.05
C4.1 AMR surveillance system	36.90	34.79
C4.2 AMR laboratory network and coordination on capacity	71.22	55.57
C4.3 Antimicrobial control and optimization	60.59	48.76
C4.4 Improve awareness and understanding	50.00	48.09
C4.5 Antimicrobial resistance rate for important antibiotics	29.54	33.03
C5 Climate change	69.42	64.19
C5.1 Mitigation and adaptation capacity	39.09	28.24
C5.2 Climate change risks	87.34	80.87
C5.3 Health outcome	83.94	85.41

Latvia

Europe & Central Asia | High income

61.09 Index **033**/160
Score

Global average: 54.82

Regional average: 60.26

Income group average: 61.66

Country performance: 61.09

Missing rate in GOHI database: 8.30%

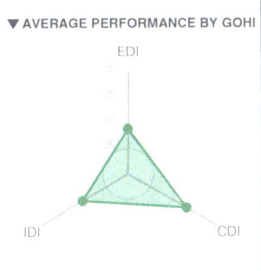

▼ AVERAGE PERFORMANCE BY GOHI

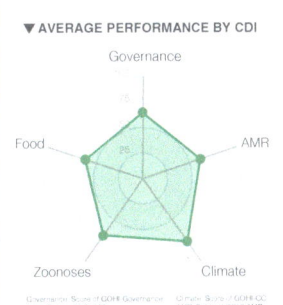

▼ AVERAGE PERFORMANCE BY CDI

	Country Score	Global Average
A External drivers index	44.30	40.45
A1 Earth system	68.02	56.21
A1.1 Land	72.97	36.41
A1.2 Forest	61.52	43.43
A1.3 Water	49.70	58.09
A1.4 Air	86.48	71.93
A1.5 Natural disasters	66.26	64.65
A2 Institutional system	53.63	46.01
A2.1 Justice	63.57	57.89
A2.2 Governance	45.15	35.58
A3 Economical system	19.16	24.62
A3.1 Finance	20.32	34.35
A3.2 Work	38.15	38.58
A4 Sociological system	37.37	37.70
A4.1 Demographic	39.18	46.31
A4.2 Education	28.57	28.26
A4.3 Inequalities	46.85	40.28
A5 Technological system	43.34	37.72
A5.1 Transport	4.92	6.54
A5.2 Technology adoption	55.58	41.23
A5.3 Consumption and production	65.75	62.53
B Intrinsic drivers index	53.08	58.01
B1 Human health	70.90	72.35
B1.1 Health coverage	60.07	58.65
B1.2 Diseases burden	65.20	79.83
B1.3 Injury and violence	89.58	80.75
B2 Animal health and ecosystem diversity	57.54	56.58
B2.1 Animal epidemic disease	95.38	94.57
B2.2 Wildlife and marine life biodiversity	19.70	18.59
B3 Environmental health	32.42	46.87
B3.1 Air quality and climate change	34.06	53.72
B3.2 Environmental biodiversity	46.05	44.05
B3.3 Environmental resources	18.14	44.25

	Country Score	Global Average
C Core drivers index	66.72	57.25
C1 Governance	64.89	56.51
C1.1 Participation	45.80	41.70
C1.3 Transparency	83.70	65.15
C1.4 Responsiveness	33.35	44.42
C1.5 Consensus oriented	94.41	86.45
C1.6 Equity and inclusiveness	99.28	73.61
C1.7 Effectiveness and efficiency	39.13	28.38
C1.8 Political support	58.56	55.89
C2 Zoonotic diseases	76.49	66.06
C2.1 Source of infection	71.56	69.22
C2.2 Route of transmission	80.53	59.30
C2.3 Targeted population	77.65	59.90
C2.4 Capacity building	70.34	72.85
C2.5 Case studies	82.83	85.89
C3 Food security	61.83	52.89
C3.1 Food demand and supply	63.25	59.53
C3.2 Food safety	83.88	69.36
C3.3 Nutrition	81.61	67.17
C3.4 Natural and social circumstances	60.81	51.54
C3.5 Government support and response	19.62	16.85
C4 Antimicrobial resistance	61.32	44.05
C4.1 AMR surveillance system	58.88	34.79
C4.2 AMR laboratory network and coordination capacity	79.96	55.57
C4.3 Antimicrobial control and optimization	71.13	48.76
C4.4 Improve awareness and understanding	60.94	48.09
C4.5 Antimicrobial resistance rate for important antibiotics	35.68	33.03
C5 Climate change	69.04	64.19
C5.1 Mitigation and adaptation capacity	30.75	28.24
C5.2 Climate change risks	90.07	80.87
C5.3 Health outcome	88.38	85.41

Scores are normalized (0-100, where 100 = most favorable)

Lithuania

Europe & Central Asia | **High income**

Index Score **034**/160

Global average: 54.82

Regional average: 60.26

Income group average: 61.66

Country performance: 60.95

Missing rate in GOHI database: 13.40%

▼ AVERAGE PERFORMANCE BY GOHI

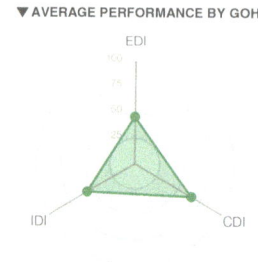

▼ AVERAGE PERFORMANCE BY CDI

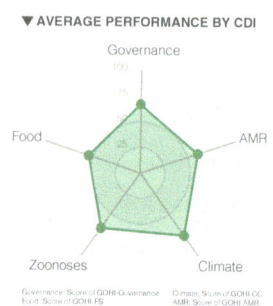

	Country Score	Global Average
A External drivers index	46.03	40.45
A1 Earth system	67.62	56.21
A1.1 Land	76.31	36.41
A1.2 Forest	49.48	43.43
A1.3 Water	54.50	58.09
A1.4 Air	86.11	71.93
A1.5 Natural disasters	66.65	64.65
A2 Institutional system	58.76	46.01
A2.1 Justice	70.12	57.89
A2.2 Governance	49.08	35.58
A3 Economical system	20.89	24.62
A3.1 Finance	24.50	34.35
A3.2 Work	38.60	38.58
A4 Sociological system	38.15	37.70
A4.1 Demographic	38.88	46.31
A4.2 Education	30.14	28.26
A4.3 Inequalities	47.83	40.28
A5 Technological system	44.74	37.72
A5.1 Transport	1.16	6.54
A5.2 Technology adoption	63.63	41.23
A5.3 Consumption and production	65.03	62.53
B Intrinsic drivers index	55.76	58.01
B1 Human health	71.38	72.35
B1.1 Health coverage	63.01	58.65
B1.2 Diseases burden	63.99	79.83
B1.3 Injury and violence	89.31	80.75
B2 Animal health and ecosystem diversity	51.99	56.58
B2.1 Animal epidemic disease	96.78	94.57
B2.2 Wildlife and marine life biodiversity	7.20	18.59
B3 Environmental health	45.60	46.87
B3.1 Air quality and climate change	55.43	53.72
B3.2 Environmental biodiversity	36.12	44.05
B3.3 Environmental resources	46.64	44.25

	Country Score	Global Average
C Core drivers index	65.49	57.25
C1 Governance	67.33	56.51
C1.1 Participation	33.91	41.70
C1.3 Transparency	84.90	65.15
C1.4 Responsiveness	58.30	44.42
C1.5 Consensus oriented	86.91	86.45
C1.6 Equity and inclusiveness	99.09	73.61
C1.7 Effectiveness and efficiency	40.40	28.38
C1.8 Political support	67.79	55.89
C2 Zoonotic diseases	75.90	68.06
C2.1 Source of infection	83.65	69.22
C2.2 Route of transmission	68.75	59.30
C2.3 Targeted population	73.58	59.90
C2.4 Capacity building	71.80	72.85
C2.5 Case studies	83.20	85.89
C3 Food security	61.17	52.89
C3.1 Food demand and supply	58.87	59.53
C3.2 Food safety	88.67	69.36
C3.3 Nutrition	74.38	67.17
C3.4 Natural and social circumstances	60.54	51.54
C3.5 Government support and response	23.38	16.85
C4 Antimicrobial resistance	54.87	44.05
C4.1 AMR surveillance system	43.71	34.79
C4.2 AMR laboratory network and coordination capacity	59.76	55.57
C4.3 Antimicrobial control and optimization	70.15	48.76
C4.4 Improve awareness and understanding	68.75	48.09
C4.5 Antimicrobial resistance rate for important antibiotics	31.99	33.03
C5 Climate change	67.27	64.19
C5.1 Mitigation and adaptation capacity	28.13	28.24
C5.2 Climate change risks	86.17	80.87
C5.3 Health outcome	89.54	85.41

Scores are normalized (0-100, where 100 = most favorable)

Cyprus
Europe & Central Asia | High income

60.47 Index Score **035**/160

Global average: 54.82

Regional average: 60.26

Income group average: 61.66

Country performance: 60.47

Missing rate in GOHI database: 13.00%

▼ AVERAGE PERFORMANCE BY GOHI

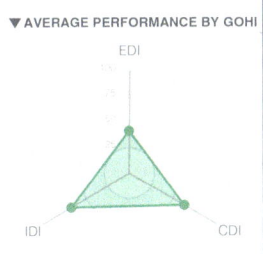

▼ AVERAGE PERFORMANCE BY CDI

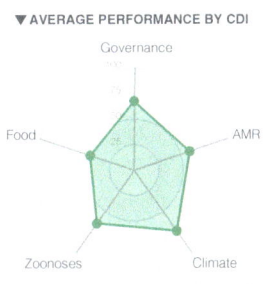

	Country Score	Global Average
A External drivers index	41.67	40.45
A1 Earth system	54.78	56.21
A1.1 Land	18.35	36.41
A1.2 Forest	40.57	43.43
A1.3 Water	64.61	58.09
A1.4 Air	74.57	71.93
A1.5 Natural disasters	66.66	64.65
A2 Institutional system	51.92	46.01
A2.1 Justice	63.48	57.89
A2.2 Governance	42.07	35.58
A3 Economical system	21.80	24.62
A3.1 Finance	26.25	34.35
A3.2 Work	39.43	38.58
A4 Sociological system	36.74	37.70
A4.1 Demographic	38.88	46.31
A4.2 Education	25.73	28.26
A4.3 Inequalities	48.74	40.28
A5 Technological system	43.10	37.72
A5.1 Transport	2.03	6.54
A5.2 Technology adoption	60.77	41.23
A5.3 Consumption and production	62.35	62.53
B Intrinsic drivers index	67.49	58.01
B1 Human health	84.79	72.35
B1.1 Health coverage	74.97	58.65
B1.2 Diseases burden	87.64	79.83
B1.3 Injury and violence	94.34	80.75
B2 Animal health and ecosystem diversity	49.64	58.58
B2.1 Animal epidemic disease	95.68	94.57
B2.2 Wildlife and marine life biodiversity	3.60	18.59
B3 Environmental health	70.08	46.87
B3.1 Air quality and climate change	84.15	53.72
B3.2 Environmental biodiversity	55.40	44.05
B3.3 Environmental resources	72.80	44.25

	Country Score	Global Average
C Core drivers index	62.98	57.25
C1 Governance	67.88	56.51
C1.1 Participation	56.68	41.70
C1.3 Transparency	80.80	65.15
C1.4 Responsiveness	41.65	44.42
C1.5 Consensus oriented	96.01	86.45
C1.6 Equity and inclusiveness	94.03	73.61
C1.7 Effectiveness and efficiency	46.60	28.38
C1.8 Political support	59.39	55.89
C2 Zoonotic diseases	73.82	68.06
C2.1 Source of infection	98.33	69.22
C2.2 Route of transmission	49.35	59.30
C2.3 Targeted population	74.25	59.90
C2.4 Capacity building	67.17	72.85
C2.5 Case studies	83.16	85.89
C3 Food security	59.81	52.89
C3.1 Food demand and supply	58.76	59.53
C3.2 Food safety	86.55	69.36
C3.3 Nutrition	78.87	67.17
C3.4 Natural and social circumstances	56.74	51.54
C3.5 Government support and response	18.12	16.85
C4 Antimicrobial resistance	46.88	44.05
C4.1 AMR surveillance system	51.06	34.79
C4.2 AMR laboratory network and coordination on capacity	48.05	55.57
C4.3 Antimicrobial control and optimization	56.68	48.76
C4.4 Improve awareness and understanding	48.44	48.09
C4.5 Antimicrobial resistance rate for important antibiotics	30.17	33.03
C5 Climate change	64.73	64.19
C5.1 Mitigation and adaptation capacity	26.82	28.24
C5.2 Climate change risks	84.22	80.87
C5.3 Health outcome	85.11	85.41

Scores are normalized (0-100, where 100 = most favorable)

Russia
Europe & Central Asia | **Upper middle income**

Index Score **036**/160

Global average: 54.82

Regional average: 60.26

Income group average: 54.54

Country performance: 60.44

Missing rate in GOHI database: 21.00%

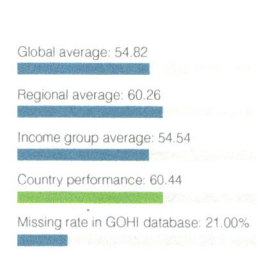

▼ AVERAGE PERFORMANCE BY GOHI

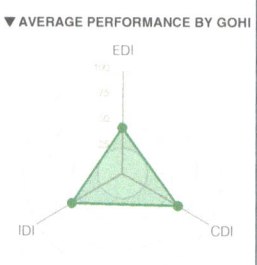

▼ AVERAGE PERFORMANCE BY CDI

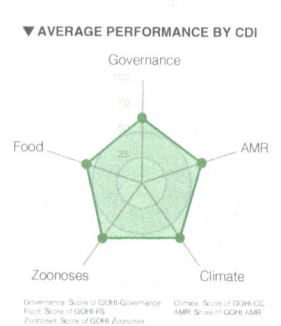

	Country Score	Global Average
A External drivers index	44.64	40.45
A1 Earth system	73.53	56.21
A1.1 Land	71.50	36.41
A1.2 Forest	79.60	43.43
A1.3 Water	75.53	58.09
A1.4 Air	70.25	71.93
A1.5 Natural disasters	66.65	64.65
A2 Institutional system	44.56	46.01
A2.1 Justice	60.22	57.89
A2.2 Governance	31.23	35.58
A3 Economical system	24.10	24.62
A3.1 Finance	32.39	34.35
A3.2 Work	39.32	38.58
A4 Sociological system	39.21	37.70
A4.1 Demographic	44.30	46.31
A4.2 Education	29.59	26.26
A4.3 Inequalities	46.02	40.28
A5 Technological system	41.78	37.72
A5.1 Transport	2.75	6.54
A5.2 Technology adoption	61.50	41.23
A5.3 Consumption and production	57.06	62.53
B Intrinsic drivers index	59.19	58.01
B1 Human health	67.67	72.35
B1.1 Health coverage	58.00	58.65
B1.2 Diseases burden	64.25	79.83
B1.3 Injury and violence	82.82	80.75
B2 Animal health and ecosystem diversity	53.40	56.58
B2.1 Animal epidemic disease	97.46	94.57
B2.2 Wildlife and marine life biodiversity	9.35	18.59
B3 Environmental health	58.28	46.87
B3.1 Air quality and climate change	63.75	53.72
B3.2 Environmental biodiversity	58.05	44.05
B3.3 Environmental resources	54.80	44.25

Scores are normalized (0-100, where 100 = most favorable)

	Country Score	Global Average
C Core drivers index	64.25	57.25
C1 Governance	63.85	56.51
C1.1 Participation	82.39	41.70
C1.3 Transparency	78.20	65.15
C1.4 Responsiveness	25.00	44.42
C1.5 Consensus oriented	99.63	86.45
C1.6 Equity and inclusiveness	97.59	73.61
C1.7 Effectiveness and efficiency	15.47	28.38
C1.8 Political support	48.68	55.89
C2 Zoonotic diseases	66.57	68.06
C2.1 Source of infection	67.62	69.22
C2.2 Route of transmission	58.62	59.30
C2.3 Targeted population	52.74	59.90
C2.4 Capacity building	81.25	72.85
C2.5 Case studies	79.36	85.89
C3 Food security	64.25	52.89
C3.1 Food demand and supply	75.12	59.53
C3.2 Food safety	87.18	69.36
C3.3 Nutrition	72.71	67.17
C3.4 Natural and social circumstances	61.00	51.54
C3.5 Government support and response	25.22	16.85
C4 Antimicrobial resistance	58.85	44.05
C4.1 AMR surveillance system	52.21	34.79
C4.2 AMR laboratory network and coordinati on capacity	91.46	55.57
C4.3 Antimicrobial control and optimization	55.76	48.76
C4.4 Improve awareness and understanding	73.44	48.09
C4.5 Antimicrobial resistance rate for important antibiotics	21.41	33.03
C5 Climate change	67.45	64.19
C5.1 Mitigation and adaptation capacity	36.05	28.24
C5.2 Climate change risks	76.37	80.87
C5.3 Health outcome	91.96	85.41

Luxembourg
Europe & Central Asia | High income

Index Score **037**/160

60.39

Global average: 54.82

Regional average: 60.26

Income group average: 61.66

Country performance: 60.39

Missing rate in GOHI database: 11.60%

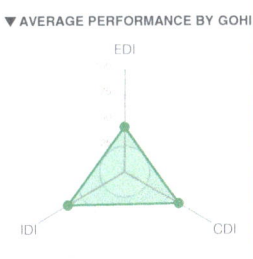

▼ AVERAGE PERFORMANCE BY GOHI

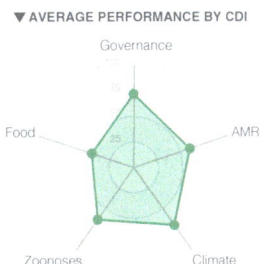

▼ AVERAGE PERFORMANCE BY CDI

	Country Score	Global Average
A External drivers index	44.01	40.45
A1 Earth system	50.38	56.21
A1.1 Land	27.61	36.41
A1.2 Forest	47.47	43.43
A1.3 Water	42.59	58.09
A1.4 Air	65.36	71.93
A1.5 Natural disasters	66.67	64.65
A2 Institutional system	61.12	46.01
A2.1 Justice	67.50	57.89
A2.2 Governance	55.69	35.58
A3 Economical system	27.88	24.62
A3.1 Finance	42.45	34.35
A3.2 Work	39.17	38.58
A4 Sociological system	40.61	37.70
A4.1 Demographic	42.75	46.31
A4.2 Education	32.09	28.26
A4.3 Inequalities	49.34	40.28
A5 Technological system	40.06	37.72
A5.1 Transport	7.59	6.54
A5.2 Technology adoption	71.10	41.23
A5.3 Consumption and production	37.71	62.53
B Intrinsic drivers index	66.22	58.01
B1 Human health	81.90	72.35
B1.1 Health coverage	80.45	58.65
B1.2 Diseases burden	83.88	79.83
B1.3 Injury and violence	83.86	80.75
B2 Animal health and ecosystem diversity	51.54	56.58
B2.1 Animal epidemic disease	93.68	94.57
B2.2 Wildlife and marine life biodiversity	9.40	18.59
B3 Environmental health	67.21	46.87
B3.1 Air quality and climate change	79.20	53.72
B3.2 Environmental biodiversity	53.15	44.05
B3.3 Environmental resources	71.32	44.25

	Country Score	Global Average
C Core drivers index	62.65	57.25
C1 Governance	72.22	56.51
C1.1 Participation	85.83	41.70
C1.3 Transparency	78.20	65.15
C1.4 Responsiveness	33.35	44.42
C1.5 Consensus oriented	97.58	86.45
C1.6 Equity and inclusiveness	99.15	73.61
C1.7 Effectiveness and efficiency	28.13	28.38
C1.8 Political support	83.33	55.89
C2 Zoonotic diseases	69.87	68.06
C2.1 Source of infection	71.95	69.22
C2.2 Route of transmission	68.14	59.30
C2.3 Targeted population	51.74	59.90
C2.4 Capacity building	76.82	72.85
C2.5 Case studies	84.67	85.89
C3 Food security	60.39	52.89
C3.1 Food demand and supply	76.57	59.53
C3.2 Food safety	87.14	69.36
C3.3 Nutrition	73.15	67.17
C3.4 Natural and social circumstances	63.30	51.54
C3.5 Government support and response	1.79	16.85
C4 Antimicrobial resistance	44.98	44.05
C4.1 AMR surveillance system	30.16	34.79
C4.2 AMR laboratory network and coordination capacity	52.95	55.57
C4.3 Antimicrobial control and optimization	49.88	48.76
C4.4 Improve awareness and understanding	50.00	48.09
C4.5 Antimicrobial resistance rate for important antibiotics	41.92	33.03
C5 Climate change	63.38	64.19
C5.1 Mitigation and adaptation capacity	34.11	28.24
C5.2 Climate change risks	75.61	80.87
C5.3 Health outcome	82.33	85.41

Scores are normalized (0-100, where 100 = most favorable)

Mexico

Latin America & Caribbean | Upper middle income

60.36 Index Score 038/160

Global average: 54.82

Regional average: 55.08

Income group average: 54.54

Country performance: 60.36

Missing rate in GOHI database: 10.90%

▼ AVERAGE PERFORMANCE BY GOHI

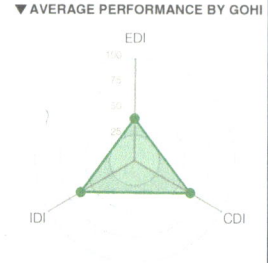

▼ AVERAGE PERFORMANCE BY CDI

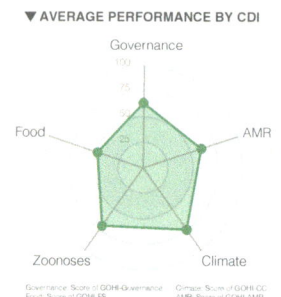

	Country Score	Global Average
A External drivers index	41.27	40.45
A1 Earth system	60.14	56.21
A1.1 Land	28.90	36.41
A1.2 Forest	48.70	43.43
A1.3 Water	65.86	58.09
A1.4 Air	81.52	71.93
A1.5 Natural disasters	66.64	64.65
A2 Institutional system	38.53	46.01
A2.1 Justice	48.25	57.89
A2.2 Governance	30.25	35.58
A3 Economical system	27.19	24.62
A3.1 Finance	41.06	34.35
A3.2 Work	38.61	38.58
A4 Sociological system	38.44	37.70
A4.1 Demographic	50.33	46.31
A4.2 Education	26.04	28.26
A4.3 Inequalities	41.14	40.28
A5 Technological system	42.04	37.72
A5.1 Transport	2.03	6.54
A5.2 Technology adoption	50.13	41.23
A5.3 Consumption and production	70.20	62.53
B Intrinsic drivers index	62.69	53.01
B1 Human health	70.10	72.35
B1.1 Health coverage	63.79	58.65
B1.2 Diseases burden	86.45	79.83
B1.3 Injury and violence	62.17	80.75
B2 Animal health and ecosystem diversity	59.77	56.58
B2.1 Animal epidemic disease	93.15	94.57
B2.2 Wildlife and marine life biodiversity	26.40	18.59
B3 Environmental health	60.09	46.87
B3.1 Air quality and climate change	69.79	53.72
B3.2 Environmental biodiversity	59.00	44.05
B3.3 Environmental resources	53.30	44.25

	Country Score	Global Average
C Core drivers index	64.05	57.25
C1 Governance	63.57	56.51
C1.1 Participation	45.72	41.70
C1.3 Transparency	87.50	65.15
C1.4 Responsiveness	54.15	44.42
C1.5 Consensus oriented	93.53	86.45
C1.6 Equity and inclusiveness	61.53	73.61
C1.7 Effectiveness and efficiency	31.27	28.38
C1.8 Political support	71.32	55.89
C2 Zoonotic diseases	74.99	68.06
C2.1 Source of infection	90.45	69.22
C2.2 Route of transmission	72.05	59.30
C2.3 Targeted population	45.49	59.90
C2.4 Capacity building	79.36	72.85
C2.5 Case studies	88.03	85.89
C3 Food security	61.57	52.89
C3.1 Food demand and supply	59.18	59.53
C3.2 Food safety	83.90	69.36
C3.3 Nutrition	82.18	67.17
C3.4 Natural and social circumstances	55.88	51.54
C3.5 Government support and response	26.70	16.85
C4 Antimicrobial resistance	48.64	44.05
C4.1 AMR surveillance system	33.91	34.79
C4.2 AMR laboratory network and coordination capacity	63.98	55.57
C4.3 Antimicrobial control and optimization	54.81	48.76
C4.4 Improve awareness and understanding	48.44	48.09
C4.5 Antimicrobial resistance rate for important antibiotics	42.06	33.03
C5 Climate change	70.55	64.19
C5.1 Mitigation and adaptation capacity	41.45	28.24
C5.2 Climate change risks	86.92	80.87
C5.3 Health outcome	85.41	85.41

Scores are normalized (0-100, where 100 = most favorable)

Costa Rica

Latin America & Caribbean | Upper middle income

60.12 | Index Score **039**/160

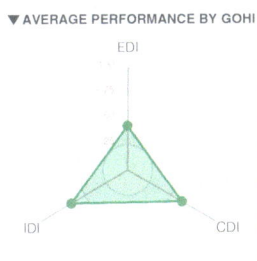

▼ AVERAGE PERFORMANCE BY GOHI

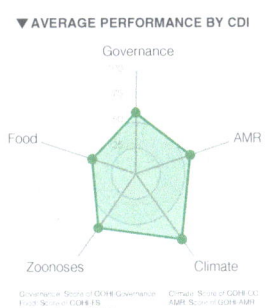

▼ AVERAGE PERFORMANCE BY CDI

Global average: 54.82

Regional average: 55.08

Income group average: 54.54

Country performance: 60.12

Missing rate in GOHI database: 11.60%

	Country Score	Global Average
A External drivers index	43.32	40.45
A1 Earth system	61.69	56.21
A1.1 Land	20.96	36.41
A1.2 Forest	57.78	43.43
A1.3 Water	68.14	58.09
A1.4 Air	87.65	71.93
A1.5 Natural disasters	63.47	64.65
A2 Institutional system	49.77	46.01
A2.1 Justice	60.58	57.89
A2.2 Governance	40.57	35.58
A3 Economical system	24.65	24.62
A3.1 Finance	36.48	34.35
A3.2 Work	35.95	38.58
A4 Sociological system	36.95	37.70
A4.1 Demographic	45.49	46.31
A4.2 Education	27.77	28.26
A4.3 Inequalities	39.26	40.28
A5 Technological system	43.55	37.72
A5.1 Transport	3.36	6.54
A5.2 Technology adoption	55.50	41.23
A5.3 Consumption and production	67.89	62.53
B Intrinsic drivers index	65.89	58.01
B1 Human health	83.54	72.35
B1.1 Health coverage	87.13	58.65
B1.2 Diseases burden	88.29	79.83
B1.3 Injury and violence	77.74	80.75
B2 Animal health and ecosystem diversity	58.68	56.58
B2.1 Animal epidemic disease	99.11	94.57
B2.2 Wildlife and marine life biodiversity	18.25	18.59
B3 Environmental health	57.43	46.87
B3.1 Air quality and climate change	75.70	53.72
B3.2 Environmental biodiversity	45.70	44.05
B3.3 Environmental resources	52.64	44.25

Scores are normalized (0-100, where 100 = most favorable)

	Country Score	Global Average
C Core drivers index	62.49	57.25
C1 Governance	60.13	56.51
C1.1 Participation	30.29	41.70
C1.3 Transparency	79.80	65.15
C1.4 Responsiveness	58.30	44.42
C1.5 Consensus oriented	95.27	86.45
C1.6 Equity and inclusiveness	70.96	73.61
C1.7 Effectiveness and efficiency	35.07	28.38
C1.8 Political support	51.23	55.89
C2 Zoonotic diseases	79.92	68.06
C2.1 Source of infection	85.18	69.22
C2.2 Route of transmission	71.56	59.30
C2.3 Targeted population	75.60	59.90
C2.4 Capacity building	82.57	72.85
C2.5 Case studies	88.20	85.89
C3 Food security	58.60	52.89
C3.1 Food demand and supply	64.96	59.53
C3.2 Food safety	85.39	69.36
C3.3 Nutrition	74.63	67.17
C3.4 Natural and social circumstances	52.23	51.54
C3.5 Government support and response	15.79	16.85
C4 Antimicrobial resistance	46.80	44.05
C4.1 AMR surveillance system	32.46	34.79
C4.2 AMR laboratory network and coordination on capacity	60.74	55.57
C4.3 Antimicrobial control and optimization	45.42	48.76
C4.4 Improve awareness and understanding	54.69	48.09
C4.5 Antimicrobial resistance rate for important antibiotics	40.71	33.03
C5 Climate change	65.91	64.19
C5.1 Mitigation and adaptation capacity	23.40	28.24
C5.2 Climate change risks	89.91	80.87
C5.3 Health outcome	86.40	85.41

Croatia
Europe & Central Asia | **High income**

 Index Score **040**/160

Global average: 54.82

Regional average: 60.26

Income group average: 61.66

Country performance: 60.12

Missing rate in GOHI database: 12.30%

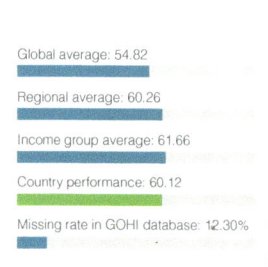
▼ AVERAGE PERFORMANCE BY GOHI

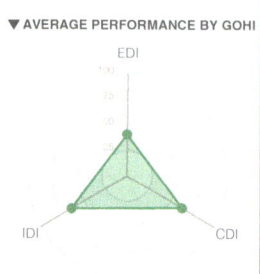

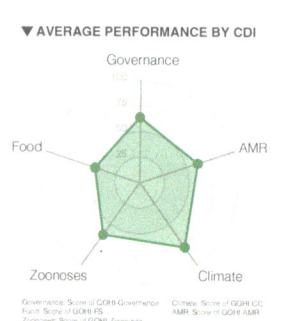
▼ AVERAGE PERFORMANCE BY CDI

	Country Score	Global Average
A External drivers index	40.78	40.45
A1 Earth system	55.94	56.21
A1.1 Land	33.98	36.41
A1.2 Forest	49.48	43.43
A1.3 Water	45.75	58.09
A1.4 Air	80.72	71.93
A1.5 Natural disasters	64.93	64.65
A2 Institutional system	49.48	46.01
A2.1 Justice	60.08	57.89
A2.2 Governance	40.45	35.58
A3 Economical system	18.36	24.62
A3.1 Finance	20.08	34.35
A3.2 Work	35.77	38.58
A4 Sociological system	37.11	37.70
A4.1 Demographic	34.98	46.31
A4.2 Education	30.65	28.26
A4.3 Inequalities	47.98	40.28
A5 Technological system	43.02	37.72
A5.1 Transport	3.23	6.54
A5.2 Technology adoption	56.32	41.23
A5.3 Consumption and production	65.59	62.53
B Intrinsic drivers index	64.50	58.01
B1 Human health	76.65	72.35
B1.1 Health coverage	67.24	58.65
B1.2 Diseases burden	71.74	79.83
B1.3 Injury and violence	93.29	80.75
B2 Animal health and ecosystem diversity	57.42	56.58
B2.1 Animal epidemic disease	96.84	94.57
B2.2 Wildlife and marine life biodiversity	18.00	18.59
B3 Environmental health	61.39	46.87
B3.1 Air quality and climate change	54.33	53.72
B3.2 Environmental biodiversity	57.95	44.05
B3.3 Environmental resources	73.76	44.25

	Country Score	Global Average
C Core drivers index	63.37	57.25
C1 Governance	64.18	56.51
C1.1 Participation	51.72	41.70
C1.3 Transparency	68.40	65.15
C1.4 Responsiveness	35.40	44.42
C1.5 Consensus oriented	94.11	86.45
C1.6 Equity and inclusiveness	94.62	73.61
C1.7 Effectiveness and efficiency	37.27	28.38
C1.8 Political support	67.71	55.89
C2 Zoonotic diseases	78.09	68.06
C2.1 Source of infection	85.93	69.22
C2.2 Route of transmission	74.51	59.30
C2.3 Targeted population	74.23	59.90
C2.4 Capacity building	72.55	72.85
C2.5 Case studies	82.84	85.89
C3 Food security	61.91	52.59
C3.1 Food demand and supply	59.59	59.53
C3.2 Food safety	83.99	69.36
C3.3 Nutrition	76.81	67.17
C3.4 Natural and social circumstances	55.35	51.54
C3.5 Government support and response	33.83	16.85
C4 Antimicrobial resistance	44.98	44.05
C4.1 AMR surveillance system	37.81	34.79
C4.2 AMR laboratory network and coordinati on capacity	68.31	55.57
C4.3 Antimicrobial control and optimization	58.76	48.76
C4.4 Improve awareness and understanding	43.75	48.09
C4.5 Antimicrobial resistance rate for important antibiotics	30.10	33.03
C5 Climate change	63.21	64.19
C5.1 Mitigation and adaptation capacity	26.25	28.24
C5.2 Climate change risks	77.83	80.87
C5.3 Health outcome	87.48	85.41

Scores are normalized (0-100, where 100 = most favorable)

Estonia

Europe & Central Asia | High income

 Index Score **041**/160

59.99

Global average: 54.82

Regional average: 60.26

Income group average: 61.66

Country performance: 59.99

Missing rate in GOHI database: 7.60%

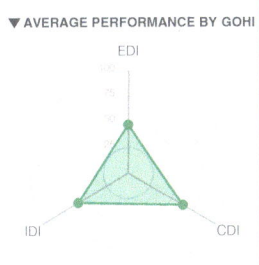

▼ AVERAGE PERFORMANCE BY GOHI

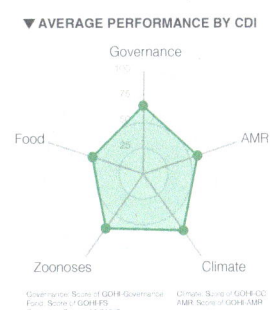

▼ AVERAGE PERFORMANCE BY CDI

	Country Score	Global Average
A External drivers index	47.51	40.45
A1 Earth system	69.61	56.21
A1.1 Land	62.02	36.41
A1.2 Forest	62.98	43.43
A1.3 Water	65.82	58.09
A1.4 Air	86.02	71.93
A1.5 Natural disasters	64.18	64.65
A2 Institutional system	61.96	46.01
A2.1 Justice	76.94	57.89
A2.2 Governance	49.20	35.58
A3 Economical system	20.37	24.62
A3.1 Finance	22.00	34.35
A3.2 Work	39.34	38.58
A4 Sociological system	38.39	37.70
A4.1 Demographic	37.46	46.31
A4.2 Education	31.70	28.26
A4.3 Inequalities	48.20	40.28
A5 Technological system	47.24	37.72
A5.1 Transport	17.33	6.54
A5.2 Technology adoption	65.58	41.23
A5.3 Consumption and production	55.63	62.53
B Intrinsic drivers index	58.73	58.01
B1 Human health	78.20	72.35
B1.1 Health coverage	70.09	58.65
B1.2 Diseases burden	72.35	79.83
B1.3 Injury and violence	94.51	80.75
B2 Animal health and ecosystem diversity	55.99	56.58
B2.1 Animal epidemic disease	91.09	94.57
B2.2 Wildlife and marine life biodiversity	20.90	18.59
B3 Environmental health	43.76	46.87
B3.1 Air quality and climate change	59.65	53.72
B3.2 Environmental biodiversity	49.45	44.05
B3.3 Environmental resources	23.52	44.25

	Country Score	Global Average
C Core drivers index	67.00	57.25
C1 Governance	64.18	56.51
C1.1 Participation	21.89	41.70
C1.3 Transparency	86.10	65.15
C1.4 Responsiveness	50.00	44.42
C1.5 Consensus oriented	99.00	86.45
C1.6 Equity and inclusiveness	99.18	73.61
C1.7 Effectiveness and efficiency	42.53	28.38
C1.8 Political support	70.32	55.89
C2 Zoonotic diseases	68.74	68.06
C2.1 Source of infection	64.21	69.22
C2.2 Route of transmission	75.26	59.30
C2.3 Targeted population	49.66	59.90
C2.4 Capacity building	73.17	72.85
C2.5 Case studies	84.09	85.89
C3 Food security	58.38	52.89
C3.1 Food demand and supply	62.34	59.53
C3.2 Food safety	80.25	69.36
C3.3 Nutrition	77.78	67.17
C3.4 Natural and social circumstances	63.31	51.54
C3.5 Government support and response	8.20	16.85
C4 Antimicrobial resistance	54.40	44.05
C4.1 AMR surveillance system	40.26	34.79
C4.2 AMR laboratory network and coordination capacity	63.11	55.57
C4.3 Antimicrobial control and optimization	57.53	48.76
C4.4 Improve awareness and understanding	62.50	48.09
C4.5 Antimicrobial resistance rate for important antibiotics	48.63	33.03
C5 Climate change	66.08	64.19
C5.1 Mitigation and adaptation capacity	32.26	28.24
C5.2 Climate change risks	80.18	80.87
C5.3 Health outcome	87.79	85.41

Scores are normalized (0-100, where 100 = most favorable)

Slovakia

Europe & Central Asia | High income

59.88 Index Score **042**/160

Global average: 54.82

Regional average: 60.26

Income group average: 61.66

Country performance: 59.88

Missing rate in GOHI database: 17.80%

▼ AVERAGE PERFORMANCE BY GOHI

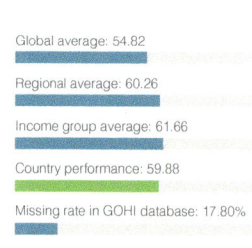

▼ AVERAGE PERFORMANCE BY CDI

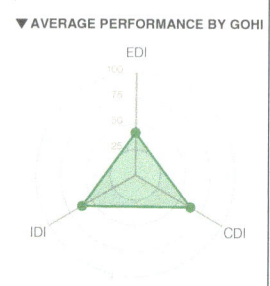

	Country Score	Global Average
A External drivers index	41.46	40.45
A1 Earth system	55.58	56.21
A1.1 Land	28.70	36.41
A1.2 Forest	49.89	43.43
A1.3 Water	41.76	58.09
A1.4 Air	86.07	71.93
A1.5 Natural disasters	66.67	64.65
A2 Institutional system	50.70	46.01
A2.1 Justice	59.86	57.89
A2.2 Governance	42.89	35.58
A3 Economical system	20.46	24.62
A3.1 Finance	23.49	34.35
A3.2 Work	38.45	38.58
A4 Sociological system	38.13	37.70
A4.1 Demographic	37.33	46.31
A4.2 Education	30.36	28.26
A4.3 Inequalities	49.23	40.28
A5 Technological system	42.44	37.72
A5.1 Transport	1.78	6.54
A5.2 Technology adoption	59.74	41.23
A5.3 Consumption and production	61.69	62.53
B Intrinsic drivers index	61.59	53.01
B1 Human health	79.08	72.35
B1.1 Health coverage	68.85	58.65
B1.2 Diseases burden	76.60	79.83
B1.3 Injury and violence	94.21	80.75
B2 Animal health and ecosystem diversity	55.64	56.58
B2.1 Animal epidemic disease	97.96	94.57
B2.2 Wildlife and marine life biodiversity	13.32	18.59
B3 Environmental health	51.91	46.87
B3.1 Air quality and climate change	61.87	53.72
B3.2 Environmental biodiversity	43.68	44.05
B3.3 Environmental resources	51.75	44.25

Scores are normalized (0-100, where 100 = most favorable)

	Country Score	Global Average
C Core drivers index	63.56	57.25
C1 Governance	66.03	56.51
C1.1 Participation	32.65	41.70
C1.3 Transparency	70.72	65.15
C1.4 Responsiveness	52.05	44.42
C1.5 Consensus oriented	90.03	86.45
C1.6 Equity and inclusiveness	97.11	73.61
C1.7 Effectiveness and efficiency	45.20	28.38
C1.8 Political support	74.45	55.89
C2 Zoonotic diseases	76.47	68.06
C2.1 Source of infection	84.59	69.22
C2.2 Route of transmission	66.98	59.30
C2.3 Targeted population	79.23	59.90
C2.4 Capacity building	70.46	72.85
C2.5 Case studies	82.84	85.89
C3 Food security	52.84	52.89
C3.1 Food demand and supply	66.25	59.53
C3.2 Food safety	76.06	69.36
C3.3 Nutrition	52.81	67.17
C3.4 Natural and social circumstances	58.19	51.54
C3.5 Government support and response	10.90	16.85
C4 Antimicrobial resistance	56.54	44.05
C4.1 AMR surveillance system	32.61	34.79
C4.2 AMR laboratory network and coordination capacity	87.73	55.57
C4.3 Antimicrobial control and optimization	64.37	48.76
C4.4 Improve awareness and understanding	60.94	48.09
C4.5 Antimicrobial resistance rate for important antibiotics	37.06	33.03
C5 Climate change	65.70	64.19
C5.1 Mitigation and adaptation capacity	26.82	28.24
C5.2 Climate change risks	81.50	80.87
C5.3 Health outcome	90.79	85.41

Turkey
Europe & Central Asia | Upper middle income

59.66 Index Score **043**/160

Global average: 54.82

Regional average: 60.26

Income group average: 54.54

Country performance: 59.66

Missing rate in GOHI database: 15.90%

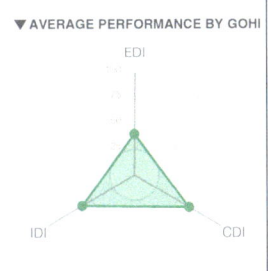

▼ AVERAGE PERFORMANCE BY GOHI

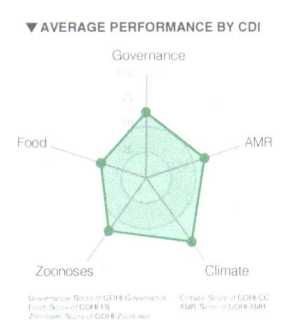

▼ AVERAGE PERFORMANCE BY CDI

	Country Score	Global Average
A External drivers index	40.22	40.45
A1 Earth system	50.42	56.21
A1.1 Land	24.20	36.41
A1.2 Forest	44.73	43.43
A1.3 Water	51.14	58.09
A1.4 Air	61.98	71.93
A1.5 Natural disasters	66.11	64.65
A2 Institutional system	42.16	46.01
A2.1 Justice	55.96	57.89
A2.2 Governance	30.41	35.58
A3 Economical system	26.92	24.62
A3.1 Finance	43.61	34.35
A3.2 Work	34.49	38.58
A4 Sociological system	39.96	37.70
A4.1 Demographic	45.45	46.31
A4.2 Education	31.52	28.26
A4.3 Inequalities	44.76	40.28
A5 Technological system	41.64	37.72
A5.1 Transport	3.43	6.54
A5.2 Technology adoption	49.70	41.23
A5.3 Consumption and production	67.90	62.53
B Intrinsic drivers index	61.09	58.01
B1 Human health	82.82	72.35
B1.1 Health coverage	70.17	58.65
B1.2 Diseases burden	88.47	79.83
B1.3 Injury and violence	92.34	80.75
B2 Animal health and ecosystem diversity	53.67	56.58
B2.1 Animal epidemic disease	96.58	94.57
B2.2 Wildlife and marine life biodiversity	10.75	18.59
B3 Environmental health	48.63	46.87
B3.1 Air quality and climate change	71.65	53.72
B3.2 Environmental biodiversity	28.05	44.05
B3.3 Environmental resources	47.66	44.25

	Country Score	Global Average
C Core drivers index	64.48	57.25
C1 Governance	66.03	56.51
C1.1 Participation	46.36	41.70
C1.3 Transparency	84.60	65.15
C1.4 Responsiveness	50.00	44.42
C1.5 Consensus oriented	95.49	86.45
C1.6 Equity and inclusiveness	80.15	73.61
C1.7 Effectiveness and efficiency	41.07	28.38
C1.8 Political support	53.70	55.89
C2 Zoonotic diseases	77.82	68.06
C2.1 Source of infection	82.60	69.22
C2.2 Route of transmission	70.10	59.30
C2.3 Targeted population	77.67	59.90
C2.4 Capacity building	76.17	72.85
C2.5 Case studies	85.27	85.89
C3 Food security	62.29	52.89
C3.1 Food demand and supply	61.44	59.53
C3.2 Food safety	85.69	69.36
C3.3 Nutrition	90.70	67.17
C3.4 Natural and social circumstances	52.82	51.54
C3.5 Government support and response	20.80	16.85
C4 Antimicrobial resistance	47.55	44.05
C4.1 AMR surveillance system	45.71	34.79
C4.2 AMR laboratory network and coordination on capacity	46.76	55.57
C4.3 Antimicrobial control and optimization	60.75	48.76
C4.4 Improve awareness and understanding	59.38	48.09
C4.5 Antimicrobial resistance rate for important antibiotics	25.18	33.03
C5 Climate change	64.38	64.19
C5.1 Mitigation and adaptation capacity	29.55	28.24
C5.2 Climate change risks	80.15	80.87
C5.3 Health outcome	95.39	85.41

Scores are normalized (0-100, where 100 = most favorable)

Philippines
East Asia & Pacific | Lower middle income

 Index Score **044**/160

Global average: 54.82

Regional average: 56.52

Income group average: 51.29

Country performance: 59.45

Missing rate in GOHI database: 12.30%

▼ AVERAGE PERFORMANCE BY GOHI

▼ AVERAGE PERFORMANCE BY CDI

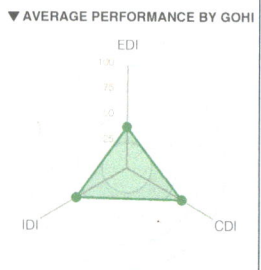

Governance: Score of GOHI-Governance   Climate: Score of GOHI-CC
Food: Score of GOHI-FS   AMR: Score of GOHI-AMR
Zoonoses: Score of GOHI-Zoonoses

	Country Score	Global Average
A External drivers index	39.98	40.45
A1 Earth system	58.64	56.21
A1.1 Land	20.24	36.41
A1.2 Forest	42.64	43.43
A1.3 Water	72.19	58.09
A1.4 Air	86.93	71.93
A1.5 Natural disasters	57.62	64.65
A2 Institutional system	39.73	46.01
A2.1 Justice	47.42	57.89
A2.2 Governance	33.18	35.58
A3 Economical system	27.21	24.62
A3.1 Finance	41.21	34.35
A3.2 Work	38.52	38.58
A4 Sociological system	35.79	37.70
A4.1 Demographic	46.23	46.31
A4.2 Education	25.59	28.26
A4.3 Inequalities	37.26	40.28
A5 Technological system	38.55	37.72
A5.1 Transport	1.21	6.54
A5.2 Technology adoption	37.18	41.23
A5.3 Consumption and production	74.00	62.53
B Intrinsic drivers index	59.00	58.01
B1 Human health	73.08	72.35
B1.1 Health coverage	50.09	58.65
B1.2 Diseases burden	86.88	79.83
B1.3 Injury and violence	84.47	80.75
B2 Animal health and ecosystem diversity	62.13	56.58
B2.1 Animal epidemic disease	90.36	94.57
B2.2 Wildlife and marine life biodiversity	33.90	18.59
B3 Environmental health	43.59	46.87
B3.1 Air quality and climate change	44.01	53.72
B3.2 Environmental biodiversity	41.05	44.05
B3.3 Environmental resources	47.04	44.25

	Country Score	Global Average
C Core drivers index	60.48	57.25
C1 Governance	66.03	56.51
C1.1 Participation	46.09	41.70
C1.3 Transparency	75.70	65.15
C1.4 Responsiveness	54.20	44.42
C1.5 Consensus oriented	98.31	86.45
C1.6 Equity and inclusiveness	63.96	73.61
C1.7 Effectiveness and efficiency	33.80	28.38
C1.8 Political support	51.32	55.89
C2 Zoonotic diseases	76.57	68.06
C2.1 Source of infection	77.93	69.22
C2.2 Route of transmission	76.86	59.30
C2.3 Targeted population	68.71	59.90
C2.4 Capacity building	73.72	72.85
C2.5 Case studies	87.02	85.89
C3 Food security	56.39	52.89
C3.1 Food demand and supply	61.46	59.53
C3.2 Food safety	79.73	69.36
C3.3 Nutrition	66.86	67.17
C3.4 Natural and social circumstances	50.42	51.54
C3.5 Government support and response	23.47	16.85
C4 Antimicrobial resistance	57.29	44.05
C4.1 AMR surveillance system	50.07	34.79
C4.2 AMR laboratory network and coordination on capacity	61.01	55.57
C4.3 Antimicrobial control and optimization	69.29	48.76
C4.4 Improve awareness and understanding	68.75	48.09
C4.5 Antimicrobial resistance rate for important antibiotics	37.32	33.03
C5 Climate change	69.07	64.19
C5.1 Mitigation and adaptation capacity	30.44	28.24
C5.2 Climate change risks	92.69	80.87
C5.3 Health outcome	86.19	85.41

Scores are normalized (0-100, where 100 = most favorable)

Israel

Middle East & North Africa | **High income**

59.38 Index
Score **045**/160

Global average: 54.82

Regional average: 53.57

Income group average: 61.66

Country performance: 59.38

Missing rate in GOHI database: 20.30%

▼ AVERAGE PERFORMANCE BY GOHI

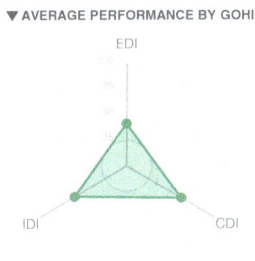

▼ AVERAGE PERFORMANCE BY CDI

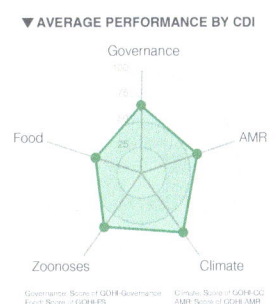

	Country Score	Global Average
A External drivers index	41.64	40.45
A1 Earth system	47.25	56.21
A1.1 Land	19.93	36.41
A1.2 Forest	35.70	43.43
A1.3 Water	39.81	58.09
A1.4 Air	72.51	71.93
A1.5 Natural disasters	63.59	64.65
A2 Institutional system	54.19	46.01
A2.1 Justice	70.06	57.89
A2.2 Governance	40.67	35.58
A3 Economical system	25.68	24.62
A3.1 Finance	36.64	34.35
A3.2 Work	39.19	38.58
A4 Sociological system	41.96	37.70
A4.1 Demographic	40.51	46.31
A4.2 Education	37.89	28.26
A4.3 Inequalities	48.93	40.28
A5 Technological system	39.10	37.72
A5.1 Transport	9.07	6.54
A5.2 Technology adoption	45.46	41.23
A5.3 Consumption and production	59.91	62.53
B Intrinsic drivers index	60.71	58.01
B1 Human health	89.11	72.35
B1.1 Health coverage	89.29	58.65
B1.2 Diseases burden	91.43	79.83
B1.3 Injury and violence	96.32	80.75
B2 Animal health and ecosystem diversity	60.68	56.58
B2.1 Animal epidemic disease	93.56	94.57
B2.2 Wildlife and marine life biodiversity	27.80	18.59
B3 Environmental health	34.17	46.87
B3.1 Air quality and climate change	39.87	53.72
B3.2 Environmental biodiversity	41.73	44.05
B3.3 Environmental resources	21.96	44.25

	Country Score	Global Average
C Core drivers index	66.59	57.25
C1 Governance	66.03	56.51
C1.1 Participation	76.71	41.70
C1.3 Transparency	78.10	65.15
C1.4 Responsiveness	41.65	44.42
C1.5 Consensus oriented	98.55	86.45
C1.6 Equity and inclusiveness	80.67	73.61
C1.7 Effectiveness and efficiency	25.27	28.38
C1.8 Political support	65.16	55.89
C2 Zoonotic diseases	72.18	68.06
C2.1 Source of infection	70.22	69.22
C2.2 Route of transmission	77.65	59.30
C2.3 Targeted population	46.55	59.90
C2.4 Capacity building	84.24	72.85
C2.5 Case studies	85.08	85.89
C3 Food security	60.16	52.89
C3.1 Food demand and supply	66.01	59.53
C3.2 Food safety	67.80	69.36
C3.3 Nutrition	86.72	67.17
C3.4 Natural and social circumstances	67.20	51.54
C3.5 Government support and response	13.06	16.85
C4 Antimicrobial resistance	49.21	44.05
C4.1 AMR surveillance system	36.90	34.79
C4.2 AMR laboratory network and coordination capacity	50.65	55.57
C4.3 Antimicrobial control and optimization	63.52	48.76
C4.4 Improve awareness and understanding	50.00	48.09
C4.5 Antimicrobial resistance rate for important antibiotics	44.97	33.03
C5 Climate change	65.53	64.19
C5.1 Mitigation and adaptation capacity	33.00	28.24
C5.2 Climate change risks	80.11	80.87
C5.3 Health outcome	85.48	85.41

Scores are normalized (0-100, where 100 = most favorable)

Uruguay

Latin America & Caribbean | High income

 59.12 | Index Score **046**/160

Global average: 54.82

Regional average: 55.08

Income group average: 61.66

Country performance: 59.12

Missing rate in GOHI database: 21.00%

▼ AVERAGE PERFORMANCE BY GOHI

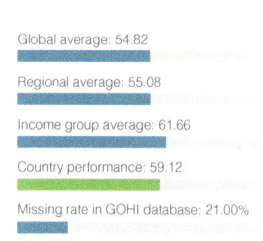

▼ AVERAGE PERFORMANCE BY CDI

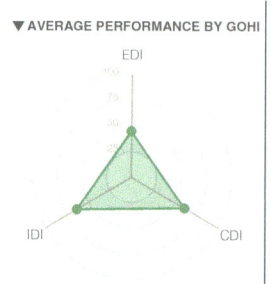

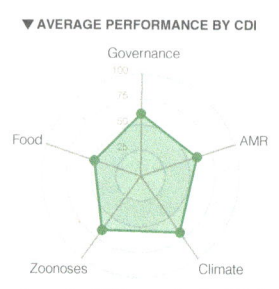

Governance: Score of GOHI-Governance   Climate: Score of GOHI-CC
Food: Score of GOHI-FS   AMR: Score of GOHI-AMR
Zoonoses: Score of GOHI-Zoonoses

	Country Score	Global Average
A External drivers index	44.98	40.45
A1 Earth system	64.40	56.21
A1.1 Land	66.60	36.41
A1.2 Forest	38.59	43.43
A1.3 Water	51.91	58.09
A1.4 Air	92.69	71.93
A1.5 Natural disasters	64.83	64.65
A2 Institutional system	61.77	46.01
A2.1 Justice	77.07	57.89
A2.2 Governance	48.75	35.58
A3 Economical system	22.33	24.62
A3.1 Finance	28.67	34.35
A3.2 Work	38.13	38.58
A4 Sociological system	38.12	37.70
A4.1 Demographic	46.62	46.31
A4.2 Education	27.81	28.26
A4.3 Inequalities	41.96	40.28
A5 Technological system	38.29	37.72
A5.1 Transport	6.17	6.54
A5.2 Technology adoption	39.94	41.23
A5.3 Consumption and production	65.88	62.53
B Intrinsic drivers index	63.82	58.01
B1 Human health	76.40	72.35
B1.1 Health coverage	80.01	58.65
B1.2 Diseases burden	74.53	79.83
B1.3 Injury and violence	76.97	80.75
B2 Animal health and ecosystem diversity	53.90	56.58
B2.1 Animal epidemic disease	97.45	94.57
B2.2 Wildlife and marine life biodiversity	10.35	18.59
B3 Environmental health	63.08	46.87
B3.1 Air quality and climate change	75.94	53.72
B3.2 Environmental biodiversity	40.35	44.05
B3.3 Environmental resources	74.88	44.25

	Country Score	Global Average
C Core drivers index	61.14	57.25
C1 Governance	60.94	56.51
C1.1 Participation	34.18	41.70
C1.3 Transparency	66.80	65.15
C1.4 Responsiveness	41.65	44.42
C1.5 Consensus oriented	97.58	86.45
C1.6 Equity and inclusiveness	87.19	73.61
C1.7 Effectiveness and efficiency	38.93	28.38
C1.8 Political support	60.27	55.89
C2 Zoonotic diseases	88.63	68.06
C2.1 Source of infection	93.64	69.22
C2.2 Route of transmission	36.63	59.30
C2.3 Targeted population	60.88	59.90
C2.4 Capacity building	73.83	72.85
C2.5 Case studies	86.97	85.89
C3 Food security	60.31	52.89
C3.1 Food demand and supply	53.87	59.53
C3.2 Food safety	86.21	69.36
C3.3 Nutrition	78.48	67.17
C3.4 Natural and social circumstances	62.20	51.54
C3.5 Government support and response	20.80	16.85
C4 Antimicrobial resistance	49.03	44.05
C4.1 AMR surveillance system	29.55	34.79
C4.2 AMR laboratory network and coordinati on capacity	62.75	55.57
C4.3 Antimicrobial control and optimization	65.35	48.76
C4.4 Improve awareness and understanding	53.12	48.09
C4.5 Antimicrobial resistance rate for important antibiotics	34.35	33.03
C5 Climate change	65.96	64.19
C5.1 Mitigation and adaptation capacity	29.56	28.24
C5.2 Climate change risks	84.24	80.87
C5.3 Health outcome	86.10	85.41

Scores are normalized (0-100, where 100 = most favorable)

Hungary

Europe & Central Asia | High income

58.69 Index 047/160
       Score

Global average: 54.82

Regional average: 60.26

Income group average: 61.66

Country performance: 58.69

Missing rate in GOHI database: 12.00%

▼ AVERAGE PERFORMANCE BY GOHI

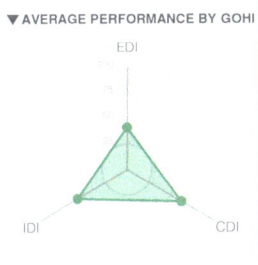

▼ AVERAGE PERFORMANCE BY CDI

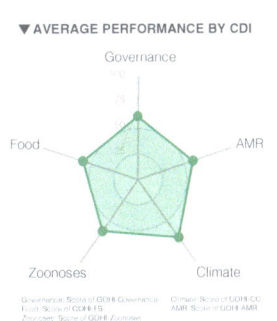

	Country Score	Global Average
A External drivers index	41.52	40.45
A1 Earth system	55.85	56.21
A1.1 Land	53.84	36.41
A1.2 Forest	42.77	43.43
A1.3 Water	34.79	58.09
A1.4 Air	79.80	71.93
A1.5 Natural disasters	66.54	64.65
A2 Institutional system	49.96	46.01
A2.1 Justice	59.45	57.89
A2.2 Governance	41.88	35.58
A3 Economical system	19.64	24.62
A3.1 Finance	21.00	34.35
A3.2 Work	38.86	38.58
A4 Sociological system	39.35	37.70
A4.1 Demographic	39.43	46.31
A4.2 Education	33.66	28.26
A4.3 Inequalities	46.72	40.28
A5 Technological system	42.81	37.72
A5.1 Transport	2.46	6.54
A5.2 Technology adoption	57.15	41.23
A5.3 Consumption and production	64.85	62.53
B Intrinsic drivers index	57.52	58.01
B1 Human health	72.25	72.35
B1.1 Health coverage	60.45	58.65
B1.2 Diseases burden	67.67	79.83
B1.3 Injury and violence	90.83	80.75
B2 Animal health and ecosystem diversity	57.67	56.58
B2.1 Animal epidemic disease	98.20	94.57
B2.2 Wildlife and marine life biodiversity	17.13	18.59
B3 Environmental health	44.39	46.87
B3.1 Air quality and climate change	56.77	53.72
B3.2 Environmental biodiversity	37.35	44.05
B3.3 Environmental resources	40.39	44.25

	Country Score	Global Average
C Core drivers index	62.78	57.25
C1 Governance	62.21	56.51
C1.1 Participation	22.71	41.70
C1.3 Transparency	84.80	65.15
C1.4 Responsiveness	41.65	44.42
C1.5 Consensus oriented	95.33	86.45
C1.6 Equity and inclusiveness	93.08	73.61
C1.7 Effectiveness and efficiency	29.20	28.38
C1.8 Political support	68.68	55.89
C2 Zoonotic diseases	70.53	68.06
C2.1 Source of infection	82.23	69.22
C2.2 Route of transmission	66.66	59.30
C2.3 Targeted population	49.67	59.90
C2.4 Capacity building	71.89	72.85
C2.5 Case studies	83.52	85.89
C3 Food security	59.32	52.89
C3.1 Food demand and supply	67.13	59.53
C3.2 Food safety	77.75	69.36
C3.3 Nutrition	80.47	67.17
C3.4 Natural and social circumstances	59.35	51.54
C3.5 Government support and response	11.89	16.85
C4 Antimicrobial resistance	58.96	44.05
C4.1 AMR surveillance system	52.21	34.79
C4.2 AMR laboratory network and coordination on capacity	75.33	55.57
C4.3 Antimicrobial control and optimization	71.21	48.76
C4.4 Improve awareness and understanding	60.94	48.09
C4.5 Antimicrobial resistance rate for important antibiotics	35.09	33.03
C5 Climate change	62.65	64.19
C5.1 Mitigation and adaptation capacity	27.90	28.24
C5.2 Climate change risks	75.95	80.87
C5.3 Health outcome	86.01	85.41

Scores are normalized (0-100, where 100 = most favorable)

Belarus

Europe & Central Asia | Upper middle income

58.63 Index Score **048**/160

Global average: 54.82

Regional average: 60.26

Income group average: 54.54

Country performance: 58.63

Missing rate in GOHI database: 13.40%

▼ AVERAGE PERFORMANCE BY GOHI

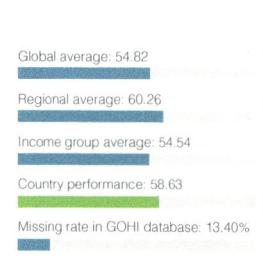

▼ AVERAGE PERFORMANCE BY CDI

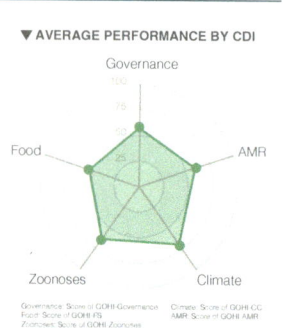

	Country Score	Global Average
A External drivers index	40.79	40.45
A1 Earth system	63.76	56.21
A1.1 Land	66.58	36.41
A1.2 Forest	53.10	43.43
A1.3 Water	53.12	58.09
A1.4 Air	76.90	71.93
A1.5 Natural disasters	65.35	64.65
A2 Institutional system	34.68	46.01
A2.1 Justice	46.03	57.89
A2.2 Governance	25.00	35.58
A3 Economical system	24.52	24.62
A3.1 Finance	31.90	34.35
A3.2 Work	41.33	38.58
A4 Sociological system	39.13	37.70
A4.1 Demographic	42.68	46.31
A4.2 Education	29.07	28.26
A4.3 Inequalities	48.27	40.28
A5 Technological system	41.85	37.72
A5.1 Transport	0.36	6.54
A5.2 Technology adoption	56.27	41.23
A5.3 Consumption and production	64.85	62.53
B Intrinsic drivers index	61.47	58.01
B1 Human health	72.10	72.35
B1.1 Health coverage	60.56	58.65
B1.2 Diseases burden	66.15	79.83
B1.3 Injury and violence	91.79	80.75
B2 Animal health and ecosystem diversity	54.96	56.58
B2.1 Animal epidemic disease	96.01	94.57
B2.2 Wildlife and marine life biodiversity	13.90	18.59
B3 Environmental health	59.20	46.87
B3.1 Air quality and climate change	73.05	53.72
B3.2 Environmental biodiversity	42.30	44.05
B3.3 Environmental resources	64.04	44.25

	Country Score	Global Average
C Core drivers index	61.93	57.25
C1 Governance	58.67	56.51
C1.1 Participation	18.61	41.70
C1.3 Transparency	77.10	65.15
C1.4 Responsiveness	45.80	44.42
C1.5 Consensus oriented	94.11	86.45
C1.6 Equity and inclusiveness	98.58	73.61
C1.7 Effectiveness and efficiency	36.53	28.38
C1.8 Political support	39.97	55.89
C2 Zoonotic diseases	70.98	68.06
C2.1 Source of infection	73.23	69.22
C2.2 Route of transmission	60.71	59.30
C2.3 Targeted population	68.96	59.90
C2.4 Capacity building	70.88	72.85
C2.5 Case studies	88.83	85.89
C3 Food security	61.14	52.89
C3.1 Food demand and supply	63.11	59.53
C3.2 Food safety	88.67	69.36
C3.3 Nutrition	70.66	67.17
C3.4 Natural and social circumstances	53.23	51.54
C3.5 Government support and response	30.02	16.85
C4 Antimicrobial resistance	53.67	44.05
C4.1 AMR surveillance system	40.65	34.79
C4.2 AMR laboratory network and coordination capacity	69.76	55.57
C4.3 Antimicrobial control and optimization	56.06	48.76
C4.4 Improve awareness and understanding	82.81	48.09
C4.5 Antimicrobial resistance rate for important antibiotics	19.06	33.03
C5 Climate change	64.78	64.19
C5.1 Mitigation and adaptation capacity	27.29	28.24
C5.2 Climate change risks	80.47	80.87
C5.3 Health outcome	88.54	85.41

Scores are normalized (0-100, where 100 = most favorable)

Indonesia

East Asia & Pacific | Lower middle income

58.6 | Index Score **049**/160

Global average: 54.82

Regional average: 56.52

Income group average: 51.29

Country performance: 58.60

Missing rate in GOHI database: 10.10%

▼ AVERAGE PERFORMANCE BY GOHI

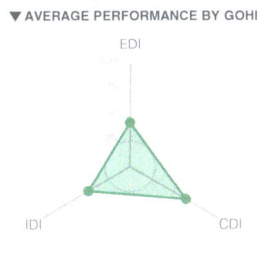

▼ AVERAGE PERFORMANCE BY CDI

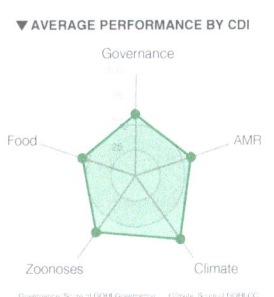

	Country Score	Global Average
A External drivers index	43.33	40.45
A1 Earth system	64.97	56.21
A1.1 Land	30.30	36.41
A1.2 Forest	31.29	43.43
A1.3 Water	96.00	58.09
A1.4 Air	84.32	71.93
A1.5 Natural disasters	65.59	64.65
A2 Institutional system	45.98	46.01
A2.1 Justice	56.50	57.89
A2.2 Governance	37.02	35.58
A3 Economical system	27.76	24.62
A3.1 Finance	41.20	34.35
A3.2 Work	40.36	38.58
A4 Sociological system	35.87	37.70
A4.1 Demographic	47.78	46.31
A4.2 Education	24.87	28.26
A4.3 Inequalities	36.74	40.28
A5 Technological system	42.07	37.72
A5.1 Transport	1.07	6.54
A5.2 Technology adoption	48.05	41.23
A5.3 Consumption and production	73.30	62.53
B Intrinsic drivers index	48.40	58.01
B1 Human health	71.76	72.35
B1.1 Health coverage	51.42	58.65
B1.2 Diseases burden	84.51	79.83
B1.3 Injury and violence	81.53	80.75
B2 Animal health and ecosystem diversity	59.31	56.58
B2.1 Animal epidemic disease	97.96	94.57
B2.2 Wildlife and marine life biodiversity	20.65	18.59
B3 Environmental health	15.61	46.87
B3.1 Air quality and climate change	99.70	53.72
B3.2 Environmental biodiversity	15.40	44.05
B3.3 Environmental resources	21.92	44.25

	Country Score	Global Average
C Core drivers index	64.42	67.25
C1 Governance	60.62	56.51
C1.1 Participation	47.54	41.70
C1.3 Transparency	72.20	65.15
C1.4 Responsiveness	37.50	44.42
C1.5 Consensus oriented	92.71	86.45
C1.6 Equity and inclusiveness	60.01	73.61
C1.7 Effectiveness and efficiency	44.20	28.38
C1.8 Political support	70.21	55.89
C2 Zoonotic diseases	76.93	68.06
C2.1 Source of infection	81.19	69.22
C2.2 Route of transmission	70.59	59.30
C2.3 Targeted population	72.53	59.90
C2.4 Capacity building	78.36	72.85
C2.5 Case studies	84.81	85.89
C3 Food security	59.28	52.89
C3.1 Food demand and supply	68.57	59.53
C3.2 Food safety	75.72	69.36
C3.3 Nutrition	61.57	67.17
C3.4 Natural and social circumstances	54.69	51.54
C3.5 Government support and response	35.92	16.85
C4 Antimicrobial resistance	56.63	44.05
C4.1 AMR surveillance system	60.41	34.79
C4.2 AMR laboratory network and coordination on capacity	57.48	55.57
C4.3 Antimicrobial control and optimization	71.13	48.76
C4.4 Improve awareness and understanding	62.50	48.09
C4.5 Antimicrobial resistance rate for important antibiotics	31.65	33.03
C5 Climate change	68.66	64.19
C5.1 Mitigation and adaptation capacity	29.61	28.24
C5.2 Climate change risks	91.95	80.87
C5.3 Health outcome	86.49	85.41

Scores are normalized (0-100, where 100 = most favorable)

Malta

Middle East & North Africa | High income

58.32 Index Score **050**/160

Global average: 54.82

Regional average: 53.57

Income group average: 61.66

Country performance: 58.32

Missing rate in GOHI database: 17.40%

▼ AVERAGE PERFORMANCE BY GOHI

▼ AVERAGE PERFORMANCE BY CDI

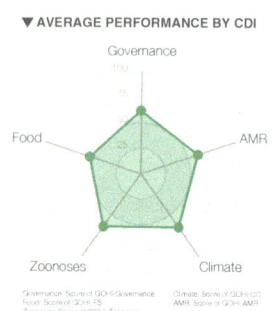

	Country Score	Global Average
A External drivers index	43.40	40.45
A1 Earth system	54.22	56.21
A1.1 Land	18.76	36.41
A1.2 Forest	30.12	43.43
A1.3 Water	60.55	58.09
A1.4 Air	86.46	71.93
A1.5 Natural disasters	63.65	64.65
A2 Institutional system	52.05	46.01
A2.1 Justice	61.10	57.89
A2.2 Governance	44.34	35.58
A3 Economical system	21.97	24.62
A3.1 Finance	26.39	34.35
A3.2 Work	39.81	38.58
A4 Sociological system	38.54	37.70
A4.1 Demographic	43.41	46.31
A4.2 Education	27.88	28.26
A4.3 Inequalities	46.97	40.28
A5 Technological system	50.22	37.72
A5.1 Transport	29.05	6.54
A5.2 Technology adoption	64.83	41.23
A5.3 Consumption and production	54.48	62.53
B Intrinsic drivers index	59.69	58.01
B1 Human health	85.43	72.35
B1.1 Health coverage	81.19	58.65
B1.2 Diseases burden	82.40	79.83
B1.3 Injury and violence	95.29	80.75
B2 Animal health and ecosystem diversity	60.94	56.58
B2.1 Animal epidemic disease	91.48	94.57
B2.2 Wildlife and marine life biodiversity	30.40	18.59
B3 Environmental health	34.52	46.87
B3.1 Air quality and climate change	46.73	53.72
B3.2 Environmental biodiversity	36.70	44.05
B3.3 Environmental resources	21.16	44.25

Scores are normalized (0-100, where 100 = most favorable)

	Country Score	Global Average
C Core drivers index	61.79	57.25
C1 Governance	68.03	56.51
C1.1 Participation	39.61	41.70
C1.3 Transparency	74.60	65.15
C1.4 Responsiveness	18.75	44.42
C1.5 Consensus oriented	94.89	86.45
C1.6 Equity and inclusiveness	95.70	73.61
C1.7 Effectiveness and efficiency	22.60	28.38
C1.8 Political support	88.52	55.89
C2 Zoonotic diseases	65.10	68.06
C2.1 Source of infection	61.28	69.22
C2.2 Route of transmission	57.67	59.30
C2.3 Targeted population	50.59	59.90
C2.4 Capacity building	77.32	72.85
C2.5 Case studies	88.28	85.89
C3 Food security	60.82	52.89
C3.1 Food demand and supply	62.39	59.53
C3.2 Food safety	80.68	69.36
C3.3 Nutrition	81.39	67.17
C3.4 Natural and social circumstances	54.44	51.54
C3.5 Government support and response	25.18	16.85
C4 Antimicrobial resistance	54.05	44.05
C4.1 AMR surveillance system	44.71	34.79
C4.2 AMR laboratory network and coordination capacity	67.41	55.57
C4.3 Antimicrobial control and optimization	58.61	48.76
C4.4 Improve awareness and understanding	59.38	48.09
C4.5 Antimicrobial resistance rate for important antibiotics	40.12	33.03
C5 Climate change	64.22	64.19
C5.1 Mitigation and adaptation capacity	32.92	28.24
C5.2 Climate change risks	81.50	80.87
C5.3 Health outcome	80.20	85.41

Peru

Latin America & Caribbean | Upper middle income

 Index Score **051**/160

Global average: 54.82

Regional average: 55.08

Income group average: 54.54

Country performance: 58.24

Missing rate in GOHI database: 12.00%

▼ AVERAGE PERFORMANCE BY GOHI

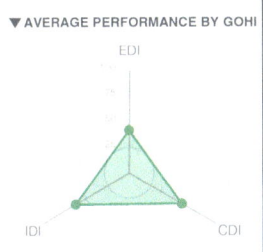

▼ AVERAGE PERFORMANCE BY CDI

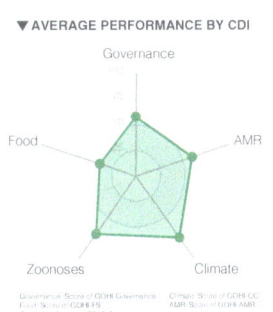

	Country Score	Global Average
A External drivers index	42.07	40.45
A1 Earth system	63.44	56.21
A1.1 Land	31.96	36.41
A1.2 Forest	41.42	43.43
A1.3 Water	87.57	58.09
A1.4 Air	76.85	71.93
A1.5 Natural disasters	66.00	64.65
A2 Institutional system	42.00	46.01
A2.1 Justice	51.93	57.89
A2.2 Governance	33.55	35.58
A3 Economical system	25.82	24.62
A3.1 Finance	34.97	34.35
A3.2 Work	41.77	38.58
A4 Sociological system	37.26	37.70
A4.1 Demographic	48.18	46.31
A4.2 Education	26.65	28.26
A4.3 Inequalities	38.74	40.28
A5 Technological system	41.87	37.72
A5.1 Transport	2.07	6.54
A5.2 Technology adoption	47.61	41.23
A5.3 Consumption and production	72.15	62.53
B Intrinsic drivers index	62.24	58.01
B1 Human health	84.47	72.35
B1.1 Health coverage	75.12	58.65
B1.2 Diseases burden	92.62	79.83
B1.3 Injury and violence	88.23	80.75
B2 Animal health and ecosystem diversity	66.65	56.58
B2.1 Animal epidemic disease	97.19	94.57
B2.2 Wildlife and marine life biodiversity	36.10	18.59
B3 Environmental health	37.48	46.87
B3.1 Air quality and climate change	33.50	53.72
B3.2 Environmental biodiversity	39.20	44.05
B3.3 Environmental resources	40.88	44.25

	Country Score	Global Average
C Core drivers index	60.88	57.25
C1 Governance	58.30	56.51
C1.1 Participation	14.70	41.70
C1.3 Transparency	68.80	65.15
C1.4 Responsiveness	66.65	44.42
C1.5 Consensus oriented	93.78	86.45
C1.6 Equity and inclusiveness	58.46	73.61
C1.7 Effectiveness and efficiency	31.60	28.38
C1.8 Political support	74.14	55.89
C2 Zoonotic diseases	74.93	68.06
C2.1 Source of infection	80.06	69.22
C2.2 Route of transmission	61.16	59.30
C2.3 Targeted population	77.24	59.90
C2.4 Capacity building	77.46	72.85
C2.5 Case studies	84.18	85.89
C3 Food security	60.32	52.89
C3.1 Food demand and supply	61.01	59.53
C3.2 Food safety	86.85	69.36
C3.3 Nutrition	75.88	67.17
C3.4 Natural and social circumstances	55.82	51.54
C3.5 Government support and response	22.04	16.85
C4 Antimicrobial resistance	39.24	44.05
C4.1 AMR surveillance system	27.41	34.79
C4.2 AMR laboratory network and coordination on capacity	63.19	55.57
C4.3 Antimicrobial control and optimization	41.44	48.76
C4.4 Improve awareness and understanding	37.50	48.09
C4.5 Antimicrobial resistance rate for important antibiotics	26.67	33.03
C5 Climate change	70.28	64.19
C5.1 Mitigation and adaptation capacity	33.48	28.24
C5.2 Climate change risks	91.18	80.87
C5.3 Health outcome	88.32	85.41

Scores are normalized (0-100, where 100 = most favorable)

Colombia

Latin America & Caribbean | **Upper middle income**

58.16 Index Score **052**/160

Global average: 54.82

Regional average: 55.08

Income group average: 54.54

Country performance: 58.16

Missing rate in GOHI database: 7.60%

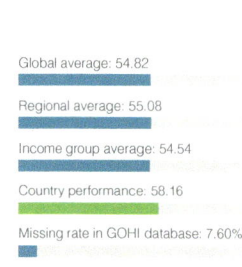

▼ AVERAGE PERFORMANCE BY GOHI

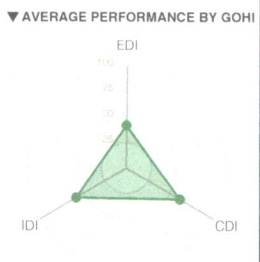

▼ AVERAGE PERFORMANCE BY CDI

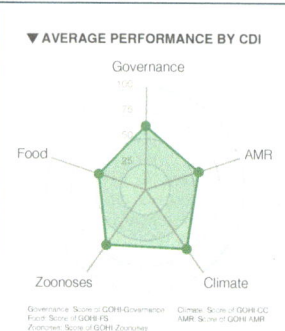

	Country Score	Global Average
A External drivers index	41.85	40.45
A1 Earth system	68.72	56.21
A1.1 Land	33.05	36.41
A1.2 Forest	48.54	43.43
A1.3 Water	96.67	58.09
A1.4 Air	83.44	71.93
A1.5 Natural disasters	66.51	64.65
A2 Institutional system	40.33	46.01
A2.1 Justice	49.03	57.89
A2.2 Governance	32.91	35.58
A3 Economical system	24.66	24.62
A3.1 Finance	35.81	34.35
A3.2 Work	37.50	38.58
A4 Sociological system	36.72	37.70
A4.1 Demographic	49.48	46.31
A4.2 Education	25.88	28.26
A4.3 Inequalities	36.39	40.28
A5 Technological system	38.66	37.72
A5.1 Transport	1.42	6.54
A5.2 Technology adoption	39.11	41.23
A5.3 Consumption and production	72.16	62.53
B Intrinsic drivers index	58.52	58.01
B1 Human health	76.18	72.35
B1.1 Health coverage	76.34	58.65
B1.2 Diseases burden	90.81	79.83
B1.3 Injury and violence	63.70	80.75
B2 Animal health and ecosystem diversity	54.40	56.58
B2.1 Animal epidemic disease	92.49	94.57
B2.2 Wildlife and marine life biodiversity	16.30	18.59
B3 Environmental health	46.74	46.87
B3.1 Air quality and climate change	36.59	53.72
B3.2 Environmental biodiversity	54.00	44.05
B3.3 Environmental resources	51.04	44.25

Scores are normalized (0-100, where 100 = most favorable)

	Country Score	Global Average
C Core drivers index	61.70	57.25
C1 Governance	62.38	56.51
C1.1 Participation	78.91	41.70
C1.3 Transparency	73.80	65.15
C1.5 Responsiveness	41.65	44.42
C1.5 Consensus oriented	90.64	86.45
C1.6 Equity and inclusiveness	58.39	73.61
C1.7 Effectiveness and efficiency	33.27	28.38
C1.8 Political support	60.03	55.89
C2 Zoonotic diseases	71.85	68.06
C2.1 Source of infection	81.93	69.22
C2.2 Route of transmission	45.08	59.30
C2.3 Targeted population	74.68	59.90
C2.4 Capacity building	79.88	72.85
C2.5 Case studies	88.38	85.89
C3 Food security	56.88	52.89
C3.1 Food demand and supply	59.25	59.53
C3.2 Food safety	84.47	69.36
C3.3 Nutrition	72.39	67.17
C3.4 Natural and social circumstances	51.12	51.54
C3.5 Government support and response	17.15	16.85
C4 Antimicrobial resistance	49.60	44.05
C4.1 AMR surveillance system	35.06	34.79
C4.2 AMR laboratory network and coordination on capacity	60.86	55.57
C4.3 Antimicrobial control and optimization	63.40	48.76
C4.4 Improve awareness and understanding	48.44	48.09
C4.5 Antimicrobial resistance rate for important antibiotics	40.24	33.03
C5 Climate change	67.12	64.19
C5.1 Mitigation and adaptation capacity	29.88	28.24
C5.2 Climate change risks	90.27	80.87
C5.3 Health outcome	83.23	85.41

Romania

Europe & Central Asia | High income

 Index Score **053**/160

Global average: 54.82

Regional average: 60.26

Income group average: 61.66

Country performance: 57.65

Missing rate in GOHI database: 9.80%

▼ AVERAGE PERFORMANCE BY GOHI

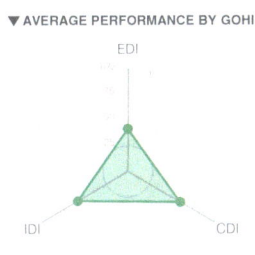

▼ AVERAGE PERFORMANCE BY CDI

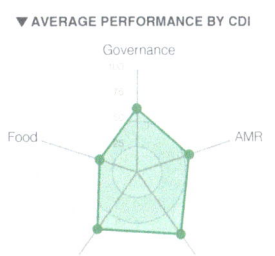

	Country Score	Global Average
A External drivers index	41.66	40.45
A1 Earth system	58.21	56.21
A1.1 Land	51.21	36.41
A1.2 Forest	45.99	43.43
A1.3 Water	40.23	58.09
A1.4 Air	83.52	71.93
A1.5 Natural disasters	66.67	64.65
A2 Institutional system	52.50	46.01
A2.1 Justice	66.27	57.89
A2.2 Governance	40.77	35.58
A3 Economical system	20.00	24.62
A3.1 Finance	23.85	34.35
A3.2 Work	36.48	38.58
A4 Sociological system	34.78	37.70
A4.1 Demographic	35.99	46.31
A4.2 Education	27.69	28.26
A4.3 Inequalities	42.70	40.28
A5 Technological system	42.82	37.72
A5.1 Transport	1.63	6.54
A5.2 Technology adoption	54.33	41.23
A5.3 Consumption and production	68.53	62.53
B Intrinsic drivers index	58.64	58.01
B1 Human health	73.96	72.35
B1.1 Health coverage	62.53	58.65
B1.2 Diseases burden	70.84	79.83
B1.3 Injury and violence	90.60	80.75
B2 Animal health and ecosystem diversity	67.08	56.58
B2.1 Animal epidemic disease	94.02	94.57
B2.2 Wildlife and marine life biodiversity	40.15	18.59
B3 Environmental health	37.25	46.87
B3.1 Air quality and climate change	35.03	53.72
B3.2 Environmental biodiversity	47.00	44.05
B3.3 Environmental resources	30.84	44.25

Scores are normalized (0-100, where 100 = most favorable)

	Country Score	Global Average
C Core drivers index	60.91	57.25
C1 Governance	62.61	56.51
C1.1 Participation	50.10	41.70
C1.3 Transparency	77.50	65.15
C1.4 Responsiveness	25.00	44.42
C1.5 Consensus oriented	95.62	86.45
C1.6 Equity and inclusiveness	84.38	73.61
C1.7 Effectiveness and efficiency	40.80	28.38
C1.8 Political support	64.88	55.89
C2 Zoonotic diseases	75.45	68.06
C2.1 Source of infection	78.15	69.22
C2.2 Route of transmission	70.58	59.30
C2.3 Targeted population	79.30	59.90
C2.4 Capacity building	67.11	72.85
C2.5 Case studies	83.75	85.89
C3 Food security	56.10	52.89
C3.1 Food demand and supply	65.93	59.53
C3.2 Food safety	62.63	69.36
C3.3 Nutrition	79.34	67.17
C3.4 Natural and social circumstances	56.44	51.54
C3.5 Government support and response	16.17	16.85
C4 Antimicrobial resistance	39.87	44.05
C4.1 AMR surveillance system	23.81	34.79
C4.2 AMR laboratory network and coordination capacity	39.52	55.57
C4.3 Antimicrobial control and optimization	58.74	48.76
C4.4 Improve awareness and understanding	51.46	48.09
C4.5 Antimicrobial resistance rate for important antibiotics	25.71	33.03
C5 Climate change	69.08	64.19
C5.1 Mitigation and adaptation capacity	36.93	28.24
C5.2 Climate change risks	81.81	80.87
C5.3 Health outcome	90.60	85.41

Viet Nam

East Asia & Pacific | Lower middle income

 57.63 **Index Score 054**/160

Global average: 54.82

Regional average: 56.52

Income group average: 51.29

Country performance: 57.63

Missing rate in GOHI database: 25.40%

▼ AVERAGE PERFORMANCE BY GOHI

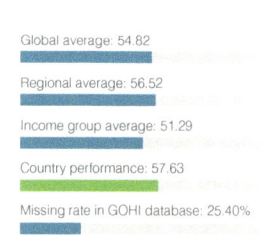

▼ AVERAGE PERFORMANCE BY CDI

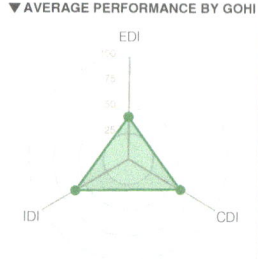

	Country Score	Global Average
A External drivers index	56.93	40.45
A1 Earth system	64.97	56.21
A1.1 Land	29.78	36.41
A1.2 Forest	51.48	43.43
A1.3 Water	51.16	58.09
A1.4 Air	80.62	71.93
A1.5 Natural disasters	65.83	64.65
A2 Institutional system	45.98	46.01
A2.1 Justice	57.07	57.89
A2.2 Governance	36.95	35.58
A3 Economical system	27.76	24.62
A3.1 Finance	27.82	34.35
A3.2 Work	42.68	38.58
A4 Sociological system	35.87	37.70
A4.1 Demographic	42.08	46.31
A4.2 Education	33.82	28.26
A4.3 Inequalities	42.13	40.28
A5 Technological system	42.07	37.72
A5.1 Transport	1.49	6.54
A5.2 Technology adoption	50.88	41.23
A5.3 Consumption and production	69.22	62.53
B Intrinsic drivers index	61.93	58.01
B1 Human health	73.45	72.35
B1.1 Health coverage	63.53	58.65
B1.2 Diseases burden	85.41	79.83
B1.3 Injury and violence	73.65	80.75
B2 Animal health and ecosystem diversity	60.66	56.58
B2.1 Animal epidemic disease	94.73	94.57
B2.2 Wildlife and marine life biodiversity	26.60	18.59
B3 Environmental health	53.55	46.87
B3.1 Air quality and climate change	73.35	53.72
B3.2 Environmental biodiversity	52.55	44.05
B3.3 Environmental resources	36.36	44.25

Scores are normalized (0-100, where 100 = most favorable)

	Country Score	Global Average
C Core drivers index	60.22	57.25
C1 Governance	57.79	56.51
C1.1 Participation	47.94	41.70
C1.3 Transparency	76.33	65.15
C1.4 Responsiveness	43.75	44.42
C1.5 Consensus oriented	93.75	86.45
C1.6 Equity and inclusiveness	57.99	73.61
C1.7 Effectiveness and efficiency	35.20	28.38
C1.8 Political support	49.58	55.89
C2 Zoonotic diseases	78.18	68.06
C2.1 Source of infection	79.05	69.22
C2.2 Route of transmission	74.64	59.30
C2.3 Targeted population	73.06	59.90
C2.4 Capacity building	77.88	72.85
C2.5 Case studies	89.55	85.89
C3 Food security	65.09	52.89
C3.1 Food demand and supply	68.52	59.53
C3.2 Food safety	83.76	69.36
C3.3 Nutrition	79.69	67.17
C3.4 Natural and social circumstances	51.76	51.54
C3.5 Government support and response	41.73	16.85
C4 Antimicrobial resistance	29.59	44.05
C4.1 AMR surveillance system	22.51	34.79
C4.2 AMR laboratory and coordination capacity	44.06	55.57
C4.3 Antimicrobial control and optimization	22.16	48.76
C4.4 Improve awareness and understanding	17.19	48.09
C4.5 Antimicrobial resistance rate for important antibiotics	42.04	33.03
C5 Climate change	67.67	64.19
C5.1 Mitigation and adaptation capacity	31.96	28.24
C5.2 Climate change risks	85.11	80.87
C5.3 Health outcome	88.00	85.41

Qatar

Middle East & North Africa | High income

57.52 Index Score **055**/160

Global average: 54.82

Regional average: 53.57

Income group average: 61.66

Country performance: 57.52

Missing rate in GOHI database: 20.30%

▼ AVERAGE PERFORMANCE BY GOHI

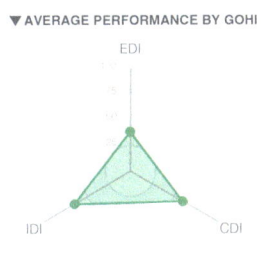

▼ AVERAGE PERFORMANCE BY CDI

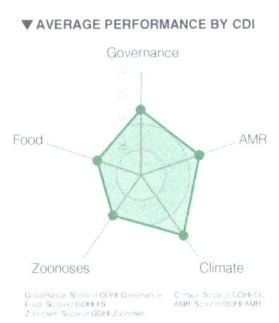

	Country Score	Global Average
A External drivers index	38.52	40.45
A1 Earth system	29.89	56.21
A1.1 Land	24.61	36.41
A1.2 Forest	33.33	43.43
A1.3 Water	32.91	58.09
A1.4 Air	0.00	71.93
A1.5 Natural disasters	66.53	64.65
A2 Institutional system	54.37	46.01
A2.1 Justice	65.35	57.89
A2.2 Governance	45.01	35.58
A3 Economical system	28.94	24.62
A3.1 Finance	43.55	34.35
A3.2 Work	41.31	38.58
A4 Sociological system	37.14	37.70
A4.1 Demographic	47.61	46.31
A4.2 Education	25.80	28.26
A4.3 Inequalities	40.77	40.28
A5 Technological system	42.25	37.72
A5.1 Transport	50.00	6.54
A5.2 Technology adoption	51.78	41.23
A5.3 Consumption and production	25.37	62.53
B Intrinsic drivers index	65.03	58.01
B1 Human health	85.58	72.35
B1.1 Health coverage	70.14	58.65
B1.2 Diseases burden	97.08	79.83
B1.3 Injury and violence	92.12	80.75
B2 Animal health and ecosystem diversity	54.61	56.58
B2.1 Animal epidemic disease	97.36	94.57
B2.2 Wildlife and marine life biodiversity	11.85	18.59
B3 Environmental health	56.88	46.87
B3.1 Air quality and climate change	58.85	53.72
B3.2 Environmental biodiversity	39.55	44.05
B3.3 Environmental resources	73.96	44.25

	Country Score	Global Average
C Core drivers index	59.97	57.25
C1 Governance	64.23	56.51
C1.1 Participation	48.55	41.70
C1.3 Transparency	63.00	65.15
C1.4 Responsiveness	50.00	44.42
C1.5 Consensus oriented	94.02	86.45
C1.6 Equity and inclusiveness	85.78	73.61
C1.7 Effectiveness and efficiency	40.73	28.38
C1.8 Political support	67.54	55.89
C2 Zoonotic diseases	73.50	68.06
C2.1 Source of infection	84.93	69.22
C2.2 Route of transmission	49.82	59.30
C2.3 Targeted population	76.09	59.90
C2.4 Capacity building	74.47	72.85
C2.5 Case studies	90.83	85.89
C3 Food security	63.19	52.89
C3.1 Food demand and supply	72.77	59.53
C3.2 Food safety	83.83	69.36
C3.3 Nutrition	73.07	67.17
C3.4 Natural and social circumstances	53.78	51.54
C3.5 Government support and response	32.49	16.85
C4 Antimicrobial resistance	46.87	44.05
C4.1 AMR surveillance system	28.01	34.79
C4.2 AMR laboratory network and coordinati on capacity	72.11	55.57
C4.3 Antimicrobial control and optimization	46.16	48.76
C4.4 Improve awareness and understanding	53.12	48.09
C4.5 Antimicrobial resistance rate for important antibiotics	34.95	33.03
C5 Climate change	49.16	64.19
C5.1 Mitigation and adaptation capacity	28.88	28.24
C5.2 Climate change risks	54.79	80.87
C5.3 Health outcome	65.30	85.41

Scores are normalized (0-100, where 100 = most favorable)

Poland

Europe & Central Asia | **High income**

57.51 Index **056**/160
       Score

Global average: 54.82

Regional average: 60.26

Income group average: 61.66

Country performance: 57.51

Missing rate in GOHI database: 7.20%

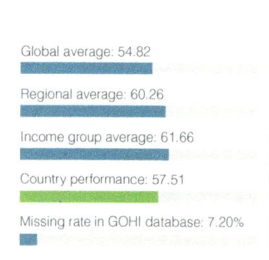

▼ AVERAGE PERFORMANCE BY GOHI

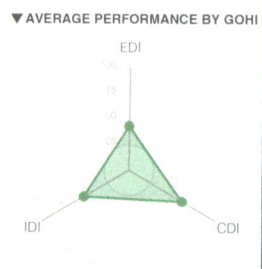

▼ AVERAGE PERFORMANCE BY CDI

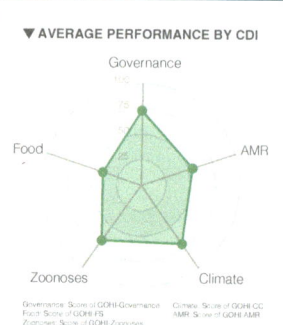

	Country Score	Global Average
A External drivers index	43.15	40.45
A1 Earth system	58.24	56.21
A1.1 Land	43.68	36.41
A1.2 Forest	45.85	43.43
A1.3 Water	61.37	58.09
A1.4 Air	67.92	71.93
A1.5 Natural disasters	66.66	64.65
A2 Institutional system	52.90	46.01
A2.1 Justice	65.84	57.89
A2.2 Governance	41.87	35.58
A3 Economical system	20.88	24.62
A3.1 Finance	24.58	34.35
A3.2 Work	38.46	38.58
A4 Sociological system	38.48	37.70
A4.1 Demographic	37.57	46.31
A4.2 Education	31.91	28.26
A4.3 Inequalities	48.12	40.28
A5 Technological system	45.24	37.72
A5.1 Transport	1.66	6.54
A5.2 Technology adoption	65.13	41.23
A5.3 Consumption and production	64.51	62.53
B Intrinsic drivers index	52.47	58.01
B1 Human health	77.50	72.35
B1.1 Health coverage	66.44	58.65
B1.2 Diseases burden	76.38	79.83
B1.3 Injury and violence	92.04	80.75
B2 Animal health and ecosystem diversity	50.85	56.58
B2.1 Animal epidemic disease	94.70	94.57
B2.2 Wildlife and marine life biodiversity	7.00	18.59
B3 Environmental health	30.65	46.87
B3.1 Air quality and climate change	23.35	53.72
B3.2 Environmental biodiversity	40.45	44.05
B3.3 Environmental resources	29.08	44.25

	Country Score	Global Average
C Core drivers index	61.89	57.25
C1 Governance	73.16	56.51
C1.1 Participation	78.93	41.70
C1.3 Transparency	89.10	65.15
C1.4 Responsiveness	45.80	44.42
C1.5 Consensus oriented	99.33	86.45
C1.6 Equity and inclusiveness	98.48	73.61
C1.7 Effectiveness and efficiency	35.27	28.38
C1.8 Political support	65.19	55.89
C2 Zoonotic diseases	71.13	68.06
C2.1 Source of infection	79.41	69.22
C2.2 Route of transmission	58.00	59.30
C2.3 Targeted population	68.48	59.90
C2.4 Capacity building	69.37	72.85
C2.5 Case studies	85.42	85.89
C3 Food security	54.75	52.89
C3.1 Food demand and supply	65.58	59.53
C3.2 Food safety	61.27	69.36
C3.3 Nutrition	81.18	67.17
C3.4 Natural and social circumstances	52.03	51.54
C3.5 Government support and response	13.70	16.85
C4 Antimicrobial resistance	40.85	44.05
C4.1 AMR surveillance system	43.02	34.79
C4.2 AMR laboratory network and coordinati on capacity	45.82	55.57
C4.3 Antimicrobial control and optimization	49.74	48.76
C4.4 Improve awareness and understanding	32.81	48.09
C4.5 Antimicrobial resistance rate for important antibiotics	32.85	33.03
C5 Climate change	67.33	64.19
C5.1 Mitigation and adaptation capacity	32.04	28.24
C5.2 Climate change risks	82.58	80.87
C5.3 Health outcome	89.41	85.41

Scores are normalized (0-100, where 100 = most favorable)

United Arab Emirates
Middle East & North Africa | High income

57.42 | Index Score **057**/160

Global average: 54.82

Regional average: 53.57

Income group average: 61.66

Country performance: 57.42

Missing rate in GOHI database: 17.80%

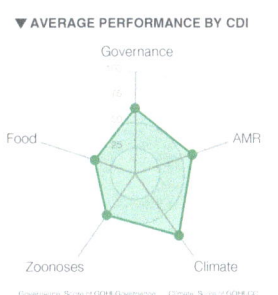

▼ AVERAGE PERFORMANCE BY GOHI

▼ AVERAGE PERFORMANCE BY CDI

	Country Score	Global Average
A External drivers index	43.75	40.45
A1 Earth system	33.03	56.21
A1.1 Land	22.26	36.41
A1.2 Forest	31.24	43.43
A1.3 Water	33.34	58.09
A1.4 Air	20.91	71.93
A1.5 Natural disasters	60.99	64.65
A2 Institutional system	55.95	46.01
A2.1 Justice	68.92	57.89
A2.2 Governance	44.90	35.58
A3 Economical system	37.52	24.82
A3.1 Finance	64.49	34.35
A3.2 Work	43.36	38.50
A4 Sociological system	39.77	37.70
A4.1 Demographic	47.36	46.31
A4.2 Education	22.70	28.26
A4.3 Inequalities	46.93	40.28
A5 Technological system	52.50	37.72
A5.1 Transport	50.00	6.54
A5.2 Technology adoption	69.50	41.23
A5.3 Consumption and production	37.30	62.53
B Intrinsic drivers index	61.12	58.01
B1 Human health	78.29	72.35
B1.1 Health coverage	70.11	58.65
B1.2 Diseases burden	89.86	79.83
B1.3 Injury and violence	77.26	80.75
B2 Animal health and ecosystem diversity	59.02	56.58
B2.1 Animal epidemic disease	97.44	94.57
B2.2 Wildlife and marine life biodiversity	20.60	18.59
B3 Environmental health	47.91	46.87
B3.1 Air quality and climate change	49.82	53.72
B3.2 Environmental biodiversity	42.50	44.05
B3.3 Environmental resources	52.86	44.25

Scores are normalized (0-100, where 100 = most favorable)

	Country Score	Global Average
C Core drivers index	59.58	57.25
C1 Governance	64.30	56.51
C1.1 Participation	83.53	41.70
C1.3 Transparency	59.70	65.15
C1.4 Responsiveness	43.75	44.42
C1.5 Consensus oriented	94.58	86.45
C1.6 Equity and inclusiveness	70.48	73.61
C1.7 Effectiveness and efficiency	34.33	28.38
C1.8 Political support	63.76	55.89
C2 Zoonotic diseases	75.16	68.06
C2.1 Source of infection	73.99	69.22
C2.2 Route of transmission	60.68	59.30
C2.3 Targeted population	70.01	59.90
C2.4 Capacity building	81.84	72.85
C2.5 Case studies	91.48	85.89
C3 Food security	61.49	52.89
C3.1 Food demand and supply	70.88	59.53
C3.2 Food safety	87.38	69.36
C3.3 Nutrition	68.83	67.17
C3.4 Natural and social circumstances	56.48	51.54
C3.5 Government support and response	23.87	16.85
C4 Antimicrobial resistance	43.52	44.05
C4.1 AMR surveillance system	26.80	34.79
C4.2 AMR laboratory network and coordinati on capacity	43.47	55.57
C4.3 Antimicrobial control and optimization	65.39	48.76
C4.4 Improve awareness and understanding	42.19	48.09
C4.5 Antimicrobial resistance rate for important antibiotics	39.76	33.03
C5 Climate change	50.37	64.19
C5.1 Mitigation and adaptation capacity	28.80	28.24
C5.2 Climate change risks	57.69	80.87
C5.3 Health outcome	66.16	85.41

India

South Asia | Lower middle income

57.17 Index **058**/160
      Score

Global average: 54.82

Regional average: 51.61

Income group average: 51.29

Country performance: 57.17

Missing rate in GOHI database: 12.30%

▼ AVERAGE PERFORMANCE BY GOHI

▼ AVERAGE PERFORMANCE BY CDI

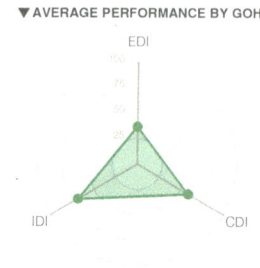

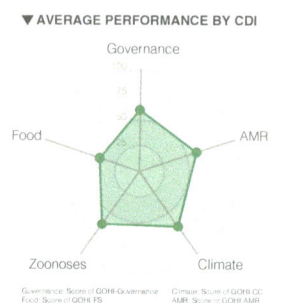

Governance: Score of GOHI-Governance   Climate: Score of GOHI-CC
Food: Score of GOHI-FS   AMR: Score of GOHI-AMR
Zoonoses: Score of GOHI-Zoonoses

	Country Score	Global Average
A External drivers index	36.60	40.45
A1 Earth system	52.60	56.21
A1.1 Land	27.90	36.41
A1.2 Forest	42.48	43.43
A1.3 Water	74.09	58.09
A1.4 Air	46.27	71.93
A1.5 Natural disasters	66.07	64.65
A2 Institutional system	39.34	46.01
A2.1 Justice	44.45	57.89
A2.2 Governance	34.99	35.58
A3 Economical system	18.91	24.62
A3.1 Finance	20.25	34.35
A3.2 Work	37.40	38.58
A4 Sociological system	36.34	37.70
A4.1 Demographic	46.49	46.31
A4.2 Education	28.90	28.26
A4.3 Inequalities	34.54	40.28
A5 Technological system	35.81	37.72
A5.1 Transport	0.25	6.54
A5.2 Technology adoption	30.68	41.23
A5.3 Consumption and production	73.51	62.53
B Intrinsic drivers index	68.55	59.01
B1 Human health	69.36	72.35
B1.1 Health coverage	45.51	58.65
B1.2 Diseases burden	79.68	79.83
B1.3 Injury and violence	85.00	80.75
B2 Animal health and ecosystem diversity	62.93	56.58
B2.1 Animal epidemic disease	97.11	94.57
B2.2 Wildlife and marine life biodiversity	28.75	18.59
B3 Environmental health	75.43	46.87
B3.1 Air quality and climate change	85.35	53.72
B3.2 Environmental biodiversity	67.20	44.05
B3.3 Environmental resources	76.02	44.25

	Country Score	Global Average
C Core drivers index	59.04	57.25
C1 Governance	60.17	56.51
C1.1 Participation	45.81	41.70
C1.3 Transparency	70.40	65.15
C1.4 Responsiveness	52.05	44.42
C1.5 Consensus oriented	97.45	86.45
C1.6 Equity and inclusiveness	59.62	73.61
C1.7 Effectiveness and efficiency	43.53	28.38
C1.8 Political support	52.30	55.89
C2 Zoonotic diseases	66.80	68.06
C2.1 Source of infection	66.24	69.22
C2.2 Route of transmission	78.28	59.30
C2.3 Targeted population	70.20	59.90
C2.4 Capacity building	78.79	72.85
C2.5 Case studies	30.88	85.89
C3 Food security	60.22	52.89
C3.1 Food demand and supply	71.25	59.53
C3.2 Food safety	70.85	69.36
C3.3 Nutrition	60.87	67.17
C3.4 Natural and social circumstances	56.86	51.54
C3.5 Government support and response	41.29	16.85
C4 Antimicrobial resistance	42.47	44.05
C4.1 AMR surveillance system	35.82	34.79
C4.2 AMR laboratory network and coordination capacity	66.39	55.57
C4.3 Antimicrobial control and optimization	44.18	48.76
C4.4 Improve awareness and understanding	45.31	48.09
C4.5 Antimicrobial resistance rate for important antibiotics	20.66	33.03
C5 Climate change	64.01	64.19
C5.1 Mitigation and adaptation capacity	37.13	28.24
C5.2 Climate change risks	76.26	80.87
C5.3 Health outcome	80.59	85.41

Scores are normalized (0-100, where 100 = most favorable)

Oman

Middle East & North Africa | High income

57.11 Index Score **059**/160

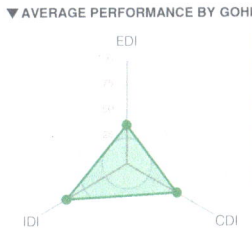

Global average: 54.82

Regional average: 53.57

Income group average: 61.66

Country performance: 57.11

Missing rate in GOHI database: 18.10%

▼ AVERAGE PERFORMANCE BY GOHI

▼ AVERAGE PERFORMANCE BY CDI

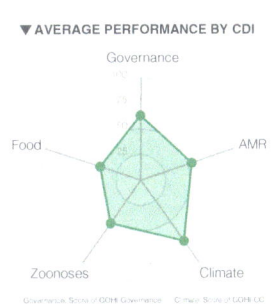

	Country Score	Global Average
A External drivers index	37.81	40.45
A1 Earth system	43.86	56.21
A1.1 Land	26.96	36.41
A1.2 Forest	29.65	43.43
A1.3 Water	57.88	58.09
A1.4 Air	35.53	71.93
A1.5 Natural disasters	66.67	64.65
A2 Institutional system	45.37	46.01
A2.1 Justice	56.23	57.89
A2.2 Governance	36.12	35.58
A3 Economical system	27.26	24.62
A3.1 Finance	39.46	34.35
A3.2 Work	40.86	38.58
A4 Sociological system	38.08	37.70
A4.1 Demographic	49.59	46.31
A4.2 Education	24.08	28.26
A4.3 Inequalities	43.43	40.28
A5 Technological system	34.50	37.72
A5.1 Transport	7.62	6.54
A5.2 Technology adoption	42.20	41.23
A5.3 Consumption and production	51.07	62.53
B Intrinsic drivers index	70.96	58.01
B1 Human health	82.71	72.35
B1.1 Health coverage	63.52	58.65
B1.2 Diseases burden	95.57	79.83
B1.3 Injury and violence	91.54	80.75
B2 Animal health and ecosystem diversity	55.56	56.58
B2.1 Animal epidemic disease	87.33	94.57
B2.2 Wildlife and marine life biodiversity	23.80	18.59
B3 Environmental health	76.82	46.87
B3.1 Air quality and climate change	96.20	53.72
B3.2 Environmental biodiversity	51.00	44.05
B3.3 Environmental resources	85.60	44.25

	Country Score	Global Average
C Core drivers index	58.11	57.25
C1 Governance	63.42	56.51
C1.1 Participation	49.29	41.70
C1.3 Transparency	58.50	65.15
C1.4 Responsiveness	58.30	44.42
C1.5 Consensus oriented	98.54	86.45
C1.6 Equity and inclusiveness	88.82	73.61
C1.7 Effectiveness and efficiency	32.53	28.38
C1.8 Political support	57.95	55.89
C2 Zoonotic diseases	74.09	68.06
C2.1 Source of infection	72.89	69.22
C2.2 Route of transmission	58.49	59.30
C2.3 Targeted population	76.87	59.90
C2.4 Capacity building	82.88	72.85
C2.5 Case studies	88.83	85.89
C3 Food security	54.79	52.89
C3.1 Food demand and supply	60.70	59.53
C3.2 Food safety	68.04	69.36
C3.3 Nutrition	68.06	67.17
C3.4 Natural and social circumstances	49.46	51.54
C3.5 Government support and response	27.70	16.85
C4 Antimicrobial resistance	43.22	44.05
C4.1 AMR surveillance system	36.21	34.79
C4.2 AMR laboratory network and coordination on capacity	37.78	55.57
C4.3 Antimicrobial control and optimization	66.37	48.76
C4.4 Improve awareness and understanding	50.00	48.09
C4.5 Antimicrobial resistance rate for important antibiotics	25.73	33.03
C5 Climate change	52.71	64.19
C5.1 Mitigation and adaptation capacity	25.70	28.24
C5.2 Climate change risks	66.29	80.87
C5.3 Health outcome	67.73	85.41

Scores are normalized (0-100, where 100 = most favorable)

Saudi Arabia
Middle East & North Africa | **High income**

56.49 | Index Score **060**/160

Global average: 54.82

Regional average: 53.57

Income group average: 61.66

Country performance: 56.49

Missing rate in GOHI database: 15.20%

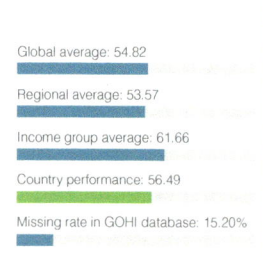

▼ AVERAGE PERFORMANCE BY GOHI

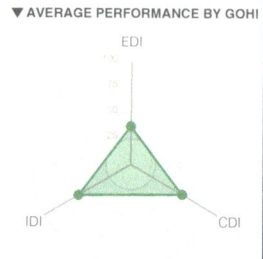

▼ AVERAGE PERFORMANCE BY CDI

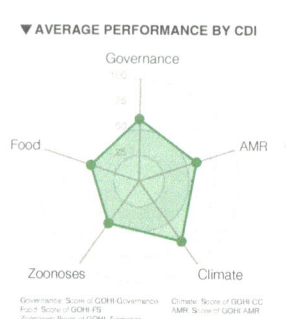

	Country Score	Global Average
A External drivers index	**37.23**	**40.45**
A1 Earth system	35.68	56.21
A1.1 Land	32.39	36.41
A1.2 Forest	33.46	43.43
A1.3 Water	33.37	58.09
A1.4 Air	18.39	71.93
A1.5 Natural disasters	66.41	64.65
A2 Institutional system	44.79	46.01
A2.1 Justice	61.89	57.89
A2.2 Governance	30.22	35.58
A3 Economical system	27.36	24.62
A3.1 Finance	41.51	34.35
A3.2 Work	38.64	38.58
A4 Sociological system	39.38	37.70
A4.1 Demographic	46.14	46.31
A4.2 Education	29.83	28.26
A4.3 Inequalities	44.21	40.28
A5 Technological system	38.94	37.72
A5.1 Transport	5.49	6.54
A5.2 Technology adoption	59.75	41.23
A5.3 Consumption and production	48.01	62.53
B Intrinsic drivers index	**61.12**	**58.01**
B1 Human health	77.24	72.35
B1.1 Health coverage	71.06	58.65
B1.2 Diseases burden	92.02	79.83
B1.3 Injury and violence	70.98	80.75
B2 Animal health and ecosystem diversity	55.33	56.58
B2.1 Animal epidemic disease	95.91	94.57
B2.2 Wildlife and marine life biodiversity	14.75	18.59
B3 Environmental health	52.65	46.87
B3.1 Air quality and climate change	46.71	53.72
B3.2 Environmental biodiversity	79.55	44.05
B3.3 Environmental resources	33.30	44.25

	Country Score	Global Average
C Core drivers index	**59.67**	**57.25**
C1 Governance	60.78	56.51
C1.1 Participation	19.28	41.70
C1.3 Transparency	63.40	65.15
C1.4 Responsiveness	43.75	44.42
C1.5 Consensus oriented	95.16	86.45
C1.6 Equity and inclusiveness	89.62	73.61
C1.7 Effectiveness and efficiency	45.00	28.38
C1.8 Political support	69.27	55.89
C2 Zoonotic diseases	73.02	68.06
C2.1 Source of infection	73.18	69.22
C2.2 Route of transmission	54.23	59.30
C2.3 Targeted population	73.01	59.90
C2.4 Capacity building	85.92	72.85
C2.5 Case studies	89.89	85.89
C3 Food security	60.40	52.89
C3.1 Food demand and supply	65.60	59.53
C3.2 Food safety	66.31	69.36
C3.3 Nutrition	77.91	67.17
C3.4 Natural and social circumstances	62.82	51.54
C3.5 Government support and response	29.37	16.85
C4 Antimicrobial resistance	50.65	44.05
C4.1 AMR surveillance system	39.66	34.79
C4.2 AMR laboratory network and coordination on capacity	69.26	55.57
C4.3 Antimicrobial control and optimization	59.73	48.76
C4.4 Improve awareness and understanding	60.94	48.09
C4.5 Antimicrobial resistance rate for important antibiotics	23.67	33.03
C5 Climate change	51.63	64.19
C5.1 Mitigation and adaptation capacity	32.37	28.24
C5.2 Climate change risks	56.67	80.87
C5.3 Health outcome	67.42	85.41

Scores are normalized (0-100, where 100 = most favorable)

Panama

Latin America & Caribbean | **High income**

 **Index Score 061** /160

Global average: 54.82

Regional average: 55.08

Income group average: 61.66

Country performance: 56.40

Missing rate in GOHI database: 21.70%

▼ AVERAGE PERFORMANCE BY GOHI

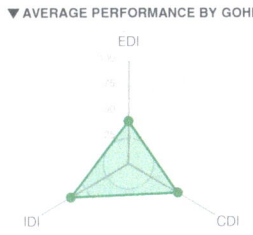

▼ AVERAGE PERFORMANCE BY CDI

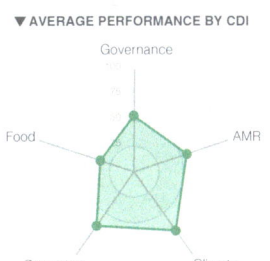

Governance: Score of GOHI Governance   Climate: Score of GOHI CC
Food: Score of GOHI FS   AMR: Score of GOHI AMR
Zoonoses: Score of GOHI Zoonoses

	Country Score	Global Average
A External drivers index	41.83	40.45
A1 Earth system	62.18	56.21
A1.1 Land	29.30	36.41
A1.2 Forest	47.87	43.43
A1.3 Water	68.11	58.09
A1.4 Air	88.74	71.93
A1.5 Natural disasters	66.10	64.65
A2 Institutional system	46.77	46.01
A2.1 Justice	57.24	57.89
A2.2 Governance	37.85	35.58
A3 Economical system	24.10	24.62
A3.1 Finance	34.29	34.35
A3.2 Work	36.89	38.58
A4 Sociological system	35.51	37.70
A4.1 Demographic	44.03	46.31
A4.2 Education	27.08	28.26
A4.3 Inequalities	38.86	40.28
A5 Technological system	40.62	37.72
A5.1 Transport	11.93	6.54
A5.2 Technology adoption	40.41	41.23
A5.3 Consumption and production	67.00	62.53
B Intrinsic drivers index	66.62	58.01
B1 Human health	84.45	72.35
B1.1 Health coverage	84.30	58.65
B1.2 Diseases burden	91.39	79.83
B1.3 Injury and violence	80.21	80.75
B2 Animal health and ecosystem diversity	62.64	56.58
B2.1 Animal epidemic disease	95.19	94.57
B2.2 Wildlife and marine life biodiversity	30.10	18.59
B3 Environmental health	54.80	46.87
B3.1 Air quality and climate change	57.04	53.72
B3.2 Environmental biodiversity	47.43	44.05
B3.3 Environmental resources	61.59	44.25

	Country Score	Global Average
C Core drivers index	57.21	57.25
C1 Governance	55.01	56.51
C1.1 Participation	20.63	41.70
C1.3 Transparency	59.60	65.15
C1.4 Responsiveness	58.30	44.42
C1.5 Consensus oriented	98.58	86.45
C1.6 Equity and inclusiveness	66.79	73.61
C1.7 Effectiveness and efficiency	26.07	28.38
C1.8 Political support	55.14	55.89
C2 Zoonotic diseases	71.47	68.06
C2.1 Source of infection	80.46	69.22
C2.2 Route of transmission	65.40	59.30
C2.3 Targeted population	45.05	59.90
C2.4 Capacity building	83.60	72.85
C2.5 Case studies	87.40	85.89
C3 Food security	56.32	52.89
C3.1 Food demand and supply	66.63	59.53
C3.2 Food safety	86.43	69.36
C3.3 Nutrition	67.13	67.17
C3.4 Natural and social circumstances	50.36	51.54
C3.5 Government support and response	11.06	16.85
C4 Antimicrobial resistance	36.22	44.05
C4.1 AMR surveillance system	22.35	34.79
C4.2 AMR laboratory network and coordination capacity	37.76	55.57
C4.3 Antimicrobial control and optimization	57.51	48.76
C4.4 Improve awareness and understanding	31.25	48.09
C4.5 Antimicrobial resistance rate for important antibiotics	32.25	33.03
C5 Climate change	65.65	64.19
C5.1 Mitigation and adaptation capacity	23.44	28.24
C5.2 Climate change risks	87.82	80.87
C5.3 Health outcome	87.70	85.41

Scores are normalized (0-100, where 100 = most favorable)

Cuba

Latin America & Caribbean | Upper middle income

56.34 Index **062**/160
Score

Global average: 54.82

Regional average: 55.08

Income group average: 54.54

Country performance: 56.34

Missing rate in GOHI database: 27.20%

▼ AVERAGE PERFORMANCE BY GOHI

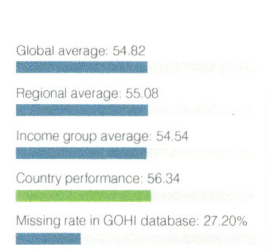

▼ AVERAGE PERFORMANCE BY CDI

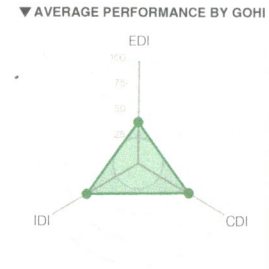

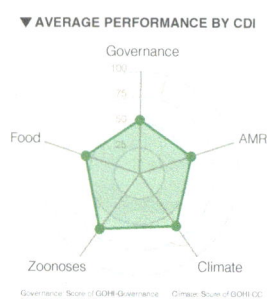

	Country Score	Global Average
A External drivers index	40.54	40.45
A1 Earth system	63.04	56.21
A1.1 Land	42.65	36.41
A1.2 Forest	46.16	43.43
A1.3 Water	65.48	58.09
A1.4 Air	85.22	71.93
A1.5 Natural disasters	66.54	64.65
A2 Institutional system	41.60	46.01
A2.1 Justice	50.68	57.89
A2.2 Governance	33.86	35.58
A3 Economical system	23.76	24.62
A3.1 Finance	30.85	34.35
A3.2 Work	40.12	38.58
A4 Sociological system	36.53	37.70
A4.1 Demographic	42.27	46.31
A4.2 Education	27.84	28.26
A4.3 Inequalities	41.39	40.28
A5 Technological system	37.77	37.72
A5.1 Transport	2.87	6.54
A5.2 Technology adoption	36.69	41.23
A5.3 Consumption and production	70.70	62.53
B Intrinsic drivers index	60.64	53.01
B1 Human health	79.47	72.35
B1.1 Health coverage	73.44	58.65
B1.2 Diseases burden	76.98	79.83
B1.3 Injury and violence	90.40	80.75
B2 Animal health and ecosystem diversity	58.46	56.58
B2.1 Animal epidemic disease	92.96	94.57
B2.2 Wildlife and marine life biodiversity	23.95	18.59
B3 Environmental health	45.83	46.87
B3.1 Air quality and climate change	64.44	53.72
B3.2 Environmental biodiversity	32.65	44.05
B3.3 Environmental resources	41.78	44.25

	Country Score	Global Average
C Core drivers index	58.83	57.25
C1 Governance	52.56	56.51
C1.1 Participation	51.04	41.70
C1.3 Transparency	66.67	65.15
C1.4 Responsiveness	25.00	44.42
C1.5 Consensus oriented	89.90	86.45
C1.6 Equity and inclusiveness	71.49	73.61
C1.7 Effectiveness and efficiency	15.20	28.38
C1.8 Political support	48.60	55.89
C2 Zoonotic diseases	63.64	68.06
C2.1 Source of infection	69.42	69.22
C2.2 Route of transmission	44.28	59.30
C2.3 Targeted population	49.55	59.90
C2.4 Capacity building	76.29	72.85
C2.5 Case studies	90.74	85.89
C3 Food security	55.17	52.89
C3.1 Food demand and supply	58.58	59.53
C3.2 Food safety	76.41	69.36
C3.3 Nutrition	73.40	67.17
C3.4 Natural and social circumstances	49.53	51.54
C3.5 Government support and response	17.92	16.85
C4 Antimicrobial resistance	56.56	44.05
C4.1 AMR surveillance system	48.16	34.79
C4.2 AMR laboratory network and coordination capacity	70.22	55.57
C4.3 Antimicrobial control and optimization	67.36	48.76
C4.4 Improve awareness and understanding	65.62	48.09
C4.5 Antimicrobial resistance rate for important antibiotics	31.41	33.03
C5 Climate change	67.39	64.19
C5.1 Mitigation and adaptation capacity	30.87	28.24
C5.2 Climate change risks	88.32	80.87
C5.3 Health outcome	85.03	85.41

Scores are normalized (0-100, where 100 = most favorable)

Armenia
Europe & Central Asia | Upper middle income

56.22 Index Score **063**/160

Global average: 54.82

Regional average: 60.26

Income group average: 54.54

Country performance: 56.22

Missing rate in GOHI database: 19.90%

▼ AVERAGE PERFORMANCE BY GOHI

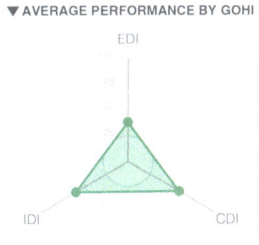

▼ AVERAGE PERFORMANCE BY CDI

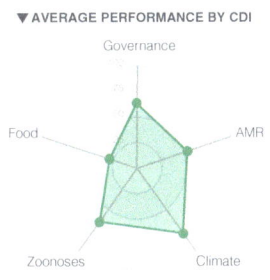

	Country Score	Global Average
A External drivers index	38.57	40.45
A1 Earth system	53.26	56.21
A1.1 Land	24.00	36.41
A1.2 Forest	38.41	43.43
A1.3 Water	58.52	58.09
A1.4 Air	72.28	71.93
A1.5 Natural disasters	65.37	64.65
A2 Institutional system	46.40	46.01
A2.1 Justice	57.51	57.89
A2.2 Governance	36.93	35.58
A3 Economical system	21.99	24.62
A3.1 Finance	30.11	34.35
A3.2 Work	35.17	38.58
A4 Sociological system	36.12	37.70
A4.1 Demographic	43.37	46.31
A4.2 Education	24.67	28.26
A4.3 Inequalities	42.87	40.26
A5 Technological system	35.06	37.72
A5.1 Transport	0.54	6.54
A5.2 Technology adoption	36.36	41.23
A5.3 Consumption and production	65.21	62.53
B Intrinsic drivers index	60.72	58.01
B1 Human health	72.75	72.35
B1.1 Health coverage	55.75	58.65
B1.2 Diseases burden	81.79	79.83
B1.3 Injury and violence	82.93	80.75
B2 Animal health and ecosystem diversity	57.90	56.58
B2.1 Animal epidemic disease	97.58	94.57
B2.2 Wildlife and marine life biodiversity	18.22	18.59
B3 Environmental health	53.36	46.87
B3.1 Air quality and climate change	57.45	53.72
B3.2 Environmental biodiversity	66.50	44.05
B3.3 Environmental resources	37.74	44.25

	Country Score	Global Average
C Core drivers index	59.08	57.25
C1 Governance	64.02	56.51
C1.1 Participation	17.51	41.70
C1.3 Transparency	82.20	65.15
C1.4 Responsiveness	75.00	44.42
C1.5 Consensus oriented	95.61	86.45
C1.6 Equity and inclusiveness	83.06	73.61
C1.7 Effectiveness and efficiency	40.00	28.38
C1.8 Political support	54.75	55.89
C2 Zoonotic diseases	79.50	68.06
C2.1 Source of infection	83.53	69.22
C2.2 Route of transmission	73.73	59.30
C2.3 Targeted population	78.75	59.90
C2.4 Capacity building	79.26	72.85
C2.5 Case studies	84.07	85.89
C3 Food security	53.92	52.89
C3.1 Food demand and supply	58.84	59.53
C3.2 Food safety	73.47	69.36
C3.3 Nutrition	68.06	67.17
C3.4 Natural and social circumstances	48.59	51.54
C3.5 Government support and response	20.64	16.85
C4 Antimicrobial resistance	29.68	44.05
C4.1 AMR surveillance system	10.10	34.79
C4.2 AMR laboratory network and coordination on capacity	30.94	55.57
C4.3 Antimicrobial control and optimization	40.44	48.76
C4.4 Improve awareness and understanding	45.31	48.09
C4.5 Antimicrobial resistance rate for important antibiotics	21.58	33.03
C5 Climate change	65.53	64.19
C5.1 Mitigation and adaptation capacity	29.25	28.24
C5.2 Climate change risks	81.86	80.87
C5.3 Health outcome	87.46	85.41

Scores are normalized (0-100, where 100 = most favorable)

South Africa

Sub-Saharan Africa | Upper middle income

Index Score **064**/160

Global average: 54.82

Regional average: 48.03

Income group average: 54.54

Country performance: 56.18

Missing rate in GOHI database: 16.70%

▼ AVERAGE PERFORMANCE BY GOHI

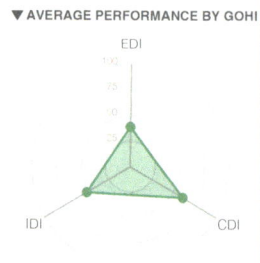

▼ AVERAGE PERFORMANCE BY CDI

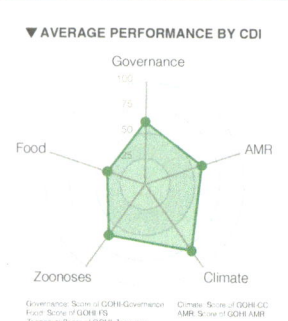

Governance: Score of GOHI-Governance   Climate: Score of GOHI-CC
Food: Score of GOHI-FS   AMR: Score of GOHI-AMR
Zoonoses: Score of GOHI-Zoonoses

	Country Score	Global Average
A External drivers index	39.04	40.45
A1 Earth system	50.69	56.21
A1.1 Land	32.17	36.41
A1.2 Forest	40.56	43.43
A1.3 Water	58.30	58.09
A1.4 Air	64.48	71.93
A1.5 Natural disasters	49.70	64.65
A2 Institutional system	46.91	46.01
A2.1 Justice	61.71	57.89
A2.2 Governance	34.30	35.58
A3 Economical system	17.62	24.62
A3.1 Finance	22.25	34.35
A3.2 Work	30.55	38.58
A4 Sociological system	41.90	37.70
A4.1 Demographic	55.53	46.31
A4.2 Education	31.50	28.26
A4.3 Inequalities	40.02	40.28
A5 Technological system	38.08	37.72
A5.1 Transport	1.83	6.54
A5.2 Technology adoption	43.44	41.23
A5.3 Consumption and production	65.62	62.53
B Intrinsic drivers index	51.06	58.01
B1 Human health	54.99	72.35
B1.1 Health coverage	50.86	58.65
B1.2 Diseases burden	67.96	79.83
B1.3 Injury and violence	47.82	80.75
B2 Animal health and ecosystem diversity	61.07	56.58
B2.1 Animal epidemic disease	95.68	94.57
B2.2 Wildlife and marine life biodiversity	26.45	18.59
B3 Environmental health	38.73	46.87
B3.1 Air quality and climate change	38.13	53.72
B3.2 Environmental biodiversity	54.18	44.05
B3.3 Environmental resources	25.07	44.25

Scores are normalized (0-100, where 100 = most favorable)

	Country Score	Global Average
C Core drivers index	61.20	57.25
C1 Governance	61.20	56.51
C1.1 Participation	46.03	41.70
C1.3 Transparency	73.50	65.15
C1.4 Responsiveness	18.30	44.42
C1.5 Consensus oriented	93.89	86.45
C1.6 Equity and inclusiveness	69.40	73.61
C1.7 Effectiveness and efficiency	33.20	28.38
C1.8 Political support	54.09	55.89
C2 Zoonotic diseases	80.51	68.06
C2.1 Source of infection	96.21	69.22
C2.2 Route of transmission	66.91	59.30
C2.3 Targeted population	77.23	59.90
C2.4 Capacity building	78.20	72.85
C2.5 Case studies	85.35	85.89
C3 Food security	60.15	52.89
C3.1 Food demand and supply	69.08	59.53
C3.2 Food safety	85.31	69.36
C3.3 Nutrition	68.20	67.17
C3.4 Natural and social circumstances	54.09	51.54
C3.5 Government support and response	24.07	16.85
C4 Antimicrobial resistance	39.94	44.05
C4.1 AMR surveillance system	26.11	34.79
C4.2 AMR laboratory network and coordination on capacity	56.89	55.57
C4.3 Antimicrobial control and optimization	44.24	48.76
C4.4 Improve awareness and understanding	34.38	48.09
C4.5 Antimicrobial resistance rate for important antibiotics	38.09	33.03
C5 Climate change	61.97	64.19
C5.1 Mitigation and adaptation capacity	24.06	28.24
C5.2 Climate change risks	75.25	80.87
C5.3 Health outcome	88.49	85.41

Georgia

Europe & Central Asia | Upper middle income

55.95 Index Score **065**/160

Global average: 54.82

Regional average: 60.26

Income group average: 54.54

Country performance: 55.95

Missing rate in GOHI database: 12.70%

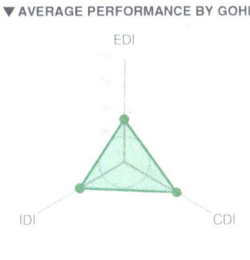

▼ AVERAGE PERFORMANCE BY GOHI

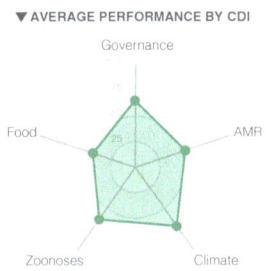

▼ AVERAGE PERFORMANCE BY CDI

	Country Score	Global Average
A External drivers index	41.89	40.45
A1 Earth system	58.41	56.21
A1.1 Land	15.49	36.41
A1.2 Forest	51.86	43.43
A1.3 Water	64.48	58.09
A1.4 Air	84.04	71.93
A1.5 Natural disasters	66.63	64.65
A2 Institutional system	53.36	46.01
A2.1 Justice	67.26	57.89
A2.2 Governance	41.52	35.58
A3 Economical system	23.75	24.62
A3.1 Finance	32.68	34.35
A3.2 Work	37.78	38.58
A4 Sociological system	34.61	37.70
A4.1 Demographic	39.65	46.31
A4.2 Education	25.44	28.26
A4.3 Inequalities	40.91	40.28
A5 Technological system	39.32	37.72
A5.1 Transport	2.26	6.54
A5.2 Technology adoption	50.89	41.23
A5.3 Consumption and production	61.20	62.53
B Intrinsic drivers index	51.27	58.01
B1 Human health	70.19	72.35
B1.1 Health coverage	53.92	58.65
B1.2 Diseases burden	70.53	79.83
B1.3 Injury and violence	88.26	80.75
B2 Animal health and ecosystem diversity	53.87	56.58
B2.1 Animal epidemic disease	95.64	94.57
B2.2 Wildlife and marine life biodiversity	12.10	18.59
B3 Environmental health	31.30	46.87
B3.1 Air quality and climate change	32.24	53.72
B3.2 Environmental biodiversity	35.35	44.05
B3.3 Environmental resources	27.26	44.25

	Country Score	Global Average
C Core drivers index	60.18	57.25
C1 Governance	65.58	56.51
C1.1 Participation	46.39	41.70
C1.3 Transparency	80.10	65.15
C1.4 Responsiveness	66.70	44.42
C1.5 Consensus oriented	96.13	86.45
C1.6 Equity and inclusiveness	71.65	73.61
C1.7 Effectiveness and efficiency	29.33	28.38
C1.8 Political support	68.75	55.89
C2 Zoonotic diseases	71.44	68.06
C2.1 Source of infection	68.73	69.22
C2.2 Route of transmission	83.19	59.30
C2.3 Targeted population	48.82	59.90
C2.4 Capacity building	75.49	72.85
C2.5 Case studies	80.09	85.89
C3 Food security	53.83	52.89
C3.1 Food demand and supply	62.04	59.53
C3.2 Food safety	76.83	69.36
C3.3 Nutrition	72.23	67.17
C3.4 Natural and social circumstances	47.66	51.54
C3.5 Government support and response	9.87	16.85
C4 Antimicrobial resistance	45.37	44.05
C4.1 AMR surveillance system	36.60	34.79
C4.2 AMR laboratory network and coordination on capacity	49.24	55.57
C4.3 Antimicrobial control and optimization	47.13	48.76
C4.4 Improve awareness and understanding	64.06	48.09
C4.5 Antimicrobial resistance rate for important antibiotics	29.81	33.03
C5 Climate change	63.28	64.19
C5.1 Mitigation and adaptation capacity	26.20	28.24
C5.2 Climate change risks	77.55	80.87
C5.3 Health outcome	88.00	85.41

Scores are normalized (0-100, where 100 = most favorable)

Iran
Middle East & North Africa | Lower middle income

55.84   Index **066**/160
Score

Global average: 54.82

Regional average: 53.57

Income group average: 51.29

Country performance: 55.84

Missing rate in GOHI database: 24.30%

▼ AVERAGE PERFORMANCE BY GOHI

▼ AVERAGE PERFORMANCE BY CDI

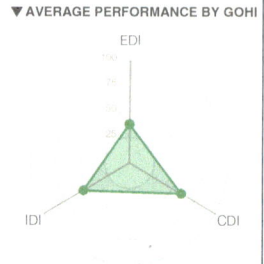

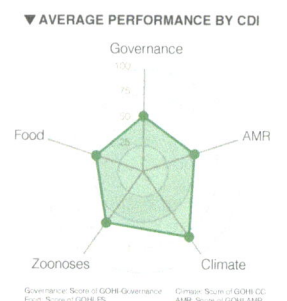

	Country Score	Global Average
A External drivers index	39.04	40.45
A1 Earth system	37.91	56.21
A1.1 Land	20.10	36.41
A1.2 Forest	35.92	43.43
A1.3 Water	61.75	58.09
A1.4 Air	70.02	71.93
A1.5 Natural disasters	61.63	64.65
A2 Institutional system	33.56	46.01
A2.1 Justice	43.93	57.89
A2.2 Governance	24.73	35.58
A3 Economical system	24.31	24.62
A3.1 Finance	33.19	34.35
A3.2 Work	38.98	38.58
A4 Sociological system	38.18	37.70
A4.1 Demographic	48.08	46.31
A4.2 Education	28.59	28.26
A4.3 Inequalities	39.50	40.28
A5 Technological system	41.81	37.72
A5.1 Transport	0.48	6.54
A5.2 Technology adoption	55.93	41.23
A5.3 Consumption and production	64.98	62.53
B Intrinsic drivers index	54.24	58.01
B1 Human health	80.15	72.35
B1.1 Health coverage	81.23	58.65
B1.2 Diseases burden	89.21	79.83
B1.3 Injury and violence	72.43	80.75
B2 Animal health and ecosystem diversity	57.85	56.58
B2.1 Animal epidemic disease	95.51	94.57
B2.2 Wildlife and marine life biodiversity	20.20	18.59
B3 Environmental health	26.38	46.87
B3.1 Air quality and climate change	20.36	53.72
B3.2 Environmental biodiversity	32.40	44.05
B3.3 Environmental resources	27.18	44.25

	Country Score	Global Average
C Core drivers index	60.21	57.25
C1 Governance	54.06	56.51
C1.1 Participation	14.89	41.70
C1.3 Transparency	69.20	65.15
C1.4 Responsiveness	54.20	44.42
C1.5 Consensus oriented	93.19	86.45
C1.6 Equity and inclusiveness	78.01	73.61
C1.7 Effectiveness and efficiency	27.60	28.38
C1.8 Political support	41.30	55.89
C2 Zoonotic diseases	79.69	68.06
C2.1 Source of infection	93.29	69.22
C2.2 Route of transmission	64.59	59.30
C2.3 Targeted population	78.09	59.90
C2.4 Capacity building	78.96	72.85
C2.5 Case studies	86.46	85.89
C3 Food security	54.66	52.89
C3.1 Food demand and supply	61.47	59.53
C3.2 Food safety	68.29	69.36
C3.3 Nutrition	70.46	67.17
C3.4 Natural and social circumstances	46.25	51.54
C3.5 Government support and response	26.84	16.85
C4 Antimicrobial resistance	49.58	44.05
C4.1 AMR surveillance system	45.71	34.79
C4.2 AMR laboratory network and coordination capacity	65.51	55.57
C4.3 Antimicrobial control and optimization	53.99	48.76
C4.4 Improve awareness and understanding	60.94	48.09
C4.5 Antimicrobial resistance rate for important antibiotics	21.76	33.03
C5 Climate change	62.81	64.19
C5.1 Mitigation and adaptation capacity	42.32	28.24
C5.2 Climate change risks	70.21	60.87
C5.3 Health outcome	77.81	85.41

Scores are normalized (0-100, where 100 = most favorable)

Kazakhstan
Europe & Central Asia | Upper middle income

 Index Score **067**/160

▼ AVERAGE PERFORMANCE BY GOHI

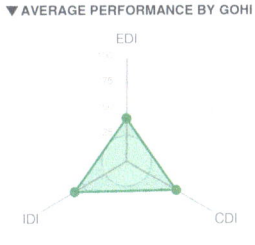

▼ AVERAGE PERFORMANCE BY CDI

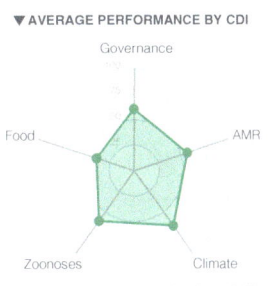

Global average: 54.82

Regional average: 60.26

Income group average: 54.54

Country performance: 55.70

Missing rate in GOHI database: 19.60%

	Country Score	Global Average
A External drivers index	42.00	40.45
A1 Earth system	60.34	56.21
A1.1 Land	86.75	36.41
A1.2 Forest	35.97	43.43
A1.3 Water	51.68	58.09
A1.4 Air	59.57	71.93
A1.5 Natural disasters	66.36	64.65
A2 Institutional system	42.81	46.01
A2.1 Justice	54.95	57.89
A2.2 Governance	32.46	35.58
A3 Economical system	30.88	24.62
A3.1 Finance	49.87	34.35
A3.2 Work	39.77	38.58
A4 Sociological system	35.80	37.70
A4.1 Demographic	42.25	46.31
A4.2 Education	23.34	28.26
A4.3 Inequalities	44.80	40.26
A5 Technological system	40.16	37.72
A5.1 Transport	1.30	6.54
A5.2 Technology adoption	54.91	41.23
A5.3 Consumption and production	60.47	62.53
B Intrinsic drivers index	61.16	58.01
B1 Human health	74.15	72.35
B1.1 Health coverage	59.79	58.65
B1.2 Diseases burden	76.96	79.83
B1.3 Injury and violence	87.95	80.75
B2 Animal health and ecosystem diversity	55.90	56.58
B2.1 Animal epidemic disease	97.89	94.57
B2.2 Wildlife and marine life biodiversity	13.91	18.59
B3 Environmental health	55.29	46.87
B3.1 Air quality and climate change	75.35	53.72
B3.2 Environmental biodiversity	43.65	44.05
B3.3 Environmental resources	48.54	44.25

	Country Score	Global Average
C Core drivers index	57.45	57.25
C1 Governance	60.72	56.51
C1.1 Participation	29.03	41.70
C1.3 Transparency	78.60	65.15
C1.4 Responsiveness	50.00	44.42
C1.5 Consensus oriented	94.93	86.45
C1.6 Equity and inclusiveness	79.52	73.61
C1.7 Effectiveness and efficiency	33.73	28.38
C1.8 Political support	59.23	55.89
C2 Zoonotic diseases	66.94	68.06
C2.1 Source of infection	83.44	69.22
C2.2 Route of transmission	32.88	59.30
C2.3 Targeted population	68.95	59.90
C2.4 Capacity building	78.99	72.85
C2.5 Case studies	82.14	85.89
C3 Food security	56.88	52.89
C3.1 Food demand and supply	61.74	59.53
C3.2 Food safety	83.62	69.36
C3.3 Nutrition	64.58	67.17
C3.4 Natural and social circumstances	55.80	51.54
C3.5 Government support and response	18.66	16.85
C4 Antimicrobial resistance	39.84	44.05
C4.1 AMR surveillance system	28.58	34.79
C4.2 AMR laboratory network and coordinati on capacity	57.96	55.57
C4.3 Antimicrobial control and optimization	37.83	48.76
C4.4 Improve awareness and understanding	40.62	48.09
C4.5 Antimicrobial resistance rate for important antibiotics	34.18	33.03
C5 Climate change	61.06	64.19
C5.1 Mitigation and adaptation capacity	27.53	28.24
C5.2 Climate change risks	68.44	80.87
C5.3 Health outcome	89.05	85.41

Scores are normalized (0-100, where 100 = most favorable)

Nicaragua
Latin America & Caribbean | Lower middle income

55.66 Index Score **068**/160

Global average: 54.82

Regional average: 55.08

Income group average: 51.29

Country performance: 55.66

Missing rate in GOHI database: 19.60%

▼ AVERAGE PERFORMANCE BY GOHI

▼ AVERAGE PERFORMANCE BY CDI

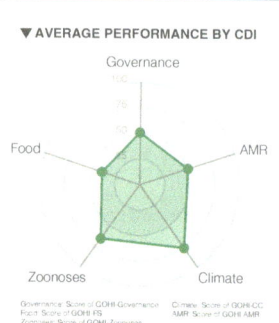

	Country Score	Global Average
A External drivers index	38.25	40.45
A1 Earth system	61.10	56.21
A1.1 Land	38.17	36.41
A1.2 Forest	36.68	43.43
A1.3 Water	67.25	58.09
A1.4 Air	86.90	71.93
A1.5 Natural disasters	65.42	64.65
A2 Institutional system	34.56	46.01
A2.1 Justice	46.89	57.89
A2.2 Governance	24.06	35.58
A3 Economical system	25.31	24.62
A3.1 Finance	36.76	34.35
A3.2 Work	37.81	38.58
A4 Sociological system	35.89	37.70
A4.1 Demographic	46.00	46.31
A4.2 Education	25.50	28.26
A4.3 Inequalities	37.99	40.28
A5 Technological system	34.36	37.72
A5.1 Transport	1.89	6.54
A5.2 Technology adoption	27.63	41.23
A5.3 Consumption and production	70.90	62.53
B Intrinsic drivers index	66.53	58.01
B1 Human health	81.87	72.35
B1.1 Health coverage	73.95	58.65
B1.2 Diseases burden	91.00	79.83
B1.3 Injury and violence	83.14	80.75
B2 Animal health and ecosystem diversity	53.64	56.58
B2.1 Animal epidemic disease	91.09	94.57
B2.2 Wildlife and marine life biodiversity	16.20	18.59
B3 Environmental health	66.10	46.87
B3.1 Air quality and climate change	74.20	53.72
B3.2 Environmental biodiversity	51.75	44.05
B3.3 Environmental resources	74.36	44.25

	Country Score	Global Average
C Core drivers index	56.95	57.25
C1 Governance	51.04	56.51
C1.1 Participation	15.76	41.70
C1.3 Transparency	51.70	65.15
C1.4 Responsiveness	47.90	44.42
C1.5 Consensus oriented	96.47	86.45
C1.6 Equity and inclusiveness	62.93	73.61
C1.7 Effectiveness and efficiency	36.00	28.38
C1.8 Political support	46.53	55.89
C2 Zoonotic diseases	76.76	68.06
C2.1 Source of infection	77.23	69.22
C2.2 Route of transmission	74.32	59.30
C2.3 Targeted population	62.31	59.90
C2.4 Capacity building	82.24	72.85
C2.5 Case studies	92.24	85.89
C3 Food security	51.12	52.89
C3.1 Food demand and supply	49.75	59.53
C3.2 Food safety	83.45	69.36
C3.3 Nutrition	57.37	67.17
C3.4 Natural and social circumstances	51.24	51.54
C3.5 Government support and response	13.80	16.85
C4 Antimicrobial resistance	39.62	44.05
C4.1 AMR surveillance system	25.19	34.79
C4.2 AMR laboratory network and coordination on capacity	45.49	55.57
C4.3 Antimicrobial control and optimization	48.97	48.76
C4.4 Improve awareness and understanding	51.56	48.09
C4.5 Antimicrobial resistance rate for important antibiotics	26.89	33.03
C5 Climate change	65.81	64.19
C5.1 Mitigation and adaptation capacity	23.92	28.24
C5.2 Climate change risks	87.13	80.87
C5.3 Health outcome	88.37	85.41

Scores are normalized (0-100, where 100 = most favorable)

Mongolia

East Asia & Pacific | **Lower middle income**

55.44 Index Score **069**/160

Global average: 54.82

Regional average: 56.52

Income group average: 51.29

Country performance: 55.44

Missing rate in GOHI database: 23.20%

▼ AVERAGE PERFORMANCE BY GOHI

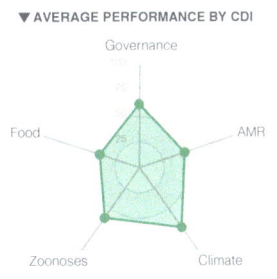

▼ AVERAGE PERFORMANCE BY CDI

	Country Score	Global Average
A External drivers index	42.63	40.45
A1 Earth system	63.81	56.21
A1.1 Land	72.05	36.41
A1.2 Forest	52.70	43.43
A1.3 Water	66.98	58.09
A1.4 Air	57.56	71.93
A1.5 Natural disasters	65.43	64.65
A2 Institutional system	44.15	46.01
A2.1 Justice	54.67	57.89
A2.2 Governance	35.18	35.58
A3 Economical system	27.38	24.62
A3.1 Finance	42.13	34.35
A3.2 Work	37.90	38.58
A4 Sociological system	37.50	37.70
A4.1 Demographic	47.17	46.31
A4.2 Education	25.59	28.26
A4.3 Inequalities	42.09	40.28
A5 Technological system	40.52	37.72
A5.1 Transport	0.66	6.54
A5.2 Technology adoption	49.78	41.23
A5.3 Consumption and production	67.32	62.53
B Intrinsic drivers index	58.12	58.01
B1 Human health	67.71	72.35
B1.1 Health coverage	52.58	58.65
B1.2 Diseases burden	74.84	79.83
B1.3 Injury and violence	77.77	80.75
B2 Animal health and ecosystem diversity	51.80	56.58
B2.1 Animal epidemic disease	94.14	94.57
B2.2 Wildlife and marine life biodiversity	9.45	18.59
B3 Environmental health	56.63	46.87
B3.1 Air quality and climate change	70.68	53.72
B3.2 Environmental biodiversity	42.07	44.05
B3.3 Environmental resources	58.84	44.25

Scores are normalized (0-100, where 100 = most favorable)

	Country Score	Global Average
C Core drivers index	57.65	57.25
C1 Governance	62.33	56.51
C1.1 Participation	12.15	41.70
C1.3 Transparency	76.30	65.15
C1.4 Responsiveness	58.35	44.42
C1.5 Consensus oriented	95.41	86.45
C1.6 Equity and inclusiveness	97.83	73.61
C1.7 Effectiveness and efficiency	38.53	28.38
C1.8 Political support	57.72	55.89
C2 Zoonotic diseases	72.60	68.06
C2.1 Source of infection	63.38	69.22
C2.2 Route of transmission	73.15	59.30
C2.3 Targeted population	72.81	59.90
C2.4 Capacity building	71.77	72.85
C2.5 Case studies	86.78	85.89
C3 Food security	48.65	52.89
C3.1 Food demand and supply	48.73	59.53
C3.2 Food safety	62.38	69.36
C3.3 Nutrition	73.04	67.17
C3.4 Natural and social circumstances	48.02	51.54
C3.5 Government support and response	11.07	16.85
C4 Antimicrobial resistance	42.45	44.05
C4.1 AMR surveillance system	29.55	34.79
C4.2 AMR laboratory network and coordination capacity	58.50	55.57
C4.3 Antimicrobial control and optimization	50.04	48.76
C4.4 Improve awareness and understanding	40.62	48.09
C4.5 Antimicrobial resistance rate for important antibiotics	33.52	33.03
C5 Climate change	61.00	64.19
C5.1 Mitigation and adaptation capacity	28.14	28.24
C5.2 Climate change risks	72.02	80.87
C5.3 Health outcome	84.69	85.41

Morocco

Middle East & North Africa | Lower middle income

55.38 | Index Score **070**/160

Global average: 54.82

Regional average: 53.57

Income group average: 51.29

Country performance: 55.38

Missing rate in GOHI database: 15.20%

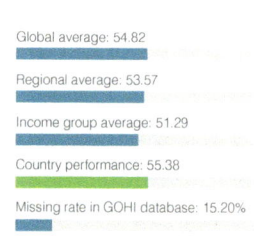

▼ AVERAGE PERFORMANCE BY GOHI

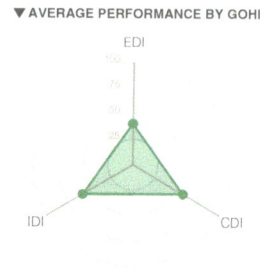

▼ AVERAGE PERFORMANCE BY CDI

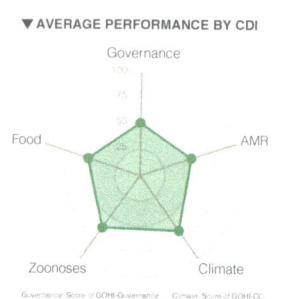

	Country Score	Global Average
A External drivers index	40.15	40.45
A1 Earth system	55.45	56.21
A1.1 Land	28.48	36.41
A1.2 Forest	38.16	43.43
A1.3 Water	63.30	58.09
A1.4 Air	72.37	71.93
A1.5 Natural disasters	66.66	64.65
A2 Institutional system	43.81	48.01
A2.1 Justice	60.62	57.89
A2.2 Governance	29.50	35.58
A3 Economical system	21.97	24.62
A3.1 Finance	31.41	34.35
A3.2 Work	33.46	38.58
A4 Sociological system	36.13	37.70
A4.1 Demographic	45.66	46.31
A4.2 Education	27.46	28.26
A4.3 Inequalities	36.66	40.28
A5 Technological system	43.36	37.72
A5.1 Transport	1.40	6.54
A5.2 Technology adoption	51.42	41.23
A5.3 Consumption and production	73.32	62.53
B Intrinsic drivers index	58.47	59.01
B1 Human health	73.29	72.35
B1.1 Health coverage	59.42	58.65
B1.2 Diseases burden	77.15	79.83
B1.3 Injury and violence	85.51	80.75
B2 Animal health and ecosystem diversity	56.56	56.58
B2.1 Animal epidemic disease	96.52	94.57
B2.2 Wildlife and marine life biodiversity	16.60	18.59
B3 Environmental health	47.33	46.87
B3.1 Air quality and climate change	48.01	53.72
B3.2 Environmental biodiversity	44.65	44.05
B3.3 Environmental resources	50.78	44.25

Scores are normalized (0-100, where 100 = most favorable)

	Country Score	Global Average
C Core drivers index	56.03	57.25
C1 Governance	51.44	56.51
C1.1 Participation	18.45	41.70
C1.3 Transparency	59.00	65.15
C1.4 Responsiveness	41.65	44.42
C1.5 Consensus oriented	93.19	86.45
C1.6 Equity and inclusiveness	71.94	73.61
C1.7 Effectiveness and efficiency	16.20	28.38
C1.8 Political support	59.66	55.89
C2 Zoonotic diseases	67.15	68.06
C2.1 Source of infection	71.06	69.22
C2.2 Route of transmission	60.98	59.30
C2.3 Targeted population	43.24	59.90
C2.4 Capacity building	80.80	72.85
C2.5 Case studies	86.39	85.89
C3 Food security	54.14	52.89
C3.1 Food demand and supply	54.77	59.53
C3.2 Food safety	70.07	69.36
C3.3 Nutrition	70.23	67.17
C3.4 Natural and social circumstances	54.02	51.54
C3.5 Government support and response	21.61	16.85
C4 Antimicrobial resistance	54.59	44.06
C4.1 AMR surveillance system	71.05	34.79
C4.2 AMR laboratory network and coordination capacity	45.69	55.57
C4.3 Antimicrobial control and optimization	54.68	48.76
C4.4 Improve awareness and understanding	65.62	48.09
C4.5 Antimicrobial resistance rate for important antibiotics	35.92	33.03
C5 Climate change	63.60	64.19
C5.1 Mitigation and adaptation capacity	21.70	28.24
C5.2 Climate change risks	84.80	80.87
C5.3 Health outcome	86.24	85.41

Bhutan
South Asia | **Lower middle income**

55.31 Index 071 /160
Score

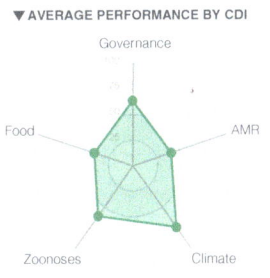

Global average: 54.82

Regional average: 51.61

Income group average: 51.29

Country performance: 55.31

Missing rate in GOHI database: 23.20%

▼ AVERAGE PERFORMANCE BY GOHI

▼ AVERAGE PERFORMANCE BY CDI

	Country Score	Global Average
A External drivers index	41.93	40.45
A1 Earth system	58.16	56.21
A1.1 Land	12.65	36.41
A1.2 Forest	74.91	43.43
A1.3 Water	67.80	58.09
A1.4 Air	63.80	71.93
A1.5 Natural disasters	66.61	64.65
A2 Institutional system	52.68	46.01
A2.1 Justice	65.18	57.89
A2.2 Governance	42.04	35.58
A3 Economical system	23.67	24.62
A3.1 Finance	29.77	34.35
A3.2 Work	41.19	38.58
A4 Sociological system	35.39	37.70
A4.1 Demographic	46.15	46.31
A4.2 Education	24.75	28.26
A4.3 Inequalities	37.09	40.28
A5 Technological system	39.72	37.72
A5.1 Transport	5.60	6.54
A5.2 Technology adoption	44.09	41.23
A5.3 Consumption and production	66.34	62.53
B Intrinsic drivers index	62.07	58.01
B1 Human health	76.46	72.35
B1.1 Health coverage	58.58	58.65
B1.2 Diseases burden	86.78	79.83
B1.3 Injury and violence	86.33	80.75
B2 Animal health and ecosystem diversity	62.53	56.58
B2.1 Animal epidemic disease	93.86	94.57
B2.2 Wildlife and marine life biodiversity	31.20	18.59
B3 Environmental health	49.09	46.87
B3.1 Air quality and climate change	59.80	53.72
B3.2 Environmental biodiversity	56.45	44.05
B3.3 Environmental resources	32.52	44.25

	Country Score	Global Average
C Core drivers index	56.68	57.25
C1 Governance	63.81	56.51
C1.1 Participation	74.96	41.70
C1.3 Transparency	52.00	65.15
C1.4 Responsiveness	75.00	44.42
C1.5 Consensus oriented	93.50	86.45
C1.6 Equity and inclusiveness	56.57	73.61
C1.7 Effectiveness and efficiency	47.00	28.38
C1.8 Political support	47.67	55.89
C2 Zoonotic diseases	74.84	68.06
C2.1 Source of infection	68.24	69.22
C2.2 Route of transmission	72.87	59.30
C2.3 Targeted population	71.10	59.90
C2.4 Capacity building	76.46	72.85
C2.5 Case studies	91.37	85.89
C3 Food security	41.10	52.89
C3.1 Food demand and supply	56.78	59.53
C3.2 Food safety	55.40	69.36
C3.3 Nutrition	40.67	67.17
C3.4 Natural and social circumstances	49.33	51.54
C3.5 Government support and response	3.29	16.85
C4 Antimicrobial resistance	41.44	44.05
C4.1 AMR surveillance system	36.21	34.79
C4.2 AMR laboratory network and coordination on capacity	53.05	55.57
C4.3 Antimicrobial control and optimization	47.03	48.76
C4.4 Improve awareness and understanding	43.75	48.09
C4.5 Antimicrobial resistance rate for important antibiotics	27.16	33.03
C5 Climate change	61.23	64.19
C5.1 Mitigation and adaptation capacity	20.06	28.24
C5.2 Climate change risks	79.72	80.87
C5.3 Health outcome	85.77	85.41

Scores are normalized (0-100, where 100 = most favorable)

Egypt
Middle East & North Africa | Lower middle income

55.12 Index **072**/160 Score

Global average: 54.82

Regional average: 53.57

Income group average: 51.29

Country performance: 55.12

Missing rate in GOHI database: 18.50%

▼ AVERAGE PERFORMANCE BY GOHI

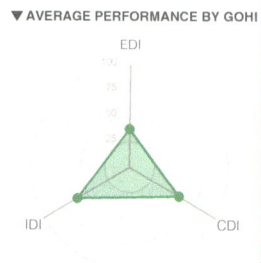

▼ AVERAGE PERFORMANCE BY CDI

	Country Score	Global Average
A External drivers index	37.51	40.45
A1 Earth system	43.12	56.21
A1.1 Land	51.27	36.41
A1.2 Forest	33.34	43.43
A1.3 Water	23.27	58.09
A1.4 Air	45.47	71.93
A1.5 Natural disasters	66.66	64.65
A2 Institutional system	46.70	46.01
A2.1 Justice	63.64	57.89
A2.2 Governance	32.27	35.58
A3 Economical system	25.68	24.62
A3.1 Finance	38.41	34.35
A3.2 Work	36.94	38.58
A4 Sociological system	36.47	37.70
A4.1 Demographic	43.41	46.31
A4.2 Education	30.28	28.26
A4.3 Inequalities	36.69	40.28
A5 Technological system	35.56	37.72
A5.1 Transport	0.52	6.54
A5.2 Technology adoption	31.57	41.23
A5.3 Consumption and production	71.62	62.53
B Intrinsic drivers index	61.15	58.01
B1 Human health	76.98	72.35
B1.1 Health coverage	55.50	58.65
B1.2 Diseases burden	86.93	79.83
B1.3 Injury and violence	90.85	80.75
B2 Animal health and ecosystem diversity	54.65	56.58
B2.1 Animal epidemic disease	99.51	94.57
B2.2 Wildlife and marine life biodiversity	9.80	18.59
B3 Environmental health	53.66	46.87
B3.1 Air quality and climate change	65.91	53.72
B3.2 Environmental biodiversity	50.50	44.05
B3.3 Environmental resources	46.20	44.25

Scores are normalized (0-100, where 100 = most favorable)

	Country Score	Global Average
C Core drivers index	56.68	57.25
C1 Governance	58.93	56.51
C1.1 Participation	72.83	41.70
C1.3 Transparency	74.10	65.15
C1.4 Responsiveness	22.90	44.42
C1.5 Consensus oriented	97.07	86.45
C1.6 Equity and inclusiveness	73.15	73.61
C1.7 Effectiveness and efficiency	13.80	28.38
C1.8 Political support	58.69	55.89
C2 Zoonotic diseases	78.99	68.06
C2.1 Source of infection	82.95	69.22
C2.2 Route of transmission	73.59	59.30
C2.3 Targeted population	73.40	59.90
C2.4 Capacity building	80.61	72.85
C2.5 Case studies	87.05	85.89
C3 Food security	55.59	52.89
C3.1 Food demand and supply	62.10	59.53
C3.2 Food safety	82.95	69.36
C3.3 Nutrition	65.95	67.17
C3.4 Natural and social circumstances	48.15	51.54
C3.5 Government support and response	18.79	16.85
C4 Antimicrobial resistance	31.07	44.05
C4.1 AMR surveillance system	16.31	34.79
C4.2 AMR laboratory network and coordination capacity	51.29	55.57
C4.3 Antimicrobial control and optimization	30.93	48.76
C4.4 Improve awareness and understanding	42.19	48.09
C4.5 Antimicrobial resistance rate for important antibiotics	14.65	33.03
C5 Climate change	60.82	64.19
C5.1 Mitigation and adaptation capacity	25.03	28.24
C5.2 Climate change risks	77.44	80.87
C5.3 Health outcome	81.82	85.41

Serbia

Europe & Central Asia | **Upper middle income**

 Index Score **073**/160

Global average: 54.82

Regional average: 60.26

Income group average: 54.54

Country performance: 55.03

Missing rate in GOHI database: 16.70%

▼ AVERAGE PERFORMANCE BY GOHI

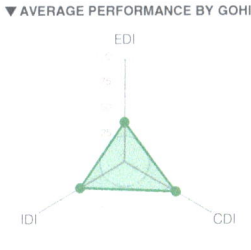

▼ AVERAGE PERFORMANCE BY CDI

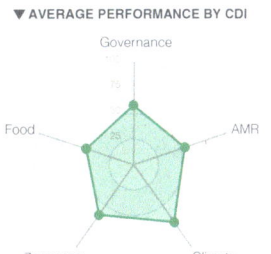

	Country Score	Global Average
A External drivers index	38.74	40.45
A1 Earth system	53.48	56.21
A1.1 Land	43.51	36.41
A1.2 Forest	46.30	43.43
A1.3 Water	42.13	58.09
A1.4 Air	67.11	71.93
A1.5 Natural disasters	66.67	64.65
A2 Institutional system	45.93	46.01
A2.1 Justice	58.88	57.89
A2.2 Governance	34.91	35.58
A3 Economical system	16.42	24.62
A3.1 Finance	14.50	34.35
A3.2 Work	36.37	38.58
A4 Sociological system	36.53	37.70
A4.1 Demographic	36.93	46.31
A4.2 Education	29.28	28.26
A4.3 Inequalities	45.57	40.28
A5 Technological system	41.37	37.72
A5.1 Transport	0.76	6.54
A5.2 Technology adoption	53.39	41.23
A5.3 Consumption and production	66.01	62.53
B Intrinsic drivers index	52.60	58.01
B1 Human health	74.41	72.35
B1.1 Health coverage	61.85	58.65
B1.2 Diseases burden	70.60	79.83
B1.3 Injury and violence	93.02	80.75
B2 Animal health and ecosystem diversity	52.19	56.58
B2.1 Animal epidemic disease	94.27	94.57
B2.2 Wildlife and marine life biodiversity	10.11	18.59
B3 Environmental health	32.81	46.87
B3.1 Air quality and climate change	39.16	53.72
B3.2 Environmental biodiversity	40.30	44.05
B3.3 Environmental resources	19.96	44.25

	Country Score	Global Average
C Core drivers index	59.23	57.25
C1 Governance	58.39	56.51
C1.1 Participation	16.55	41.70
C1.3 Transparency	75.80	65.15
C1.4 Responsiveness	39.55	44.42
C1.5 Consensus oriented	96.69	86.45
C1.6 Equity and inclusiveness	96.17	73.61
C1.7 Effectiveness and efficiency	33.67	28.38
C1.8 Political support	50.27	55.89
C2 Zoonotic diseases	70.00	68.06
C2.1 Source of infection	82.81	69.22
C2.2 Route of transmission	55.30	59.30
C2.3 Targeted population	66.62	59.90
C2.4 Capacity building	65.53	72.85
C2.5 Case studies	83.74	85.89
C3 Food security	55.12	52.89
C3.1 Food demand and supply	60.63	59.53
C3.2 Food safety	81.01	69.36
C3.3 Nutrition	67.72	67.17
C3.4 Natural and social circumstances	51.61	51.54
C3.5 Government support and response	14.62	16.85
C4 Antimicrobial resistance	31.07	44.05
C4.1 AMR surveillance system	39.07	34.79
C4.2 AMR laboratory network and coordination capacity	62.74	55.57
C4.3 Antimicrobial control and optimization	70.11	48.76
C4.4 Improve awareness and understanding	64.06	48.09
C4.5 Antimicrobial resistance rate for important antibiotics	19.28	33.03
C5 Climate change	61.12	64.19
C5.1 Mitigation and adaptation capacity	23.64	28.24
C5.2 Climate change risks	74.06	80.87
C5.3 Health outcome	87.50	85.41

Scores are normalized (0-100, where 100 = most favorable)

Paraguay
Latin America & Caribbean | Upper middle income

54.93 | Index Score **074**/160

Global average: 54.82

Regional average: 55.08

Income group average: 54.54

Country performance: 54.93

Missing rate in GOHI database: 18.80%

▼ AVERAGE PERFORMANCE BY GOHI

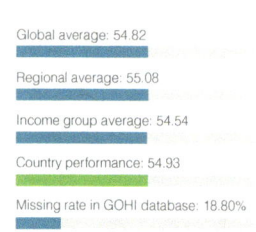

▼ AVERAGE PERFORMANCE BY CDI

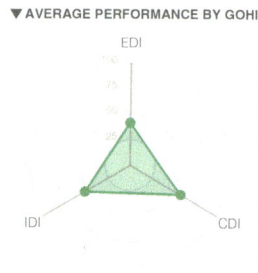

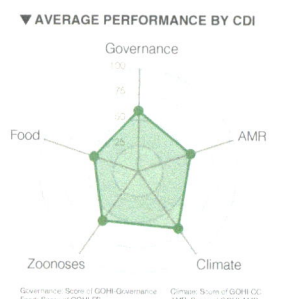

Governance: Score of GOHI-Governance   Climate: Score of GOHI-CC
Food: Score of GOHI-FS   AMR: Score of GOHI-AMR
Zoonoses: Score of GOHI-Zoonoses

	Country Score	Global Average
A External drivers index	41.67	40.45
A1 Earth system	65.85	56.21
A1.1 Land	77.83	36.41
A1.2 Forest	43.25	43.43
A1.3 Water	45.11	58.09
A1.4 Air	92.32	71.93
A1.5 Natural disasters	65.96	64.65
A2 Institutional system	37.35	46.01
A2.1 Justice	42.29	57.89
A2.2 Governance	33.15	35.58
A3 Economical system	27.99	24.62
A3.1 Finance	41.16	34.35
A3.2 Work	41.18	38.58
A4 Sociological system	36.10	37.70
A4.1 Demographic	47.75	46.31
A4.2 Education	26.13	28.26
A4.3 Inequalities	35.90	40.28
A5 Technological system	41.03	37.72
A5.1 Transport	5.95	6.54
A5.2 Technology adoption	47.51	41.23
A5.3 Consumption and production	66.35	62.53
B Intrinsic drivers index	52.66	58.01
B1 Human health	75.22	72.35
B1.1 Health coverage	62.96	58.65
B1.2 Diseases burden	88.90	79.83
B1.3 Injury and violence	76.08	80.75
B2 Animal health and ecosystem diversity	54.34	56.58
B2.1 Animal epidemic disease	99.77	94.57
B2.2 Wildlife and marine life biodiversity	8.91	18.59
B3 Environmental health	30.00	46.87
B3.1 Air quality and climate change	40.13	53.72
B3.2 Environmental biodiversity	23.85	44.05
B3.3 Environmental resources	26.94	44.25

	Country Score	Global Average
C Core drivers index	56.42	57.25
C1 Governance	59.24	56.51
C1.1 Participation	36.62	41.70
C1.3 Transparency	61.10	65.15
C1.4 Responsiveness	66.65	44.42
C1.5 Consensus oriented	99.51	86.45
C1.6 Equity and inclusiveness	69.78	73.61
C1.7 Effectiveness and efficiency	29.20	28.38
C1.8 Political support	51.82	55.89
C2 Zoonotic diseases	69.22	68.06
C2.1 Source of infection	81.51	69.22
C2.2 Route of transmission	43.50	59.30
C2.3 Targeted population	73.24	59.90
C2.4 Capacity building	70.65	72.85
C2.5 Case studies	86.32	85.89
C3 Food security	55.45	52.89
C3.1 Food demand and supply	58.70	59.53
C3.2 Food safety	84.11	69.36
C3.3 Nutrition	71.84	67.17
C3.4 Natural and social circumstances	54.52	51.54
C3.5 Government support and response	8.08	16.85
C4 Antimicrobial resistance	46.74	44.05
C4.1 AMR surveillance system	30.46	34.79
C4.2 AMR laboratory network and coordination capacity	71.25	55.57
C4.3 Antimicrobial control and optimization	55.62	48.76
C4.4 Improve awareness and understanding	48.44	48.09
C4.5 Antimicrobial resistance rate for important antibiotics	27.93	33.03
C5 Climate change	60.43	64.19
C5.1 Mitigation and adaptation capacity	24.65	28.24
C5.2 Climate change risks	75.23	80.87
C5.3 Health outcome	83.25	85.41

Scores are normalized (0-100, where 100 = most favorable)

North Macedonia

Europe & Central Asia | Upper middle income

 Index 075/160
Score

Global average: 54.82

Regional average: 60.26

Income group average: 54.54

Country performance: 54.72

Missing rate in GOHI database: 25.70%

▼ AVERAGE PERFORMANCE BY GOHI

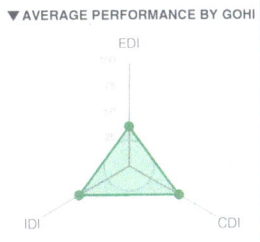

▼ AVERAGE PERFORMANCE BY CDI

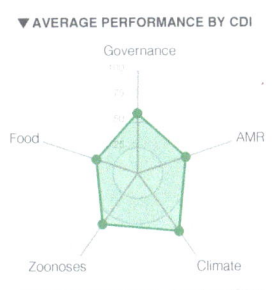

	Country Score	Global Average
A External drivers index	38.58	40.45
A1 Earth system	57.14	56.21
A1.1 Land	27.15	36.41
A1.2 Forest	49.95	43.43
A1.3 Water	59.66	58.09
A1.4 Air	77.72	71.93
A1.5 Natural disasters	63.53	64.65
A2 Institutional system	46.33	46.01
A2.1 Justice	55.17	57.89
A2.2 Governance	38.80	35.58
A3 Economical system	18.42	24.62
A3.1 Finance	21.28	34.35
A3.2 Work	34.48	38.58
A4 Sociological system	35.99	37.70
A4.1 Demographic	39.64	46.31
A4.2 Education	25.22	28.26
A4.3 Inequalities	45.96	40.28
A5 Technological system	35.01	37.72
A5.1 Transport	1.17	6.54
A5.2 Technology adoption	33.52	41.23
A5.3 Consumption and production	67.40	62.53
B Intrinsic drivers index	57.91	58.01
B1 Human health	75.99	72.35
B1.1 Health coverage	62.37	58.65
B1.2 Diseases burden	74.22	79.83
B1.3 Injury and violence	93.69	80.75
B2 Animal health and ecosystem diversity	53.36	56.58
B2.1 Animal epidemic disease	95.22	94.57
B2.2 Wildlife and marine life biodiversity	11.50	18.59
B3 Environmental health	46.14	46.87
B3.1 Air quality and climate change	54.11	53.72
B3.2 Environmental biodiversity	52.58	44.05
B3.3 Environmental resources	54.11	44.25

	Country Score	Global Average
C Core drivers index	57.54	57.25
C1 Governance	58.76	56.51
C1.1 Participation	15.51	41.70
C1.3 Transparency	72.00	65.15
C1.4 Responsiveness	43.75	44.42
C1.5 Consensus oriented	94.71	86.45
C1.6 Equity and inclusiveness	97.66	73.61
C1.7 Effectiveness and efficiency	32.80	28.38
C1.8 Political support	54.92	55.89
C2 Zoonotic diseases	70.62	68.06
C2.1 Source of infection	82.66	69.22
C2.2 Route of transmission	65.32	59.30
C2.3 Targeted population	46.50	59.90
C2.4 Capacity building	72.76	72.85
C2.5 Case studies	88.69	85.89
C3 Food security	51.35	52.89
C3.1 Food demand and supply	54.91	59.53
C3.2 Food safety	60.21	69.36
C3.3 Nutrition	75.45	67.17
C3.4 Natural and social circumstances	49.96	51.54
C3.5 Government support and response	16.21	18.85
C4 Antimicrobial resistance	44.27	44.05
C4.1 AMR surveillance system	41.57	34.79
C4.2 AMR laboratory network and coordinati on capacity	46.57	55.57
C4.3 Antimicrobial control and optimization	47.18	48.76
C4.4 Improve awareness and understanding	68.75	48.09
C4.5 Antimicrobial resistance rate for important antibiotics	17.30	33.03
C5 Climate change	61.87	64.19
C5.1 Mitigation and adaptation capacity	26.83	28.24
C5.2 Climate change risks	75.68	80.87
C5.3 Health outcome	84.91	85.41

Scores are normalized (0-100, where 100 = most favorable)

Bulgaria

Europe & Central Asia | **Upper middle income**

54.62 Index Score **076**/160

Global average: 54.82

Regional average: 60.26

Income group average: 54.54

Country performance: 54.62

Missing rate in GOHI database: 10.10%

▼ AVERAGE PERFORMANCE BY GOHI

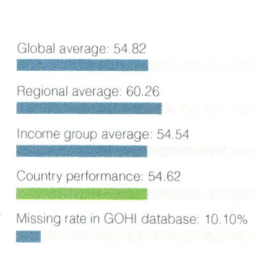

▼ AVERAGE PERFORMANCE BY CDI

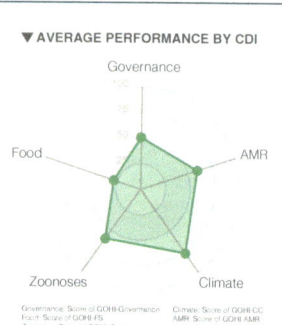

Governance: Score of GOHI-Governance   Climate: Score of GOHI-CC
Food: Score of GOHI-FS   AMR: Score of GOHI-AMR
Zoonoses: Score of GOHI-Zoonoses

	Country Score	Global Average
A External drivers index	43.19	40.45
A1 Earth system	63.10	56.21
A1.1 Land	52.90	36.41
A1.2 Forest	49.02	43.43
A1.3 Water	63.52	58.09
A1.4 Air	76.75	71.93
A1.5 Natural disasters	66.66	64.65
A2 Institutional system	49.63	46.01
A2.1 Justice	62.72	57.89
A2.2 Governance	38.49	35.58
A3 Economical system	23.77	24.62
A3.1 Finance	32.98	34.35
A3.2 Work	37.46	38.58
A4 Sociological system	37.71	37.70
A4.1 Demographic	42.47	46.31
A4.2 Education	28.77	28.26
A4.3 Inequalities	44.03	40.28
A5 Technological system	41.72	37.72
A5.1 Transport	2.57	6.54
A5.2 Technology adoption	55.53	41.23
A5.3 Consumption and production	63.18	62.53
B Intrinsic drivers index	59.93	58.01
B1 Human health	68.76	72.35
B1.1 Health coverage	55.15	58.65
B1.2 Diseases burden	61.63	79.83
B1.3 Injury and violence	91.59	80.75
B2 Animal health and ecosystem diversity	56.59	56.58
B2.1 Animal epidemic disease	98.28	94.57
B2.2 Wildlife and marine life biodiversity	14.90	18.59
B3 Environmental health	56.25	46.87
B3.1 Air quality and climate change	56.93	53.72
B3.2 Environmental biodiversity	56.25	44.05
B3.3 Environmental resources	57.26	44.25

	Country Score	Global Average
C Core drivers index	55.91	57.25
C1 Governance	50.77	56.51
C1.1 Participation	19.35	41.70
C1.3 Transparency	82.30	65.15
C1.4 Responsiveness	41.65	44.42
C1.5 Consensus oriented	7.35	86.45
C1.6 Equity and inclusiveness	96.63	73.61
C1.7 Effectiveness and efficiency	40.73	28.38
C1.8 Political support	67.39	55.89
C2 Zoonotic diseases	77.57	68.06
C2.1 Source of infection	81.66	69.22
C2.2 Route of transmission	76.77	59.30
C2.3 Targeted population	65.60	59.90
C2.4 Capacity building	83.38	72.85
C2.5 Case studies	81.18	85.89
C3 Food security	60.13	52.89
C3.1 Food demand and supply	65.89	59.53
C3.2 Food safety	83.75	69.36
C3.3 Nutrition	74.44	67.17
C3.4 Natural and social circumstances	56.18	51.54
C3.5 Government support and response	20.37	16.85
C4 Antimicrobial resistance	28.42	44.05
C4.1 AMR surveillance system	13.25	34.79
C4.2 AMR laboratory network and coordinati on capacity	38.22	55.57
C4.3 Antimicrobial control and optimization	47.93	48.76
C4.4 Improve awareness and understanding	12.50	48.09
C4.5 Antimicrobial resistance rate for important antibiotics	30.19	33.03
C5 Climate change	60.14	64.19
C5.1 Mitigation and adaptation capacity	22.35	28.24
C5.2 Climate change risks	73.51	80.87
C5.3 Health outcome	86.39	85.41

Scores are normalized (0-100, where 100 = most favorable)

Moldova

Europe & Central Asia | **Upper middle income**

54.47 | Index Score **077**/160

Global average: 54.82

Regional average: 60.26

Income group average: 54.54

Country performance: 54.47

Missing rate in GOHI database: 25.00%

▼ AVERAGE PERFORMANCE BY GOHI

▼ AVERAGE PERFORMANCE BY CDI

	Country Score	Global Average
A External drivers index	39.01	40.45
A1 Earth system	61.15	56.21
A1.1 Land	41.54	36.41
A1.2 Forest	37.89	43.43
A1.3 Water	59.25	58.09
A1.4 Air	91.26	71.93
A1.5 Natural disasters	66.05	64.65
A2 Institutional system	44.25	46.01
A2.1 Justice	59.69	57.89
A2.2 Governance	31.09	35.58
A3 Economical system	18.98	24.82
A3.1 Finance	16.68	34.35
A3.2 Work	42.14	38.58
A4 Sociological system	33.47	37.70
A4.1 Demographic	39.61	46.31
A4.2 Education	24.99	28.26
A4.3 Inequalities	37.60	40.28
A5 Technological system	37.22	37.72
A5.1 Transport	0.86	6.54
A5.2 Technology adoption	39.51	41.23
A5.3 Consumption and production	68.03	62.53
B Intrinsic drivers index	58.16	58.01
B1 Human health	73.74	72.35
B1.1 Health coverage	56.72	58.65
B1.2 Diseases burden	75.06	79.83
B1.3 Injury and violence	91.69	80.75
B2 Animal health and ecosystem diversity	54.31	56.58
B2.1 Animal epidemic disease	95.98	94.57
B2.2 Wildlife and marine life biodiversity	12.64	18.59
B3 Environmental health	48.20	46.87
B3.1 Air quality and climate change	65.80	53.72
B3.2 Environmental biodiversity	51.80	44.05
B3.3 Environmental resources	28.46	44.25

Scores are normalized (0-100, where 100 = most favorable)

	Country Score	Global Average
C Core drivers index	57.03	57.26
C1 Governance	56.26	56.51
C1.1 Participation	12.43	41.70
C1.3 Transparency	79.30	65.15
C1.4 Responsiveness	41.65	44.42
C1.5 Consensus oriented	88.74	86.45
C1.6 Equity and inclusiveness	93.58	73.61
C1.7 Effectiveness and efficiency	30.67	28.38
C1.8 Political support	47.48	55.89
C2 Zoonotic diseases	71.26	68.06
C2.1 Source of infection	75.27	69.22
C2.2 Route of transmission	82.22	59.30
C2.3 Targeted population	42.03	59.90
C2.4 Capacity building	71.13	72.85
C2.5 Case studies	83.79	85.89
C3 Food security	53.28	52.89
C3.1 Food demand and supply	51.59	59.53
C3.2 Food safety	80.83	69.36
C3.3 Nutrition	74.52	67.17
C3.4 Natural and social circumstances	47.04	51.54
C3.5 Government support and response	12.40	16.85
C4 Antimicrobial resistance	34.63	44.05
C4.1 AMR surveillance system	17.00	34.79
C4.2 AMR laboratory network and coordination capacity	35.36	55.57
C4.3 Antimicrobial control and optimization	55.64	48.76
C4.4 Improve awareness and understanding	48.44	48.09
C4.5 Antimicrobial resistance rate for important antibiotics	16.71	33.03
C5 Climate change	68.53	64.19
C5.1 Mitigation and adaptation capacity	33.20	28.24
C5.2 Climate change risks	88.05	80.87
C5.3 Health outcome	86.41	85.41

Ecuador
Latin America & Caribbean | Upper middle income

 54.36 Index Score **078**/160

Global average: 54.82

Regional average: 55.08

Income group average: 54.54

Country performance: 54.36

Missing rate in GOHI database: 14.90%

▼ AVERAGE PERFORMANCE BY GOHI

▼ AVERAGE PERFORMANCE BY CDI

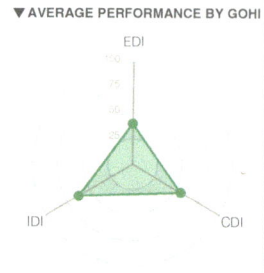

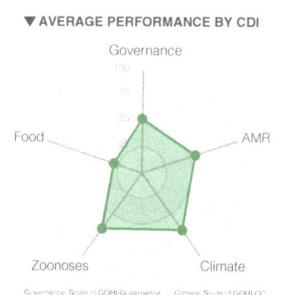

	Country Score	Global Average
A External drivers index	39.78	40.45
A1 Earth system	61.25	56.21
A1.1 Land	26.51	36.41
A1.2 Forest	44.90	43.43
A1.3 Water	73.09	58.09
A1.4 Air	84.40	71.93
A1.5 Natural disasters	66.76	64.65
A2 Institutional system	42.60	46.01
A2.1 Justice	54.06	57.89
A2.2 Governance	32.83	35.58
A3 Economical system	22.63	24.62
A3.1 Finance	28.10	34.35
A3.2 Work	39.84	38.58
A4 Sociological system	36.45	37.70
A4.1 Demographic	45.57	46.31
A4.2 Education	27.43	28.26
A4.3 Inequalities	37.87	40.28
A5 Technological system	35.96	37.72
A5.1 Transport	0.92	6.54
A5.2 Technology adoption	32.18	41.23
A5.3 Consumption and production	71.80	62.53
B Intrinsic drivers index	62.58	59.01
B1 Human health	79.61	72.35
B1.1 Health coverage	73.82	58.65
B1.2 Diseases burden	88.54	79.83
B1.3 Injury and violence	78.87	80.75
B2 Animal health and ecosystem diversity	62.16	56.58
B2.1 Animal epidemic disease	98.22	94.57
B2.2 Wildlife and marine life biodiversity	26.10	18.59
B3 Environmental health	47.86	46.87
B3.1 Air quality and climate change	66.75	53.72
B3.2 Environmental biodiversity	48.80	44.05
B3.3 Environmental resources	29.48	44.25

	Country Score	Global Average
C Core drivers index	55.64	57.25
C1 Governance	53.09	56.51
C1.1 Participation	18.41	41.70
C1.3 Transparency	72.90	65.15
C1.4 Responsiveness	52.05	44.42
C1.5 Consensus oriented	86.70	86.45
C1.6 Equity and inclusiveness	55.62	73.61
C1.7 Effectiveness and efficiency	31.93	28.38
C1.8 Political support	54.04	55.89
C2 Zoonotic diseases	69.44	68.06
C2.1 Source of infection	69.31	69.22
C2.2 Route of transmission	66.40	59.30
C2.3 Targeted population	48.80	59.90
C2.4 Capacity building	79.59	72.85
C2.5 Case studies	89.54	85.89
C3 Food security	56.41	52.89
C3.1 Food demand and supply	66.53	59.53
C3.2 Food safety	83.55	69.36
C3.3 Nutrition	61.42	67.17
C3.4 Natural and social circumstances	54.27	51.54
C3.5 Government support and response	16.29	16.85
C4 Antimicrobial resistance	29.79	44.05
C4.1 AMR surveillance system	26.87	34.79
C4.2 AMR laboratory network and coordination capacity	39.55	55.57
C4.3 Antimicrobial control and optimization	30.87	48.76
C4.4 Improve awareness and understanding	21.88	48.09
C4.5 Antimicrobial resistance rate for important antibiotics	29.77	33.03
C5 Climate change	67.89	64.19
C5.1 Mitigation and adaptation capacity	22.59	28.24
C5.2 Climate change risks	92.38	80.87
C5.3 Health outcome	90.78	85.41

Scores are normalized (0-100, where 100 = most favorable)

Albania

Europe & Central Asia | Upper middle income

 Index **079**/160
Score

54.14

▼ AVERAGE PERFORMANCE BY GOHI

▼ AVERAGE PERFORMANCE BY CDI

Global average: 54.82

Regional average: 60.26

Income group average: 54.54

Country performance: 54.14

Missing rate in GOHI database: 22.50%

	Country Score	Global Average
A External drivers index	40.10	40.45
A1 Earth system	58.61	56.21
A1.1 Land	24.40	36.41
A1.2 Forest	46.30	43.43
A1.3 Water	62.96	58.09
A1.4 Air	89.93	71.93
A1.5 Natural disasters	61.96	64.65
A2 Institutional system	43.37	46.01
A2.1 Justice	50.42	57.89
A2.2 Governance	37.36	35.58
A3 Economical system	19.20	24.62
A3.1 Finance	21.61	34.35
A3.2 Work	36.62	38.58
A4 Sociological system	36.50	37.70
A4.1 Demographic	40.37	46.31
A4.2 Education	26.41	28.26
A4.3 Inequalities	45.31	40.28
A5 Technological system	42.85	37.72
A5.1 Transport	15.12	6.54
A5.2 Technology adoption	45.83	41.23
A5.3 Consumption and production	65.07	62.53
B Intrinsic drivers index	61.86	58.01
B1 Human health	77.39	72.35
B1.1 Health coverage	61.41	58.65
B1.2 Diseases burden	84.37	79.83
B1.3 Injury and violence	88.74	80.75
B2 Animal health and ecosystem diversity	59.29	56.58
B2.1 Animal epidemic disease	94.26	94.57
B2.2 Wildlife and marine life biodiversity	24.32	18.59
B3 Environmental health	50.76	46.87
B3.1 Air quality and climate change	68.75	53.72
B3.2 Environmental biodiversity	44.05	44.05
B3.3 Environmental resources	41.02	44.25

Scores are normalized (0-100, where 100 = most favorable)

	Country Score	Global Average
C Core drivers index	55.44	57.25
C1 Governance	47.44	56.51
C1.1 Participation	13.69	41.70
C1.3 Transparency	75.40	65.15
C1.4 Responsiveness	66.65	44.42
C1.5 Consensus oriented	7.27	86.45
C1.6 Equity and inclusiveness	77.96	73.61
C1.7 Effectiveness and efficiency	33.33	28.38
C1.8 Political support	57.81	55.89
C2 Zoonotic diseases	78.98	68.06
C2.1 Source of infection	93.67	69.22
C2.2 Route of transmission	71.18	59.30
C2.3 Targeted population	75.81	59.90
C2.4 Capacity building	66.15	72.85
C2.5 Case studies	87.22	85.89
C3 Food security	60.24	52.89
C3.1 Food demand and supply	65.03	59.53
C3.2 Food safety	82.71	69.36
C3.3 Nutrition	81.98	67.17
C3.4 Natural and social circumstances	49.79	51.54
C3.5 Government support and response	21.71	16.85
C4 Antimicrobial resistance	30.17	44.05
C4.1 AMR surveillance system	16.54	34.79
C4.2 AMR laboratory network and coordination on capacity	48.11	55.57
C4.3 Antimicrobial control and optimization	25.07	48.76
C4.4 Improve awareness and understanding	25.00	48.09
C4.5 Antimicrobial resistance rate for important antibiotics	36.11	33.03
C5 Climate change	58.10	64.19
C5.1 Mitigation and adaptation capacity	23.98	28.24
C5.2 Climate change risks	78.89	80.87
C5.3 Health outcome	73.19	85.41

Kenya
Sub-Saharan Africa | Lower middle income

54.01 | **Index Score 080**/160

Global average: 54.82

Regional average: 48.03

Income group average: 51.29

Country performance: 54.01

Missing rate in GOHI database: 18.50%

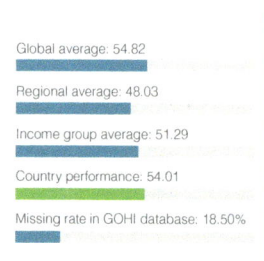

▼ AVERAGE PERFORMANCE BY GOHI

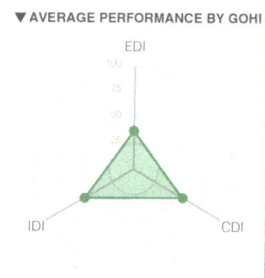

▼ AVERAGE PERFORMANCE BY CDI

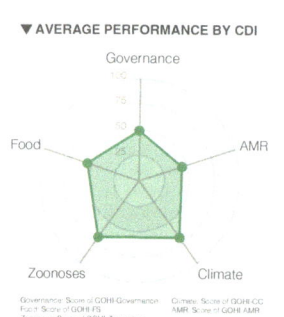

	Country Score	Global Average
A External drivers index	37.35	40.45
A1 Earth system	55.35	56.21
A1.1 Land	30.47	36.41
A1.2 Forest	36.06	43.43
A1.3 Water	53.64	58.09
A1.4 Air	86.94	71.93
A1.5 Natural disasters	59.98	64.65
A2 Institutional system	38.98	46.01
A2.1 Justice	50.86	57.89
A2.2 Governance	28.85	35.58
A3 Economical system	22.85	24.62
A3.1 Finance	28.82	34.35
A3.2 Work	29.66	38.58
A4 Sociological system	35.86	37.70
A4.1 Demographic	50.29	46.31
A4.2 Education	25.62	28.26
A4.3 Inequalities	32.93	40.28
A5 Technological system	33.72	37.72
A5.1 Transport	0.46	6.54
A5.2 Technology adoption	29.83	41.23
A5.3 Consumption and production	68.05	62.53
B Intrinsic drivers index	57.50	58.01
B1 Human health	66.29	72.35
B1.1 Health coverage	43.26	58.65
B1.2 Diseases burden	84.27	79.83
B1.3 Injury and violence	73.35	80.75
B2 Animal health and ecosystem diversity	57.09	56.58
B2.1 Animal epidemic disease	95.47	94.57
B2.2 Wildlife and marine life biodiversity	18.70	18.59
B3 Environmental health	50.86	46.87
B3.1 Air quality and climate change	64.30	53.72
B3.2 Environmental biodiversity	44.35	44.05
B3.3 Environmental resources	45.46	44.25

	Country Score	Global Average
C Core drivers index	56.88	57.25
C1 Governance	48.93	56.51
C1.1 Participation	41.04	41.70
C1.3 Transparency	54.50	65.15
C1.4 Responsiveness	29.15	44.42
C1.5 Consensus oriented	95.99	86.45
C1.6 Equity and inclusiveness	51.44	73.61
C1.7 Effectiveness and efficiency	22.80	28.38
C1.8 Political support	47.61	55.89
C2 Zoonotic diseases	69.10	68.06
C2.1 Source of infection	61.58	69.22
C2.2 Route of transmission	70.47	59.30
C2.3 Targeted population	64.49	59.90
C2.4 Capacity building	69.06	72.85
C2.5 Case studies	84.42	85.89
C3 Food security	44.77	52.89
C3.1 Food demand and supply	44.97	59.53
C3.2 Food safety	56.13	69.36
C3.3 Nutrition	56.38	67.17
C3.4 Natural and social circumstances	37.80	51.54
C3.5 Government support and response	28.57	16.85
C4 Antimicrobial resistance	54.82	44.05
C4.1 AMR surveillance system	40.11	34.79
C4.2 AMR laboratory network and coordination on capacity	75.10	55.57
C4.3 Antimicrobial control and optimization	61.56	48.76
C4.4 Improve awareness and understanding	68.75	48.09
C4.5 Antimicrobial resistance rate for important antibiotics	28.59	33.03
C5 Climate change	68.77	64.19
C5.1 Mitigation and adaptation capacity	23.58	26.24
C5.2 Climate change risks	88.73	80.87
C5.3 Health outcome	96.10	85.41

Scores are normalized (0-100, where 100 = most favorable)

Ukraine

Europe & Central Asia | Lower middle income

Index Score **081** /160

Global average: 54.82

Regional average: 60.26

Income group average: 51.29

Country performance: 53.99

Missing rate in GOHI database: 10.50%

▼ AVERAGE PERFORMANCE BY GOHI

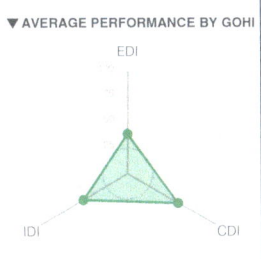

▼ AVERAGE PERFORMANCE BY CDI

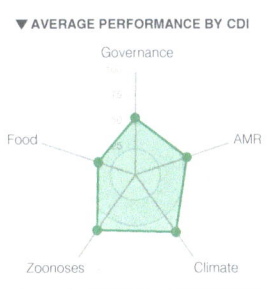

	Country Score	Global Average
A External drivers index	38.97	40.45
A1 Earth system	62.36	56.21
A1.1 Land	73.83	36.41
A1.2 Forest	40.47	43.43
A1.3 Water	43.66	58.09
A1.4 Air	83.63	71.93
A1.5 Natural disasters	66.66	64.65
A2 Institutional system	41.20	46.01
A2.1 Justice	55.72	57.89
A2.2 Governance	28.84	35.58
A3 Economical system	17.05	24.62
A3.1 Finance	16.11	34.35
A3.2 Work	36.44	38.58
A4 Sociological system	37.68	37.70
A4.1 Demographic	43.29	46.31
A4.2 Education	28.03	28.26
A4.3 Inequalities	43.95	40.28
A5 Technological system	36.53	37.72
A5.1 Transport	0.68	6.54
A5.2 Technology adoption	38.74	41.23
A5.3 Consumption and production	66.96	62.53
B Intrinsic drivers index	51.70	58.01
B1 Human health	65.63	72.35
B1.1 Health coverage	52.66	58.65
B1.2 Diseases burden	57.20	79.83
B1.3 Injury and violence	89.00	80.75
B2 Animal health and ecosystem diversity	57.01	56.58
B2.1 Animal epidemic disease	99.16	94.57
B2.2 Wildlife and marine life biodiversity	14.85	18.59
B3 Environmental health	34.04	46.87
B3.1 Air quality and climate change	30.82	53.72
B3.2 Environmental biodiversity	45.20	44.05
B3.3 Environmental resources	27.14	44.25

	Country Score	Global Average
C Core drivers index	57.87	57.25
C1 Governance	55.90	56.51
C1.1 Participation	19.06	41.70
C1.3 Transparency	72.50	65.15
C1.4 Responsiveness	25.00	44.42
C1.5 Consensus oriented	96.96	86.45
C1.6 Equity and inclusiveness	96.80	73.61
C1.7 Effectiveness and efficiency	30.60	28.38
C1.8 Political support	50.40	55.89
C2 Zoonotic diseases	69.66	68.06
C2.1 Source of infection	71.66	69.22
C2.2 Route of transmission	55.25	59.30
C2.3 Targeted population	74.94	59.90
C2.4 Capacity building	70.03	72.85
C2.5 Case studies	83.58	85.89
C3 Food security	55.80	52.89
C3.1 Food demand and supply	62.32	59.53
C3.2 Food safety	78.38	69.36
C3.3 Nutrition	64.14	67.17
C3.4 Natural and social circumstances	58.81	51.54
C3.5 Government support and response	14.32	16.85
C4 Antimicrobial resistance	39.84	44.05
C4.1 AMR surveillance system	16.31	34.79
C4.2 AMR laboratory network and coordination capacity	70.50	55.57
C4.3 Antimicrobial control and optimization	44.25	48.76
C4.4 Improve awareness and understanding	42.19	48.09
C4.5 Antimicrobial resistance rate for important antibiotics	25.93	33.03
C5 Climate change	67.47	64.19
C5.1 Mitigation and adaptation capacity	30.75	28.24
C5.2 Climate change risks	83.99	80.87
C5.3 Health outcome	89.72	85.41

Scores are normalized (0-100, where 100 = most favorable)

Sri Lanka
South Asia | Lower middle income

53.88   Index Score **082**/160

Global average: 54.82

Regional average: 51.61

Income group average: 51.29

Country performance: 53.88

Missing rate in GOHI database: 15.90%

▼ AVERAGE PERFORMANCE BY GOHI

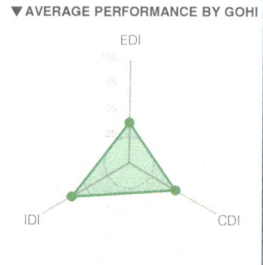

▼ AVERAGE PERFORMANCE BY CDI

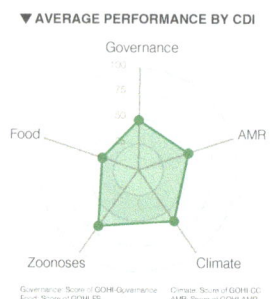

	Country Score	Global Average
A External drivers index	39.27	40.45
A1 Earth system	55.22	56.21
A1.1 Land	27.59	36.41
A1.2 Forest	24.49	43.43
A1.3 Water	60.64	58.09
A1.4 Air	86.51	71.93
A1.5 Natural disasters	65.42	64.65
A2 Institutional system	42.25	46.01
A2.1 Justice	50.82	57.89
A2.2 Governance	34.95	35.58
A3 Economical system	27.28	24.62
A3.1 Finance	40.59	34.35
A3.2 Work	39.51	38.58
A4 Sociological system	32.97	37.70
A4.1 Demographic	31.98	46.31
A4.2 Education	27.86	28.26
A4.3 Inequalities	40.82	40.28
A5 Technological system	38.64	37.72
A5.1 Transport	1.54	6.54
A5.2 Technology adoption	36.94	41.23
A5.3 Consumption and production	74.21	62.53
B Intrinsic drivers index	66.90	53.01
B1 Human health	75.67	72.35
B1.1 Health coverage	63.96	58.65
B1.2 Diseases burden	82.90	79.83
B1.3 Injury and violence	82.43	80.75
B2 Animal health and ecosystem diversity	65.01	56.58
B2.1 Animal epidemic disease	92.13	94.57
B2.2 Wildlife and marine life biodiversity	37.90	18.59
B3 Environmental health	62.04	46.87
B3.1 Air quality and climate change	54.41	53.72
B3.2 Environmental biodiversity	49.60	44.05
B3.3 Environmental resources	83.98	44.25

	Country Score	Global Average
C Core drivers index	57.87	57.25
C1 Governance	48.68	56.51
C1.1 Participation	16.32	41.70
C1.3 Transparency	72.60	65.15
C1.4 Responsiveness	35.40	44.42
C1.5 Consensus oriented	93.49	86.45
C1.6 Equity and inclusiveness	50.69	73.61
C1.7 Effectiveness and efficiency	16.13	28.38
C1.8 Political support	56.13	55.89
C2 Zoonotic diseases	61.95	68.06
C2.1 Source of infection	44.02	69.22
C2.2 Route of transmission	67.69	59.30
C2.3 Targeted population	43.37	59.90
C2.4 Capacity building	74.25	72.85
C2.5 Case studies	90.26	85.89
C3 Food security	52.97	52.89
C3.1 Food demand and supply	65.16	59.53
C3.2 Food safety	56.64	69.36
C3.3 Nutrition	73.08	67.17
C3.4 Natural and social circumstances	48.03	51.54
C3.5 Government support and response	21.92	16.85
C4 Antimicrobial resistance	38.36	44.05
C4.1 AMR surveillance system	24.96	34.79
C4.2 AMR laboratory network and coordination capacity	56.86	55.57
C4.3 Antimicrobial control and optimization	44.31	48.76
C4.4 Improve awareness and understanding	37.50	48.09
C4.5 Antimicrobial resistance rate for important antibiotics	28.16	33.03
C5 Climate change	68.24	64.19
C5.1 Mitigation and adaptation capacity	27.80	28.24
C5.2 Climate change risks	93.82	80.87
C5.3 Health outcome	85.16	85.41

Scores are normalized (0-100, where 100 = most favorable)

Ghana
Sub-Saharan Africa | Lower middle income

53.73 Index Score **083**/160

Global average: 54.82

Regional average: 48.03

Income group average: 51.29

Country performance: 53.73

Missing rate in GOHI database: 18.80%

▼ AVERAGE PERFORMANCE BY GOHI

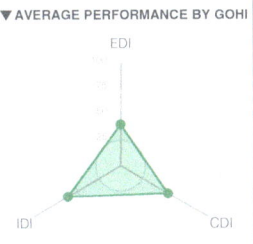

▼ AVERAGE PERFORMANCE BY CDI

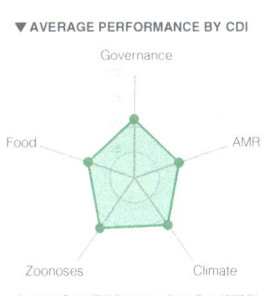

	Country Score	Global Average
A External drivers index	40.41	40.45
A1 Earth system	52.31	56.21
A1.1 Land	33.31	36.41
A1.2 Forest	47.40	43.43
A1.3 Water	51.33	58.09
A1.4 Air	59.97	71.93
A1.5 Natural disasters	66.67	64.65
A2 Institutional system	47.36	46.01
A2.1 Justice	60.25	57.89
A2.2 Governance	36.39	35.58
A3 Economical system	24.64	24.62
A3.1 Finance	34.45	34.35
A3.2 Work	38.50	38.58
A4 Sociological system	38.42	37.70
A4.1 Demographic	54.00	46.31
A4.2 Education	28.93	28.26
A4.3 Inequalities	33.12	40.28
A5 Technological system	39.32	37.72
A5.1 Transport	3.42	6.54
A5.2 Technology adoption	42.86	41.23
A5.3 Consumption and production	68.40	62.53
B Intrinsic drivers index	61.38	58.01
B1 Human health	62.42	72.35
B1.1 Health coverage	38.50	58.65
B1.2 Diseases burden	80.59	79.83
B1.3 Injury and violence	70.07	80.75
B2 Animal health and ecosystem diversity	55.19	56.58
B2.1 Animal epidemic disease	95.99	94.57
B2.2 Wildlife and marine life biodiversity	14.40	18.59
B3 Environmental health	68.38	46.87
B3.1 Air quality and climate change	63.03	53.72
B3.2 Environmental biodiversity	53.20	44.05
B3.3 Environmental resources	90.98	44.25

Scores are normalized (0-100, where 100 = most favorable)

	Country Score	Global Average
C Core drivers index	54.68	57.25
C1 Governance	57.52	56.51
C1.1 Participation	42.18	41.70
C1.3 Transparency	62.00	65.15
C1.4 Responsiveness	41.65	44.42
C1.5 Consensus oriented	94.72	86.45
C1.6 Equity and inclusiveness	73.40	73.61
C1.7 Effectiveness and efficiency	24.00	28.38
C1.8 Political support	64.69	55.89
C2 Zoonotic diseases	57.56	68.06
C2.1 Source of infection	50.96	69.22
C2.2 Route of transmission	44.84	59.30
C2.3 Targeted population	45.47	59.90
C2.4 Capacity building	72.01	72.85
C2.5 Case studies	88.38	85.89
C3 Food security	48.14	52.89
C3.1 Food demand and supply	56.34	59.53
C3.2 Food safety	53.58	69.36
C3.3 Nutrition	61.38	67.17
C3.4 Natural and social circumstances	47.25	51.54
C3.5 Government support and response	22.15	16.85
C4 Antimicrobial resistance	50.28	44.05
C4.1 AMR surveillance system	58.50	34.79
C4.2 AMR laboratory network and coordination on capacity	54.79	55.57
C4.3 Antimicrobial control and optimization	51.86	48.76
C4.4 Improve awareness and understanding	54.69	48.09
C4.5 Antimicrobial resistance rate for important antibiotics	31.55	33.03
C5 Climate change	61.12	64.19
C5.1 Mitigation and adaptation capacity	25.01	28.24
C5.2 Climate change risks	74.16	80.87
C5.3 Health outcome	86.04	85.41

Jordan

Middle East & North Africa | **Upper middle income**

53.53 Index Score **084**/160

Global average: 54.82

Regional average: 53.57

Income group average: 54.54

Country performance: 53.53

Missing rate in GOHI database: 21.70%

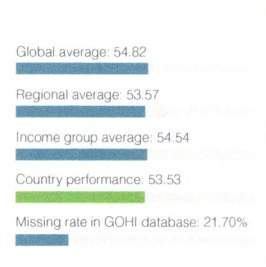

▼ AVERAGE PERFORMANCE BY GOHI

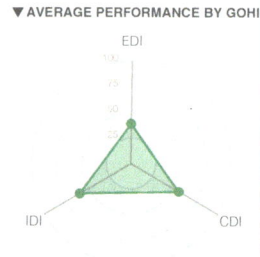

▼ AVERAGE PERFORMANCE BY CDI

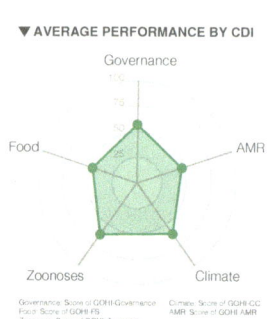

	Country Score	Global Average
A External drivers index	**38.97**	**40.45**
A1 Earth system	50.77	56.21
A1.1 Land	21.79	36.41
A1.2 Forest	33.70	43.43
A1.3 Water	49.73	58.09
A1.4 Air	75.20	71.93
A1.5 Natural disasters	66.66	64.65
A2 Institutional system	47.33	46.01
A2.1 Justice	59.96	57.89
A2.2 Governance	36.57	35.58
A3 Economical system	26.04	24.62
A3.1 Finance	38.96	34.35
A3.2 Work	37.45	38.58
A4 Sociological system	36.83	37.70
A4.1 Demographic	50.65	46.31
A4.2 Education	24.42	28.26
A4.3 Inequalities	37.37	40.28
A5 Technological system	33.91	37.72
A5.1 Transport	1.73	6.54
A5.2 Technology adoption	30.07	41.23
A5.3 Consumption and production	67.20	62.53
B Intrinsic drivers index	**59.50**	**58.01**
B1 Human health	80.60	72.35
B1.1 Health coverage	65.40	58.65
B1.2 Diseases burden	95.56	79.83
B1.3 Injury and violence	83.27	80.75
B2 Animal health and ecosystem diversity	52.48	56.58
B2.1 Animal epidemic disease	94.41	94.57
B2.2 Wildlife and marine life biodiversity	10.56	18.59
B3 Environmental health	47.23	46.87
B3.1 Air quality and climate change	62.65	53.72
B3.2 Environmental biodiversity	39.18	44.05
B3.3 Environmental resources	41.28	44.25

Scores are normalized (0-100, where 100 = most favorable)

	Country Score	Global Average
C Core drivers index	**55.34**	**57.25**
C1 Governance	57.04	56.51
C1.1 Participation	15.25	41.70
C1.3 Transparency	62.00	65.15
C1.4 Responsiveness	60.40	44.42
C1.5 Consensus oriented	97.53	86.45
C1.6 Equity and inclusiveness	84.37	73.61
C1.7 Effectiveness and efficiency	34.87	28.38
C1.8 Political support	44.88	55.89
C2 Zoonotic diseases	62.06	68.06
C2.1 Source of infection	69.25	69.22
C2.2 Route of transmission	43.73	59.30
C2.3 Targeted population	51.94	59.90
C2.4 Capacity building	69.32	72.85
C2.5 Case studies	86.21	85.89
C3 Food security	47.59	52.89
C3.1 Food demand and supply	54.47	59.53
C3.2 Food safety	75.77	69.36
C3.3 Nutrition	46.62	67.17
C3.4 Natural and social circumstances	52.34	51.54
C3.5 Government support and response	8.74	16.85
C4 Antimicrobial resistance	47.35	44.05
C4.1 AMR surveillance system	50.15	34.79
C4.2 AMR laboratory network and coordination on capacity	63.85	55.57
C4.3 Antimicrobial control and optimization	41.44	48.76
C4.4 Improve awareness and understanding	54.69	48.09
C4.5 Antimicrobial resistance rate for important antibiotics	26.60	33.03
C5 Climate change	62.74	64.19
C5.1 Mitigation and adaptation capacity	27.15	28.24
C5.2 Climate change risks	81.25	80.87
C5.3 Health outcome	81.73	85.41

Rwanda

Sub-Saharan Africa | Low income

53.11 Index Score **085**/160

Global average: 54.82

Regional average: 48.03

Income group average: 46.63

Country performance: 53.11

Missing rate in GOHI database: 22.50%

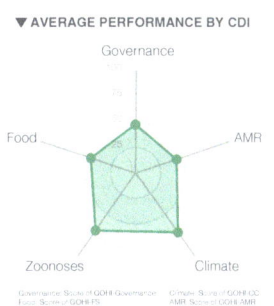

▼ AVERAGE PERFORMANCE BY GOHI

EDI

IDI

CDI

▼ AVERAGE PERFORMANCE BY CDI

Governance

Food

AMR

Zoonoses

Climate

Governance Score of GOHI-Governance   Climate Score of GOHI-UC
Food Score of GOHI-FS   AMR Score of GOHI-AMR
Zoonoses Score of GOHI-Zoonoses

	Country Score	Global Average
A External drivers index	38.79	40.45
A1 Earth system	51.86	56.21
A1.1 Land	15.68	36.41
A1.2 Forest	37.62	43.43
A1.3 Water	55.79	58.09
A1.4 Air	75.67	71.93
A1.5 Natural disasters	65.66	64.65
A2 Institutional system	49.62	46.01
A2.1 Justice	62.57	57.89
A2.2 Governance	38.59	35.58
A3 Economical system	27.92	24.62
A3.1 Finance	42.59	34.35
A3.2 Work	39.13	38.58
A4 Sociological system	34.11	37.70
A4.1 Demographic	42.79	46.31
A4.2 Education	25.06	28.26
A4.3 Inequalities	36.07	40.28
A5 Technological system	30.44	37.72
A5.1 Transport	0.10	6.54
A5.2 Technology adoption	20.64	41.23
A5.3 Consumption and production	68.18	62.53
B Intrinsic drivers index	54.93	58.01
B1 Human health	68.43	72.35
B1.1 Health coverage	47.60	58.65
B1.2 Diseases burden	85.18	79.83
B1.3 Injury and violence	74.58	80.75
B2 Animal health and ecosystem diversity	55.20	56.58
B2.1 Animal epidemic disease	95.42	94.57
B2.2 Wildlife and marine life biodiversity	14.99	18.59
B3 Environmental health	42.81	46.87
B3.1 Air quality and climate change	45.21	53.72
B3.2 Environmental biodiversity	31.55	44.05
B3.3 Environmental resources	52.98	44.25

	Country Score	Global Average
C Core drivers index	55.87	57.25
C1 Governance	47.58	56.51
C1.1 Participation	12.75	41.70
C1.3 Transparency	67.30	65.15
C1.4 Responsiveness	27.10	44.42
C1.5 Consensus oriented	95.02	86.45
C1.6 Equity and inclusiveness	57.51	73.61
C1.7 Effectiveness and efficiency	26.73	28.38
C1.8 Political support	46.67	55.89
C2 Zoonotic diseases	72.18	68.06
C2.1 Source of infection	76.75	69.22
C2.2 Route of transmission	61.55	59.30
C2.3 Targeted population	60.62	59.90
C2.4 Capacity building	78.10	72.85
C2.5 Case studies	90.83	85.89
C3 Food security	43.44	52.89
C3.1 Food demand and supply	47.20	59.53
C3.2 Food safety	63.92	69.36
C3.3 Nutrition	51.90	67.17
C3.4 Natural and social circumstances	43.83	51.54
C3.5 Government support and response	10.33	16.85
C4 Antimicrobial resistance	47.79	44.05
C4.1 AMR surveillance system	40.20	34.79
C4.2 AMR laboratory network and coordination capacity	62.79	55.57
C4.3 Antimicrobial control and optimization	73.18	48.76
C4.4 Improve awareness and understanding	45.31	48.09
C4.5 Antimicrobial resistance rate for important antibiotics	17.46	33.03
C5 Climate change	69.92	64.19
C5.1 Mitigation and adaptation capacity	21.88	28.24
C5.2 Climate change risks	90.56	80.87
C5.3 Health outcome	99.44	85.41

Scores are normalized (0-100, where 100 = most favorable)

Cote d'Ivoire
Sub-Saharan Africa | Lower middle income

 **53.1** Index **086**/160
Score

Global average: 54.82

Regional average: 48.03

Income group average: 51.29

Country performance: 53.10

Missing rate in GOHI database: 28.60%

▼ AVERAGE PERFORMANCE BY GOHI

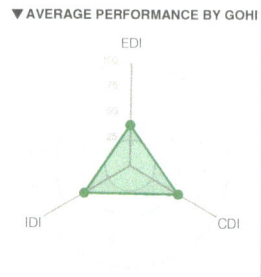

▼ AVERAGE PERFORMANCE BY CDI

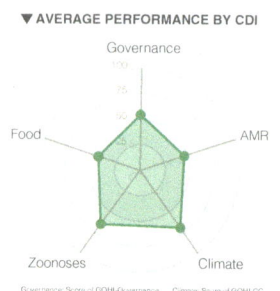

Governance Score of GOHI-Governance   Climate: Score of GOHI-CC
Food: Score of GOHI-FS   AMR: Score of GOHI-AMR
Zoonoses: Score of GOHI-Zoonoses

	Country Score	Global Average
A External drivers index	39.66	40.45
A1 Earth system	50.66	56.21
A1.1 Land	43.77	36.41
A1.2 Forest	38.78	43.43
A1.3 Water	53.64	58.09
A1.4 Air	49.42	71.93
A1.5 Natural disasters	65.42	64.65
A2 Institutional system	41.24	46.01
A2.1 Justice	54.02	57.89
A2.2 Governance	30.36	35.58
A3 Economical system	26.23	24.62
A3.1 Finance	38.12	34.35
A3.2 Work	39.16	38.58
A4 Sociological system	43.06	37.70
A4.1 Demographic	60.52	46.31
A4.2 Education	29.85	28.26
A4.3 Inequalities	40.52	40.28
A5 Technological system	37.12	37.72
A5.1 Transport	2.00	6.54
A5.2 Technology adoption	35.54	41.23
A5.3 Consumption and production	70.76	62.53
B Intrinsic drivers index	53.84	58.01
B1 Human health	61.31	72.35
B1.1 Health coverage	30.82	58.65
B1.2 Diseases burden	75.37	79.83
B1.3 Injury and violence	79.58	80.75
B2 Animal health and ecosystem diversity	56.17	56.58
B2.1 Animal epidemic disease	92.69	94.57
B2.2 Wildlife and marine life biodiversity	19.65	18.59
B3 Environmental health	45.69	46.87
B3.1 Air quality and climate change	56.36	53.72
B3.2 Environmental biodiversity	56.85	44.05
B3.3 Environmental resources	25.24	44.25

Scores are normalized (0-100, where 100 = most favorable)

	Country Score	Global Average
C Core drivers index	55.91	57.25
C1 Governance	54.50	56.51
C1.1 Participation	43.01	41.70
C1.3 Transparency	56.10	65.15
C1.4 Responsiveness	58.30	44.42
C1.5 Consensus oriented	90.13	86.45
C1.6 Equity and inclusiveness	61.36	73.61
C1.7 Effectiveness and efficiency	21.67	28.38
C1.8 Political support	50.93	55.89
C2 Zoonotic diseases	69.48	68.06
C2.1 Source of infection	69.29	69.22
C2.2 Route of transmission	68.68	59.30
C2.3 Targeted population	54.24	59.90
C2.4 Capacity building	70.55	72.85
C2.5 Case studies	89.19	85.89
C3 Food security	46.53	52.89
C3.1 Food demand and supply	52.56	59.53
C3.2 Food safety	45.15	69.36
C3.3 Nutrition	63.15	67.17
C3.4 Natural and social circumstances	51.50	51.54
C3.5 Government support and response	20.26	16.85
C4 Antimicrobial resistance	43.46	44.05
C4.1 AMR surveillance system	26.11	34.79
C4.2 AMR laboratory network and coordination capacity	71.73	55.57
C4.3 Antimicrobial control and optimization	45.22	48.76
C4.4 Improve awareness and understanding	40.62	48.09
C4.5 Antimicrobial resistance rate for important antibiotics	33.62	33.03
C5 Climate change	65.65	64.19
C5.1 Mitigation and adaptation capacity	24.86	28.24
C5.2 Climate change risks	79.70	80.87
C5.3 Health outcome	94.39	85.41

Lebanon

Middle East & North Africa | Lower middle income

 53.03 | Index Score **087**/160

Global average: 54.82

Regional average: 53.57

Income group average: 51.29

Country performance: 53.03

Missing rate in GOHI database: 18.50%

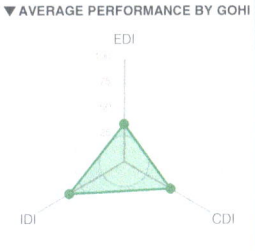
▼ AVERAGE PERFORMANCE BY GOHI

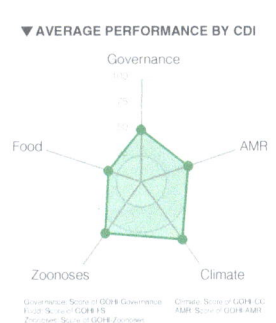
▼ AVERAGE PERFORMANCE BY CDI

	Country Score	Global Average
A External drivers index	36.86	40.45
A1 Earth system	51.32	56.21
A1.1 Land	7.05	36.41
A1.2 Forest	38.53	43.43
A1.3 Water	62.05	58.09
A1.4 Air	73.73	71.93
A1.5 Natural disasters	65.85	64.65
A2 Institutional system	32.73	46.01
A2.1 Justice	39.68	57.89
A2.2 Governance	26.82	35.58
A3 Economical system	23.83	24.62
A3.1 Finance	33.94	34.35
A3.2 Work	36.45	38.58
A4 Sociological system	38.03	37.70
A4.1 Demographic	46.56	46.31
A4.2 Education	28.21	28.26
A4.3 Inequalities	41.18	40.28
A5 Technological system	38.37	37.72
A5.1 Transport	2.41	6.54
A5.2 Technology adoption	42.57	41.23
A5.3 Consumption and production	66.85	62.53
B Intrinsic drivers index	64.21	58.01
B1 Human health	79.50	72.35
B1.1 Health coverage	69.44	58.65
B1.2 Diseases burden	86.58	79.83
B1.3 Injury and violence	84.88	80.75
B2 Animal health and ecosystem diversity	52.66	56.58
B2.1 Animal epidemic disease	94.12	94.57
B2.2 Wildlife and marine life biodiversity	11.20	18.59
B3 Environmental health	62.42	46.87
B3.1 Air quality and climate change	62.04	53.72
B3.2 Environmental biodiversity	50.05	44.05
B3.3 Environmental resources	77.06	44.25

	Country Score	Global Average
C Core drivers index	53.98	57.25
C1 Governance	50.99	56.51
C1.1 Participation	18.06	41.70
C1.3 Transparency	51.90	65.15
C1.4 Responsiveness	58.30	44.42
C1.5 Consensus oriented	81.41	86.45
C1.6 Equity and inclusiveness	82.67	73.61
C1.7 Effectiveness and efficiency	24.73	28.38
C1.8 Political support	39.86	55.89
C2 Zoonotic diseases	70.27	68.06
C2.1 Source of infection	61.67	69.22
C2.2 Route of transmission	72.75	59.30
C2.3 Targeted population	74.68	59.90
C2.4 Capacity building	59.82	72.85
C2.5 Case studies	85.59	85.89
C3 Food security	49.91	52.89
C3.1 Food demand and supply	61.26	59.53
C3.2 Food safety	62.20	69.36
C3.3 Nutrition	64.95	67.17
C3.4 Natural and social circumstances	42.25	51.54
C3.5 Government support and response	18.87	16.85
C4 Antimicrobial resistance	35.08	44.05
C4.1 AMR surveillance system	23.11	34.79
C4.2 AMR laboratory network and coordinati on capacity	46.70	55.57
C4.3 Antimicrobial control and optimization	32.71	48.76
C4.4 Improve awareness and understanding	42.19	48.09
C4.5 Antimicrobial resistance rate for important antibiotics	30.70	33.03
C5 Climate change	62.75	64.19
C5.1 Mitigation and adaptation capacity	25.58	28.24
C5.2 Climate change risks	82.94	80.87
C5.3 Health outcome	81.62	85.41

Scores are normalized (0-100, where 100 = most favorable)

Jamaica

Latin America & Caribbean | **Upper middle income**

52.99 Index Score **088**/160

Global average: 54.82

Regional average: 55.08

Income group average: 54.54

Country performance: 52.99

Missing rate in GOHI database: 22.80%

▼ AVERAGE PERFORMANCE BY GOHI

▼ AVERAGE PERFORMANCE BY CDI

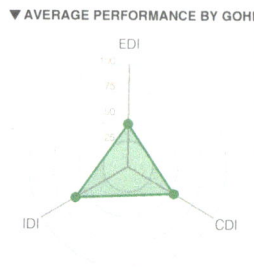

Governance: Score of GOHI-Governance   Climate: Score of GOHI-CC
Food: Score of GOHI-FS   AMR: Score of GOHI-AMR
Zoonoses: Score of GOHI-Zoonoses

	Country Score	Global Average
A External drivers index	41.73	40.45
A1 Earth system	60.62	56.21
A1.1 Land	20.48	36.41
A1.2 Forest	54.76	43.43
A1.3 Water	65.92	58.09
A1.4 Air	87.89	71.93
A1.5 Natural disasters	63.76	64.65
A2 Institutional system	48.87	46.01
A2.1 Justice	62.43	57.89
A2.2 Governance	37.32	35.58
A3 Economical system	22.27	24.62
A3.1 Finance	28.20	34.35
A3.2 Work	38.51	38.58
A4 Sociological system	36.34	37.70
A4.1 Demographic	46.25	46.31
A4.2 Education	25.31	28.26
A4.3 Inequalities	39.53	40.28
A5 Technological system	40.52	37.72
A5.1 Transport	19.36	6.54
A5.2 Technology adoption	34.64	41.23
A5.3 Consumption and production	65.85	62.53
B Intrinsic drivers index	61.15	58.01
B1 Human health	65.14	72.35
B1.1 Health coverage	64.76	58.65
B1.2 Diseases burden	86.45	79.83
B1.3 Injury and violence	46.19	80.75
B2 Animal health and ecosystem diversity	59.66	56.58
B2.1 Animal epidemic disease	93.88	94.57
B2.2 Wildlife and marine life biodiversity	25.45	18.59
B3 Environmental health	60.51	46.87
B3.1 Air quality and climate change	52.40	53.72
B3.2 Environmental biodiversity	51.30	44.05
B3.3 Environmental resources	79.66	44.25

	Country Score	Global Average
C Core drivers index	53.56	57.25
C1 Governance	50.37	56.51
C1.1 Participation	42.79	41.70
C1.3 Transparency	54.60	65.15
C1.4 Responsiveness	41.65	44.42
C1.5 Consensus oriented	65.61	86.45
C1.6 Equity and inclusiveness	63.64	73.61
C1.7 Effectiveness and efficiency	19.40	28.38
C1.8 Political support	64.87	55.89
C2 Zoonotic diseases	65.67	68.06
C2.1 Source of infection	55.88	69.22
C2.2 Route of transmission	66.87	59.30
C2.3 Targeted population	47.07	59.90
C2.4 Capacity building	79.81	72.85
C2.5 Case studies	86.80	85.89
C3 Food security	52.51	52.89
C3.1 Food demand and supply	65.33	59.53
C3.2 Food safety	67.43	69.36
C3.3 Nutrition	72.85	67.17
C3.4 Natural and social circumstances	44.70	51.54
C3.5 Government support and response	12.23	16.85
C4 Antimicrobial resistance	33.13	44.05
C4.1 AMR surveillance system	17.30	34.79
C4.2 AMR laboratory network and coordination on capacity	48.74	55.57
C4.3 Antimicrobial control and optimization	32.81	48.76
C4.4 Improve awareness and understanding	31.25	48.09
C4.5 Antimicrobial resistance rate for important antibiotics	35.54	33.03
C5 Climate change	65.21	64.19
C5.1 Mitigation and adaptation capacity	21.87	28.24
C5.2 Climate change risks	87.99	80.87
C5.3 Health outcome	87.74	85.41

Scores are normalized (0-100, where 100 = most favorable)

Kyrgyzstan
Europe & Central Asia | Upper middle income country

Index Score **089**/160 · 52.92

Global average: 54.82

Regional average: 60.26

Income group average: 52.92

Country performance: 52.92

Missing rate in GOHI database: 23.60%

▼ AVERAGE PERFORMANCE BY GOHI

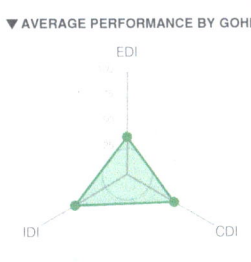

▼ AVERAGE PERFORMANCE BY CDI

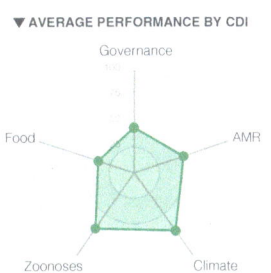

	Country Score	Global Average
A External drivers index	36.70	40.45
A1 Earth system	53.80	56.21
A1.1 Land	18.03	36.41
A1.2 Forest	27.21	43.43
A1.3 Water	63.29	58.09
A1.4 Air	82.41	71.93
A1.5 Natural disasters	66.67	64.65
A2 Institutional system	38.16	46.01
A2.1 Justice	50.97	57.89
A2.2 Governance	27.24	35.58
A3 Economical system	22.48	24.62
A3.1 Finance	28.39	34.35
A3.2 Work	38.96	38.58
A4 Sociological system	34.98	37.70
A4.1 Demographic	42.44	46.31
A4.2 Education	24.31	28.26
A4.3 Inequalities	40.48	40.28
A5 Technological system	34.08	37.72
A5.1 Transport	0.91	6.54
A5.2 Technology adoption	30.68	41.23
A5.3 Consumption and production	67.82	62.53
B Intrinsic drivers index	61.11	58.01
B1 Human health	77.06	72.35
B1.1 Health coverage	58.03	58.65
B1.2 Diseases burden	87.37	79.83
B1.3 Injury and violence	88.10	80.75
B2 Animal health and ecosystem diversity	51.34	56.58
B2.1 Animal epidemic disease	94.15	94.57
B2.2 Wildlife and marine life biodiversity	8.53	18.59
B3 Environmental health	56.80	46.87
B3.1 Air quality and climate change	73.50	53.72
B3.2 Environmental biodiversity	44.50	44.05
B3.3 Environmental resources	54.12	44.25

	Country Score	Global Average
C Core drivers index	54.58	57.25
C1 Governance	44.43	56.51
C1.1 Participation	13.01	41.70
C1.3 Transparency	57.07	65.15
C1.4 Responsiveness	33.35	44.42
C1.5 Consensus oriented	64.39	86.45
C1.6 Equity and inclusiveness	76.91	73.61
C1.7 Effectiveness and efficiency	28.47	28.38
C1.8 Political support	37.83	55.89
C2 Zoonotic diseases	70.33	68.06
C2.1 Source of infection	80.57	69.22
C2.2 Route of transmission	60.60	59.30
C2.3 Targeted population	53.35	59.90
C2.4 Capacity building	76.22	72.85
C2.5 Case studies	85.48	85.89
C3 Food security	52.71	52.89
C3.1 Food demand and supply	64.70	59.53
C3.2 Food safety	72.39	69.36
C3.3 Nutrition	62.29	67.17
C3.4 Natural and social circumstances	50.65	51.54
C3.5 Government support and response	13.52	16.85
C4 Antimicrobial resistance	37.99	44.05
C4.1 AMR surveillance system	31.01	34.79
C4.2 AMR laboratory network and coordination capacity	55.31	55.57
C4.3 Antimicrobial control and optimization	33.84	48.76
C4.4 Improve awareness and understanding	51.56	48.09
C4.5 Antimicrobial resistance rate for important antibiotics	18.24	33.03
C5 Climate change	67.58	64.19
C5.1 Mitigation and adaptation capacity	28.93	28.24
C5.2 Climate change risks	81.56	80.87
C5.3 Health outcome	94.31	85.41

Scores are normalized (0-100, where 100 = most favorable)

Uganda
Sub-Saharan Africa | Low income

52.85 Index Score **090**/160

Global average: 54.82

Regional average: 48.03

Income group average: 46.63

Country performance: 52.85

Missing rate in GOHI database: 22.50%

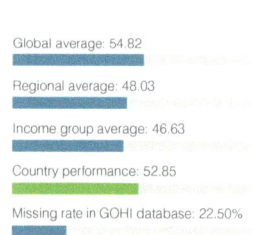

▼ AVERAGE PERFORMANCE BY GOHI

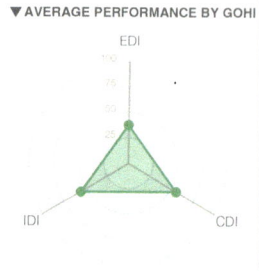

▼ AVERAGE PERFORMANCE BY CDI

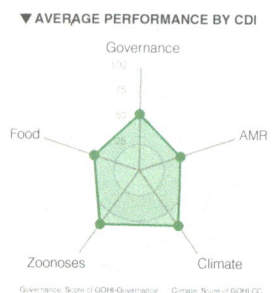

	Country Score	Global Average
A External drivers index	37.58	40.45
A1 Earth system	53.28	56.21
A1.1 Land	33.23	36.41
A1.2 Forest	26.90	43.43
A1.3 Water	55.16	58.09
A1.4 Air	76.45	71.93
A1.5 Natural disasters	66.46	64.65
A2 Institutional system	39.47	46.01
A2.1 Justice	49.71	57.89
A2.2 Governance	30.74	35.58
A3 Economical system	27.04	24.62
A3.1 Finance	39.13	34.35
A3.2 Work	40.56	38.58
A4 Sociological system	36.73	37.70
A4.1 Demographic	48.34	46.31
A4.2 Education	30.82	28.26
A4.3 Inequalities	31.26	40.28
A5 Technological system	31.38	37.72
A5.1 Transport	13.41	6.54
A5.2 Technology adoption	16.40	41.23
A5.3 Consumption and production	63.18	62.53
B Intrinsic drivers index	55.66	58.01
B1 Human health	60.72	72.35
B1.1 Health coverage	35.42	58.65
B1.2 Diseases burden	81.43	79.83
B1.3 Injury and violence	67.14	80.75
B2 Animal health and ecosystem diversity	62.30	56.58
B2.1 Animal epidemic disease	96.84	94.57
B2.2 Wildlife and marine life biodiversity	27.76	18.59
B3 Environmental health	45.65	46.87
B3.1 Air quality and climate change	61.26	53.72
B3.2 Environmental biodiversity	50.23	44.05
B3.3 Environmental resources	26.85	44.25

Scores are normalized (0-100, where 100 = most favorable)

	Country Score	Global Average
C Core drivers index	55.58	57.25
C1 Governance	54.95	56.51
C1.1 Participation	41.71	41.70
C1.3 Transparency	67.60	65.15
C1.4 Responsiveness	50.00	44.42
C1.5 Consensus oriented	97.56	86.45
C1.6 Equity and inclusiveness	48.65	73.61
C1.7 Effectiveness and efficiency	29.53	28.38
C1.8 Political support	49.62	55.89
C2 Zoonotic diseases	67.43	68.06
C2.1 Source of infection	44.34	69.22
C2.2 Route of transmission	79.14	59.30
C2.3 Targeted population	60.97	59.90
C2.4 Capacity building	73.15	72.85
C2.5 Case studies	85.80	85.89
C3 Food security	43.35	52.89
C3.1 Food demand and supply	47.64	59.53
C3.2 Food safety	47.62	69.36
C3.3 Nutrition	56.27	67.17
C3.4 Natural and social circumstances	47.21	51.54
C3.5 Government support and response	18.02	16.85
C4 Antimicrobial resistance	47.05	44.05
C4.1 AMR surveillance system	42.41	34.79
C4.2 AMR laboratory network and coordinati on capacity	57.43	55.57
C4.3 Antimicrobial control and optimization	51.88	48.76
C4.4 Improve awareness and understanding	48.44	48.09
C4.5 Antimicrobial resistance rate for important antibiotics	35.09	33.03
C5 Climate change	65.73	64.19
C5.1 Mitigation and adaptation capacity	18.55	28.24
C5.2 Climate change risks	82.51	80.87
C5.3 Health outcome	96.13	85.41

Tunisia

Middle East & North Africa | Lower middle income

 52.75 Index Score **091**/160

Global average: 54.82

Regional average: 53.57

Income group average: 51.29

Country performance: 52.75

Missing rate in GOHI database: 19.60%

▼ AVERAGE PERFORMANCE BY GOHI

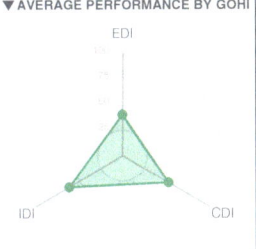

▼ AVERAGE PERFORMANCE BY CDI

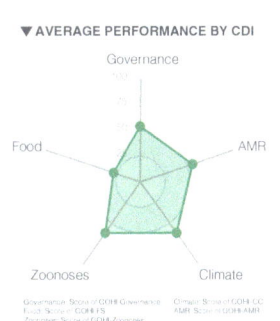

	Country Score	Global Average
A External drivers index	40.31	40.45
A1 Earth system	56.67	56.21
A1.1 Land	43.42	36.41
A1.2 Forest	35.05	43.43
A1.3 Water	56.46	58.09
A1.4 Air	74.91	71.93
A1.5 Natural disasters	66.66	64.65
A2 Institutional system	43.81	46.01
A2.1 Justice	57.36	57.89
A2.2 Governance	32.26	35.58
A3 Economical system	28.17	24.62
A3.1 Finance	43.63	34.35
A3.2 Work	38.62	38.58
A4 Sociological system	37.44	37.70
A4.1 Demographic	45.93	46.31
A4.2 Education	26.44	28.26
A4.3 Inequalities	42.18	40.28
A5 Technological system	35.47	37.72
A5.1 Transport	1.34	6.54
A5.2 Technology adoption	36.53	41.23
A5.3 Consumption and production	65.50	62.53
B Intrinsic drivers index	62.32	58.01
B1 Human health	78.76	72.35
B1.1 Health coverage	67.26	58.65
B1.2 Diseases burden	88.07	79.83
B1.3 Injury and violence	83.33	80.75
B2 Animal health and ecosystem diversity	53.39	56.58
B2.1 Animal epidemic disease	94.23	94.57
B2.2 Wildlife and marine life biodiversity	12.55	18.59
B3 Environmental health	56.71	46.87
B3.1 Air quality and climate change	77.15	53.72
B3.2 Environmental biodiversity	50.65	44.05
B3.3 Environmental resources	44.04	44.25

	Country Score	Global Average
C Core drivers index	53.24	57.25
C1 Governance	54.53	56.51
C1.1 Participation	26.33	41.70
C1.3 Transparency	64.10	65.15
C1.4 Responsiveness	35.40	44.42
C1.5 Consensus oriented	97.23	86.45
C1.6 Equity and inclusiveness	76.34	73.61
C1.7 Effectiveness and efficiency	32.20	28.38
C1.8 Political support	50.14	55.89
C2 Zoonotic diseases	62.19	68.06
C2.1 Source of infection	69.67	69.22
C2.2 Route of transmission	37.60	59.30
C2.3 Targeted population	51.31	59.90
C2.4 Capacity building	79.46	72.85
C2.5 Case studies	86.21	85.89
C3 Food security	56.14	52.89
C3.1 Food demand and supply	48.93	59.53
C3.2 Food safety	88.50	69.36
C3.3 Nutrition	72.45	67.17
C3.4 Natural and social circumstances	54.22	51.54
C3.5 Government support and response	16.59	16.85
C4 Antimicrobial resistance	29.04	44.05
C4.1 AMR surveillance system	24.80	34.79
C4.2 AMR laboratory network and coordination capacity	27.02	55.57
C4.3 Antimicrobial control and optimization	27.96	48.76
C4.4 Improve awareness and understanding	35.94	48.09
C4.5 Antimicrobial resistance rate for important antibiotics	29.46	33.03
C5 Climate change	62.21	64.19
C5.1 Mitigation and adaptation capacity	23.45	28.24
C5.2 Climate change risks	81.68	80.87
C5.3 Health outcome	83.38	85.41

Scores are normalized (0-100, where 100 = most favorable)

Myanmar

East Asia & Pacific | Lower middle income

52.68 **Index Score 092**/160

Global average: 54.82

Regional average: 56.52

Income group average: 51.29

Country performance: 52.68

Missing rate in GOHI database: 20.30%

▼ AVERAGE PERFORMANCE BY GOHI

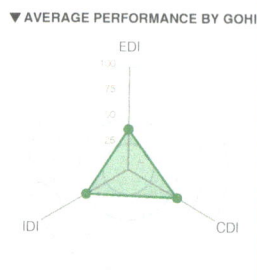

▼ AVERAGE PERFORMANCE BY CDI

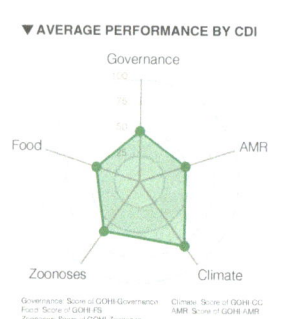

	Country Score	Global Average
A External drivers index	39.15	40.45
A1 Earth system	59.46	56.21
A1.1 Land	31.08	36.41
A1.2 Forest	30.16	43.43
A1.3 Water	77.22	58.09
A1.4 Air	79.91	71.93
A1.5 Natural disasters	65.95	64.65
A2 Institutional system	32.38	46.01
A2.1 Justice	48.00	57.89
A2.2 Governance	19.07	35.58
A3 Economical system	31.75	24.62
A3.1 Finance	52.62	34.35
A3.2 Work	39.19	38.58
A4 Sociological system	37.43	37.70
A4.1 Demographic	48.17	46.31
A4.2 Education	29.87	28.26
A4.3 Inequalities	35.13	40.28
A5 Technological system	34.72	37.72
A5.1 Transport	0.09	6.54
A5.2 Technology adoption	31.69	41.23
A5.3 Consumption and production	69.42	62.53
B Intrinsic drivers index	49.89	58.01
B1 Human health	66.55	72.35
B1.1 Health coverage	43.97	58.65
B1.2 Diseases burden	80.73	79.83
B1.3 Injury and violence	76.95	80.75
B2 Animal health and ecosystem diversity	55.71	56.58
B2.1 Animal epidemic disease	93.37	94.57
B2.2 Wildlife and marine life biodiversity	18.05	18.59
B3 Environmental health	25.90	46.87
B3.1 Air quality and climate change	18.95	53.72
B3.2 Environmental biodiversity	40.50	44.05
B3.3 Environmental resources	19.02	44.25

	Country Score	Global Average
C Core drivers index	56.58	57.25
C1 Governance	49.37	56.51
C1.1 Participation	29.57	41.70
C1.3 Transparency	63.80	65.15
C1.4 Responsiveness	43.75	44.42
C1.5 Consensus oriented	66.88	86.45
C1.6 Equity and inclusiveness	62.00	73.61
C1.7 Effectiveness and efficiency	23.93	28.38
C1.8 Political support	55.63	55.89
C2 Zoonotic diseases	78.14	68.06
C2.1 Source of infection	74.14	69.22
C2.2 Route of transmission	80.55	59.30
C2.3 Targeted population	73.35	59.90
C2.4 Capacity building	77.55	72.85
C2.5 Case studies	87.04	85.89
C3 Food security	48.72	52.89
C3.1 Food demand and supply	59.65	59.53
C3.2 Food safety	57.34	69.36
C3.3 Nutrition	67.62	67.17
C3.4 Natural and social circumstances	49.14	51.54
C3.5 Government support and response	9.83	16.85
C4 Antimicrobial resistance	46.07	44.05
C4.1 AMR surveillance system	34.21	34.79
C4.2 AMR laboratory network and coordinati on capacity	55.38	55.57
C4.3 Antimicrobial control and optimization	52.04	48.76
C4.4 Improve awareness and understanding	57.81	48.09
C4.5 Antimicrobial resistance rate for important antibiotics	30.89	33.03
C5 Climate change	60.71	64.19
C5.1 Mitigation and adaptation capacity	17.09	28.24
C5.2 Climate change risks	81.72	80.87
C5.3 Health outcome	85.17	85.41

Scores are normalized (0-100, where 100 = most favorable)

El Salvador

Latin America & Caribbean | Lower middle income

Index **093**/160
Score

52.62

Global average: 54.82

Regional average: 55.08

Income group average: 51.29

Country performance: 52.62

Missing rate in GOHI database: 17.80%

▼ AVERAGE PERFORMANCE BY GOHI

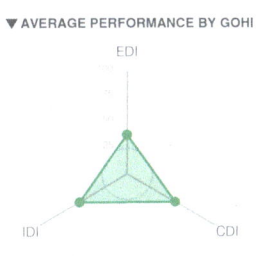

▼ AVERAGE PERFORMANCE BY CDI

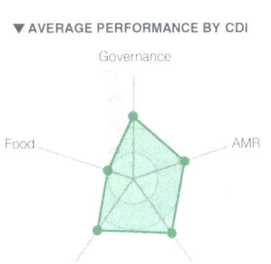

	Country Score	Global Average
A External drivers index	38.50	40.45
A1 Earth system	54.31	56.21
A1.1 Land	25.12	36.41
A1.2 Forest	33.05	43.43
A1.3 Water	53.25	58.09
A1.4 Air	84.68	71.93
A1.5 Natural disasters	66.66	64.65
A2 Institutional system	43.13	46.01
A2.1 Justice	55.87	57.89
A2.2 Governance	32.28	35.58
A3 Economical system	23.70	24.62
A3.1 Finance	32.05	34.35
A3.2 Work	38.41	38.58
A4 Sociological system	36.05	37.70
A4.1 Demographic	49.31	46.31
A4.2 Education	23.78	28.26
A4.3 Inequalities	37.04	40.28
A5 Technological system	35.30	37.72
A5.1 Transport	1.67	6.54
A5.2 Technology adoption	41.88	41.23
A5.3 Consumption and production	59.20	62.53
B Intrinsic drivers index	55.46	58.01
B1 Human health	63.77	72.35
B1.1 Health coverage	72.12	58.65
B1.2 Diseases burden	87.28	79.83
B1.3 Injury and violence	33.85	80.75
B2 Animal health and ecosystem diversity	56.02	56.58
B2.1 Animal epidemic disease	96.04	94.57
B2.2 Wildlife and marine life biodiversity	16.00	18.59
B3 Environmental health	48.26	46.87
B3.1 Air quality and climate change	60.36	53.72
B3.2 Environmental biodiversity	48.80	44.05
B3.3 Environmental resources	37.08	44.25

Scores are normalized (0-100, where 100 = most favorable)

	Country Score	Global Average
C Core drivers index	55.09	57.25
C1 Governance	61.42	56.51
C1.1 Participation	60.04	41.70
C1.3 Transparency	68.80	65.15
C1.4 Responsiveness	45.80	44.42
C1.5 Consensus oriented	95.98	86.45
C1.6 Equity and inclusiveness	70.73	73.61
C1.7 Effectiveness and efficiency	39.60	28.38
C1.8 Political support	49.02	55.89
C2 Zoonotic diseases	68.23	68.06
C2.1 Source of infection	68.64	69.22
C2.2 Route of transmission	55.83	59.30
C2.3 Targeted population	42.21	59.90
C2.4 Capacity building	84.35	72.85
C2.5 Case studies	90.07	85.89
C3 Food security	55.44	52.89
C3.1 Food demand and supply	60.08	59.53
C3.2 Food safety	86.70	69.36
C3.3 Nutrition	74.25	67.17
C3.4 Natural and social circumstances	49.19	51.54
C3.5 Government support and response	6.97	16.85
C4 Antimicrobial resistance	26.87	44.05
C4.1 AMR surveillance system	13.25	34.79
C4.2 AMR laboratory network and coordination on capacity	37.49	55.57
C4.3 Antimicrobial control and optimization	27.48	48.76
C4.4 Improve awareness and understanding	25.00	48.09
C4.5 Antimicrobial resistance rate for important antibiotics	31.16	33.03
C5 Climate change	62.61	64.19
C5.1 Mitigation and adaptation capacity	23.79	28.24
C5.2 Climate change risks	85.52	80.87
C5.3 Health outcome	80.41	85.41

Dominican Republic

Latin America & Caribbean | Upper middle income

52.39 Index Score **094**/160

Global average: 54.82

Regional average: 55.08

Income group average: 54.54

Country performance: 52.39

Missing rate in GOHI database: 14.90%

▼ AVERAGE PERFORMANCE BY GOHI

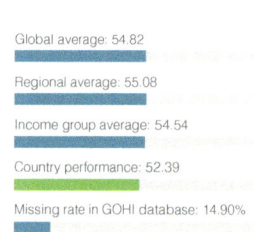

▼ AVERAGE PERFORMANCE BY CDI

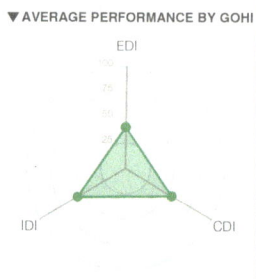

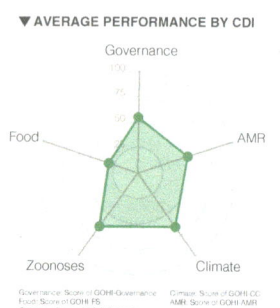

Governance: Score of GOHI-Governance   Climate: Score of GOHI-CC
Food: Score of GOHI-FS   AMR: Score of GOHI-AMR
Zoonoses: Score of GOHI-Zoonoses

	Country Score	Global Average
A External drivers index	40.50	40.45
A1 Earth system	59.99	56.21
A1.1 Land	23.71	36.41
A1.2 Forest	50.42	43.43
A1.3 Water	64.06	58.09
A1.4 Air	85.70	71.93
A1.5 Natural disasters	66.64	64.65
A2 Institutional system	44.53	46.01
A2.1 Justice	54.62	57.89
A2.2 Governance	35.94	35.58
A3 Economical system	26.76	24.62
A3.1 Finance	39.96	34.35
A3.2 Work	38.67	38.58
A4 Sociological system	37.09	37.70
A4.1 Demographic	52.05	46.31
A4.2 Education	24.20	28.26
A4.3 Inequalities	36.97	40.28
A5 Technological system	34.11	37.72
A5.1 Transport	2.68	6.54
A5.2 Technology adoption	31.92	41.23
A5.3 Consumption and production	65.03	62.53
B Intrinsic drivers index	56.11	58.01
B1 Human health	63.46	72.35
B1.1 Health coverage	66.76	58.65
B1.2 Diseases burden	85.20	79.83
B1.3 Injury and violence	40.34	80.75
B2 Animal health and ecosystem diversity	61.61	56.58
B2.1 Animal epidemic disease	84.01	94.57
B2.2 Wildlife and marine life biodiversity	39.20	18.59
B3 Environmental health	44.97	46.87
B3.1 Air quality and climate change	54.52	53.72
B3.2 Environmental biodiversity	34.40	44.05
B3.3 Environmental resources	47.36	44.25

Scores are normalized (0-100, where 100 = most favorable)

	Country Score	Global Average
C Core drivers index	54.15	57.25
C1 Governance	54.49	56.51
C1.1 Participation	12.95	41.70
C1.3 Transparency	63.90	65.15
C1.4 Responsiveness	58.30	44.42
C1.5 Consensus oriented	98.17	86.45
C1.6 Equity and inclusiveness	58.79	73.61
C1.7 Effectiveness and efficiency	33.53	28.38
C1.8 Political support	56.48	55.89
C2 Zoonotic diseases	65.40	68.06
C2.1 Source of infection	67.98	69.22
C2.2 Route of transmission	33.35	59.30
C2.3 Targeted population	76.93	59.90
C2.4 Capacity building	75.02	72.85
C2.5 Case studies	89.75	85.89
C3 Food security	53.11	52.89
C3.1 Food demand and supply	53.66	59.53
C3.2 Food safety	80.80	69.36
C3.3 Nutrition	72.07	67.17
C3.4 Natural and social circumstances	52.30	51.54
C3.5 Government support and response	6.74	16.85
C4 Antimicrobial resistance	30.84	44.05
C4.1 AMR surveillance system	15.31	34.79
C4.2 AMR laboratory network and coordination capacity	48.69	55.57
C4.3 Antimicrobial control and optimization	31.81	48.76
C4.4 Improve awareness and understanding	26.56	48.09
C4.5 Antimicrobial resistance rate for important antibiotics	31.85	33.03
C5 Climate change	65.26	64.19
C5.1 Mitigation and adaptation capacity	21.27	28.24
C5.2 Climate change risks	87.56	80.87
C5.3 Health outcome	88.92	85.41

Brunei Darussalam

East Asia & Pacific | High income

52.37 Index Score **095**/160

Global average: 54.82

Regional average: 56.52

Income group average: 61.66

Country performance: 52.37

Missing rate in GOHI database: 30.80%

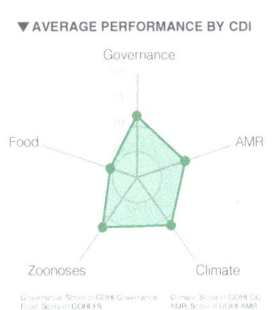

▼AVERAGE PERFORMANCE BY GOHI

EDI

IDI   CDI

▼AVERAGE PERFORMANCE BY CDI

Governance

Food   AMR

Zoonoses   Climate

	Country Score	Global Average
A External drivers index	39.36	40.45
A1 Earth system	50.86	56.21
A1.1 Land	24.51	36.41
A1.2 Forest	43.20	43.43
A1.3 Water	66.56	58.09
A1.4 Air	48.66	71.93
A1.5 Natural disasters	66.25	64.65
A2 Institutional system	46.88	46.01
A2.1 Justice	49.59	57.89
A2.2 Governance	44.58	35.58
A3 Economical system	28.45	24.62
A3.1 Finance	44.07	34.35
A3.2 Work	39.03	38.58
A4 Sociological system	35.35	37.70
A4.1 Demographic	39.71	46.31
A4.2 Education	25.75	28.26
A4.3 Inequalities	42.95	40.28
A5 Technological system	35.24	37.72
A5.1 Transport	11.05	6.54
A5.2 Technology adoption	47.01	41.23
A5.3 Consumption and production	45.20	62.53
B Intrinsic drivers index	63.63	58.01
B1 Human health	81.86	72.35
B1.1 Health coverage	66.31	58.65
B1.2 Diseases burden	90.96	79.83
B1.3 Injury and violence	90.77	80.75
B2 Animal health and ecosystem diversity	52.13	58.58
B2.1 Animal epidemic disease	92.56	94.57
B2.2 Wildlife and marine life biodiversity	11.70	18.59
B3 Environmental health	58.84	46.87
B3.1 Air quality and climate change	80.85	53.72
B3.2 Environmental biodiversity	39.60	44.05
B3.3 Environmental resources	57.84	44.25

	Country Score	Global Average
C Core drivers index	52.59	57.25
C1 Governance	60.53	56.51
C1.1 Participation	24.80	41.70
C1.3 Transparency	60.17	65.15
C1.4 Responsiveness	58.30	44.42
C1.5 Consensus oriented	94.20	86.45
C1.6 Equity and inclusiveness	81.52	73.61
C1.7 Effectiveness and efficiency	43.00	28.38
C1.8 Political support	61.75	55.89
C2 Zoonotic diseases	58.58	68.06
C2.1 Source of infection	42.04	69.22
C2.2 Route of transmission	57.66	59.30
C2.3 Targeted population	52.59	59.90
C2.4 Capacity building	64.68	72.85
C2.5 Case studies	86.80	85.89
C3 Food security	51.80	52.89
C3.1 Food demand and supply	63.84	59.53
C3.2 Food safety	73.33	69.36
C3.3 Nutrition	60.69	67.17
C3.4 Natural and social circumstances	56.58	51.54
C3.5 Government support and response	4.54	16.85
C4 Antimicrobial resistance	28.88	44.05
C4.1 AMR surveillance system	23.66	34.79
C4.2 AMR laboratory network and coordination on capacity	44.55	55.57
C4.3 Antimicrobial control and optimization	14.47	48.76
C4.4 Improve awareness and understanding	20.31	48.09
C4.5 Antimicrobial resistance rate for important antibiotics	41.38	33.03
C5 Climate change	60.82	64.19
C5.1 Mitigation and adaptation capacity	21.13	28.24
C5.2 Climate change risks	86.40	80.87
C5.3 Health outcome	76.76	85.41

Scores are normalized (0-100, where 100 = most favorable)

Ethiopia
Sub-Saharan Africa | Low income

52.01 Index Score **096**/160

Global average: 54.82

Regional average: 48.03

Income group average: 46.63

Country performance: 52.01

Missing rate in GOHI database: 19.20%

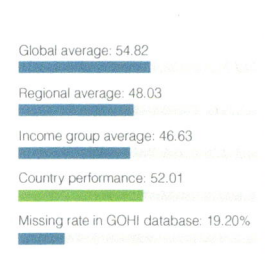

▼ AVERAGE PERFORMANCE BY GOHI

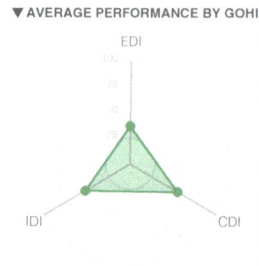

▼ AVERAGE PERFORMANCE BY CDI

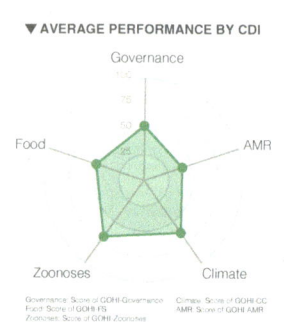

	Country Score	Global Average
A External drivers index	37.08	40.45
A1 Earth system	54.75	56.21
A1.1 Land	28.04	36.41
A1.2 Forest	28.69	43.43
A1.3 Water	66.16	58.09
A1.4 Air	77.58	71.93
A1.5 Natural disasters	62.01	64.65
A2 Institutional system	35.79	46.01
A2.1 Justice	48.19	57.89
A2.2 Governance	25.22	35.58
A3 Economical system	26.91	24.62
A3.1 Finance	45.45	34.35
A3.2 Work	41.14	38.58
A4 Sociological system	33.81	37.70
A4.1 Demographic	46.52	46.31
A4.2 Education	25.14	28.26
A4.3 Inequalities	30.70	40.28
A5 Technological system	31.46	37.72
A5.1 Transport	0.29	6.54
A5.2 Technology adoption	26.32	41.23
A5.3 Consumption and production	65.16	62.53
B Intrinsic drivers index	53.11	58.01
B1 Human health	61.60	72.35
B1.1 Health coverage	33.92	58.65
B1.2 Diseases burden	85.06	79.83
B1.3 Injury and violence	67.69	80.75
B2 Animal health and ecosystem diversity	57.84	56.58
B2.1 Animal epidemic disease	89.44	94.57
B2.2 Wildlife and marine life biodiversity	26.25	18.59
B3 Environmental health	41.48	46.87
B3.1 Air quality and climate change	58.45	53.72
B3.2 Environmental biodiversity	24.80	44.05
B3.3 Environmental resources	42.46	44.25

	Country Score	Global Average
C Core drivers index	55.07	57.25
C1 Governance	53.31	56.51
C1.1 Participation	39.12	41.70
C1.3 Transparency	53.60	65.15
C1.4 Responsiveness	66.65	44.42
C1.5 Consensus oriented	66.43	86.45
C1.6 Equity and inclusiveness	63.52	73.61
C1.7 Effectiveness and efficiency	29.27	28.38
C1.8 Political support	54.57	55.89
C2 Zoonotic diseases	63.92	68.06
C2.1 Source of infection	51.33	69.22
C2.2 Route of transmission	66.01	59.30
C2.3 Targeted population	60.79	59.90
C2.4 Capacity building	77.05	72.85
C2.5 Case studies	69.50	85.89
C3 Food security	40.69	52.89
C3.1 Food demand and supply	42.78	59.53
C3.2 Food safety	59.76	69.36
C3.3 Nutrition	59.04	67.17
C3.4 Natural and social circumstances	28.68	51.54
C3.5 Government support and response	13.22	16.85
C4 Antimicrobial resistance	50.47	44.05
C4.1 AMR surveillance system	47.31	34.79
C4.2 AMR laboratory network and coordination capacity	56.94	55.57
C4.3 Antimicrobial control and optimization	50.92	48.76
C4.4 Improve awareness and understanding	64.06	48.09
C4.5 Antimicrobial resistance rate for important antibiotics	33.12	33.03
C5 Climate change	68.52	64.19
C5.1 Mitigation and adaptation capacity	27.68	28.24
C5.2 Climate change risks	83.91	80.87
C5.3 Health outcome	96.07	85.41

Scores are normalized (0-100, where 100 = most favorable)

Kuwait
Middle East & North Africa | **High income**

Index Score **097** /160

Global average: 54.82

Regional average: 53.57

Income group average: 61.66

Country performance: 51.98

Missing rate in GOHI database: 23.60%

▼ AVERAGE PERFORMANCE BY GOHI

EDI

IDI

CDI

▼ AVERAGE PERFORMANCE BY CDI

Governance

Food

AMR

Zoonoses

Climate

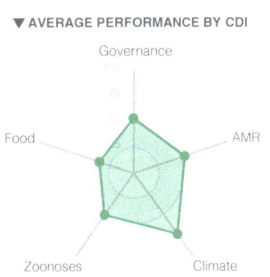

	Country Score	Global Average
A External drivers index	32.83	40.45
A1 Earth system	23.24	56.21
A1.1 Land	24.19	36.41
A1.2 Forest	33.42	43.43
A1.3 Water	0.00	58.09
A1.4 Air	5.68	71.93
A1.5 Natural disasters	66.62	64.65
A2 Institutional system	46.26	46.01
A2.1 Justice	61.30	57.89
A2.2 Governance	33.45	35.58
A3 Economical system	20.35	24.62
A3.1 Finance	24.06	34.35
A3.2 Work	37.36	38.58
A4 Sociological system	36.86	37.70
A4.1 Demographic	46.51	46.31
A4.2 Education	24.06	28.26
A4.3 Inequalities	42.65	40.28
A5 Technological system	37.45	37.72
A5.1 Transport	7.55	6.54
A5.2 Technology adoption	68.08	41.23
A5.3 Consumption and production	33.18	62.53
B Intrinsic drivers index	59.93	58.01
B1 Human health	82.87	72.35
B1.1 Health coverage	69.73	58.65
B1.2 Diseases burden	95.72	79.83
B1.3 Injury and violence	85.67	80.75
B2 Animal health and ecosystem diversity	56.81	56.58
B2.1 Animal epidemic disease	95.83	94.57
B2.2 Wildlife and marine life biodiversity	17.80	18.59
B3 Environmental health	41.92	46.87
B3.1 Air quality and climate change	45.20	53.72
B3.2 Environmental biodiversity	42.40	44.05
B3.3 Environmental resources	39.44	44.25

	Country Score	Global Average
C Core drivers index	54.35	57.25
C1 Governance	53.81	56.51
C1.1 Participation	20.41	41.70
C1.3 Transparency	64.20	65.15
C1.4 Responsiveness	33.35	44.42
C1.5 Consensus oriented	95.61	86.45
C1.6 Equity and inclusiveness	86.42	73.61
C1.7 Effectiveness and efficiency	16.40	28.38
C1.8 Political support	59.96	55.89
C2 Zoonotic diseases	74.09	68.06
C2.1 Source of infection	86.18	69.22
C2.2 Route of transmission	49.67	59.30
C2.3 Targeted population	78.21	59.90
C2.4 Capacity building	75.32	72.85
C2.5 Case studies	89.46	85.89
C3 Food security	54.55	52.89
C3.1 Food demand and supply	68.54	59.53
C3.2 Food safety	63.78	69.36
C3.3 Nutrition	69.31	67.17
C3.4 Natural and social circumstances	47.65	51.54
C3.5 Government support and response	23.48	16.85
C4 Antimicrobial resistance	36.32	44.05
C4.1 AMR surveillance system	31.24	34.79
C4.2 AMR laboratory network and coordinati on capacity	23.52	55.57
C4.3 Antimicrobial control and optimization	39.52	48.76
C4.4 Improve awareness and understanding	59.38	48.09
C4.5 Antimicrobial resistance rate for important antibiotics	27.96	33.03
C5 Climate change	50.66	64.19
C5.1 Mitigation and adaptation capacity	28.52	28.24
C5.2 Climate change risks	54.04	80.87
C5.3 Health outcome	70.96	85.41

Scores are normalized (0-100, where 100 = most favorable)

Bangladesh
South Asia | Lower middle income

51.75 Index Score **098**/160

Global average: 54.82

Regional average: 51.61

Income group average: 51.29

Country performance: 51.75

Missing rate in GOHI database: 16.70%

▼ AVERAGE PERFORMANCE BY GOHI

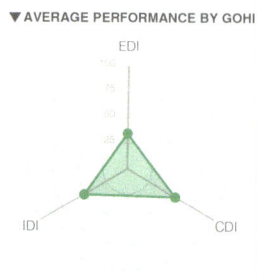

▼ AVERAGE PERFORMANCE BY CDI

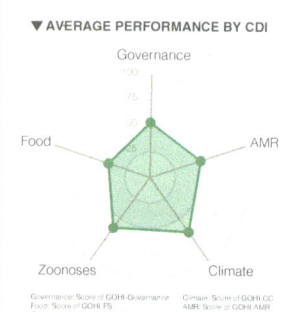

Governance Score of GOHI-Governance
Food: Score of GOHI-FS
Zoonoses: Score of GOHI-Zoonoses
Climate: Score of GOHI-CC
AMR: Score of GOHI-AMR

	Country Score	Global Average
A External drivers index	34.45	40.45
A1 Earth system	44.41	56.21
A1.1 Land	27.28	36.41
A1.2 Forest	38.70	43.43
A1.3 Water	37.42	58.09
A1.4 Air	52.64	71.93
A1.5 Natural disasters	65.70	64.65
A2 Institutional system	33.53	46.01
A2.1 Justice	37.61	57.89
A2.2 Governance	30.05	35.58
A3 Economical system	21.81	24.62
A3.1 Finance	25.88	34.35
A3.2 Work	39.92	38.58
A4 Sociological system	36.45	37.70
A4.1 Demographic	45.34	46.31
A4.2 Education	30.44	28.26
A4.3 Inequalities	34.22	40.28
A5 Technological system	36.07	37.72
A5.1 Transport	0.07	6.54
A5.2 Technology adoption	30.50	41.23
A5.3 Consumption and production	74.62	62.53
B Intrinsic drivers index	50.56	58.01
B1 Human health	72.50	72.35
B1.1 Health coverage	46.31	58.65
B1.2 Diseases burden	87.53	79.83
B1.3 Injury and violence	85.84	80.75
B2 Animal health and ecosystem diversity	61.02	56.58
B2.1 Animal epidemic disease	91.98	94.67
B2.2 Wildlife and marine life biodiversity	30.05	18.59
B3 Environmental health	19.69	46.87
B3.1 Air quality and climate change	16.23	53.72
B3.2 Environmental biodiversity	26.15	44.05
B3.3 Environmental resources	17.30	44.25

	Country Score	Global Average
C Core drivers index	55.68	57.25
C1 Governance	53.81	56.51
C1.1 Participation	45.82	41.70
C1.3 Transparency	58.10	65.15
C1.4 Responsiveness	50.00	44.42
C1.5 Consensus oriented	94.33	86.45
C1.6 Equity and inclusiveness	53.07	73.61
C1.7 Effectiveness and efficiency	29.13	28.38
C1.8 Political support	46.21	55.89
C2 Zoonotic diseases	66.47	68.06
C2.1 Source of infection	60.61	69.22
C2.2 Route of transmission	64.40	59.30
C2.3 Targeted population	48.48	59.90
C2.4 Capacity building	79.11	72.85
C2.5 Case studies	87.78	85.89
C3 Food security	53.18	52.89
C3.1 Food demand and supply	67.81	59.53
C3.2 Food safety	60.00	69.36
C3.3 Nutrition	60.58	67.17
C3.4 Natural and social circumstances	54.45	51.54
C3.5 Government support and response	23.08	16.85
C4 Antimicrobial resistance	43.68	44.05
C4.1 AMR surveillance system	28.01	34.79
C4.2 AMR laboratory network and coordination capacity	62.66	55.57
C4.3 Antimicrobial control and optimization	44.29	48.76
C4.4 Improve awareness and understanding	45.31	48.09
C4.5 Antimicrobial resistance rate for important antibiotics	38.12	33.03
C5 Climate change	61.70	64.19
C5.1 Mitigation and adaptation capacity	19.62	28.24
C5.2 Climate change risks	81.08	80.87
C5.3 Health outcome	86.26	85.41

Scores are normalized (0-100, where 100 = most favorable)

Mauritius
Sub-Saharan Africa | Upper middle income

 **Index Score 099**/160

Global average: 54.82

Regional average: 48.03

Income group average: 54.54

Country performance: 51.73

Missing rate in GOHI database: 18.50%

▼ AVERAGE PERFORMANCE BY GOHI

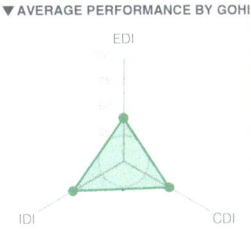

▼ AVERAGE PERFORMANCE BY CDI

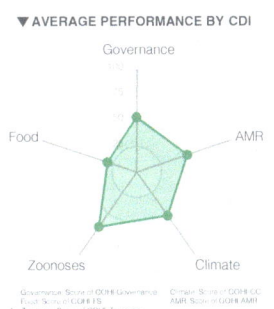

	Country Score	Global Average
A External drivers index	42.32	40.45
A1 Earth system	58.13	56.21
A1.1 Land	24.37	36.41
A1.2 Forest	40.55	43.43
A1.3 Water	65.10	58.09
A1.4 Air	85.25	71.93
A1.5 Natural disasters	64.54	64.65
A2 Institutional system	54.02	46.01
A2.1 Justice	63.52	57.89
A2.2 Governance	45.92	35.58
A3 Economical system	22.25	24.62
A3.1 Finance	30.63	34.35
A3.2 Work	35.37	38.58
A4 Sociological system	35.25	37.70
A4.1 Demographic	39.99	46.31
A4.2 Education	26.43	28.26
A4.3 Inequalities	41.40	40.26
A5 Technological system	41.95	37.72
A5.1 Transport	16.31	6.54
A5.2 Technology adoption	41.84	41.23
A5.3 Consumption and production	65.42	62.53
B Intrinsic drivers index	58.69	58.01
B1 Human health	73.46	72.35
B1.1 Health coverage	58.63	58.65
B1.2 Diseases burden	76.25	79.83
B1.3 Injury and violence	87.73	80.75
B2 Animal health and ecosystem diversity	66.49	56.58
B2.1 Animal epidemic disease	93.73	94.57
B2.2 Wildlife and marine life biodiversity	39.25	18.59
B3 Environmental health	37.87	46.87
B3.1 Air quality and climate change	36.71	53.72
B3.2 Environmental biodiversity	46.00	44.05
B3.3 Environmental resources	32.06	44.25

Scores are normalized (0-100, where 100 = most favorable)

	Country Score	Global Average
C Core drivers index	52.18	57.25
C1 Governance	53.87	56.51
C1.1 Participation	17.85	41.70
C1.3 Transparency	75.90	65.15
C1.4 Responsiveness	58.30	44.42
C1.5 Consensus oriented	95.69	86.45
C1.6 Equity and inclusiveness	48.19	73.61
C1.7 Effectiveness and efficiency	22.33	28.38
C1.8 Political support	58.82	55.89
C2 Zoonotic diseases	53.17	68.06
C2.1 Source of infection	48.59	69.22
C2.2 Route of transmission	61.89	59.30
C2.3 Targeted population	49.00	59.90
C2.4 Capacity building	18.84	72.85
C2.5 Case studies	89.08	85.89
C3 Food security	54.79	52.89
C3.1 Food demand and supply	66.92	59.53
C3.2 Food safety	68.31	69.36
C3.3 Nutrition	67.11	67.17
C3.4 Natural and social circumstances	46.11	51.54
C3.5 Government support and response	25.53	16.85
C4 Antimicrobial resistance	31.39	44.05
C4.1 AMR surveillance system	21.51	34.79
C4.2 AMR laboratory network and coordination capacity	38.19	55.57
C4.3 Antimicrobial control and optimization	31.77	48.76
C4.4 Improve awareness and understanding	35.94	48.09
C4.5 Antimicrobial resistance rate for important antibiotics	29.52	33.03
C5 Climate change	66.45	64.19
C5.1 Mitigation and adaptation capacity	27.11	28.24
C5.2 Climate change risks	85.84	80.87
C5.3 Health outcome	88.40	85.41

Azerbaijan
Europe & Central Asia | **Upper middle income**

51.61 Index Score **100**/160

Global average: 54.82

Regional average: 60.26

Income group average: 54.54

Country performance: 51.61

Missing rate in GOHI database: 19.60%

▼ AVERAGE PERFORMANCE BY GOHI

▼ AVERAGE PERFORMANCE BY CDI
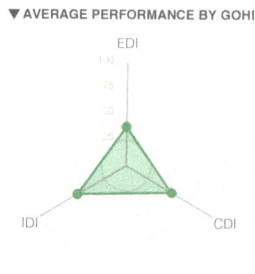

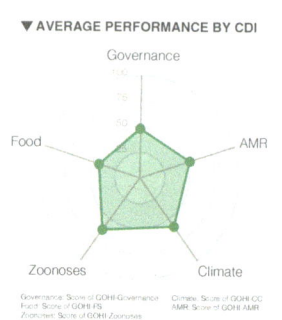

Governance: Score of GOHI-Governance   Climate: Score of GOHI-CC
Food: Score of GOHI-FS   AMR: Score of GOHI-AMR
Zoonoses: Score of GOHI-Zoonoses

	Country Score	Global Average
A External drivers index	38.10	40.45
A1 Earth system	50.80	56.21
A1.1 Land	32.25	36.41
A1.2 Forest	38.88	43.43
A1.3 Water	37.08	58.09
A1.4 Air	75.85	71.93
A1.5 Natural disasters	66.66	64.65
A2 Institutional system	41.18	46.01
A2.1 Justice	55.11	57.89
A2.2 Governance	29.32	35.58
A3 Economical system	26.16	24.62
A3.1 Finance	37.17	34.35
A3.2 Work	40.13	38.58
A4 Sociological system	36.81	37.70
A4.1 Demographic	46.78	46.31
A4.2 Education	24.51	28.26
A4.3 Inequalities	41.59	40.28
A5 Technological system	35.52	37.72
A5.1 Transport	0.79	6.54
A5.2 Technology adoption	33.31	41.23
A5.3 Consumption and production	69.46	62.53
B Intrinsic drivers index	56.88	58.01
B1 Human health	74.03	72.35
B1.1 Health coverage	49.27	58.65
B1.2 Diseases burden	82.38	79.83
B1.3 Injury and violence	92.68	80.75
B2 Animal health and ecosystem diversity	50.89	56.58
B2.1 Animal epidemic disease	89.63	94.57
B2.2 Wildlife and marine life biodiversity	12.15	18.59
B3 Environmental health	47.43	46.87
B3.1 Air quality and climate change	61.05	53.72
B3.2 Environmental biodiversity	52.15	44.05
B3.3 Environmental resources	30.52	44.25

	Country Score	Global Average
C Core drivers index	53.36	57.25
C1 Governance	48.21	56.51
C1.1 Participation	46.06	41.70
C1.3 Transparency	68.10	65.15
C1.4 Responsiveness	50.00	44.42
C1.5 Consensus oriented	6.78	86.45
C1.6 Equity and inclusiveness	78.93	73.61
C1.7 Effectiveness and efficiency	35.00	28.38
C1.8 Political support	52.63	55.89
C2 Zoonotic diseases	59.30	68.06
C2.1 Source of infection	63.47	69.22
C2.2 Route of transmission	31.88	59.30
C2.3 Targeted population	51.50	59.90
C2.4 Capacity building	79.48	72.85
C2.5 Case studies	86.10	85.89
C3 Food security	52.97	52.89
C3.1 Food demand and supply	65.80	59.53
C3.2 Food safety	86.06	69.36
C3.3 Nutrition	57.32	67.17
C3.4 Natural and social circumstances	49.31	51.54
C3.5 Government support and response	6.39	16.85
C4 Antimicrobial resistance	43.13	44.05
C4.1 AMR surveillance system	36.90	34.79
C4.2 AMR laboratory network and coordination capacity	40.57	55.57
C4.3 Antimicrobial control and optimization	51.85	48.76
C4.4 Improve awareness and understanding	60.94	48.09
C4.5 Antimicrobial resistance rate for important antibiotics	25.39	33.03
C5 Climate change	63.34	64.19
C5.1 Mitigation and adaptation capacity	24.06	28.24
C5.2 Climate change risks	78.18	80.87
C5.3 Health outcome	89.71	85.41

Scores are normalized (0-100, where 100 = most favorable)

Belize

Latin America & Caribbean | **Upper middle income**

51.51 **Index Score 101** /160

Global average: 54.82

Regional average: 55.08

Income group average: 54.54

Country performance: 51.51

Missing rate in GOHI database: 23.90%

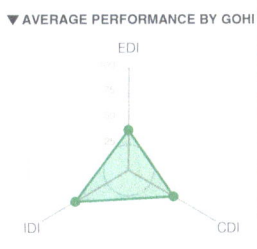

▼ AVERAGE PERFORMANCE BY GOHI

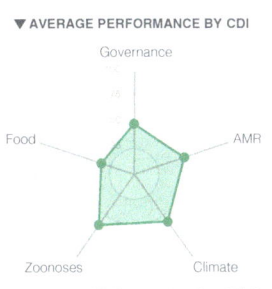

▼ AVERAGE PERFORMANCE BY CDI

	Country Score	Global Average
A External drivers index	39.39	40.45
A1 Earth system	61.69	56.21
A1.1 Land	45.32	36.41
A1.2 Forest	54.02	43.43
A1.3 Water	56.91	58.09
A1.4 Air	79.91	71.93
A1.5 Natural disasters	66.60	64.65
A2 Institutional system	41.32	46.01
A2.1 Justice	54.31	57.89
A2.2 Governance	30.26	35.58
A3 Economical system	23.49	24.62
A3.1 Finance	30.66	34.35
A3.2 Work	39.45	38.58
A4 Sociological system	35.98	37.70
A4.1 Demographic	44.71	46.31
A4.2 Education	25.56	28.26
A4.3 Inequalities	39.71	40.28
A5 Technological system	34.45	37.72
A5.1 Transport	7.30	6.54
A5.2 Technology adoption	31.33	41.23
A5.3 Consumption and production	62.42	62.53
B Intrinsic drivers index	61.96	58.01
B1 Human health	75.04	72.35
B1.1 Health coverage	63.11	58.65
B1.2 Diseases burden	88.86	79.83
B1.3 Injury and violence	75.41	80.75
B2 Animal health and ecosystem diversity	56.33	56.58
B2.1 Animal epidemic disease	90.81	94.57
B2.2 Wildlife and marine life biodiversity	21.85	18.59
B3 Environmental health	56.38	46.87
B3.1 Air quality and climate change	68.80	53.72
B3.2 Environmental biodiversity	60.80	44.05
B3.3 Environmental resources	41.24	44.25

Scores are normalized (0-100, where 100 = most favorable)

	Country Score	Global Average
C Core drivers index	51.73	57.25
C1 Governance	49.82	56.51
C1.1 Participation	42.39	41.70
C1.3 Transparency	58.80	65.15
C1.4 Responsiveness	18.75	44.42
C1.5 Consensus oriented	97.83	86.45
C1.6 Equity and inclusiveness	74.21	73.61
C1.7 Effectiveness and efficiency	13.40	28.38
C1.8 Political support	41.95	55.89
C2 Zoonotic diseases	57.63	68.06
C2.1 Source of infection	67.47	69.22
C2.2 Route of transmission	42.22	59.30
C2.3 Targeted population	31.32	59.90
C2.4 Capacity building	70.26	72.85
C2.5 Case studies	87.16	85.89
C3 Food security	53.72	52.89
C3.1 Food demand and supply	58.09	59.53
C3.2 Food safety	80.58	69.36
C3.3 Nutrition	71.35	67.17
C3.4 Natural and social circumstances	49.25	51.54
C3.5 Government support and response	9.34	16.85
C4 Antimicrobial resistance	35.02	44.05
C4.1 AMR surveillance system	29.10	34.79
C4.2 AMR laboratory network and coordination on capacity	53.20	55.57
C4.3 Antimicrobial control and optimization	37.59	48.76
C4.4 Improve awareness and understanding	26.56	48.09
C4.5 Antimicrobial resistance rate for important antibiotics	28.67	33.03
C5 Climate change	61.77	64.19
C5.1 Mitigation and adaptation capacity	20.30	28.24
C5.2 Climate change risks	85.23	80.87
C5.3 Health outcome	81.66	85.41

Botswana
Sub-Saharan Africa | Upper middle income

 51.46 **Index Score 102**/160

Global average: 54.82

Regional average: 48.03

Income group average: 54.54

Country performance: 51.46

Missing rate in GOHI database: 23.90%

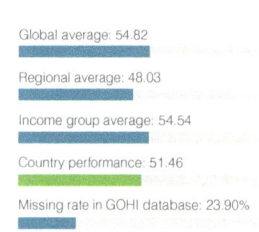
▼ AVERAGE PERFORMANCE BY GOHI

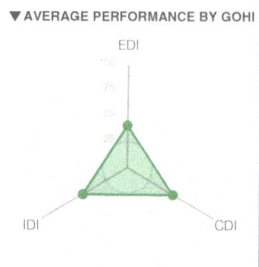
▼ AVERAGE PERFORMANCE BY CDI

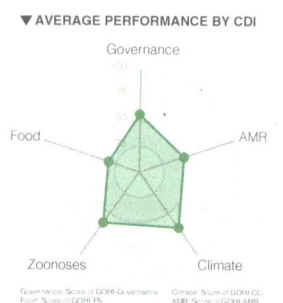

Governance Score of GOHI-Governance   Climate Score of GOHI-CC
Food: Score of GOHI-FS   AMR: Score of GOHI-AMR
Zoonoses: Score of GOHI-Zoonoses

	Country Score	Global Average
A External drivers index	41.30	40.45
A1 Earth system	57.83	56.21
A1.1 Land	52.19	36.41
A1.2 Forest	56.92	43.43
A1.3 Water	39.77	58.09
A1.4 Air	78.66	71.93
A1.5 Natural disasters	59.00	64.65
A2 Institutional system	50.40	46.01
A2.1 Justice	65.30	57.89
A2.2 Governance	37.71	35.58
A3 Economical system	21.02	24.62
A3.1 Finance	28.20	34.35
A3.2 Work	34.35	38.58
A4 Sociological system	39.65	37.70
A4.1 Demographic	58.91	46.31
A4.2 Education	24.22	28.26
A4.3 Inequalities	37.94	40.28
A5 Technological system	37.58	37.72
A5.1 Transport	10.44	6.54
A5.2 Technology adoption	35.76	41.23
A5.3 Consumption and production	64.21	62.53
B Intrinsic drivers index	52.57	58.01
B1 Human health	58.52	72.35
B1.1 Health coverage	42.24	58.65
B1.2 Diseases burden	70.80	79.83
B1.3 Injury and violence	64.29	80.75
B2 Animal health and ecosystem diversity	51.34	56.58
B2.1 Animal epidemic disease	95.50	94.67
B2.2 Wildlife and marine life biodiversity	7.18	18.59
B3 Environmental health	49.44	46.87
B3.1 Air quality and climate change	50.67	53.72
B3.2 Environmental biodiversity	74.05	44.05
B3.3 Environmental resources	25.10	44.25

Scores are normalized (0-100, where 100 = most favorable)

	Country Score	Global Average
C Core drivers index	53.45	57.25
C1 Governance	56.39	56.51
C1.1 Participation	44.69	41.70
C1.3 Transparency	57.30	65.15
C1.4 Responsiveness	25.00	44.42
C1.5 Consensus oriented	92.94	86.45
C1.6 Equity and inclusiveness	72.13	73.61
C1.7 Effectiveness and efficiency	35.67	28.38
C1.8 Political support	67.00	55.89
C2 Zoonotic diseases	67.88	68.06
C2.1 Source of infection	75.54	69.22
C2.2 Route of transmission	46.37	59.30
C2.3 Targeted population	70.85	59.90
C2.4 Capacity building	67.54	72.85
C2.5 Case studies	88.48	85.89
C3 Food security	47.19	52.89
C3.1 Food demand and supply	53.54	59.53
C3.2 Food safety	69.61	69.36
C3.3 Nutrition	51.43	67.17
C3.4 Natural and social circumstances	45.20	51.54
C3.5 Government support and response	16.17	16.85
C4 Antimicrobial resistance	32.68	44.05
C4.1 AMR surveillance system	12.40	34.79
C4.2 AMR laboratory network and coordination capacity	39.19	55.57
C4.3 Antimicrobial control and optimization	40.40	48.76
C4.4 Improve awareness and understanding	37.50	48.09
C4.5 Antimicrobial resistance rate for important antibiotics	33.89	33.03
C5 Climate change	61.70	64.19
C5.1 Mitigation and adaptation capacity	24.47	28.24
C5.2 Climate change risks	77.51	80.87
C5.3 Health outcome	84.97	85.41

Laos

East Asia & Pacific | Lower middle income

51.38 **Index Score 103**/160

Global average: 54.82

Regional average: 56.52

Income group average: 51.29

Country performance: 51.38

Missing rate in GOHI database: 29.30%

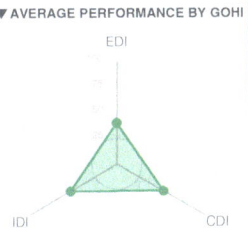

▼ AVERAGE PERFORMANCE BY GOHI

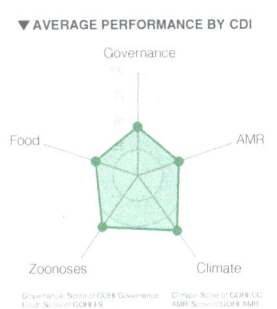

▼ AVERAGE PERFORMANCE BY CDI

	Country Score	Global Average
A External drivers index	40.24	40.45
A1 Earth system	62.16	56.21
A1.1 Land	29.24	36.41
A1.2 Forest	69.03	43.43
A1.3 Water	56.18	58.09
A1.4 Air	84.79	71.93
A1.5 Natural disasters	65.83	64.65
A2 Institutional system	41.98	46.01
A2.1 Justice	54.63	57.89
A2.2 Governance	31.20	35.58
A3 Economical system	25.55	24.62
A3.1 Finance	35.62	34.35
A3.2 Work	40.05	38.58
A4 Sociological system	35.67	37.70
A4.1 Demographic	49.64	46.31
A4.2 Education	25.49	28.26
A4.3 Inequalities	33.11	40.28
A5 Technological system	35.83	37.72
A5.1 Transport	4.23	6.54
A5.2 Technology adoption	37.07	41.23
A5.3 Consumption and production	63.36	62.53
B Intrinsic drivers index	53.74	58.01
B1 Human health	67.09	72.35
B1.1 Health coverage	41.95	58.65
B1.2 Diseases burden	83.12	79.83
B1.3 Injury and violence	78.23	80.75
B2 Animal health and ecosystem diversity	55.57	58.58
B2.1 Animal epidemic disease	92.40	94.57
B2.2 Wildlife and marine life biodiversity	18.73	18.59
B3 Environmental health	40.20	46.87
B3.1 Air quality and climate change	43.11	53.72
B3.2 Environmental biodiversity	45.10	44.05
B3.3 Environmental resources	33.62	44.25

	Country Score	Global Average
C Core drivers index	53.30	57.25
C1 Governance	47.63	56.51
C1.1 Participation	19.07	41.70
C1.3 Transparency	54.10	65.15
C1.4 Responsiveness	43.75	44.42
C1.5 Consensus oriented	87.87	86.45
C1.6 Equity and inclusiveness	63.69	73.61
C1.7 Effectiveness and efficiency	12.53	28.38
C1.8 Political support	53.79	55.89
C2 Zoonotic diseases	67.31	68.06
C2.1 Source of infection	44.24	69.22
C2.2 Route of transmission	70.01	59.30
C2.3 Targeted population	67.73	59.90
C2.4 Capacity building	73.85	72.85
C2.5 Case studies	91.16	85.89
C3 Food security	44.19	52.89
C3.1 Food demand and supply	51.37	59.53
C3.2 Food safety	50.38	69.36
C3.3 Nutrition	57.75	67.17
C3.4 Natural and social circumstances	49.43	51.54
C3.5 Government support and response	12.00	16.85
C4 Antimicrobial resistance	45.34	44.05
C4.1 AMR surveillance system	26.41	34.79
C4.2 AMR laboratory network and coordinati on capacity	72.90	55.57
C4.3 Antimicrobial control and optimization	44.21	48.76
C4.4 Improve awareness and understanding	42.19	48.09
C4.5 Antimicrobial resistance rate for important antibiotics	40.99	33.03
C5 Climate change	62.63	64.19
C5.1 Mitigation and adaptation capacity	26.56	28.24
C5.2 Climate change risks	78.35	80.87
C5.3 Health outcome	84.89	85.41

Scores are normalized (0-100, where 100 = most favorable)

Algeria
Middle East & North Africa | **Lower middle income**

Index Score **104**/160

Global average: 54.82

Regional average: 53.57

Income group average: 51.29

Country performance: 51.24

Missing rate in GOHI database: 22.10%

▼ AVERAGE PERFORMANCE BY GOHI

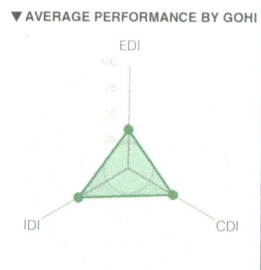
▼ AVERAGE PERFORMANCE BY CDI

	Country Score	Global Average
A External drivers index	37.75	40.45
A1 Earth system	54.42	56.21
A1.1 Land	39.86	36.41
A1.2 Forest	33.72	43.43
A1.3 Water	55.23	58.09
A1.4 Air	70.45	71.93
A1.5 Natural disasters	66.58	64.65
A2 Institutional system	38.00	46.01
A2.1 Justice	26.01	57.89
A2.2 Governance	22.65	35.58
A3 Economical system	23.22	24.62
A3.1 Finance	31.71	34.35
A3.2 Work	37.24	38.58
A4 Sociological system	37.19	37.70
A4.1 Demographic	46.16	46.31
A4.2 Education	26.54	28.26
A4.3 Inequalities	40.94	40.28
A5 Technological system	35.94	37.72
A5.1 Transport	0.35	6.54
A5.2 Technology adoption	33.07	41.23
A5.3 Consumption and production	71.33	62.53
B Intrinsic drivers index	58.81	58.01
B1 Human health	79.71	72.35
B1.1 Health coverage	70.08	58.65
B1.2 Diseases burden	90.24	79.83
B1.3 Injury and violence	81.21	80.75
B2 Animal health and ecosystem diversity	54.67	56.58
B2.1 Animal epidemic disease	95.59	94.57
B2.2 Wildlife and marine life biodiversity	13.75	18.59
B3 Environmental health	43.84	46.87
B3.1 Air quality and climate change	64.14	53.72
B3.2 Environmental biodiversity	23.20	44.05
B3.3 Environmental resources	45.50	44.25

	Country Score	Global Average
C Core drivers index	52.44	57.25
C1 Governance	50.61	56.51
C1.1 Participation	14.28	41.70
C1.3 Transparency	55.10	65.15
C1.4 Responsiveness	35.40	44.42
C1.5 Consensus oriented	95.44	86.45
C1.6 Equity and inclusiveness	81.52	73.61
C1.7 Effectiveness and efficiency	21.33	28.38
C1.8 Political support	52.59	55.89
C2 Zoonotic diseases	65.14	68.06
C2.1 Source of infection	66.29	69.22
C2.2 Route of transmission	32.88	59.30
C2.3 Targeted population	76.94	59.90
C2.4 Capacity building	81.04	72.85
C2.5 Case studies	84.77	85.89
C3 Food security	55.05	52.89
C3.1 Food demand and supply	58.24	59.53
C3.2 Food safety	84.02	69.36
C3.3 Nutrition	66.33	67.17
C3.4 Natural and social circumstances	51.91	51.54
C3.5 Government support and response	14.17	16.85
C4 Antimicrobial resistance	28.46	44.05
C4.1 AMR surveillance system	23.14	34.79
C4.2 AMR laboratory network and coordinati on capacity	44.48	55.57
C4.3 Antimicrobial control and optimization	19.19	48.76
C4.4 Improve awareness and understanding	22.92	48.09
C4.5 Antimicrobial resistance rate for important antibiotics	32.57	33.03
C5 Climate change	60.66	64.19
C5.1 Mitigation and adaptation capacity	23.53	28.24
C5.2 Climate change risks	83.72	80.87
C5.3 Health outcome	77.19	85.41

Scores are normalized (0-100, where 100 = most favorable)

Uzbekistan

Europe & Central Asia | Lower middle income

 **Index Score** 105/160

51.19

Global average: 54.82

Regional average: 60.26

Income group average: 51.29

Country performance: 51.19

Missing rate in GOHI database: 22.10%

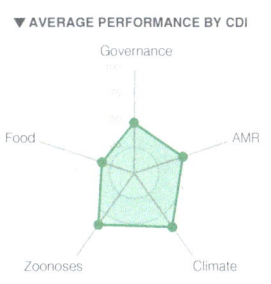

▼ AVERAGE PERFORMANCE BY GOHI

▼ AVERAGE PERFORMANCE BY CDI

Scores are normalized (0-100, where 100 = most favorable)

	Country Score	Global Average
A External drivers index	36.90	40.45
A1 Earth system	44.28	56.21
A1.1 Land	31.81	36.41
A1.2 Forest	25.31	43.43
A1.3 Water	27.47	58.09
A1.4 Air	68.52	71.93
A1.5 Natural disasters	66.67	64.65
A2 Institutional system	38.80	46.01
A2.1 Justice	52.06	57.89
A2.2 Governance	27.51	35.58
A3 Economical system	29.44	24.62
A3.1 Finance	47.18	34.35
A3.2 Work	30.38	38.58
A4 Sociological system	37.07	37.70
A4.1 Demographic	44.63	46.31
A4.2 Education	25.95	28.26
A4.3 Inequalities	43.05	40.28
A5 Technological system	34.90	37.72
A5.1 Transport	0.30	6.54
A5.2 Technology adoption	31.11	41.23
A5.3 Consumption and production	70.36	62.53
B Intrinsic drivers index	56.36	58.01
B1 Human health	75.76	72.35
B1.1 Health coverage	58.41	58.65
B1.2 Diseases burden	82.93	79.83
B1.3 Injury and violence	88.25	80.75
B2 Animal health and ecosystem diversity	51.33	56.58
B2.1 Animal epidemic disease	93.56	94.57
B2.2 Wildlife and marine life biodiversity	9.09	18.59
B3 Environmental health	43.71	46.87
B3.1 Air quality and climate change	65.18	53.72
B3.2 Environmental biodiversity	16.75	44.05
B3.3 Environmental resources	50.52	44.25

	Country Score	Global Average
C Core drivers index	53.14	57.25
C1 Governance	49.38	56.51
C1.1 Participation	25.47	41.70
C1.3 Transparency	54.90	65.15
C1.4 Responsiveness	50.00	44.42
C1.5 Consensus oriented	88.74	86.45
C1.6 Equity and inclusiveness	67.10	73.61
C1.7 Effectiveness and efficiency	15.33	28.38
C1.8 Political support	44.11	55.89
C2 Zoonotic diseases	65.59	68.06
C2.1 Source of infection	83.06	69.22
C2.2 Route of transmission	43.89	59.30
C2.3 Targeted population	54.52	59.90
C2.4 Capacity building	76.13	72.85
C2.5 Case studies	77.18	85.89
C3 Food security	52.35	52.89
C3.1 Food demand and supply	63.72	59.53
C3.2 Food safety	68.32	69.36
C3.3 Nutrition	64.56	67.17
C3.4 Natural and social circumstances	53.71	51.54
C3.5 Government support and response	11.43	16.85
C4 Antimicrobial resistance	34.66	44.05
C4.1 AMR surveillance system	8.80	34.79
C4.2 AMR laboratory network and coordination on capacity	42.25	55.57
C4.3 Antimicrobial control and optimization	48.99	48.76
C4.4 Improve awareness and understanding	48.44	48.09
C4.5 Antimicrobial resistance rate for important antibiotics	24.84	33.03
C5 Climate change	62.87	64.19
C5.1 Mitigation and adaptation capacity	26.56	28.24
C5.2 Climate change risks	75.38	80.87
C5.3 Health outcome	88.57	85.41

Maldives
South Asia | Upper middle income

51.03 | Index **Score 106**/160

Global average: 54.82

Regional average: 51.61

Income group average: 54.54

Country performance: 51.03

Missing rate in GOHI database: 32.20%

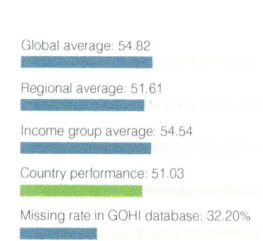
▼ AVERAGE PERFORMANCE BY GOHI

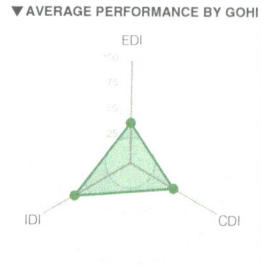

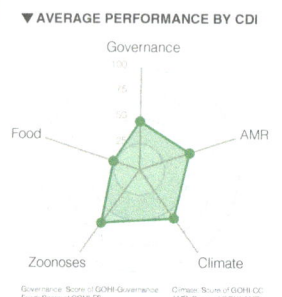
▼ AVERAGE PERFORMANCE BY CDI

	Country Score	Global Average
A External drivers index	39.17	40.45
A1 Earth system	56.13	56.21
A1.1 Land	25.34	36.41
A1.2 Forest	23.20	43.43
A1.3 Water	65.51	58.09
A1.4 Air	87.48	71.93
A1.5 Natural disasters	66.46	64.65
A2 Institutional system	43.84	46.01
A2.1 Justice	55.72	57.89
A2.2 Governance	33.72	35.58
A3 Economical system	25.23	24.62
A3.1 Finance	35.29	34.35
A3.2 Work	39.40	38.58
A4 Sociological system	34.59	37.70
A4.1 Demographic	37.36	46.31
A4.2 Education	25.27	28.26
A4.3 Inequalities	43.67	40.28
A5 Technological system	36.06	37.72
A5.1 Transport	7.93	6.54
A5.2 Technology adoption	35.69	41.23
A5.3 Consumption and production	62.08	62.53
B Intrinsic drivers index	64.90	53.01
B1 Human health	87.81	72.35
B1.1 Health coverage	80.52	58.65
B1.2 Diseases burden	95.24	79.83
B1.3 Injury and violence	90.33	80.75
B2 Animal health and ecosystem diversity	64.95	56.58
B2.1 Animal epidemic disease	93.05	94.57
B2.2 Wildlife and marine life biodiversity	36.85	18.59
B3 Environmental health	43.92	46.87
B3.1 Air quality and climate change	58.55	53.72
B3.2 Environmental biodiversity	27.25	44.05
B3.3 Environmental resources	47.28	44.25

	Country Score	Global Average
C Core drivers index	50.38	57.25
C1 Governance	47.23	56.51
C1.1 Participation	16.00	41.70
C1.3 Transparency	52.90	65.15
C1.4 Responsiveness	41.65	44.42
C1.5 Consensus oriented	83.18	86.45
C1.6 Equity and inclusiveness	67.16	73.61
C1.7 Effectiveness and efficiency	19.27	28.38
C1.8 Political support	50.43	55.89
C2 Zoonotic diseases	58.99	68.06
C2.1 Source of infection	67.54	69.22
C2.2 Route of transmission	59.28	59.30
C2.3 Targeted population	47.60	59.90
C2.4 Capacity building	33.76	72.85
C2.5 Case studies	87.41	85.89
C3 Food security	52.45	52.89
C3.1 Food demand and supply	72.67	59.53
C3.2 Food safety	76.24	69.36
C3.3 Nutrition	61.09	67.17
C3.4 Natural and social circumstances	46.22	51.54
C3.5 Government support and response	6.02	16.85
C4 Antimicrobial resistance	27.47	44.05
C4.1 AMR surveillance system	10.34	34.79
C4.2 AMR laboratory network and coordination capacity	29.71	55.57
C4.3 Antimicrobial control and optimization	36.47	48.76
C4.4 Improve awareness and understanding	35.94	48.09
C4.5 Antimicrobial resistance rate for important antibiotics	24.89	33.03
C5 Climate change	64.66	64.19
C5.1 Mitigation and adaptation capacity	24.86	28.24
C5.2 Climate change risks	85.81	80.87
C5.3 Health outcome	85.27	85.41

Scores are normalized (0-100, where 100 = most favorable)

Tanzania

Sub-Saharan Africa | Lower middle income

Index **107**/160
Score

50.96

Global average: 54.82

Regional average: 48.03

Income group average: 51.29

Country performance: 50.96

Missing rate in GOHI database: 27.50%

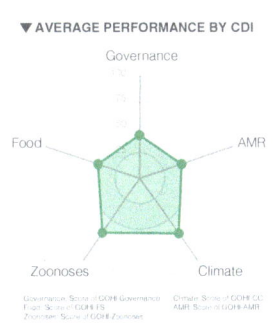

▼ AVERAGE PERFORMANCE BY GOHI

EDI

IDI   CDI

▼ AVERAGE PERFORMANCE BY CDI

Governance

Food   AMR

Zoonoses   Climate

	Country Score	Global Average
A External drivers index	37.20	40.45
A1 Earth system	53.55	56.21
A1.1 Land	31.49	36.41
A1.2 Forest	32.81	43.43
A1.3 Water	56.13	58.09
A1.4 Air	73.79	71.93
A1.5 Natural disasters	65.98	64.65
A2 Institutional system	38.89	46.01
A2.1 Justice	47.60	57.89
A2.2 Governance	31.46	35.58
A3 Economical system	22.84	24.62
A3.1 Finance	29.12	34.35
A3.2 Work	39.24	38.58
A4 Sociological system	38.94	37.70
A4.1 Demographic	47.57	46.31
A4.2 Education	29.80	28.26
A4.3 Inequalities	41.08	40.28
A5 Technological system	31.79	37.72
A5.1 Transport	1.90	6.54
A5.2 Technology adoption	20.35	41.23
A5.3 Consumption and production	70.82	62.53
B Intrinsic drivers index	55.76	58.01
B1 Human health	64.24	72.35
B1.1 Health coverage	42.36	58.65
B1.2 Diseases burden	77.92	79.83
B1.3 Injury and violence	74.38	80.75
B2 Animal health and ecosystem diversity	58.83	56.58
B2.1 Animal epidemic disease	92.60	94.57
B2.2 Wildlife and marine life biodiversity	25.05	18.59
B3 Environmental health	45.91	46.87
B3.1 Air quality and climate change	50.17	53.72
B3.2 Environmental biodiversity	70.30	44.05
B3.3 Environmental resources	18.66	44.25

	Country Score	Global Average
C Core drivers index	52.88	57.25
C1 Governance	42.35	56.51
C1.1 Participation	12.38	41.70
C1.3 Transparency	58.10	65.15
C1.4 Responsiveness	8.35	44.42
C1.5 Consensus oriented	94.86	86.45
C1.6 Equity and inclusiveness	44.66	73.61
C1.7 Effectiveness and efficiency	29.13	28.38
C1.8 Political support	48.94	55.89
C2 Zoonotic diseases	67.20	68.06
C2.1 Source of infection	62.61	69.22
C2.2 Route of transmission	62.69	59.30
C2.3 Targeted population	61.31	59.90
C2.4 Capacity building	70.19	72.85
C2.5 Case studies	86.05	85.89
C3 Food security	44.96	52.89
C3.1 Food demand and supply	45.33	59.53
C3.2 Food safety	55.34	69.36
C3.3 Nutrition	51.54	67.17
C3.4 Natural and social circumstances	51.11	51.54
C3.5 Government support and response	21.50	16.85
C4 Antimicrobial resistance	45.15	44.05
C4.1 AMR surveillance system	42.11	34.79
C4.2 AMR laboratory network and coordination capacity	59.64	55.57
C4.3 Antimicrobial control and optimization	42.39	48.76
C4.4 Improve awareness and understanding	50.00	48.09
C4.5 Antimicrobial resistance rate for important antibiotics	31.59	33.03
C5 Climate change	66.24	64.19
C5.1 Mitigation and adaptation capacity	17.46	28.24
C5.2 Climate change risks	85.97	80.87
C5.3 Health outcome	97.29	85.41

Scores are normalized (0-100, where 100 = most favorable)

Cambodia

East Asia & Pacific | **Lower middle income**

50.94 **Index Score 108**/160

Global average: 54.82

Regional average: 56.52

Income group average: 51.29

Country performance: 50.94

Missing rate in GOHI database: 17.00%

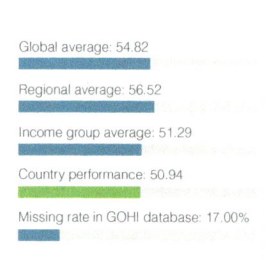

▼ AVERAGE PERFORMANCE BY GOHI

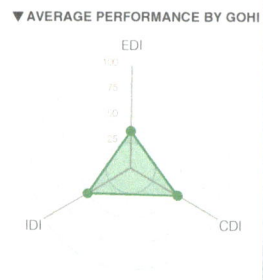

▼ AVERAGE PERFORMANCE BY CDI

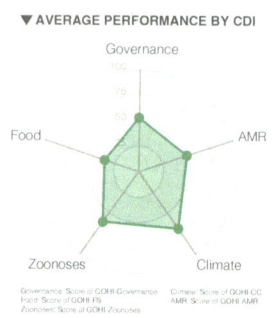

	Country Score	Global Average
A External drivers index	36.10	40.45
A1 Earth system	54.33	56.21
A1.1 Land	39.42	36.41
A1.2 Forest	30.30	43.43
A1.3 Water	43.61	58.09
A1.4 Air	85.19	71.93
A1.5 Natural disasters	66.60	64.65
A2 Institutional system	37.60	48.01
A2.1 Justice	48.00	57.89
A2.2 Governance	28.74	35.58
A3 Economical system	23.21	24.62
A3.1 Finance	29.78	34.35
A3.2 Work	39.65	38.58
A4 Sociological system	33.55	37.70
A4.1 Demographic	42.29	46.31
A4.2 Education	25.47	28.26
A4.3 Inequalities	34.19	40.28
A5 Technological system	31.83	37.72
A5.1 Transport	0.84	6.54
A5.2 Technology adoption	30.94	41.23
A5.3 Consumption and production	61.01	62.53
B Intrinsic drivers index	50.33	58.01
B1 Human health	62.73	72.35
B1.1 Health coverage	51.14	58.65
B1.2 Diseases burden	83.62	79.83
B1.3 Injury and violence	55.33	80.75
B2 Animal health and ecosystem diversity	55.97	56.58
B2.1 Animal epidemic disease	95.29	94.57
B2.2 Wildlife and marine life biodiversity	16.65	18.59
B3 Environmental health	33.80	46.87
B3.1 Air quality and climate change	44.67	53.72
B3.2 Environmental biodiversity	37.75	44.05
B3.3 Environmental resources	20.02	44.25

Scores are normalized (0-100, where 100 = most favorable)

	Country Score	Global Average
C Core drivers index	54.39	57.25
C1 Governance	52.80	56.51
C1.1 Participation	73.63	41.70
C1.3 Transparency	56.20	65.15
C1.4 Responsiveness	31.25	44.42
C1.5 Consensus oriented	94.68	86.45
C1.6 Equity and inclusiveness	54.30	73.61
C1.7 Effectiveness and efficiency	13.87	28.38
C1.8 Political support	45.66	55.89
C2 Zoonotic diseases	69.24	68.06
C2.1 Source of infection	53.49	69.22
C2.2 Route of transmission	68.40	59.30
C2.3 Targeted population	67.17	59.90
C2.4 Capacity building	75.06	72.85
C2.5 Case studies	91.47	85.89
C3 Food security	51.37	52.89
C3.1 Food demand and supply	57.39	59.53
C3.2 Food safety	74.78	69.36
C3.3 Nutrition	65.50	67.17
C3.4 Natural and social circumstances	50.24	51.54
C3.5 Government support and response	8.91	16.85
C4 Antimicrobial resistance	36.25	44.05
C4.1 AMR surveillance system	25.56	34.79
C4.2 AMR laboratory network and coordination capacity	50.09	55.57
C4.3 Antimicrobial control and optimization	27.92	48.76
C4.4 Improve awareness and understanding	43.75	48.09
C4.5 Antimicrobial resistance rate for important antibiotics	33.09	33.03
C5 Climate change	61.15	64.19
C5.1 Mitigation and adaptation capacity	21.71	28.24
C5.2 Climate change risks	81.43	80.87
C5.3 Health outcome	82.17	85.41

Honduras

Latin America & Caribbean | Lower middle income

 **Index Score 109**/160

Global average: 54.82

Regional average: 55.08

Income group average: 51.29

Country performance: 50.61

Missing rate in GOHI database: 24.60%

▼ AVERAGE PERFORMANCE BY GOHI

▼ AVERAGE PERFORMANCE BY CDI

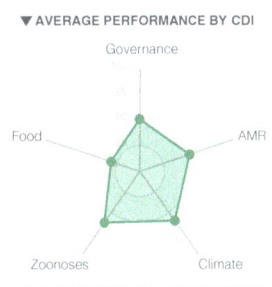

	Country Score	Global Average
A External drivers index	37.15	40.45
A1 Earth system	57.93	56.21
A1.1 Land	24.19	36.41
A1.2 Forest	35.75	43.43
A1.3 Water	67.21	58.09
A1.4 Air	84.49	71.93
A1.5 Natural disasters	66.65	64.65
A2 Institutional system	35.90	46.01
A2.1 Justice	49.42	57.89
A2.2 Governance	24.39	35.58
A3 Economical system	25.59	24.62
A3.1 Finance	37.83	34.35
A3.2 Work	37.37	38.58
A4 Sociological system	34.89	37.70
A4.1 Demographic	48.32	46.31
A4.2 Education	24.49	28.26
A4.3 Inequalities	33.23	40.28
A5 Technological system	31.46	37.72
A5.1 Transport	1.33	6.54
A5.2 Technology adoption	28.01	41.23
A5.3 Consumption and production	62.47	62.53
B Intrinsic drivers index	57.69	58.01
B1 Human health	66.04	72.35
B1.1 Health coverage	59.88	58.65
B1.2 Diseases burden	90.14	79.83
B1.3 Injury and violence	50.10	80.75
B2 Animal health and ecosystem diversity	60.86	56.58
B2.1 Animal epidemic disease	95.32	94.57
B2.2 Wildlife and marine life biodiversity	26.40	18.59
B3 Environmental health	47.91	46.87
B3.1 Air quality and climate change	52.51	53.72
B3.2 Environmental biodiversity	54.72	44.05
B3.3 Environmental resources	37.95	44.25

	Country Score	Global Average
C Core drivers index	51.92	57.25
C1 Governance	51.28	56.51
C1.1 Participation	36.87	41.70
C1.3 Transparency	61.20	65.15
C1.4 Responsiveness	52.05	44.42
C1.5 Consensus oriented	99.48	86.45
C1.6 Equity and inclusiveness	51.00	73.61
C1.7 Effectiveness and efficiency	11.47	28.38
C1.8 Political support	46.91	55.89
C2 Zoonotic diseases	60.22	68.06
C2.1 Source of infection	66.58	69.22
C2.2 Route of transmission	35.17	59.30
C2.3 Targeted population	48.65	59.90
C2.4 Capacity building	76.23	72.85
C2.5 Case studies	89.04	85.89
C3 Food security	53.51	52.89
C3.1 Food demand and supply	51.96	59.53
C3.2 Food safety	82.47	69.36
C3.3 Nutrition	69.39	67.17
C3.4 Natural and social circumstances	50.33	51.54
C3.5 Government support and response	13.39	16.85
C4 Antimicrobial resistance	30.83	44.05
C4.1 AMR surveillance system	20.36	34.79
C4.2 AMR laboratory network and coordinati on capacity	37.10	55.57
C4.3 Antimicrobial control and optimization	32.74	48.76
C4.4 Improve awareness and understanding	25.00	48.09
C4.5 Antimicrobial resistance rate for important antibiotics	38.96	33.03
C5 Climate change	62.37	64.19
C5.1 Mitigation and adaptation capacity	14.95	28.24
C5.2 Climate change risks	84.19	80.87
C5.3 Health outcome	89.85	85.41

Scores are normalized (0-100, where 100 = most favorable)

Eswatini
Sub-Saharan Africa | Lower middle income

50.51 **Index Score 110**/160

Global average: 54.82

Regional average: 48.03

Income group average: 51.29

Country performance: 50.51

Missing rate in GOHI database: 28.30%

▼ AVERAGE PERFORMANCE BY GOHI

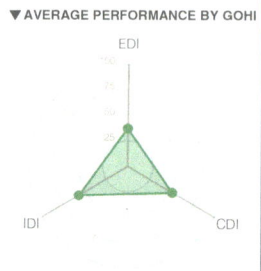

▼ AVERAGE PERFORMANCE BY CDI

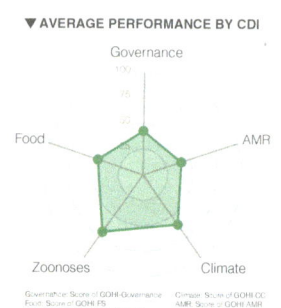

Governance Score of GOHI-Governance   Climate Score of GOHI-CC
Food: Score of GOHI-FS   AMR Score of GOHI-AMR
Zoonotes: Score of GOHI-Zoonoses

	Country Score	Global Average
A External drivers index	37.02	40.45
A1 Earth system	53.35	56.21
A1.1 Land	21.79	36.41
A1.2 Forest	48.52	43.43
A1.3 Water	47.04	58.09
A1.4 Air	77.61	71.93
A1.5 Natural disasters	66.67	64.65
A2 Institutional system	40.49	46.01
A2.1 Justice	55.77	57.89
A2.2 Governance	27.47	35.58
A3 Economical system	20.98	24.62
A3.1 Finance	27.56	34.35
A3.2 Work	35.03	38.58
A4 Sociological system	36.58	37.70
A4.1 Demographic	52.98	46.31
A4.2 Education	23.58	28.26
A4.3 Inequalities	34.96	40.28
A5 Technological system	33.68	37.72
A5.1 Transport	6.72	6.54
A5.2 Technology adoption	26.59	41.23
A5.3 Consumption and production	65.57	62.53
B Intrinsic drivers index	57.40	59.01
B1 Human health	53.05	72.35
B1.1 Health coverage	34.47	58.65
B1.2 Diseases burden	60.80	79.83
B1.3 Injury and violence	65.48	80.75
B2 Animal health and ecosystem diversity	56.01	56.58
B2.1 Animal epidemic disease	90.96	94.57
B2.2 Wildlife and marine life biodiversity	21.05	18.59
B3 Environmental health	64.89	46.87
B3.1 Air quality and climate change	68.95	53.72
B3.2 Environmental biodiversity	50.60	44.05
B3.3 Environmental resources	77.10	44.25

Scores are normalized (0-100, where 100 = most favorable)

	Country Score	Global Average
C Core drivers index	51.87	57.25
C1 Governance	42.96	56.51
C1.1 Participation	17.92	41.70
C1.3 Transparency	47.20	65.15
C1.4 Responsiveness	35.40	44.42
C1.5 Consensus oriented	88.26	86.45
C1.6 Equity and inclusiveness	53.12	73.61
C1.7 Effectiveness and efficiency	10.60	28.38
C1.8 Political support	48.23	55.89
C2 Zoonotic diseases	60.38	68.06
C2.1 Source of infection	61.08	69.22
C2.2 Route of transmission	50.48	59.30
C2.3 Targeted population	39.34	59.90
C2.4 Capacity building	73.81	72.85
C2.5 Case studies	87.49	85.89
C3 Food security	40.72	52.89
C3.1 Food demand and supply	47.48	59.53
C3.2 Food safety	45.41	69.36
C3.3 Nutrition	52.89	67.17
C3.4 Natural and social circumstances	50.82	51.54
C3.5 Government support and response	6.99	16.85
C4 Antimicrobial resistance	48.10	44.05
C4.1 AMR surveillance system	40.50	34.79
C4.2 AMR laboratory network and coordination capacity	68.97	55.57
C4.3 Antimicrobial control and optimization	51.94	48.76
C4.4 Improve awareness and understanding	53.12	48.09
C4.5 Antimicrobial resistance rate for important antibiotics	25.97	33.03
C5 Climate change	69.56	64.19
C5.1 Mitigation and adaptation capacity	33.85	28.24
C5.2 Climate change risks	84.10	80.87
C5.3 Health outcome	92.85	85.41

Montenegro
Europe & Central Asia | Upper middle income

50.49 Index Score **111**/160

Global average: 54.82

Regional average: 60.26

Income group average: 54.54

Country performance: 50.49

Missing rate in GOHI database: 23.20%

▼ AVERAGE PERFORMANCE BY GOHI

EDI / IDI / CDI

▼ AVERAGE PERFORMANCE BY CDI

Governance / Food / AMR / Zoonoses / Climate

	Country Score	Global Average
A External drivers index	41.81	40.45
A1 Earth system	59.78	56.21
A1.1 Land	24.27	36.41
A1.2 Forest	62.05	43.43
A1.3 Water	64.23	58.09
A1.4 Air	77.10	71.93
A1.5 Natural disasters	63.84	64.65
A2 Institutional system	47.02	46.01
A2.1 Justice	59.24	57.89
A2.2 Governance	36.61	35.58
A3 Economical system	21.59	24.62
A3.1 Finance	28.22	34.35
A3.2 Work	36.22	38.58
A4 Sociological system	36.31	37.70
A4.1 Demographic	38.95	46.31
A4.2 Education	25.93	28.26
A4.3 Inequalities	46.90	40.28
A5 Technological system	44.36	37.72
A5.1 Transport	8.07	6.54
A5.2 Technology adoption	61.40	41.23
A5.3 Consumption and production	59.90	62.53
B Intrinsic drivers index	52.31	58.01
B1 Human health	74.10	72.35
B1.1 Health coverage	62.02	58.65
B1.2 Diseases burden	70.58	79.83
B1.3 Injury and violence	91.94	80.75
B2 Animal health and ecosystem diversity	53.09	56.58
B2.1 Animal epidemic disease	88.97	94.57
B2.2 Wildlife and marine life biodiversity	17.20	18.59
B3 Environmental health	31.33	46.87
B3.1 Air quality and climate change	10.02	53.72
B3.2 Environmental biodiversity	49.45	44.05
B3.3 Environmental resources	25.48	44.25

	Country Score	Global Average
C Core drivers index	51.99	57.25
C1 Governance	52.37	56.51
C1.1 Participation	14.61	41.70
C1.3 Transparency	67.00	65.15
C1.4 Responsiveness	35.40	44.42
C1.5 Consensus oriented	78.19	86.45
C1.6 Equity and inclusiveness	81.74	73.61
C1.7 Effectiveness and efficiency	33.40	28.38
C1.8 Political support	56.26	55.89
C2 Zoonotic diseases	63.56	68.06
C2.1 Source of infection	69.84	69.22
C2.2 Route of transmission	36.17	59.30
C2.3 Targeted population	74.61	59.90
C2.4 Capacity building	67.98	72.85
C2.5 Case studies	80.69	85.89
C3 Food security	50.34	52.89
C3.1 Food demand and supply	66.35	59.53
C3.2 Food safety	63.09	69.36
C3.3 Nutrition	65.10	67.17
C3.4 Natural and social circumstances	43.07	51.54
C3.5 Government support and response	14.08	16.85
C4 Antimicrobial resistance	33.87	44.05
C4.1 AMR surveillance system	18.15	34.79
C4.2 AMR laboratory network and coordination on capacity	42.57	55.57
C4.3 Antimicrobial control and optimization	53.61	48.76
C4.4 Improve awareness and understanding	31.25	48.09
C4.5 Antimicrobial resistance rate for important antibiotics	23.76	33.03
C5 Climate change	58.47	64.19
C5.1 Mitigation and adaptation capacity	16.99	28.24
C5.2 Climate change risks	80.02	80.87
C5.3 Health outcome	80.17	85.41

Scores are normalized (0-100, where 100 = most favorable)

Tajikistan

Europe & Central Asia | **Lower middle income**

50.39　**Index Score 112**/160

Global average: 54.82

Regional average: 60.26

Income group average: 51.29

Country performance: 50.39

Missing rate in GOHI database: 27.50%

▼ AVERAGE PERFORMANCE BY GOHI

▼ AVERAGE PERFORMANCE BY CDI

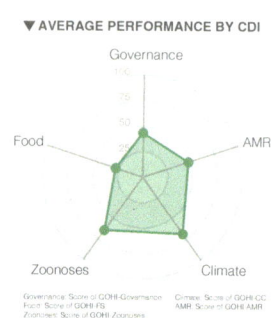

Governance Score of GOHI-Governance　　Climate: Score of GOHI-CC
Food: Score of GOHI-FS　　　　　　　　AMR: Score of GOHI-AMR
Zoonoses: Score of GOHI-Zoonoses

	Country Score	Global Average
A External drivers index	36.45	40.45
A1 Earth system	47.95	56.21
A1.1 Land	6.58	36.41
A1.2 Forest	28.91	43.43
A1.3 Water	56.61	58.09
A1.4 Air	72.22	71.93
A1.5 Natural disasters	66.45	64.65
A2 Institutional system	34.47	46.01
A2.1 Justice	49.96	57.89
A2.2 Governance	21.28	35.58
A3 Economical system	30.89	24.62
A3.1 Finance	50.91	34.35
A3.2 Work	38.47	38.58
A4 Sociological system	34.73	37.70
A4.1 Demographic	43.12	46.31
A4.2 Education	23.74	28.26
A4.3 Inequalities	39.58	40.28
A5 Technological system	34.21	37.72
A5.1 Transport	0.50	6.54
A5.2 Technology adoption	30.72	41.23
A5.3 Consumption and production	68.53	62.53
B Intrinsic drivers index	61.40	56.01
B1 Human health	75.15	72.35
B1.1 Health coverage	56.13	58.65
B1.2 Diseases burden	86.72	79.83
B1.3 Injury and violence	84.89	80.75
B2 Animal health and ecosystem diversity	52.05	56.58
B2.1 Animal epidemic disease	96.86	94.57
B2.2 Wildlife and marine life biodiversity	7.23	18.59
B3 Environmental health	58.85	46.87
B3.1 Air quality and climate change	73.10	53.72
B3.2 Environmental biodiversity	43.05	44.05
B3.3 Environmental resources	62.18	44.25

	Country Score	Global Average
C Core drivers index	50.87	57.25
C1 Governance	43.34	56.51
C1.1 Participation	13.56	41.70
C1.3 Transparency	55.80	65.15
C1.4 Responsiveness	35.40	44.42
C1.5 Consensus oriented	54.81	86.45
C1.6 Equity and inclusiveness	85.13	73.61
C1.7 Effectiveness and efficiency	29.40	28.38
C1.8 Political support	29.26	55.89
C2 Zoonotic diseases	69.05	68.06
C2.1 Source of infection	80.19	69.22
C2.2 Route of transmission	42.80	59.30
C2.3 Targeted population	72.24	59.90
C2.4 Capacity building	73.55	72.85
C2.5 Case studies	86.50	85.89
C3 Food security	48.15	52.89
C3.1 Food demand and supply	52.37	59.53
C3.2 Food safety	69.06	69.36
C3.3 Nutrition	59.95	67.17
C3.4 Natural and social circumstances	46.56	51.54
C3.5 Government support and response	12.82	16.85
C4 Antimicrobial resistance	28.55	44.05
C4.1 AMR surveillance system	18.91	34.79
C4.2 AMR laboratory network and coordination capacity	47.18	55.57
C4.3 Antimicrobial control and optimization	15.44	48.76
C4.4 Improve awareness and understanding	42.19	48.09
C4.5 Antimicrobial resistance rate for important antibiotics	19.02	33.03
C5 Climate change	64.73	64.19
C5.1 Mitigation and adaptation capacity	24.30	28.24
C5.2 Climate change risks	76.88	80.87
C5.3 Health outcome	94.96	85.41

Scores are normalized (0-100, where 100 = most favorable)

Bolivia

Latin America & Caribbean | Lower middle income

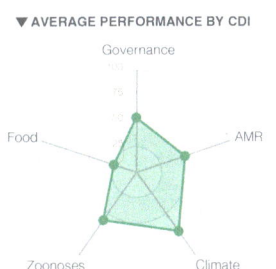

50.28 | Index Score **113**/160

▼ AVERAGE PERFORMANCE BY GOHI

▼ AVERAGE PERFORMANCE BY CDI

Global average: 54.82

Regional average: 55.08

Income group average: 51.29

Country performance: 50.28

Missing rate in GOHI database: 27.20%

	Country Score	Global Average
A External drivers index	**38.06**	**40.45**
A1 Earth system	**61.69**	**56.21**
A1.1 Land	54.79	36.41
A1.2 Forest	61.84	43.43
A1.3 Water	46.09	58.09
A1.4 Air	79.60	71.93
A1.5 Natural disasters	63.39	64.65
A2 Institutional system	**30.44**	**46.01**
A2.1 Justice	41.16	57.89
A2.2 Governance	21.32	35.58
A3 Economical system	**25.53**	**24.62**
A3.1 Finance	33.76	34.35
A3.2 Work	42.32	38.58
A4 Sociological system	**38.86**	**37.70**
A4.1 Demographic	54.09	46.31
A4.2 Education	27.00	28.26
A4.3 Inequalities	37.08	40.28
A5 Technological system	**33.78**	**37.72**
A5.1 Transport	0.74	6.54
A5.2 Technology adoption	30.40	41.23
A5.3 Consumption and production	67.40	62.53
B Intrinsic drivers index	**52.87**	**58.01**
B1 Human health	**72.84**	**72.35**
B1.1 Health coverage	58.81	58.65
B1.2 Diseases burden	84.29	79.83
B1.3 Injury and violence	77.62	80.75
B2 Animal health and ecosystem diversity	**53.73**	**56.58**
B2.1 Animal epidemic disease	93.90	94.57
B2.2 Wildlife and marine life biodiversity	13.57	18.59
B3 Environmental health	**33.64**	**46.87**
B3.1 Air quality and climate change	22.37	53.72
B3.2 Environmental biodiversity	47.80	44.05
B3.3 Environmental resources	31.78	44.25

	Country Score	Global Average
C Core drivers index	**52.38**	**57.25**
C1 Governance	**53.69**	**56.51**
C1.1 Participation	48.72	41.70
C1.3 Transparency	62.70	65.15
C1.4 Responsiveness	35.40	44.42
C1.5 Consensus oriented	97.82	86.45
C1.6 Equity and inclusiveness	65.54	73.61
C1.7 Effectiveness and efficiency	20.13	28.38
C1.8 Political support	45.53	55.89
C2 Zoonotic diseases	**71.63**	**68.06**
C2.1 Source of infection	74.83	69.22
C2.2 Route of transmission	54.11	59.30
C2.3 Targeted population	75.74	59.90
C2.4 Capacity building	74.71	72.85
C2.5 Case studies	87.32	85.89
C3 Food security	**51.64**	**52.89**
C3.1 Food demand and supply	58.92	59.53
C3.2 Food safety	67.50	69.36
C3.3 Nutrition	71.20	67.17
C3.4 Natural and social circumstances	53.76	51.54
C3.5 Government support and response	6.82	16.85
C4 Antimicrobial resistance	**24.06**	**44.05**
C4.1 AMR surveillance system	23.81	34.79
C4.2 AMR laboratory network and coordinati on capacity	31.54	55.57
C4.3 Antimicrobial control and optimization	27.88	48.76
C4.4 Improve awareness and understanding	7.81	48.09
C4.5 Antimicrobial resistance rate for important antibiotics	29.26	33.03
C5 Climate change	**58.24**	**64.19**
C5.1 Mitigation and adaptation capacity	12.99	28.24
C5.2 Climate change risks	82.45	80.87
C5.3 Health outcome	81.05	85.41

Scores are normalized (0-100, where 100 = most favorable)

Senegal
Sub-Saharan Africa | **Lower middle income**

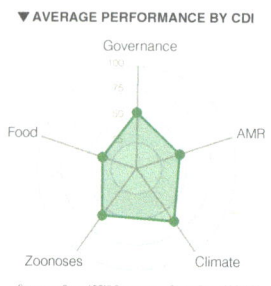 **Index Score 114**/160

50.17

Global average: 54.82

Regional average: 48.03

Income group average: 51.29

Country performance: 50.17

Missing rate in GOHI database: 22.10%

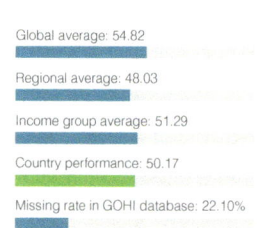
▼ AVERAGE PERFORMANCE BY GOHI

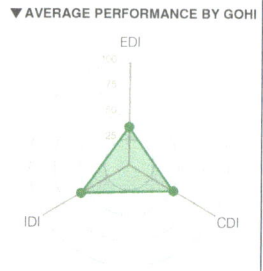
▼ AVERAGE PERFORMANCE BY CDI

Governance: Score of GOHI-Governance   Climate: Score of GOHI-CC
Food: Score of GOHI-FS   AMR: Score of GOHI-AMR
Zoonoses: Score of GOHI-Zoonoses

	Country Score	Global Average
A External drivers index	36.98	40.45
A1 Earth system	48.00	56.21
A1.1 Land	38.12	36.41
A1.2 Forest	27.20	43.43
A1.3 Water	54.60	58.09
A1.4 Air	55.32	71.93
A1.5 Natural disasters	59.01	64.65
A2 Institutional system	46.08	46.01
A2.1 Justice	60.39	57.89
A2.2 Governance	33.89	35.58
A3 Economical system	24.61	24.62
A3.1 Finance	33.92	34.35
A3.2 Work	39.06	38.58
A4 Sociological system	34.64	37.70
A4.1 Demographic	48.76	46.31
A4.2 Education	24.75	28.26
A4.3 Inequalities	31.51	40.28
A5 Technological system	31.56	37.72
A5.1 Transport	1.85	6.54
A5.2 Technology adoption	26.62	41.23
A5.3 Consumption and production	63.73	62.53
B Intrinsic drivers index	56.14	58.01
B1 Human health	61.92	72.35
B1.1 Health coverage	40.31	58.65
B1.2 Diseases burden	82.78	79.83
B1.3 Injury and violence	64.55	80.75
B2 Animal health and ecosystem diversity	54.92	56.58
B2.1 Animal epidemic disease	94.89	94.57
B2.2 Wildlife and marine life biodiversity	14.95	18.59
B3 Environmental health	53.28	46.87
B3.1 Air quality and climate change	46.89	53.72
B3.2 Environmental biodiversity	64.65	44.05
B3.3 Environmental resources	49.92	44.25

Scores are normalized (0-100, where 100 = most favorable)

	Country Score	Global Average
C Core drivers index	51.69	57.25
C1 Governance	54.96	56.51
C1.1 Participation	33.35	41.70
C1.3 Transparency	63.60	65.15
C1.4 Responsiveness	58.35	44.42
C1.5 Consensus oriented	92.29	86.45
C1.6 Equity and inclusiveness	63.53	73.61
C1.7 Effectiveness and efficiency	17.07	28.38
C1.8 Political support	56.52	55.89
C2 Zoonotic diseases	64.14	68.06
C2.1 Source of infection	64.85	69.22
C2.2 Route of transmission	57.62	59.30
C2.3 Targeted population	46.34	59.90
C2.4 Capacity building	72.56	72.85
C2.5 Case studies	87.08	85.89
C3 Food security	45.27	52.89
C3.1 Food demand and supply	42.26	59.53
C3.2 Food safety	59.13	69.36
C3.3 Nutrition	54.87	67.17
C3.4 Natural and social circumstances	47.39	51.54
C3.5 Government support and response	22.68	16.85
C4 Antimicrobial resistance	35.58	44.05
C4.1 AMR surveillance system	33.00	34.79
C4.2 AMR laboratory network and coordinati on capacity	45.48	55.57
C4.3 Antimicrobial control and optimization	18.36	48.76
C4.4 Improve awareness and understanding	42.19	48.09
C4.5 Antimicrobial resistance rate for important antibiotics	38.86	33.03
C5 Climate change	57.33	64.19
C5.1 Mitigation and adaptation capacity	18.29	28.24
C5.2 Climate change risks	71.57	80.87
C5.3 Health outcome	83.87	85.41

Iraq
Middle East & North Africa | **Upper middle income**

50.13 **Index Score 115**/160

Global average: 54.82

Regional average: 53.57

Income group average: 54.54

Country performance: 50.13

Missing rate in GOHI database: 18.50%

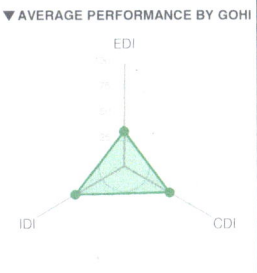

▼ AVERAGE PERFORMANCE BY GOHI

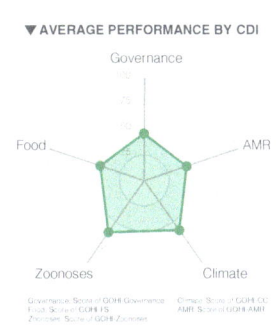

▼ AVERAGE PERFORMANCE BY CDI

	Country Score	Global Average
A External drivers index	33.97	40.45
A1 Earth system	42.85	56.21
A1.1 Land	30.66	36.41
A1.2 Forest	26.68	43.43
A1.3 Water	40.95	58.09
A1.4 Air	57.95	71.93
A1.5 Natural disasters	53.35	64.65
A2 Institutional system	33.47	46.01
A2.1 Justice	50.77	57.89
A2.2 Governance	18.73	35.58
A3 Economical system	22.40	24.62
A3.1 Finance	34.18	34.35
A3.2 Work	31.37	38.58
A4 Sociological system	36.97	37.70
A4.1 Demographic	49.99	46.31
A4.2 Education	26.52	28.26
A4.3 Inequalities	35.84	40.28
A5 Technological system	34.18	37.72
A5.1 Transport	0.19	6.54
A5.2 Technology adoption	27.98	41.23
A5.3 Consumption and production	71.54	62.53
B Intrinsic drivers index	56.27	58.01
B1 Human health	72.91	72.35
B1.1 Health coverage	51.37	58.65
B1.2 Diseases burden	91.64	79.83
B1.3 Injury and violence	77.91	80.75
B2 Animal health and ecosystem diversity	58.35	56.58
B2.1 Animal epidemic disease	93.62	94.57
B2.2 Wildlife and marine life biodiversity	23.08	18.59
B3 Environmental health	39.26	46.87
B3.1 Air quality and climate change	31.35	53.72
B3.2 Environmental biodiversity	47.15	44.05
B3.3 Environmental resources	40.48	44.25

	Country Score	Global Average
C Core drivers index	52.26	57.25
C1 Governance	46.08	56.51
C1.1 Participation	18.34	41.70
C1.3 Transparency	34.80	65.15
C1.4 Responsiveness	35.40	44.42
C1.5 Consensus oriented	94.94	86.45
C1.6 Equity and inclusiveness	67.45	73.61
C1.7 Effectiveness and efficiency	8.07	28.38
C1.8 Political support	63.59	55.89
C2 Zoonotic diseases	60.55	68.06
C2.1 Source of infection	72.03	69.22
C2.2 Route of transmission	33.00	59.30
C2.3 Targeted population	49.99	59.90
C2.4 Capacity building	76.87	72.85
C2.5 Case studies	83.88	85.89
C3 Food security	45.65	52.89
C3.1 Food demand and supply	50.46	59.53
C3.2 Food safety	56.92	69.36
C3.3 Nutrition	56.87	67.17
C3.4 Natural and social circumstances	54.86	51.54
C3.5 Government support and response	9.13	16.85
C4 Antimicrobial resistance	47.23	44.05
C4.1 AMR surveillance system	36.51	34.79
C4.2 AMR laboratory network and coordination capacity	63.24	55.57
C4.3 Antimicrobial control and optimization	54.79	48.76
C4.4 Improve awareness and understanding	57.81	48.09
C4.5 Antimicrobial resistance rate for important antibiotics	23.78	33.03
C5 Climate change	62.98	64.19
C5.1 Mitigation and adaptation capacity	35.51	28.24
C5.2 Climate change risks	78.80	80.87
C5.3 Health outcome	76.53	85.41

Scores are normalized (0-100, where 100 = most favorable)

Trinidad and Tobago
Latin America & Caribbean | High income

Index Score 116/160

50.04

Global average: 54.82

Regional average: 55.08

Income group average: 61.66

Country performance: 50.04

Missing rate in GOHI database: 23.90%

▼ AVERAGE PERFORMANCE BY GOHI

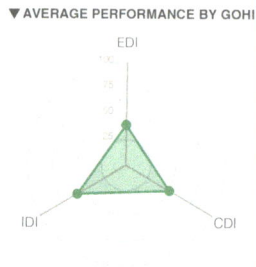

▼ AVERAGE PERFORMANCE BY CDI

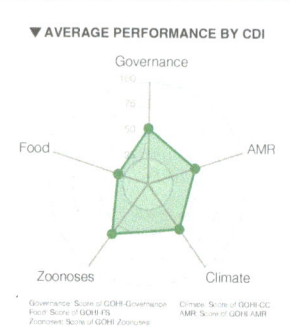

Governance: Score of GOHI-Governance   Climate: Score of GOHI-CC
Food: Score of GOHI-FS   AMR: Score of GOHI-AMR
Zoonoses: Score of GOHI-Zoonoses

	Country Score	Global Average
A External drivers index	39.37	40.45
A1 Earth system	53.76	56.21
A1.1 Land	23.72	36.41
A1.2 Forest	50.78	43.43
A1.3 Water	65.21	58.09
A1.4 Air	58.98	71.93
A1.5 Natural disasters	64.11	64.65
A2 Institutional system	48.65	46.01
A2.1 Justice	61.71	57.89
A2.2 Governance	37.89	35.58
A3 Economical system	26.90	24.62
A3.1 Finance	41.29	34.35
A3.2 Work	37.37	38.58
A4 Sociological system	35.01	37.70
A4.1 Demographic	43.00	46.31
A4.2 Education	24.33	28.26
A4.3 Inequalities	39.91	40.28
A5 Technological system	32.31	37.72
A5.1 Transport	3.59	6.54
A5.2 Technology adoption	41.59	41.23
A5.3 Consumption and production	48.95	62.53
B Intrinsic drivers index	57.27	58.01
B1 Human health	67.00	72.35
B1.1 Health coverage	62.61	58.65
B1.2 Diseases burden	78.11	79.83
B1.3 Injury and violence	62.31	80.75
B2 Animal health and ecosystem diversity	56.77	56.58
B2.1 Animal epidemic disease	95.30	94.57
B2.2 Wildlife and marine life biodiversity	18.25	18.59
B3 Environmental health	49.76	46.87
B3.1 Air quality and climate change	70.95	53.72
B3.2 Environmental biodiversity	31.62	44.05
B3.3 Environmental resources	48.21	44.25

Scores are normalized (0-100, where 100 = most favorable)

	Country Score	Global Average
C Core drivers index	50.70	57.25
C1 Governance	54.53	56.51
C1.1 Participation	46.92	41.70
C1.3 Transparency	42.10	65.15
C1.4 Responsiveness	58.30	44.42
C1.5 Consensus oriented	96.55	86.45
C1.6 Equity and inclusiveness	70.56	73.61
C1.7 Effectiveness and efficiency	17.93	28.38
C1.8 Political support	49.37	55.89
C2 Zoonotic diseases	54.84	68.06
C2.1 Source of infection	66.66	69.22
C2.2 Route of transmission	37.85	59.30
C2.3 Targeted population	25.87	59.90
C2.4 Capacity building	68.96	72.85
C2.5 Case studies	85.67	85.89
C3 Food security	50.22	52.89
C3.1 Food demand and supply	63.38	59.53
C3.2 Food safety	61.29	69.36
C3.3 Nutrition	68.87	67.17
C3.4 Natural and social circumstances	45.30	51.54
C3.5 Government support and response	12.27	16.85
C4 Antimicrobial resistance	31.52	44.05
C4.1 AMR surveillance system	11.10	34.79
C4.2 AMR laboratory network and coordination on capacity	33.59	55.57
C4.3 Antimicrobial control and optimization	41.25	48.76
C4.4 Improve awareness and understanding	31.25	48.09
C4.5 Antimicrobial resistance rate for important antibiotics	40.43	33.03
C5 Climate change	60.96	64.19
C5.1 Mitigation and adaptation capacity	24.54	28.24
C5.2 Climate change risks	74.47	80.87
C5.3 Health outcome	85.72	85.41

Fiji
East Asia & Pacific | Upper middle income

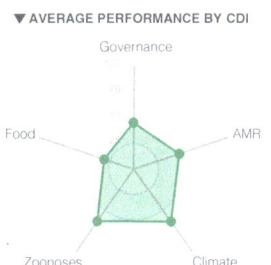

49.99 **Index Score 117** /160

▼ AVERAGE PERFORMANCE BY GOHI

▼ AVERAGE PERFORMANCE BY CDI

Global average: 54.82

Regional average: 56.52

Income group average: 54.54

Country performance: 49.99

Missing rate in GOHI database: 31.50%

	Country Score	Global Average
A External drivers index	41.81	40.45
A1 Earth system	63.93	56.21
A1.1 Land	34.86	36.41
A1.2 Forest	57.58	43.43
A1.3 Water	67.11	58.09
A1.4 Air	90.23	71.93
A1.5 Natural disasters	59.29	64.65
A2 Institutional system	46.12	46.01
A2.1 Justice	55.00	57.89
A2.2 Governance	38.56	35.58
A3 Economical system	23.01	24.62
A3.1 Finance	29.55	34.35
A3.2 Work	39.29	38.58
A4 Sociological system	37.34	37.70
A4.1 Demographic	49.00	46.31
A4.2 Education	25.19	28.26
A4.3 Inequalities	39.98	40.28
A5 Technological system	38.65	37.72
A5.1 Transport	11.86	6.54
A5.2 Technology adoption	36.06	41.23
A5.3 Consumption and production	65.73	62.53
B Intrinsic drivers index	54.52	53.01
B1 Human health	67.48	72.35
B1.1 Health coverage	48.34	58.65
B1.2 Diseases burden	75.00	79.83
B1.3 Injury and violence	81.13	80.75
B2 Animal health and ecosystem diversity	61.88	56.58
B2.1 Animal epidemic disease	92.61	94.57
B2.2 Wildlife and marine life biodiversity	31.15	18.59
B3 Environmental health	35.87	46.87
B3.1 Air quality and climate change	47.63	53.72
B3.2 Environmental biodiversity	28.87	44.05
B3.3 Environmental resources	32.19	44.25

Scores are normalized (0-100, where 100 = most favorable)

	Country Score	Global Average
C Core drivers index	50.73	57.25
C1 Governance	45.55	56.51
C1.1 Participation	13.54	41.70
C1.3 Transparency	57.60	65.15
C1.4 Responsiveness	35.40	44.42
C1.5 Consensus oriented	63.64	86.45
C1.6 Equity and inclusiveness	57.15	73.61
C1.7 Effectiveness and efficiency	37.47	28.38
C1.8 Political support	54.05	55.89
C2 Zoonotic diseases	63.87	68.06
C2.1 Source of infection	71.71	69.22
C2.2 Route of transmission	33.91	59.30
C2.3 Targeted population	64.13	59.90
C2.4 Capacity building	74.30	72.85
C2.5 Case studies	89.79	85.89
C3 Food security	48.75	52.89
C3.1 Food demand and supply	60.74	59.53
C3.2 Food safety	55.86	69.36
C3.3 Nutrition	70.33	67.17
C3.4 Natural and social circumstances	47.11	51.54
C3.5 Government support and response	9.69	16.85
C4 Antimicrobial resistance	31.39	44.05
C4.1 AMR surveillance system	26.65	34.79
C4.2 AMR laboratory network and coordination on capacity	28.36	55.57
C4.3 Antimicrobial control and optimization	29.78	48.76
C4.4 Improve awareness and understanding	48.44	48.09
C4.5 Antimicrobial resistance rate for important antibiotics	23.74	33.03
C5 Climate change	63.60	64.19
C5.1 Mitigation and adaptation capacity	20.14	28.24
C5.2 Climate change risks	88.90	80.87
C5.3 Health outcome	83.69	85.41

Barbados
Latin America & Caribbean | High income

49.83 Index **118**/160
       Score

▼ AVERAGE PERFORMANCE BY GOHI
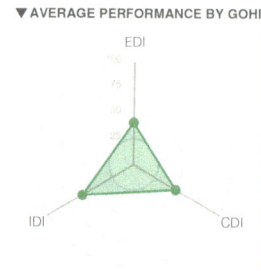

▼ AVERAGE PERFORMANCE BY CDI
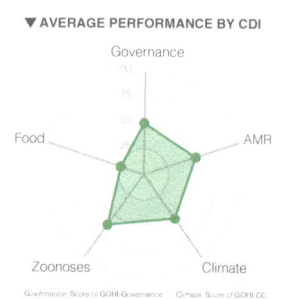

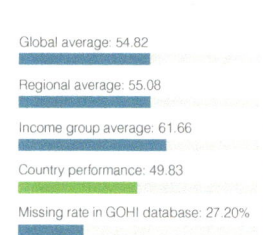

Global average: 54.82

Regional average: 55.08

Income group average: 61.66

Country performance: 49.83

Missing rate in GOHI database: 27.20%

	Country Score	Global Average
A External drivers index	41.09	40.45
A1 Earth system	55.44	56.21
A1.1 Land	22.04	36.41
A1.2 Forest	38.83	43.43
A1.3 Water	60.07	58.09
A1.4 Air	81.18	71.93
A1.5 Natural disasters	65.75	64.65
A2 Institutional system	52.04	46.01
A2.1 Justice	56.54	57.89
A2.2 Governance	48.20	35.58
A3 Economical system	28.18	24.62
A3.1 Finance	43.84	34.35
A3.2 Work	38.41	38.58
A4 Sociological system	33.52	37.70
A4.1 Demographic	34.06	46.31
A4.2 Education	25.72	28.26
A4.3 Inequalities	43.14	40.28
A5 Technological system	36.25	37.72
A5.1 Transport	4.42	6.54
A5.2 Technology adoption	42.68	41.23
A5.3 Consumption and production	58.65	62.53
B Intrinsic drivers index	60.21	58.01
B1 Human health	76.74	72.35
B1.1 Health coverage	68.11	58.65
B1.2 Diseases burden	80.15	79.83
B1.3 Injury and violence	84.29	80.75
B2 Animal health and ecosystem diversity	52.28	56.58
B2.1 Animal epidemic disease	89.41	94.57
B2.2 Wildlife and marine life biodiversity	15.15	18.59
B3 Environmental health	53.45	46.87
B3.1 Air quality and climate change	82.65	53.72
B3.2 Environmental biodiversity	24.75	44.05
B3.3 Environmental resources	54.56	44.25

	Country Score	Global Average
C Core drivers index	49.31	57.25
C1 Governance	50.37	56.51
C1.1 Participation	14.31	41.70
C1.3 Transparency	47.20	65.15
C1.4 Responsiveness	41.65	44.42
C1.5 Consensus oriented	87.76	86.45
C1.6 Equity and inclusiveness	83.58	73.61
C1.7 Effectiveness and efficiency	20.27	28.38
C1.8 Political support	57.79	55.89
C2 Zoonotic diseases	53.59	68.06
C2.1 Source of infection	71.05	69.22
C2.2 Route of transmission	37.90	59.30
C2.3 Targeted population	50.80	59.90
C2.4 Capacity building	27.62	72.85
C2.5 Case studies	84.76	85.89
C3 Food security	54.80	52.89
C3.1 Food demand and supply	70.11	59.53
C3.2 Food safety	60.44	69.36
C3.3 Nutrition	76.11	67.17
C3.4 Natural and social circumstances	46.73	51.54
C3.5 Government support and response	20.63	16.85
C4 Antimicrobial resistance	24.35	44.05
C4.1 AMR surveillance system	15.24	34.79
C4.2 AMR laboratory network and coordination capacity	32.29	55.57
C4.3 Antimicrobial control and optimization	26.54	48.76
C4.4 Improve awareness and understanding	21.88	48.09
C4.5 Antimicrobial resistance rate for important antibiotics	25.72	33.03
C5 Climate change	61.47	64.19
C5.1 Mitigation and adaptation capacity	23.53	28.24
C5.2 Climate change risks	82.35	80.87
C5.3 Health outcome	80.39	85.41

Scores are normalized (0-100, where 100 = most favorable)

Zambia
Sub-Saharan Africa | Low income

Index Score **119**/160

▼ AVERAGE PERFORMANCE BY GOHI

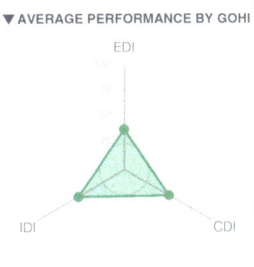

▼ AVERAGE PERFORMANCE BY CDI

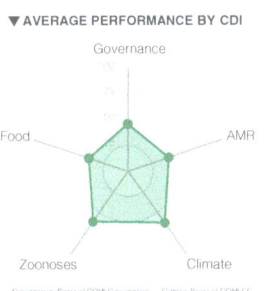

Global average: 54.82

Regional average: 48.03

Income group average: 46.63

Country performance: 49.73

Missing rate in GOHI database: 22.80%

	Country Score	Global Average
A External drivers index	39.49	40.45
A1 Earth system	59.35	56.21
A1.1 Land	39.72	36.41
A1.2 Forest	44.93	43.43
A1.3 Water	59.91	58.09
A1.4 Air	83.28	71.93
A1.5 Natural disasters	59.93	64.65
A2 Institutional system	41.76	46.01
A2.1 Justice	54.00	57.89
A2.2 Governance	31.34	35.58
A3 Economical system	22.42	24.62
A3.1 Finance	28.89	34.35
A3.2 Work	38.14	38.58
A4 Sociological system	39.24	37.70
A4.1 Demographic	55.89	46.31
A4.2 Education	29.38	28.26
A4.3 Inequalities	33.20	40.28
A5 Technological system	34.69	37.72
A5.1 Transport	23.00	6.54
A5.2 Technology adoption	21.73	41.23
A5.3 Consumption and production	58.68	62.53
B Intrinsic drivers index	53.61	58.01
B1 Human health	60.63	72.35
B1.1 Health coverage	38.55	58.65
B1.2 Diseases burden	78.05	79.83
B1.3 Injury and violence	66.53	80.75
B2 Animal health and ecosystem diversity	58.33	56.58
B2.1 Animal epidemic disease	98.66	94.57
B2.2 Wildlife and marine life biodiversity	18.00	18.59
B3 Environmental health	43.70	46.87
B3.1 Air quality and climate change	39.91	53.72
B3.2 Environmental biodiversity	50.42	44.05
B3.3 Environmental resources	42.09	44.25

	Country Score	Global Average
C Core drivers index	51.06	57.25
C1 Governance	46.40	56.51
C1.1 Participation	22.19	41.70
C1.3 Transparency	59.00	65.15
C1.4 Responsiveness	43.75	44.42
C1.5 Consensus oriented	96.06	86.45
C1.6 Equity and inclusiveness	47.47	73.61
C1.7 Effectiveness and efficiency	11.20	28.38
C1.8 Political support	45.16	55.89
C2 Zoonotic diseases	62.80	68.06
C2.1 Source of infection	51.75	69.22
C2.2 Route of transmission	50.51	59.30
C2.3 Targeted population	66.09	59.90
C2.4 Capacity building	69.83	72.85
C2.5 Case studies	88.72	85.89
C3 Food security	43.85	52.89
C3.1 Food demand and supply	51.72	59.53
C3.2 Food safety	54.90	69.36
C3.3 Nutrition	53.05	67.17
C3.4 Natural and social circumstances	50.05	51.54
C3.5 Government support and response	9.54	16.85
C4 Antimicrobial resistance	41.76	44.05
C4.1 AMR surveillance system	32.61	34.79
C4.2 AMR laboratory network and coordinati on capacity	55.87	55.57
C4.3 Antimicrobial control and optimization	47.05	48.76
C4.4 Improve awareness and understanding	35.94	48.09
C4.5 Antimicrobial resistance rate for important antibiotics	37.31	33.03
C5 Climate change	61.17	64.19
C5.1 Mitigation and adaptation capacity	13.10	28.24
C5.2 Climate change risks	76.44	80.87
C5.3 Health outcome	95.83	85.41

Scores are normalized (0-100, where 100 = most favorable)

Pakistan
South Asia | Lower middle income

49.7 Index Score 120/160

Global average: 54.82

Regional average: 51.61

Income group average: 51.29

Country performance: 49.70

Missing rate in GOHI database: 13.80%

▼ AVERAGE PERFORMANCE BY GOHI

▼ AVERAGE PERFORMANCE BY CDI

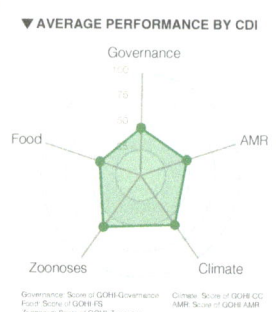

Governance: Score of GOHI-Governance   Climate: Score of GOHI-CC
Food: Score of GOHI-FS   AMR: Score of GOHI-AMR
Zoonoses: Score of GOHI-Zoonoses

	Country Score	Global Average
A External drivers index	34.82	40.45
A1 Earth system	41.81	56.21
A1.1 Land	24.91	36.41
A1.2 Forest	31.41	43.43
A1.3 Water	33.42	58.09
A1.4 Air	52.68	71.93
A1.5 Natural disasters	66.39	64.65
A2 Institutional system	35.92	46.01
A2.1 Justice	43.96	57.89
A2.2 Governance	29.07	35.58
A3 Economical system	25.38	24.62
A3.1 Finance	37.51	34.35
A3.2 Work	37.09	38.58
A4 Sociological system	37.41	37.70
A4.1 Demographic	52.62	46.31
A4.2 Education	27.44	28.26
A4.3 Inequalities	33.17	40.28
A5 Technological system	33.56	37.72
A5.1 Transport	0.11	6.54
A5.2 Technology adoption	23.52	41.23
A5.3 Consumption and production	74.41	62.53
B Intrinsic drivers index	53.34	58.01
B1 Human health	65.33	72.35
B1.1 Health coverage	35.49	58.65
B1.2 Diseases burden	76.29	79.83
B1.3 Injury and violence	86.20	80.75
B2 Animal health and ecosystem diversity	55.98	56.58
B2.1 Animal epidemic disease	92.66	94.57
B2.2 Wildlife and marine life biodiversity	19.30	18.59
B3 Environmental health	40.32	46.87
B3.1 Air quality and climate change	51.45	53.72
B3.2 Environmental biodiversity	33.50	44.05
B3.3 Environmental resources	37.24	44.25

	Country Score	Global Average
C Core drivers index	52.15	57.25
C1 Governance	46.35	56.51
C1.1 Participation	14.48	41.70
C1.3 Transparency	60.70	65.15
C1.4 Responsiveness	22.90	44.42
C1.5 Consensus oriented	96.27	86.45
C1.6 Equity and inclusiveness	64.68	73.61
C1.7 Effectiveness and efficiency	14.00	28.38
C1.8 Political support	51.44	55.89
C2 Zoonotic diseases	59.91	68.06
C2.1 Source of infection	58.26	69.22
C2.2 Route of transmission	61.27	59.30
C2.3 Targeted population	39.34	59.90
C2.4 Capacity building	69.99	72.85
C2.5 Case studies	75.02	85.89
C3 Food security	49.07	52.89
C3.1 Food demand and supply	59.25	59.53
C3.2 Food safety	50.32	69.36
C3.3 Nutrition	53.71	67.17
C3.4 Natural and social circumstances	54.06	51.54
C3.5 Government support and response	28.02	16.85
C4 Antimicrobial resistance	43.05	44.05
C4.1 AMR surveillance system	57.05	34.79
C4.2 AMR laboratory network and coordination capacity	65.12	55.57
C4.3 Antimicrobial control and optimization	27.94	48.76
C4.4 Improve awareness and understanding	42.19	48.09
C4.5 Antimicrobial resistance rate for important antibiotics	22.94	33.03
C5 Climate change	62.90	64.19
C5.1 Mitigation and adaptation capacity	30.17	28.24
C5.2 Climate change risks	79.51	80.87
C5.3 Health outcome	80.93	85.41

Scores are normalized (0-100, where 100 = most favorable)

Guyana

Latin America & Caribbean | **Upper middle income**

Index Score 121/160

Global average: 54.82

Regional average: 55.08

Income group average: 54.54

Country performance: 49.69

Missing rate in GOHI database: 27.20%

▼ AVERAGE PERFORMANCE BY GOHI

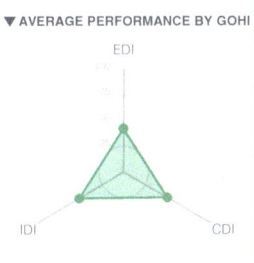

▼ AVERAGE PERFORMANCE BY CDI

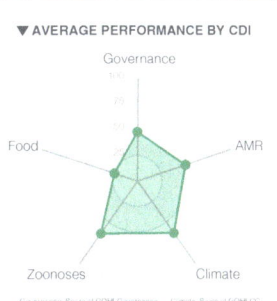

	Country Score	Global Average
A External drivers index	42.51	40.45
A1 Earth system	73.21	56.21
A1.1 Land	84.71	36.41
A1.2 Forest	66.67	43.43
A1.3 Water	66.52	58.09
A1.4 Air	80.05	71.93
A1.5 Natural disasters	63.13	64.65
A2 Institutional system	44.26	46.01
A2.1 Justice	58.40	57.89
A2.2 Governance	32.20	35.58
A3 Economical system	24.99	24.62
A3.1 Finance	36.53	34.35
A3.2 Work	37.03	38.58
A4 Sociological system	34.73	37.70
A4.1 Demographic	44.82	46.31
A4.2 Education	24.15	28.26
A4.3 Inequalities	37.11	40.28
A5 Technological system	35.37	37.72
A5.1 Transport	7.50	6.54
A5.2 Technology adoption	32.16	41.23
A5.3 Consumption and production	64.10	62.53
B Intrinsic drivers index	52.37	58.01
B1 Human health	61.42	72.35
B1.1 Health coverage	55.83	58.65
B1.2 Diseases burden	61.28	79.83
B1.3 Injury and violence	69.01	80.75
B2 Animal health and ecosystem diversity	52.93	56.58
B2.1 Animal epidemic disease	92.56	94.57
B2.2 Wildlife and marine life biodiversity	13.30	18.59
B3 Environmental health	44.34	46.87
B3.1 Air quality and climate change	59.70	53.72
B3.2 Environmental biodiversity	52.25	44.05
B3.3 Environmental resources	22.40	44.25

Scores are normalized (0-100, where 100 = most favorable)

	Country Score	Global Average
C Core drivers index	50.66	57.25
C1 Governance	48.29	56.51
C1.1 Participation	20.16	41.70
C1.3 Transparency	41.50	65.15
C1.4 Responsiveness	41.65	44.42
C1.5 Consensus oriented	96.15	86.45
C1.6 Equity and inclusiveness	71.05	73.61
C1.7 Effectiveness and efficiency	15.07	28.38
C1.8 Political support	50.44	55.89
C2 Zoonotic diseases	63.17	68.06
C2.1 Source of infection	57.79	69.22
C2.2 Route of transmission	49.61	59.30
C2.3 Targeted population	49.66	59.90
C2.4 Capacity building	84.22	72.85
C2.5 Case studies	88.01	85.89
C3 Food security	51.82	52.89
C3.1 Food demand and supply	42.71	59.53
C3.2 Food safety	71.87	69.36
C3.3 Nutrition	76.73	67.17
C3.4 Natural and social circumstances	58.11	51.54
C3.5 Government support and response	9.66	16.85
C4 Antimicrobial resistance	24.62	44.05
C4.1 AMR surveillance system	13.04	34.79
C4.2 AMR laboratory network and coordination on capacity	32.80	55.57
C4.3 Antimicrobial control and optimization	33.26	48.76
C4.4 Improve awareness and understanding	18.75	48.09
C4.5 Antimicrobial resistance rate for important antibiotics	25.25	33.03
C5 Climate change	63.79	64.19
C5.1 Mitigation and adaptation capacity	22.60	28.24
C5.2 Climate change risks	82.86	80.87
C5.3 Health outcome	87.83	85.41

Mali
Sub-Saharan Africa | Low income

49.49 Index Score **122**/160

Global average: 54.82

Regional average: 48.03

Income group average: 46.63

Country performance: 49.49

Missing rate in GOHI database: 21.70%

▼ AVERAGE PERFORMANCE BY GOHI

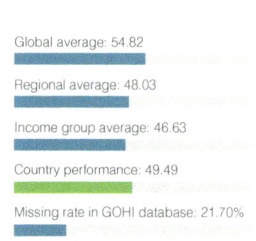

▼ AVERAGE PERFORMANCE BY CDI

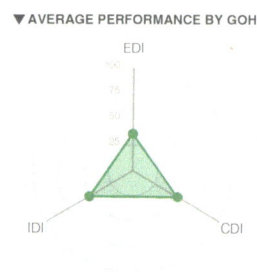

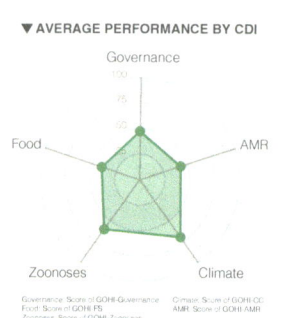

	Country Score	Global Average
A External drivers index	36.08	40.45
A1 Earth system	50.36	56.21
A1.1 Land	50.49	36.41
A1.2 Forest	34.67	43.43
A1.3 Water	50.36	58.09
A1.4 Air	50.82	71.93
A1.5 Natural disasters	63.24	64.65
A2 Institutional system	38.19	46.01
A2.1 Justice	50.72	57.89
A2.2 Governance	23.82	35.58
A3 Economical system	25.50	24.62
A3.1 Finance	36.62	34.35
A3.2 Work	38.62	38.58
A4 Sociological system	36.10	37.70
A4.1 Demographic	60.49	46.31
A4.2 Education	21.09	26.26
A4.3 Inequalities	28.01	40.28
A5 Technological system	32.24	37.72
A5.1 Transport	8.87	6.54
A5.2 Technology adoption	22.31	41.23
A5.3 Consumption and production	63.77	62.53
B Intrinsic drivers index	51.05	58.01
B1 Human health	52.38	72.35
B1.1 Health coverage	23.21	58.65
B1.2 Diseases burden	65.46	79.83
B1.3 Injury and violence	70.07	80.75
B2 Animal health and ecosystem diversity	50.77	56.58
B2.1 Animal epidemic disease	95.12	94.57
B2.2 Wildlife and marine life biodiversity	6.43	18.59
B3 Environmental health	51.53	46.87
B3.1 Air quality and climate change	67.04	53.72
B3.2 Environmental biodiversity	55.65	44.05
B3.3 Environmental resources	33.46	44.25

Scores are normalized (0-100, where 100 = most favorable)

	Country Score	Global Average
C Core drivers index	52.11	57.25
C1 Governance	47.58	56.51
C1.1 Participation	15.39	41.70
C1.3 Transparency	51.90	65.15
C1.4 Responsiveness	41.65	44.42
C1.5 Consensus oriented	94.58	86.45
C1.6 Equity and inclusiveness	58.92	73.61
C1.7 Effectiveness and efficiency	8.53	28.38
C1.8 Political support	62.06	55.89
C2 Zoonotic diseases	69.53	68.06
C2.1 Source of infection	67.18	69.22
C2.2 Route of transmission	65.47	59.30
C2.3 Targeted population	61.71	59.90
C2.4 Capacity building	73.13	72.85
C2.5 Case studies	85.89	85.89
C3 Food security	42.99	52.89
C3.1 Food demand and supply	36.82	59.53
C3.2 Food safety	71.74	69.36
C3.3 Nutrition	59.95	67.17
C3.4 Natural and social circumstances	33.51	51.54
C3.5 Government support and response	12.94	16.85
C4 Antimicrobial resistance	40.13	44.05
C4.1 AMR surveillance system	35.30	34.79
C4.2 AMR laboratory network and coordination capacity	68.45	55.57
C4.3 Antimicrobial control and optimization	35.63	48.76
C4.4 Improve awareness and understanding	28.12	48.09
C4.5 Antimicrobial resistance rate for important antibiotics	33.16	33.03
C5 Climate change	60.50	64.19
C5.1 Mitigation and adaptation capacity	24.94	28.24
C5.2 Climate change risks	74.74	80.87
C5.3 Health outcome	83.65	85.41

Burkina Faso

Sub-Saharan Africa | Low income

Index Score **123**/160

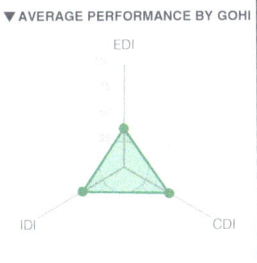

▼ AVERAGE PERFORMANCE BY GOHI

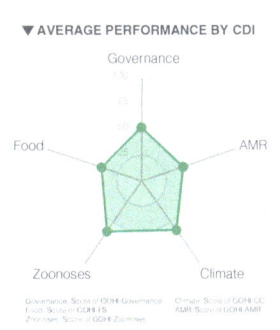

▼ AVERAGE PERFORMANCE BY CDI

Global average: 54.82

Regional average: 48.03

Income group average: 46.63

Country performance: 49.49

Missing rate in GOHI database: 20.70%

	Country Score	Global Average
A External drivers index	37.77	40.45
A1 Earth system	53.09	56.21
A1.1 Land	43.96	36.41
A1.2 Forest	30.98	43.43
A1.3 Water	63.83	58.09
A1.4 Air	56.47	71.93
A1.5 Natural disasters	63.84	64.65
A2 Institutional system	40.54	46.01
A2.1 Justice	55.20	57.89
A2.2 Governance	28.05	35.58
A3 Economical system	23.83	24.62
A3.1 Finance	31.49	34.35
A3.2 Work	39.53	38.58
A4 Sociological system	36.75	37.70
A4.1 Demographic	56.29	46.31
A4.2 Education	25.25	28.26
A4.3 Inequalities	29.59	40.28
A5 Technological system	34.62	37.72
A5.1 Transport	20.78	6.54
A5.2 Technology adoption	18.61	41.23
A5.3 Consumption and production	63.73	62.53
B Intrinsic drivers index	48.41	58.01
B1 Human health	50.05	72.35
B1.1 Health coverage	31.41	58.65
B1.2 Diseases burden	65.39	79.83
B1.3 Injury and violence	54.88	80.75
B2 Animal health and ecosystem diversity	54.73	56.58
B2.1 Animal epidemic disease	97.02	94.57
B2.2 Wildlife and marine life biodiversity	12.45	18.59
B3 Environmental health	41.91	46.87
B3.1 Air quality and climate change	63.05	53.72
B3.2 Environmental biodiversity	44.10	44.05
B3.3 Environmental resources	19.84	44.25

	Country Score	Global Average
C Core drivers index	52.35	57.25
C1 Governance	52.46	56.51
C1.1 Participation	66.07	41.70
C1.3 Transparency	53.60	65.15
C1.4 Responsiveness	41.65	44.42
C1.5 Consensus oriented	85.05	86.45
C1.6 Equity and inclusiveness	61.23	73.61
C1.7 Effectiveness and efficiency	11.80	28.38
C1.8 Political support	47.83	55.89
C2 Zoonotic diseases	59.99	68.06
C2.1 Source of infection	48.50	69.22
C2.2 Route of transmission	67.52	59.30
C2.3 Targeted population	32.03	59.90
C2.4 Capacity building	73.57	72.85
C2.5 Case studies	85.64	85.89
C3 Food security	44.70	52.89
C3.1 Food demand and supply	44.75	59.53
C3.2 Food safety	57.57	69.36
C3.3 Nutrition	54.54	67.17
C3.4 Natural and social circumstances	46.35	51.54
C3.5 Government support and response	20.29	16.85
C4 Antimicrobial resistance	43.29	44.05
C4.1 AMR surveillance system	47.55	34.79
C4.2 AMR laboratory network and coordination capacity	49.02	55.57
C4.3 Antimicrobial control and optimization	47.09	48.76
C4.4 Improve awareness and understanding	42.19	48.09
C4.5 Antimicrobial resistance rate for important antibiotics	30.60	33.03
C5 Climate change	61.50	64.19
C5.1 Mitigation and adaptation capacity	24.27	28.24
C5.2 Climate change risks	77.13	80.87
C5.3 Health outcome	84.96	85.41

Scores are normalized (0-100, where 100 = most favorable)

Turkmenistan

Europe & Central Asia | Upper middle income

49.42 Index Score **124**/160

Global average: 54.82

Regional average: 60.26

Income group average: 54.54

Country performance: 49.42

Missing rate in GOHI database: 28.60%

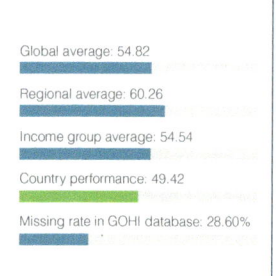

▼ AVERAGE PERFORMANCE BY GOHI

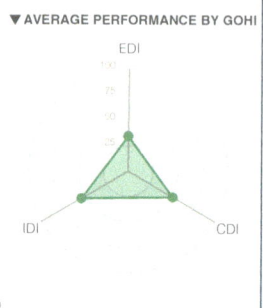

▼ AVERAGE PERFORMANCE BY CDI

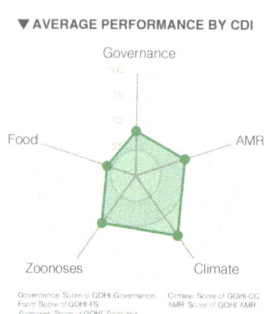

	Country Score	Global Average
A External drivers index	34.18	40.45
A1 Earth system	46.46	56.21
A1.1 Land	51.88	36.41
A1.2 Forest	36.56	43.43
A1.3 Water	23.51	58.09
A1.4 Air	57.27	71.93
A1.5 Natural disasters	65.95	64.65
A2 Institutional system	25.74	46.01
A2.1 Justice	34.70	57.89
A2.2 Governance	18.11	35.58
A3 Economical system	28.37	24.62
A3.1 Finance	41.38	34.35
A3.2 Work	42.15	38.58
A4 Sociological system	37.78	37.70
A4.1 Demographic	50.41	46.31
A4.2 Education	26.53	28.26
A4.3 Inequalities	38.15	40.28
A5 Technological system	32.57	37.72
A5.1 Transport	0.60	6.54
A5.2 Technology adoption	33.88	41.23
A5.3 Consumption and production	60.36	62.53
B Intrinsic drivers index	54.20	58.01
B1 Human health	73.86	72.35
B1.1 Health coverage	58.13	58.65
B1.2 Diseases burden	81.72	79.83
B1.3 Injury and violence	83.97	80.75
B2 Animal health and ecosystem diversity	52.82	56.58
B2.1 Animal epidemic disease	96.30	94.57
B2.2 Wildlife and marine life biodiversity	9.34	18.59
B3 Environmental health	37.55	46.87
B3.1 Air quality and climate change	49.76	53.72
B3.2 Environmental biodiversity	14.75	44.05
B3.3 Environmental resources	49.28	44.25

	Country Score	Global Average
C Core drivers index	51.67	57.25
C1 Governance	43.42	56.51
C1.1 Participation	14.11	41.70
C1.3 Transparency	23.50	65.15
C1.4 Responsiveness	16.65	44.42
C1.5 Consensus oriented	98.18	86.45
C1.6 Equity and inclusiveness	93.08	73.61
C1.7 Effectiveness and efficiency	18.80	28.38
C1.8 Political support	39.58	55.89
C2 Zoonotic diseases	73.00	68.06
C2.1 Source of infection	81.18	69.22
C2.2 Route of transmission	48.83	59.30
C2.3 Targeted population	77.89	59.90
C2.4 Capacity building	77.44	72.85
C2.5 Case studies	89.50	85.89
C3 Food security	52.23	52.89
C3.1 Food demand and supply	65.95	59.53
C3.2 Food safety	60.84	69.36
C3.3 Nutrition	72.34	67.17
C3.4 Natural and social circumstances	53.17	51.54
C3.5 Government support and response	8.85	16.85
C4 Antimicrobial resistance	30.59	44.05
C4.1 AMR surveillance system	13.12	34.79
C4.2 AMR laboratory network and coordination capacity	45.41	55.57
C4.3 Antimicrobial control and optimization	20.21	48.76
C4.4 Improve awareness and understanding	45.31	48.09
C4.5 Antimicrobial resistance rate for important antibiotics	28.88	33.03
C5 Climate change	57.88	64.19
C5.1 Mitigation and adaptation capacity	24.12	28.24
C5.2 Climate change risks	63.69	80.87
C5.3 Health outcome	87.58	85.41

Scores are normalized (0-100, where 100 = most favorable)

Nepal
South Asia | Lower middle income

49.35 Index Score **125**/160

▼ AVERAGE PERFORMANCE BY GOHI

▼ AVERAGE PERFORMANCE BY CDI

Global average: 54.82

Regional average: 51.61

Income group average: 51.29

Country performance: 49.35

Missing rate in GOHI database: 21.00%

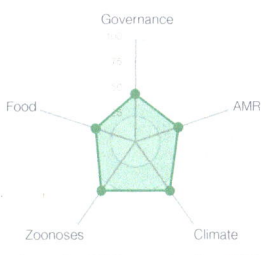

	Country Score	Global Average
A External drivers index	35.82	40.45
A1 Earth system	48.70	56.21
A1.1 Land	6.17	36.41
A1.2 Forest	49.49	43.43
A1.3 Water	67.26	58.09
A1.4 Air	49.19	71.93
A1.5 Natural disasters	65.68	64.65
A2 Institutional system	40.84	46.01
A2.1 Justice	52.26	57.89
A2.2 Governance	31.10	35.58
A3 Economical system	21.78	24.62
A3.1 Finance	25.81	34.35
A3.2 Work	39.89	38.58
A4 Sociological system	35.61	37.70
A4.1 Demographic	44.69	46.31
A4.2 Education	29.47	28.26
A4.3 Inequalities	33.31	40.28
A5 Technological system	32.20	37.72
A5.1 Transport	0.33	6.54
A5.2 Technology adoption	24.10	41.23
A5.3 Consumption and production	69.58	62.53
B Intrinsic drivers index	55.36	58.01
B1 Human health	69.03	72.35
B1.1 Health coverage	44.15	58.65
B1.2 Diseases burden	83.08	79.83
B1.3 Injury and violence	81.96	80.75
B2 Animal health and ecosystem diversity	60.87	56.58
B2.1 Animal epidemic disease	97.37	94.57
B2.2 Wildlife and marine life biodiversity	24.37	18.59
B3 Environmental health	37.86	46.87
B3.1 Air quality and climate change	43.94	53.72
B3.2 Environmental biodiversity	50.32	44.05
B3.3 Environmental resources	20.47	44.25

	Country Score	Global Average
C Core drivers index	50.93	57.25
C1 Governance	46.87	56.51
C1.1 Participation	19.94	41.70
C1.3 Transparency	53.60	65.15
C1.4 Responsiveness	31.25	44.42
C1.5 Consensus oriented	94.09	86.45
C1.6 Equity and inclusiveness	62.67	73.61
C1.7 Effectiveness and efficiency	19.20	28.38
C1.8 Political support	47.34	55.89
C2 Zoonotic diseases	59.71	68.06
C2.1 Source of infection	49.64	69.22
C2.2 Route of transmission	57.27	59.30
C2.3 Targeted population	47.92	59.90
C2.4 Capacity building	64.41	72.85
C2.5 Case studies	89.20	85.89
C3 Food security	46.32	52.89
C3.1 Food demand and supply	59.84	59.53
C3.2 Food safety	49.50	69.36
C3.3 Nutrition	68.80	67.17
C3.4 Natural and social circumstances	47.19	51.54
C3.5 Government support and response	6.26	16.85
C4 Antimicrobial resistance	42.46	44.05
C4.1 AMR surveillance system	30.31	34.79
C4.2 AMR laboratory network and coordinati on capacity	57.67	55.57
C4.3 Antimicrobial control and optimization	47.97	48.76
C4.4 Improve awareness and understanding	43.75	48.09
C4.5 Antimicrobial resistance rate for important antibiotics	32.61	33.03
C5 Climate change	59.68	64.19
C5.1 Mitigation and adaptation capacity	16.40	28.24
C5.2 Climate change risks	75.48	80.87
C5.3 Health outcome	88.96	85.41

Scores are normalized (0-100, where 100 = most favorable)

Nigeria
Sub-Saharan Africa | Lower middle income

Index Score **126**/160

49.35

Global average: 54.82

Regional average: 48.03

Income group average: 51.29

Country performance: 49.35

Missing rate in GOHI database: 18.10%

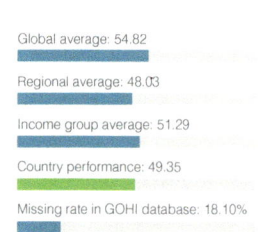

▼ AVERAGE PERFORMANCE BY GOHI

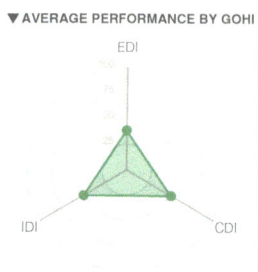

▼ AVERAGE PERFORMANCE BY CDI

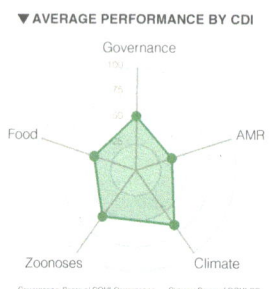

Governance Score of GOHI-Governance   Climate Score of GOHI-CC
Food Score in GOHI-FS   AMR Score of GOHI-AMR
Zoonoses Score of GOHI-Zoonoses

	Country Score	Global Average
A External drivers index	38.50	40.45
A1 Earth system	49.93	56.21
A1.1 Land	35.81	36.41
A1.2 Forest	31.38	43.43
A1.3 Water	61.82	58.09
A1.4 Air	49.16	71.93
A1.5 Natural disasters	66.66	64.65
A2 Institutional system	38.00	46.01
A2.1 Justice	54.54	57.89
A2.2 Governance	23.92	35.58
A3 Economical system	29.98	24.62
A3.1 Finance	48.19	34.35
A3.2 Work	38.88	38.58
A4 Sociological system	44.40	37.70
A4.1 Demographic	64.59	46.31
A4.2 Education	30.30	28.26
A4.3 Inequalities	39.90	40.28
A5 Technological system	30.19	37.72
A5.1 Transport	0.00	6.54
A5.2 Technology adoption	22.19	41.23
A5.3 Consumption and production	65.94	62.53
B Intrinsic drivers index	50.36	58.01
B1 Human health	55.12	72.35
B1.1 Health coverage	21.63	58.65
B1.2 Diseases burden	73.57	79.83
B1.3 Injury and violence	71.85	80.75
B2 Animal health and ecosystem diversity	57.71	56.58
B2.1 Animal epidemic disease	96.28	94.57
B2.2 Wildlife and marine life biodiversity	19.15	18.59
B3 Environmental health	39.76	46.87
B3.1 Air quality and climate change	20.27	53.72
B3.2 Environmental biodiversity	79.80	44.05
B3.3 Environmental resources	20.42	44.25

Scores are normalized (0-100, where 100 = most favorable)

	Country Score	Global Average
C Core drivers index	51.53	57.25
C1 Governance	52.93	56.51
C1.1 Participation	41.93	41.70
C1.3 Transparency	53.60	65.15
C1.4 Responsiveness	58.30	44.42
C1.5 Consensus oriented	95.93	86.45
C1.6 Equity and inclusiveness	53.98	73.61
C1.7 Effectiveness and efficiency	18.33	28.38
C1.8 Political support	48.45	55.89
C2 Zoonotic diseases	66.45	68.06
C2.1 Source of infection	64.45	69.22
C2.2 Route of transmission	55.11	59.30
C2.3 Targeted population	69.24	59.90
C2.4 Capacity building	72.62	72.85
C2.5 Case studies	78.17	85.89
C3 Food security	37.95	52.89
C3.1 Food demand and supply	49.95	59.53
C3.2 Food safety	26.72	69.36
C3.3 Nutrition	64.34	67.17
C3.4 Natural and social circumstances	31.86	51.54
C3.5 Government support and response	16.89	16.85
C4 Antimicrobial resistance	44.00	44.05
C4.1 AMR surveillance system	27.71	34.79
C4.2 AMR laboratory network and coordination capacity	53.36	55.57
C4.3 Antimicrobial control and optimization	46.10	48.76
C4.4 Improve awareness and understanding	60.94	48.09
C4.5 Antimicrobial resistance rate for important antibiotics	31.89	33.03
C5 Climate change	56.51	64.19
C5.1 Mitigation and adaptation capacity	19.57	28.24
C5.2 Climate change risks	70.87	80.87
C5.3 Health outcome	80.81	85.41

Zimbabwe

Sub-Saharan Africa | Lower middle income

 Index Score **127**/160

Global average: 54.82

Regional average: 48.03

Income group average: 51.29

Country performance: 49.10

Missing rate in GOHI database: 24.60%

▼ AVERAGE PERFORMANCE BY GOHI

▼ AVERAGE PERFORMANCE BY CDI

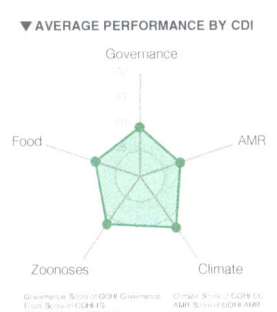

	Country Score	Global Average
A External drivers index	36.17	40.45
A1 Earth system	56.44	56.21
A1.1 Land	38.85	36.41
A1.2 Forest	41.35	43.43
A1.3 Water	51.30	58.09
A1.4 Air	86.95	71.93
A1.5 Natural disasters	54.73	64.65
A2 Institutional system	31.27	46.01
A2.1 Justice	42.08	57.89
A2.2 Governance	22.06	35.58
A3 Economical system	22.25	24.62
A3.1 Finance	27.02	34.35
A3.2 Work	39.94	38.58
A4 Sociological system	38.01	37.70
A4.1 Demographic	54.74	46.31
A4.2 Education	28.73	28.26
A4.3 Inequalities	31.12	40.28
A5 Technological system	32.87	37.72
A5.1 Transport	5.55	6.54
A5.2 Technology adoption	21.67	41.23
A5.3 Consumption and production	69.30	62.53
B Intrinsic drivers index	49.50	58.01
B1 Human health	56.56	72.35
B1.1 Health coverage	37.15	58.65
B1.2 Diseases burden	72.74	79.83
B1.3 Injury and violence	61.51	80.75
B2 Animal health and ecosystem diversity	56.04	56.58
B2.1 Animal epidemic disease	90.91	94.57
B2.2 Wildlife and marine life biodiversity	21.17	18.59
B3 Environmental health	37.39	46.87
B3.1 Air quality and climate change	38.10	53.72
B3.2 Environmental biodiversity	55.45	44.05
B3.3 Environmental resources	19.76	44.25

	Country Score	Global Average
C Core drivers index	51.88	57.25
C1 Governance	48.25	56.51
C1.1 Participation	17.16	41.70
C1.3 Transparency	61.70	65.15
C1.4 Responsiveness	52.05	44.42
C1.5 Consensus oriented	95.35	86.45
C1.6 Equity and inclusiveness	52.29	73.61
C1.7 Effectiveness and efficiency	16.73	28.38
C1.8 Political support	42.44	55.89
C2 Zoonotic diseases	62.44	68.06
C2.1 Source of infection	50.77	69.22
C2.2 Route of transmission	67.45	59.30
C2.3 Targeted population	39.58	59.90
C2.4 Capacity building	74.35	72.85
C2.5 Case studies	88.00	85.89
C3 Food security	43.67	52.89
C3.1 Food demand and supply	47.79	59.53
C3.2 Food safety	57.57	69.36
C3.3 Nutrition	56.16	67.17
C3.4 Natural and social circumstances	46.44	51.54
C3.5 Government support and response	10.39	16.85
C4 Antimicrobial resistance	47.73	44.05
C4.1 AMR surveillance system	51.84	34.79
C4.2 AMR laboratory network and coordination on capacity	63.40	55.57
C4.3 Antimicrobial control and optimization	51.96	48.76
C4.4 Improve awareness and understanding	40.62	48.09
C4.5 Antimicrobial resistance rate for important antibiotics	30.83	33.03
C5 Climate change	58.05	64.19
C5.1 Mitigation and adaptation capacity	19.09	28.24
C5.2 Climate change risks	80.04	80.87
C5.3 Health outcome	76.78	85.41

Scores are normalized (0-100, where 100 = most favorable)

Bahrain
Middle East & North Africa | High income

49.09 Index Score **128**/160

Global average: 54.82

Regional average: 53.57

Income group average: 61.66

Country performance: 49.09

Missing rate in GOHI database: 24.60%

▼ AVERAGE PERFORMANCE BY GOHI

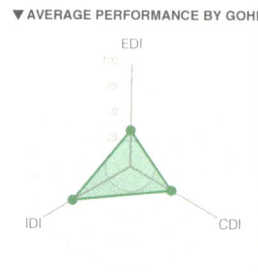
▼ AVERAGE PERFORMANCE BY CDI

Governance: Score of GOHI-Governance   Climate: Score of GOHI-CC
Food: Score of GOHI-FS   AMR: Score of GOHI-AMR
Zoonoses: Score of GOHI-Zoonoses

	Country Score	Global Average
A External drivers index	35.14	40.45
A1 Earth system	27.37	56.21
A1.1 Land	23.95	36.41
A1.2 Forest	22.51	43.43
A1.3 Water	24.39	58.09
A1.4 Air	7.09	71.93
A1.5 Natural disasters	66.35	64.65
A2 Institutional system	44.40	46.01
A2.1 Justice	49.70	57.89
A2.2 Governance	39.88	35.58
A3 Economical system	25.18	24.62
A3.1 Finance	33.08	34.35
A3.2 Work	42.02	38.58
A4 Sociological system	38.42	37.70
A4.1 Demographic	46.45	46.31
A4.2 Education	28.14	28.26
A4.3 Inequalities	42.76	40.28
A5 Technological system	40.32	37.72
A5.1 Transport	11.41	6.54
A5.2 Technology adoption	64.70	41.23
A5.3 Consumption and production	41.58	62.53
B Intrinsic drivers index	66.93	58.01
B1 Human health	81.34	72.35
B1.1 Health coverage	67.56	58.65
B1.2 Diseases burden	89.99	79.83
B1.3 Injury and violence	88.93	80.75
B2 Animal health and ecosystem diversity	58.80	56.58
B2.1 Animal epidemic disease	98.14	94.57
B2.2 Wildlife and marine life biodiversity	19.45	18.59
B3 Environmental health	62.68	46.87
B3.1 Air quality and climate change	67.35	53.72
B3.2 Environmental biodiversity	57.65	44.05
B3.3 Environmental resources	64.94	44.25

	Country Score	Global Average
C Core drivers index	47.96	57.25
C1 Governance	35.13	56.51
C1.1 Participation	18.51	41.70
C1.3 Transparency	54.50	65.15
C1.4 Responsiveness	58.35	44.42
C1.5 Consensus oriented	3.23	86.45
C1.6 Equity and inclusiveness	65.33	73.61
C1.7 Effectiveness and efficiency	21.47	28.38
C1.8 Political support	24.51	55.89
C2 Zoonotic diseases	64.67	68.06
C2.1 Source of infection	69.95	69.22
C2.2 Route of transmission	54.81	59.30
C2.3 Targeted population	50.87	59.90
C2.4 Capacity building	68.20	72.85
C2.5 Case studies	86.41	85.89
C3 Food security	49.95	52.89
C3.1 Food demand and supply	61.62	59.53
C3.2 Food safety	62.62	69.36
C3.3 Nutrition	61.58	67.17
C3.4 Natural and social circumstances	49.90	51.54
C3.5 Government support and response	14.02	16.85
C4 Antimicrobial resistance	38.74	44.05
C4.1 AMR surveillance system	14.70	34.79
C4.2 AMR laboratory network and coordination on capacity	41.36	55.57
C4.3 Antimicrobial control and optimization	52.79	48.76
C4.4 Improve awareness and understanding	56.25	48.09
C4.5 Antimicrobial resistance rate for important antibiotics	28.61	33.03
C5 Climate change	51.38	64.19
C5.1 Mitigation and adaptation capacity	25.17	28.24
C5.2 Climate change risks	63.38	80.87
C5.3 Health outcome	67.15	85.41

Scores are normalized (0-100, where 100 = most favorable)

Gabon

Sub-Saharan Africa | Upper middle income

49.03 Index Score **129**/160

Global average: 54.82

Regional average: 48.03

Income group average: 54.54

Country performance: 49.03

Missing rate in GOHI database: 29.30%

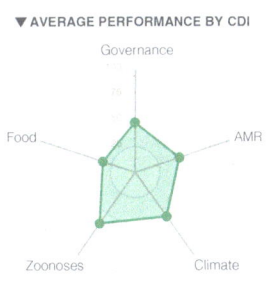

▼ AVERAGE PERFORMANCE BY GOHI

▼ AVERAGE PERFORMANCE BY CDI

	Country Score	Global Average
A External drivers index	42.26	40.45
A1 Earth system	70.97	56.21
A1.1 Land	46.78	36.41
A1.2 Forest	100.00	43.43
A1.3 Water	68.82	58.09
A1.4 Air	72.48	71.93
A1.5 Natural disasters	64.10	64.65
A2 Institutional system	39.02	46.01
A2.1 Justice	49.77	57.89
A2.2 Governance	29.86	35.58
A3 Economical system	24.63	24.62
A3.1 Finance	37.11	34.35
A3.2 Work	35.11	38.58
A4 Sociological system	39.47	37.70
A4.1 Demographic	58.81	46.31
A4.2 Education	24.58	28.26
A4.3 Inequalities	36.97	40.28
A5 Technological system	37.20	37.72
A5.1 Transport	13.92	6.54
A5.2 Technology adoption	31.70	41.23
A5.3 Consumption and production	64.10	62.53
B Intrinsic drivers index	54.13	58.01
B1 Human health	62.19	72.35
B1.1 Health coverage	45.31	58.65
B1.2 Diseases burden	81.27	79.83
B1.3 Injury and violence	61.88	80.75
B2 Animal health and ecosystem diversity	51.21	56.58
B2.1 Animal epidemic disease	96.41	94.57
B2.2 Wildlife and marine life biodiversity	6.00	18.59
B3 Environmental health	50.62	46.87
B3.1 Air quality and climate change	55.37	53.72
B3.2 Environmental biodiversity	56.48	44.05
B3.3 Environmental resources	41.53	44.25

	Country Score	Global Average
C Core drivers index	49.33	57.25
C1 Governance	48.89	56.51
C1.1 Participation	45.00	41.70
C1.3 Transparency	28.10	65.15
C1.4 Responsiveness	25.00	44.42
C1.5 Consensus oriented	94.66	86.45
C1.6 Equity and inclusiveness	77.83	73.61
C1.7 Effectiveness and efficiency	11.47	28.38
C1.8 Political support	60.16	55.89
C2 Zoonotic diseases	53.73	68.06
C2.1 Source of infection	53.73	69.22
C2.2 Route of transmission	33.70	59.30
C2.3 Targeted population	39.87	59.90
C2.4 Capacity building	69.51	72.85
C2.5 Case studies	87.20	85.89
C3 Food security	47.25	52.69
C3.1 Food demand and supply	52.39	59.53
C3.2 Food safety	65.98	69.36
C3.3 Nutrition	62.01	67.17
C3.4 Natural and social circumstances	47.54	51.54
C3.5 Government support and response	8.33	16.85
C4 Antimicrobial resistance	34.31	44.05
C4.1 AMR surveillance system	38.14	34.79
C4.2 AMR laboratory network and coordination on capacity	59.50	55.57
C4.3 Antimicrobial control and optimization	24.99	48.76
C4.4 Improve awareness and understanding	17.19	48.09
C4.5 Antimicrobial resistance rate for important antibiotics	31.73	33.03
C5 Climate change	62.11	64.19
C5.1 Mitigation and adaptation capacity	14.92	28.24
C5.2 Climate change risks	86.27	80.87
C5.3 Health outcome	87.02	85.41

Scores are normalized (0-100, where 100 = most favorable)

Namibia

Sub-Saharan Africa | Upper middle income

Index Score **130**/160 48.93

Global average: 54.82

Regional average: 48.03

Income group average: 54.54

Country performance: 48.93

Missing rate in GOHI database: 21.70%

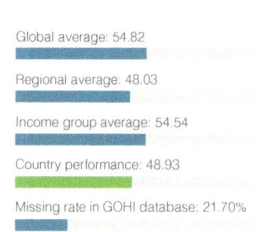

▼ AVERAGE PERFORMANCE BY GOHI

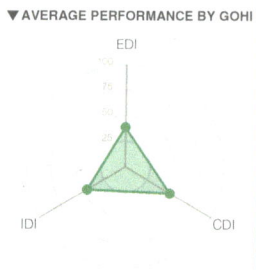

▼ AVERAGE PERFORMANCE BY CDI

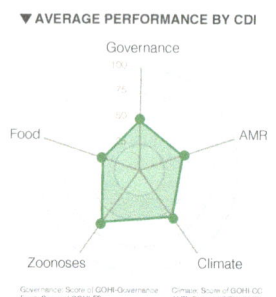

Governance: Score of GOHI-Governance   Climate: Score of GOHI-CC
Food: Score of GOHI-FS   AMR: Score of GOHI-AMR
Zoonoses: Score of GOHI-Zoonoses

	Country Score	Global Average
A External drivers index	38.77	40.45
A1 Earth system	57.82	56.21
A1.1 Land	67.25	36.41
A1.2 Forest	31.22	43.43
A1.3 Water	38.53	58.09
A1.4 Air	81.97	71.93
A1.5 Natural disasters	66.65	64.65
A2 Institutional system	47.15	46.01
A2.1 Justice	63.06	57.89
A2.2 Governance	33.59	35.58
A3 Economical system	16.50	24.62
A3.1 Finance	16.20	34.35
A3.2 Work	34.49	38.58
A4 Sociological system	39.45	37.70
A4.1 Demographic	55.31	46.31
A4.2 Education	26.19	28.26
A4.3 Inequalities	38.77	40.28
A5 Technological system	32.94	37.72
A5.1 Transport	1.67	6.54
A5.2 Technology adoption	26.93	41.23
A5.3 Consumption and production	67.65	62.53
B Intrinsic drivers index	44.76	58.01
B1 Human health	63.49	72.35
B1.1 Health coverage	44.59	58.65
B1.2 Diseases burden	78.90	79.83
B1.3 Injury and violence	68.91	80.75
B2 Animal health and ecosystem diversity	52.32	56.58
B2.1 Animal epidemic disease	89.88	94.57
B2.2 Wildlife and marine life biodiversity	14.75	18.59
B3 Environmental health	19.84	46.87
B3.1 Air quality and climate change	20.88	53.72
B3.2 Environmental biodiversity	23.90	44.05
B3.3 Environmental resources	15.34	44.25

Scores are normalized (0-100, where 100 = most favorable)

	Country Score	Global Average
C Core drivers index	52.18	57.25
C1 Governance	50.04	56.51
C1.1 Participation	44.91	41.70
C1.3 Transparency	52.20	65.15
C1.4 Responsiveness	25.00	44.42
C1.5 Consensus oriented	93.25	86.45
C1.6 Equity and inclusiveness	63.13	73.61
C1.7 Effectiveness and efficiency	17.07	28.38
C1.8 Political support	54.71	55.89
C2 Zoonotic diseases	58.44	68.06
C2.1 Source of infection	56.56	69.22
C2.2 Route of transmission	40.20	59.30
C2.3 Targeted population	46.92	59.90
C2.4 Capacity building	76.97	72.85
C2.5 Case studies	85.87	85.89
C3 Food security	47.65	52.89
C3.1 Food demand and supply	56.93	59.53
C3.2 Food safety	55.85	69.36
C3.3 Nutrition	61.21	67.17
C3.4 Natural and social circumstances	48.88	51.54
C3.5 Government support and response	15.35	16.85
C4 Antimicrobial resistance	39.67	44.05
C4.1 AMR surveillance system	37.60	34.79
C4.2 AMR laboratory network and coordination on capacity	45.79	55.57
C4.3 Antimicrobial control and optimization	37.51	48.76
C4.4 Improve awareness and understanding	40.62	48.09
C4.5 Antimicrobial resistance rate for important antibiotics	36.81	33.03
C5 Climate change	65.31	64.19
C5.1 Mitigation and adaptation capacity	28.92	28.24
C5.2 Climate change risks	79.99	80.87
C5.3 Health outcome	89.01	85.41

Sudan

Sub-Saharan Africa | Low income

Index Score **131**/160 48.57

Global average: 54.82

Regional average: 48.03

Income group average: 46.63

Country performance: 48.57

Missing rate in GOHI database: 30.10%

▼ AVERAGE PERFORMANCE BY GOHI

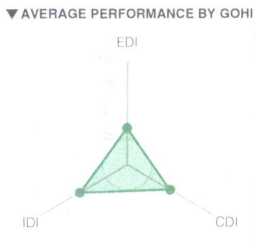

▼ AVERAGE PERFORMANCE BY CDI

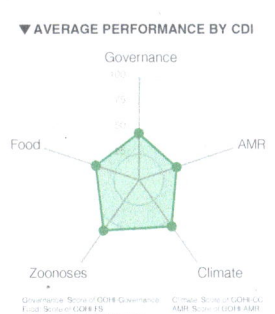

	Country Score	Global Average
A External drivers index	35.87	40.45
A1 Earth system	46.79	56.21
A1.1 Land	57.10	36.41
A1.2 Forest	26.36	43.43
A1.3 Water	25.73	58.09
A1.4 Air	59.92	71.93
A1.5 Natural disasters	66.09	64.65
A2 Institutional system	33.41	46.01
A2.1 Justice	50.81	57.89
A2.2 Governance	18.58	35.58
A3 Economical system	28.33	24.62
A3.1 Finance	45.45	34.35
A3.2 Work	36.87	38.58
A4 Sociological system	37.08	37.70
A4.1 Demographic	49.46	46.31
A4.2 Education	31.28	28.26
A4.3 Inequalities	30.61	40.28
A5 Technological system	33.72	37.72
A5.1 Transport	22.58	6.54
A5.2 Technology adoption	15.74	41.23
A5.3 Consumption and production	62.41	62.53
B Intrinsic drivers index	55.31	58.01
B1 Human health	65.62	72.35
B1.1 Health coverage	39.45	58.65
B1.2 Diseases burden	85.99	79.83
B1.3 Injury and violence	73.42	80.75
B2 Animal health and ecosystem diversity	55.06	56.58
B2.1 Animal epidemic disease	98.12	94.57
B2.2 Wildlife and marine life biodiversity	12.00	18.59
B3 Environmental health	46.93	46.87
B3.1 Air quality and climate change	54.74	53.72
B3.2 Environmental biodiversity	50.92	44.05
B3.3 Environmental resources	36.55	44.25

	Country Score	Global Average
C Core drivers index	49.79	57.25
C1 Governance	45.74	58.51
C1.1 Participation	18.39	41.70
C1.3 Transparency	39.20	65.15
C1.4 Responsiveness	50.00	44.42
C1.5 Consensus oriented	90.29	86.45
C1.6 Equity and inclusiveness	72.68	73.61
C1.7 Effectiveness and efficiency	5.73	28.38
C1.8 Political support	43.91	55.89
C2 Zoonotic diseases	56.67	68.06
C2.1 Source of infection	55.41	69.22
C2.2 Route of transmission	46.95	59.30
C2.3 Targeted population	37.74	59.90
C2.4 Capacity building	72.61	72.65
C2.5 Case studies	81.11	85.89
C3 Food security	40.55	52.89
C3.1 Food demand and supply	36.72	59.53
C3.2 Food safety	61.56	69.36
C3.3 Nutrition	56.76	67.17
C3.4 Natural and social circumstances	32.11	51.54
C3.5 Government support and response	15.60	16.85
C4 Antimicrobial resistance	45.73	44.05
C4.1 AMR surveillance system	25.11	34.79
C4.2 AMR laboratory network and coordination capacity	71.19	55.57
C4.3 Antimicrobial control and optimization	37.55	48.76
C4.4 Improve awareness and understanding	56.25	48.09
C4.5 Antimicrobial resistance rate for important antibiotics	38.55	33.03
C5 Climate change	61.61	64.19
C5.1 Mitigation and adaptation capacity	25.86	28.24
C5.2 Climate change risks	73.09	80.87
C5.3 Health outcome	87.75	85.41

Scores are normalized (0-100, where 100 = most favorable)

Mozambique

Sub-Saharan Africa | Low income

Index Score **132**/160

Global average: 54.82

Regional average: 48.03

Income group average: 46.63

Country performance: 48.46

Missing rate in GOHI database: 19.90%

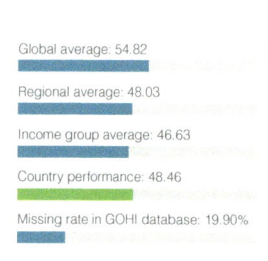

▼ AVERAGE PERFORMANCE BY GOHI

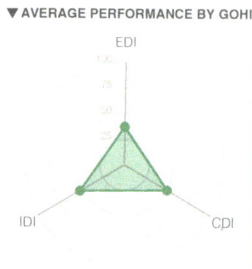

▼ AVERAGE PERFORMANCE BY CDI

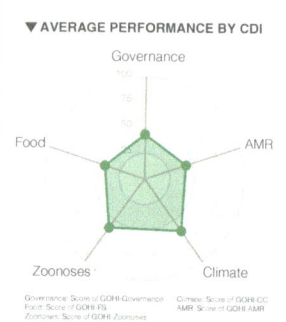

Governance: Score of GOHI-Governance   Climate: Score of GOHI-CC
Food: Score of GOHI-FS   AMR: Score of GOHI-AMR
Zoonoses: Score of GOHI-Zoonoses

	Country Score	Global Average
A External drivers index	37.17	40.45
A1 Earth system	56.85	56.21
A1.1 Land	36.93	36.41
A1.2 Forest	45.59	43.43
A1.3 Water	50.19	58.09
A1.4 Air	87.91	71.93
A1.5 Natural disasters	55.04	64.65
A2 Institutional system	34.40	46.01
A2.1 Justice	47.24	57.89
A2.2 Governance	23.46	35.58
A3 Economical system	25.12	24.62
A3.1 Finance	36.36	34.35
A3.2 Work	37.68	38.58
A4 Sociological system	37.63	37.70
A4.1 Demographic	56.44	46.31
A4.2 Education	26.40	28.26
A4.3 Inequalities	30.95	40.28
A5 Technological system	31.88	37.72
A5.1 Transport	12.48	6.54
A5.2 Technology adoption	12.45	41.23
A5.3 Consumption and production	69.56	62.53
B Intrinsic drivers index	51.89	58.01
B1 Human health	55.95	72.35
B1.1 Health coverage	28.50	58.65
B1.2 Diseases burden	66.89	79.83
B1.3 Injury and violence	74.15	80.75
B2 Animal health and ecosystem diversity	67.51	56.58
B2.1 Animal epidemic disease	95.98	94.57
B2.2 Wildlife and marine life biodiversity	39.05	18.59
B3 Environmental health	33.78	46.87
B3.1 Air quality and climate change	44.73	53.72
B3.2 Environmental biodiversity	18.35	44.05
B3.3 Environmental resources	39.28	44.25

	Country Score	Global Average
C Core drivers index	50.16	57.25
C1 Governance	43.48	56.51
C1.1 Participation	14.67	41.70
C1.3 Transparency	56.20	65.15
C1.4 Responsiveness	50.00	44.42
C1.5 Consensus oriented	65.29	86.45
C1.6 Equity and inclusiveness	49.79	73.61
C1.7 Effectiveness and efficiency	19.87	28.38
C1.8 Political support	48.57	55.89
C2 Zoonotic diseases	63.19	68.06
C2.1 Source of infection	53.92	69.22
C2.2 Route of transmission	68.81	59.30
C2.3 Targeted population	35.65	59.90
C2.4 Capacity building	77.01	72.85
C2.5 Case studies	87.76	85.89
C3 Food security	43.51	52.89
C3.1 Food demand and supply	44.34	59.53
C3.2 Food safety	76.86	69.36
C3.3 Nutrition	54.67	67.17
C3.4 Natural and social circumstances	27.99	51.54
C3.5 Government support and response	13.71	16.85
C4 Antimicrobial resistance	41.67	44.05
C4.1 AMR surveillance system	35.15	34.79
C4.2 AMR laboratory network and coordination capacity	52.38	55.57
C4.3 Antimicrobial control and optimization	47.24	48.76
C4.4 Improve awareness and understanding	34.38	48.09
C4.5 Antimicrobial resistance rate for important antibiotics	39.20	33.03
C5 Climate change	59.63	64.19
C5.1 Mitigation and adaptation capacity	25.91	28.24
C5.2 Climate change risks	76.31	80.87
C5.3 Health outcome	78.48	85.41

Scores are normalized (0-100, where 100 = most favorable)

Timor-Leste

East Asia & Pacific | Lower middle income

48.33 **Index Score** **133**/160

Global average: 54.82

Regional average: 56.52

Income group average: 51.29

Country performance: 48.33

Missing rate in GOHI database: 27.50%

▼ AVERAGE PERFORMANCE BY GOHI

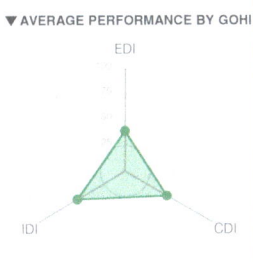

▼ AVERAGE PERFORMANCE BY CDI

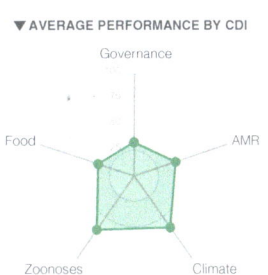

	Country Score	Global Average
A External drivers index	39.37	40.45
A1 Earth system	59.79	56.21
A1.1 Land	26.91	36.41
A1.2 Forest	47.83	43.43
A1.3 Water	64.68	58.09
A1.4 Air	83.93	71.93
A1.5 Natural disasters	66.11	64.65
A2 Institutional system	44.17	46.01
A2.1 Justice	57.46	57.89
A2.2 Governance	32.85	35.58
A3 Economical system	23.89	24.62
A3.1 Finance	30.97	34.35
A3.2 Work	40.42	38.58
A4 Sociological system	34.03	37.70
A4.1 Demographic	42.99	46.31
A4.2 Education	25.18	28.26
A4.3 Inequalities	35.42	40.28
A5 Technological system	34.96	37.72
A5.1 Transport	5.98	6.54
A5.2 Technology adoption	30.57	41.23
A5.3 Consumption and production	66.11	62.53
B Intrinsic drivers index	55.77	58.01
B1 Human health	71.42	72.35
B1.1 Health coverage	44.39	58.65
B1.2 Diseases burden	86.61	79.83
B1.3 Injury and violence	85.44	80.75
B2 Animal health and ecosystem diversity	58.81	56.58
B2.1 Animal epidemic disease	92.97	94.57
B2.2 Wildlife and marine life biodiversity	24.65	18.59
B3 Environmental health	38.76	46.87
B3.1 Air quality and climate change	34.76	53.72
B3.2 Environmental biodiversity	33.35	44.05
B3.3 Environmental resources	49.34	44.25

	Country Score	Global Average
C Core drivers index	48.55	57.25
C1 Governance	33.08	56.51
C1.1 Participation	49.16	41.70
C1.3 Transparency	51.00	65.15
C1.4 Responsiveness	6.25	44.42
C1.5 Consensus oriented	27.24	86.45
C1.6 Equity and inclusiveness	57.28	73.61
C1.7 Effectiveness and efficiency	11.60	28.38
C1.8 Political support	29.03	55.89
C2 Zoonotic diseases	62.61	68.06
C2.1 Source of infection	49.84	69.22
C2.2 Route of transmission	44.84	59.30
C2.3 Targeted population	71.90	59.90
C2.4 Capacity building	71.77	72.85
C2.5 Case studies	90.44	85.89
C3 Food security	44.83	52.89
C3.1 Food demand and supply	58.52	59.53
C3.2 Food safety	69.81	69.36
C3.3 Nutrition	47.29	67.17
C3.4 Natural and social circumstances	45.92	51.54
C3.5 Government support and response	2.61	16.85
C4 Antimicrobial resistance	38.41	44.05
C4.1 AMR surveillance system	42.65	34.79
C4.2 AMR laboratory network and coordination capacity	39.05	55.57
C4.3 Antimicrobial control and optimization	27.88	48.76
C4.4 Improve awareness and understanding	56.25	48.09
C4.5 Antimicrobial resistance rate for important antibiotics	26.21	33.03
C5 Climate change	65.51	64.19
C5.1 Mitigation and adaptation capacity	18.11	28.24
C5.2 Climate change risks	92.13	80.87
C5.3 Health outcome	88.27	85.41

Scores are normalized (0-100, where 100 = most favorable)

Seychelles
Sub-Saharan Africa | High income

48.18 Index **134**/160
Score

▼ **AVERAGE PERFORMANCE BY GOHI**

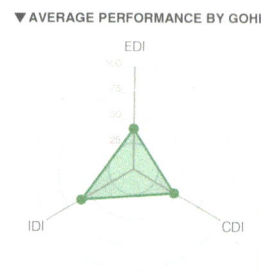

▼ **AVERAGE PERFORMANCE BY CDI**

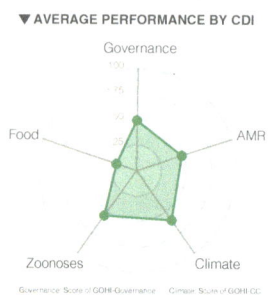

Global average: 54.82

Regional average: 48.03

Income group average: 61.66

Country performance: 48.18

Missing rate in GOHI database: 31.50%

	Country Score	Global Average
A External drivers index	**39.44**	**40.45**
A1 Earth system	**51.74**	**56.21**
A1.1 Land	2.37	36.41
A1.2 Forest	27.32	43.43
A1.3 Water	65.72	58.09
A1.4 Air	84.01	71.93
A1.5 Natural disasters	66.32	64.65
A2 Institutional system	**53.70**	**46.01**
A2.1 Justice	64.98	57.89
A2.2 Governance	44.10	35.58
A3 Economical system	**25.53**	**24.62**
A3.1 Finance	35.68	34.35
A3.2 Work	39.90	38.58
A4 Sociological system	**35.07**	**37.70**
A4.1 Demographic	42.83	46.31
A4.2 Education	25.17	28.26
A4.3 Inequalities	39.22	40.28
A5 Technological system	**31.15**	**37.72**
A5.1 Transport	5.99	6.54
A5.2 Technology adoption	43.36	41.23
A5.3 Consumption and production	41.53	62.53
B Intrinsic drivers index	**60.48**	**59.01**
B1 Human health	**74.91**	**72.35**
B1.1 Health coverage	60.91	58.65
B1.2 Diseases burden	80.41	79.83
B1.3 Injury and violence	85.67	80.75
B2 Animal health and ecosystem diversity	**59.56**	**56.58**
B2.1 Animal epidemic disease	92.47	94.57
B2.2 Wildlife and marine life biodiversity	26.65	18.59
B3 Environmental health	**48.80**	**46.87**
B3.1 Air quality and climate change	53.43	53.72
B3.2 Environmental biodiversity	43.20	44.05
B3.3 Environmental resources	51.26	44.25

Scores are normalized (0-100, where 100 = most favorable)

	Country Score	Global Average
C Core drivers index	**47.20**	**57.25**
C1 Governance	**49.33**	**56.51**
C1.1 Participation	49.42	41.70
C1.3 Transparency	48.60	65.15
C1.4 Responsiveness	27.10	44.42
C1.5 Consensus oriented	96.84	86.45
C1.6 Equity and inclusiveness	66.73	73.61
C1.7 Effectiveness and efficiency	22.93	28.38
C1.8 Political support	33.69	55.89
C2 Zoonotic diseases	**60.40**	**68.06**
C2.1 Source of infection	73.36	69.22
C2.2 Route of transmission	36.60	59.30
C2.3 Targeted population	46.07	59.90
C2.4 Capacity building	71.68	72.85
C2.5 Case studies	85.48	85.89
C3 Food security	**47.73**	**52.89**
C3.1 Food demand and supply	68.22	59.53
C3.2 Food safety	64.12	69.36
C3.3 Nutrition	59.55	67.17
C3.4 Natural and social circumstances	43.82	51.54
C3.5 Government support and response	2.97	16.85
C4 Antimicrobial resistance	**21.34**	**44.05**
C4.1 AMR surveillance system	11.74	34.79
C4.2 AMR laboratory network and coordination on capacity	29.53	55.57
C4.3 Antimicrobial control and optimization	13.69	48.76
C4.4 Improve awareness and understanding	25.00	48.09
C4.5 Antimicrobial resistance rate for important antibiotics	26.73	33.03
C5 Climate change	**54.88**	**64.19**
C5.1 Mitigation and adaptation capacity	25.18	28.24
C5.2 Climate change risks	80.07	80.87
C5.3 Health outcome	61.06	85.41

Guatemala

Latin America & Caribbean | Upper middle income

Index Score **135**/160

48.03

Global average: 54.82

Regional average: 55.08

Income group average: 54.54

Country performance: 48.03

Missing rate in GOHI database: 15.90%

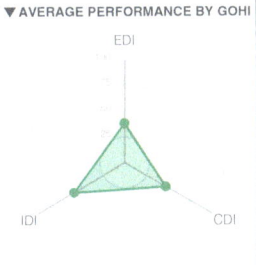

▼ AVERAGE PERFORMANCE BY GOHI

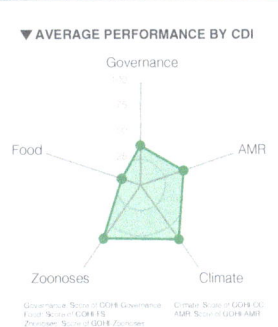

▼ AVERAGE PERFORMANCE BY CDI

	Country Score	Global Average
A External drivers index	38.52	40.45
A1 Earth system	55.74	56.21
A1.1 Land	22.49	36.41
A1.2 Forest	36.24	43.43
A1.3 Water	63.09	58.09
A1.4 Air	80.38	71.93
A1.5 Natural disasters	66.55	64.65
A2 Institutional system	36.97	46.01
A2.1 Justice	45.67	57.89
A2.2 Governance	29.56	35.58
A3 Economical system	25.64	24.62
A3.1 Finance	36.00	34.35
A3.2 Work	39.85	38.58
A4 Sociological system	35.80	37.70
A4.1 Demographic	48.44	46.31
A4.2 Education	25.44	28.26
A4.3 Inequalities	34.99	40.28
A5 Technological system	38.47	37.72
A5.1 Transport	3.71	6.54
A5.2 Technology adoption	42.74	41.23
A5.3 Consumption and production	65.76	62.53
B Intrinsic drivers index	59.14	58.01
B1 Human health	69.66	72.35
B1.1 Health coverage	62.51	58.65
B1.2 Diseases burden	87.93	79.83
B1.3 Injury and violence	60.65	80.75
B2 Animal health and ecosystem diversity	59.21	56.58
B2.1 Animal epidemic disease	91.67	94.57
B2.2 Wildlife and marine life biodiversity	26.75	18.59
B3 Environmental health	50.34	46.87
B3.1 Air quality and climate change	71.75	53.72
B3.2 Environmental biodiversity	32.40	44.05
B3.3 Environmental resources	48.40	44.25

	Country Score	Global Average
C Core drivers index	47.51	57.25
C1 Governance	38.94	56.51
C1.1 Participation	55.71	41.70
C1.3 Transparency	61.00	65.15
C1.4 Responsiveness	35.40	44.42
C1.5 Consensus oriented	1.13	86.45
C1.6 Equity and inclusiveness	56.98	73.61
C1.7 Effectiveness and efficiency	11.67	28.38
C1.8 Political support	50.67	55.89
C2 Zoonotic diseases	65.98	68.06
C2.1 Source of infection	64.79	69.22
C2.2 Route of transmission	62.09	59.30
C2.3 Targeted population	47.42	59.90
C2.4 Capacity building	74.42	72.85
C2.5 Case studies	74.89	85.89
C3 Food security	46.45	52.89
C3.1 Food demand and supply	49.91	59.53
C3.2 Food safety	72.07	69.36
C3.3 Nutrition	67.84	67.17
C3.4 Natural and social circumstances	30.53	51.54
C3.5 Government support and response	11.89	16.85
C4 Antimicrobial resistance	20.28	44.05
C4.1 AMR surveillance system	11.33	34.79
C4.2 AMR laboratory network and coordination on capacity	30.01	55.57
C4.3 Antimicrobial control and optimization	16.38	48.76
C4.4 Improve awareness and understanding	20.31	48.09
C4.5 Antimicrobial resistance rate for important antibiotics	23.35	33.03
C5 Climate change	65.15	64.19
C5.1 Mitigation and adaptation capacity	23.57	28.24
C5.2 Climate change risks	85.36	80.87
C5.3 Health outcome	88.48	85.41

Scores are normalized (0-100, where 100 = most favorable)

Madagascar
Sub-Saharan Africa | **Low income**

47.92 | Index Score **136**/160

Global average: 54.82

Regional average: 48.03

Income group average: 46.63

Country performance: 47.92

Missing rate in GOHI database: 25.70%

▼ AVERAGE PERFORMANCE BY GOHI

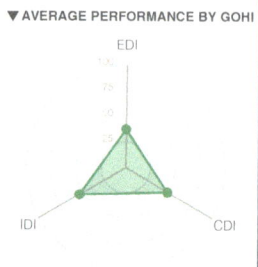
▼ AVERAGE PERFORMANCE BY CDI

	Country Score	Global Average
A External drivers index	37.42	40.45
A1 Earth system	59.21	56.21
A1.1 Land	29.05	36.41
A1.2 Forest	24.92	43.43
A1.3 Water	71.11	58.09
A1.4 Air	90.45	71.93
A1.5 Natural disasters	66.66	64.65
A2 Institutional system	37.98	46.01
A2.1 Justice	48.34	57.89
A2.2 Governance	29.16	35.58
A3 Economical system	26.36	24.62
A3.1 Finance	38.98	34.35
A3.2 Work	38.49	38.58
A4 Sociological system	36.94	37.70
A4.1 Demographic	50.88	46.31
A4.2 Education	26.37	28.26
A4.3 Inequalities	34.92	40.28
A5 Technological system	26.63	37.72
A5.1 Transport	0.01	6.54
A5.2 Technology adoption	13.45	41.23
A5.3 Consumption and production	64.48	62.53
B Intrinsic drivers index	53.59	58.01
B1 Human health	62.10	72.35
B1.1 Health coverage	33.43	58.65
B1.2 Diseases burden	80.40	79.83
B1.3 Injury and violence	74.35	80.75
B2 Animal health and ecosystem diversity	60.89	56.58
B2.1 Animal epidemic disease	93.68	94.57
B2.2 Wildlife and marine life biodiversity	28.10	18.59
B3 Environmental health	39.41	46.87
B3.1 Air quality and climate change	54.29	53.72
B3.2 Environmental biodiversity	34.40	44.05
B3.3 Environmental resources	30.73	44.25

	Country Score	Global Average
C Core drivers index	48.91	57.25
C1 Governance	45.01	56.51
C1.1 Participation	27.39	41.70
C1.3 Transparency	52.00	65.15
C1.4 Responsiveness	29.15	44.42
C1.5 Consensus oriented	92.88	86.45
C1.6 Equity and inclusiveness	37.48	73.61
C1.7 Effectiveness and efficiency	26.67	28.38
C1.8 Political support	49.48	55.89
C2 Zoonotic diseases	56.36	68.06
C2.1 Source of infection	47.85	69.22
C2.2 Route of transmission	56.61	59.30
C2.3 Targeted population	34.73	59.90
C2.4 Capacity building	65.82	72.85
C2.5 Case studies	86.06	85.89
C3 Food security	32.95	52.89
C3.1 Food demand and supply	50.40	59.53
C3.2 Food safety	35.57	69.36
C3.3 Nutrition	40.00	67.17
C3.4 Natural and social circumstances	31.99	51.54
C3.5 Government support and response	6.80	16.85
C4 Antimicrobial resistance	43.76	44.05
C4.1 AMR surveillance system	52.12	34.79
C4.2 AMR laboratory network and coordination on capacity	55.32	55.57
C4.3 Antimicrobial control and optimization	36.74	48.76
C4.4 Improve awareness and understanding	39.06	48.09
C4.5 Antimicrobial resistance rate for important antibiotics	35.52	33.03
C5 Climate change	68.79	64.19
C5.1 Mitigation and adaptation capacity	22.60	28.24
C5.2 Climate change risks	89.86	80.87
C5.3 Health outcome	96.00	85.41

Scores are normalized (0-100, where 100 = most favorable)

Guinea
Sub-Saharan Africa | Low income

 Index Score **137**/160

Global average: 54.82

Regional average: 48.03

Income group average: 46.63

Country performance: 47.82

Missing rate in GOHI database: 30.80%

▼ AVERAGE PERFORMANCE BY GOHI

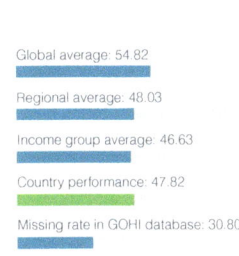

▼ AVERAGE PERFORMANCE BY CDI

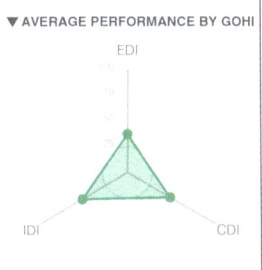

	Country Score	Global Average
A External drivers index	37.64	40.45
A1 Earth system	54.07	56.21
A1.1 Land	40.71	36.41
A1.2 Forest	25.03	43.43
A1.3 Water	70.12	58.09
A1.4 Air	59.75	71.93
A1.5 Natural disasters	66.24	64.65
A2 Institutional system	38.08	46.01
A2.1 Justice	50.52	57.89
A2.2 Governance	27.49	35.58
A3 Economical system	25.03	24.62
A3.1 Finance	34.27	34.35
A3.2 Work	40.02	38.58
A4 Sociological system	39.70	37.70
A4.1 Demographic	60.58	46.31
A4.2 Education	24.71	28.26
A4.3 Inequalities	35.58	40.28
A5 Technological system	31.32	37.72
A5.1 Transport	0.68	6.54
A5.2 Technology adoption	22.66	41.23
A5.3 Consumption and production	68.19	62.53
B Intrinsic drivers index	52.47	58.01
B1 Human health	55.73	72.35
B1.1 Health coverage	25.78	56.65
B1.2 Diseases burden	68.36	79.83
B1.3 Injury and violence	74.72	80.75
B2 Animal health and ecosystem diversity	56.51	56.58
B2.1 Animal epidemic disease	96.52	94.57
B2.2 Wildlife and marine life biodiversity	16.50	18.59
B3 Environmental health	46.75	46.87
B3.1 Air quality and climate change	61.80	53.72
B3.2 Environmental biodiversity	51.33	44.05
B3.3 Environmental resources	28.54	44.25

	Country Score	Global Average
C Core drivers index	48.98	57.25
C1 Governance	41.62	56.51
C1.1 Participation	12.07	41.70
C1.3 Transparency	45.90	65.15
C1.4 Responsiveness	29.15	44.42
C1.5 Consensus oriented	92.49	86.45
C1.6 Equity and inclusiveness	56.82	73.61
C1.7 Effectiveness and efficiency	10.53	28.38
C1.8 Political support	44.40	55.89
C2 Zoonotic diseases	62.70	68.06
C2.1 Source of infection	56.17	69.22
C2.2 Route of transmission	64.90	59.30
C2.3 Targeted population	38.41	59.90
C2.4 Capacity building	72.93	72.85
C2.5 Case studies	88.57	85.89
C3 Food security	43.59	52.89
C3.1 Food demand and supply	41.60	59.53
C3.2 Food safety	62.02	69.36
C3.3 Nutrition	55.99	67.17
C3.4 Natural and social circumstances	48.63	51.54
C3.5 Government support and response	9.73	16.85
C4 Antimicrobial resistance	34.12	44.05
C4.1 AMR surveillance system	29.10	34.79
C4.2 AMR laboratory network and coordinati on capacity	50.52	55.57
C4.3 Antimicrobial control and optimization	40.38	48.76
C4.4 Improve awareness and understanding	31.25	48.09
C4.5 Antimicrobial resistance rate for important antibiotics	19.34	33.03
C5 Climate change	63.30	64.19
C5.1 Mitigation and adaptation capacity	23.55	28.24
C5.2 Climate change risks	77.07	80.87
C5.3 Health outcome	91.21	85.41

Scores are normalized (0-100, where 100 = most favorable)

Papua New Guinea

East Asia & Pacific | Lower middle income

47.77 Index Score **138**/160

Global average: 54.82

Regional average: 56.52

Income group average: 51.29

Country performance: 47.77

Missing rate in GOHI database: 28.30%

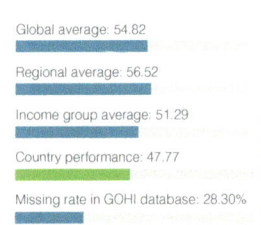

▼ AVERAGE PERFORMANCE BY GOHI

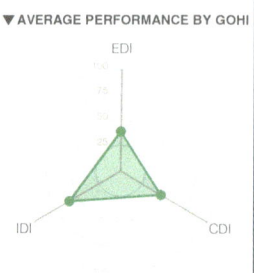

▼ AVERAGE PERFORMANCE BY CDI

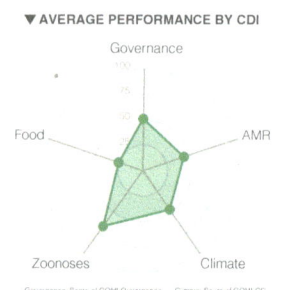

	Country Score	Global Average
A External drivers index	38.65	40.45
A1 Earth system	61.42	56.21
A1.1 Land	26.10	36.41
A1.2 Forest	48.47	43.43
A1.3 Water	79.19	58.09
A1.4 Air	81.42	71.93
A1.5 Natural disasters	58.83	64.65
A2 Institutional system	43.84	46.01
A2.1 Justice	57.22	57.89
A2.2 Governance	32.45	35.58
A3 Economical system	27.00	24.62
A3.1 Finance	40.57	34.35
A3.2 Work	38.60	38.58
A4 Sociological system	32.89	37.70
A4.1 Demographic	44.97	46.31
A4.2 Education	24.41	26.26
A4.3 Inequalities	30.23	40.28
A5 Technological system	28.08	37.72
A5.1 Transport	0.40	6.54
A5.2 Technology adoption	23.12	41.23
A5.3 Consumption and production	58.43	62.53
B Intrinsic drivers index	59.43	58.01
B1 Human health	61.45	72.35
B1.1 Health coverage	35.52	58.65
B1.2 Diseases burden	84.89	79.83
B1.3 Injury and violence	65.80	80.75
B2 Animal health and ecosystem diversity	60.77	56.58
B2.1 Animal epidemic disease	95.29	94.57
B2.2 Wildlife and marine life biodiversity	26.25	18.59
B3 Environmental health	57.86	46.87
B3.1 Air quality and climate change	71.76	53.72
B3.2 Environmental biodiversity	53.25	44.05
B3.3 Environmental resources	50.34	44.25

Scores are normalized (0-100, where 100 = most favorable)

	Country Score	Global Average
C Core drivers index	47.03	57.25
C1 Governance	50.78	56.51
C1.1 Participation	52.36	41.70
C1.3 Transparency	40.80	65.15
C1.4 Responsiveness	60.40	44.42
C1.5 Consensus oriented	95.48	86.45
C1.6 Equity and inclusiveness	51.98	73.61
C1.7 Effectiveness and efficiency	10.73	28.38
C1.8 Political support	43.72	55.89
C2 Zoonotic diseases	46.96	68.06
C2.1 Source of infection	39.10	69.22
C2.2 Route of transmission	32.55	59.30
C2.3 Targeted population	31.88	59.90
C2.4 Capacity building	61.11	72.85
C2.5 Case studies	86.74	85.89
C3 Food security	43.81	52.89
C3.1 Food demand and supply	55.93	59.53
C3.2 Food safety	54.88	69.36
C3.3 Nutrition	48.85	67.17
C3.4 Natural and social circumstances	44.72	51.54
C3.5 Government support and response	14.67	16.85
C4 Antimicrobial resistance	25.72	44.05
C4.1 AMR surveillance system	5.05	34.79
C4.2 AMR laboratory network and coordination capacity	33.52	55.57
C4.3 Antimicrobial control and optimization	18.30	48.76
C4.4 Improve awareness and understanding	34.38	48.09
C4.5 Antimicrobial resistance rate for important antibiotics	37.37	33.03
C5 Climate change	67.31	64.19
C5.1 Mitigation and adaptation capacity	21.14	28.24
C5.2 Climate change risks	89.94	80.87
C5.3 Health outcome	92.88	85.41

Sierra Leone

Sub-Saharan Africa | Low income

47.23 **Index Score 139**/160

Global average: 54.82

Regional average: 48.03

Income group average: 46.63

Country performance: 47.23

Missing rate in GOHI database: 26.10%

▼ AVERAGE PERFORMANCE BY GOHI

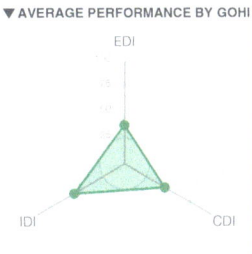

▼ AVERAGE PERFORMANCE BY CDI

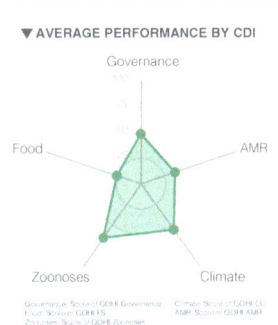

	Country Score	Global Average
A External drivers index	37.93	40.45
A1 Earth system	56.36	56.21
A1.1 Land	36.91	36.41
A1.2 Forest	48.62	43.43
A1.3 Water	69.16	58.09
A1.4 Air	55.27	71.93
A1.5 Natural disasters	66.36	64.65
A2 Institutional system	38.00	46.01
A2.1 Justice	55.19	57.89
A2.2 Governance	23.36	35.58
A3 Economical system	26.90	24.62
A3.1 Finance	39.05	34.35
A3.2 Work	40.22	38.58
A4 Sociological system	38.34	37.70
A4.1 Demographic	63.74	46.31
A4.2 Education	22.89	28.26
A4.3 Inequalities	29.68	40.28
A5 Technological system	30.03	37.72
A5.1 Transport	6.60	6.54
A5.2 Technology adoption	15.66	41.23
A5.3 Consumption and production	66.18	62.53
B Intrinsic drivers index	58.58	58.01
B1 Human health	54.45	72.35
B1.1 Health coverage	28.54	58.65
B1.2 Diseases burden	69.60	79.83
B1.3 Injury and violence	66.87	80.75
B2 Animal health and ecosystem diversity	56.28	56.58
B2.1 Animal epidemic disease	92.06	94.57
B2.2 Wildlife and marine life biodiversity	20.50	18.59
B3 Environmental health	66.80	46.87
B3.1 Air quality and climate change	77.40	53.72
B3.2 Environmental biodiversity	73.90	44.05
B3.3 Environmental resources	51.12	44.25

	Country Score	Global Average
C Core drivers index	46.60	57.25
C1 Governance	48.99	56.51
C1.1 Participation	22.11	41.70
C1.3 Transparency	52.80	65.15
C1.4 Responsiveness	58.30	44.42
C1.5 Consensus oriented	91.64	86.45
C1.6 Equity and inclusiveness	63.74	73.61
C1.7 Effectiveness and efficiency	9.27	28.38
C1.8 Political support	45.05	55.89
C2 Zoonotic diseases	55.96	68.06
C2.1 Source of infection	39.69	69.22
C2.2 Route of transmission	52.50	59.30
C2.3 Targeted population	39.52	59.90
C2.4 Capacity building	72.80	72.85
C2.5 Case studies	89.29	85.89
C3 Food security	36.40	52.89
C3.1 Food demand and supply	44.32	59.53
C3.2 Food safety	37.12	69.36
C3.3 Nutrition	49.97	67.17
C3.4 Natural and social circumstances	41.44	51.54
C3.5 Government support and response	9.16	16.85
C4 Antimicrobial resistance	25.81	44.05
C4.1 AMR surveillance system	5.05	34.79
C4.2 AMR laboratory network and coordination on capacity	43.34	55.57
C4.3 Antimicrobial control and optimization	26.11	48.76
C4.4 Improve awareness and understanding	28.12	48.09
C4.5 Antimicrobial resistance rate for important antibiotics	26.43	33.03
C5 Climate change	65.64	64.19
C5.1 Mitigation and adaptation capacity	25.65	28.24
C5.2 Climate change risks	81.77	80.87
C5.3 Health outcome	91.48	85.41

Scores are normalized (0-100, where 100 = most favorable)

Benin
Sub-Saharan Africa | Lower middle income

Index Score **140**/160

Global average: 54.82

Regional average: 48.03

Income group average: 51.29

Country performance: 47.12

Missing rate in GOHI database: 21.40%

▼ AVERAGE PERFORMANCE BY GOHI

▼ AVERAGE PERFORMANCE BY CDI

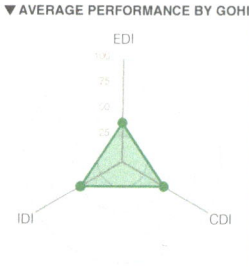

Governance: Score of GOHI-Governance   Climate: Score of GOHI-CC
Food: Score of GOHI-FS   AMR: Score of GOHI-AMR
Zoonoses: Score of GOHI-Zoonoses

	Country Score	Global Average
A External drivers index	37.88	40.45
A1 Earth system	51.53	56.21
A1.1 Land	41.64	36.41
A1.2 Forest	33.72	43.43
A1.3 Water	46.46	58.09
A1.4 Air	65.69	71.93
A1.5 Natural disasters	66.44	64.65
A2 Institutional system	42.27	46.01
A2.1 Justice	51.40	57.89
A2.2 Governance	34.48	35.58
A3 Economical system	23.00	24.62
A3.1 Finance	29.86	34.35
A3.2 Work	38.85	38.58
A4 Sociological system	39.10	37.70
A4.1 Demographic	59.29	46.31
A4.2 Education	27.02	28.26
A4.3 Inequalities	31.96	40.28
A5 Technological system	33.50	37.72
A5.1 Transport	6.00	6.54
A5.2 Technology adoption	21.39	41.23
A5.3 Consumption and production	71.05	62.53
B Intrinsic drivers index	48.94	58.01
B1 Human health	57.92	72.35
B1.1 Health coverage	25.88	58.65
B1.2 Diseases burden	73.19	79.83
B1.3 Injury and violence	76.43	80.75
B2 Animal health and ecosystem diversity	50.84	56.58
B2.1 Animal epidemic disease	91.52	94.57
B2.2 Wildlife and marine life biodiversity	10.15	18.59
B3 Environmental health	39.55	46.87
B3.1 Air quality and climate change	61.15	53.72
B3.2 Environmental biodiversity	39.70	44.05
B3.3 Environmental resources	19.00	44.25

	Country Score	Global Average
C Core drivers index	48.74	57.25
C1 Governance	45.89	56.51
C1.1 Participation	12.47	41.70
C1.3 Transparency	48.00	65.15
C1.4 Responsiveness	35.40	44.42
C1.5 Consensus oriented	92.90	86.45
C1.6 Equity and inclusiveness	57.99	73.61
C1.7 Effectiveness and efficiency	23.60	28.38
C1.8 Political support	50.89	55.89
C2 Zoonotic diseases	48.69	68.06
C2.1 Source of infection	24.48	69.22
C2.2 Route of transmission	48.98	59.30
C2.3 Targeted population	30.23	59.90
C2.4 Capacity building	68.12	72.85
C2.5 Case studies	87.85	85.89
C3 Food security	47.19	52.89
C3.1 Food demand and supply	46.18	59.53
C3.2 Food safety	61.74	69.36
C3.3 Nutrition	68.93	67.17
C3.4 Natural and social circumstances	47.42	51.54
C3.5 Government support and response	11.68	16.85
C4 Antimicrobial resistance	40.48	44.05
C4.1 AMR surveillance system	34.15	34.79
C4.2 AMR laboratory network and coordination on capacity	52.82	55.57
C4.3 Antimicrobial control and optimization	35.63	48.76
C4.4 Improve awareness and understanding	42.19	48.09
C4.5 Antimicrobial resistance rate for important antibiotics	37.61	33.03
C5 Climate change	62.06	64.19
C5.1 Mitigation and adaptation capacity	22.36	28.24
C5.2 Climate change risks	78.40	80.87
C5.3 Health outcome	87.29	85.41

Scores are normalized (0-100, where 100 = most favorable)

Malawi
Sub-Saharan Africa | Low income

46.92 **Index Score 141**/160

Global average: 54.82

Regional average: 48.03

Income group average: 46.63

Country performance: 46.92

Missing rate in GOHI database: 19.90%

▼ AVERAGE PERFORMANCE BY GOHI

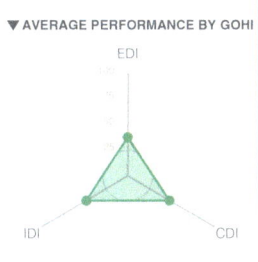

▼ AVERAGE PERFORMANCE BY CDI

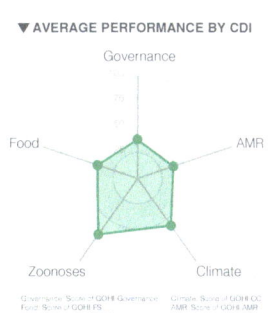

	Country Score	Global Average
A External drivers index	37.73	40.45
A1 Earth system	56.04	56.21
A1.1 Land	33.40	36.41
A1.2 Forest	21.08	43.43
A1.3 Water	63.42	58.09
A1.4 Air	84.88	71.93
A1.5 Natural disasters	65.63	64.65
A2 Institutional system	44.78	46.01
A2.1 Justice	57.17	57.89
A2.2 Governance	34.22	35.58
A3 Economical system	26.98	24.62
A3.1 Finance	40.25	34.35
A3.2 Work	38.94	38.68
A4 Sociological system	33.61	37.70
A4.1 Demographic	46.89	46.31
A4.2 Education	24.99	28.26
A4.3 Inequalities	29.78	40.28
A5 Technological system	27.24	37.72
A5.1 Transport	0.54	6.54
A5.2 Technology adoption	11.19	41.23
A5.3 Consumption and production	68.09	62.53
B Intrinsic drivers index	48.57	58.01
B1 Human health	63.43	72.35
B1.1 Health coverage	39.68	58.65
B1.2 Diseases burden	80.94	79.83
B1.3 Injury and violence	71.60	80.75
B2 Animal health and ecosystem diversity	57.36	56.58
B2.1 Animal epidemic disease	95.74	94.57
B2.2 Wildlife and marine life biodiversity	18.99	18.59
B3 Environmental health	26.39	46.87
B3.1 Air quality and climate change	33.13	53.72
B3.2 Environmental biodiversity	26.40	44.05
B3.3 Environmental resources	20.44	44.25

	Country Score	Global Average
C Core drivers index	48.57	57.25
C1 Governance	38.32	56.51
C1.1 Participation	11.33	41.70
C1.3 Transparency	56.50	65.15
C1.4 Responsiveness	18.75	44.42
C1.5 Consensus oriented	84.18	86.45
C1.6 Equity and inclusiveness	44.43	73.61
C1.7 Effectiveness and efficiency	11.53	28.38
C1.8 Political support	41.50	55.89
C2 Zoonotic diseases	57.51	68.06
C2.1 Source of infection	62.10	69.22
C2.2 Route of transmission	39.93	59.30
C2.3 Targeted population	39.72	59.90
C2.4 Capacity building	71.12	72.85
C2.5 Case studies	87.07	85.89
C3 Food security	38.61	52.89
C3.1 Food demand and supply	40.01	59.53
C3.2 Food safety	37.18	69.36
C3.3 Nutrition	57.70	67.17
C3.4 Natural and social circumstances	46.36	51.54
C3.5 Government support and response	11.79	16.85
C4 Antimicrobial resistance	42.50	44.05
C4.1 AMR surveillance system	24.96	34.79
C4.2 AMR laboratory network and coordinati on capacity	77.10	55.57
C4.3 Antimicrobial control and optimization	50.11	48.76
C4.4 Improve awareness and understanding	45.31	48.09
C4.5 Antimicrobial resistance rate for important antibiotics	15.03	33.03
C5 Climate change	68.26	64.19
C5.1 Mitigation and adaptation capacity	25.29	28.24
C5.2 Climate change risks	87.80	80.87
C5.3 Health outcome	83.76	85.41

Scores are normalized (0-100, where 100 = most favorable)

Cabo Verde

Sub-Saharan Africa | Lower middle income

46.87 Index Score **142**/160

Global average: 54.82

Regional average: 48.03

Income group average: 51.29

Country performance: 46.87

Missing rate in GOHI database: 29.30%

▼ AVERAGE PERFORMANCE BY GOHI

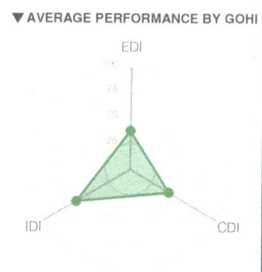

▼ AVERAGE PERFORMANCE BY CDI

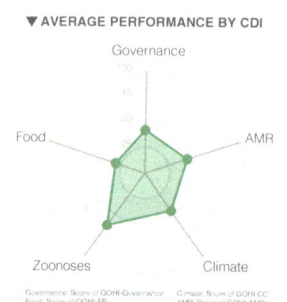

	Country Score	Global Average
A External drivers index	37.77	40.45
A1 Earth system	50.50	56.21
A1.1 Land	20.02	36.41
A1.2 Forest	37.77	43.43
A1.3 Water	66.06	58.09
A1.4 Air	55.37	71.93
A1.5 Natural disasters	66.51	64.65
A2 Institutional system	48.81	46.01
A2.1 Justice	62.35	57.89
A2.2 Governance	37.28	35.58
A3 Economical system	22.46	24.62
A3.1 Finance	29.15	34.35
A3.2 Work	37.94	38.58
A4 Sociological system	32.50	37.70
A4.1 Demographic	37.45	46.31
A4.2 Education	25.35	28.26
A4.3 Inequalities	36.22	40.28
A5 Technological system	34.59	37.72
A5.1 Transport	6.22	6.54
A5.2 Technology adoption	30.47	41.23
A5.3 Consumption and production	64.70	62.53
B Intrinsic drivers index	62.40	58.01
B1 Human health	73.32	72.35
B1.1 Health coverage	64.76	58.65
B1.2 Diseases burden	84.67	79.83
B1.3 Injury and violence	72.73	80.75
B2 Animal health and ecosystem diversity	73.37	56.58
B2.1 Animal epidemic disease	92.23	94.57
B2.2 Wildlife and marine life biodiversity	54.50	18.59
B3 Environmental health	42.41	46.87
B3.1 Air quality and climate change	49.16	53.72
B3.2 Environmental biodiversity	46.45	44.05
B3.3 Environmental resources	32.90	44.25

	Country Score	Global Average
C Core drivers index	45.21	57.25
C1 Governance	42.18	56.51
C1.1 Participation	54.11	41.70
C1.3 Transparency	54.70	65.15
C1.4 Responsiveness	58.30	44.42
C1.5 Consensus oriented	1.21	86.45
C1.6 Equity and inclusiveness	75.53	73.61
C1.7 Effectiveness and efficiency	25.27	28.38
C1.8 Political support	26.10	55.89
C2 Zoonotic diseases	45.36	68.06
C2.1 Source of infection	45.86	69.22
C2.2 Route of transmission	26.27	59.30
C2.3 Targeted population	48.25	59.90
C2.4 Capacity building	30.99	72.85
C2.5 Case studies	88.79	85.89
C3 Food security	44.87	52.99
C3.1 Food demand and supply	50.76	59.53
C3.2 Food safety	81.47	69.36
C3.3 Nutrition	50.50	67.17
C3.4 Natural and social circumstances	39.85	51.54
C3.5 Government support and response	1.80	16.85
C4 Antimicrobial resistance	30.70	44.05
C4.1 AMR surveillance system	21.13	34.79
C4.2 AMR laboratory network and coordination capacity	33.06	55.57
C4.3 Antimicrobial control and optimization	31.67	48.76
C4.4 Improve awareness and understanding	40.62	48.09
C4.5 Antimicrobial resistance rate for important antibiotics	27.03	33.03
C5 Climate change	63.22	64.19
C5.1 Mitigation and adaptation capacity	24.43	28.24
C5.2 Climate change risks	83.96	80.87
C5.3 Health outcome	83.18	85.41

Scores are normalized (0-100, where 100 = most favorable)

Libya

Middle East & North Africa | **Upper middle income**

Index Score **143**/160

Global average: 54.82

Regional average: 53.57

Income group average: 54.54

Country performance: 46.49

Missing rate in GOHI database: 28.60%

▼ AVERAGE PERFORMANCE BY GOHI

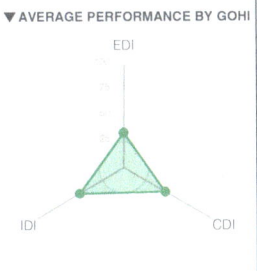

▼ AVERAGE PERFORMANCE BY CDI

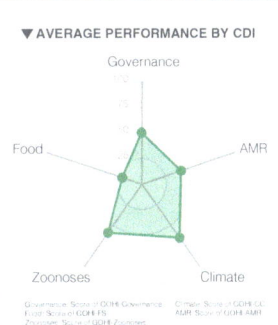

	Country Score	Global Average
A External drivers index	34.00	40.45
A1 Earth system	49.88	56.21
A1.1 Land	66.46	36.41
A1.2 Forest	25.95	43.43
A1.3 Water	33.34	58.09
A1.4 Air	58.75	71.93
A1.5 Natural disasters	65.08	64.65
A2 Institutional system	28.08	46.01
A2.1 Justice	43.41	57.89
A2.2 Governance	15.02	35.58
A3 Economical system	20.37	24.62
A3.1 Finance	25.03	34.35
A3.2 Work	36.20	38.58
A4 Sociological system	39.33	37.70
A4.1 Demographic	48.42	46.31
A4.2 Education	27.70	28.26
A4.3 Inequalities	44.23	40.28
A5 Technological system	32.35	37.72
A5.1 Transport	0.12	6.54
A5.2 Technology adoption	31.34	41.23
A5.3 Consumption and production	62.79	62.53
B Intrinsic drivers index	51.60	56.01
B1 Human health	72.32	72.35
B1.1 Health coverage	60.37	58.65
B1.2 Diseases burden	89.20	79.83
B1.3 Injury and violence	69.58	80.75
B2 Animal health and ecosystem diversity	55.28	56.58
B2.1 Animal epidemic disease	89.99	94.57
B2.2 Wildlife and marine life biodiversity	20.57	18.59
B3 Environmental health	28.77	46.87
B3.1 Air quality and climate change	51.79	53.72
B3.2 Environmental biodiversity	14.60	44.05
B3.3 Environmental resources	20.80	44.25

	Country Score	Global Average
C Core drivers index	48.05	57.25
C1 Governance	50.56	56.51
C1.1 Participation	60.22	41.70
C1.3 Transparency	21.40	65.15
C1.4 Responsiveness	41.65	44.42
C1.5 Consensus oriented	99.99	86.45
C1.6 Equity and inclusiveness	76.18	73.61
C1.7 Effectiveness and efficiency	5.20	28.38
C1.8 Political support	49.32	55.89
C2 Zoonotic diseases	65.29	68.06
C2.1 Source of infection	68.72	69.22
C2.2 Route of transmission	59.46	59.30
C2.3 Targeted population	71.05	59.90
C2.4 Capacity building	43.37	72.85
C2.5 Case studies	86.66	85.89
C3 Food security	42.46	52.89
C3.1 Food demand and supply	57.24	59.53
C3.2 Food safety	58.55	69.36
C3.3 Nutrition	43.27	67.17
C3.4 Natural and social circumstances	47.22	51.54
C3.5 Government support and response	6.00	16.85
C4 Antimicrobial resistance	21.00	44.05
C4.1 AMR surveillance system	1.30	34.79
C4.2 AMR laboratory network and coordination capacity	35.96	55.57
C4.3 Antimicrobial control and optimization	8.61	48.76
C4.4 Improve awareness and understanding	29.69	48.09
C4.5 Antimicrobial resistance rate for important antibiotics	29.42	33.03
C5 Climate change	59.08	64.19
C5.1 Mitigation and adaptation capacity	28.45	28.24
C5.2 Climate change risks	70.52	80.87
C5.3 Health outcome	80.05	85.41

Scores are normalized (0-100, where 100 = most favorable)

Cameroon

Sub-Saharan Africa | Lower middle income

 **Index Score 144**/160

46.06

Global average: 54.82

Regional average: 48.03

Income group average: 51.29

Country performance: 46.06

Missing rate in GOHI database: 23.60%

▼ AVERAGE PERFORMANCE BY GOHI

▼ AVERAGE PERFORMANCE BY CDI

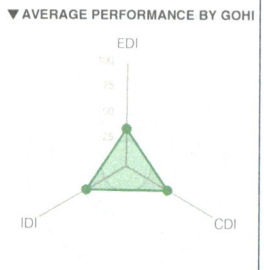

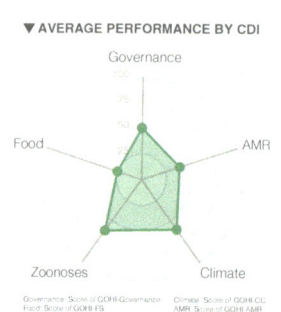

Governance: Score of GOHI-Governance   Climate: Score of GOHI-CC
Food: Score of GOHI-FS   AMR: Score of GOHI-AMR
Zoonoses: Score of GOHI-Zoonoses

	Country Score	Global Average
A External drivers index	36.44	40.45
A1 Earth system	53.70	56.21
A1.1 Land	41.90	36.41
A1.2 Forest	32.36	43.43
A1.3 Water	69.65	58.09
A1.4 Air	52.47	71.93
A1.5 Natural disasters	65.47	64.65
A2 Institutional system	34.15	46.01
A2.1 Justice	44.88	57.89
A2.2 Governance	25.00	35.58
A3 Economical system	21.95	24.62
A3.1 Finance	25.51	34.35
A3.2 Work	40.87	38.58
A4 Sociological system	39.18	37.70
A4.1 Demographic	60.15	46.31
A4.2 Education	26.94	28.26
A4.3 Inequalities	31.27	40.28
A5 Technological system	33.26	37.72
A5.1 Transport	5.69	6.54
A5.2 Technology adoption	22.52	41.23
A5.3 Consumption and production	69.46	62.53
B Intrinsic drivers index	46.67	58.01
B1 Human health	56.90	72.35
B1.1 Health coverage	25.92	58.65
B1.2 Diseases burden	75.91	79.83
B1.3 Injury and violence	70.60	80.75
B2 Animal health and ecosystem diversity	55.01	56.58
B2.1 Animal epidemic disease	96.81	94.57
B2.2 Wildlife and marine life biodiversity	13.20	18.59
B3 Environmental health	29.52	46.87
B3.1 Air quality and climate change	34.63	53.72
B3.2 Environmental biodiversity	30.55	44.05
B3.3 Environmental resources	24.26	44.25

	Country Score	Global Average
C Core drivers index	48.05	57.25
C1 Governance	50.62	56.51
C1.1 Participation	46.64	41.70
C1.3 Transparency	53.50	65.15
C1.4 Responsiveness	35.40	44.42
C1.5 Consensus oriented	96.72	86.45
C1.6 Equity and inclusiveness	55.02	73.61
C1.7 Effectiveness and efficiency	19.13	28.38
C1.8 Political support	47.90	55.89
C2 Zoonotic diseases	60.62	68.06
C2.1 Source of infection	45.92	69.22
C2.2 Route of transmission	63.44	59.30
C2.3 Targeted population	40.61	59.90
C2.4 Capacity building	75.99	72.85
C2.5 Case studies	87.11	85.89
C3 Food security	40.36	52.89
C3.1 Food demand and supply	45.69	59.53
C3.2 Food safety	37.40	69.36
C3.3 Nutrition	54.03	67.17
C3.4 Natural and social circumstances	52.02	51.54
C3.5 Government support and response	12.67	16.85
C4 Antimicrobial resistance	25.57	44.05
C4.1 AMR surveillance system	20.91	34.79
C4.2 AMR laboratory network and coordination on capacity	41.76	55.57
C4.3 Antimicrobial control and optimization	13.17	48.76
C4.4 Improve awareness and understanding	18.75	48.09
C4.5 Antimicrobial resistance rate for important antibiotics	33.27	33.03
C5 Climate change	62.10	64.19
C5.1 Mitigation and adaptation capacity	22.49	28.24
C5.2 Climate change risks	78.57	80.87
C5.3 Health outcome	87.54	85.41

Scores are normalized (0-100, where 100 = most favorable)

Togo
Sub-Saharan Africa | Low income

45.66 Index **145**/160
Score

Global average: 54.82

Regional average: 48.03

Income group average: 46.63

Country performance: 45.66

Missing rate in GOHI database: 22.80%

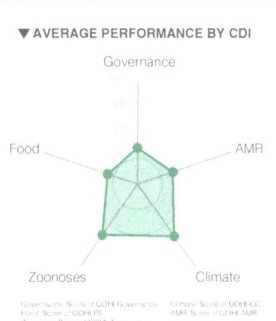

▼ AVERAGE PERFORMANCE BY GOHI

▼ AVERAGE PERFORMANCE BY CDI

	Country Score	Global Average
A External drivers index	37.76	40.45
A1 Earth system	53.44	56.21
A1.1 Land	46.03	36.41
A1.2 Forest	36.43	43.43
A1.3 Water	59.36	58.09
A1.4 Air	67.39	71.93
A1.5 Natural disasters	49.37	64.65
A2 Institutional system	38.45	46.01
A2.1 Justice	49.80	57.89
A2.2 Governance	28.79	35.58
A3 Economical system	25.82	24.62
A3.1 Finance	36.71	34.35
A3.2 Work	39.56	38.58
A4 Sociological system	36.63	37.70
A4.1 Demographic	54.66	46.31
A4.2 Education	24.38	28.26
A4.3 Inequalities	32.17	40.28
A5 Technological system	34.44	37.72
A5.1 Transport	8.14	6.54
A5.2 Technology adoption	22.66	41.23
A5.3 Consumption and production	70.55	62.53
B Intrinsic drivers index	51.76	58.01
B1 Human health	60.13	72.35
B1.1 Health coverage	32.61	58.65
B1.2 Diseases burden	77.61	79.83
B1.3 Injury and violence	71.97	80.75
B2 Animal health and ecosystem diversity	52.15	56.58
B2.1 Animal epidemic disease	93.75	94.57
B2.2 Wildlife and marine life biodiversity	10.55	18.59
B3 Environmental health	44.57	46.87
B3.1 Air quality and climate change	66.25	53.72
B3.2 Environmental biodiversity	44.65	44.05
B3.3 Environmental resources	24.16	44.25

Scores are normalized (0-100, where 100 = most favorable)

	Country Score	Global Average
C Core drivers index	45.97	57.25
C1 Governance	35.51	56.51
C1.1 Participation	14.16	41.70
C1.3 Transparency	60.90	65.15
C1.4 Responsiveness	35.40	44.42
C1.5 Consensus oriented	39.21	86.45
C1.6 Equity and inclusiveness	50.80	73.61
C1.7 Effectiveness and efficiency	12.33	28.38
C1.8 Political support	35.75	55.89
C2 Zoonotic diseases	63.45	68.06
C2.1 Source of infection	49.73	69.22
C2.2 Route of transmission	76.07	59.30
C2.3 Targeted population	34.03	59.90
C2.4 Capacity building	74.98	72.85
C2.5 Case studies	88.20	85.89
C3 Food security	38.20	52.89
C3.1 Food demand and supply	50.75	59.53
C3.2 Food safety	31.82	69.36
C3.3 Nutrition	50.70	67.17
C3.4 Natural and social circumstances	48.84	51.54
C3.5 Government support and response	8.88	16.85
C4 Antimicrobial resistance	31.90	44.05
C4.1 AMR surveillance system	17.15	34.79
C4.2 AMR laboratory network and coordinati on capacity	45.45	55.57
C4.3 Antimicrobial control and optimization	38.49	48.76
C4.4 Improve awareness and understanding	35.94	48.09
C4.5 Antimicrobial resistance rate for important antibiotics	22.45	33.03
C5 Climate change	61.79	64.19
C5.1 Mitigation and adaptation capacity	18.11	28.24
C5.2 Climate change risks	80.16	80.87
C5.3 Health outcome	88.98	85.41

Liberia

Sub-Saharan Africa | Low income

45.59 Index Score **146**/160

Global average: 54.82

Regional average: 48.03

Income group average: 46.63

Country performance: 45.59

Missing rate in GOHI database: 23.90%

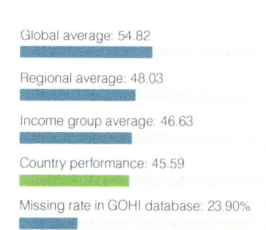

▼ AVERAGE PERFORMANCE BY GOHI

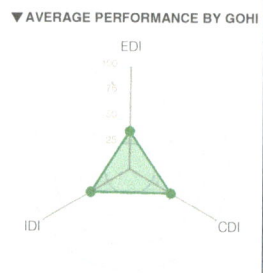

▼ AVERAGE PERFORMANCE BY CDI

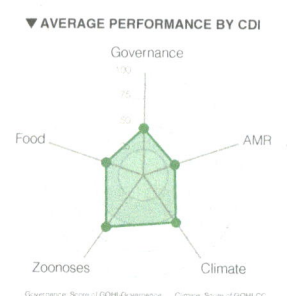

	Country Score	Global Average
A External drivers index	37.03	40.45
A1 Earth system	54.28	56.21
A1.1 Land	33.51	36.41
A1.2 Forest	45.21	43.43
A1.3 Water	65.19	58.09
A1.4 Air	55.76	71.93
A1.5 Natural disasters	66.51	64.65
A2 Institutional system	40.86	46.01
A2.1 Justice	53.12	57.89
A2.2 Governance	30.41	35.58
A3 Economical system	23.41	24.62
A3.1 Finance	29.46	34.35
A3.2 Work	40.70	38.58
A4 Sociological system	37.70	37.70
A4.1 Demographic	60.45	46.31
A4.2 Education	23.70	28.26
A4.3 Inequalities	30.17	40.28
A5 Technological system	28.91	37.72
A5.1 Transport	6.07	6.54
A5.2 Technology adoption	12.68	41.23
A5.3 Consumption and production	66.42	62.53
B Intrinsic drivers index	44.96	58.01
B1 Human health	58.83	72.35
B1.1 Health coverage	31.92	58.65
B1.2 Diseases burden	81.05	79.83
B1.3 Injury and violence	65.31	80.75
B2 Animal health and ecosystem diversity	53.77	56.58
B2.1 Animal epidemic disease	92.19	94.57
B2.2 Wildlife and marine life biodiversity	15.35	18.59
B3 Environmental health	23.64	46.87
B3.1 Air quality and climate change	32.43	53.72
B3.2 Environmental biodiversity	21.00	44.05
B3.3 Environmental resources	18.22	44.25

	Country Score	Global Average
C Core drivers index	47.64	57.25
C1 Governance	45.74	56.51
C1.1 Participation	11.48	41.70
C1.3 Transparency	49.40	65.15
C1.4 Responsiveness	33.35	44.42
C1.5 Consensus oriented	93.31	86.45
C1.6 Equity and inclusiveness	55.59	73.61
C1.7 Effectiveness and efficiency	32.47	28.38
C1.8 Political support	44.59	55.89
C2 Zoonotic diseases	57.41	68.06
C2.1 Source of infection	28.90	69.22
C2.2 Route of transmission	44.12	59.30
C2.3 Targeted population	67.62	59.90
C2.4 Capacity building	75.75	72.85
C2.5 Case studies	91.07	85.89
C3 Food security	33.58	52.89
C3.1 Food demand and supply	37.96	59.53
C3.2 Food safety	39.81	69.36
C3.3 Nutrition	41.24	67.17
C3.4 Natural and social circumstances	42.19	51.54
C3.5 Government support and response	6.71	16.85
C4 Antimicrobial resistance	39.50	44.05
C4.1 AMR surveillance system	11.25	34.79
C4.2 AMR laboratory network and coordinati on capacity	59.16	55.57
C4.3 Antimicrobial control and optimization	41.46	48.76
C4.4 Improve awareness and understanding	59.38	48.09
C4.5 Antimicrobial resistance rate for important antibiotics	26.23	33.03
C5 Climate change	63.32	64.19
C5.1 Mitigation and adaptation capacity	15.37	28.24
C5.2 Climate change risks	83.44	80.87
C5.3 Health outcome	93.07	85.41

Scores are normalized (0-100, where 100 = most favorable)

Vanuatu

East Asia & Pacific | Lower middle income

44.81 **Index Score** **147**/160

Global average: 54.82	
Regional average: 56.52	
Income group average: 51.29	
Country performance: 44.81	
Missing rate in GOHI database: 29.70%	

▼ AVERAGE PERFORMANCE BY GOHI

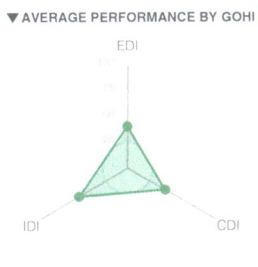

▼ AVERAGE PERFORMANCE BY CDI

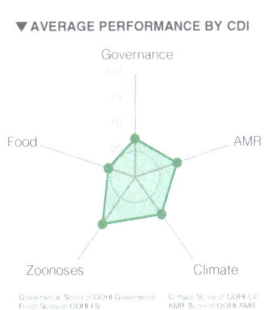

	Country Score	Global Average
A External drivers index	40.92	40.45
A1 Earth system	64.94	56.21
A1.1 Land	38.10	36.41
A1.2 Forest	60.58	43.43
A1.3 Water	65.78	58.09
A1.4 Air	86.19	71.93
A1.5 Natural disasters	65.79	64.65
A2 Institutional system	49.54	46.01
A2.1 Justice	58.55	57.89
A2.2 Governance	41.85	35.58
A3 Economical system	25.59	24.62
A3.1 Finance	34.80	34.35
A3.2 Work	41.21	38.58
A4 Sociological system	32.36	37.70
A4.1 Demographic	40.40	46.31
A4.2 Education	24.00	28.26
A4.3 Inequalities	34.16	40.28
A5 Technological system	32.17	37.72
A5.1 Transport	6.12	6.54
A5.2 Technology adoption	22.61	41.23
A5.3 Consumption and production	65.76	62.53
B Intrinsic drivers index	56.56	58.01
B1 Human health	66.16	72.35
B1.1 Health coverage	43.80	58.65
B1.2 Diseases burden	73.64	79.83
B1.3 Injury and violence	83.03	80.75
B2 Animal health and ecosystem diversity	60.18	56.58
B2.1 Animal epidemic disease	92.87	94.57
B2.2 Wildlife and marine life biodiversity	27.50	18.59
B3 Environmental health	45.04	46.87
B3.1 Air quality and climate change	58.35	53.72
B3.2 Environmental biodiversity	47.75	44.05
B3.3 Environmental resources	30.38	44.25

	Country Score	Global Average
C Core drivers index	42.88	57.25
C1 Governance	37.74	56.51
C1.1 Participation	52.09	41.70
C1.3 Transparency	40.70	65.15
C1.4 Responsiveness	35.40	44.42
C1.5 Consensus oriented	44.64	86.45
C1.6 Equity and inclusiveness	48.66	73.61
C1.7 Effectiveness and efficiency	12.93	28.38
C1.8 Political support	29.78	55.89
C2 Zoonotic diseases	45.50	68.06
C2.1 Source of infection	38.33	69.22
C2.2 Route of transmission	37.46	59.30
C2.3 Targeted population	43.81	59.90
C2.4 Capacity building	30.27	72.85
C2.5 Case studies	89.15	85.89
C3 Food security	45.32	52.89
C3.1 Food demand and supply	60.09	59.53
C3.2 Food safety	61.08	69.36
C3.3 Nutrition	57.72	67.17
C3.4 Natural and social circumstances	44.98	51.54
C3.5 Government support and response	2.73	16.85
C4 Antimicrobial resistance	28.57	44.05
C4.1 AMR surveillance system	12.87	34.79
C4.2 AMR laboratory network and coordination on capacity	31.74	55.57
C4.3 Antimicrobial control and optimization	43.31	48.76
C4.4 Improve awareness and understanding	28.12	48.09
C4.5 Antimicrobial resistance rate for important antibiotics	26.83	33.03
C5 Climate change	57.25	64.19
C5.1 Mitigation and adaptation capacity	21.73	28.24
C5.2 Climate change risks	87.83	80.87
C5.3 Health outcome	63.91	85.41

Scores are normalized (0-100, where 100 = most favorable)

Niger
Sub-Saharan Africa | Low income

44.77 Index Score **148**/160

Global average: 54.82

Regional average: 48.03

Income group average: 46.63

Country performance: 44.77

Missing rate in GOHI database: 25.70%

▼ AVERAGE PERFORMANCE BY GOHI

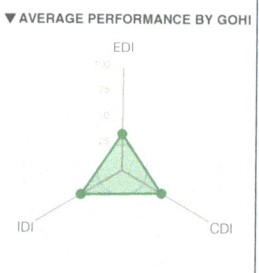

▼ AVERAGE PERFORMANCE BY CDI

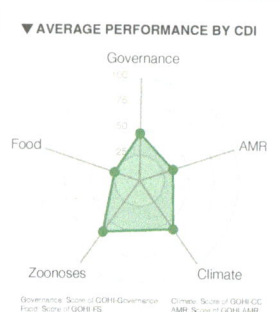

Governance: Score of GOHI-Governance   Climate: Score of GOHI-CC
Food: Score of GOHI-FS   AMR: Score of GOHI-AMR
Zoonoses: Score of GOHI-Zoonoses

	Country Score	Global Average
A External drivers index	35.54	40.45
A1 Earth system	51.84	56.21
A1.1 Land	79.09	36.41
A1.2 Forest	29.97	43.43
A1.3 Water	36.00	58.09
A1.4 Air	50.00	71.93
A1.5 Natural disasters	66.32	64.65
A2 Institutional system	39.09	46.01
A2.1 Justice	51.44	57.89
A2.2 Governance	28.58	35.58
A3 Economical system	21.42	24.62
A3.1 Finance	25.41	34.35
A3.2 Work	39.22	38.58
A4 Sociological system	35.02	37.70
A4.1 Demographic	52.91	46.31
A4.2 Education	25.43	28.26
A4.3 Inequalities	27.24	40.28
A5 Technological system	30.34	37.72
A5.1 Transport	2.30	6.54
A5.2 Technology adoption	15.37	41.23
A5.3 Consumption and production	71.33	62.53
B Intrinsic drivers index	46.35	58.01
B1 Human health	56.05	72.35
B1.1 Health coverage	26.48	58.65
B1.2 Diseases burden	66.13	79.83
B1.3 Injury and violence	77.24	80.75
B2 Animal health and ecosystem diversity	52.17	56.58
B2.1 Animal epidemic disease	91.55	94.57
B2.2 Wildlife and marine life biodiversity	12.79	18.59
B3 Environmental health	38.30	46.87
B3.1 Air quality and climate change	43.09	53.72
B3.2 Environmental biodiversity	39.90	44.05
B3.3 Environmental resources	33.08	44.25

Scores are normalized (0-100, where 100 = most favorable)

	Country Score	Global Average
C Core drivers index	45.97	57.25
C1 Governance	46.27	56.51
C1.1 Participation	16.97	41.70
C1.3 Transparency	57.00	65.15
C1.4 Responsiveness	27.10	44.42
C1.5 Consensus oriented	96.02	86.45
C1.6 Equity and inclusiveness	57.53	73.61
C1.7 Effectiveness and efficiency	20.93	28.38
C1.8 Political support	48.38	55.89
C2 Zoonotic diseases	58.76	68.06
C2.1 Source of infection	51.20	69.22
C2.2 Route of transmission	62.96	59.30
C2.3 Targeted population	35.17	59.90
C2.4 Capacity building	66.93	72.85
C2.5 Case studies	84.30	85.89
C3 Food security	35.71	52.89
C3.1 Food demand and supply	35.75	59.53
C3.2 Food safety	28.60	69.36
C3.3 Nutrition	49.95	67.17
C3.4 Natural and social circumstances	52.50	51.54
C3.5 Government support and response	11.76	16.85
C4 Antimicrobial resistance	26.66	44.05
C4.1 AMR surveillance system	22.75	34.79
C4.2 AMR laboratory network and coordination capacity	29.08	55.57
C4.3 Antimicrobial control and optimization	32.61	48.76
C4.4 Improve awareness and understanding	26.56	48.09
C4.5 Antimicrobial resistance rate for important antibiotics	22.28	33.03
C5 Climate change	62.27	64.19
C5.1 Mitigation and adaptation capacity	28.45	28.24
C5.2 Climate change risks	76.83	80.87
C5.3 Health outcome	83.42	85.41

Equatorial Guinea

Sub-Saharan Africa | Upper middle income

44.69 Index Score **149**/160

Global average: 54.82

Regional average: 48.03

Income group average: 54.54

Country performance: 44.69

Missing rate in GOHI database: 32.60%

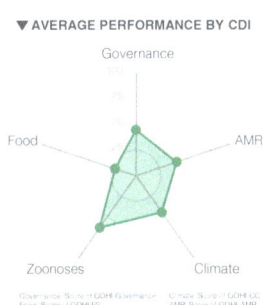

▼ AVERAGE PERFORMANCE BY GOHI

EDI

IDI

CDI

▼ AVERAGE PERFORMANCE BY CDI

Governance

Food

AMR

Zoonoses

Climate

	Country Score	Global Average
A External drivers index	37.76	40.45
A1 Earth system	57.47	56.21
A1.1 Land	30.12	36.41
A1.2 Forest	56.94	43.43
A1.3 Water	67.07	58.09
A1.4 Air	61.36	71.93
A1.5 Natural disasters	66.39	64.65
A2 Institutional system	31.64	46.01
A2.1 Justice	43.91	57.89
A2.2 Governance	21.19	35.58
A3 Economical system	24.39	24.62
A3.1 Finance	34.66	34.35
A3.2 Work	37.40	38.58
A4 Sociological system	40.98	37.70
A4.1 Demographic	62.98	46.31
A4.2 Education	25.85	28.26
A4.3 Inequalities	35.76	40.28
A5 Technological system	34.34	37.72
A5.1 Transport	4.46	6.54
A5.2 Technology adoption	26.67	41.23
A5.3 Consumption and production	69.48	62.53
B Intrinsic drivers index	54.37	58.01
B1 Human health	63.32	72.35
B1.1 Health coverage	32.61	58.65
B1.2 Diseases burden	83.97	79.83
B1.3 Injury and violence	75.29	80.75
B2 Animal health and ecosystem diversity	56.50	56.58
B2.1 Animal epidemic disease	92.05	94.57
B2.2 Wildlife and marine life biodiversity	20.95	18.59
B3 Environmental health	44.94	46.87
B3.1 Air quality and climate change	57.00	53.72
B3.2 Environmental biodiversity	34.85	44.05
B3.3 Environmental resources	44.32	44.25

	Country Score	Global Average
C Core drivers index	43.94	57.25
C1 Governance	45.07	56.51
C1.1 Participation	17.63	41.70
C1.3 Transparency	61.67	65.15
C1.4 Responsiveness	18.75	44.42
C1.5 Consensus oriented	95.56	86.45
C1.6 Equity and inclusiveness	69.20	73.61
C1.7 Effectiveness and efficiency	8.93	28.38
C1.8 Political support	43.75	55.89
C2 Zoonotic diseases	44.64	68.06
C2.1 Source of infection	27.94	69.22
C2.2 Route of transmission	31.04	59.30
C2.3 Targeted population	33.53	59.90
C2.4 Capacity building	62.61	72.85
C2.5 Case studies	87.63	85.89
C3 Food security	43.95	52.89
C3.1 Food demand and supply	52.54	59.53
C3.2 Food safety	51.62	69.36
C3.3 Nutrition	53.56	67.17
C3.4 Natural and social circumstances	47.01	51.54
C3.5 Government support and response	15.02	16.85
C4 Antimicrobial resistance	22.32	44.05
C4.1 AMR surveillance system	27.80	34.79
C4.2 AMR laboratory network and coordination on capacity	25.58	55.57
C4.3 Antimicrobial control and optimization	20.17	48.76
C4.4 Improve awareness and understanding	9.38	48.09
C4.5 Antimicrobial resistance rate for important antibiotics	28.69	33.03
C5 Climate change	63.00	64.19
C5.1 Mitigation and adaptation capacity	17.61	28.24
C5.2 Climate change risks	83.47	80.87
C5.3 Health outcome	89.82	85.41

Scores are normalized (0-100, where 100 = most favorable)

Afghanistan
South Asia | **Low income**

44.67 Index Score **150**/160

Global average: 54.82

Regional average: 51.61

Income group average: 46.63

Country performance: 44.67

Missing rate in GOHI database: 25.40%

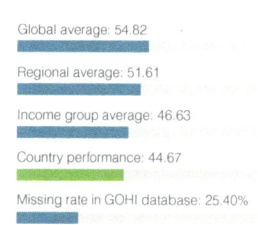

▼ AVERAGE PERFORMANCE BY GOHI

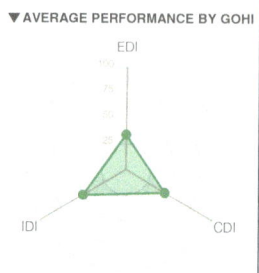

▼ AVERAGE PERFORMANCE BY CDI

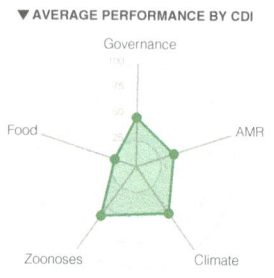

Governance: Score of GOHI-Governance   Climate: Score of GOHI-CC
Food: Score of GOHI-FS   AMR: Score of GOHI-AMR
Zoonoses: Score of GOHI-Zoonoses

	Country Score	Global Average
A External drivers index	34.04	40.45
A1 Earth system	44.05	56.21
A1.1 Land	28.14	36.41
A1.2 Forest	26.64	43.43
A1.3 Water	53.71	58.09
A1.4 Air	59.48	71.93
A1.5 Natural disasters	43.17	64.65
A2 Institutional system	34.01	46.01
A2.1 Justice	52.31	57.89
A2.2 Governance	18.41	35.58
A3 Economical system	27.22	24.62
A3.1 Finance	42.59	34.35
A3.2 Work	36.79	38.58
A4 Sociological system	34.02	37.70
A4.1 Demographic	50.20	46.31
A4.2 Education	24.28	28.26
A4.3 Inequalities	28.37	40.28
A5 Technological system	30.90	37.72
A5.1 Transport	0.00	6.54
A5.2 Technology adoption	28.76	41.23
A5.3 Consumption and production	61.29	62.53
B Intrinsic drivers index	50.32	59.01
B1 Human health	63.15	72.35
B1.1 Health coverage	30.08	58.65
B1.2 Diseases burden	79.97	79.83
B1.3 Injury and violence	81.33	80.75
B2 Animal health and ecosystem diversity	56.74	56.58
B2.1 Animal epidemic disease	94.82	94.57
B2.2 Wildlife and marine life biodiversity	18.65	18.59
B3 Environmental health	32.58	46.87
B3.1 Air quality and climate change	38.89	53.72
B3.2 Environmental biodiversity	46.25	44.05
B3.3 Environmental resources	13.60	44.25

Scores are normalized (0-100, where 100 = most favorable)

	Country Score	Global Average
C Core drivers index	45.70	57.25
C1 Governance	47.91	56.51
C1.1 Participation	44.10	41.70
C1.3 Transparency	49.80	65.15
C1.4 Responsiveness	29.15	44.42
C1.5 Consensus oriented	92.03	86.45
C1.6 Equity and inclusiveness	57.20	73.61
C1.7 Effectiveness and efficiency	14.13	28.38
C1.8 Political support	48.99	55.89
C2 Zoonotic diseases	56.66	68.06
C2.1 Source of infection	57.71	69.22
C2.2 Route of transmission	45.93	59.30
C2.3 Targeted population	42.72	59.90
C2.4 Capacity building	72.93	72.85
C2.5 Case studies	72.48	85.89
C3 Food security	39.98	52.89
C3.1 Food demand and supply	45.16	59.53
C3.2 Food safety	49.74	69.36
C3.3 Nutrition	54.04	67.17
C3.4 Natural and social circumstances	26.30	51.54
C3.5 Government support and response	24.66	16.85
C4 Antimicrobial resistance	22.85	44.05
C4.1 AMR surveillance system	2.60	34.79
C4.2 AMR laboratory network and coordination capacity	27.09	55.57
C4.3 Antimicrobial control and optimization	13.56	48.76
C4.4 Improve awareness and understanding	34.38	48.09
C4.5 Antimicrobial resistance rate for important antibiotics	36.63	33.03
C5 Climate change	60.00	64.19
C5.1 Mitigation and adaptation capacity	19.77	28.24
C5.2 Climate change risks	77.86	80.87
C5.3 Health outcome	84.18	85.41

Lesotho

Sub-Saharan Africa | Lower middle income

44.34 Index 151 /160
Score

Global average: 54.82

Regional average: 48.03

Income group average: 51.29

Country performance: 44.34

Missing rate in GOHI database: 26.10%

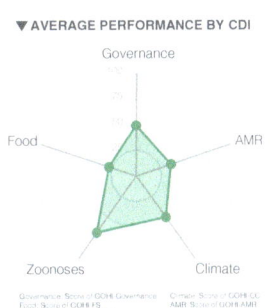

▼ AVERAGE PERFORMANCE BY GOHI

EDI

IDI   CDI

▼ AVERAGE PERFORMANCE BY CDI

Governance

Food   AMR

Zoonoses   Climate

Governance Score of GOHI-Governance   Climate Score of GOHI-CLI
Food Score of CORI-FS   AMR Score of GOHI-AMR
Zoonoses Score of GOHI-Zoonoses

	Country Score	Global Average
A External drivers index	35.83	40.45
A1 Earth system	50.47	56.21
A1.1 Land	5.10	36.41
A1.2 Forest	28.31	43.43
A1.3 Water	66.58	58.09
A1.4 Air	74.40	71.93
A1.5 Natural disasters	66.57	64.65
A2 Institutional system	38.72	46.01
A2.1 Justice	52.72	57.89
A2.2 Governance	26.79	35.58
A3 Economical system	20.27	24.62
A3.1 Finance	25.20	34.35
A3.2 Work	35.64	38.58
A4 Sociological system	38.99	37.70
A4.1 Demographic	59.81	46.31
A4.2 Education	25.16	28.26
A4.3 Inequalities	33.43	40.28
A5 Technological system	30.68	37.72
A5.1 Transport	6.22	6.54
A5.2 Technology adoption	17.72	41.23
A5.3 Consumption and production	66.33	62.53
B Intrinsic drivers index	41.99	58.01
B1 Human health	37.40	72.35
B1.1 Health coverage	15.62	58.65
B1.2 Diseases burden	26.82	79.83
B1.3 Injury and violence	70.89	80.75
B2 Animal health and ecosystem diversity	54.39	56.58
B2.1 Animal epidemic disease	91.39	94.57
B2.2 Wildlife and marine life biodiversity	17.38	18.59
B3 Environmental health	35.44	46.87
B3.1 Air quality and climate change	43.14	53.72
B3.2 Environmental biodiversity	19.60	44.05
B3.3 Environmental resources	44.66	44.25

	Country Score	Global Average
C Core drivers index	46.80	57.25
C1 Governance	49.57	56.51
C1.1 Participation	44.96	41.70
C1.3 Transparency	55.20	65.15
C1.4 Responsiveness	27.10	44.42
C1.5 Consensus oriented	96.55	86.45
C1.6 Equity and inclusiveness	68.02	73.61
C1.7 Effectiveness and efficiency	10.60	28.38
C1.8 Political support	44.60	55.89
C2 Zoonotic diseases	50.25	68.06
C2.1 Source of infection	48.79	69.22
C2.2 Route of transmission	37.97	59.30
C2.3 Targeted population	41.62	59.90
C2.4 Capacity building	45.85	72.85
C2.5 Case studies	88.86	85.89
C3 Food security	36.84	52.89
C3.1 Food demand and supply	53.46	59.53
C3.2 Food safety	46.09	69.36
C3.3 Nutrition	36.04	67.17
C3.4 Natural and social circumstances	41.80	51.54
C3.5 Government support and response	6.79	16.85
C4 Antimicrobial resistance	28.90	44.05
C4.1 AMR surveillance system	3.45	34.79
C4.2 AMR laboratory network and coordination on capacity	53.16	55.57
C4.3 Antimicrobial control and optimization	21.21	48.76
C4.4 Improve awareness and understanding	39.06	48.09
C4.5 Antimicrobial resistance rate for important antibiotics	27.63	33.03
C5 Climate change	68.77	64.19
C5.1 Mitigation and adaptation capacity	24.49	28.24
C5.2 Climate change risks	88.85	80.87
C5.3 Health outcome	95.06	85.41

Scores are normalized (0-100, where 100 = most favorable)

Burundi

Sub-Saharan Africa | Low income

44.33 Index Score **152**/160

Global average: 54.82

Regional average: 48.03

Income group average: 46.63

Country performance: 44.33

Missing rate in GOHI database: 25.40%

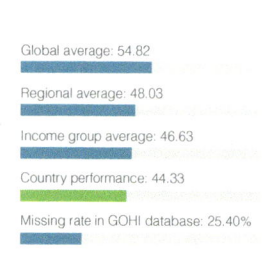

▼ AVERAGE PERFORMANCE BY GOHI

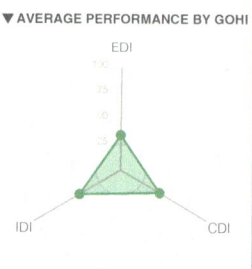

▼ AVERAGE PERFORMANCE BY CDI

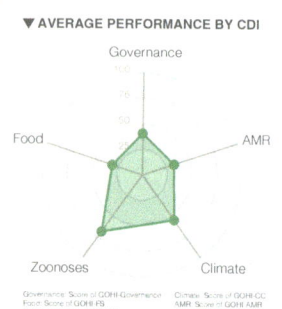

Governance: Score of GOHI-Governance
Food: Score of GOHI-FS
Zoonoses: Score of GOHI-Zoonoses
Climate: Score of GOHI-CC
AMR: Score of GOHI-AMR

	Country Score	Global Average
A External drivers index	34.17	40.45
A1 Earth system	52.89	58.21
A1.1 Land	24.11	36.41
A1.2 Forest	37.56	43.43
A1.3 Water	59.49	58.09
A1.4 Air	69.68	71.93
A1.5 Natural disasters	66.15	64.65
A2 Institutional system	33.00	46.01
A2.1 Justice	48.66	57.89
A2.2 Governance	19.66	35.58
A3 Economical system	23.77	24.62
A3.1 Finance	30.07	34.35
A3.2 Work	41.15	38.58
A4 Sociological system	33.75	37.70
A4.1 Demographic	44.72	46.31
A4.2 Education	25.15	28.26
A4.3 Inequalities	32.54	40.28
A5 Technological system	27.46	37.72
A5.1 Transport	5.77	6.54
A5.2 Technology adoption	8.62	41.23
A5.3 Consumption and production	66.62	62.53
B Intrinsic drivers index	48.32	58.01
B1 Human health	59.45	72.35
B1.1 Health coverage	35.18	56.65
B1.2 Diseases burden	77.34	79.83
B1.3 Injury and violence	67.62	80.75
B2 Animal health and ecosystem diversity	55.02	56.58
B2.1 Animal epidemic disease	92.94	94.57
B2.2 Wildlife and marine life biodiversity	17.10	18.59
B3 Environmental health	31.97	46.87
B3.1 Air quality and climate change	41.00	53.72
B3.2 Environmental biodiversity	32.25	44.05
B3.3 Environmental resources	23.62	44.25

	Country Score	Global Average
C Core drivers index	45.65	57.25
C1 Governance	40.62	56.51
C1.1 Participation	17.52	41.70
C1.3 Transparency	50.90	65.15
C1.4 Responsiveness	14.60	44.42
C1.5 Consensus oriented	98.31	86.45
C1.6 Equity and inclusiveness	48.06	73.61
C1.7 Effectiveness and efficiency	7.80	28.38
C1.8 Political support	47.17	55.89
C2 Zoonotic diseases	54.98	68.06
C2.1 Source of infection	40.03	69.22
C2.2 Route of transmission	51.17	59.30
C2.3 Targeted population	39.07	59.90
C2.4 Capacity building	73.30	72.85
C2.5 Case studies	84.52	85.89
C3 Food security	33.54	52.89
C3.1 Food demand and supply	44.03	59.53
C3.2 Food safety	26.56	69.36
C3.3 Nutrition	46.43	67.17
C3.4 Natural and social circumstances	45.00	51.54
C3.5 Government support and response	5.68	16.85
C4 Antimicrobial resistance	31.68	44.05
C4.1 AMR surveillance system	20.75	34.79
C4.2 AMR laboratory network and coordination on capacity	48.64	55.57
C4.3 Antimicrobial control and optimization	30.73	48.76
C4.4 Improve awareness and understanding	31.25	48.09
C4.5 Antimicrobial resistance rate for important antibiotics	27.05	33.03
C5 Climate change	68.95	64.19
C5.1 Mitigation and adaptation capacity	19.77	28.24
C5.2 Climate change risks	90.99	80.87
C5.3 Health outcome	98.18	85.41

Scores are normalized (0-100, where 100 = most favorable)

Dem. Rep. Congo
Sub-Saharan Africa | Low income

44.02 Index Score **153**/160

Global average: 54.82

Regional average: 48.03

Income group average: 46.63

Country performance: 44.02

Missing rate in GOHI database: 37.30%

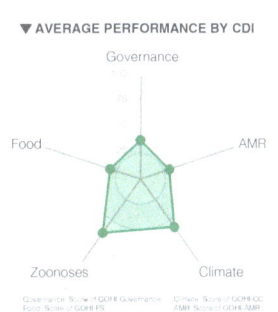

▼ AVERAGE PERFORMANCE BY GOHI

▼ AVERAGE PERFORMANCE BY CDI

	Country Score	Global Average
A External drivers index	36.46	40.45
A1 Earth system	51.04	56.21
A1.1 Land	37.48	36.41
A1.2 Forest	40.85	43.43
A1.3 Water	42.16	58.09
A1.4 Air	65.71	71.93
A1.5 Natural disasters	66.67	64.65
A2 Institutional system	35.04	46.01
A2.1 Justice	53.99	57.89
A2.2 Governance	18.91	35.58
A3 Economical system	21.22	24.62
A3.1 Finance	24.88	34.35
A3.2 Work	39.20	38.58
A4 Sociological system	44.74	37.70
A4.1 Demographic	74.72	46.31
A4.2 Education	25.61	28.26
A4.3 Inequalities	35.70	40.28
A5 Technological system	30.28	37.72
A5.1 Transport	0.00	6.54
A5.2 Technology adoption	16.05	41.23
A5.3 Consumption and production	72.53	62.53
B Intrinsic drivers index	48.33	58.01
B1 Human health	59.50	72.35
B1.1 Health coverage	30.04	58.65
B1.2 Diseases burden	79.80	79.83
B1.3 Injury and violence	70.46	80.75
B2 Animal health and ecosystem diversity	53.38	56.58
B2.1 Animal epidemic disease	92.28	94.57
B2.2 Wildlife and marine life biodiversity	14.47	18.59
B3 Environmental health	33.58	46.87
B3.1 Air quality and climate change	36.83	53.72
B3.2 Environmental biodiversity	43.00	44.05
B3.3 Environmental resources	21.94	44.25

	Country Score	Global Average
C Core drivers index	44.68	57.25
C1 Governance	38.09	56.51
C1.1 Participation	25.95	41.70
C1.3 Transparency	33.80	65.15
C1.4 Responsiveness	27.10	44.42
C1.5 Consensus oriented	82.62	86.45
C1.6 Equity and inclusiveness	44.03	73.61
C1.7 Effectiveness and efficiency	13.53	28.38
C1.8 Political support	39.58	55.89
C2 Zoonotic diseases	58.42	68.06
C2.1 Source of infection	47.96	69.22
C2.2 Route of transmission	45.19	59.30
C2.3 Targeted population	57.64	59.90
C2.4 Capacity building	71.68	72.85
C2.5 Case studies	83.24	85.89
C3 Food security	31.01	52.89
C3.1 Food demand and supply	47.44	59.53
C3.2 Food safety	39.76	69.36
C3.3 Nutrition	30.40	67.17
C3.4 Natural and social circumstances	31.63	51.54
C3.5 Government support and response	5.83	16.85
C4 Antimicrobial resistance	32.13	44.05
C4.1 AMR surveillance system	19.83	34.79
C4.2 AMR laboratory network and coordination capacity	43.09	55.57
C4.3 Antimicrobial control and optimization	30.71	48.76
C4.4 Improve awareness and understanding	43.75	48.09
C4.5 Antimicrobial resistance rate for important antibiotics	23.27	33.03
C5 Climate change	65.37	64.19
C5.1 Mitigation and adaptation capacity	22.02	28.24
C5.2 Climate change risks	81.39	80.87
C5.3 Health outcome	94.69	85.41

Scores are normalized (0-100, where 100 = most favorable)

Djibouti
Middle East & North Africa | **Lower middle income**

43.49 **Index Score 154**/160

Global average: 54.82

Regional average: 53.57

Income group average: 51.29

Country performance: 43.49

Missing rate in GOHI database: 29.00%

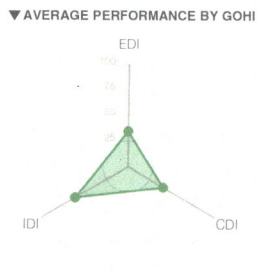
▼ AVERAGE PERFORMANCE BY GOHI

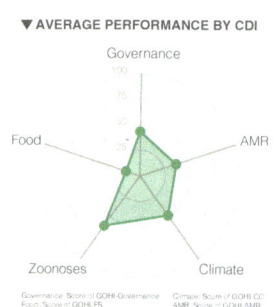
▼ AVERAGE PERFORMANCE BY CDI

	Country Score	Global Average
A External drivers index	**34.64**	**40.45**
A1 Earth system	49.00	56.21
A1.1 Land	15.35	36.41
A1.2 Forest	25.98	43.43
A1.3 Water	66.22	58.09
A1.4 Air	61.79	71.93
A1.5 Natural disasters	66.51	64.65
A2 Institutional system	33.40	46.01
A2.1 Justice	43.62	57.89
A2.2 Governance	24.70	35.58
A3 Economical system	22.47	24.62
A3.1 Finance	31.74	34.35
A3.2 Work	34.70	38.58
A4 Sociological system	37.72	37.70
A4.1 Demographic	61.72	46.31
A4.2 Education	20.80	28.26
A4.3 Inequalities	32.56	40.28
A5 Technological system	30.63	37.72
A5.1 Transport	6.22	6.54
A5.2 Technology adoption	17.66	41.23
A5.3 Consumption and production	66.23	62.53
B Intrinsic drivers index	**61.41**	**58.01**
B1 Human health	63.50	72.35
B1.1 Health coverage	34.99	58.65
B1.2 Diseases burden	80.03	79.83
B1.3 Injury and violence	77.41	80.75
B2 Animal health and ecosystem diversity	52.74	56.58
B2.1 Animal epidemic disease	92.23	94.57
B2.2 Wildlife and marine life biodiversity	13.25	18.59
B3 Environmental health	69.84	46.87
B3.1 Air quality and climate change	71.82	53.72
B3.2 Environmental biodiversity	46.65	44.05
B3.3 Environmental resources	93.16	44.25

Scores are normalized (0-100, where 100 = most favorable)

	Country Score	Global Average
C Core drivers index	**43.58**	**57.25**
C1 Governance	43.58	56.51
C1.1 Participation	34.67	41.70
C1.3 Transparency	36.60	65.15
C1.4 Responsiveness	25.00	44.42
C1.5 Consensus oriented	93.36	86.45
C1.6 Equity and inclusiveness	60.37	73.61
C1.7 Effectiveness and efficiency	11.33	28.38
C1.8 Political support	43.73	55.89
C2 Zoonotic diseases	48.00	68.06
C2.1 Source of infection	34.12	69.22
C2.2 Route of transmission	34.05	59.30
C2.3 Targeted population	34.24	59.90
C2.4 Capacity building	68.03	72.85
C2.5 Case studies	88.20	85.89
C3 Food security	37.88	52.89
C3.1 Food demand and supply	44.91	59.53
C3.2 Food safety	57.57	69.36
C3.3 Nutrition	54.60	67.17
C3.4 Natural and social circumstances	26.65	51.54
C3.5 Government support and response	5.65	16.85
C4 Antimicrobial resistance	14.75	44.05
C4.1 AMR surveillance system	5.20	34.79
C4.2 AMR laboratory network and coordination on capacity	20.55	55.57
C4.3 Antimicrobial control and optimization	7.67	48.76
C4.4 Improve awareness and understanding	12.50	48.09
C4.5 Antimicrobial resistance rate for important antibiotics	27.81	33.03
C5 Climate change	60.70	64.19
C5.1 Mitigation and adaptation capacity	26.36	28.24
C5.2 Climate change risks	83.23	80.87
C5.3 Health outcome	74.36	85.41

Solomon Islands
East Asia & Pacific | Lower middle income

Index Score **155**/160

Global average: 54.82

Regional average: 56.52

Income group average: 51.29

Country performance: 43.34

Missing rate in GOHI database: 31.50%

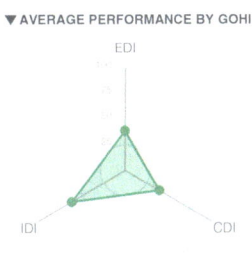

▼ AVERAGE PERFORMANCE BY GOHI

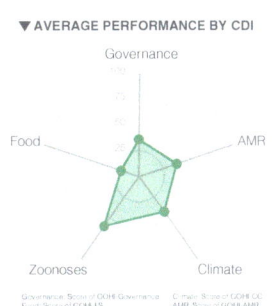

▼ AVERAGE PERFORMANCE BY CDI

	Country Score	Global Average
A External drivers index	38.92	40.45
A1 Earth system	62.74	56.21
A1.1 Land	27.63	36.41
A1.2 Forest	58.16	43.43
A1.3 Water	66.43	58.09
A1.4 Air	86.12	71.93
A1.5 Natural disasters	66.33	64.65
A2 Institutional system	41.01	46.01
A2.1 Justice	56.99	57.89
A2.2 Governance	27.39	35.58
A3 Economical system	25.21	24.62
A3.1 Finance	33.71	34.35
A3.2 Work	41.34	38.58
A4 Sociological system	30.94	37.70
A4.1 Demographic	38.41	46.31
A4.2 Education	21.63	28.26
A4.3 Inequalities	34.64	40.28
A5 Technological system	34.71	37.72
A5.1 Transport	5.77	6.54
A5.2 Technology adoption	29.57	41.23
A5.3 Consumption and production	66.40	62.53
B Intrinsic drivers index	62.43	58.01
B1 Human health	64.44	72.35
B1.1 Health coverage	45.64	58.65
B1.2 Diseases burden	67.36	79.83
B1.3 Injury and violence	82.28	80.75
B2 Animal health and ecosystem diversity	55.54	58.58
B2.1 Animal epidemic disease	92.22	94.57
B2.2 Wildlife and marine life biodiversity	18.85	18.59
B3 Environmental health	69.19	46.87
B3.1 Air quality and climate change	66.20	53.72
B3.2 Environmental biodiversity	59.30	44.05
B3.3 Environmental resources	84.16	44.25

	Country Score	Global Average
C Core drivers index	39.79	57.25
C1 Governance	36.38	56.51
C1.1 Participation	44.99	41.70
C1.3 Transparency	41.70	65.15
C1.4 Responsiveness	35.40	44.42
C1.5 Consensus oriented	33.78	86.45
C1.6 Equity and inclusiveness	51.86	73.61
C1.7 Effectiveness and efficiency	10.60	28.38
C1.8 Political support	36.34	55.89
C2 Zoonotic diseases	43.01	68.06
C2.1 Source of infection	29.10	69.22
C2.2 Route of transmission	33.05	59.30
C2.3 Targeted population	41.48	59.90
C2.4 Capacity building	37.97	72.85
C2.5 Case studies	88.97	85.89
C3 Food security	40.00	52.89
C3.1 Food demand and supply	60.41	59.53
C3.2 Food safety	41.22	69.36
C3.3 Nutrition	49.09	67.17
C3.4 Natural and social circumstances	47.13	51.54
C3.5 Government support and response	2.17	16.85
C4 Antimicrobial resistance	18.84	44.05
C4.1 AMR surveillance system	7.05	34.79
C4.2 AMR laboratory network and coordination capacity	27.60	55.57
C4.3 Antimicrobial control and optimization	15.37	48.76
C4.4 Improve awareness and understanding	17.19	48.09
C4.5 Antimicrobial resistance rate for important antibiotics	26.97	33.03
C5 Climate change	60.54	64.19
C5.1 Mitigation and adaptation capacity	14.81	28.24
C5.2 Climate change risks	92.38	80.87
C5.3 Health outcome	76.27	85.41

Scores are normalized (0-100, where 100 = most favorable)

Chad

Sub-Saharan Africa | Low income

Index Score **156**/160 · 42.88

Global average: 54.82

Regional average: 48.03

Income group average: 46.63

Country performance: 42.88

Missing rate in GOHI database: 26.10%

▼ AVERAGE PERFORMANCE BY GOHI

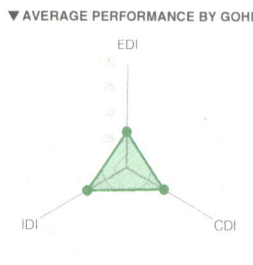

▼ AVERAGE PERFORMANCE BY CDI

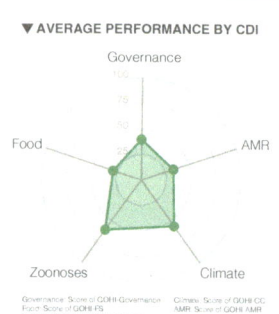

Governance: Score of GOHI-Governance   Climate: Score of GOHI-CC
Food: Score of GOHI-FS   AMR: Score of GOHI-AMR
Zoonoses: Score of GOHI-Zoonoses

	Country Score	Global Average
A External drivers index	35.09	40.45
A1 Earth system	49.28	56.21
A1.1 Land	51.51	36.41
A1.2 Forest	29.35	43.43
A1.3 Water	44.21	58.09
A1.4 Air	54.22	71.93
A1.5 Natural disasters	65.48	64.65
A2 Institutional system	34.38	46.01
A2.1 Justice	48.69	57.89
A2.2 Governance	22.19	35.58
A3 Economical system	25.92	24.62
A3.1 Finance	35.97	34.35
A3.2 Work	40.83	38.58
A4 Sociological system	37.49	37.70
A4.1 Demographic	61.17	46.31
A4.2 Education	24.46	28.26
A4.3 Inequalities	27.61	40.28
A5 Technological system	28.37	37.72
A5.1 Transport	0.62	6.54
A5.2 Technology adoption	14.44	41.23
A5.3 Consumption and production	68.01	62.53
B Intrinsic drivers index	46.27	58.01
B1 Human health	47.91	72.35
B1.1 Health coverage	10.58	58.65
B1.2 Diseases burden	62.92	79.83
B1.3 Injury and violence	71.67	80.75
B2 Animal health and ecosystem diversity	53.59	56.58
B2.1 Animal epidemic disease	92.73	94.57
B2.2 Wildlife and marine life biodiversity	14.44	18.59
B3 Environmental health	38.73	46.87
B3.1 Air quality and climate change	62.15	53.72
B3.2 Environmental biodiversity	35.70	44.05
B3.3 Environmental resources	19.52	44.25

	Country Score	Global Average
C Core drivers index	43.80	57.25
C1 Governance	39.74	56.51
C1.1 Participation	13.90	41.70
C1.3 Transparency	38.50	65.15
C1.4 Responsiveness	27.10	44.42
C1.5 Consensus oriented	93.12	86.45
C1.6 Equity and inclusiveness	55.89	73.61
C1.7 Effectiveness and efficiency	7.20	28.38
C1.8 Political support	42.47	55.89
C2 Zoonotic diseases	56.19	68.06
C2.1 Source of infection	45.97	69.22
C2.2 Route of transmission	57.19	59.30
C2.3 Targeted population	32.25	59.90
C2.4 Capacity building	69.33	72.85
C2.5 Case studies	86.15	85.89
C3 Food security	33.83	52.89
C3.1 Food demand and supply	35.03	59.53
C3.2 Food safety	25.27	69.36
C3.3 Nutrition	49.13	67.17
C3.4 Natural and social circumstances	49.19	51.54
C3.5 Government support and response	10.52	16.85
C4 Antimicrobial resistance	29.33	44.05
C4.1 AMR surveillance system	24.35	34.79
C4.2 AMR laboratory network and coordination on capacity	37.84	55.57
C4.3 Antimicrobial control and optimization	40.32	48.76
C4.4 Improve awareness and understanding	25.00	48.09
C4.5 Antimicrobial resistance rate for important antibiotics	19.12	33.03
C5 Climate change	60.64	64.19
C5.1 Mitigation and adaptation capacity	24.99	28.24
C5.2 Climate change risks	74.47	80.87
C5.3 Health outcome	84.30	85.41

Scores are normalized (0–100, where 100 = most favorable)

Mauritania
Sub-Saharan Africa | Lower middle income

42.46 Index Score **157**/160

Global average: 54.82

Regional average: 48.03

Income group average: 51.29

Country performance: 42.46

Missing rate in GOHI database: 24.30%

▼ AVERAGE PERFORMANCE BY GOHI

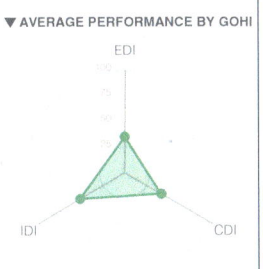

▼ AVERAGE PERFORMANCE BY CDI

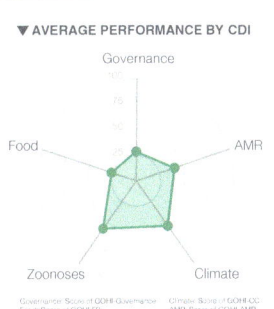

	Country Score	Global Average
A External drivers index	38.48	40.45
A1 Earth system	35.27	56.21
A1.1 Land	43.48	36.41
A1.2 Forest	51.93	43.43
A1.3 Water	26.58	58.09
A1.4 Air	33.53	71.93
A1.5 Natural disasters	49.32	64.65
A2 Institutional system	55.48	46.01
A2.1 Justice	36.66	57.89
A2.2 Governance	43.99	35.58
A3 Economical system	30.42	24.62
A3.1 Finance	26.10	34.35
A3.2 Work	39.02	38.58
A4 Sociological system	37.59	37.70
A4.1 Demographic	36.33	46.31
A4.2 Education	56.47	28.26
A4.3 Inequalities	22.34	40.28
A5 Technological system	31.74	37.72
A5.1 Transport	33.80	6.54
A5.2 Technology adoption	4.42	41.23
A5.3 Consumption and production	25.69	62.53
B Intrinsic drivers index	66.94	58.01
B1 Human health	52.01	72.35
B1.1 Health coverage	67.03	58.65
B1.2 Diseases burden	38.74	79.83
B1.3 Injury and violence	88.41	80.75
B2 Animal health and ecosystem diversity	75.97	56.58
B2.1 Animal epidemic disease	51.64	94.57
B2.2 Wildlife and marine life biodiversity	93.18	18.59
B3 Environmental health	10.10	46.87
B3.1 Air quality and climate change	38.95	53.72
B3.2 Environmental biodiversity	67.45	44.05
B3.3 Environmental resources	34.25	44.25

	Country Score	Global Average
C Core drivers index	41.79	57.25
C1 Governance	28.83	56.51
C1.1 Participation	13.58	41.70
C1.3 Transparency	48.10	65.15
C1.4 Responsiveness	29.15	44.42
C1.5 Consensus oriented	5.02	86.45
C1.6 Equity and inclusiveness	70.43	73.61
C1.7 Effectiveness and efficiency	20.13	28.38
C1.8 Political support	15.42	55.89
C2 Zoonotic diseases	54.79	68.06
C2.1 Source of infection	43.68	69.22
C2.2 Route of transmission	41.22	59.30
C2.3 Targeted population	45.77	59.90
C2.4 Capacity building	70.41	72.85
C2.5 Case studies	88.94	85.89
C3 Food security	41.40	52.89
C3.1 Food demand and supply	42.64	59.53
C3.2 Food safety	43.34	69.36
C3.3 Nutrition	60.47	67.17
C3.4 Natural and social circumstances	48.13	51.54
C3.5 Government support and response	12.40	16.85
C4 Antimicrobial resistance	26.50	44.05
C4.1 AMR surveillance system	8.65	34.79
C4.2 AMR laboratory network and coordinati on capacity	46.32	55.57
C4.3 Antimicrobial control and optimization	32.73	48.76
C4.4 Improve awareness and understanding	23.44	48.09
C4.5 Antimicrobial resistance rate for important antibiotics	21.37	33.03
C5 Climate change	58.14	64.19
C5.1 Mitigation and adaptation capacity	22.84	28.24
C5.2 Climate change risks	75.39	80.87
C5.3 Health outcome	77.95	85.41

Scores are normalized (0-100, where 100 = most favorable)

Central African Republic

Sub-Saharan Africa | Low income

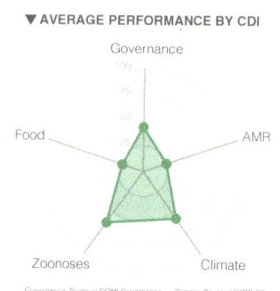

Index Score **158**/160

42.1

Global average: 54.82

Regional average: 48.03

Income group average: 46.63

Country performance: 42.10

Missing rate in GOHI database: 27.90%

▼ AVERAGE PERFORMANCE BY GOHI

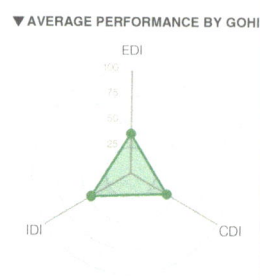

▼ AVERAGE PERFORMANCE BY CDI

	Country Score	Global Average
A External drivers index	38.48	40.45
A1 Earth system	66.70	56.21
A1.1 Land	58.21	36.41
A1.2 Forest	78.71	43.43
A1.3 Water	68.87	58.09
A1.4 Air	59.23	71.93
A1.5 Natural disasters	66.61	64.65
A2 Institutional system	34.73	46.01
A2.1 Justice	51.07	57.89
A2.2 Governance	20.81	35.58
A3 Economical system	21.19	24.62
A3.1 Finance	24.02	34.35
A3.2 Work	40.21	38.58
A4 Sociological system	39.15	37.70
A4.1 Demographic	64.44	46.31
A4.2 Education	25.42	28.26
A4.3 Inequalities	28.37	40.28
A5 Technological system	30.61	37.72
A5.1 Transport	6.37	6.54
A5.2 Technology adoption	17.37	41.23
A5.3 Consumption and production	66.34	62.53
B Intrinsic drivers index	46.33	58.01
B1 Human health	42.36	72.35
B1.1 Health coverage	9.61	58.65
B1.2 Diseases burden	52.90	79.83
B1.3 Injury and violence	65.87	80.75
B2 Animal health and ecosystem diversity	60.04	56.58
B2.1 Animal epidemic disease	93.58	94.57
B2.2 Wildlife and marine life biodiversity	26.50	18.59
B3 Environmental health	38.00	46.87
B3.1 Air quality and climate change	37.61	53.72
B3.2 Environmental biodiversity	59.95	44.05
B3.3 Environmental resources	17.60	44.25

	Country Score	Global Average
C Core drivers index	41.90	57.25
C1 Governance	43.53	56.51
C1.1 Participation	57.15	41.70
C1.3 Transparency	54.03	65.15
C1.4 Responsiveness	25.00	44.42
C1.5 Consensus oriented	65.29	86.45
C1.6 Equity and inclusiveness	55.10	73.61
C1.7 Effectiveness and efficiency	5.73	28.38
C1.8 Political support	42.41	55.89
C2 Zoonotic diseases	57.15	68.06
C2.1 Source of infection	43.47	69.22
C2.2 Route of transmission	45.60	59.30
C2.3 Targeted population	57.62	59.90
C2.4 Capacity building	65.52	72.85
C2.5 Case studies	88.04	85.89
C3 Food security	24.84	52.89
C3.1 Food demand and supply	37.08	59.53
C3.2 Food safety	25.25	69.36
C3.3 Nutrition	28.90	67.17
C3.4 Natural and social circumstances	28.32	51.54
C3.5 Government support and response	4.64	16.85
C4 Antimicrobial resistance	22.15	44.05
C4.1 AMR surveillance system	8.95	34.79
C4.2 AMR laboratory network and coordination capacity	22.26	55.57
C4.3 Antimicrobial control and optimization	39.42	48.76
C4.4 Improve awareness and understanding	12.50	48.09
C4.5 Antimicrobial resistance rate for important antibiotics	27.62	33.03
C5 Climate change	62.26	64.19
C5.1 Mitigation and adaptation capacity	26.14	28.24
C5.2 Climate change risks	74.36	80.87
C5.3 Health outcome	88.16	85.41

Scores are normalized (0-100, where 100 = most favorable)

Somalia

Sub-Saharan Africa | Low income

39.29 Index Score **159**/160

Global average: 54.82

Regional average: 48.03

Income group average: 46.63

Country performance: 39.29

Missing rate in GOHI database: 32.60%

▼ AVERAGE PERFORMANCE BY GOHI

▼ AVERAGE PERFORMANCE BY CDI

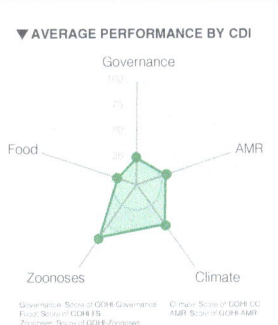

	Country Score	Global Average
A External drivers index	34.67	40.45
A1 Earth system	44.13	56.21
A1.1 Land	29.90	36.41
A1.2 Forest	26.23	43.43
A1.3 Water	45.20	58.09
A1.4 Air	74.85	71.93
A1.5 Natural disasters	33.33	64.65
A2 Institutional system	25.98	46.01
A2.1 Justice	42.97	57.89
A2.2 Governance	11.51	35.58
A3 Economical system	30.45	24.62
A3.1 Finance	51.96	34.35
A3.2 Work	35.67	38.58
A4 Sociological system	43.02	37.70
A4.1 Demographic	66.74	46.31
A4.2 Education	25.02	28.26
A4.3 Inequalities	39.60	40.28
A5 Technological system	29.76	37.72
A5.1 Transport	8.12	6.54
A5.2 Technology adoption	14.27	41.23
A5.3 Consumption and production	65.43	62.53
B Intrinsic drivers index	45.78	58.01
B1 Human health	53.12	72.35
B1.1 Health coverage	20.16	58.65
B1.2 Diseases burden	66.95	79.83
B1.3 Injury and violence	73.87	80.75
B2 Animal health and ecosystem diversity	53.25	56.58
B2.1 Animal epidemic disease	92.03	94.57
B2.2 Wildlife and marine life biodiversity	14.47	18.59
B3 Environmental health	32.35	46.87
B3.1 Air quality and climate change	64.30	53.72
B3.2 Environmental biodiversity	9.90	44.05
B3.3 Environmental resources	23.82	44.25

	Country Score	Global Average
C Core drivers index	38.78	57.25
C1 Governance	26.75	56.51
C1.1 Participation	12.26	41.70
C1.3 Transparency	19.60	65.15
C1.4 Responsiveness	18.75	44.42
C1.5 Consensus oriented	48.95	86.45
C1.6 Equity and inclusiveness	53.50	73.61
C1.7 Effectiveness and efficiency	3.00	28.38
C1.8 Political support	31.18	55.89
C2 Zoonotic diseases	50.04	68.06
C2.1 Source of infection	45.82	69.22
C2.2 Route of transmission	49.86	59.30
C2.3 Targeted population	7.59	59.90
C2.4 Capacity building	74.28	72.85
C2.5 Case studies	83.65	85.89
C3 Food security	32.16	52.89
C3.1 Food demand and supply	30.42	59.53
C3.2 Food safety	33.52	69.36
C3.3 Nutrition	63.12	67.17
C3.4 Natural and social circumstances	23.98	51.54
C3.5 Government support and response	9.77	16.85
C4 Antimicrobial resistance	20.49	44.05
C4.1 AMR surveillance system	18.68	34.79
C4.2 AMR laboratory network and coordinati on capacity	27.44	55.57
C4.3 Antimicrobial control and optimization	10.66	48.76
C4.4 Improve awareness and understanding	23.44	48.09
C4.5 Antimicrobial resistance rate for important antibiotics	22.22	33.03
C5 Climate change	66.08	64.19
C5.1 Mitigation and adaptation capacity	25.19	28.24
C5.2 Climate change risks	84.99	80.87
C5.3 Health outcome	90.06	85.41

Scores are normalized (0-100, where 100 = most favorable)

Guinea-Bissau
Sub-Saharan Africa | Low income

39.03 ⟩ Index Score **160**/160

Global average: 54.82

Regional average: 48.03

Income group average: 46.63

Country performance: 39.03

Missing rate in GOHI database: 27.50%

▼ AVERAGE PERFORMANCE BY GOHI

▼ AVERAGE PERFORMANCE BY CDI

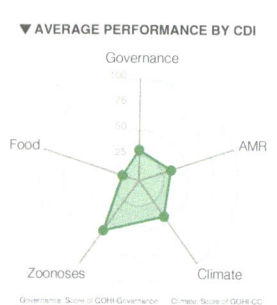

Governance: Score of GOHI Governance   Climate: Score of GOHI CC
Food: Score of GOHI FS   AMR: Score of GOHI AMR
Zoonoses: Score of GOHI Zoonoses

	Country Score	Global Average
A External drivers index	**37.50**	**40.45**
A1 Earth system	50.20	56.21
A1.1 Land	38.37	36.41
A1.2 Forest	40.89	43.43
A1.3 Water	50.48	58.09
A1.4 Air	52.96	71.93
A1.5 Natural disasters	66.21	64.65
A2 Institutional system	40.94	46.01
A2.1 Justice	57.48	57.89
A2.2 Governance	26.86	35.58
A3 Economical system	27.07	24.62
A3.1 Finance	39.63	34.35
A3.2 Work	40.02	38.58
A4 Sociological system	37.75	37.70
A4.1 Demographic	58.93	46.31
A4.2 Education	23.61	28.26
A4.3 Inequalities	32.19	40.28
A5 Technological system	31.52	37.72
A5.1 Transport	6.04	6.54
A5.2 Technology adoption	20.14	41.23
A5.3 Consumption and production	66.46	62.53
B Intrinsic drivers index	**49.12**	**58.01**
B1 Human health	54.87	72.35
B1.1 Health coverage	22.80	58.65
B1.2 Diseases burden	74.06	79.83
B1.3 Injury and violence	69.40	80.75
B2 Animal health and ecosystem diversity	57.16	56.58
B2.1 Animal epidemic disease	93.82	94.57
B2.2 Wildlife and marine life biodiversity	20.50	18.59
B3 Environmental health	36.83	46.87
B3.1 Air quality and climate change	52.34	53.72
B3.2 Environmental biodiversity	37.25	44.05
B3.3 Environmental resources	22.02	44.25

	Country Score	Global Average
C Core drivers index	**36.98**	**57.25**
C1 Governance	30.34	56.51
C1.1 Participation	50.40	41.70
C1.3 Transparency	33.40	65.15
C1.4 Responsiveness	41.65	44.42
C1.5 Consensus oriented	3.30	86.45
C1.6 Equity and inclusiveness	54.58	73.61
C1.7 Effectiveness and efficiency	7.20	28.38
C1.8 Political support	21.85	55.89
C2 Zoonotic diseases	43.40	68.06
C2.1 Source of infection	36.38	69.22
C2.2 Route of transmission	34.86	59.30
C2.3 Targeted population	5.28	59.90
C2.4 Capacity building	68.61	72.85
C2.5 Case studies	88.83	85.89
C3 Food security	34.00	52.89
C3.1 Food demand and supply	43.54	59.53
C3.2 Food safety	33.33	69.36
C3.3 Nutrition	43.60	67.17
C3.4 Natural and social circumstances	45.61	51.54
C3.5 Government support and response	3.92	16.85
C4 Antimicrobial resistance	17.32	44.05
C4.1 AMR surveillance system	18.99	34.79
C4.2 AMR laboratory network and coordination on capacity	21.36	55.57
C4.3 Antimicrobial control and optimization	3.89	48.76
C4.4 Improve awareness and understanding	15.62	48.09
C4.5 Antimicrobial resistance rate for important antibiotics	26.73	33.03
C5 Climate change	60.40	64.19
C5.1 Mitigation and adaptation capacity	18.26	28.24
C5.2 Climate change risks	79.58	80.87
C5.3 Health outcome	85.19	85.41

Scores are normalized (0-100, where 100 = most favorable)

Glossary

Abbreviations

AMR	Antimicrobial resistance
CARSS	China Antimicrobial Resistance Surveillance System
CB	Capacity building
CCR	Climate change risks
COVID-19	Coronavirus disease 2019
CS	Case studies
EARS-Net	European Antimicrobial Resistance Surveillance Network
ECDC	European Centre for Disease Prevention and Control
ECI	Ecological interventions
EDI	External drivers index
EPI	Environmental Performance Index
FAO	Food and Agriculture Organization of the United Nations
FSI	Food Sustainability Index
GAP	Global Action Plan on Antimicrobial Resistance
GDP	Gross Domestic Product
GFSI	Global Food Security Index
GHI	Global Hunger Index
GHS Index	Global Health Security Index
GLASS	Global Antimicrobial Resistance and Use Surveillance System
GOH-EDI	Global One Health index-external drivers index
GOHF	Generalizable One Health Framework
GOHI	Global One Health index
GOHI-AMR	Global One Health index-antimicrobial resistance
GOHI-CC	Global One Health index-climate change
GOHI-FS	Global One Health index-food security
GOHI-Governance	Global One Health index-governance
GOHI-IDI	Global One Health index-intrinsic drivers index
GOHI-Zoonoses	Global One Health index-zoonotic diseases
GT	Grounded theory
HDI	Human Development Index
HLPE-FSN	High-Level Panel of Experts on Food Security and Nutrition
HOC	Health outcome of climate change
IEA	International Energy Agency
IHB	Inhabitants below 5 m above sea level
IMF	International Monetary Fund
ITU	International Telecommunication Union
MAC	Mitigation and adaptation capacity
MERS	Middle East respiratory syndrome
MF	Monitoring and feedback
NR	Nature reserves
NTDs	Neglected tropical diseases
OECD	Organization for Economic Co-operation and Development
OH JPA	One Health Joint Plan of Action
OHHLEP	One Health High-Level Expert Panel
OHZDP	One Health Zoonotic Disease Prioritization
PAHO	Pan America Health Organization
RLI	Red list index
RT	Route of transmission
SARS	Severe acute respiratory syndrome
SDGs	United Nations Sustainable Development Goals

SDI	Social Development Index	UNHCR	United Nations High Commissioner for Refugees
SI	Sources of infection		
SOFI	The State of Food Security and Nutrition in the World	WFP	World Food Programme
		WHO	World Health Organization
TB	Tuberculosis	WMO	World Meteorological Organization
TP	Targeted populations		
TrACSS	Tripartite AMR country self-assessment survey	WOAH	World Organization for Animal Health
UHC	Universal health coverage	WOAH-WAHIS	World Animal Information System of World Animal Health Organization
UN	United Nations		
UNEP	United Nations Environment Programme	WTO	World Trade Organization

References

1. Centers for Disease Control and Prevention. Zoonotic diseases 2021. https://www.cdc.gov/one-health/basics/zoonoticdiseases.html. Accessed 24 Jan 2022.
2. WHO. WHO COVID-19 Dashboard 2022. https://covid19.who.int. Accessed 28 Feb 2022.
3. Sharun K, Tiwari R, Natesan S, Dhama K. SARS-CoV-2 infection in farmed minks, associated zoonotic concerns, and importance of the One Health approach during the ongoing COVID-19 pandemic. Vet Q. 2021;41(1):50–60.
4. Bulletin of the WHO. William Karesh: championing "One Health". Bull World Health Organ. 2020;98(10):652–3.
5. WHO. Tripartite and UNEP support OHHLEP's definition of "One Health" 2021. https://www.who.int/news/item/01-12-2021-tripartite-and-unep-support-ohhlep-s-definition-of-one-health. Accessed 27 Jan 2022.
6. Zhang XX, Liu JS, Han LF, Xia S, Li SZ, Li OY, et al. Towards a global One Health index: a potential assessment tool for One Health performance. Infect Dis Poverty. 2022;11(1):57.
7. Donabedian A. Evaluating the quality of medical care. Milbank Q. 2005;83(4):691–729.
8. Wang YM, Chin KS. Fuzzy analytic hierarchy process: a logarithmic fuzzy preference programming methodology. Int J Approx Reason. 2011;52(4):541–53.
9. Henderson JW. Health economics and policy. Cengage South-Western; 2022.
10. Heal MR, Kumar P, Harrison RM. Particles, air quality, policy and health. Chem Soc Rev. 2012;41(19):6606–30.
11. (OHHLEP) OHH-LEP, Adisasmito WB, Almuhairi S, Behravesh CB, Bilivogui P, Bukachi SA, et al. One Health: a new definition for a sustainable and healthy future. PLoS Pathog. 2022;18(6):e1010537.
12. Glaser BG, Strauss AL, Strutzel E. The discovery of grounded theory; strategies for qualitative research. Nurs Res. 1968;17(4):364.
13. de la Harpe S, Rijken C, Roos R. Good governance. Potchefstroom Electron Law J. 2008;11:2–15.
14. Banerji A. Global and national leadership in good governance 2015. https://www.un.org/en/chron-icle/article/global-andnational-leadership-good-governance. Accessed 16 Apr 2023.
15. Commission on Global Governance. Our global neighbourhood: the report of the Commission on Global Governance. Oxford University Press; 1995.
16. WHO. One Health joint plan of action (2022–2026): working together for the health of humans, animals, plants and the environment. 2022.
17. WHO. WHO health topic page: zoonoses 2020. https://www.who.int/news-room/fact-sheets/detail/zoonoses.
18. Karesh WB, Dobson A, Lloyd-Smith JO, Lubroth J, Dixon MA, Bennett M, et al. Ecology of zoonoses: natural and unnatural histories. Lancet. 2012;380(9857):1936–45.
19. Centers for Disease Control and Prevention. Zoonotic diseases shared between animals and people of most concern in the U.S. 2019. https://www.cdc.gov/media/releases/2019/s0506-zoonotic-diseases-shared.html#print.
20. Nakayima J, Hayashida K, Nakao R, Ishii A, Ogawa H, Nakamura I, et al. Detection and characterization of zoonotic pathogens of free-ranging nonhuman primates from Zambia. Parasit Vectors. 2014;7(1):490.
21. Gebreyes WA, Dupouy-Camet J, Newport MJ, Oliveira CJ, Schlesinger LS, Saif YM, et al. The Global One Health Paradigm: challenges and opportunities for tackling infectious diseases at the human, animal, and environment interface in low-resource settings. PLoS Negl Trop Dis. 2014;8(11):e3257.
22. Shi Z, Hu Z. A review of studies on animal reservoirs of the SARS coronavirus. Virus Res. 2008;133(1):74–87.
23. Han HJ, Yu H, Yu XJ. Evidence for zoonotic origins of Middle East respiratory syndrome coronavirus. J Gen Virol. 2016;97(2):274–80.
24. Yoo HS, Yoo D. COVID-19 and veterinarians for One Health, zoonotic- and reverse-zoonotic transmissions. J Vet Sci. 2020;21(3):e51.
25. Dhama K, Patel SK, Sharun K, Pathak M, Tiwari R, Yatoo MI, et al. SARS-CoV-2 jumping the species barrier: zoonotic lessons from SARS, MERS and recent advances to combat this pandemic virus. Travel Med Infect Dis. 2020;37:101830.

26. Shi J, Wen Z, Zhong G, Yang H, Wang C, Huang B, et al. Susceptibility of ferrets, cats, dogs, and other domesticated animals to SARS-coronavirus 2. Science. 2020;368(6494):1016–20.

27. Hale VL, Dennis PM, McBride DS, Nolting JM, Madden C, Huey D, et al. S ARS-CoV-2 infection in free-ranging white-tailed deer. Nature. 2022;602(7897):481–6.

28. Mishra A, Kumar N, Bhatia S, Aasdev A, Kanniappan S, Sekhar AT, et al. SARS-CoV-2 delta variant among Asiatic Lions, India. Emerg Infect Dis. 2021;27(10):2723–5.

29. Daszak P, Cunningham AA, Hyatt AD. Emerging infectious diseases of wild life—threats to biodiversity and human health. Science. 2000;287(5452):443–9.

30. WHO. FAO, OIE, and WHO launch a guide for countries on taking a One Health approach to addressing zoonotic diseases 2019. https://www.who.int/news/item/11-03-2019-fao-oie-and-who-launch-aguide-for-countries-on-taking-a-one-health-approach-to-addressingzoonotic-diseases.

31. WHO. One Health 2017. https://www.who.int/news-room/questions-and-answers/item/one-health.

32. Salyer SJ, Silver R, Simone K, Barton Behravesh C. Prioritizing zoonoses for global health capacity building-themes from One Health zoonotic disease workshops in 7 countries, 2014-2016. Emerg Infect Dis. 2017;23(13):S55–64.

33. Ghai RR, Wallace RM, Kile JC, Shoemaker TR, Vieira AR, Negron ME, et al. A generalizable One Health framework for the control of zoonotic diseases. Sci Rep. 2022;12(1):8588.

34. Zhao HQ, Fei SW, Yin JX, Li Q, Jiang TG, Guo ZY, et al. Assessment of performance for a key indicator of One Health: evidence based on One Health index for zoonoses in sub-Saharan Africa. Infect Dis Poverty. 2022;11(1):109.

35. WHO. One Health joint plan of action (2022–2026): working together for the health of humans, animals, plants and the environment. https://www.who.int/publications/i/item/9789240059139.

36. Godfray HC, Beddington JR, Crute IR, Haddad L, Lawrence D, Muir JF, et al. Food security: the challenge of feeding 9 billion people. Science. 2010;327(5967):812–8.

37. Lv F, Deng L, Zhang Z, Wang Z, Wu Q, Qiao J. Multiscale analysis of Leishmania. Chin J Zoonoses. 2015;31(05):462–6. (in Chinese)

38. Chen K, Wu WP, Guan YY. Advances in research on animal hosts of sustainability: a synthesis of the current concepts and empirical approaches for meeting SDGs. Sustainability. 2021;13(21)

39. Aliyu US, Ozdeser H, Cavusoglu B, Usman MAM. Food security factors affecting food security in China, 1980-2017. Environ Sci Pollut Res Int. 2021;

40. Wang LD, Chen HG, Guo JG, Zeng XJ, Hong XL, Xiong JJ, et al. A strategy to control transmission of Schistosoma japonicum in China. N Engl J Med. 2009;360(2):121–8.

41. Zhou Y, Chen Y, Jiang Q. History of human schistosomiasis (bilharziasis) in China: from discovery to elimination. Acta Parasitol. 2021;66(3):760–9.

42. United Nations Affairs. Chinese President Xi Jinping's speech at the UN: China actively participates in international anti-epidemic cooperation and strives to achieve carbon neutrality by 2060. 2020. https://news.un.org/zh/story/2020/09/1067222. Accessed 21 Aug 2022. (in Chinese).

43. Andrade L, O'Dwyer J, O'Neill E, Hynds P. Surface water flooding, groundwater contamination, and enteric disease in developed countries: a scoping review of connections and consequences. Environ Pollut. 2018;236:540–9.

44. Xinhua News Agency. China's policies and actions to address climate change. State Council Information Office; 2021. http://www.gov.cn/zhengce/2021-10/27/content_5646697.htm. Accessed 20 Aug 2022. (in Chinese).

45. One Health joint plan of action, 2022–2026: FAO; UNEP; WHO; World Organisation for Animal Health (WOAH) (founded as OIE); 2022. Accessed 14 Oct 2022.

46. Ryu S, Kim BI, Lim JS, Tan CS, Chun BC. One Health perspectives on emerging public health threats. J Prev Med Public Health. 2017;50(6):411–4.

47. Global Food Security Index (GFSI) 2023 [updated 2023-04-03T09:35:08.

48. Li GR. Research on the prevention and treatment of canine leishmaniasis—the progress of antimony in the treatment of different clinical types of canine leishmaniasis. J Prev Med Inform. 1989;05:310+08. (in Chinese)

49. Ma L, Zhai JL, Gao XH. New progress in research and development of leishmaniasis vaccine. Dermatol Bull. 2020;37(04):355–63+3. (in Chinese)

50. FAO. An introduction to the basic concepts of food security 2008. https://www.fao.org/3/al936e/al936e00.pdf. Accessed 1 Apr 2023.

51. WHO. Antimicrobial resistance 2021. https://www.who.int/news-room/fact-sheets/detail/antimicrobial-resistance.

52. Global antimicrobial resistance and use surveillance system (GLASS). 2022. https://www.who.int/data/gho/data/themes/topics/global-antimicrobial-resistance-surveillance-system-glass.

53. WHO. Global action plan on antimicrobial resistance 2016. https://www.who.int/publications/i/item/9789241509763.

54. WHO, FAO, UNEP, WOAH. Antimicrobial resistance and the United Nations sustainable development cooperation framework: guidance for United Nations country teams. Geneva: World Health Organization; 2021.

55. Laxminarayan R, Duse A, Wattal C, Zaidi AK, Wertheim HF, Sumpradit N, et al. Antibiotic resistance-the need for global solutions. Lancet Infect Dis. 2013;13(12):1057–98.

56. WHO. WHO publishes list of bacteria for which new antibiotics are urgently needed. Geneva: WHO; 2017. https://www.who.int/news/item/27-02-2017-who-publishes-list-of-bacteria-for-which-new-antibiotics-areurgently-needed.

57. Van Boeckel TP, Glennon EE, Chen D, Gilbert M, Robinson TP, Grenfell BT, et al. Reducing antimicrobial use in food animals. Science. 2017;357(6358):1350–2.

58. Tian M, He X, Feng Y, Wang W, Chen H, Gong M, et al. Pollution by antibiotics and antimicrobial resistance in livestock and poultry manure in China, and countermeasures. Antibiotics (Basel). 2021;10(5):539.

59. Hendriksen RS, Munk P, Njage P, van Bunnik B, McNally L, Lukjancenko O, et al. Global monitoring of antimicrobial resistance based on metagenomics analyses of urban sewage. Nat Commun. 2019;10(1):1124.

60. Collaborators AR. Global burden of bacterial antimicrobial resistance in 2019: a systematic analysis. Lancet. 2022;399(10325):629–55.

61. Wu D, Walsh TR, Wu Y. World antimicrobial awareness week 2021—spread awareness, stop resistance. China CDC Wkly. 2021;3(47):987–93.

62. OHHLEP. 2022. https://www.who.int/publications/m/item/one-health-theory-of-change. Accessed 27 Mar 2023.

63. de Kraker ME, Stewardson AJ, Harbarth S. Will 10 million people die a year due to antimicrobial resistance by 2050? PLoS Med. 2016;13(11): e1002184.

64. Naylor NR, Atun R, Zhu N, Kulasabanathan K, Silva S, Chatterjee A, et al. Estimating the burden of antimicrobial resistance: a systematic literature review. Antimicrob Resist Infect Control. 2018;7:58.

65. FAO, UNEP, WHO, WOAH. One Health joint plan of action (2022–2026) working together for the health of humans, animals, plants and the environment 2022.

66. Patel J, Sridhar D. The pandemic legacy of antimicrobial resistance in the USA. Lancet Microbe. 2022;3(10):e726–e7.

67. The Lancet. Humanising health and climate change. Lancet. 2018;392(10162):2326.

68. Roca Villanueva B, Beltrán Salvador M, Gómez Huelgas R. Cambio climático y salud. Rev Clin Esp. 2019;219(5):260–5.

69. Zinsstag J, Crump L, Schelling E, Hattendorf J, Maidane YO, Ali KO, et al. Climate change and One Health. FEMS Microbiol Lett. 2018;365(11):fny085.

70. McMichael C. Human mobility, climate change, and health: unpacking the connections. Lancet Planet Health. 2020;4(6):e217–8.

71. van Bergen L, Birch M. Climate change, health and armed conflict: the links that still need making. Med Confl Surviv. 2021;37(4):257–9.

72. Weeramanthri TS, Quilty S, Campbell SL. Climate, extreme heat and human health: risks and lessons for Australia. Med J Aust. 2021;215(9):393–5.

73. Wight J, Middleton J. Climate change: the greatest public health threat of the century. BMJ. 2019;365:l2371.

74. Patz JA, Thomson MC. Climate change and health: moving from theory to practice. PLoS Med. 2018;15(7):e1002628.

75. Wise J. WHO and the global health community call for urgent action on the climate crisis. BMJ. 2021;375:n2482.

76. Capon A, Corvalan C. Climate change and health: global issue, local responses. Public Health Res Pract. 2018;28(4):2841823.

77. Wu X, Lu Y, Zhou S, Chen L, Xu B. Impact of climate change on human infectious diseases: empirical evidence and human adaptation. Environ Int. 2016;86:14–23.

78. Huang C, Barnett AG, Wang X, Tong S. The impact of temperature on years of life lost in Brisbane, Australia. Nat Climate Change. 2012;2(4):265–70.

79. Luo Q, Li S, Guo Y, Han X, Jaakkola JJK. A systematic review and meta-analysis of the association between daily mean temperature and mortality in China. Environ Res. 2019;173:281–99.

80. He Y, Cheng L, Bao J, Deng S, Liao W, Wang Q, et al. Geographical disparities in the impacts of heat on diabetes mortality and the protective role of greenness in Thailand: a nationwide case-crossover analysis. Sci Tot Environ. 2020;711:135098.

81. Johnston Fay H, Henderson Sarah B, Chen Y, Randerson James T, Marlier M, DeFries Ruth S, et al. Estimated global mortality attributable to smoke from landscape fires. Environ Health Perspect. 2012;120(5):695–701.

82. Carlson CJ, Albery GF, Merow C, Trisos CH, Zipfel CM, Eskew EA, et al. Climate change increases cross-species viral transmission risk. Nature. 2022;607(7919):555–62.

83. Xiang J, Hansen A, Liu Q, Liu X, Tong MX, Sun Y, et al. Association between dengue fever incidence and meteorological factors in Guangzhou, China, 2005–2014. Environ Res. 2017;153:17–26.

84. Xiang J, Hansen A, Liu Q, Tong MX, Liu X, Sun Y, et al. Impact of meteorological factors on hemorrhagic fever with renal syndrome in 19 cities in China, 2005–2014. Sci Total Environ. 2018;636:1249–56.

85. Gage KL, Burkot TR, Eisen RJ, Hayes EB. Climate and vectorborne diseases. Am J Prev Med. 2008;35(5):436–50.

86. Githeko AK, Lindsay SW, Confalonieri UE, Patz JA. Climate change and vector-borne diseases: a regional analysis. Bull World Health Organ. 2000;78(9):1136–47.

87. Watts N, Adger WN, Ayeb-Karlsson S, Bai Y, Byass P, Campbell-Lendrum D, et al. The Lancet Countdown: tracking progress on health and climate change. Lancet. 2017;389(10074):1151–64.

88. Watts N, Amann M, Arnell N, Ayeb-Karlsson S, Belesova K, Boykoff M, et al. The 2019 report of The Lancet Countdown on health and climate change: ensuring that the health of a child born

today is not defined by a changing climate. Lancet. 2019;394(10211):1836–78.

89. Tang Y, Song T, Gao L, Yin S, Ma M, Tan Y, et al. A CRISPR-based ultrasensitive assay detects atto-molar concentrations of SARS-CoV-2 antibodies in clinical samples. Nat Commun. 2022;13(1):4667.

90. Dresser C, Gentile E, Lyons R, Sullivan K, Balsari S. Climate change and health in New England: a review of training and policy initiatives at health education institutions and professional societies. R I Med J (2013). 2021;104(9):49–54.

91. Ebi KL. Managing climate change risks is imperative for human health. Nat Rev Nephrol. 2022;18(2):74–5.

92. Fadadu RP, Jayaraman T, Teherani A. Climate and health education for medical students. Clin Teach. 2021;18(4):362–4.

93. Delpla I, Diallo TA, Keeling M, Bellefleur O. Tools and methods to include health in climate change adaptation and mitigation strategies and policies: a scoping review. Int J Environ Res Public Health. 2021;18(5):2547.

94. Sinclair JR. Importance of a One Health approach in advancing global health security and the sustainable development goals. Rev Sci Tech. 2019;38(1):145–54.

95. Chen J, He J, Bergquist R. Challenges and response to pandemics as seen in a One Health perspective. Sci One Health. 2022;1:100010.

96. Mwatondo A, Rahman-Shepherd A, Hollmann L, Chiossi S, Maina J, Kurup KK, et al. A global analysis of One Health Networks and the proliferation of One Health collaborations. Lancet. 2023;401(10376):605–16.

97. The World Bank. From panic and neglect to investing in health security: financing pandemic preparedness at a national level 2017. https://www.worldbank.org/en/topic/pandemics/publication/from-panic-neglect-to-investing-in-health-security-financing-pandemicpreparedness-at-a-national-level. Accessed 16 Apr 2023.

98. Otu A, Effa E, Meseko C, Cadmus S, Ochu C, Athingo R, et al. Africa needs to prioritize One Health approaches that focus on the environment, animal health and human health. Nat Med. 2021;27(6):943–6.

99. Zinsstag J, Kaiser-Grolimund A, Heitz-Tokpa K, Sreedharan R, Lubroth J, Caya F, et al. Advancing One human-animal-environment Health for global health security: what does the evidence say? Lancet. 2023;401(10376):591–604.

100. Schwind JS, Goldstein T, Thomas K, Mazet JAK, Smith WA, Consortium P. Capacity building efforts and perceptions for wildlife surveillance to detect zoonotic pathogens: comparing stakeholder perspectives. BMC Public Health. 2014;14(1):684.

101. Bird BH, Mazet JAK. Detection of emerging zoonotic pathogens: an integrated One Health approach. Annu Rev Anim Biosci. 2018;6(1):121–39.

102. Centers for Disease Control and Prevention. Influenza and zoonoses education among youth in agriculture 2018. https://www.cdc.gov/onehealth/in-action/influenza-and-zoonoseseducation.html. Accessed 16 Apr 2023.

103. Eliakimu ES, Mans L. Addressing inequalities toward inclusive governance for achieving One Health: a rapid review. Front Public Health. 2021;9(75):5285.

Bibliography[1]

Cheng Z, Zhou N, Zhang X, Lv C, Guo X, Zhu Y, et al. Urging health collaboration to combat antimicrobial resistance between China and B&R countries. Infect Dis Poverty. 2022;11(1):108.

Feng J, Guo Z, Ai L, Liu J, Zhang X, Cao C, et al. Establishment of an indicator framework for global One Health Intrinsic Drivers index based on the grounded theory and fuzzy analytical hierarchy-entropy weight method. Infect Dis Poverty. 2022a;11(1):121.

Feng X, Wang S, Cheng G, et al. Editorial: Needs and potential application of One Health approach in the control of vector-borne and zoonotic infectious disease. Front Microbiol. 2022b;13:1089174.

Guo Z-Y, Feng J-X, Ai L, Xue J-B, Liu J-S, Zhang X-X, et al. Assessment of integrated patterns of human-animal-environment health: a holistic and stratified analysis. Infect Dis Poverty. 2023;12(1):17.

He J, Guo Z, Yang P, et al. Social insights on the implementation of One Health in zoonosis prevention and control: a scoping review. Infect Dis Poverty. 2022;11(1):48.

Hong Z, Li L, Zhang L, et al. Elimination of schistosomiasis japonica in China: from the One Health perspective. China CDC Wkly. 2022;4(7):130–4.

Li Q, Bergquist R, Grant L, et al. Consideration of COVID-19 beyond the human-centred approach of prevention and control: the ONE-HEALTH perspective. Emerg Microbes Infect. 2022;11(1):2520–8.

Li OY, Wang X, Yang K, et al. The approaching pilot for One Health governance index. Infect Dis Poverty. 2023;12(1):16.

Miao L, Li H, Ding W, et al. Research priorities on One Health: a bibliometric analysis. Front Public Health. 2022;10:889854.

Qiang N, Gu SY, Wang XY, Zhang XX, Xia S, Zheng JX, et al. A One Health information database based on standard bibliometric analysis. Sci One Health. 2022;1:100012.

---

[1] Note: Part of the indicators utilized for previous publications have been refined with updated data. For details see special reports.

Xie Y, Li H, Liu J, Han L, Zhang X, Zhou X, et al. Climate change impacts and responses index: risks, opportunities and policy implications 2023. (in press).

Zhang XX, Liu JS, Han LF, Xia S, Li SZ, Li OY, et al. Towards a global One Health index: a potential assessment tool for One Health performance. Infect Dis Poverty. 2022a;11(1):57.

Zhang XX, Liu JS, Han LF, Simm G, Guo XK, Zhou XN. One Health: new evaluation framework launched. Nature. 2022b;604(7907):625.

Zhao HQ, Fei SW, Yin JX, Li Q, Jiang TG, Guo ZY, et al. Assessment of performance for a key indicator of One Health: evidence based on One Health index for zoonoses in sub-Saharan Africa. Infect Dis Poverty. 2022;11(1):109.

Zhou N, Cheng Z, Zhang X, Lv C, Guo C, Liu H, et al. Global antimicrobial resistance: a system-wide comprehensive investigation using the Global One Health Index. Infect Dis Poverty. 2022;11(1):92.